# Lecture Notes in Computer Science    **9408**

*Commenced Publication in 1973*
Founding and Former Series Editors:
Gerhard Goos, Juris Hartmanis, and Jan van Leeuwen

More information about this series at http://www.springer.com/series/7410

Meikang Qiu · Shouhuai Xu
Moti Yung · Haibo Zhang (Eds.)

# Network and System Security

9th International Conference, NSS 2015
New York, NY, USA, November 3–5, 2015
Proceedings

 Springer

*Editors*
Meikang Qiu
Department of Computer Science
Pace University
New York, NY
USA

Moti Yung
Department of Computer Science
Columbia University
New York, NY
USA

Shouhuai Xu
Department of Computer Science
University of Texas
San Antonio, TX
USA

Haibo Zhang
Department of Computer Science
University of Otago
Dunedin
New Zealand

ISSN 0302-9743            ISSN 1611-3349  (electronic)
Lecture Notes in Computer Science
ISBN 978-3-319-25644-3        ISBN 978-3-319-25645-0  (eBook)
DOI 10.1007/978-3-319-25645-0

Library of Congress Control Number: 2015952062

LNCS Sublibrary: SL4 – Security and Cryptology

Printed on acid-free paper

Springer International Publishing AG Switzerland is part of Springer Science+Business Media
(www.springer.com)

# Preface

This volume contains the papers presented at NSS 2015: The 9th International Conference on Network and System Security held during November 3–5, 2015, in New York City, New York, USA. NSS 2015 was organized and supported by Pace University and New York Institute of Technology (NYIT). Since its inauguration in 2007, NSS has become a highly successful series of annual international gatherings, for academic and industrial researchers and practitioners to exchange ideas in the area of network and system security. Previous editions of NSS were held in: Xi'an, China (2014); Madrid, Spain(2013); Wu Yi Shan, China (2012); Milan, Italy (2011); Melbourne, Australia; (2010); Gold Coast, Australia (2009); Shanghai, China (2008); and Dalian, China (2007).

The conference received 110 submissions. Each submission was carefully reviewed by at least three, and mostly four, Program Committee members. The Program Committee decided to accept 23 full papers and 18 short papers. The program also included three invited talks, which were given by Professor Steven M. Bellovin (Columbia University, USA), Professor Michael Reiter (University of North Carolina at Chapel Hill, USA), and Professor Gene Tsudik (University of California, Irvine, USA).

We would like to thank all authors who submitted their papers to NSS 2015, and the conference attendees for their interest and support, which made the conference possible. We further thank the Organizing Committee for their time and efforts; their support allowed us to focus on the paper selection process. We thank the Program Committee members and the external reviewers for their hard work in reviewing the submissions; the conference would not have been possible without their expert reviews. We also thank the invited speakers for enriching the program with their presentations. We thank Professor Yang Xiang, Chair of the NSS Steering Commitee, for his advice throughout the conference preparation process. Last but not least, we thank EasyChair for making the entire process of the conference convenient.

We hope you find these proceedings educational and enjoyable!

November 2015

Meikang Qiu
Shouhuai Xu
Moti Yung
Haibo Zhang

# Organization

## General Co-chairs

Meikang Qiu                Pace University, USA
Elisa Bertino              Purdue University, USA

## Program Co-charis

Shouhuai Xu                University of Texas at San Antonio, USA
Moti Yung                  Columbia University, USA
Haibo Zhang                University of Otago, New Zealand

## Local Chair

Tao Zhang                  New York Institute of Technology, USA

## Web and Publicity Chair

Qingji Zheng               Huawei Research, USA
Wenjia Li                  New York Institute of Technology, USA

## Program Committee

Rafael Accorsi             University of Freiburg, Germany
Giuseppe Ateniese          Sapienza University of Rome, Italy
Rida Bazzi                 Arizona State University, USA
Alex Biryukov              University of Luxembourg, Luxembourg
Pino Caballero Gil         Universidad de La Laguna, Spain
Bogdan Carbunar            Florida International University, USA
Songqing Chen              George Mason University, USA
Mauro Conti                University of Padua, Italy
Roberto Di Pietro          Bell Labs, USA
Cunsheng Ding              Hong Kong University of Science and Technology,
                             SAR China
Xuhua Ding                 Singapore Management University, Singapore
Alban Gabillon             University of Polynésie Française, France
Keke Gai                   Pace University, USA
Joaquin Garcia-Alfaro      Telecom SudParis, France
Weili Han                  Fudan University, China
James Joshi                University of Pittsburgh, USA
Stefan Katzenbeisser       TU Darmstadt, Germany

# Additional Reviewers

Almohri, Hussain
Anada, Hiroaki
Anand, S. Abhishek
Ariyapala, Kanishka
Awad, Amro
Banescu, Sebastian
Bardas, Alexandru G.
Barenghi, Alessandro
Beckers, Kristian
Belhaouane, Malek
Blanc, Gregory
Cazorla, Lorena
Chen, Bo
Chen, Haoyu
Costantino, Gianpiero
Dargahi, Tooska
De Gaspari, Fabio
Ding, Ding
Dinu, Dumitru Daniel
Elrakaiby, Yehia
Fereidooni, Hossien
Fernandez, Gerardo
Fromm, Alexander
Georg, Geri
Guo, Zeqing
Han, Jun
Jiang, Han
Jin, Yier
Jin, Zhe

Karvelas, Nikolaos
Kawakita, Masanori
Kelarev, Andrei
Kelbert, Florian
Le Corre, Yann
Li, Qi
Li, Qianqian
Li, Yongqiang
Li, Yuping
Li, Zhen
Liu, Fang
Lu, Jiqiang
Martín Fernández,
    Francisco
Martín-Fernández,
    Francisco
Matsumoto, Shinichi
Mohamed, Manar
Neupane, Ajaya
Nieto, Ana
Nuñez, David
Ochoa, Martín
Ognawala, Saahil
Perrin, Leo
Perrin, Léo Paul
Rao, Prasad
Ricks, Brian
Rios, Ruben
Roy, Partha Sarathi

Ruj, Sushmita
Sahay, Rishikesh
Santos-González, Iván
Saracino, Andrea
Shen, Jinan
Shirvanian, Maliheh
Shrestha, Babins
Shrestha, Prakash
Shu, Xiaokui
Spolaor, Riccardo
Sun, Wuliang
Sundaramurthy, Sathya
    Chandran
Tews, Erik
Tian, Ke
Tian, Yuan
Toumi, Khalifa
Ueshige, Yoshifumi
Velichkov, Vesselin
Wang, Daniel
Wang, Xiao
Wei, Fengguo
Wüchner, Tobias
Xu, Haitao
Zhang, Liqiang
Zhang, Pan
Zhang, Su
Zhao, Kao
Zomlot, Loai

# Contents

## Application Security

## Security Management

## Applied Cryptography

## Cryptosystems

## Short Papers: Cryptographic Mechanisms

## Short Papers: Security Mechanisms

# Wireless Security and Privacy

# Dandelion - Revealing Malicious Groups of Interest in Large Mobile Networks

Wei Wang$^{(\boxtimes)}$, Mikhail Istomin, and Jeffrey Bickford

AT&T Security Research Center, New York, USA
{wei.wang.2,mikhail.istomin,jbickford}@att.com

**Abstract.** There are an enormous number of security anomalies that occur across the Internet on a daily basis. These anomalies are typically viewed as individual security events that are manually analyzed in order to detect an attack and take action. Important characteristics of an attack may go unnoticed due to limited manual resources. Mobile attacks introduce further complexity by typically traversing multiple types of networks making correlation and detection even more challenging. In this paper, we propose a system *Dandelion*, which aims to automatically correlate individual security anomalies together to reveal an entire mobile attack campaign. The system also identifies previously unknown malicious network entities that are highly correlated. Our prototype system correlates thousands of network anomalies across both the SMS and IP networks of a large US tier-1 mobile service provider, reducing them to approximately 20 ~ 30 groups of interest a day. To demonstrate Dandelion's value, we show how our system has provided the critical information necessary to human analysts in detecting and mitigating previously unknown mobile attacks.

## 1 Introduction

The landscape of attacks in mobile networks has expanded rapidly in the past several years [3,20]. Unique features on smartphones have made attacks easier, resulting in a wide range of threats, such as voice call fraud, SMS message phishing, spyware, and other malware driven attacks [16]. Shortened URLs and limited screen sizes make phishing attacks a prime infection vector for mobile devices. Attackers have also found unique ways to monetize their malicious campaign through the use and enrollment of premium services [18] and most recently through mobile ransomware, which has plagued many third party app markets [19].

On the defense side, detecting an attack in mobile networks is typically complicated and time consuming. Attacks typically traverse through multiple different networks, such as voice, SMS, and the Internet. If detection only occurs in one type of network, the complete picture of an attack may be missed. Attacks also frequently change, rendering mitigation attempts on a single attack component useless. The mobile network is also unique in that there is zero tolerance for false positives when mitigating mobile attacks. Unlike simply blocking access

© Springer International Publishing Switzerland 2015
M. Qiu et al. (Eds.): NSS 2015, LNCS 9408, pp. 3–17, 2015.
DOI: 10.1007/978-3-319-25645-0_1

to a domain or IP address, mitigation on a mobile attack may end up canceling phone numbers or premium short code services. For this reason, it is very crucial that an attack is thoroughly studied and fully understood before any action is taken. The large volume of anomalies that must be manually investigated results in a daunting task.

There have been previous studies on detecting malicious campaigns across the Internet [8,14]. Previous work has typically relied on traditional blacklists to identify additional malicious relationships. In our case, the system is not limited by only anomalies that are known to be malicious, it can begin with potential attack components, such as third-party app download sites [16] and newly registered domains [12], so that new emerging attacks can be revealed. Though previous work on detecting threats in the mobile network solve certain aspects of the problem [4,5,7,9,21], we provide a mechanism to reveal entire attack campaigns through various types of correlation across multiple types of network data.

Motivated by the uniqueness of the problem, we propose a system named *Dandelion*. Dandelion ingests network data and security anomalies to automatically detect entire attack campaigns, including previously undiscovered malicious network entities. Correlation will be made based on relationships among *network entities*, defined as phone numbers, short codes, domains, and IP addresses. In our study, we will introduce two types of relationships, "share-user" and "share-owner". The "share-user" relationship correlates network entities within an attack campaign due to the fact that they share a significant number of infected users. Alternatively, the "share-owner" relationship correlates network entities created by the same attacker. These relationships produce a manageable number of *groups of interest* which contain network entities that are highly correlated to security anomalies. For example, users infected with a malicious app may all show network communication with a common C&C server. As a result of Dandelion, these same users are observed downloading the same application from a third-party app market, identifying the infection vector of the attack.

The contribution of the paper is twofold. First, the system can reveal previously unknown network entities that are involved in entire attack campaigns across multiple networks. This provides more meaningful information to human analysts when compared to individual security anomalies. The system has detected real malicious campaigns in a large Tier-1 US mobile network. Secondly, the system is scalable and can process billions of data records on commodity hardware. We will show how the system processes a large amount of data balancing the tradeoff between computer memory and disk storage. In practice, Dandelion reduces thousands of security anomalies across multiple networks to $20 \sim 30$ suspicious groups of interest on a daily basis. The system has successfully aided human analysts in detecting newly emerging malicious campaigns as well as the evolution of existing campaigns within the mobile network. We will present details of two real-world malicious campaigns that were discovered using Dandelion, one that turned users into an SMS gateway and the other performing mobile click fraud that has not been reported in any major social media.

## 2   Data Overview

Dandelion uses a dataset of SMS records and IP flows collected by a large US mobile carrier. All phone numbers are anonymized with randomized unique values to protect privacy. Each SMS record is simply a time-stamped tuple, indicating the source and destination anonymized phone number. IP data records, similarly, consists of time-stamped tuples indicating the anonymized phone number and the domain visited. We also use an internal Whois database [23] to collect domain registration information used to illustrate the "share-owner" relationship. To reduce the commonality between users caused by highly popular domains and SMS short-codes (i.e Google, 224444), we remove the corresponding data records from our dataset via a whitelisting process. Due to required sampling caused by volume constraints and whitelisting, our weekly dataset consists of approximately 40 million unique communication edges among 8 million unique entities. Among these, approximately 4.5 million entities represent anonymized phone numbers and 20 thousand represent domain registration email addresses. All other entities represent domains or IP addresses.

A list of security anomalies are used as input to the system. Categories of security anomalies include SMS spammers, known C&C domains/IPs, phishing sites, third-party app markets, and newly visited domains within the last 30 days. It is important to note that security anomalies are not necessarily malicious, but instead may represent network entities more likely to be used in an attack (i.e. third-party app markets, newly visited domains) [12,25].

## 3   System

Figure 1 represents the methodology of our system which will be explained in the following section. Dandelion begins with a large amount of SMS, IP data, and domain registration records which represent communication and domain ownership throughout the mobile network. Based on these records, the system identifies strong relationships between network entities by generating a *relationship graph*. The relationship graph is a graph in which nodes are network entities and an edge between two nodes represents "share-user" or "share-owner" relationships. The system then identifies nodes that are highly correlated with security anomalies through the relationship graph. This naturally reveals *groups of interest* containing newly discovered network entities that are highly correlated with security anomalies. Figure 1 summarizes how Dandelion reduces millions of data records to approximately 20 ~ 30 groups of interest, which is a manageable number for humans to investigate.

### 3.1   Relationship Graph Generation

In this section, we will explain how Dandelion generates the relationship graph from the data records. The relationship graph is a graph in which edges represent the presence of *relationships* between nodes, not direct communication. For example, in the relationship graph, a short code and domain name may have an edge

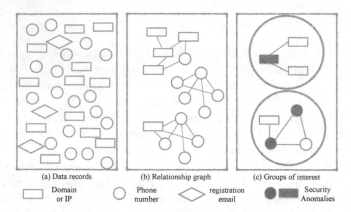

(a) Data records      (b) Relationship graph      (c) Groups of interest

☐ Domain or IP    ○ Phone number    ◇ registration email    ●■ Security Anomalies

**Fig. 1.** This figure illustrates how Dandelion begins with millions of data records and generates a relationship graph of correlated network entities. Finally, the system reveals several groups of interest with network entities highly correlated to security anomalies.

between them if they share a significant number of users in the communication graph; i.e. the same users sent an SMS message to a short code and sent IP packets to the same domain name. We define these types of edges as *share-user* edges. The other type of edge in the relationship graph is a *share-owner* edge. Two domains will have an edge between them in the relationship graph if they are registered with the same email address.

Each day, Dandelion aggregates the data records from the previous seven days to generate the relationship graph. Each edge in the relationship graph is assigned a *relationship coefficient*, or edge weight, which quantitatively measures how two entities are correlated. We compute the relationship coefficient $R(a, b)$ between two nodes $a$ and $b$. If both $a$ and $b$ are domains registered under the same email address, an edge between them is created signifying the "share-owner" relationship with relationship coefficient set to 1. Otherwise, edges between nodes are based on the "share-user" relationship, quantified by the Dice association coefficient [24]. Specifically, this is depicted using the following formula:

$$R(a, b) = \begin{cases} 1 & \text{if } a \text{ and } b \text{ are both domains sharing registration email} \\ \frac{|A \cap B|}{\min\{|A|, |B|\}} & \text{otherwise} \end{cases}$$

$$\text{with } |A| \geq \tau, |B| \geq \tau$$

where $A$ and $B$ represent the set of users that communicate with nodes $a$ and $b$ respectively, and $|\cdot|$ represents the cardinality of a set. The condition of $|A| \geq \tau, |B| \geq \tau$ is introduced to avoid correlation between nodes that have an insignificantly small number of users.

The Dice association coefficient, which uses the minimum cardinality of two sets in the denominator, ensures that relationships are maintained even if a single node is largely popular. For example, a SMS spammer may send a phishing domain to thousands of users, of which only dozens may visit. By using other similarity metrics, such as the Jaccard index, correlation between the SMS spammer and the phishing domain will be weakened and mistakenly left out of the final groups of interest.

## 3.2  Percolation on the Relationship Graph

In this section, we will show how the system starts with various *seed nodes* and propagates throughout the relationship graph to find other related nodes of interest. Seed nodes are network entities that represent potential threats, identified by security anomalies. The process will be referred to as *suspiciousness percolation* on the relationship graph. Entities that are highly correlated to these seed nodes will be revealed, displaying a holistic picture of an entire attack campaign and quickly supplying a human analyst with valuable information. Though similar approaches have been used in the past to propagate trustworthiness across the web, such as TrustRank [11], Dandelion relies on various relationships, instead of just communication, to identify strongly correlated entities across multiple networks.

There are several intuitions that are taken into consideration when designing the suspiciousness percolation algorithm. First, we percolate suspiciousness to a neighboring node by multiplying a node's suspiciousness by the edge's relationship coefficient. Suspiciousness is aggregated together for nodes with multiple neighbors with a suspiciousness score higher than zero. Nodes with multiple edges of high relationship coefficients will typically result in a higher suspiciousness score. Second, to avoid over-percolation, we normalize the relationship coefficients across the number of edges of a node. This ensures that nodes with a significantly large amount of edges do not introduce unrelated entities in the final groups of interest. Lastly, we introduce a decay factor to ensure that nodes far away from the initial seed, are less likely to be included in a group of interest.

Based on these intuitions, the *suspiciousness percolation* algorithm is designed as the following. Assume we have the complete relationship graph with $N$ nodes, represented as an adjacency matrix $\mathbf{T}$, which is square and symmetric. An off the diagonal element $t_{ij}(i \neq j)$ equals the relationship coefficient $R(i,j)$ defined as the equation from section 3.1, representing the relationship correlation between a node pair $(i,j)$. Elements on the diagonal are all ones. Finally, $M$ seed nodes are represented as set $B$. We quantify the suspiciousness score (abbreviated as score hereafter) for all nodes in the graph by a numeric vector, represented as $\mathbf{S}$, with $s_i$ (for $i \in [1, N]$) being the score for a single node $i$. Initially, all nodes will have zero scores, except for seed nodes which have scores of one ($s_i = 1$ if $i \in B$). Here ll security anomalies as treated as equally important.

The off the diagonal elements in each column of the matrix $\mathbf{T}$ are normalized to the sum of one so that the suspiciousness score of one node will be split among all edges of its neighboring nodes. The elements on the diagonal will remain to be ones. By multiplying $\mathbf{T} \times \mathbf{S}$, suspiciousness is aggregated together for nodes with multiple neighbors, thus the first intuition is satisfied. Given column $j$, if many column elements are nonzeros (meaning node $j$ has many connected nodes), then by normalizing the column coefficients to one, each coefficient will be small, penalizing nodes with a large amount of edges and avoiding over-percolation. To satisfy the third intuition, we introduce a decay factor $\beta$ which is a numeric score to reduce the impact of suspiciousness for nodes that are long distance away (measured as the number of hops) from seed nodes. The penalty will grow as a function of the number of hops from seed nodes as iteration increases. Lastly, the system will favor seed nodes by adding some suspiciousness back during each iteration via $(1-\beta) \times \mathbf{S_0}$, where $\mathbf{S_0}$ is the initial vector of seed node elements with a value of one. In this way, the original seed nodes will maintain a high score in the final result. We will iteratively compute the $\mathbf{S}$, as $\mathbf{S} = \beta \times \mathbf{T} \times \mathbf{S} + (1-\beta) \times \mathbf{S_0}$ for each iteration, to simulate suspiciousness percolating from seed nodes to all others. The convergence is measured as the Euclidean distance of $\mathbf{S}$ between two consecutive iterations. We observed that with a few number of iterations, the suspiciousness scores will converge to a stable state. The main equation for iteration may cosmetically resemble the TrustRank algorithm, but our definition for $\mathbf{T}$ is quite different as we use the relationship graph. The final output of the percolation algorithm is the vector $\mathbf{S}$, which contains suspiciousness scores for all nodes in the relationship graph.

### 3.3   Implementation

Our prototype system is running on a shared secure analysis environment that is both limited in memory and computational resources. Fortunately, generating the entire relationship graph is not necessary, as we only need to identify network entities that are highly correlated with security anomalies. Based on this fact, our prototype is implemented in a scalable way to deal with our large data set and computational constraints.

The data structure and retrieval process is overall fairly similar to the one described by Brin and Page in their original web search engine system [6]. As shown in Figure 2, we keep two separate pieces of information to represent the communication graph. The first is a file that contains all information about the various nodes, called *node records*. Each record contains the node id, name, node type, and list of neighbors. The offset of each node record from the file header is calculated for all nodes and stored within a second data structure called the

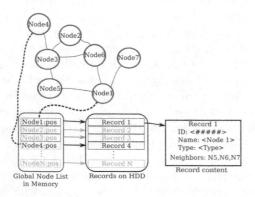

**Fig. 2.** Node list loaded in memory and node records stored on disk storage.

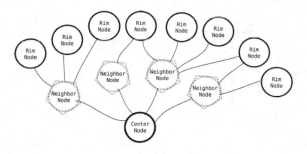

**Fig. 3.** A dandelion graph of one center node, with its rim nodes being connected through neighbor nodes.

*global node list.* This data structure contains a mapping between node id and record offset. The global node list is typically loaded into memory while the node records are stored on disk. This type of data structure avoids having to load all of the node information into memory in order to do our analysis.

We iteratively traverse the graph during the percolation stage and generate relationships on the fly. The process starts with a list of seed nodes that are obtained via the various security anomalies as mentioned in the previous sections. Small relationship graphs, their relationship coefficients, and suspiciousness are all iteratively generated through these seed nodes via *dandelion graph generation.*

The *dandelion graph,* is a very small communication graph consisting of a center node, it's neighbors, and it's neighbor's neighbors, which we define as a *rim node.* An example of a dandelion graph is shown in Figure 3. When generating the dandelion graph, the relationship coefficient, is calculated between each rim node and center node. Recall, that we are measuring relationships between two nodes that share the same entity. Once we have calculated the relationship coefficient for each pair of nodes, these values are normalized and suspiciousness is percolated to each rim node as explained in Section 3.2. Rim nodes with a suspiciousness value above a specific threshold are added to a work queue for the next iteration. Dandelion graphs will be generated for each node in the work queue iteratively until the process converges and terminates.

Once the process terminates, the traversed nodes and their edges are used to produce groups of interest. A 2D graph is rendered with nodes of various shapes and colors, as well as edges of different thickness, to help a human analyst clearly distinguish entities or catch interesting patterns. Dandelion has been successfully reducing $1500 \sim 2000$ individual security anomalies per day to approximately $25 \sim 30$ suspicious groups of interest, by analyzing 40 million data records in an average time of 100 minutes.

## 4   Evaluation and Case Studies

Due to the small number of ongoing mobile threats at any given time in the US mobile market [13], it is very difficult to evaluate the system by traditional metrics. Even with a small number of attacks, it is highly important for mobile

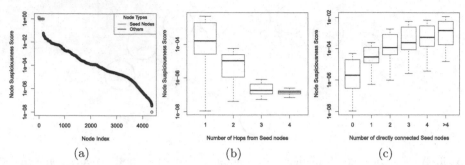

**Fig. 4.** Node suspiciousness score overview and its relationship with seed nodes.

service providers to detect and mitigate security issues that impact network reliability and customer satisfaction. We will give concrete results to prove that our findings are consistent with Dandelion's design and report several real world cases where Dandelion aided in detecting malicious activities on a Tier-1 US mobile service provider's network.

By experimenting with various parameters of Dandelion, we found that the suspiciousness percolation typically converges after 4 iterations, with the Euclidean distance between the last two iterations being less than $10^{-7}$. This observation is similar to the study in [8] where they used the maximum iteration of 5 to find p2p botnets. We also chose a value of 0.6 for the decay coefficient $\beta$ to limit the number of nodes introduced during the percolation process. Figure 4(a) is the result of the suspiciousness scores for nodes after percolation in a descending order (log-scale) during a single day's run, while other runs behave similarly. The scores associated with the seed nodes (represented in red) are higher than the ones for others. This is consistent with the design where a constant factor $1 - \beta$ ensures that the seed nodes are ranked highest in the end.

Figure 4(b) shows the boxplot of node suspiciousness scores for different numbers of hops from seed nodes in the relationship graph. The mean of the suspiciousness scores decreases as the number of hops increases. In general, the scores between the 1st and the 3rd quartiles decrease as well. This is consistent with our intuition that the the farther away from a seed node, the less likely a node should be related to it. Figure 4(c) shows node suspiciousness scores versus the number of directly connected seed nodes in the relationship graph. It represents that as the number of directly connected seed nodes increases for a node, its suspiciousness score increases.

### 4.1 Bazuc - "Free" International SMS

Our first example will demonstrate that our system can reveal interesting new pieces of information by utilizing data sources across different communication networks such as SMS and IP networks. In this case, customers downloaded an

**Fig. 5.** The relationship graph for devices infected with Bazuc (anonymized numbers in eclipse shape) share relationships with the same IP address (in box shape) which represents the C&C.

application from the Google Play store [1] which advertised itself as "Earn Money by Installing this App" [17].

**What it Does:**  The "Bazuc Earn Money" application turns a user's phone into an SMS proxy and claims to pay the user a small amount of money for each message sent. It is not clear exactly who is using the SMS proxy service, as a later report by Lookout identified that their alternative "Free International SMS" app was not functional [2]. Around the time of investigation, SMS spam detection algorithms identified an abnormal increase in international SMS activity for some customers with the Bazuc application installed. We believe the SMS proxy service was being used or resold by the authors, potentially for use in spamming campaigns.

**Analysis via Dandelion:**  The initial seed data for this analysis is the result of the SMS spam detection algorithm which generates a daily report of phone numbers with abnormal SMS behavior. The exact method and details of this algorithm are out of scope of this paper, though it is similar to various previous work on SMS spam detection [9,21]. Using this initial list of phone numbers with abnormal SMS activity as seed nodes, Dandelion automatically generates a relationship graph using both their SMS and IP traffic. On average, using a few hundred spammers as seed nodes produces $0 \sim 3$ graphs daily.

Figure 5 shows the relationship graph for users with the Bazuc application installed. This graph was initially of interest due to the fact that five users with abnormal SMS activity not only share a fair number of users, but also share

---

[1] This application was reported to Google Play due to the fact that it violates the terms of service and is no longer available via the official application market.

[2] It is important to note that we first detected this app via Dandelion in October 2013, prior to any third party reports being released.

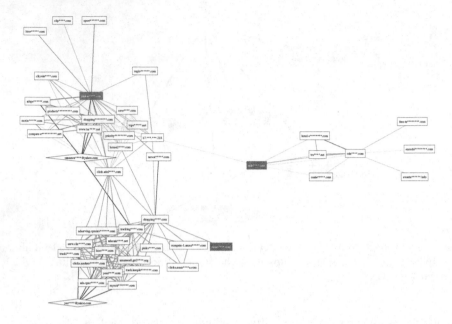

**Fig. 6.** Fake Flash player: a mobile click fraud with three groups of interest which represent the evolution of the campaign over ten months. Domains in red rectangles are download sites as seed nodes.

communication with the same IP address. It is important to note that no phone number within the graph communicated with the central IP address during the previous 20 days.

The common IP address shared among these spammers resulted in a need for immediate attention. Previous study has shown that professional SMS spamming campaigns rarely have any IP traffic, let alone communication with the same common IP address [21]. The resulting graph more closely resembles botnet-like behavior. Analysts working along with customer service representatives were able to identify that the Bazuc application was the cause of this problem. Detailed manual analysis of the application binary confirmed the central IP address as the command and control server of the application. Though in this case, Dandelion did not specifically identify the cause of the problem, we were able to help identify the set of users that were potentially impacted by similar botnet-like behavior and help analysts take action through remediation.

### 4.2   Yet Another Fake Flash Player - Mobile Ad Fraud

Our next case is an example of a malicious campaign that uses mobile traffic for monetary gain. In this case, the adversaries create a botnet of mobile devices and use them for online advertising fraud. Though not necessarily a significant impact to the provider itself, these types of malicious campaigns can be of annoyance to the customer because of advertisement pop-ups and significant background traffic, resulting in possible data overages or increased battery consumption.

**What it Does:** Over the past several years, there have been numerous cases of Android malware being encapsulated under the disguise of Adobe Flash Player. For example, the ScarePackage ransomware app claimed to be Adobe Flash Player, but locked the device and required a user to submit a payment order to unlock the phone [19]. Other types of "fake" Flash Players have had the ability to send premium SMS messages or steal sensitive information off of the device. In April 2014, Dandelion detected a similar type of malicious Flash Player application which we have called "Yet Another Fake Flash Player". This application creates a botnet for use in mobile advertising fraud and to our knowledge has not be reported in the mainstream media.

Users receive the fake flash player application either through drive by downloads or by clicking on a link to watch a video that "requires" flash. In some cases, we have seen users be redirected from pornography and live sports TV sites. When the user installs and runs the application for the first time, a background service is started and the application removes its icon from the home screen and application tray in order to hide itself. In the background, the application performs click fraud operations via URLs received by the command and control server. After multiple redirects and requests, an ad click is simulated in the background and the advertiser's website is automatically displayed on the user's device, most likely frustrating the user due to frequent random pop-ups.

**Analysis via Dandelion:** In this example, we use a different type of security event as the seed data to start the suspiciousness percolation. Because malicious applications tend to reside on third party application markets, domains hosting APK files are used as seed nodes for analysis. On average, $\sim 200$ domains are associated with third-party app downloads per day, resulting in an average of 10 groups of interest.

Over the last ten months, three different groups of interest for Yet Another Fake Flash Player have been identified via Dandelion. Figure 6 combines these groups of interest into one visualization. For privacy reasons, all domains have been obfuscated for inclusion in this paper.

Three sites, `pinkie****.com`, `mlp****.com` and `rainb****.com` (marked in red), were observed to host Android APK files and served as seed nodes to Dandelion. For example,`rainb****.com` hosted downloads for `FlashPlayer.apk`. In this case, users who visited `rainb****.com` also visited various domain names that appeared to be related to ad networks, such as `click.adol****.com` and `adscam****.net`. Domains such as `shopping****.com` and `house2****.com` appear to be normal websites by name, but their popularity within the network is significantly low. Besides the share-user relationship, Dandelion also revealed the fact that some domains were registered with the same email address. Five domains, such as `tracking****.com` and `pinkie****.com` share the same registration email of `sanamra****@yahoo.com`, while another three domains share `yes****@yahoo.com`.

Based on the syntax of domain names and their relationships, we hypothesized that this application was related to mobile advertisement fraud. To confirm this suspicion, we briefly browsed some of the domains to understand their potential role in this suspicious graph. For example, `shopping****.com` states that "This domain is used to track traffic and ensure its quality to our advertisers". Interestingly enough, `tracki****.com` also displays the same exact message, while `house2****.com` appears to be a legitimate website, but it's content is unoriginal and replicated from various places on the Internet.

To confirm our hypothesis, we downloaded the application and ran it through a static and dynamic analysis platform, which was built in-house using open source tools [1, 2]. Our analysis of the application confirmed that this graph was indeed related to a mobile click fraud campaign. On execution, the application connects to `pinks****.com`, a hard coded command and control server within the APK binary itself. This C&C server is periodically checked and obtains a search URL to `shopping****.com`. This redirects to `tracki****.com` which then redirects to the advertisement network `clicks.mam****a.com`. From here, the device is directed to `house2****.com` with a prepopulated search term, such as `partynextdoor+thirsty+download`. The device is then redirected through a series of legitimate advertisement networks until the advertiser's website is displayed to the user.

Our analysis helped confirm our hypothesis that this application was indeed being used for malicious activity. Dandelion helped identify the application as potentially suspicious and provided a list of domain names of interest that may correlate with a malicious campaign. Manual analysis was quickened due to the fact that the APK analysis could be easily correlated with what we observed in the graph as Figure 6. The graph also shows other domains involved, which may not be identified with one dynamic run. Overtime, Dandelion also allowed us to observe changes in the this click fraud campaign and have been able to track the various download sites and command and control servers.

## 5   Related Work

There have been many studies related to detecting malicious activity across the Internet using clustering approaches [8, 10, 11, 14, 15, 22]. An early work, TrustRank [11] was proposed to combat web spam by using potentially benign and trustworthy web pages to propagate a trust score across the web. Gu et. al. [10] applied clustering analysis using features extracted from network traffic to reveal groups of botnets. Li et. al. [14] crawl millions of seed URLs, both benign and malicious, to identify previously unknown domains and IP addresses that are dedicated to malicious web activity. Nadji et al [22] used malicious domains and IP addresses to build a graph of malicious and related entities using historical DNS data. Under the argument of "guilty by association", a mutual contact graph-based clustering is proposed to detect P2P bots in network flow traffic by Coskun et al [8]. Though similar in nature to these works, Dandelion specifically focuses on the unique characteristics of mobile attacks, which typically span multiple types of networks.

There has been recent work specifically dedicated to detecting malicious activities in mobile networks [4,5,7,9,21]. Corinna et al. proposed a pioneer idea to combat fraudsters in mobile networks [7]. By tracking the communication graph evolving over time, the algorithm can detect fraudsters changing from one account to another. Authors in [9] identified SMS spam with similar content using Bloom filters, while [21] identified spammers by studying their communication patterns compared with legitimate users. These studies aimed to identify only one aspect of malicious activity, rather than revealing entire malicious campaigns. Finally, closest to our work, Boggs et al. detect emergent malicious campaigns by finding groups of abnormal entities in mobile networks [5]. An anomalous behavior is taken into account only when a large number of network users exhibit the same anomaly thereby reducing the false positives. Complementary to this work, Dandelion focuses on correlating mobile network entities together by using multiple types of relationships.

## 6  Limitations and Future Work

In this section, we will address several limitations that we found while testing the system on real world data. The first limitation is that the system may include "benign" entities in groups. Such entities could be new services emerging in the network. Another limitation is that highly distributed attacks might avoid detection if connectivity for each entity is significantly low. Lastly, if some stages of an attack are related to popular entities, such as social media sites, these entities may not appear in a group of interest. It is important to note that other stages of this type of attack will still be revealed by Dandelion.

In the future, we would like to continue to extend Dandelion in several ways. Once Dandelion is used by more analysts, we would like to incorporate feedback from human analysts to remove nodes that are identified as legitimate from the relationship graph. Newly confirmed malicious entities can also be added back into the system to further expand the list of malicious entities. Because the system can help observe groups over time, we would like to automatically detect changes to attack campaigns to effectively mitigate threats as soon as possible. For example, if a malicious domain name is blacklisted and quickly replaced by another one, Dandelion would detect this new domain in the attack campaign.

## 7  Conclusion

In this paper, we propose a system that uses multiple relationships across different types of networks to correlate network entities and security anomalies into groups of interest. These groups of interest represent an entire attack campaign and help human analysts observe the complete picture of an attack, rather than looking into individual anomalies one by one. Dandelion has successfully revealed attacks in a large mobile network. The system has greatly increased the efficiency of human analysts by shortening the time of detection and providing information required for attack mitigation. Over time, we would like to continue to improve Dandelion by incorporating other sources of malicious information as well as extend to other types of networks and data.

# References

1. Androguard. https://github.com/androguard/androguard
2. Droidbox. http://code.google.com/p/droidbox/
3. Anti-Phishing Working Group: Global phishing survey: trends and domain name use in 2014. http://goo.gl/cfPCEY
4. Baliga, A., Bickford, J., Daswani, N.: Triton: A carrier-based approach for detecting and mitigating mobile malware. Journal of Cyber Security **3**(2), 1–30 (2012)
5. Boggs, N., Wang, W., Mathur, S., Coskun, B., Pincock, C.: Discovery of emergent malicious campaigns in cellular networks. In: Proceedings of the 29th Annual Computer Security Applications Conference, ACSAC 2013, pp. 29–38. ACM, New York (2013)
6. Brin, S., Page, L.: The anatomy of a large-scale hypertextual web search engine. In: Seventh International World-Wide Web Conference (1998)
7. Cortes, C., Pregibon, D., Volinsky, C.: Communities of interest. In: Hoffmann, F., Hand, D.J., Adams, N., Fisher, D., Guimaraes, G. (eds.) IDA 2001. LNCS, vol. 2189, pp. 105–114. Springer, Heidelberg (2001)
8. Coskun, B., Dietrich, S., Memon, N.: Friends of an enemy: identifying local members of peer-to-peer botnets using mutual contacts. In: Proc. of the 26 Annual Computer Security Applications Conference (ACSAC) (2010)
9. Coskun, B., Giura, P.: Mitigating SMS spam by online detection of repetitive near-duplicate messages. In: IEEE ICC 2012 Symposium on Communication and Information Systems Security (2012)
10. Gu, G., Perdisci, R., Zhang, J., Lee, W., et al.: Botminer: clustering analysis of network traffic for protocol-and structure-independent botnet detection. In: USENIX Security Symposium, pp. 139–154 (2008)
11. Gyöngyi, Z., Garcia-Molina, H., Pedersen, J.: Combating web spam with trustrank. In: 13th International Conference on Very Large Data Bases, pp. 576–587 (2004)
12. He, Y., Zhong, Z., Krasser, S., Tang, Y.: Mining dns for malicious domain registrations. In: CollaborateCom, pp. 1–6. IEEE (2010)
13. Lever, C., Antonakakis, M., Reaves, B., Traynor, P., Lee., W.: The core of the matter: analyzing malicious traffic in cellular carriers. In: Proceedings of the ISOC Network & Distributed System Security Symposium (NDSS) (2013)
14. Li, Z., Alrwais, S., Xie, Y., Yu, F., Wang, X.: Finding the linchpins of the dark web: a study on topologically dedicated hosts on malicious web infrastructures. In: 2013 IEEE Symposium on Security and Privacy, pp. 112–126 (2013)
15. Li, Z., Zhang, K., Xie, Y., Yu, F., Wang, X.: Knowing your enemy: understanding and detecting malicious web advertising. In: 2012 ACM Conference on Computer and Communications Security, pp. 674–686 (2012)
16. Lookout: 2014 mobile threat report. http://goo.gl/9aYO9B
17. Lookout: Security alert: Shoot the bulk messenger. https://blog.lookout.com/blog/2013/12/19/shoot-the-bulk-messenger/
18. Lookout: You are a winner! or are you? the walmart gift card scam. http://goo.gl/WX6ps.

19. Lookout: U.S. targeted by coercive mobile ransomware impersonating the FBI, July 2014. https://blog.lookout.com/blog/2014/07/16/scarepakage
20. McAfee: Mcafee labs threats report. http://mcafee.com/us/resources/reports/rp-quarterly-threat-q3-2014.pdf
21. Murynets, I., Piqueras Jover, R.: Crime scene investigation: Sms spam data analysis. In: Proceedings of the 2012 ACM Conference on Internet Measurement Conference, pp. 441–452 (2012)
22. Nadji, Y., Antonakakis, M., Perdisci, R., Lee, W.: Connected colors: unveiling the structure of criminal networks. In: Stolfo, S.J., Stavrou, A., Wright, C.V. (eds.) RAID 2013. LNCS, vol. 8145, pp. 390–410. Springer, Heidelberg (2013)
23. Wikipedia: Whois. http://en.wikipedia.org/wiki/Whois
24. Wolda, H.: Similarity indices, sample size and diversity. Oecologia **50**(3), 296–302 (1981)
25. Yadav, S., Reddy, A.K.K., Reddy, A.N., Ranjan, S.: Detecting algorithmically generated malicious domain names. In: Proceedings of the 10th ACM SIGCOMM Conference on Internet Measurement, pp. 48–61 (2010)

# Distance-Based Trustworthiness Assessment for Sensors in Wireless Sensor Networks

Jongho Won[✉] and Elisa Bertino

Computer Science, Purdue University, West Lafayette, Indiana, USA
{won12,bertino}@purdue.edu
https://cs.purdue.edu

**Abstract.** Wireless Sensor Networks (WSNs) have been substituting for human senses to make human lives better by monitoring the environment and providing intelligence. Collected sensor data are used to make decisions as a human does. Therefore, providing trustworthy sensor data is crucial to make correct decisions. However, faulty sensors can give incorrect information. In addition, since sensors are usually deployed in unattended areas and can be compromised, cryptographic approaches are insufficient. To address this problem, we propose a distance-based trustworthiness assessment scheme. In our scheme, a centralized trust assessment module outputs an absolute trust score of each sensed value and the trust score of each sensor. The trust scores of sensed values are calculated based on the differences of sensed values provided by a sensor and its neighbors and the physical distances from the neighbors. Our simulation results show that our scheme outputs practical and accurate trust scores in a realistic environment where the sensed values of interest gradually change over the monitored areas.

**Keywords:** Trustworthiness assessment in wireless sensor networks · Sensor trust assessment · Sensor trust management

## 1 Introduction

Along with the advance in sensors, network technologies and embedded devices, sensor nodes in Wireless Sensor Networks (WSNs) have now become tiny and inexpensive. In the near future, WSNs will behave as a digital skin providing a virtual sense for physical environments. Collected sensed data can be utilized for many critical tasks ranging from military tasks to civilian tasks such as surveillance, fire detection, industrial facility monitoring and soil monitoring for precision agriculture. In such applications, hundreds to thousands of tiny sensor nodes are densely deployed and large amounts of sensed data are collected. The collected sensed data are then used to make critical decisions.

However, since sensors are usually made with cheap hardware and deployed in unattended hostile areas, they are exposed to the risks of being compromised by attackers. Once sensor nodes are compromised, they may endanger the system by injecting malicious false data. In addition, as pointed out in [5], in real

© Springer International Publishing Switzerland 2015
M. Qiu et al. (Eds.): NSS 2015, LNCS 9408, pp. 18–31, 2015.
DOI: 10.1007/978-3-319-25645-0_2

applications, lots of incorrect sensed data are reported by faulty sensors. There-fore, providing indications about the trustworthiness of collected data to data users is crucial in order for these users to make correct decisions.

Approaches to score sensors or sensed data based on reputation or trust man-agement schemes have been proposed. Such approaches can be categorized into *distributed* and *centralized* approaches. In the distributed approaches [5,7,9], each sensor has its own trust management module which evaluates the trust scores of its neighbors. On the other hand, centralized approaches [6] assess the trustworthiness of all sensors using the collected sensed data from the system perspective. Since WSNs are self-organized and cooperatively operated in a dis-tributed manner for networking or data aggregation, many schemes have focused on how each sensor node builds trust scores about its neighbors. For example, each sensor counts selfish routing misbehavior of its neighbors or compares its sensed value with the sensed values of its neighbors. Then, each sensor node establishes the trust scores of neighbors from its own point of view. While a distributed approach is best suited for local decisions such as routing and data aggregation, a centralized approach is required in order to make decisions from the perspective of system operations. For example, by using the trust scores about sensors, system administrators can execute corrective follow-up actions such as replacing faulty or abnormal sensors, i.e. sensors with low trust scores, with new sensors. In this paper, we focus on the centralized approach.

Although previous approaches provide effective methodologies for trustwor-thiness assessment of sensors in WSNs, none of them have taken into account the physical distances among each pair of sensors for calculating their trust scores. In this work, we focus on the fact that the closer two sensors are, the more consistent their sensed values are. A centralized trust assessment module then computes absolute trust scores of sensors based on their sensed values and their physical distances. The simulation results show that our trustworthiness assessment scheme provides practical and accurate trust scores in realistic envi-ronments where the sensed values of interest gradually change over the monitored areas.

The rest of the paper is organized as follows. Section 2 discusses related work and Section 3 introduces some motivating examples. Section 4 presents our distance-based trustworthiness assessment scheme. Section 5 reports the simulation results and Section 6 outlines conclusions and future work.

## 2    Related Work

The self-organizing nature of WSNs calls for distributed trust management schemes [5,7,9]. Zhang et al. [9] proposed a trust-based framework for secure data aggregation. The trustworthiness of each sensor in one cluster is evaluated by using an information theoretic metrics under the assumption that multiple nodes in one cluster sense the mean of the physical environment parameter of interest independently. Probst et al. [7] presented a trust establishment scheme based on computing statistical trust and a confidence interval around the trust based on direct and indirect experiences of neighbor's behavior. Ganeriwal et al. [5] proposed a framework by which each sensor node maintains reputation metrics for neighbors. Using an outlier detection algorithm, the actions of neighbors are classified as either cooperative or noncooperative and then the classification results are given as input to a beta reputation system for the trust representation of neighbors. Notice that such distributed schemes require additional memory and computational resources for sensors. Furthermore, using such schemes for already deployed WSNs is difficult since they require software updates all sensor nodes.

Lim et al. [6] proposed a centralized scheme which evaluates the trust score of values and nodes based on the sensed values and their provenance. The trust score of a sensed value and the trust score of a sensor node periodically evolve according to a cyclic framework by affecting each other. The scheme assumes that the set of sensed values which are affected by an event can be determined. Also, it assumes that the set of sensed values are equally affected by the event. Based on these assumptions, the scheme calculates the mean ($\mu$) and standard deviation ($\sigma$) of all sensed values which are affected by the same event. Using $\mu$ and $\sigma$, the distribution is modeled as a normal distribution $\mathcal{N}(\mu, \sigma)$. Then, each sensed value is scored based on the distribution. That is, the closer the sensed value provided by a sensor is to the mean, the higher trust score is assigned to the sensor. However, in ordinary monitoring applications, this approach has four problems. First, defining an event may be impossible in many applications or contexts. Second, determining the set of sensed values which are affected by an event is difficult. Third, even if we can identify an event and the sensors affected by the event, the event does not equally affect all these sensors. Fourth, the scheme assigns relative trust scores to sensors since the scores are calculated based on the distribution. That is, even though all sensors are working well, low trust scores may be assigned to some sensors. These problems are discussed in detail in Section 3.

Unlike [6], in this paper, we do not consider the provenance of a sensed value. In [6], when a sensed value passes through intermediate sensor nodes, the trust score of the sensed value is dominated by the worst node with the smallest trust score since a malicious intermediate node may change the sensed value passing the node. However, this assumption is too conservative since, as discussed in [5], abnormal sensed values can be generated due to other reasons such as a low voltage level, a faulty sensor module or abnormal natural phenomenon. We believe that compromised nodes can be detected by distributed schemes [5,8][1].

None of the previous approaches take into account the correlation between sensed values and their physical distances in the computation of the trust scores. The physical distances between sensors are known by the system administrator since location information of sensors as well as their sensed values are important factors to be considered for decisions.

---

[1] Notice that distributed schemes can be combined with centralized schemes to make the system more robust.

## 3    Motivating Examples

The typical applications of WSNs monitor large areas with hundreds or thousands of sensors. In these applications, the sensed values reported by sensors at a specific area may be very different from the sensed values reported by sensors at a different area. For instance, consider the situation where sensors monitor the temperature in a forest reserve as shown in Fig. 1. At night all sensors may

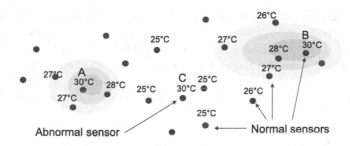

**Fig. 1.** An illustration of WSNs monitoring temperature

provide similar temperature values. However, in the daytime, the temperature values may differ according to the presence of direct sunlight or the angle between the sun's rays and the surface. Assume that sensor $A$ and $B$ are normal, but sensor $C$ is abnormal. Sensor $A$ and sensor $B$ give a temperature of 30°C while most of sensors, except sensor $C$, give a temperature of under 30°C. In this situation, we cannot determine the set of sensors which are affected by an event. If possible, the sensors may not be equally influenced by the event. Nonetheless, if

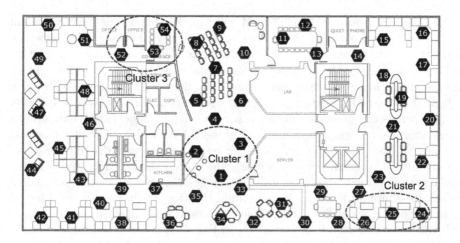

**Fig. 2.** The topology of sensors in the Intel lab

we define this kind of situation (without a specific event) as an 'event' and utilize the normal distribution-based approach [6], the event will include the entire sensed values. As a result, low trust scores will be assigned to sensor $A$ and $B$ even if the values they provide are correct. Their trust scores may increase at night since all sensors may provide similar temperature values and trust scores are periodically re-assessed. However, the trust scores of sensor $A$ and $B$ will eventually become low throughout the cyclic procedure if temperature values at sensor $A$ and $B$ are higher than others in every daytime since such bad effects are accumulated.

This phenomenon can be verified in a real test-bed experiment. We analyzed the data collected from 54 sensors deployed in the Intel Berkeley Research lab [1]. As shown in Fig. 2, we focused on 9 sensors in three different areas. Sensor 1, 2 and 3 (cluster 1) are located in the center of the lab. Sensor 24, 25 and 26 (cluster 2) are located at the corner of the lab and sensor 52, 53 and 54 (cluster 3) are located in a conference room. Fig. 3(a) shows the temperature values of

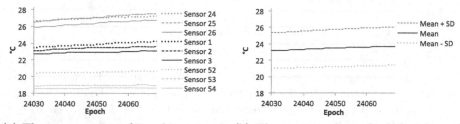

(a) The temperature values of 9 sensors in 3 different areas

(b) The mean and standard deviation of temperature values from 54 sensors

**Fig. 3.** Intel lab data from 9:13 AM to 9:32 AM

the 9 sensors from 9:13 AM to 9:32 AM and Fig. 3(b) shows the mean value and standard deviation of temperature values generated by all sensors. The sensors in cluster 1 output temperature values near the mean while the sensors in cluster 2 and 3 output temperature values far from the mean value. These differences are due to various factors such as heat from PCs, the positions of air-conditioners or heat from the sun. Such experimental results confirm two facts. First, even though there is no specific event, some sensors output higher/lower temperature values than the mean plus/minus the standard deviation. Therefore, sensors in cluster 2 and 3 will get low trust scores if the normal distribution-based approach [6] is utilized. Second, sensors which are close to each other produce similar outputs due to the heat diffusion process. Although we did not include the results of humidity due to the page limit, the same phenomena were observed.

In this paper, we utilize the fact that the sensed value of a sensor is consistent with the sensed values of its neighbors. In Fig. 1, the trustworthiness of sensor $A$ and sensor $B$ is supported by their neighbors, while the trustworthiness of sensor $C$ is not supported by its neighbors.

## 4    Distance-Based Trustworthiness Assessment

In this section, we present our distance-based trustworthiness assessment for sensors based on their sensed values and their physical distances.

### 4.1    Overview of the Scheme

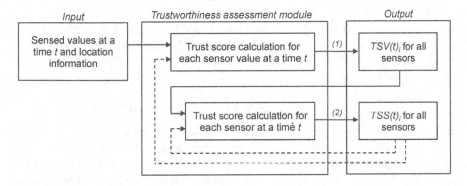

**Fig. 4.** Overview of the trust score calculation procedure. $TSV(t)_i$ is the trust score of the sensed value generated by sensor $i$ at a time $t$. $TSS(t)_i$ is the trust score of sensor $i$ at a time $t$.

Our trustworthiness assessment has two steps. In the first step, the trust score of each sensed value generated by sensor $i$ at a time $t$, i.e., $TSV(t)_i$, is calculated by using as input: all sensed values at a time $t$, sensor location information, and the previous trust scores. In the second step, the trust score of sensor $i$ at a time $t$, i.e., $TSS(t)_i$, is calculated using the previous trust score of sensor $i$, i.e., $TSS(t-1)_i$, and $TSV(t)_i$. The trust scores of sensors evolve through this cyclic framework as time passes. The trust scores in our scheme range in the interval [0,1].

### 4.2    Details of the Scheme

In the first step, the trust score of a sensed value generated by sensor $i$, $TSV(t)_i$, is derived by calculating the weighted mean ($\tau$) of differences between the value of sensor $i$ and the values of the $i$'s neighbors as follows:

$$TSV(t)_i = \frac{1}{1+|\tau|}, \quad \tau = \frac{\sum_{j=0}^{n} \frac{(v(t)_i - v(t)_j) \times TSS(t-1)_j^{\beta}}{d_{i,j}^{\alpha}}}{\sum_{j=0}^{n} \frac{TSS(t-1)_j^{\beta}}{d_{i,j}^{\alpha}}}, \tag{1}$$

where $n$ is the number of neighbors of sensor $i$, $v(t)_i$ is the sensed value provided by sensor $i$ at a time $t$ and $d_{i,j}$ is the distance between $i$ and $j$. There are two weighting factors. One is the distance between sensor $i$ and its neighbors and the other is the trust score of sensor $i$'s neighbors. $\alpha$ ($\geq 0$) is a system parameter which controls the effect of $d_{i,j}$. The bigger $\alpha$ is, the larger the influence of the neighbors which are close to $i$ becomes. $\beta$ ($\geq 0$) is also a system parameter which controls the effect of the previous trust score of the neighbor, i.e., $TSS(t-1)_j$. The bigger $\beta$ is, the larger the influence of the neighbors with high trust scores becomes. If $\alpha$ and $\beta$ are 0, $\tau$ is just the mean of value differences regardless of $d_{i,j}$ and $TSS(t-1)_j$, respectively. If the sensed value $v(t)_i$ is consistent with the sensed values of its neighbor, $TSV(t)_i$ becomes close to 1. Otherwise, $TSV(t)_i$ becomes close to 0.

In the second step, to obtain the trust score of sensor $i$ at a time $t$, i.e., $TSS(t)_i$, the current trust score of the sensed value provided by sensor $i$, i.e., $TSV(t)_i$, and the previously accumulated historic score $TSS(t-1)_i$ are taken into account as follows:

$$TSS(t)_i = w \times TSV(t)_i + (1-w) \times TSS(t-1)_i, (0 \leq w \leq 1), \qquad (2)$$

where constant $w$ represents how fast the trust score of the sensor evolves as the cycle is repeated. The larger $w$ is, the more important the recent trust scores are. In other words, if $w$ is large, the trust score of a sensor will evolve fast. In contrast, if $w$ is small, the trust score of a sensor will evolve slowly. Fig. 5 shows

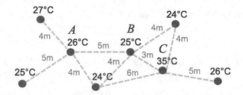

**Fig. 5.** Example scenario. Dashed lines represent neighbor relationships.

an example scenario at a time $t$ when $\alpha$ and $\beta$ are both 1 and $w$ is 0.5. Assume that the initial $TSS(t)$s of all sensors are 0.5 at the time $t$ and the sensed values do not change throughout this example. Also, assume that sensor $A$ and sensor $B$ are normal, whereas sensor $C$ is abnormal. At the time $t$, $TSV(t)_A$, $TSV(t)_B$ and $TSV(t)_C$ are 0.58, 0.25 and 0.09, respectively. Sensor $A$ provides the sensed value with the highest trust score since the sensed value is consistent with the sensed values of its neighbors, whereas sensor $C$ provides the sensed value with the lowest trust score since the sensed value is not consistent with the sensed values of its neighbors. Notice that $TSV(t)_B$ is much lower than $TSV(t)_A$ even though $TSV(t)_B$ is also normal since one of its close neighbors, that is, sensor $C$ provides the abnormal sensed value (35°C). However, $TSV(t+\delta)_B$ eventually becomes high as $\delta$ increases due to the following reason. $TSS(t+\delta)_C$ becomes low as $\delta$ increases and thus, when $TSV(t+\delta)_B$ is calculated, the sensed value of sensor $C$ is taken into account to a slight extent (see Eq. 1). In this example, at the time $t+3$, $TSV(t+3)_A$, $TSV(t+3)_B$ and $TSV(t+3)_C$ evolve to 0.58, 0.55 and 0.09, respectively. The trust score of the sensed value provided by sensor $B$ increases from 0.25 to 0.55, and thus the trust score of sensor $B$ also increases.

## 4.3 Minimum Trust Score of a Normal Sensed Value

Our trustworthiness assessment scheme generates absolute trust scores for sensed values. Under the assumption that a physical phenomenon gradually changes over a physical space, we can derive the minimum trust score of a sensed value $TSV_{min}$ produced by a normal sensor at a time specific $t$. To obtain $TSV_{min}$, we consider the case in which a normal sensor $i$ is located at the peak of a physical phenomenon as shown in Fig. 6. For instance, imagine that a sensor is located at a heat source such as a heater. We assume that the monitoring value decreases

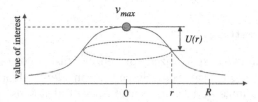

**Fig. 6.** An illustration which shows that a normal sensor $i$ is at the peak of the monitoring values ($r = 0$). $v_{max}$ is the highest value and $r$ is the distance from the peak point. $U(r, t)$ is a monotonic increasing function of $r$ until $r \leq R$ at a time $t$.

from the peak value, i.e., $v_{max}$, according to a monotonic increasing function $U(r, t)$. For instance, if $U(r, t)$ is the heat equation, the function is a parabolic partial differential equation describing the distribution of heat in a given region over time [4]. For this analysis, we assume that $U(r, t)$ equally increases in any direction as $r$ ($\leq R$) increases. $R$ is the maximum distance within which sensors are considered as neighbors of sensor $i$. We also assume that sensors are evenly deployed and $\beta$ is 0. We only consider sensors on the inside of the deployed area since sensors at the border of the area have fewer neighbors. Then, $TSV(t)_i$ is calculated as follows:

$$TSV(t)_i = \frac{1}{1 + |\tau'|}, \tag{3}$$

$$\tau' = \frac{\int_0^R \frac{U(r,t) \times \rho \times 2\pi r}{r^\alpha} dr}{\int_0^R \frac{\rho \times 2\pi r}{r^\alpha} dr} = \frac{\int_0^R \frac{U(r,t)}{r^{\alpha-1}} dr}{\int_0^R \frac{1}{r^{\alpha-1}} dr}, \tag{4}$$

where $\rho$ is the density of sensors. If we set $\alpha$ to 1 and the maximum gradient of $U(r, t)$ is $\gamma$ ($\gamma > 0$) at a time $t$, then $\tau'$ is less than or equal to $\frac{\gamma \times R}{2}$ as follows:

$$\tau' = \frac{\int_0^R U(r,t) dr}{\int_0^R dr} \leq \frac{\int_0^R \gamma \times r dr}{\int_0^R dr} = \frac{\gamma \times R}{2}. \tag{5}$$

Therefore, $TSV(t)_i$ must be greater than or equal to $\frac{2}{2+\gamma R}$.

$$TSV(t)_i \geq TSV_{min} = \frac{1}{1 + \frac{\gamma R}{2}} = \frac{2}{2 + \gamma R} \tag{6}$$

For instance, if $R$ is 70 (m) and $\gamma$ is 0.05 (°C/$m$), the minimum trust score of a normal value sensor should be greater than 0.36. Therefore, if the trust score of a sensed value is greater than 0.36, the sensed value can be considered as a trustworthy one.

## 5    Simulation

In this section, we present our performance evaluation through simulations. We first describe the simulation settings, and then present the simulation results.

### 5.1    Simulation Setting

We developed a simulator specialized for sensor trust assessment and focused on the performance of our algorithm. Since the considered algorithms are purely based on sensor readings and their locations, we did not use general network simulators such as TOSSIM [3] and NS-2 [2].

For the simulations, 250 sensors are randomly deployed in a 400m×400m area. $n$ IDs are assigned to the sensors from 0 to 249 as shown in Fig. 7. Sensors from 0 to 229 are normal, while sensors from 230 to 249 are abnormal. Each sensor reports 100 temperature values at a time $t$ ($0 \leq t \leq 99$). Both $\alpha$ and $\beta$ are set to 1 and $w$ is set to 0.2. A temperature value of a normal sensor is sampled from the normal distribution with the mean of 25 and the standard deviation of 2, i.e., $\mathcal{N}(25, 2)$.

The maximum neighbor range $R$ is set to 70m, which means that the neighbors of sensor $i$ are the sensors within 70m of sensor $i$. Sensors at the center of the area have approximately 24 neighbors, while sensors at the corners have approximately 6 neighbors. If $R$ is too small, the accuracy of trust scores becomes low since only a few neighbors might be taken into account in order to compute the trust score of a sensor. As $R$ increases, the accuracy increases with the increased computational cost. However, if $R$ becomes larger than a certain level, the accuracy improvement becomes limited since distant neighbors scarcely affect the trust score of a sensor.

A heat source is located at (300, 300) and the mean temperature of the peak point is set to 45°C. From the peak point, the temperature linearly decreases with the gradient of 0.05 (°C/$m$). If the distance from the peak point is greater than 400m, the temperature does not decrease. Thus, in our simulation, $TSV_{min}$ is 0.36. We varied two parameters $\Delta_{mean}$ and $\Delta_{sd}$ for abnormal sensors. $\Delta_{mean}$ and $\Delta_{sd}$ are added to the mean and the standard deviation of the normal distribution of a normal sensor, respectively. That is, temperature values of an abnormal sensor are sampled from $\mathcal{N}(25 + \Delta_{mean}, 2 + \Delta_{sd})$.

Throughout the simulations, we compare two schemes: our scheme and the normal distribution-based scheme. The normal distribution-based scheme calculates the trust score of a sensed value based on the normal distribution which is modeled by using all sensed values at each time as in [6,9].

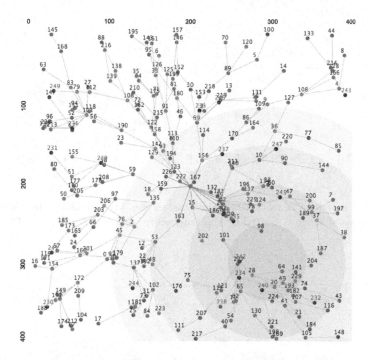

**Fig. 7.** Simulation topology

## 5.2   Simulation Result

First, we obtained the trust scores of sensors when all sensors are correctly working, i.e, $\delta_{mean} = 0$ and $\delta_{sd} = 0$.

Fig. 8 shows the sorted trust scores of all sensors when the normal distribution-based scheme is used. Even if there is no abnormal sensor, some sensors get low trust scores since the trust scores are relative. As a result, the administrator of the WSNs cannot distinguish whether there are abnormal sensors in the network or not.

However, since our scheme outputs absolute trust scores (see Fig. 9). the administrator of the WSNs can distinguish whether there are abnormal sensors in the network or not under the assumption he/she knows the minimum trust score. Notice that, in this scenario, 26 sensors have lower trust scores than $TSV_{min}$ (=0.36) even though all sensors are normal due to the following reasons. First, the sensors are not perfectly evenly-deployed and some sensors do not have enough neighbors. Second, the sensed values are generated with the standard deviation of 2. Thus, the overall trust scores are lowered. In real applications, $TSV_{min}$ may be estimated at the time of the initial deployment when all sensors are working correctly. If the administrator successfully obtains $TSV_{min}$ for his/her application, he/she can distinguish normal sensors from abnormal sensors and execute follow-up actions such as replacing sensors with trust scores under $TSV_{min}$ with new sensors.

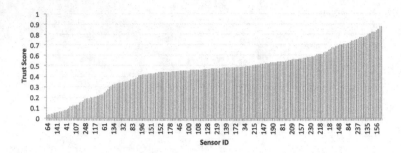

**Fig. 8.** Trust scores of sensors when the trust scores are calculated by the normal distribution-based scheme. Sorted by the trust score ($\delta_{mean} = 0$ and $\delta_{sd} = 0$)

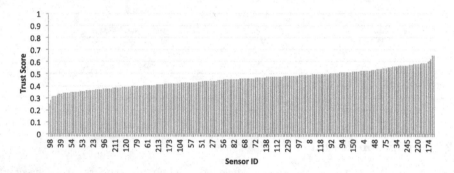

**Fig. 9.** Trust scores of sensors when the trust scores are calculated by our scheme. Sorted by the trust score ($\delta_{mean} = 0$ and $\delta_{sd} = 0$)

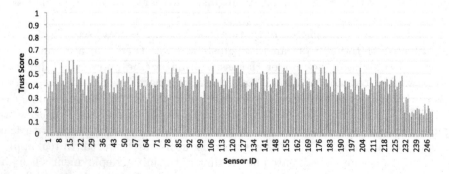

**Fig. 10.** Trust scores of sensors when the trust scores are calculated by our scheme. Sorted by the ID ($\delta_{mean} = 5$ and $\delta_{sd} = 0$)

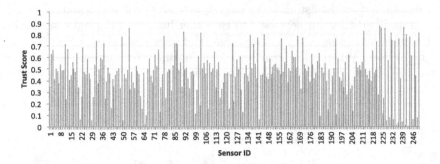

**Fig. 11.** Trust scores of sensors when the trust scores are calculated by the normal distribution-based scheme, Sorted by the ID ($\delta_{mean} = 5$ and $\delta_{sd} = 0$)

Fig. 10 and Fig. 11 show the trust scores of the all sensors when our scheme and the normal distribution-based scheme are used, respectively; $\delta_{mean}$ is set to 5 and $\delta_{sd}$ is set to 0. As shown in Fig. 10, when our scheme is utilized, the trust scores of the sensors from 230 to 249 are distinctly lower than the trust scores of the normal sensors. However, when the normal distribution-based scheme is used, sensors near the peak location get low trust scores since the sensed values provided by them are far from the mean, while sensors at the middle of the slope get higher trust scores than others since they are close to the mean.

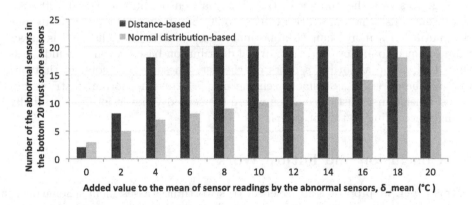

**Fig. 12.** Comparison between our scheme and the normal distribution-based scheme when $\delta_{mean}$ varies from 0 to 20

Fig. 12 shows the number of the abnormal sensors (sensors from 230 to 249) on the bottom 20 trust score sensor list when $\delta_{mean}$ varies from 0 to 20. When all sensors are correctly working, in our scheme, 2 abnormal sensors are included on the bottom 20 list. However, when $\delta_{mean}$ is only 4, our scheme includes 18 abnormal sensors on the list and when $\delta_{mean}$ is 6, all the 20 abnormal sensors are included on the list by our scheme. On the other hand, the normal distribution-based scheme cannot include as many abnormal sensors on the bottom 20 list as our scheme does. When $\delta_{mean}$ reaches 20, the normal distribution-based scheme can include all the 20 abnormal sensors on the list.

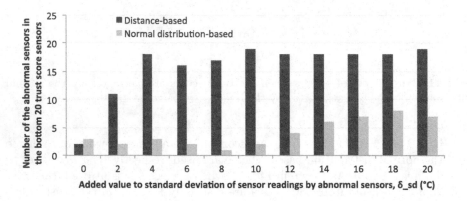

**Fig. 13.** Comparison between our scheme and the normal distribution-based scheme when $\delta_{sd}$ varies from 0 to 20

Fig. 13 shows the number of the abnormal sensors on the bottom 20 trust score sensor list when $\delta_{sd}$ varies from 0 to 20. Similarly to the prior result, our scheme includes more than 16 abnormal sensors on the list when $\delta_{sd}$ is larger than or equal to 4. However, the normal distribution-based scheme includes less than half of the abnormal sensors on the list. These results confirm that our distance-based trust assessment scheme outperforms the normal distribution-based scheme in realistic scenarios where the sensed value of interest gradually changes according to the locations.

## 6    Conclusion and Future Work

In this paper, we propose a novel sensor trustworthiness assessment scheme using the distances between sensors. In the cyclic framework, the trust score of a sensed value is evaluated based on the fact the sensed values are correlated with their positions. In the first step, the trust score of a sensed value is calculated using the sensed values of its neighbors, their trust scores and the distances from the neighbors. Then, the trust score of a sensor evolves at each time by taking the new trust score of its sensed value into account. Our simulation results confirm that our trustworthiness assessment scheme provides practical and accurate trust scores of sensors in a realistic scenario. As future work, we plan to investigate extensions of our approach to reliably assess sensor trustworthiness in presence of collusion attacks. We also plan to investigate how our approach needs to be extended/modified with dealing with different physical phenomena.

**Acknowledgments.** The work reported in this paper has been partially supported by the Purdue Cyber Center and by the National Science Foundation under grant CNS-1111512.

# References

1. Intel lab data. http://db.csail.mit.edu/labdata/labdata.html
2. ns2. http://www.isi.edu/nsnam/ns/
3. Tossim. http://tinyos.stanford.edu/tinyos-wiki/index.php/tossim
4. Cannon, J.R.: The one-dimensional heat equation (1984)
5. Ganeriwal, S., Balzano, L.K., Srivastava, M.B.: Reputation-based framework for high integrity sensor networks. ACM Trans. Sen. Netw. 4(3), 15:1–15:37 (2008)
6. Lim, H.-S., Moon, Y.-S., Bertino, E.: Provenance-based trustworthiness assessment in sensor networks. In: Proceedings of the Seventh International Workshop on Data Management for Sensor Networks, DMSN 2010, pp. 2–7. ACM, New York (2010)
7. Probst, M., Kasera, S.: Statistical trust establishment in wireless sensor networks. In: 2007 International Conference on Parallel and Distributed Systems, vol. 2, pp. 1–8, December 2007
8. Zhang, Q., Yu, T., Ning, P.: A framework for identifying compromised nodes in wireless sensor networks. ACM Trans. Inf. Syst. Secur. 11(3), 12:1–12:37 (2008)
9. Zhang, W., Das, S., Liu, Y.: A trust based framework for secure data aggregation in wireless sensor networks. In: 2006 3rd Annual IEEE Communications Society on Sensor and Ad Hoc Communications and Networks, SECON 2006, vol. 1, pp. 60–69, September 2006

# Isolation of Multiple Anonymous Attackers in Mobile Networks

Brian Ricks$^{(\boxtimes)}$ and Patrick Tague

Carnegie Mellon University, Mountain View, USA
{brian.ricks,patrick.tague}@sv.cmu.edu

**Abstract.** Many mobile wireless networks unintentionally provide opportunity for attackers to launch anonymous attacks or spoof other users, often without fear of being caught. It's often ideal for network carriers to block all traffic from an attacker, not just the attack traffic, for example to stop any concurrent attacks which cannot be detected by the carrier. We present an approach to detect common attacks at the access point, and leverage this with packet clustering to block all traffic originating from attackers during an attack. To achieve packet clustering, we utilize received signal strength at the access point to properly cluster attack packets according to each unique attacker, and further classify all other packets according to these clusters. Our approach is designed with attacker and legitimate user mobility in mind, low memory overhead, and is scalable to many simultaneous attackers. Our experimental results show very high classification accuracy, sensitivity and specificity.

## 1 Introduction

Preventing malicious behavior is an important challenge for network carriers. Such behavior can not only be detrimental to a carrier's legitimate customers, but can also be a liability issue for the carrier if such attacks are traced back to the carrier network as the source. While in traditional networks blocking such a malicious user may have entailed simply blocking the interface to which that user is connected, the problem becomes more difficult in modern wireless networks, where users are not physically connected to the network, but rather wirelessly connected to *access points* (APs). To further complicate the situation, wireless users are often mobile, such as with cellular networks, and they may hop between different access points in the carrier network.

Mobile networks which support and serve users using public shared key, or open networks, have additional challenges. In these networks, users are trusted simply if they know the shared key, or users are not trusted at all. Often times authentication reduces to mapping parameters to users, such as MAC address or IP address. As such mappings are easily spoofed by an attacker, for example using MAC addresses is basically an honor system type approach, it in essence reduces the network to one which comprises anonymous users. In other words, under a network environment of weak authentication or no authentication at all, we can treat the users as anonymous. Not only can this result in attackers

M. Qiu et al. (Eds.): NSS 2015, LNCS 9408, pp. 32–45, 2015.
DOI: 10.1007/978-3-319-25645-0_3

launching attacks in which the carrier network does not know the source, but it also opens the door for attackers to spoof legitimate users during an attack. This culminates into the question: "I, as a mobile network carrier, can detect an ongoing attack, but I don't know from whom the attack is originating. How can I completely block such an anonymous attacker from my network while they are being malicious? And can I do this without accidentally blocking legitimate users?"

We take an approach to answer these questions by first looking back at why some common attacks are difficult to detect accurately, and how next generation architectures may help us to defeat the attacks in ways that are not possible in traditional networks. Then we take a look at some additional properties of next generation mobile networks that may help us to block all traffic from attackers while they are launching attacks over such networks.

Our approach can be broken down into two steps. The first step is attack detection near the sources of attacks, as opposed to the target server or edge routers, exploiting the architecture common to next generation mobile networks. Our approach brings the detectors as close as possible to the end users: right at the first hop. We show how to detect with very high accuracy common flooding attacks which rely on source IP spoofing, such as TCP SYN flooding attacks, by using cross-layer packet header inspection, a feature of next generation mobile networks. As TCP SYN flooding attacks are well researched in the literature, we will use that attack class as a case study in this paper.

The second step is attacker isolation, based on clustering of the ongoing attack(s). For this step we utilize *Received Signal Strength Indicator (RSSI)* to classify all anonymous traffic through the AP as either belonging to an attacker or to a benign user. This is achieved without the carrier network ever knowing the identity of the attacker(s). Blocking all attacker traffic is beneficial to the carrier network as the attacker may be launching concurrent attacks, not all of which the network carrier may be able to detect. This approach works for multiple attackers launching concurrent attacks, and can provide information in terms of the total number of unique attackers launching attacks at any given time.

We validate our approach through rigorous experimentation, which gives very promising results, with very high classification accuracy, sensitivity and specificity both for attacker traffic and user traffic. We further show that our approach is easily deployable, with few parameters, all of which can be tweaked within a broad range without affecting classification accuracy significantly. This allows for quicker deployment without optimal parameter tuning.

The rest of the paper is organized as follows: Section 2 covers relevant background, including related work. Section 3 gives an overview of our approach, divided into detection and isolation steps. Section 4 provides a methodology of our experimental process, results, and in-depth analysis of the results. Section 5 presents some challenges and limitations of our current approach, and finally, Section 6 summarizes our work.

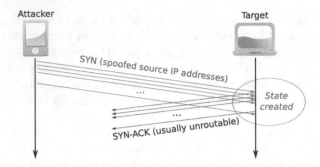

**Fig. 1.** Illustration of a SYN Flooding attack. State is created each time a SYN packet with a unique source IP address is received at the target.

## 2   Preliminaries

Here we define important background and discuss relevant related work.

### 2.1   SYN Flooding Attacks

A *SYN Flooding* attack is class of TCP-based denial-of-service attacks, with the end goal of the attacker to disrupt service at the target TCP server. The attacker accomplishes this by exploiting the natural flow of the three-way TCP connection handshake. Under normal circumstances, a TCP connection is established using the following high-level description:

- The client sends a SYN packet to the TCP server. The TCP server, upon receiving this packet, creates state called a *half-open connection*.
- The TCP server sends back a SYN-ACK packet to the client. The TCP server uses the source IP address of the SYN packet as the destination IP address of the SYN-ACK packet.
- The client, upon receipt of the SYN-ACK packet, sends to the TCP server an ACK packet. This completes the connection, and the half-open connection state at the TCP server is deleted.

The attacker exploits the first step, by sending many SYN packets at once, with the goal of creating one half-open connection state at the TCP server for each SYN packet sent. To accomplish this, the attacker spoofs the source IP address of all generated SYN packets: a different, unique source IP address per SYN packet. If the attacker can send enough SYN packets, the half-open connection buffer will completely fill up before some timeout period, potentially denying service to legitimate clients trying to establish a TCP connection.

Detection of SYN flooding attacks traditionally has utilized statistical methods to model the flooding behavior. In Wang et al. [11] and Ling et al. [6], many of the same assumptions are utilized as our approach, such as cross-layer packet header inspection and detector placement near the source.[1] In Wang et al. [11], SYN flooding attacks are detected by correlating SYN/FIN packet pairs. Their approach however is reliant on the attacker not being aware of the method of detection, and the detector can be defeated by simply generating SYN/FIN pairs to defeat the statistical correlation. Their approach focuses specifically on TCP SYN flooding attacks, and not on attacker isolation.

In Ling et al. [6], ratio of SYN and SYN+ACK packets at an edge router are used to detect a possible SYN flooding attack coming from an intranet connected to the edge router. If an anomaly is detected, then source IP addresses of potentially malicious SYN packets are checked for reachability. While the approach has low computational overhead, it maintains state, and thus an attacker could attack the detection system not only by stateholding attacks, but by inducing the system to ping many potential end hosts for reachability, which could result in a detection system induced denial-of service.

Xiao et al. [13] assumes the detector at the destination TCP server. Their approach also assumes that half-open connections are either due to network congestion or a SYN flooding attack, and similar to Ling et al.[6] uses probing to detect potential SYN floods from suspicious half-open connections. This implies additional bandwidth overhead, though their approach tries to limit attacks on the detection system by sampling a subset of half-open connections as more half-open connections are added to the TCP server.

## 2.2   Received Signal Strength

Received Signal Strength Indicator, or *RSSI*, is a measurement, taken at a wireless receiver, of the perceived power of an incoming radio signal.[2] RSSI measurements are unitless but correspond to measurements in mW or dBm, and the higher the value, the stronger the received signal. In the real-world, accuracy of RSSI measurements can vary greatly from vendor to vendor [1,7].

In this paper, we refer to *per-packet RSSI*, defined as the RSSI measurement taken during the preamble stage of the last 802.11 frame received which comprises a single IP packet. Note that additional noise present during measurement, for example from other transmitters, should not arbitrarily affect the resulting per-packet RSSI value, as any additional signal strong enough to do so should result in a collision with the incoming frame and resulting loss of that frame.

Previous work using RSSI as a metric mostly falls into the category of spatial localization [9,12]. Our work departs in that we are using RSSI not to locate the attacker spatially, but to isolate the attacker's traffic from the network. Sheng et al. [8] uses RSSI measurements to detect MAC address spoofing, however their assumptions would not be suitable in an environment where attacker mobility is present, as any assumptions on attacker mobility could be easily defeated by an attacker by changing their mobility patterns.

---

[1] Here detector placement is at edge routers, which will be one hop away from possible intranets, but usually not one hop away from the users themselves.

[2] By "incoming radio signal", we mean the *strongest* incoming radio signal within the receiving band for a receiver.

Yang et al. [14] and Faria and Cheriton [2] also use RSSI measurements to detect attacks, but factor in mobility. Yang et al. [14] uses a binary partitioning scheme and thresholding to detect spoofing attacks, but requires a training phase, making real-time selective packet blocking difficult. Faria and Cheriton [2] uses multiple concurrent RSSI values from APs and applies sets of user-defined rules to the resulting tuples, called *signalprints*, to detect both spoofing and flooding attacks, though this does not extend to attacker isolation specifically.

## 3   Blocking Anonymous Attackers During an Attack

We discuss our approach for blocking anonymous attackers during an attack by breaking it down into two parts: detection of common attacks, and the isolation of potential attacker traffic. Figure 2 gives an illustration of our approach deployed on a generic mobile network.

### 3.1   Detecting Common Attacks at the Carrier Network

A *common attack* is a well-known attack whose origins are traditionally in the global internet. These attacks normally assume that the network architecture is that of the global internet, a static, wired network of computers. Indeed, the IP protocol suite which drives the internet was built upon these same assumptions.

One goal of common attack detection in next-generation mobile networks is to leverage additional information, and exploit physical constraints within these networks to build a new set of network assumptions which can then be applied to possibly detect such attacks. We currently build our network assumptions based on two characteristics present in next-generation mobile networks:

- Leveraging cross-layer opportunities afforded to us through next generation architectures that do not follow the strict separation of OSI layers [5, 6, 11]. This allows us to probe specific higher layers, such as the network and transport layers, from lower layers, such as the MAC or physical layer.
- Exploiting specific network topology present in these mobile networks. Users wirelessly connect via access points (APs) to the network, making the APs one hop away from the users. Placing detectors at the APs has three distinct advantages. First, the task of attack detection is distributed to multiple entities (APs) within the network as opposed to a centralized entity. Second, detector placement at the APs provides opportunity for reduced overhead in only detecting attacks feasible in their locality. Third, this placement puts the detectors under the jurisdiction of the carrier, as opposed to possibly many entities if placing them outside the carrier network at edge routers [6, 11]. This makes such a solution more viable to real-world deployment.

These characteristics can be applied to extract information from higher layer packet headers at lower layers, and from a specific point in the carrier network to classify a packet as benign or a potential attack packet (Figure 2).

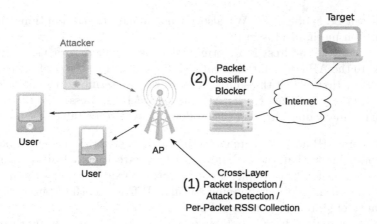

**Fig. 2.** Example mobile network with our approach deployed. The attacker and users are mobile, connected to the AP shown. The AP incorporates the attack detection step of the approach ((**1**) - Section 3.1), while the Packet Classifier handles packet classification and blocking ((**2**) - Section 3.2).

The advantages are two-fold: first, cross-layer packet header inspection allows lower layers a global view of an incoming packet. Second, higher layer packet header information may have specific context at a specific point in the carrier network, but this context may be lost by the time the packet reaches its destination. For example, if such context is in the transport layer and specific to nodes that are not the source or destination, then cross-layer header inspection must be leveraged to extract the contextual information.

To illustrate this approach to packet detection, we discuss a common class of attacks: those which utilize source IP spoofing.

**Attacks Utilizing Source IP Address Spoofing.** This class of attacks usually falls into the category of denial-of-service attacks, and relies on the attacker spoofing the source IP address of packets they generate, to give the appearance of many packets from seemingly many users. The goal is to deny service to legitimate users by exhaustion of some resource, for example server resources or bandwidth. SYN flooding (Section 2.1) and ICMP flood attacks are two well-known examples of denial-of-service attacks which utilize source IP address spoofing.

Our approach works in the following way. Each time an AP receives a packet, a quick cross-layer check is applied to verify that the source IP address of the packet is assigned to a user currently connected to that AP. Traditionally APs are layer 2 devices, and thus do not check (or understand) layer 3 header information. In a cross-layer environment however, no such constraint exists, and thus the AP is trusted for layer 3 inspection. In this case, the detector only needs to understand the layer 3 (network) header. Note that in anonymous environments, there may be no reliable way to differentiate users, as IP addresses or MAC addresses can be spoofed [3]. We also do not make any assumptions that an authentication mechanism is in place.[3]

If the source IP address is determined to be assigned to a user currently connected to the AP (we call this a *valid* IP address), then the packet is deemed not malicious. However, if the source IP address is determined to not belong to any user currently assigned to the AP (an *invalid* IP address), then the packet is potentially malicious. However, the following are also possible:

- If the source IP address belongs to the carrier network's subnet, then there is a probability that the AP may not be aware that a legitimate user is connected to it. For example, a configuration error between APs may have resulted in a mobile user hopping to this AP from another, but without an exchange of state between the APs.
- If the source IP address is outside the carrier network's subnet, then there may be a configuration issue with the user.

To increase our confidence that a potentially malicious packet correlates to an attack, the detector temporarily saves state related to this packet. Then within a small window, if another packet is deemed potentially malicious, it is compared against the previous packet state that was saved. If the source IP addresses do not match, then we deem that an attack is underway. If the source IP addresses match, then the temporary packet state is deleted and new state saved for the current packet. This guarantees that the detector only stores state related to one packet at a time, preventing stateholding attacks against the detector [4].

### 3.2 Isolating Attacker Traffic

While detection of the attacker's malicious activities is good to block those activities specifically, this still won't prevent an attacker from performing other activities, and otherwise using the network during an attack. While it may be beneficial for a carrier to completely block an attacker during an attempted attack for many reasons, one important reason is that an attacker may be launching concurrent attacks, not all of which may be detectable by the carrier network.

In traditional wired networks, blocking an attacker completely from the first hop is trivial. Simply block the interface which the attacker is connected on.[4] However, in wireless networks, all users connected to an AP share the same physical medium, and thus we must utilize other information to correlate an attacker's malicious packets with other traffic originating from the attacker. The anonymous environment and potential mobility of users further complicates this. The carrier network does not know where any of the users physically are located outside the APs that they are connected to.

---

[3] Any authentication mechanism deployed can be used to provide further information to our approach, but an authentication mechanism may also be vulnerable to defeat, and such a discussion is outside the scope of this paper.

[4] Furthermore, when the attacker changes its logical identity, it appears as a new interface, so the L2/L3 linkage is broken.

To solve these problems, we employ an approach that leverages layer 1 information provided at the AP. More specifically, each time an AP receives a packet, providing that it is determined that an attack is underway (Section 3.1), the per-packet RSSI value is recorded. This value is then used to classify the packet as originating from an attacker or other. If the origination is from an attacker, then the packet is dropped.

**The Clustering Procedure.** Our clustering procedure forms clusters based on attack packet RSSI value similarity. The clusters themselves represent a single unique attacker's most recently transmitted attack packet; thus each cluster only has a single data point at any given time, keeping the memory footprint low. We don't keep older data points because of the temporal dependency between an attacker's movement and transmission of packets: older packets simply do not reflect the current mobility state of an attacker.

In an ideal environment, one in which all users are stationary and there is no drift in RSSI measurements, clusters would only comprise members whose RSSI values are identical. However in real-world mobile networks, we have to factor in both attacker mobility and RSSI measurement drift [1,7].

Similarity of two attack packets require a *similarity metric*, to quantify the similarity, and a *similarity threshold*, to provide binary classification (does an attack belong to a cluster or not?). We formally define the similarity metric, $s_{ij}$, as

$$s_{ij} = |PKT_i^{RSSI} - CLS_j^{RSSI}|, \tag{1}$$

where $PKT_i^{RSSI}$ is the per-packet RSSI of attack packet $i$ we are classifying as measured by the AP, and $CLS_j^{RSSI}$ is the most recent per-packet RSSI measurement, taken by the AP, that was assigned to cluster $j$.

We formally define our similarity threshold, $e_{ij}$, as

$$e_{ij} = \Delta t_{ij} * d_u + d_{ap}, \tag{2}$$

where $\Delta t_{ij}$ is the time difference between the timestamp of a new attack packet $i$ recorded at the AP and the timestamp of cluster $j$, $d_u$ is a drift constant which models RSSI drift due to user mobility, and $d_{ap}$ is a drift constant related to RSSI sampling precision at the AP. For stationary users, $e_{ij}$ reduces to a constant term $e_{ij} = d_{ap}$. An attack packet is assigned to the first cluster $j$ in which $s_{ij} <= e_{ij}$. If an attack packet does not meet this criteria for any cluster, a new cluster is created, and the packet assigned to it.

Non-attacker packets are classified using the same approach, except we do not actually assign them to a cluster. Only attack packets (packets detected from the steps in Section 3.1 for example) are assigned to clusters after classification.

When attack packets are first detected for a new attack, we do not consider these packets as comprising an attack until a certain number of *sequential* packets have been assigned to the same cluster (the packets themselves are still dropped as they are invalid). Two attack packets are considered sequential if they are both assigned to the same cluster. We consider an attack to have started when

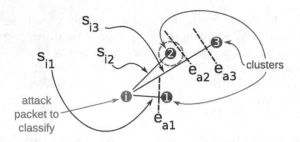

**Fig. 3.** Illustration of the clustering procedure. An attack packet is assigned to the first cluster $j$ in which $s_{ij} <= e_{ij}$. The goal is not to find the 'closest' cluster, but whether the attack packet belongs to an existing cluster or a new one. In this figure, the solid line segments represent $s_{ij}$, with shorter line segments representing greater similarity. Dashed line segments represent $e_{ij}$, with greater distance from attack packet $i$ representing a larger threshold. Visually, $s_{ij} > e_{ij}$ if the dashed line segment for cluster $j$ resides between the cluster and attack packet $i$. Here, attack packet $i$ would be assigned to cluster 2. The key is that similarity alone does not determine cluster assignment, but the relationship between packet RSSI similarity and user mobility.

the number of sequential packets observed, $p_{num}$, reaches a threshold parameter, $c_{pre}$. More formally, an attack is considered ongoing when $p_{num} > c_{pre}$.

Clusters are not permanent: a threshold parameter, $c_{to}$, is used to determine when an attack is no longer ongoing (ceases to exist). If no new attack packets have been assigned to a cluster within $c_{to}$, then the cluster is deleted. More formally, if an attack packet is assigned to a cluster at time $t$, then another attack packet must be assigned to the same cluster at some future time $t_{next}$, such that $t_{next} < (t + c_{to})$.

Note that our clustering procedure is independent of the detection approach. As long as there is some method to differentiate attack packets from all other packets, this clustering procedure (and the traffic isolation approach in general) can be used.

## 4    Experiments

Here we present our experimental methodology and results from our experiments.

### 4.1    Methodology

We implemented our approach in the OMNeT++ simulation framework [10]. We modeled a WiFi network with a single AP, and variable attackers and other mobile users of the network. While WiFi networks are not next-generation in themselves, all the basic building blocks for our required architecture are included in OMNeT++'s Inet WiFi simulation models. We extended these models with various support which we needed, such as cross-layer packet inspection.

We ran a total of five experiments on the simulated mobile network, each one increasing the number of attackers and benign users. The first scenario served as

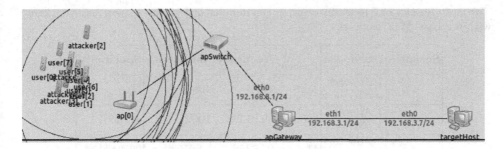

**Fig. 4.** Scenario 5 at $t = 0$. Notice that all the attackers and users are grouped tightly together. They all move southbound at differing velocities. The attackers are shown in red.

a baseline, with only a single attacker. The other 4 scenarios consisted of between 1-4 attackers, and 5-8 benign users. Each scenario was executed for 120 seconds. The parameters were set as follows: $d_u = 0.1$, $d_{ap} = 0$, $c_{pre} = 2$, $c_{to} = 1s$.

The attackers each launched SYN flooding attacks, with a start time of anywhere between 1-4 seconds. This was done intentionally to illustrate the progression of individual attacker detection (Figure 8). Both the attackers and benign users send a steady stream of UDP traffic.

Both the attackers and benign users are mobile, with velocities randomly selected from a uniform distribution of the range 0.2-2.5 m/s. This roughly corresponds to a range between a slow walk to a brisk jog. All attackers and benign users remain at their originally selected velocities throughout a scenario.

The following list explains the metrics used for interpreting the results:

- **Accuracy:** The percentage of correct classifications of all traffic.
- **Sensitivity:** The percentage of correct classifications of traffic originating from attackers. The complement of this is the false negative rate.
- **Specificity:** The percentage of correct classifications of traffic originating from benign users. The complement of this is the false positive rate.

### 4.2   Experimental Results

Table 1 gives an overview of the classification tests performed against our approach. Some highlights include a 100% accuracy rate when only an attacker is present. This provides a good baseline to make sure $d_u$ is set high enough to properly put all attack packets into the correct clusters. In the case of a single attacker, there should only be one cluster. Even as we add more attackers, and more benign users, the accuracy, sensitivity, and specificity remain very high.

Figure 5 illustrates the $e_{ij}$ and $s_{ij}$ plots for the scenario 1 TCP SYN packets from the attacker. $s_{ij}$ correlates to the path the attacker is following, in this case a straight line. We set $d_u$ high enough as to compensate for the attacker's mobility, as can be seen by the relation of the $s_{ij}$ and $e_{ij}$ plots in Figure 5. Setting $d_u$ (or $d_{ap}$) too high can result in a higher false positive rate.

**Table 1.** Results of 5 scenarios varying the number of legitimate users and attackers within a basic WiFi network.

| Scenario | Description | Total Packets | Accuracy | Sensitivity | Specificity |
|----------|-------------|---------------|----------|-------------|-------------|
| 1 | *1 Attacker 0 Users* | 1186 | 100% | 100% | N/A |
| 2 | *1 Attacker 5 Users* | 9080 | 99.912% | 100% | 99.899% |
| 3 | *2 Attackers 5 Users* | 11258 | 97.735% | 94.059% | 99.406% |
| 4 | *3 Attackers 5 Users* | 12360 | 98.115% | 95.887% | 99.513% |
| 5 | *4 Attackers 8 Users* | 18580 | 99.128% | 99.215% | 99.086% |

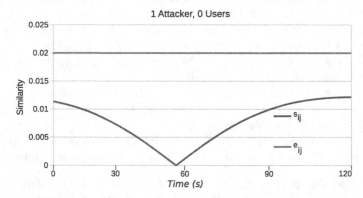

**Fig. 5.** $e_{ij}$ (orange - top) and $s_{ij}$ (blue - bottom) plots for scenario 1.

False positives can occur when an attacker is transmitting an attack packet at nearly the same time as a benign user transmitting a packet, and the per-packet RSSI readings of both packets are very close, resulting in a low $s_{ij}$. As can be seen from in Figure 6, this does not occur very often, though the probability of this occurring does increase slightly as the number of benign users increases. Adding another point of reference, such as another AP nearby, can dramatically lower the false positive rate.

False negatives can occur when $d_u$ is set too low. For example, if we set $d_u = 0.2$ and rerun scenario 3, our sensitivity increases from 94.059% to 98.294%. The reason is that $d_u$ cannot always fully compensate for all attacker mobility, such as if an attacker is moving faster than anticipated, or sending attack traffic much slower than what is expected for the attack type. The trade-off is often a lower specificity, in this case decreasing from 99.406% to 98.798%.

Figure 8 shows the number of attacker clusters versus time, for scenario 5. The 4 attackers start the SYN flooding attack at slightly offset start times from

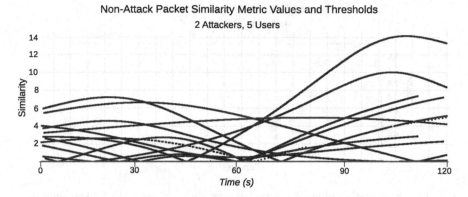

Fig. 6. $e_{ij}$ (red - bottom) and $s_{ij}$ (blue) versus time during scenario 3 for benign user packets. Notice that because the $s_{ij}$ plots are above the similarity thresholds, these packets will not be classified as originating from an attacker.

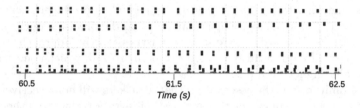

Fig. 7. $e_{ij}$ (red - bottom - circles) and $s_{ij}$ (blue - squares) of a 2 second zoomed in section of Figure 6

one another, resulting in the steep slope at the beginning of the graph. There is a one-to-one correspondence between attackers and clusters. In cases where $d_u$ is set artificially low (or $d_{ap}$ in some cases), many more clusters than attackers may be created at specific times, resulting in a very large decrease in accuracy.

## 5   Limitations and Future Work

Our current approach is limited to blocking attacker traffic during an ongoing attack. We are currently working on extending this approach to predict malicious user traffic after an attack has ceased. This will allow for the approach to continuing blocking multiple concurrent attacks which may actually be ongoing after the detectable attacks have ceased.

It is possible that a carrier network's subnet will be so large that an attacker could successfully launch an attack only using source IP addresses that are within this subnet. However such a technique is easily defeatable by the carrier network, by simply giving APs access to a lookup table with all currently allocated IP addresses and to which AP these users are currently connected to. Any mismatch would indicate an invalid source IP address with a particular AP.

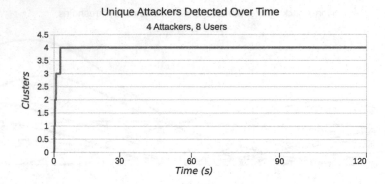

**Fig. 8.** Graph of the number of clusters versus time for scenario 5. The number of clusters corresponds to the number of unique attackers. Notice how the calculated number of clusters remains at 4 once all 4 attackers are detected.

The accuracy of attacker traffic isolation is dependent on the physical medium in which the wireless signals propagate, and also on the precision of the measurements themselves. While $d_{ap}$ introduces robustness to the approach, imprecise measurements will require this parameter to be increased, which comes at a cost of a potentially higher false positive rate.

Another limitation is the assumption that attackers will not selectively adjust transmit power during an attack to separate their attack traffic from their benign traffic, as seen from the AP. Various solutions are being actively explored, such as using additional passive sensors to record RSSI measurements to supplement the measurements from the AP. Related to this is the real-world environment in general. We believe our approach is robust given APs which record RSSI accurately and precisely, and adding passive sensors for RSSI measurement should provide additional robustness against the non-ideal medium of the real-world. Experimentation on our physical network testbed is planned as future work.

## 6    Conclusion

We introduced an approach to isolate mobile attacker traffic during attacks originating from next generation mobile networks. This approach works under the assumption that all users of the network are either anonymous, such as networks relying on shared public key, or can defeat any authentication scheme deployed on the network to spoof other benign users. Our approach uses a combination of detecting common attacks at the access points, and clustering of attack traffic using RSSI to form clusters corresponding to unique attackers. Performing packet classification over these clusters resulted in a vast majority of attacker-originated traffic being successfully blocked, with very little legitimate user traffic blocked. Our approach is scalable up to many mobile attackers and users.

# References

1. Chen, Y., Terzis, A.: On the mechanisms and effects of calibrating RSSI measurements for 802.15.4 radios. In: Silva, J.S., Krishnamachari, B., Boavida, F. (eds.) EWSN 2010. LNCS, vol. 5970, pp. 256–271. Springer, Heidelberg (2010)
2. Faria, D.B., Cheriton, D.R.: Detecting identity-based attacks in wireless networks using signalprints. In: Proceedings of the 5th ACM Workshop on Wireless Security. WiSe 2006, pp. 43–52. ACM, New York (2006)
3. Guo, F., Chiueh, T.: Sequence number-based MAC address spoof detection. In: Valdes, A., Zamboni, D. (eds.) RAID 2005. LNCS, vol. 3858, pp. 309–329. Springer, Heidelberg (2006)
4. Handley, M., Paxson, V., Kreibich, C.: Network intrusion detection: evasion, traffic normalization, and end-to-end protocol semantics. In: Proceedings of the 10th Conference on USENIX Security Symposium. SSYM 2001, vol. 10, pp. 9–9. USENIX Association, Berkeley (2001). http://dl.acm.org/citation.cfm?id=1267612.1267621
5. Iannucci, B., Tague, P., Mengshoel, O.J., Lohn, J.: Crossmobile: A cross-layer architecture for next-generation wireless systems. Tech. Rep. CMU-SV-14-001, Carnegie Institute of Technology (March 2014)
6. Ling, Y., Gu, Y., Wei, G.: Detect syn flooding attack in edge routers. International Journal of Security and its Applications 3(1) (January 2009)
7. Lui, G., Gallagher, T., Li, B., Dempster, A., Rizos, C.: Differences in RSSI readings made by different wi-fi chipsets: a limitation of WLAN localization. In: 2011 International Conference on Localization and GNSS (ICL-GNSS), pp. 53–57, June 2011
8. Sheng, Y., Tan, K., Chen, G., Kotz, D., Campbell, A.: Detecting 802.11 MAC layer spoofing using received signal strength. In: The 27th Conference on Computer Communications. INFOCOM 2008. IEEE, April 2008
9. Sugano, M.: Indoor localization system using RSSI measurement of wireless sensor network based on zigbee standard. In: Wireless and Optical Communications, pp. 1–6. IASTED/ACTA Press (2006)
10. Varga, A., Hornig, R.: An overview of the omnet++ simulation environment. In: Proceedings of the 1st International Conference on Simulation Tools and Techniques for Communications, Networks and Systems & Workshops. Simutools 2008, pp. 60:1–60:10. ICST (Institute for Computer Sciences, Social-Informatics and Telecommunications Engineering), Brussels, Belgium (2008)
11. Wang, H., Zhang, D., Shin, K.: Detecting SYN flooding attacks. In: Proceedings of IEEE INFOCOM, vol. 3, pp. 1530–1539 (2002)
12. Wessels, A., Wang, X., Laur, R., Lang, W.: Dynamic indoor localization using multilateration with RSSI in wireless sensor networks for transport logistics. Procedia Engineering 5, 220–223 (2010). eurosensor XXIV Conference
13. Xiao, B., Chen, W., He, Y., Sha, E.H.M.: An active detecting method against SYN flooding attack. In: The 11th IEEE International Conference on Parallel and Distributed Systems (ICPADS 2005), vol. 1, pp. 709–715, July 2005
14. Yang, J., Chen, Y., Trappe, W.: Detecting spoofing attacks in mobile wireless environments. In: 6th Annual IEEE Communications Society Conference on Sensor, Mesh and Ad Hoc Communications and Networks. SECON 2009, pp. 1–9, June 2009

# No Place to Hide that Bytes Won't Reveal: Sniffing Location-Based Encrypted Traffic to Track a User's Position

Giuseppe Ateniese, Briland Hitaj[✉], Luigi Vincenzo Mancini,
Nino Vincenzo Verde, and Antonio Villani

Dipartimento di Informatica, Università di Roma "La Sapienza",
Via Salaria 113, 00198 Rome, Italy
{ateniese,hitaj,mancini,verde,villani}@di.uniroma1.it
http://www.di.uniroma1.it/

**Abstract.** News reports of the last few years indicated that several intelligence agencies are able to monitor large networks or entire portions of the Internet backbone. Such a powerful adversary has only recently been considered by the academic literature.

In this paper, we propose a new adversary model for Location Based Services (LBSs). The model takes into account an unauthorized third party, different from the LBS provider itself, that wants to infer the location and monitor the movements of a LBS user. We show that such an adversary can extrapolate the position of a target user by just analyzing the size and the timing of the encrypted traffic exchanged between that user and the LBS provider. We performed a thorough analysis of a widely deployed location based app that comes pre-installed with many Android devices: GoogleNow. The results are encouraging and highlight the importance of devising more effective countermeasures against powerful adversaries to preserve the privacy of LBS users.

**Keywords:** Location-based services · Network traffic analysis · GoogleNow · Privacy · Mobile devices

## 1 Introduction

Modern surveillance systems that track the movements of cellphone users are more sophisticated than ever. Intelligence agencies can easily locate the cell tower used by a target and find his location. According to a Washington Post article [5], it is possible to exploits security vulnerabilities in the network used by mobile carriers around the world to provide services to their traveling customers. This network is called the Signaling System 7 (SS7) and once access to it is obtained, it is possible to track the location of anyone in the world and learn whether a person is walking down a specific street, driving, or taking a flight. When the approximate location of a target is known, *stingrays* [3] (or *fake towers*) can be used to redirect calls, monitor Internet traffic, steal phone's data, and even install malware.

© Springer International Publishing Switzerland 2015
M. Qiu et al. (Eds.): NSS 2015, LNCS 9408, pp. 46–59, 2015.
DOI: 10.1007/978-3-319-25645-0_4

These attacks, however, are active and (partially) intrusive. In particular, they are not completely stealthy and leave traces. Indeed, queries to the SS7 network can be logged and phones could be configured by experts to detect stingrays (e.g., IMSI-Catcher Detector on Android phones). In addition, these attacks can only be carried out in cooperation with vendors, mobile carriers, or ISPs. Often the target is in a foreign country and special permissions or agreements must be in place to be able to track his movements.

In this paper we show that it is possible to locate the position of a cellphone by simply monitoring the traffic of certain phone applications that provide location-based services (LBS). Clearly this is simple if the traffic is in the clear, but our main contribution is to show that it is possible to track users even when the traffic is properly encrypted. We believe our method will have significant implications in the way location-based services are provided. LBSs are often accessed through apps that will be referred to as *Location Based Apps* or LBAs. LBAs are used to find friends and restaurants nearby, to locate points of interest, to check public transport timetables and even to search for deals or special offers. Several physical retailers (e.g., Best Buy, Kohls), also deploy location-based promotions to push notifications while the consumer is in or near the store. TripAdvisor, Booking.com and weather forecasting applications are other examples of LBAs.

It is difficult to protect the privacy of users while at the same time provide useful LBSs. It is possible to obfuscate the exact position of a user but these obfuscation techniques are rarely adopted by vendors (location data is too valuable to them). Moreover, customers appreciate services or information they receive and do not seem concerned about sharing their location data with LBS providers.

The contribution of our paper is to show that any third party can infer a user's position by just analyzing the encrypted traffic from that user to the LBS provider. This can be performed in a non-intrusive way, without leaving any traces. For instance, an intelligence organization could monitor routers belonging to some Autonomous System (AS) traversed by LBS's packets and this would be enough to infer a target's position in a foreign country without involving that country's ISPs, mobile carriers, or any other local entities. Encryption or NAT'd addresses do not help much in this scenario. Indeed, we leverage results of previous works on analysis on encrypted traffic which already highlighted the possibility of identifying apps installed on a device [11,22], or the presence of a specific user within a network [23].

Another important point to consider in this context is that current LBAs have started to adopt push technology solutions to send "the right information at the right time" [14]. This is the maxim of the GoogleNow app which comes pre-installed on most Android devices and provides several services that are tied to the user's position. Several LBAs that come preinstalled on a phone do not even ask permission to use location data. The adoption of push technology implies that the user is continuously tracked by the LBS provider, even when the app runs in the background [6].

*Contributions.* In this work we put forward a new privacy problem related to LBSs. We introduce a new adversary model for LBSs and propose a technique that unauthorized third parties may use to infer the position of a target user. Furthermore, we analyze one of the most popular LBAs, GoogleNow, and we show that the analysis of its encrypted network traffic reveals the position of a user with high accuracy. This research is inevitably controversial. The method we developed could be used to undetectably monitor movements of users and abuse their privacy rights. However, it should be considered as a warning to the research community to spur more research in the area and come up with effective countermeasures.

*Organization.* The rest of this paper is organized as follows. In Sect. 2, we introduce the adversary model. In Sect. 3, we detail the different phases of the attack. In particular, Sect. 3.1 explains the method used by the adversary to collect the relevant data from the LBS provider. Then, Sect. 3.2 details the data analysis approach that can be used to infer user locations. Sect. 4 and 4.4 respectively report on the results achieved when analyzing GoogleNow, and on the strategy to select the points that should be monitored by the attacker. In Sect. 5, we review previous work. Finally, in Sect. 6 we draw the conclusions and discuss some possible future works.

## 2    The Adversary Model

We assume the existence of an adversary $\mathcal{A}$ that can sniff the network traffic of a mobile device. The adversary does not need to intercept the entire network traffic but just the packets that are exchanged between the LBA and the LBS provider. The adversary may do so by compromising one of the network devices of any AS that routes the information between the mobile device and the LBS. We assume that the adversary does not want to be detected, and therefore he does not compromise the mobile device nor change the content of network packets. It is well-known that the NSA can identify users around the world of specific services (such as TOR) by detecting packet "fingerprints" and monitoring large portions of the Internet. NSA accomplishes this by collaborating mainly with US telecoms firms under various programs [4].

We assume that the adversary is able to identify and isolate the network traffic of the user he is interested in, and, among those packets, he is able to identify and isolate packets that are generated by the LBA. The adversary is able to determine where discrete communications begin and end (such as the download of updated information from the LBS). This is possible, for example, by observing typical communication patterns of the LBA. Note that if the network traffic is not encrypted, then our adversary may trivially inspect the packet content and determine the location of the mobile device. Therefore, we assume that the network traffic exchanged between the mobile device and the LBS is encrypted via SSL/TLS. Furthermore, we assume that the LBS provider does not use any mechanisms to protect the privacy of its users, such as k-anonymity cloaking, etc. This assumption is based on the fact that current LBS providers do not implement these mechanisms.

To launch the traffic analysis attack that we consider in this paper, the adversary must build a knowledge base that summarizes the network traffic exchanged between the LBA and the LBS when the mobile device is located in certain locations of interest. We assume that the adversary can collect this data by using bogus accounts and virtual mobile devices.

## 3    The Attack

In this section, we detail the approach used by the adversary to infer the actual position of a target user. The entire approach can be logically divided into two steps: the *data collection* phase, and the *candidate locations selection*. The aim of the *data collection* phase is to collect enough information from the LBS provider to learn how different locations can be distinguished from each other. During this phase, the adversary builds up its knowledge base that will later be used to infer the most probable locations the target can be found in. For the sake of simplicity, we will assume that the LBS sends the same information to all users in the same location. Taking into account that the LBS may send personalized information to its users is left as future work.

### 3.1    Data Collection

Suppose that the adversary is interested in localizing users in a given area. First, the adversary logically divides the entire area in $n$ subareas, and arbitrarily chooses a point in each subarea as a representative for that location. The size of the subareas is chosen according to the desired accuracy and the granularity of the information provided by the LBS. Hence, the adversary comes with a set of point locations $\mathcal{L} = \{l_1, l_2, \ldots l_n\}$.

Then, the adversary collects data from the LBS about all the locations in $\mathcal{L}$. This can be accomplished by using the same LBA of regular users and by spoofing the GPS coordinates pretending to be in each location $l_i$ for $1 \leq i \leq n$. The adversary periodically performs the procedure above to learn the traffic pattern of the LBS over time (e.g., data sent by the LBS may change according to daily or weekly trends).

The network traffic that the adversary collects is used to build its knowledge base. The following steps are performed during this phase:

**Prefiltering:** The network traffic is analyzed with a network protocol analyzer, and only the packets directed towards, or coming from, the network of the LBS are preserved.

**Knowledge Base Record Composition:** For each location $l_i$ that is monitored, the adversary adds a record in its knowledge base composed of the following fields:

- *Location ID* (*LocID* for brevity in the following): An identifier of the probed location $l_i \in \mathcal{L}$.

**Table 1.** Example of the adversary knowledge base, user dataset related to a user position during time, and possible guesses.

| Adversary Knowledge Base | | | User Dataset | | |
|---|---|---|---|---|---|
| LocID | Bytes | Timestamp | LocID | Bytes | Timestamp |
| 1 | 35780 | 1399743000 | ? | 35780 | 1399743000 |
| 2 | 30780 | 1399743000 | ? | 35780 | 1399743020 |
| * | * | * | ? | 36780 | 1399743040 |
| * | * | * | ? | 36780 | 1399743060 |
| 1 | 36780 | 1399743060 | ? | 30784 | 1399743080 |
| 2 | 30784 | 1399743060 | ? | 30784 | 1399743100 |

- *Bytes*: The total size in bytes of the transmitted and received encrypted packets that belong to the same TLS/SSL session.
- *Timestamp*: The timestamp of the first packet of the TLS/SSL session.

An example of knowledge base that the adversary would create is reported on the left of Table 1.

### 3.2   Selection of the Candidate Locations

To track a user's position, the adversary relies upon only two fields: the sum of the exchanged bytes of a TLS/SSL session and the timestamp. This information is derived from the header of the packets, which is not encrypted by the SSL protocol. To learn the position of a given user $U$ at time $t_0$, it is enough for the adversary to collect the communication traffic between the user's LBA and the LBS between time $t_0 - t$ and $t_0$. For each TLS/SSL session, $\mathcal{A}$ calculates the fields described above and creates the user dataset. This is shown on the right of Table 1.

At any given moment, each location is potentially characterized by a fixed amount of bytes. As such, the adversary determines the candidate locations by analyzing those locations that have generated an amount of bytes similar to the entries of the user dataset. Namely, suppose that $\mathcal{A}$ wants to determine the position of the user $U$ at time $t_0$. $\mathcal{A}$ builds a filtered adversary knowledge base containing only the instances of the knowledge base such that their timestamps fall within the time frame $[t_0 - t, t_0]$. The size of the time frame depends on the specific LBA and LBS taken into consideration, and on the typical behavior of the user. We assume that, within the targeted time frame, the user does not move from his location. The adversary restricts the number of possible locations studying the statistical distribution of the filtered adversary knowledge base and the user dataset.

In the experiments, we will consider also the case of time-misalignment between the filtered adversary knowledge base and user dataset. This case is useful when the adversary is not able to collect data during the time frame $[t_0 - t, t_0]$.

In such a case, the adversary may use a different time frame $[t_0 - t - \delta, t_0 - \delta]$, for a given $\delta > 0$.

The adversary may use a statistical distance measure to quantify the distance between the samples of the user dataset, and the samples of the filtered adversary knowledge base, for each possible location. This will allow $\mathcal{A}$ to settle on a list of candidate locations where the user was at time $t_0$.

Several statistical distance measures can be used for this purpose. However, in the experimental section, we will show that our approach is accurate even when using a very simple distance metric. Let us indicate with $\bar{x}$ the user dataset, with $\bar{y}$ the filtered adversary knowledge base, and with $\mathcal{L}$ the set of all possible locations. Furthermore, with the notation $\bar{y}[l_i]$ we refer to the subset of the adversary knowledge base $\bar{y}$ related to an individual location $l_i \in \mathcal{L}$. In other words, $\bar{y}[l_i]$ contains all the instances of the filtered adversary knowledge base such that the field *LocID* is equal to $l_i$. Then the adversary will select a candidate location set $\mathcal{S}$ of size $k$ in the following way:

$$\min_{\substack{\mathcal{S} \subseteq \mathcal{L} \\ |\mathcal{S}|=k}} \sum_{l_i \in \mathcal{S}} d(\bar{x}, \bar{y}[l_i]) , \tag{1}$$

where $d(\bar{x}, \bar{y}[l_i])$ indicates some statistical distance measure between $\bar{x}$ and $\bar{y}[l_i]$. In the experiments, we used the following definition of distance: $d(\bar{x}, \bar{y}[l_i]) = |m(\bar{x}) - m(\bar{y}[l_i])|$, where $m(\cdot)$ is the median function. Once the size $k$ is fixed, Equation 1 allows to select a candidate location set $\mathcal{S}$ of size $k$, composed of the locations $l_i$ that minimize the overall distance between $\bar{x}$ and $\bar{y}[l_i]$.

## 4    Experiments and Results

To prove the feasibility and the accuracy of our approach, we performed a thorough analysis of one of the most popular and advanced LBAs: GoogleNow. GoogleNow is an application provided by Google which comes preinstalled with the vast majority of Android devices [14]. It is also available on iOS, Google Glass and even on Android Wear devices. GoogleNow is not only a LBA, but it acts also as a personal assistant by providing personalized information to the user. User-based and location-based information are sent together within the same encrypted traffic. However, we will show that the use of encrypted communications does not hinder the process of identifying user locations as long as some of the GoogleNow user's preferences are known a priori.

GoogleNow app operates regardless of the interactions with its users, and independently determines when information should be downloaded from the LBS server [13] (unless a refresh is forced by the user). We can therefore speculate that GoogleNow app periodically sends the GPS location of the user to the LBS (Google servers). The LBS then replies with the information related to the GPS position sent by the GoogleNow app (e.g., nearby restaurants, bus stops, and/or images of the location). We confirmed this by installing the GoogleNow app on an Android X86 Virtual Machine (VM) and extracting the data exchanged between our VM and Google servers via a man-in-the-middle proxy. This experiment confirmed that the GoogleNow app sends the GPS coordinates of the user but also much more data, including the information currently displayed by the app on the smartphone.

## 4.1   Data Collection of GoogleNow Data

We performed a location spoofing attack to collect the encrypted network traffic exchanged by the GoogleNow app and the Google servers, and to build the adversary knowledge base as described in Sect. 3.1. Each spoofed GPS user location corresponds to a point the adversary is interested in monitoring. We used the mitm-proxy software for this task [1] configured as a transparent proxy on a network of Androidx86 Virtual Machines run in a Virtualbox hypervisor on a Linux host. Each VM has been configured with a different user account. We configured different preferences for each account to determine to what extent Google personalizes the data sent to each user. Because of space restrictions, we report on the results achieved for a single configuration of the user preferences, that is the one where the user settled its home and work locations only. Similar results were achieved for the other accounts that we analyzed and will be reported in the full version of this paper.

GPS locations exchanged between the app and the server are encrypted within SSL, thus we performed a man-in-the-middle attack. To this aim, a self-signed certificate was copied into each VM and added to the Android's root certificates. In this way, the SSL traffic was decrypted and we found out that GoogleNow uses a protocol called Protobuf as data interchange format [2]. This protocol was designed by Google to be smaller and faster than XML. By analyzing the data structure of the protobuf messages that were intercepted by the mitm-proxy, we were able to identify the fields that contain the latitude and longitude of the user. These fields are sent to the Google servers in all the HTTPS requests that contains the following string within the URL: "tg/fe/request".

We collected data about an area of two square kilometers positioned in the center of a large European city. The adversary simulated the presence of its dummy users in the area by moving them on a grid of $5 \times 10$ points (50 different *LocID* in total). The location (i,j) of the grid is identified by the label i_j. Sect. 4.4 provides the motivation behind the selection of these parameters. In order to collect a large amount of data in a short time range, rather than changing the user position of the VM through a MockLocationProvider and then wait for a GoogleNow genuine request, the adversary replayed a request containing the "tg/fe/request" string in the URL several times, modifying the actual position with every point of the grid. The network traffic intercepted by the proxy has been used to feed the knowledge base of the adversary.

For the experiments we had to simulate the target users as well. Therefore, during the same period of three weeks, different VMs have been configured with distinct user accounts. Users moved into the monitored area, and their respective traffic was collected and stored separately. Clearly, this last step will not be performed when tracing real users.

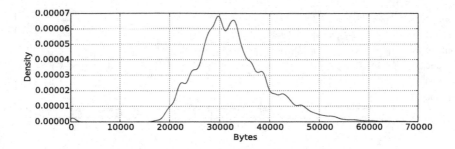

**Fig. 1.** Probability Distribution of the Bytes exchanged between the GoogleNow app and the Google servers.

## 4.2   Exploratory Data Analysis

In this section, we analyze the collected data to improve our understanding of the GoogleNow traffic dataset. This exploratory data analysis is performed over the data collected for an account that has been configured by only specifying home and work locations. All the remaining user profiles that we analyzed show a very similar behavior. Figure 1 reports on the probability distribution of the bytes per SSL session exchanged between the GoogleNow app and the Google servers during the entire monitored period. On average, 32,604 bytes were exchanged per session, with a standard deviation of 7,518. The minimum recorded value is equal to 80, while the maximum is equal to 83,831 bytes. The median is 31,804 bytes, while lower and upper quartiles are equal to 27,791 and 36,520, respectively.

To determine whether the bytes exchanged between the GoogleNow app and the Google servers might be useful to identify the actual location of the user, we analyzed the statistical distribution of the bytes exchanged in each monitored location. Figure 2 shows the boxplots diagram for all the 50 locations of the adversary knowledge base. The boxes extend from the lower to the upper quartile values of the data, with a line at the median. The whiskers extend from the boxes indicating variability outside the lower and upper quartiles. Figure 2a shows the statistical distribution of the bytes received in all the locations during the entire period of collection (3 weeks). Figure 2b was obtained while analyzing only one hour of traffic randomly selected among the three weeks. Note that in Fig. 2a, all the locations show a similar behavior. They have a mean value that is rarely greater than 40,000 and lesser than 20,000. The variance is very high, and lower and upper quartiles are quite far from the median value. With statistical distributions so similar to each other, it might be difficult to infer the actual location of a user. We quickly realized that the time of the day has a great influence on the information provided by GoogleNow, thus we limited the analysis to a period of time one hour long, randomly selected among the three weeks period. Figure 2b shows the boxplot diagram related to this subset of data. It can be observed that almost all the locations have a very tight variance. First and third quartile are very close to each other. Furthermore, once a particular

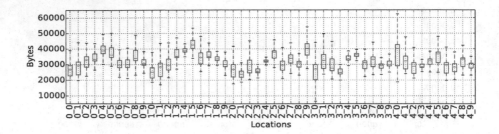

(a) Analysis of the entire adversary knowledge base (3-weeks of traffic).

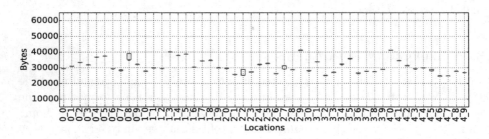

(b) Analysis of only a random hour of the adversary knowledge base.

**Fig. 2.** Statistical distribution of the bytes exchanged between the GoogleNow app and the Google servers per monitored location.

size is selected, only a few locations may have produced it. This is the main reason that led us to consider the time as an important parameter in our analysis.

*Daily Pattern.* During the exploratory data analysis, we realized that the amount of bytes exchanged between GoogleNow and the Google servers follows a daily pattern distribution. In particular, during daily hours it ranges from 26,000 to 32,000 bytes, whereas during the night it falls down in the interval between 22,000 and 24,000 bytes. In Sect. 4.3, we will show how this daily pattern influences the accuracy results.

## 4.3   Accuracy Results

In the following, we will report on the results of the tests that we performed on the collected dataset. All the experiments presented next represent the average of 10,000 tests. In each test, the adversary tries to infer the position of a user. The $k$-identifiability of a tested user position is defined as 1 if the actual position of the user is within the set $S$ of $k$ candidate locations selected with the approach described in Sect. 3.2. Otherwise $k$-identifiability is defined as 0. Thus, the $k$-accuracy is the average of the $k$-identifiability values of each tested instance [17].

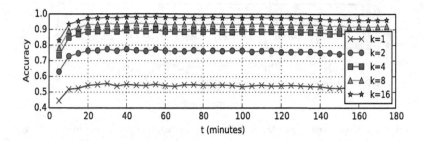

**Fig. 3.** Accuracy of Locations Sets: effect upon accuracy of varying $k$ (size of the candidate locations set) and $t$ (size of the time frame).

In Fig. 3, we show the $k$-accuracy of a user location when varying $k$ and $t$, where $k$ is the size of the candidate locations set and $t$ is the size of time frame used to filter the adversary knowledge base. Observe that for $k = 8$, we reach a value close to 95% with a time frame of only 20 minutes. The behavior of the $k$-accuracy is asymptotic and it reaches a value close to the maximum already at around $t = 20$. In other words, the adversary has to analyze only 20 minutes of traffic to reach the best accuracy performance, independently of the value $k$ selected. Other combinations of $k$ and $t$ also provide reasonable accuracy performance. For instance, for $k = 8$, 5 minutes of traffic are enough to reach an accuracy of 79%, which is quite remarkable.

In Fig. 4, we show the effect of varying $\delta$, that is the difference of time between the filtered adversary knowledge base and the user dataset. In general, larger delays result in lower accuracy. However, the figure shows a cyclic behavior that reflects the daily activity highlighted in Sect. 4.2. Thus, if the adversary does not have in its knowledge base instances that fall in the same time frame of the user dataset, then it is better to use a filtered knowledge base that is one day older (1440 minutes) than one that is only 12 hours older (720 minutes). Indeed, in the former case the accuracy is slightly below 60%, while in the latter case it is around 12% only. The figure also shows a decrease of the peaks that are in correspondence of every 24 hours. This is mainly due to the fact that the information provided by the app is being constantly updated, and it becomes obsolete after a few days.

### 4.4 Granularity of the Monitored Area

In the experiments that we reported in Sect. 4, the adversary monitored 50 points that were distributed within an area of two square kilometers. Each point represented therefore a square area of 200 $m^2$. The adversary arbitrarily chooses one point within this square as a representative. However, the granularity of 200 $m^2$ does not necessarily match the granularity adopted by GoogleNow: if the granularity of GoogleNow is finer, then there are points within the area that

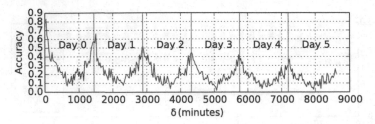

**Fig. 4.** Accuracy of Locations Sets: Effect upon accuracy of varying $\delta$ (time delay between the filtered adversary knowledge base and the user dataset). ($k = 4$, $t = 60$)

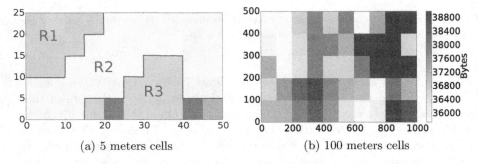

**Fig. 5.** Heat-matrices for different sizes of the cells

have not been considered during the collection phase; on the other hand, if the granularity of GoogleNow is coarser, then several different points may become indistinguishable, thus impeding detection.

We performed an additional experiment to learn the granularity used by Google services in a given area. To this aim, we run the data collection phase using different granularities: 5, 10, 25 and 100 $m^2$. The number of points is fixed to 50 in all cases considered. Each square was probed once every 5 minutes and we calculated the median of the exchanged bytes. Figure 5 shows the results achieved for the two extreme values that we used: 5 and 100 $m^2$. In Fig. 5a, it is possible to easily identify three different regions with a similar amount of bytes exchanged (they are indicated with $R1$, $R2$, $R3$). In Fig. 5b, a cell represents an area of 100 $m^2$. Even in this case there exist regions containing more than one indistinguishable square. The shapes of these regions are irregular since they depend on the location, on the importance, and on the number of the points of interests that fall in those areas.

The result of this analysis is that the granularity of GoogleNow in the particular region we analyzed is dynamic and ranges from 5 $m^2$ to 100 $m^2$. Thus the most appropriate granularity should be selected to find the right balance between performance (data collection) and detection accuracy. Our experiments were run with 200 $m^2$ in our target region because the detection accuracy was very high regardless and this allowed us to speed up data collection (the entire area could be monitored every 5 minutes) and avoid overloading GoogleNow servers with our requests.

## 5   Related Work

The closest research areas to this work, are traffic analysis and location obfuscation. In the following, both of them will be briefly described.

*Traffic Analysis* is devoted to exploiting observable features in an encrypted traffic to infer information about the content of the communication. For instance, [9,20] leverage observables such as the timing and the exchanged bytes to discover communication patterns that can be used to break the anonymity or the confidentiality of the communication. The majority of the work in this area has been conducted over HTTPS protocol [17,16,19,18], even though other protocols such as VoIP [24] have been analyzed as well. A variety of techniques such as Naive Bayes classifiers, Jaccard's coefficient [17], common text mining techniques applied to the normalized frequency distribution of observable IP packets [16] or vector machine classifier [19] have been adopted and applied to traffic analysis in order to identify which website the target user had accessed. These techniques work even if the communication is encrypted or anonymized through networks such as Tor. Indeed, [19] achieved an astonishing accuracy of 97% in these cases. Several countermeasures have also been devised [18,17,25]. They work by manipulating packet size, web object size, flow size, and the timing of the packets to hinder traffic analysis. Unfortunately, these countermeasures have significant performance drawbacks [17] and some of them are particularly vulnerable to simple attacks [12] that exploit the coarse features of traffic (e.g., total time and bandwidth).

*Location Obfuscation* aims at hiding the exact geographical location of the user from the LBSs. Considering both location information accuracy and privacy, [8] introduces the concept of relevance which is used to protect the location information of users together with other obfuscation operators. In [15], the authors propose to adjust the resolution of location information along spatial or temporal dimensions to meet specific anonymity constraints. In [10], a peer-to-peer method is proposed where users cooperate to hide their real location from the LBS. Another approach proposed in [7] consists of adding controlled noise to the user's location to obtain an approximate version of it which is then sent to the LBS. An obfuscation technique is proposed in [21] for a number of sensitive data, including IP addresses of users, this tecnique provides formal confidentiality guarantees under realistic assumptions about the adversary's knowledge.

## 6   Conclusions

In this paper, we introduced a new adversary model for Location Based Services. The model takes into account an unauthorized third party, different from the LBS provider itself, that wants to infer the position of a LBS user. We analyzed one of the most popular location based apps available on Android, that is

GoogleNow, and we have shown that our adversary can infer the position of a user with an accuracy of almost 90% through a statistical analysis of the user's encrypted network traffic.

**Acknowledgments.** This work has been partially supported by the European Commission H2020 under the SUNFISH project, N.644666, and by the European Commission Directorate General Home Affairs, under the GAINS project, HOME/2013/CIPS/AG/4000005057.

# References

1. Man in the middle proxy. https://mitmproxy.org/
2. Protocol buffers - google's data interchange format (2008). https://github.com/google/protobuf
3. Meet the machines that steal your phone's data — ars technica (2013). http://tinyurl.com/o9vd4u9
4. Schneier on security: How the nsa attacks tor/firefox users with quantum and foxacid (2013). http://tinyurl.com/n84axpz
5. For sale: Systems that can secretly track where cellphone users go around the globe - the washington post (2014). http://tinyurl.com/kuazdjs
6. Your location has been shared 5398 times (2015). http://tinyurl.com/nuh6w4e
7. Andrés, M.E., Bordenabe, N.E., Chatzikokolakis, K., Palamidessi, C.: Geo-indistinguishability: differential privacy for location-based systems. In: Proc. of the 2013 ACM SIGSAC Conference on Computer and Communications Security, CCS 2013, pp. 901–914. ACM, New York (2013)
8. Ardagna, C.A., Cremonini, M., De Capitani di Vimercati, S., Samarati, P.: An obfuscation-based approach for protecting location privacy. IEEE Transactions on Dependable and Secure Computing **8**(1), 13–27 (2011)
9. Berthold, O., Federrath, H., Köhntopp, M.: Project anonymity and unobservability in the internet. In: Proc. of the Tenth Conference on Computers, Freedom and Privacy: Challenging the Assumptions, CFP 2000, pp. 57–65. ACM, New York (2000)
10. Chow, C.-Y., Mokbel, M.F., Liu, X.: A peer-to-peer spatial cloaking algorithm for anonymous location-based service. In: Proc. of the 14th Annual ACM International Symposium on Advances in Geographic Information Systems, GIS 2006, pp. 171–178. ACM, New York (2006)
11. Conti, M., Mancini, L.V., Spolaor, R., Verde, N.V.: Can't you hear me knocking: Identification of user actions on android apps via traffic analysis. In: Proceedings of the 5th ACM Conference on Data and Application Security and Privacy, CODASPY 2015, pp. 297–304. ACM, New York (2015)
12. Dyer, K.P., Coull, S.E., Ristenpart, T., Shrimpton, T.: Peek-a-boo, i still see you: Why efficient traffic analysis countermeasures fail. In: Proc. of the 2012 IEEE Symposium on Security and Privacy, SP 2012, pp. 332–346. IEEE Computer Society, Washington (2012)
13. Google.com. Add or remove now cards (2015). http://tinyurl.com/ppy4svc
14. Google.com. Google now (2015). https://www.google.com/landing/now

15. Gruteser, M., Grunwald, D.: Anonymous usage of location-based services through spatial and temporal cloaking. In: Proc. of the 1st International Conference on Mobile Systems, Applications and Services, MobiSys 2003, pp. 31–42. ACM, New York (2003)

16. Herrmann, D., Wendolsky, R., Federrath, H.: Website fingerprinting: attacking popular privacy enhancing technologies with the multinomial naive-bayes classifier. In: Proc. of the 2009 ACM Workshop on Cloud Computing Security, CCSW 2009, pp. 31–42. ACM, New York (2009)

17. Liberatore, M., Levine, B.N.: Inferring the source of encrypted http connections. In: Proc. of the 13th ACM Conference on Computer and Communications Security. ACM, New York (2006)

18. Luo, X., Zhou, P., Chan, E.W.W., Lee, W., Chang, R.K.C., Perdisci, R.: Httpos: Sealing information leaks with browser-side obfuscation of encrypted flows. In: Proc. Network and Distributed Systems Symposium (NDSS). The Internet Society (2011)

19. Panchenko, A., Niessen, L., Zinnen, A., Engel, T.: Website fingerprinting in onion routing based anonymization networks. In: Proc. of the 10th Annual ACM Workshop on Privacy in the Electronic Society, WPES 2011, pp. 103–114. ACM, New York (2011)

20. Raymond, J.-F.: Traffic analysis: protocols, attacks, design issues, and open problems. In: Federrath, H. (ed.) Anonymity 2000. LNCS, vol. 2009, pp. 10–29. Springer, Heidelberg (2001)

21. Riboni, D., Villani, A., Vitali, D., Bettini, C., Mancini, L.V.: Obfuscation of sensitive data for incremental release of network flows. IEEE/ACM Transactions on Networking **23**(2), 672–686 (2015)

22. Stöber, T., Frank, M., Schmitt, J., Martinovic, I.: Who do you sync you are?: smartphone fingerprinting via application behaviour. In: Proc. of ACM WiSec (2013)

23. Verde, N.V., Ateniese, G., Gabrielli, E., Mancini, L.V., Spognardi, A.: No nat'd user left behind: fingerprinting users behind nat from netflow records alone. In: Proc. of the 2014 IEEE 34th International Conference on Distributed Computing Systems, ICDCS 2014, pp. 218–227. IEEE Computer Society, Madrid (2014)

24. Wright, C.V., Ballard, L., Coull, S.E., Monrose, F., Masson, G.M.: Spot me if you can: Uncovering spoken phrases in encrypted voip conversations. In: Proc. of the 2008 IEEE Symposium on Security and Privacy, SP 2008, pp. 35–49. IEEE Computer Society, Washington (2008)

25. Wright, C.V., Coull, S.E., Monrose, F.: Traffic morphing: an efficient defense against statistical traffic analysis. In: Proc. of the 16th Network and Distributed Security Symposium, pp. 237–250. IEEE (2009)

# Smartphone Security

# Compartmentation Policies for Android Apps: A Combinatorial Optimization Approach

Guillermo Suarez-Tangil, Juan E. Tapiador$^{(\boxtimes)}$, and Pedro Peris-Lopez

Department of Computer Science, Universidad Carlos III de Madrid, Leganes, Spain
guillermo.suarez.tangil@uc3m.es, guillermo.suarez-tangil@rhul.ac.uk,
{jestevez,pperis}@inf.uc3m.es

**Abstract.** Some smartphone platforms such as Android have a distinctive message passing system that allows for sophisticated interactions among app components, both within and across app boundaries. This gives rise to various security and privacy risks, including not only intentional collusion attacks via permission re-delegation but also inadvertent disclosure of information and service misuse through confused deputy attacks. In this paper, we revisit the perils of app coexistence in the same platform and propose a risk mitigation mechanism based on segregating apps into isolated groups following classical security compartmentation principles. Compartments can be implemented using lightweight approaches such as Inter-Component Communication (ICC) firewalling or through virtualization, effectively fencing off each group of apps. We then leverage recent works on quantified risk metrics for Android apps to couch compartmentation as a combinatorial optimization problem akin to the classical bin packing or knapsack problems. We study a number of simple yet effective numerical optimization heuristics, showing that very good compartmentation solutions can be obtained for the problem sizes expected in current's mobile environments.

**Keywords:** Smartphone security · Permission based security · Malware · Collusion attacks · Risk assessment

## 1 Introduction

Android's security model is substantially different from that of standard desktop operating systems, as it was designed to better fit the architecture and intended usage of smartphones. The device is seen as a platform with a number of available services, such as storage, networking, and a collection of sensors [1]. Access to each service is provided through a system API freely available to apps yet restricted with a permission system. Thus, an app must request the appropriate permission in its manifest in order to gain access to protected API calls. Permissions can be also used by apps to control interactions among components, for instance by specifying which privileges a caller must have in order to use a component. Recent studies by Felt et al. on the effectiveness of permission systems in smartphone platforms conclude that they are quite effective at protecting users [2]. However, in the case of Android it has been pointed out that apps often

© Springer International Publishing Switzerland 2015
M. Qiu et al. (Eds.): NSS 2015, LNCS 9408, pp. 63–77, 2015.
DOI: 10.1007/978-3-319-25645-0_5

request a significant amount of permissions identified as potentially dangerous. This exposes users to frequent warnings, which drastically reduces effectiveness.

Android apps are considered mutually distrusted and are isolated from each other. Thus, each app has its own process and can access its own data only. Despite this isolation, Android provides the developer with a rich inter-application message passing system. This pursues several goals, including to facilitate component reuse and inter-application collaboration. In Android, developers are encouraged to leverage existing data and services offered by other apps, which is achieved by dividing an app into components and then exchanging information within the app boundaries—ICC, or Inter-Component Communication—and across applications—IPC, or Inter-Process Communication. This is mostly achieved through *intents*, which can be thought of as messages that allow implicit and explicit communication among components.

**The Perils of Coexistence.** The Android app interaction model creates numerous security risks [3]. A careless developer may accidentally expose functionality that another (malicious) app can exploit to, for instance, trick it into performing an undesirable action. Thus, vulnerable apps can unintentionally provide attackers an interface to privileged resources in what is known as a *confused deputy attack*. Additionally, in a compromised device messages exchanged between two components could be intercepted, stopped, and/or replaced by others, as they are generally not encrypted or authenticated.

Deliberate collusion attacks are not only possible but also quite simple to implement. Two or more malicious apps can cooperate to violate security policies in the so-called *permission re-delegation attacks* [4]. Permission re-delegation takes place when an app with sufficient permissions performs a privileged task that is requested by another app that does not have those permissions, which effectively undermines the user-approved permission system. To further complicate matters, a sophisticated attacker might not even rely on the IPC/ICC subsystem, but on covert channels as a substitute to the official communication interface. This would provide colluding apps with an alternative—and most likely unnoticed—vehicle to exchange information. Chandra et al. [5] have recently conducted a comprehensive study of such covert channels in smartphones, showing that they abound and that some of them offer reasonable bandwidth. More generally, apps with networking privileges can also use communication channels external to the smartphone to exchange information.

**Related Work.** Countering attacks that exploit inter-app communications is a challenging task [6]. Bugiel et al. introduced in [7] a framework called TrustDroid to separate trusted from untrusted applications into domains, firewalling ICC messages among domains. Partly based on this concept, Samsung has recently released the KNOX Container [8], so that apps and data inside a container are isolated from apps outside it. According to Samsung, KNOX is intended to facilitate the coexistence of work and personal content on the same device, this being a more lightweight solution than using a separate virtual machine (VM) for each compartment. Interested readers can find in [9] an overview of recent progress in virtualization techniques for mobile systems.

Monitoring and enforcing restrictions on app interactions has been a major research theme almost since the first Android releases. Dietz et al. introduce in [10] *Quire*, a signature-based scheme that allows developers to specify local (ICC) and remote (RPC) communication restrictions. Other proposals such as Taint-Droid [11], AppFence [12], or XManDroid [13] closely monitor apps to enforce given security policies. While the first two use dynamic taint analysis to prevent data leakage and protect user's privacy, the latter extends Android's security architecture to prevent privilege escalation attacks at runtime.

**Motivation and Contribution.** A common theme in all the solutions discussed above is that app segregation is ultimately driven by a user-defined policy. But delegating such a burden to users can only result in a very limited protection, since policy making is unanimously recognized as a difficult task. Users hardly understand the repercussions of granting an app a given set of permissions, let alone those of all possible combinations of apps. Furthermore, policies will likely be user- and even context-specific, so a one-size-fits-all approach does not seem a sensible choice either. Lastly, the problem of leveraging covert channels for command, control, and communication among colluding apps is yet to be addressed. Isolation is generally recognized as one of the most economic and effective ways to dismantle covert channels, but then again it is unclear which apps should be set apart from which others without totally disrupting the very purpose of inter-app communication.

In a related but different area, risk analysis techniques such as [14–18] have recently gained much attention as attractive mechanisms to effectively signal potential threats and better communicate them to final users. Most of such techniques are essentially based on deriving a numerical score from various app features, generally its permissions. Motivated by the discussion provided above, in this paper we make the following contributions:

1. We argue that current risk assessment schemes based on examining apps in isolation can only offer a limited vision of the actual risk, since they fail to model the perils of app coexistence in security models such as that of Android. Ideally, risk assessment should be redefined to extend its scope to all apps residing in the platform, possibly considering dynamic contextual variables too. To formalize this, we introduce an *Unrestricted Collusion (UC)* model that captures these points in a very simple way.
2. We reuse existing risk scoring techniques and adapt them to the UC model. Simple experiments with typical apps show that, for instance, as little as 10 apps may pose a risk level higher than that the risk obtained for 75% of well-known malware instances.
3. We then revisit the classical idea of risk mitigation through compartmentation (as in, e.g., the Brewer-Nash model [19]), a notion that has been used for decades both in corporations and by the intelligence community, and is implicit in some of the works that have addressed the problem of app

isolation. However, considering the complexities and limitations that policy making entails, we use quantified risk metrics to formulate the problem as a class of mathematical optimization problems known as *packing problems*. This addresses the compartmentation problem in a very effective way while reducing user involvement to a bare minimum.

4. We explore 14 heuristics for two practical settings—risk minimization given a fixed number of compartments per mobile terminal, and minimization of the number of compartments given a maximum tolerable risk level for each of them. Our experimental results show that the problem is practically tractable for the sizes involved in current mobile's environments.

5. Lastly, we introduce a freely available online service called DroidSack that implements app compartmentation as introduced in this paper.

## 2   A Quantified Risk Model for App Colocation

### 2.1   Risk Scoring Functions for Individual Apps

Several proposals have recently addressed the design of mechanisms to palliate the ineffective way in which permissions are used to communicate potential risks to the user [14]. Wang et al. introduced in [20] DroidRisk, a permission-based quantitative risk assessment metric for Android apps. DroidRisk draws inspiration from standard methods in quantitative risk assessment and associates with each app $a$ the risk quantity

$$R(a) = \sum_i R(p_i) = \sum_i L(p_i)I(p_i), \tag{1}$$

where $R(p_i)$ is the risk level of permission $p_i$, $L(p_i)$ and $I(p_i)$ are the likelihood and the impact of permission $p_i$, respectively, and the sum is taken over all requested permissions. The likelihoods $L(p_i)$ are empirically estimated by applying Bayes' rule to a dataset of benign and malicious apps. As for the impacts $I(p_i)$, they are set to 1 for normal permissions and to 1.5 for dangerous ones. These values are also empirically chosen so as to maximize discrimination between goodware and malware.

Similar mechanisms are presented by Peng et al. in [16] and then further explored in an extended version of that paper by Gates et al. in [17]. Here the authors develop various risk scoring functions also based on the set of permissions an app requests, including probabilistic generative models such as Basic Naive Bayes (BNB), Naive Bayes with informative Priors (PNB), Mixture of Naive Bayes (MNB), and Hierarchical Mixture of Naive Bayes (HMNB). The work presented in [17] also explores a related approach in which the rarity of permissions—computed as the logarithm of the associated probability—is used to construct risk metrics. Each app $a$ is modeled as a pair $a = [c_i, x_i = (x_{i,1}, \ldots, x_{i,M})]$, where $c_i$ is the category of the app, $M$ is the number of permissions, and $x_i$ a binary vector indicating which permissions the app requests.

Two risk metrics are introduced. The first is called the Rarity Based Risk Score (RS) and associates with each app the number

$$RS(\boldsymbol{x_i}) = \sum_{m=1}^{M} x_{i,m} \cdot \ln\left(\frac{N}{c_m}\right), \tag{2}$$

where $N$ is the total number of apps. A variant called Rarity Based Risk Score with Scaling (RSS) is also explored. It uses scaling factors $w_n$ to penalize high risk permissions more than low risk ones

$$RRS(\boldsymbol{x_i}) = \sum_{m=1}^{M} x_{i,m} \cdot w_m \cdot \ln\left(\frac{N}{c_m}\right). \tag{3}$$

Other proposals, such as the work reported in [15,18,21], introduce more complex risk assessment mechanisms and consider factors other than permissions, such as *intents* or the presence of native code, among others.

## 2.2   Extending Risk Scoring to App Compartments

**Feature-Based Risk Scores.** Essentially all the risk scoring mechanisms proposed so far represent an app $\boldsymbol{a}$ as a feature set

$$\boldsymbol{a} \longleftrightarrow \phi_{\boldsymbol{a}} = \{f_1, \ldots, f_M\}, \tag{4}$$

where each $f_i$ is a feature associated with a particular *risk factor*, i.e., an aspect of the app which is relevant when measuring the risk it poses. Permissions are, by far, the most common risk factors considered by existing risk assessment metrics. Thus, most risk metrics represent $\phi_{\boldsymbol{a}}$ as a binary vector in which a one in the $i$-th position means that the app requests permission $p_i$, and vice versa.

Risk quantification is effectively done by some scoring function $\rho(\boldsymbol{a})$ returning, in general, a positive real number proportional to the amount of risk posed by $\boldsymbol{a}$. As discussed in [16], it is reasonable to assume that risk scoring functions are *monotonic*. In our feature-based framework, monotonocity for a risk scoring function $\rho$ means that, if $\phi_{\boldsymbol{a}}$ and $\phi_{\boldsymbol{b}}$ are the feature sets associated with apps $\boldsymbol{a}$ and $\boldsymbol{b}$, then

$$\phi_{\boldsymbol{a}} \subseteq \phi_{\boldsymbol{b}} \Rightarrow \rho(\boldsymbol{a}) \leq \rho(\boldsymbol{b}). \tag{5}$$

That is, adding risk factors to an app does not decrease risk.

**The Unrestricted Collusion (UC) Model.** We now consider the problem of measuring the risk of a set of apps $\{\boldsymbol{a}_1, \ldots, \boldsymbol{a}_N\}$ running on the same device. This strongly depends on the particular platform used. We will assume a rather permissive co-existence model such as the one provided by Android, in which collusion is facilitated not only by side channels, but also directly (re-delegation attacks) and indirectly (confused deputy attacks) by the IPC subsystem. Thus, we define an Unrestricted Collusion (UC) model as follows: in terms of risk, a set of apps running on the same platform can be viewed as a single app whose risk factors are the union of the risk factors of the constituent apps. More formally:

$$\{a_1, \ldots, a_N\} \longmapsto \phi_{a_1, \ldots, a_N} = \bigcup_{i=1}^{N} \phi_{a_i}. \tag{6}$$

In practical terms, the UC model states that apps can communicate with each other without restrictions. Thus, if one of them has been granted permission to access a particular resource, all of them can also access that resource via the first app. We believe the UC model is reasonable for the current smartphone ecosystem dominated by social, gaming, and sport apps that are increasingly supporting resource sharing and other forms of interactions with each other.

Abusing notation $\rho(\{a_1, \ldots, a_N\})$ can be computed by any feature-based risk scoring function for individual apps by just applying it to the union of all feature sets of the integrating apps. A priori, it is unclear what the relationship between $\rho(\{a_1, \ldots, a_N\})$ and $\{\rho(a_1), \ldots, \rho(a_N)\}$ should be. For example, both DroidRisk—expression (1)—, RS—expression (2)—, and RSS—expression (3)—are "sublinear", in the sense that they have the subadditivity property

$$\rho(\bigcup_{i=1}^{N} a_i) \leq \sum_{i=1}^{N} \rho(a_i). \tag{7}$$

Note that this will not generally hold for nonlinear risk scoring, e.g, those based on subsets of risk factors. Sublinear risk scoring functions are relevant for a class of compartmentation heuristics developed later in Section 3.

## 2.3   An Empirical Analysis of Colocation Risk

We first conducted an empirical evaluation of the risk metrics discussed above in order to assess the risk of colocated apps in the UC model. We implemented DroidRisk [20] and the RS and RSS metrics proposed in [17]. In all cases, parameters were estimated using a dataset composed of over 15K apps from the Google Play market and over 15K malicious apps from VirusShare. Each app in the dataset was preprocessed and transformed into its corresponding feature vector with the permission-related information so as to train each risk model. Overall, our results show risks distributions very similar to those reported in the original papers and confirm that permission-based risk metrics offer a fair degree of discrimination between goodware and malware.

We next considered the case of a platform hosting $N \in \{10, 20, 30, 40, 50\}$ colluding apps and measured the risk of the entire group. The choice of this range is motivated by a 2014 report from Nielsen establishing that smartphone owners use between 20 and 30 apps on a regular basis [22]. For each value of $N$, we randomly selected a group of apps from our dataset of non-malicious apps, computed the risk of the set, and repeated the experiment 1000 times. Fig. 1 shows the risk using DroidRisk and RS/RSS as underlying risk metrics. For a better understanding of the implications of colluding attacks in terms of

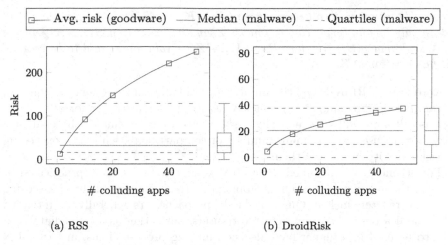

(a) RSS                              (b) DroidRisk

**Fig. 1.** Quantified risk of collusion for different number of apps

quantified risk, each plot is accompanied by the risk distribution of malware. The results suggest that, for instance, just 10 apps pose a risk level higher than 75% of the malware according to the RSS metric. The figures vary when using DroidRisk, yet the fundamentals are the same. Overall, as the number of apps increases so does the risk. As expected, risk growth slows down after certain number of apps since the likelihood of acquiring more risk factors for the group (e.g., additional permissions) gets lower.

## 3    Optimal Risk Compartmentation Policies

### 3.1    Two Compartmentation Problems

Our scheme relies on a quantified risk-driven compartmentation policy. That means that, in principle, there are no predefined conflict of interest classes, as in the classical Brewer-Nash model, nor any other enforceable mandatory controls. Contrarily, compartmentation is implemented by computing the risk of a group of apps coexisting in the same compartment and checking whether this is acceptable or not. Note that, in doing so, compartmentation takes place with minimal user intervention.

We consider two different settings in which app compartmentation can occur. The first one, called the RISKPACK problem, models a scenario in which it is feasible to define a notion of a *maximum tolerable risk*, this being an upper bound to the risk that each compartment can assume. For simplicity, we assume that all compartments have the same risk capacity. This can be straightforwardly extended to the general case in which the user can define compartments with different risk bounds.

**Definition 1 (RISKPACK).** *Given a set $A$ of $N$ apps, for each $S \subseteq A$ a risk measure $\rho(S) \in \mathbb{Z}^+$, a finite set $K$ of $N$ compartments, and a maximum tolerable* risk $\tau \in \mathbb{Z}^+$ *common to all compartments* $k \in \boldsymbol{K}$, *the RISKPACK problem is to find an integer number of compartments* $Z$ *and a* $Z$-*partition* $\boldsymbol{S}_1, \ldots, \boldsymbol{S}_Z$ *of the set* $\boldsymbol{A}$ *such that* $\rho(\boldsymbol{S}_i) \leq \tau$ *for all* $i = 1, \ldots, Z$. *A solution is said to be optimal if it has a minimal* $Z$.

Note that in RISKPACK the number of available compartments is equal to the number of apps, and it is implicitly assumed that $\rho(\boldsymbol{a}) \leq \tau$ for all $\boldsymbol{a} \in \boldsymbol{A}$. That is, all apps will be eventually assigned to a compartment, the challenge being how to use the minimum number of compartments while not exceeding the risk capacity in none of them.

The second problem, called RISKMIN, is intended for a more practical situation, in the following sense. On the one hand, the semantics of the risk scoring functions are often unclear. Quantified risk approaches are generally not intended as final indicators to be communicated to users, but rather as intermediate variables to be used in a higher lever decision making process. Thus, in RISKMIN the focus is not on each compartment's risk value in absolute terms but rather on minimizing it. On the other hand, instead of assuming that a pool of as many as necessary compartments is available, we assume a fixed, and possibly small, number of them. This is more commensurate with current smartphones' capabilities, since it is unrealistic to assume they will soon be able to support a substantial number of virtual machines.

**Definition 2 (RISKMIN).** *Given a set* $\boldsymbol{A}$ *of* $N$ *apps, for each* $\boldsymbol{S} \subseteq \boldsymbol{A}$ *a risk measure* $\rho(\boldsymbol{S}) \in \mathbb{Z}^+$, *and a finite set* $\boldsymbol{K}$ *of* $M \leq N$ *compartments, the RISKMIN problem is to find a* $Z$-*partition* $\boldsymbol{S}_1, \ldots, \boldsymbol{S}_Z$ *of the set* $\boldsymbol{A}$ *such that* $\sum\limits_{i=1}^{Z} \rho(\boldsymbol{S}_i)$ *is minimal. Other target functions are possible, for example minimizing* $\max_i \rho(\boldsymbol{S}_i)$.

For simplicity, a detailed discussion on how to introduce restrictions such as these in our model is left out of this paper. Nonetheless, we anticipate that most problem solving strategies would be able to deal with them straightforwardly.

**Online vs Offline Packing.** As in the case of many classical packing problems, it seems reasonable to consider two versions in which compartmentation can take place. In the *online* setting, apps must be installed in a compartment one at a time, without considering which the next app(s) would be. Contrarily, in an *offline* setting all apps are given upfront. It is easy to prove that the online problem is more difficult and that there is no algorithm that always gets the optimal solution.

## 3.2   Complexity Analysis and Heuristics

RISKPACK is a variant of the combinatorial optimization Bin-Packing Problem (BPP) [23]. There is, however one significant difference: while in BPP the space in a bin occupied by two objects is the sum of their sizes, in RISKPACK there might not be an straightforward relationship between the risk of two apps put together and the risks of each one of them isolated. When the risk scoring function is sublinear, RISKPACK reduces to the VM (Virtual Machine) packing problem recently explored by Sindelar et al. in [24], in which several virtual machines jointly packed in a server share memory pages and, therefore, occupy less space than the sum of their individual sizes.

The RISKMIN problem is a variant of the Multiple Subset Sum (MSS) problem, and can be also seen as a Multiple Knapsack Problem (KPP) if compartments with different risk tolerances are assumed [23]. As in the case of RISKPACK, the key difference is that risk aggregation by the scoring function might not be additive. As discussed in the next section, this can negatively impact the ability to develop efficient approximations.

Both RISKPACK and RISKMIN are NP-hard since they contain the BPP and the MSS/MKP, respectively, as special cases when the risk scoring function is strictly additive in the sense that

$$\rho(\bigcup_{i=1}^{N} \boldsymbol{a}_i) = \sum_{i=1}^{N} \rho(\boldsymbol{a}_i). \tag{8}$$

Furthermore, a direct reformulation of the results provided in [24] determines that, for arbitrary (i.e., nonlinear) risk scoring function, RISKMIN is hard to approximate, whereas for the case of RISKPACK the question is open. Despite this hardness result, we will later see that standard heuristic strategies attain sufficiently good solutions for many instances that arise in practice.

Even though BPP and MSS/MKP are known to be NP-hard, excellent solutions to large instances can be obtained by relatively simple algorithms. Many heuristics have been developed for both problems, often resulting in solvers that provide fast but generally suboptimal solutions. We have adapted some of those heuristics to our risk packing/minimization problems, and also explored others commonly used in minimization problems. In total, we explored 14 different heuristics. A short description of each of them is provided in Table 1. The implementation in all cases is straightforward.

## 4 Experimentation

### 4.1 RISKPACK

We first obtained a risk score model of our dataset for RS, RSS, and DroidRisk as described in Section 2. Then, we computed the number of compartments required to fit $N \in \{10, 30, 50\}$ apps given a *maximum tolerable risk* $\tau \in [0, 1]$. In all the risk metrics used it is possible to compute the maximum attainable risk for a set of apps. This allows us to express risk as a percentage relative to the maximum, which is arguably a more understandable communication instrument for users. For each number of compartments $N$, we randomly selected a group of apps from our dataset of non-malicious apps, repeating the experiment 1000

**Table 1.** Heuristics for the RISKPACK and RISKMIN problems.

| | Heuristic | Description |
|---|---|---|
| RISKPACK | NF | *Next Fit.* When processing the next app, see if it fits in the same compartment as the last app. Start a new empty compartment if it does not. |
| | FF | *First Fit.* As NF but rather than checking just the last compartment, check all previous compartments. |
| | BF | *Best Fit.* Place the app in the tightest compartment, i.e., in the spot so that the smallest residual risk is left. |
| | CF | *Cheapest Fit.* Place the app in the compartment in which it causes the lowest risk increment. |
| | FFD | *First Fit Decreasing.* Offline analog of FF. Sort the apps in decreasing order of risk and then apply FF. |
| | BFD | *Best Fit Decreasing.* Offline analog of BF. Sort the apps in decreasing order of risk and then apply BF. |
| | CFD | *Cheapest Fit Decreasing.* Offline analog of CF. Sort the apps in decreasing order of risk and then apply CFD. |
| RISKMIN | HC | *Hill Climbing.* Start with a random assignment of apps to compartments. Pick one app randomly and move it to a randomly chosen compartment. Keep it there if the overall risk decreases; otherwise undo the move. Repeat until no improvement is achieved for $L$ consecutive moves. |
| | MR | *Minimum Risk.* Place the app in the compartment with minimum risk. |
| | B$^\star$ | *Best Risk.* Place the app in an empty compartment, if any. Otherwise, place it in a compartment in which it causes no risk increment, if possible. Otherwise, place it where it causes the highest risk increment. |
| | CR$^\star$ | *Cheapest Risk.* Place the app in an empty compartment, if any. Otherwise, place it in a compartment in which it causes no risk increment, if possible. Otherwise, place it where it causes the lowest risk increment. |
| | MRD$^\star$ | *Minimum Risk Decreasing.* Place the app in an empty compartment, if any. Otherwise, place it in a compartment in which it causes no risk increment, if possible. Otherwise, place it in the compartment with lowest risk. |
| | BRD$^\star$ | *Best Risk Decreasing$^\star$.* Offline analog of B$^\star$. Sort the apps in decreasing order and then apply B$^\star$. |
| | CRD$^\star$ | *Cheapest Risk Decreasing$^\star$.* Offline analog of C$^\star$. Sort the apps in decreasing order and then apply C$^\star$. |

times, testing all heuristics described in Table 1 for the selected group of apps. Due to space restrictions, Fig. 2 only shows the results reported using RSS and DroidRisk (DR). RS yields very similar results to RSS.

Results show that apps can be segregated into a small number of compartments with a very low risk tolerance each. For instance, 10 apps require just 2-4 compartments for a maximum risk tolerance of 1%-2%, increasing to around 10 compartments for 50 apps. Interestingly, the risk vs. number of compartment relation is not linear: while a massive risk reduction can be done with just 2 or 3 compartments, further reducing the risk translates into an exponential increase on the number of compartments. Additionally, note that the number of compartments strongly depends on the risk metric used. For instance, a user that could only afford a 2% of the overall risk when installing 10 apps requires around 2 compartments with RSS but over 8 with DroidRisk. Some heuristics such as FF and FFD consistently outperform across settings and in all scenarios.

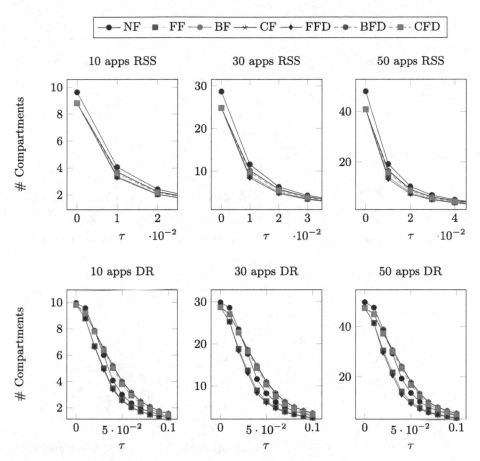

**Fig. 2.** Solutions for the RISKPACK problem using different heuristics: number of compartments used for a maximum tolerable risk $\tau$.

These heuristics are known to behave well in classical combinatorial packing problems, so this does not come as a surprise.

## 4.2  RISKMIN

We tested RISKMIN solvers using the same experimental setting described above. Based on this, we computed the risk reported by the platform given a fixed amount of compartments. For the sake of simplicity, we assume that the risk of the platform is determined by the compartment with higher risk. Fig. 3 shows the results obtained using RSS and DroidRisk (DR). As in the case of RISKPACK, the overall risk can be effectively minimized even when using a small number of compartments. From all heuristics tested, MRD, MR, and HC perform better than the others. Note the duality among the curves in Figs. 2 and 3. Unlike RISKPACK, however, the performance of the different heuristics

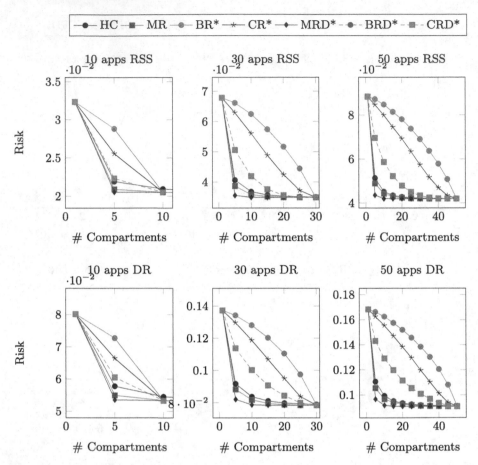

**Fig. 3.** Solutions for the RISKMIN problem using different heuristics: residual risk vs. number of available compartments.

varies significantly. For instance, MRD$^\star$ achieves a risk of $10^{-2}$ with 30 apps and 10 compartments in DroidRisk (DR), while BR$^\star$ attains about 0.13 in the same setting.

## 4.3  DroidSack: An Online Compartmentation Service

We have implemented a freely available online service called DroidSack that offers app compartmentation as introduced in this paper. The service is exposed through a REST HTTP-based API publicly available[1]. The API comprises two services, `GET RISKPACK` and `GET RISKMIN`, which implement solvers for the two problems. In the current version, apps are provided through their full names from the Google Play market. The service connects to the market, retrieves

---

[1] http://www.seg.inf.uc3m.es/DroidSack

the app, and extract the manifest to compute the risk. Candidate solutions are returned as JSON objects. Detailed instructions on how to use it along with a basic HTML interface for manual usage are provided in the URL given above.

## 5 Conclusions and Future Work

In this paper, we have revisited the security problems derived from app coexistence in mobile platforms such as Android. To counter them, we have adopted a compartmentation approach driven by a quantified risk assessment metric. We have introduced a collusion model that facilitates extending existing risk metrics for smartphone apps to sets of apps. We have then posed two combinatorial optimization problems for two practical settings and discussed our experimental results with simple yet effective numerical optimization heuristics. Overall, our results suggest that very good compartmentation solutions can be obtained quite efficiently for the sizes expected in current's mobile environments.

Our proposal presents a number of limitations that should be tackled in future work. For instance, we deliberately do not consider app collusion via Internet. We believe that, although a perfectly valid mechanism to share resources, this problem should be addressed by different means—e.g., by system-level monitoring and firewalling. Similarly, we have only considered permissions as the only type of risk factor, since it is the most common feature used by existing risk assessment metrics. However, considering additional aspects of an app such as IPC calls might provide a more precise assessment of the risk and should be further studied. Finally, dynamic reallocation policies, as opposed to re-solving the problem again with different inputs, might be worth-exploring. For example, such reallocation policies would be interesting when using context-driven risk measures in which the risk of an app changes as the context varies.

**Acknowledgments.** We are very grateful to the anonymous reviewers for constructive feedback and insightful suggestions. This work was supported by the MINECO grant TIN2013-46469-R (SPINY: Security and Privacy in the Internet of You) and the CAM grant S2013/ICE-3095 (CIBERDINE: Cybersecurity, Data, and Risks).

## References

1. Suarez-Tangil, G., Tapiador, J.E., Peris, P., Ribagorda, A.: Evolution, detection and analysis of malware for smart devices. IEEE Communications Surveys & Tutorials **16**(2), 961–987 (2014)
2. Felt, A.P., Greenwood, K., Wagner, D.: The effectiveness of application permissions. In: USENIX Web Application Development. WebApps 2011, p. 7 (2011)
3. Chin, E., Felt, A., Greenwood, K., Wagner, D.: Analyzing inter-application communication in android. In: Mobile Sys., Apps., and Services, pp. 239–252. ACM (2011)
4. Felt, A., Wang, H., Moshchuk, A., Hanna, S., Chin, E.: Permission re-delegation: attacks and defenses. In: USENIX Security Symposium, pp. 1–16 (2011)

5. Chandra, S., Lin, Z., Kundu, A., Khan, L.: Towards a systematic study of the covert channel attacks in smartphones. Univ. of Texas, Technical report (2014)
6. Fang, Z., Han, W., Li, Y.: Permission based android security: Issues and countermeasures. Computers & Security **43**, 205–218 (2014)
7. Bugiel, S., Davi, L., Dmitrienko, A., Heuser, S., Sadeghi, A.R., Shastry, B.: Practical and lightweight domain isolation on android. In: Security and Privacy in Smartphones and Mobile Devices. SPSM 2011, pp. 51–62. ACM, New York (2011)
8. Samsung: White paper: An overview of samsung knox (April 2013). http://www.samsung.com/es/business-images/resource/white-paper/2014/02/Samsung_KNOX_whitepaper-0.pdf
9. Jaramillo, D., Furht, B., Agarwal, A.: Mobile virtualization technologies. In: Virtualization Techniques for Mobile Systems, pp. 5–20. Springer (2014)
10. Dietz, M., Shekhar, S., Pisetsky, Y., Shu, A., Wallach, D.S.: QUIRE: lightweight provenance for smart phone operating systems. In: USENIX Security, p. 16 (2011)
11. Enck, W., Gilbert, P., Chun, B., Cox, L., Jung, J., McDaniel, P., Sheth, A.: Taintdroid: an information-flow tracking system for realtime privacy monitoring on smartphones. In: USENIX OS Design and Implementation, pp. 1–6 (2010)
12. Hornyack, P., Han, S., Jung, J., Schechter, S., Wetherall, D.: These aren't the droids you're looking for: retrofitting android to protect data from imperious applications. In: Computer and Communications Security, pp. 639–652. ACM (2011)
13. Bugiel, S., Davi, L., Dmitrienko, A., Fischer, T., Sadeghi, A.: Xmandroid: A new android evolution to mitigate privilege escalation attacks. Technical report, Technische Universitat Darmstadt (2011)
14. Felt, A.P., Finifter, M., Chin, E., Hanna, S., Wagner, D.: A survey of mobile malware in the wild. In: Proceedings of the 1st ACM Workshop on Security and Privacy in Smartphones and Mobile Devices. SPSM 2011, NY, USA, pp. 3–14 (2011)
15. Grace, M., Zhou, Y., Zhang, Q., Zou, S., Jiang, X.: Riskranker: scalable and accurate zero-day android malware detection. In: Proceedings of the 10th International Conference on Mobile Systems, Applications, and Services, pp. 281–294. ACM (2012)
16. Peng, H., Gates, C., Sarma, B., Li, N., Qi, Y., Potharaju, R., Nita-Rotaru, C., Molloy, I.: Using probabilistic generative models for ranking risks of android apps. In: Computer and Communications Security, pp. 241–252. ACM (2012)
17. Gates, C., Li, N., Peng, H., Sarma, B., Qi, Y., Potharaju, R., Nita-Rotaru, C., Molloy, I.: Generating summary risk scores for mobile applications. IEEE Transactions on Dependable and Secure Computing **11**(3), 238–251 (2014)
18. Wang, W., Wang, X., Feng, D., Liu, J., Han, Z., Zhang, X.: Exploring permission-induced risk in android applications for malicious application detection. IEEE Transactions on Information Forensics and Security **9**(11), 1869–1882 (2014)
19. Brewer, D.F.C., Nash, M.J.: The chinese wall security policy. In: IEEE Symposium on Security and Privacy, Oakland, CA, USA, 206–214 (1989)
20. Wang, Y., Zheng, J., Sun, C., Mukkamala, S.: Quantitative security risk assessment of android permissions and applications. In: Wang, L., Shafiq, B. (eds.) DBSec 2013. LNCS, vol. 7964, pp. 226–241. Springer, Heidelberg (2013)
21. Chakradeo, S., Reaves, B., Traynor, P., Enck, W.: Mast: triage for market-scale mobile malware analysis. In: Security and Privacy in Wireless and Mobile Networks. WiSec 2013, pp. 13–24. ACM, NY (2013)

22. Nielsen: Smartphones: so many apps, so much time (July 2014). (last visited October 2014)
23. Martello, S., Toth, P.: Knapsack Problems: Algorithms and Computer Implementations. J. Wiley & Sons (1990)
24. Sindelar, M., Sitaraman, R.K., Shenoy, P.J.: Sharing-aware algorithms for virtual machine colocation. In: ACM Symposium on Parallelism in Algorithms and Architectures, pp. 367–378 (2011)

# Android Botnets: What URLs are Telling Us

Andi Fitriah Abdul Kadir[✉], Natalia Stakhanova, and Ali Akbar Ghorbani

Faculty of Computer Science, University of New Brunswick,
Fredericton, New Brunswick, Canada
{andi.fitriah,natalia.stakhanova,ghorbani}@unb.ca

**Abstract.** Botnets have traditionally been seen as a threat to personal computers; however, the recent shift to mobile platforms resulted in a wave of new botnets. Due to its popularity, Android mobile Operating System became the most targeted platform. In spite of rising numbers, there is a significant gap in understanding the nature of mobile botnets and their communication characteristics. In this paper, we address this gap and provide a deep analysis of Command and Control (C&C) and built-in URLs of Android botnets detected since the first appearance of the Android platform. By combining both static and dynamic analyses with visualization, we uncover the relationships between the majority of the analyzed botnet families and offer an insight into each malicious infrastructure. As a part of this study we compile and offer to the research community a dataset containing 1929 samples representing 14 Android botnet families.

**Keywords:** Android botnet · Malware · URL · Visualization

## 1 Introduction

The proliferation of mobile platforms in our daily lives has quickly brought mobile malware to the forefront of security concerns. Almost non-existent before the official release of the Android platform in 2008, nowadays mobile malware is a serious threat to modern mobile devices. Among them, mobile botnets are quickly gaining the attention of the research community. The recent report published by Sophos [2] noted the sophistication and highly stealthy nature of rapidly appearing mobile botnets.

Although the first studies in this domain only offered proof of concept models of mobile botnets, they identified the potential of the mobile platform for creating more sophisticated and stealthy botnets [26]. Indeed, the resource-constraint environment of smartphones, which are unable to afford computationally intensive operations presents significant challenges to the development of solutions for their detection. Botnets in the mobile environment have to be resource-aware to continue their operation and remain undetected. This effectively forces mobile botnets to curtail their communication to a minimum and leverage alternative hard-to-detect channels (e.g., audio/video sensors [18], SMS/MMS [16,27,19,26]).

© Springer International Publishing Switzerland 2015
M. Qiu et al. (Eds.): NSS 2015, LNCS 9408, pp. 78–91, 2015.
DOI: 10.1007/978-3-319-25645-0_6

Mobility also opens up new avenues for old attacks. Mobile phones are a rich source of sensitive information, traditionally not available to stationary computers (e.g., location information, user's activities). This creates an opportunity for new context-aware mobile botnets to be able to exfiltrate information typically not monitored by traditional detection systems. General detection of mobile malware and in particular detection of mobile botnets have been extensively studied in the last several years [25,14,15,11,10]. Aiming to address specific features of the existing botnets, these studies appear isolated and give patchy solutions to an ever growing problem. This disparity stems from a lack of solid understanding of modern mobile botnets functionality and specifics differentiating them from their traditional counterparts. In this work we aim to address this gap and offer an insight into the most popular mobile botnet families. We analyze 14 Android botnet families detected in the wild since 2010. Given an unprecedented growth of Android malware and botnets (98% of all mobile malware [13]), in this study we focus primarily on the Android platform. Our goal is to provide a deep understanding of Android botnets' characteristics that will facilitate the development of advanced mobile botnet detection approaches.

The contribution of our work is three-fold. First, we conduct a thorough investigation of the Android botnet families, their characteristics and communication behaviour. Second, through static and dynamic analysis, we extract and visualize all embedded URLs, including the obfuscated URLs. During our analysis, we identify hidden encryption keys stored within the samples that allow us to reveal previously unknown features of Android botnets which are currently used to avoid detection. This analysis not only allows us to demonstrate the relationships between botnet families, but also helps us to illustrate the C&C communication patterns. Finally, we release the accumulated dataset containing 1929 botnet samples to the research community. To the best of our knowledge, this study is the first of its kind that offers a thorough analysis of mobile botnets' URLs on the Android platform.

The rest of the paper is organized as follows: Section 2 presents the related work on Android botnets and Section 3 discusses the collected dataset. Section 4 presents the approach we used to analyze the URLs of the Android botnets. Section 5 presents the discovered trends. Finally, Section 6 concludes the paper with some remarks about the implication of the work.

## 2    Related Work

With rapid advancement of botnets and mobile device security quickly becoming an urgent necessity, researchers have focused their attention on this problem. One of the first attempts to illustrate the potential impact of a small-size mobile botnet was offered by Traynor et al. [24]. It was quickly followed by a series of studies introducing more advanced and powerful mobile botnet designs capable of significant damage: Andbot, a botnet exploiting URL fluxstrategy [26], Android botnet based on Google's Cloud to Device Messaging (C2DM) service [28], Android botnet leveraging out-of-bound communication channels (i.e., audio, ambient light, and magnetic field) [18], mobile multi-targeted bot-net [17]. Realization of mobile botnet attacks' potential triggered the development of defence techniques, many of which specifically targeted individual characteristics of botnets  [23,14,11,16,27,19,10,25,15].

We provide these approaches with an understanding of the Android botnet communication characteristics and thus provide tools to improve the effectiveness of botnet analysis. One of the techniques we employ in our study is visualization. Visualization has been seen as beneficial in many domains including mobile security. One of the first works in this area was offered by Barrera et al. [12]. The authors employed visualization to observe and analyze permission usage in malicious Android applications. This work was followed by Luoshi et al. [22] where the authors used the Gephi visualization tool for detecting Android malware by investigating the relationships between Android function calls and their paths. The recent work by Hosseinkhani et al. [21] introduced Papilio, a new visualization technique for illustrating real-world Android application permissions. In the context of our study, we adopt visualization to investigate URLs of Android botnets.

## 3   Dataset

To provide a comprehensive evaluation of Android botnets, we gathered a large collection of Android botnet samples representing 14 botnet families. These families represent early and mature versions of Android botnets that are chosen primarily due to their popularity. The summary of these families characteristics are provided in Table 1. Our accumulated dataset combines botnet samples from the Android Genome Malware project [30], malware security blog [1], VirusTotal [3] and samples provided by a well-known anti-malware vendor. Overall, our dataset includes 1929 samples of Android application package (APK) spanning a period from 2010 (the first appearance of Android botnet) to 2014. This dataset covers a large number of existing Android botnets, which reflects the current status of Android Malware. Figure 1 illustrates the cumulative growth of samples in our dataset. We have noticed that even though the first botnet was discovered in 2010, there are few samples that have been created earlier (this is witnessed by the creation dates on the ZIP files) than the official discovery date in 2008, as depicted in Figure 1. This indicates that these botnets were unknown or unlabelled until they were discoved in 2010. We have released the accumulated dataset to the research community at http://www.unb.ca/research/iscx/dataset/index.html

## 4   Extracting URLs

Traditionally, URLs are either contained in the file meta-data (e.g., the application links for updates) or embedded in malware code as plain text or obfuscated strings. URLs from meta-data are easily extracted with a simple regular

**Table 1.** Android botnet characteristics

| Botnet Family | Year | Market Origin | C&C Type | Target Country | Backdoor | Data Theft | Drive-by Download | Exploit technique | Infected SMS | Mobile Banking Attack | Ransomware | Repackaged Application | Social Engineering | Trojanised Application |
|---|---|---|---|---|---|---|---|---|---|---|---|---|---|---|
| Wroba | 2014 | 3rd-party | SMS/HTTP | Korea | | | | | | ✓ | ✓ | | | ✓ |
| Pletor | 2014 | 3rd-party | SMS/HTTP | | | | | | | | | ✓ | | ✓ |
| Sandroid | 2014 | 3rd-party | SMS | MiddleEast | | | | | | ✓ | ✓ | | | ✓ |
| NotCompatible | 2014 | forged site | HTTP | | | | ✓ | ✓ | | | | | | |
| MisoSMS | 2013 | 3rd-party | Email | Korea | ✓ | ✓ | | | | | | | | ✓ |
| Bmaster | 2012 | 3rd-party | HTTP | China | ✓ | ✓ | | | | | | ✓ | | |
| RootSmart | 2012 | 3rd-party | HTTP | China | ✓ | ✓ | | | | | | ✓ | | |
| TigerBot | 2012 | 3rd-party | SMS | | ✓ | ✓ | | | | | | | | ✓ |
| AnserverBot | 2011 | official | HTTP | | ✓ | | | | ✓ | | | | ✓ | |
| DroidDream | 2011 | official | HTTP | | ✓ | ✓ | ✓ | | | | | ✓ | | ✓ |
| NickySpy | 2011 | 3rd-party | SMS | | ✓ | | | | | | | ✓ | | |
| PJapps | 2011 | 3rd-party | HTTP | | | | | | | | | ✓ | | ✓ |
| Geinimi | 2010 | 3rd-party | HTTP | China | ✓ | ✓ | | | | | | ✓ | | |
| Zitmo | 2010 | 3rd-party | SMS | Europe | | | | | ✓ | ✓ | | ✓ | ✓ | |

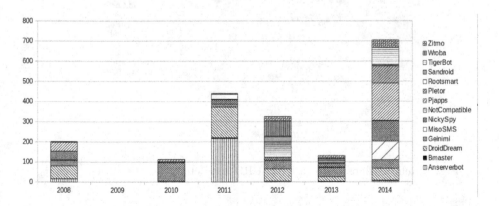

**Fig. 1.** The yearly breakdown of the collected Android botnet families

expression-based search. We refer to these extracted meta-data URLs as built-in URLs. To obtain URLs, we employ both static and dynamic analyses. The combination of static and dynamic analyses is necessary here as many botnets

**Table 2.** Overview of the extracted URLs

| Botnet Family | Total samples | Static analysis(URL) | | Dynamic analysis(URL) | | Similar URL |
|---|---|---|---|---|---|---|
| | | Total | Unique | Total | Unique | |
| Anserverbot | 244 | 903 | 130 | 289 974 | 115 | 21 |
| Bmaster | 6 | 148 | 69 | 4480 | 43 | 7 |
| DroidDream | 363 | 6 451 | 850 | 4 443 219 | 502 | 21 |
| Geinimi | 264 | 1 548 | 406 | 342 760 | 181 | 11 |
| MisoSMS | 100 | 450 | 60 | 179 907 | 224 | 9 |
| NickySpy | 199 | 5 402 | 411 | 34 303 | 171 | 24 |
| NotCompatible | 76 | 72 200 | 24 | 10 875 | 5 | 0 |
| PJapps | 244 | 4 783 | 676 | 182 932 | 200 | 13 |
| Pletor | 85 | 307 | 37 | 17 181 | 12 | 8 |
| Rootsmart | 28 | 486 | 16 | 64 | 14 | 0 |
| Sandroid | 44 | 1 305 | 218 | 2 566 | 179 | 11 |
| TigerBot | 96 | 555 | 47 | 6 188 | 35 | 4 |
| Wroba | 100 | 2 372 | 31 | NA | NA | NA |
| Zitmo | 80 | 7 648 | 74 | 158 508 | 138 | 26 |
| **Total** | 1 929 | 104 558 | 3 049 | 5 672 957 | 1 819 | 155 |

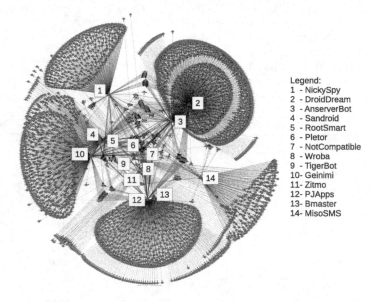

Legend:
1 - NickySpy
2 - DroidDream
3 - AnserverBot
4 - Sandroid
5 - RootSmart
6 - Pletor
7 - NotCompatible
8 - Wroba
9 - TigerBot
10- Geinimi
11- Zitmo
12- PJApps
13- Bmaster
14- MisoSMS

**Fig. 2.** Relationships between 4 713 URLs extracted from the botnet dataset

(especially with advanced capabilities) will hide URLs from static analysis. A sophisticated botnet would hide its malicious intent and avoid putting C&C URLs as meta-data. Dynamic analysis, on the other hand, forces a botnet sample to reveal these hidden URLs.

In the static analysis, we have customized scripts that leverage regular expressions and keywords such as *http, password, key, DES*. We looked at the similar keyword pattern between each family. For instance, searching the *const-string* keyword can give us more results of URLs than the plain *http* keyword. By examining the existing pattern for each botnet family, we managed to extract even the encoded URLs. This is obtained by using binary code searching. Searching binary code, however, requires disassembly of APK file and analysis of *.dex* file bytecode. Using the *baksmali* disassembler, we retrieved bytecode from each sample and string portion of its data section. We referred to domains and IP addresses extracted from the data section part of the code as C&C URLs. To confirm the discovery of the C&C URLs, we followed several patterns from the existing reports such as the use of port 8080 in their communications (which can be clearly seen in the URLs).

The dynamic analysis was conducted using Anubis [9], a web-based malware analysis tool. Anubis provides both static and dynamic analysis reports which cover the following aspects of APK files: activities, services, broadcast receivers, required permissions, used permissions, features, URLs, file operations, network operations, crypto operations, started services, and native libraries loaded. In this research, we focus primarily on the analysis of the URLs. We have extracted all the URLs from the collected xml files generated by Anubis except for the Wroba family (due to the Anubis startup-dependency issues). Following the described procedure, we extracted over 5 million of URLs (5, 777, 515) from our collected dataset (see Table 2). This resulted in 4 868 unique URLs; 155 of them are overlapping, which reduces the overall unique URLs to 4 713. Among them, we discovered 47 are the C&C URLs and the remaining 4 666 are the built-in URLs. Visualizing this information gives a high-level understanding of the relationships between botnet families. This is clearly seen in Figure 2 that displays all the unique URLs extracted from the 14 botnet families. As the visualization shows, there is a significant sharing of URL resources between seemingly isolated botnet families.

## 5    Analyzing URL Patterns

### 5.1    Resource Sharing among Botnet Families

One interesting aspect of the analyzed botnet families is the sharing of resources, i.e., not only the same URLs are being reused within and across families, but also encryption keys employed to obfuscate these addresses. Moreover, they are also sharing the same nameservers as shown in Figure 3.

*Built-in vs C&C URLs.* The sharing of URLs is clearly visible in Venn diagrams illustrating the relationships between the built-in and C&C URLs. While there is no overlap between C&C and built-in URLs, there is a clear reuse within each category. For instance, as Figure 4 shows, all the families are linked to each other through a significant reuse of built-in URLs. This might be an indication of legitimate resources being a main vehicle of botnet malware. This is also confirmed by the scanning results, as only a minor portion of these built-in URLs are malicious. It should be noted that the same pattern exists between the built-in and C&C URLs, which shows that the DroidDream is a subset of

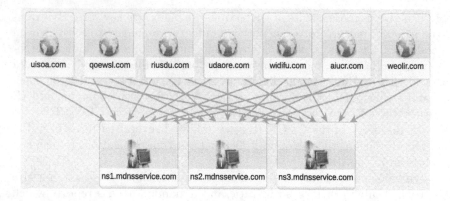

**Fig. 3.** Examples of nameservers sharing of C&C domains for the Geinimi Family

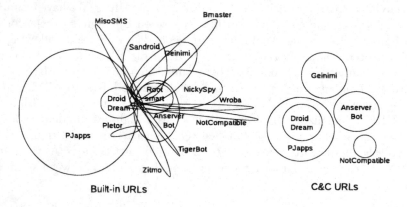

**Fig. 4.** Built-in and C&C URL relationships

the PJapps family. Based on this finding, we can infer that even though there is no URL similarity between the built-in and C&C URLs, they employ the same pattern, which might be an indication that the DroidDream family is actually the evolution of the PJapps family.

*Interfamily Relationships.* We observed the following types of relationships between employed addresses within the same family:

- one-to-one: when an APK file is associated with a single URL.
- one-to-many: when an APK file contains many URLs
- many-to-many: when many APK files are associated with many URLs.

Figure 5 illustrates these types of C&C URL-relationships. For instance, PJapps adopted a one-to-one relationship where it uses a single URL to pull down a command. Geinimi botnet uses a one-to-many relationship to make several attempts to connect to multiple C&C servers (up to 10 distinct URLs).

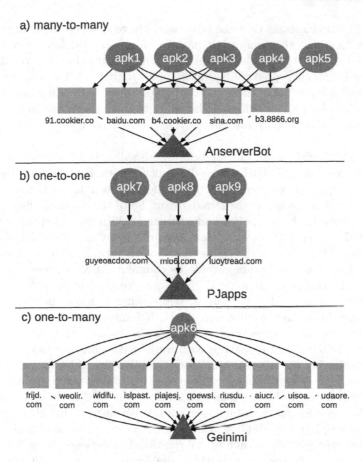

**Fig. 5.** Types of C&C URL-relationships discovered

AnserverBot, on the other hand, employed the many-to-many relationship where various APK files used the same set of URLs (up to 3 distinct URLs) to communicate with C&C servers. However, we also noticed that some families such as PJapps and DroidDream adopted multiple relationships in communicating with their C&C servers.

Furthermore, there is also a significant relationship between the C&C URLs and their encryption pattern within the same family. For instance, all of 365 APK files in the DroidDream family adopted the same technique for encrypting the C&C URLs. This botnet family stored the hardcoded URLs in the same folder and defined the key to decrypt these URLs in the Java code with the keyword of *PASSWORD_CRYPT_KEY*. A previous report by McAfee in 2011 [4] discovered that DroidDream variants save the encrypted configuration using the file name *prefer.dat* in the Asset folder. The samples we analyzed use *sense.tcd* and *small.use* to store the same DES decryption/encryption key as before -

*DDH#X%L.* This indicates that the botmasters have changed the configuration file without changing the encryption pattern (file path and key). Specifically, we discovered that 253 APK files stored their configuration in *sense.tcd* file, 148 samples saved their encrypted configuration in *prefer.dat* file, and only 4 samples used the *small.use* file. All of these 405 APK files linked to the same set of URLs (up to 7 distinct URLs) and adopted the many-to-many URL relationship. This demonstrates that botnets commonly recycle their resources.

*Intrafamily Relationships.* In our analysis we also discovered a significant relationship between the C&C URLs from different families. By searching and visualizing the encryption, we found 101 APK files of the PJapps family applied the same encryption technique as DroidDream, 88 of them stored their encryption configuration in the *prefer.dat* and another 13 APK files used the *sense.tcd* file.Both used the same DES decryption/encryption key as before, *DDH#X%L.* To further investigate, we checked these APKs with VirusTotal to see the results of its detection. The results are diverse as different APKs showed a different detection ratio. However, we noticed that some vendors such as Sophos consistently detect these APKs as PJapps, while other vendors such as F-secure declared these APKs as DroidDream. As both families appeared in the same year, we infer that this is an example of malware evolution where the botmasters replicate the APK file and repackage with improved techniques to evade detection. By scrutinizing the newest samples of DroidDream and PJapps, we found a new pair of DES decryption/encryption keys (*pG3NÔ8f?* and *G#R%AP̂H?*) which are different from the previously seen keys. None of these keys matches the encrypted files (*prefer.dat, small.use, sense.tcd*). We suspect that this is another improvement employed by the bot master in the newer versions of malware.

Moreover, there is also a significant relationship between the C&C URLs and their proxy information within the same family. By visualizing the proxy numbers, we noted that the same set of URLs shares the same proxy numbers. For example, all of the 7-set C&C URLs in a DroidDream family use the same proxy numbers in uploading (proxy number 7) and feeding (proxy number 9) the C&C server. On the other hand, a different 2-set of URLs is also linked to another proxy (proxy number 2). Specifically, this proxy information comes together with the C&C URLs that we have decrypted using DES encryption.

## 5.2   C&C Addresses Obfuscation

One of the techniques employed by Android malware to prevent detection and the subsequent analysis is the obfuscation of C&C servers' addresses. There have been a number of methods reported in the past (e.g., plain text Java file in the DroidKungFu family [30]). Here we offer an overview of the techniques we observed in Android botnets.

*Encryption.* Note that as well as the AnserverBot family that used encoding scheme to dodge detection as previously reported by Zhou and Jiang [30], other

**Table 3.** Overview of the employed encryption techniques

| Botnet Family | Total Encrypted URL | Encryption types | | | | |
|---|---|---|---|---|---|---|
| | | Rot-10 | XOR | DES | AES | Base64 |
| AnserverBot | 141 | 2 | 0 | 32 | 99 | 8 |
| Bmaster | 11 | 0 | 7 | 0 | 4 | 0 |
| DroidDream | 104 | 9 | 1 | 11 | 78 | 5 |
| Geinimi | 46 | 4 | 0 | 10 | 29 | 3 |
| MisoSMS | 2 | 0 | 0 | 0 | 1 | 1 |
| NotCompatible | 145 | 0 | 0 | 32 | 113 | 0 |
| Nickispy | 4 | 0 | 0 | 0 | 1 | 3 |
| PJapps | 27 | 11 | 0 | 7 | 1 | 8 |
| Pletor | 81 | 0 | 0 | 0 | 81 | 0 |
| Rootsmart | 25 | 0 | 0 | 0 | 25 | 0 |
| Sandroid | 2 | 0 | 0 | 0 | 9 | 2 |
| TigerBot | 23 | 0 | 0 | 0 | 0 | 23 |
| Wroba | 3 | 0 | 0 | 0 | 3 | 0 |
| Zitmo | 11 | 0 | 0 | 3 | 8 | 0 |
| **Total** | 625 | 26 | 8 | 95 | 452 | 53 |

families such as Geinimi, PJapps, and DroidDream have also adopted an encryption algorithm in their APK Botnet. A summary of the encrypted URLs and their corresponding encoding algorithms is given in Table 3.

In essence, AnserverBot adapts the popular Base64 scheme with a custom index table. PJapps customized this encoding scheme, employing Base64 with a pattern of skipping every other letter in strings. DroidDream on the other hand, employed both encoding and encrypting techniques such as XOR cipher, ROT-10 cipher, Advanced Encryption Standard (AES), and Data Encryption Standard (DES) algorithm provided with its three different keys of encryption: $DDH\#X\%LT?$, $pG3N\tilde{O}8f?$, and $G\#R\%A\hat{P}H?$.

*Exploiting DNS.* Another interesting finding of C&C URL pattern is on the Domain Name System (DNS). We found that the C&C URLs exploit its DNS by adopting the Domain Generation Algorithm (DGA) and the URL obfuscation techniques. Table 4 lists 3 types of URL obfuscation techniques commonly used by attackers [20]. Accordingly, the C&C URLs in the collected dataset used the following types: Type I - obfuscating the host with an IP address, Type III - obfuscating with the large hostname, and, Type IV - unknown or misspelled domain. However, the behavior of Type II - obfuscating the host with another domain is not found in our dataset. In a similar way, the C&C URLs are used the DGA technique as rendezvous points with their C&C servers. As such, out of 47 C&C URLs that we have extracted, 33 of them have employed the DGA. For example in the DroidDream family, the domain names of the C&C URLs (http://ju5o.com/zpmq.jsp,http://mlo6.com/owxnf.jsp,http://ya3k.com/bksy.jsp) contain both random characters and numbers, which indicates the use of DGA.

**Table 4.** Commonly used URL obfuscation techniques

| TYPE | Descriptive examples | Family |
|------|----------------------|--------|
| I | http://184.105.245.17:8080/GMServer/GMServlet&PJapps | |
| III | http://91.cookier.co.cc:8080/jk_center/91/ad.xml | AnserverBot |
| IV | www.qoewsl.com:8080; | Geimini |

*Utilizing Public Blog.* A previous technical report of AnserverBot in 2011 [29] claimed that Anserverbot was the first one in Android Malware history that used public blogs as its C&C servers to deliver commands to bot clients. According to the authors, if the connection to the C&C server is not successful, the botnet will start connecting to the public blog for the updated C&C server and then use this as a new C&C server. Moreover, the information about new C&C servers is being published on a public blog (as encrypted postings) and the C&C URLs are hard-coded using Base64 scheme (with a custom index table). Based on this information, we employed customized scripts that leverage regular expressions to search for C&C URLs. Through this search, we extracted 830 C&C URLs (8 unique URLs) from the 243 APKs of the AnserverBot family that exploit public blogs. As Figure 5 shows, all these APKs have adopted many-to-many relationships. For instance, both of these URLs from *baidu.com* and *91.cookier.co.cc* link to the same 175 APKs. This shows that the AnserverBot has a limited number of public blogs to be used as C&C servers.

### 5.3   Detection of Botnet Samples

All of the analyzed samples were collected from various sources and initially labeled as botnet malware. To measure the effectiveness of modern anti-virus scanners we analyzed the collected samples using the VirusTotal service [3]. Since the VirusTotal service incorporates a large selection of anti-virus scanners, which use different detection strategies, we identify the number of scanners that detect our samples as botnet, together with their average detection rate. The results are encouraging as the majority of our samples were recognized correctly with a few exceptions. For example, a low detection rate, 86%, was obtained for Sandroid family that appeared fairly recently (in 2014). All the older families, for the most part, were detected. Note that none of the families were recognized by all existing anti-virus solutions.

We also looked at the maliciousness of the extracted URLs. Out of the 4 713 URLs (built-in and C&C) we extracted, 516 of them were detected as malicious: 27 out of 47 C&C URLs and 489 out of 4 666 built-in URLs. Surprisingly, some benign domains such as *maps.google, news.google*, and *Androids-market* were detected as malicious when provided as complete URLs. As expected, not all the C&C URLs considered as malicious are up-to-date. Considering the first appearance of some of these botnets (2010), we assume that the domain names might be reused by someone else for legitimate purposes. In this study, we are not conducting further analysis on these particular C&C domain names. However, if we look into the domain-level, most of the non-malicious URLs have adopted the DGA technique in their DNS. To further illustrate the malicious URL relationships, we visualized these URLs based on their families.

We also cross-checked the extracted URLs with several well-known blacklists [5,8,7,6] as listed in Table 5. Interestingly, we found no matches with the extracted URLs. Even though many of the analyzed families are date back to 2010 and 2011, these botnet URLs are still not a part of these blacklists. Another point to make here is the reuse of the URLs; as our analysis shows, although Android botnets share many URLs, all of them are different from those used by other malware.

**Table 5.** Cross-check with blacklists

| Name | Total URL/domain | Total URL Detected |
|---|---|---|
| Malware Domain Blocklist | 24 070 | 0 |
| Shalla Blacklist | 179 593 | 0 |
| URL Blacklist | 242 548 | 0 |
| Zeus Tracker | 785 187 | 0 |
| **Total** | 1 231 398 | 0 |

# 6   Conclusion

In this work, we have looked at improved methods of Android botnet behavioural analysis based on URL analysis. We have also shown the major differences between Android botnet URLs and the benign ones and showed their relationship with blacklists and anti-virus scanners. We have discovered that Android botnets tend to encrypt various types of data including the URLs of C&C servers, the method names to be invoked, the file path of the payloads, and even the content of the payloads to prevent them from being reverse engineered. We confirmed that the mobile botnets are evolving and becoming more sophisticated; thus, the samples from 2012 till the recent ones are more dynamic. Most of the URLs of these samples are hard coded in the Malware but created on the fly. However, by focusing on the string pattern extraction and visualization through static and dynamic analysis, we have managed to extract and decode these URLs. Through this study, we were able to identify the variety of encryption techniques used by bot masters. This is achieved by extracting the strings and visualizing each apk file from its botnet family as well as the mappings between the URLs.

**Acknowledgments.** This research has been partially supported by the New Brunswick Innovation Foundation under research grant RAI 2015-090. The authors also gratefully acknowledge funding from International Islamic University Malaysia (IIUM) and would like to thank Alip Aswalip for sharing the malware samples.

# References

1. Mobile malware mini dump. http://contagiominidump.blogspot.ca/ (accessed April 1, 2015)
2. Security threat trends. https://www.sophos.com/en-us/threat-center/medialibrary /PDFs/other/sophos-trends-and-predictions-2015.pdf (accessed August 1, 2015)
3. Virus total. https://www.virustotal.com/en/ (accessed June 12, 2015)
4. Android malware: Past, present, and future. http://www.locked.com/sites/ default/files/android-malware-past-present-future-wp.pdf (accessed June 7, 2015)
5. Malware Blocklist. http://www.malwaredomains.com/ (accessed March 5, 2015)
6. Shalla's blacklists. http://www.shallalist.de/ (accessed March 5, 2015)
7. Url blacklist. http://www.urlblacklist.com/ (accessed March 5, 2015)
8. Zeus tracker. https://zeustracker.abuse.ch/blocklist.php (accessed March 5, 2015)
9. Anubis: web-based malware analysis for unknown binaries. https://anubis.iseclab. org/ (accessed May 30, 2015)
10. Abdelrahman, O.H., Gelenbe, E., Görbil, G., Oklander, B.: Mobile network anomaly detection and mitigation: the NEMESYS approach. In: Information Sciences and Systems 2013, pp. 429–438. Springer (2013)
11. Alzahrani, A.J., Ghorbani, A.A.: SMS mobile botnet detection using a multi-agent system: research in progress. In: Proceedings of the 1st International Workshop on Agents and CyberSecurity, pp. 2:1–2:8. ACM, New York (2014)
12. Barrera, D., Kayacik, H.G., van Oorschot, P.C., Somayaji, A.: A methodology for empirical analysis of permission-based security models and its application to Android. In: Proceedings of the 17th ACM Conference on Computer and Communications Security, pp. 73–84. ACM, New York (2010)
13. Chebyshev, V., Unuchek, R.: Mobile malware evolution. https://securelist. com/analysis/kaspersky-security-bulletin/58335/mobile-malware-evolution-2013/ (accessed March 5, 2015)
14. Choi, B., Choi, S.K., Cho, K.: Detection of mobile botnet using VPN. In: Proceedings of the 2013 Seventh International Conference on Innovative Mobile and Internet Services in Ubiquitous Computing, pp. 142–148. IEEE Computer Society, Washington (2013)
15. Feizollah, A., Anuar, N.B., Salleh, R., Amalina, F., Maarof, R.R., Shamshirband, S.: A study of machine learning classifiers for anomaly-based mobile botnet detection. Malaysian Journal of Computer Science 26(4) (2014)
16. Geng, G., Xu, G., Zhang, M., Yang, Y., Yang, G.: An improved SMS based heterogeneous mobile botnet model. In: 2011 IEEE International Conference on Information and Automation (ICIA), pp. 198–202, June 2011
17. Hamon, V.: Android botnets for multi-targeted attacks. Journal of Computer Virology and Hacking Techniques, 1–10 (2014)
18. Hasan, R., Saxena, N., Haleviz, T., Zawoad, S., Rinehart, D.: Sensing-enabled channels for hard-to-detect command and control of mobile devices. In: Proceedings of the 8th ACM SIGSAC Symposium on Information. Computer and Communications Security, pp. 469–480. ACM, New York (2013)
19. Hua, J., Sakurai, K.: A SMS-based mobile botnet using flooding algorithm. In: Ardagna, C.A., Zhou, J. (eds.) WISTP 2011. LNCS, vol. 6633, pp. 264–279. Springer, Heidelberg (2011)
20. Le, A., Markopoulou, A., Faloutsos, M.: Phishdef:url names say it all. In: 2011 Proceedings IEEE INFOCOM, pp. 191–195. IEEE (2011)

21. Loorak, M.H., Fong, P.W.L., Carpendale, S.: Papilio: Visualizing Android Application Permissions. Computer Graphics Forum **33**(3), 391–400 (2014). http://diglib.eg.org/EG/CGF/volume33/issue3/v33i3pp391-400.pdf
22. Luoshi, Z., Yan, N., Xiao, W., Zhaoguo, W., Yibo, X.: A3: automatic analysis of android malware. In: 1st International Workshop on Cloud Computing and Information Security. Atlantis Press (2013)
23. Pieterse, H., Olivier, M.: Android botnets on the rise: trends and characteristics. In: Information Security for South Africa (ISSA), pp. 1–5, August 2012
24. Traynor, P., Lin, M., Ongtang, M., Rao, V., Jaeger, T., McDaniel, P., La Porta, T.: On cellular botnets: measuring the impact of malicious devices on a cellular network core. In: Proceedings of the 16th ACM Conference on Computer and Communications Security, pp. 223–234. ACM, New York (2009)
25. Vural, I., Venter, H.: Mobile botnet detection using network forensics. In: Berre, A.J., Gómez-Pérez, A., Tutschku, K., Fensel, D. (eds.) FIS 2010. LNCS, vol. 6369, pp. 57–67. Springer, Heidelberg (2010)
26. Xiang, C., Binxing, F., Lihua, Y., Xiaoyi, L., Tianning, Z.: Andbot: towards advanced mobile botnets. In: Proceedings of the 4th USENIX Conference on Large-scale Exploits and Emergent Threats, p. 11. USENIX Association, Berkeley (2011)
27. Zeng, Y., Shin, K.G., Hu, X.: Design of SMS commanded-and-controlled and p2p-structured mobile botnets. In: Proceedings of the Fifth ACM Conference on Security and Privacy in Wireless and Mobile Networks, pp. 137–148. ACM, New York (2012)
28. Zhao, S., Lee, P.P.C., Lui, J.C.S., Guan, X., Ma, X., Tao, J.: Cloud-based push-styled mobile botnets: a case study of exploiting the cloud to device messaging service. In: Proceedings of the 28th Annual Computer Security Applications Conference, pp. 119–128. ACM, New York (2012)
29. Zhou, Y., Jiang, X.: An analysis of the Anserverbot trojan. Tech. rep., Technical report, NQ Mobile Security Research Center (2011)
30. Zhou, Y., Jiang, X.: Dissecting android malware: characterization and evolution. In: 2012 IEEE Symposium on Security and Privacy (SP), pp. 95–109, May 2012

# Systems Security

# Unraveling the Security Puzzle: A Distributed Framework to Build Trust in FPGAs

Devu Manikantan Shila[1], Vivek Venugopalan[1(✉)], and Cameron D. Patterson[2]

[1] United Technologies Research Center, 411 Silver Lane, E Hartford, CT, USA
{manikad,venugov}@utrc.utc.com
[2] Bradley Department of ECE, Virginia Tech, Blacksburg, VA, USA
cdp@vt.edu

**Abstract.** Extensive use of third party IP cores (e.g., HDL, netlist) and open source tools in the FPGA application design and development process in conjunction with the inadequate bitstream protection measures have raised crucial security concerns in the past for reconfigurable hardware systems. Designing high fidelity and secure methodologies for FPGAs are still infancy and in particular, there are almost no concrete methods/techniques that can ensure trust in FPGA applications not entirely designed and/or developed in a trusted environment. This work strongly suggests the need for an anomaly detection capability within the FPGAs that can continuously monitor the behavior of the underlying FPGA IP cores and the communication activities of IP cores with other IP cores or peripherals for any abnormalities. To capture this need, we propose a technique called FIDelity Enhancing Security (FIDES) methodology for FPGAs that uses a combination of access control policies and behavior learning techniques for anomaly detection. FIDES essentially comprises of two components: (i) *Trusted Wrappers*, a layer of monitors with sensing capabilities distributed across the FPGA fabric; these wrappers embed the output of each IP core $i$ with a tag $\tau_i$ according to the pre-defined security policy $\Pi$ and also verifies the embeddings of each input to the IP core to detect any violation of policies. The use of tagging and tracking enables us to capture the normal interactions of each IP core with its environment (e.g., other IP cores, memory, OS or I/O ports). *Trusted Wrappers* also monitors the statistical properties exhibited by each IP core module on execution such as power consumption, number of clock cycles and timing variations to detect any anomalous operations; (ii) a *Trusted Anchor* that monitors the communication between the IP cores and the peripherals with regard to the centralized security policies $\Psi$ as well as the statistical properties produced by the peripherals. To thwart an adversary from tampering or disabling the proposed security components during the deployment stage, our architecture generates a secure bitstream blob consisting of the IP cores, Trusted Wrappers and Trusted Anchor, secured using public key cryptography. We implemented FIDES architecture on a Xilinx Zynq 7020 device running a red-black system comprising of sensitive and non-sensitive IP cores. Our results show that the FIDES implementation leads to only 1-2% overhead in terms of the logic resources per wrapper

M. Qiu et al. (Eds.): NSS 2015, LNCS 9408, pp. 95–111, 2015.
DOI: 10.1007/978-3-319-25645-0_7

and incurs minimal latency per wrapper for tag verification and embedding. On the other hand, as compared to the baseline implementation, when all the communications within the system are routed to the Trusted Anchor for centralized policy checking and verification, a latency of 1.5X clock cycles is observed; this clearly manifests the advantage of using distributed wrappers as opposed to centralized policy checking.

# 1   Introduction

Due to the size, weight and power (SWaP) advantages, FPGA (Field Programmable Gate Array) devices are the primary source for both computation and communication tasks in various mission and safety critical embedded systems such as smart grid, embedded and network encryption, avionics, tactical radios, satellite communications, finance and banking, and homeland security. While the benefits of FPGAs are great, hardware security is now emerging as a serious concern for FPGAs due to the extensive use of third party IP cores/functions (e.g., HDL, netlist), open source tools (e.g., CAD) and unauthenticated configuration bitstreams in the application design and development process. For instance, efforts [22], [17], [2] show how one can exploit various vulnerable stages of the hardware lifecycle to inject stealthy malwares ('Trojans') into the ASIC and FPGA devices. Evidence of the existence of Trojans in the forms of backdoors in military grade and wireless communication devices are also shown in [21]. Typically, an FPGA application encompass a collection of intellectual property (IP) cores and soft-core processors which are in turn glued together to implement specific functionalities within a system. In many cases, the IP cores (available in the form of HDL, netlist or bitstream) are procured from multiple third-party vendors with varying trust levels which provides ample opportunities for an adversary to inject hardware Trojans. A successful triggering of one such Trojan could create chaos in civilian infrastructure (aerospace, transportation or energy domain), sabotage critical military applications and missions, disable missile and weapon systems, leak sensitive information or provide backdoor access to highly secure systems. Enforcing hardware security at the device level and system level is very critical, which in turn has motivated defense agencies such as DARPA and IARPA to launch innovative programs such as Supply chain Hardware Integrity for Electronics Defense (SHIELD) [6] and Trusted Integrated Chips (TIC) [15].

Besides these programs, a handful of research efforts along the tangents of detecting and identifying the Trojans in hardware have been proposed. The techniques presented in works such as UCI [10], VeriTrust [25], FANCI [23] and HaTCh [9] essentially focus on the idea of identifying and flagging unused or suspicious Trojan wires within a design. In HaTCh [9], for instance, authors use functional testing on the IP cores to identify all the list of unused wire combinations and augments additional tagging circuitry to the IP cores so as to keep track of the suspicious wires; as soon as a malicious wire is activated, the tagging circuitry will raise an exception to prevent the Trojan from depicting malicious behavior. A major drawback with all these approaches is the assumption that the source code of the IP core design is available to the end consumers in HDL/netlist format and hence, often neglect the scenarios where the consumers have access only to the configuration bitstreams (*"hard IP cores"*). Proof-Carrying Codes [16] are also proposed where the IP vendor will construct a formal proof of the design adhering to certain security properties, which will be later verified by IP consumer to ensure that design is free from modifications. The proof is used to detect anomalies if the design has been tampered during deployment. However, this approach does not deal with trust in the source code, as the proof can be generated for malicious code. Besides the overhead involved in creating huge proofs for even smaller codes, loop holes can also occur while defining many security properties.

In contrary to above efforts, the concepts presented in [1], [11], and [3] assumes a *"blackbox"* methodology where no assumption is made on the availability of the source code and are perhaps closest to our design. In [1], authors propose an application-dependent security infrastructure monitoring datapath signals for illegal behaviors. This approach adds reconfigurable Design-for-Enabling-Security (DEFENSE) logic to the functional design to implement a centralized run-time security monitor. The hardware-based monitors are configurable finite-state machines (FSMs) that check the current set of signals for the properties specified by the designer. Huffmire *et al.* [11] propose a memory protection mechanism by designing and implementing policy-driven memory protection techniques using reconfigurable hardware. Their work develops an access policy language that precisely describes the fine-grained memory separation of modules on an FPGA and a policy compiler that converts the specified memory access policies into enforcement hardware modules. This memory access policy mechanism is then integrated into the hardware-based centralized reference monitor to detect malicious memory accesses at run-time. The use of centralized monitors not only affects the scalability of the security mechanisms in [12], [13], [14] but also makes it vulnerable to classic communication attacks such as spoofing, Man-in-the-Middle (MITM) that enables an attacker to spoof or tamper the signals/messages to the centralized monitor, as indicated by [20], [18]. Another drawback of these approaches is the inability to identify the malicious IP cores that conforms to the access control policies but deviates from the normal execution behavior; e.g., a malicious encryption IP core instead of encrypting the data when triggered leaks the secret key. In such scenarios, monitoring the normal execution behavior of IP cores and peripherals such as number of clock cycles, total power consumption in real-time can be used to detect any abnormalities.

**Motivation and Contribution.** The addition of third party IP cores and the use of open source tools in the design and development process renders an FPGA application vulnerable to hardware Trojan based attacks. There are currently no concrete methods/techniques that can be easily instrumented into the FPGAs and provide trust guarantees in FPGA applications which are not completely developed in a trusted environment. The security methods currently available have the following shortcomings: (a) requires low level knowledge of the IP core design; (b) vulnerable to traditional communication attacks such as spoofing and MITM; (c) centralized approach; and (d) inability to detect functional behavior deviation. Moreover most existing solutions overlook the communication activities and functional behavior of IP core which in turn plays an important role in actually carrying out the attack. This paper addresses such a significant loophole by proposing a secure communication framework and behavior monitoring module that can reliably thwart hardware Trojan based attacks.

Motivated by the shortcomings in the existing works, we strongly argue the need for an anomaly detection capability within the FPGAs that can be easily instrumented with the application and continuously monitor the underlying IP core behavior and also the access activities of IP cores with other IP cores or peripherals for any signs of abnormalities. To capture this need, we propose a technique called FIDelity Enhancing Security (FIDES) methodology for FPGAs that uses a combination of access control policies and behavior learning techniques for anomaly detection. FIDES essentially comprises of two components: (i) *Trusted Wrappers*, a layer of monitors with sensing capabilities distributed across the FPGA fabric; these wrappers stamp the output of each IP core $i$ with a tag $\tau_i$ according to the pre-defined security policy $\Pi_i$ and also verifies the embeddings of each input to the IP core to detect any violation of policies. The use of tagging and tracking enables us to capture the generalized interactions of each IP core with its environment (e.g., other IP cores, memory, OS or I/O ports). *Trusted Wrappers* also monitors the statistical properties exhibited by each IP core functions on execution such as power consumption, number of clock cycles and timing variations to detect any anomalous operations; (ii) a *Trusted Anchor* that monitors the communication between the IP cores and the peripherals with regard to the centralized security policies $\Psi$ and the statistical properties produced by the peripherals.

We prototyped FIDES architecture on a Xilinx Zynq 7020 device, that consists of a hard fused ARM core and an Artix FPGA. The Trusted Wrapper is implemented in hardware logic and monitors the communication and execution behavior of IP core in a distributed manner. The Trusted Anchor is mapped to the ARM core and controls the communication of the IP cores with the external peripherals (enabled to thwart leakage of sensitive information) and provides behavioral monitoring of the peripherals (enabled to thwart covert attacks). We target FIDES architecture on a Xilinx Zynq 7020 device implemented with a red-black system comprising of sensitive and non-sensitive IP cores. Our results show that FIDES implementation leads to only 1-2% overhead in terms of the logic resources/wrapper and incurs minimal latency/wrapper for tag verification and embedding. On the other hand, as compared to the baseline implementation, when all the communications within the system are routed to the Trusted Anchor for centralized policy checking and verification, a latency of 1.5X clock cycles is observed; this clearly manifests the advantage of using distributed wrappers as opposed to centralized policy checking

To the best of our knowledge, we first design and implement a distributed and secure anomaly detection framework for FPGAs that can identify abnormal FPGA behaviors (hardware Trojans) in real-time.

**Roadmap**: Section 2 provides the detailed description of the FIDES methodology along with the description of the adversary/threat model and the system design of the distributed information model. The hardware implementation of the FIDES architecture is described in Section 3 with the results presented in Section 4. Section 5 concludes this work.

## 2    Proposed Security Framework

This paper proposes a novel, distributed and secure methodology for enhancing trust in FPGA applications designed or developed under untrusted environments called FIDES (FIDelity Enhancing Security methodology) named after the Greek God of Trust. FIDES essentially relies on the use of two major approaches: (a) *decentralized information flow control* (DIFC) model that enables safe and distributed information flows between various elements of FPGA such as IP cores, physical memory and registers by annotating/tagging each data item with its sensitivity level and the identity of the participating entities; and (b) *statistical learning techniques* that learns the normal functional behavior of IP cores, peripherals defined as *conformant core behavior* ($\mathcal{CCB}$) during the FPGA application integration/testing stage and leverages the learned $\mathcal{CCB}$ model to detect any anomalous behavior deviations in run-time.

In the sequel, we will initially present the adversary and threat model and then discuss the detailed FIDES system design in section 2.2. Table 1 presents the summary of various notations used for describing the FIDES design.

**Table 1.** Table of Notations

| Notation | Meaning |
| --- | --- |
| $< Core >_i^s$ | Sensitive IP core $i$ |
| $< Core >_i^{ns}$ | Non-sensitive IP core $i$ |
| $W_i$ | Trusted Wrapper assigned to $< Core >_i$ |
| $\mathcal{TA}$ | Trusted Anchor |
| $\Pi_i$ | User-defined policies for $< Core >_i$ |
| $\Psi$ | User-defined policies at $\mathcal{TA}$ |
| $\tau_i$ | Tags assigned to $< Core >_i$ |
| $\sigma_i$ | $< Core >_i$ functional behavior signature |
| $\mathcal{M}^S$ ,$\mathcal{M}^N$ | Sensitive and Non-sensitive memory regions |
| $\alpha$ | Characteristics of IP core ($\mathcal{S},\mathcal{N},\mathcal{E}$) |

### 2.1    Adversary and Threat Model

Majority of the efforts show that various layers of the FPGA lifecycle ranging from design to final deployment stage are vulnerable to Trojan intrusions.

This work assumes trusted FPGA application integration and testing stage however untrusted design, development and deployment stage due to the immense involvement of the third party IP cores, CAD tools and also, easily accessible FPGA configuration bit streams. With this assumption, a more realistic adversary model is considered: (i) at design and development stage, the Trojan might be present in the third party IP core or CAD tool, or might be inserted by a rogue designer during the design process; (ii) at deployment stage, the Trojan might be injected into the FPGA configuration bitstream. A handful of works along the lines of cryptographic defenses (e.g., use of bitstream signatures [5], design obfuscation [4]) have been proposed to thwart tampering attacks on FPGA bitstream. FIDES architecture will leverage those existing defenses based on asymmetric cryptography.

Embedded systems often contains a mixture of critical and non-critical applications residing on the same platform. Any intentional or accidental fault on the operation of the critical application could have an impact on safety, or could cause large financial or social loss. It is therefore necessary to thwart the non-critical components from interrupting or compromising the critical operations. This paper considers a similar scenario called the red-black system implemented in FPGA that will encompass multiple IP cores procured from various third party vendors with different sensitivity levels. In such a system, two distinct kinds of IP core (*Core*) sensitivity levels are considered: (a) IP core that accesses and processes critical and sensitive information (e.g., network encryption) called *sensitive core* ($< Core >_i^s$) and (b) IP core that accesses and processes less critical and sensitive information called *non-sensitive core* ($< Core >_i^{ns}$).

Proper segregation between the sensitive and non-sensitive operations should be realized so that an untrusted IP core will be thwarted from accessing the shared resources (e.g., memory, peripherals) and transmit the information to the outside world via a covert channel (e.g., secret unnoticeable channels) or a normal channel (e.g., send sensitive cryptographic information by mixing with the noise levels or encrypting with the attacker-known keys). With regard to the red-black system design, we derive the attack scenarios given by ([A1] - [A4]) and propose the security policy requirements addressed by ([R1] - [R4]).

### Attack Scenarios

A1. $< Core >_i^s$ *accesses the critical and sensitive information and export the information to the outside world*

A2. $< Core >_i^{ns}$ *accesses the critical and sensitive information and export the information to the outside world*

A3. $< Core >_i^{ns}$ *uses trusted* $< Core >_j^s$ *as a conduit (a Man-in-the-middle) to access sensitive regions and export the information to the outside world*

A4. *Malicious IP core spoof as a legitimate core and access application resources*

## Security Requirements

R1. $< Core >_i^{ns}$ shall be prevented from accessing and processing the sensitive information

R2. Cores shall be restricted from accessing the peripherals directly to limit export of data.

R3. The information flow between $< Core >_i^{ns}$ and $< Core >_i^s$ shall be restricted or performed in the presence of a security officer.

R4. The statistical properties of each $< Core >_i$ shall be measured and monitored to detect any anomalous functional behavior deviations

## 2.2 System Design

**Initialization phase:** During the FPGA application integration/testing stage, the following components will be generated by the end consumer: (a) *Trusted Wrapper* $(W_i)$ - a thin layer of hardware logic that interface with each IP core $< Core >_i$ and manages/monitors the communication activities of $< Core >_i$ with other cores $(< Core >_j$, where $j \neq i)$; (b) *Trusted Anchor* $(\mathcal{TA})$ - a centralized security officer, implemented in ARM, that manages/monitors the communication of the IP cores with the external world (I/O Peripherals) according to the pre-defined security policy $\Psi$; (c) *Tagged Physical Memory* - a partitioned memory with *tags* annotated to the data denoting their sensitivity level; and (d) *Secure Bitstream Blob* - a cryptographically signed bitstream blob containing $W_i$; $\forall i \in \mathbb{S}$, where $\mathbb{S}$ represents the set of IP cores and $\mathcal{TA}$ modules with the private key $(K-)$ of the end consumer; the signed blob together with the public key $(K+)$ will be loaded into the memory. A hash of the $(K+)$ will be also loaded into the trusted region within the processor to thwart any attempts to modify the bitstream signatures. The use of cryptographic signatures will prevent an adversary from subverting the protection schemes included within the configuration bitstream. The complete architecture of FIDES is presented in Figure 1. FIDES specifically provides three functionalities:

- **Prevention**: The use of asymmetric cryptographic signatures prevents unauthorized tampering of bitstreams (disabling or modifying the protection schemes) built with the proposed protection schemes (Trusted Wrappers and Anchor).
- **Detection**: The combination of Trusted Wrappers and Trusted Anchor detects any unauthorized communication (e.g., non-sensitive IP core accessing sensitive memory regions or communicating with sensitive IP cores) and anomalous execution of IP cores and peripherals.
- **Response**: On detection of an attack, the framework responds by logging the details of the attack in the *Logging buffer* and communicating to the external world for further diagnostics.

FIDES specifically *prevents* unauthorized modification of bitstreams through the use of asymmetric cryptographic signatures and detects any unauthorized communication and execution behavior of IP cores and peripherals through the use of Trusted Anchor and Trusted Wrappers. In the sequel, we present the various approaches used by FIDES to enable these security protections.

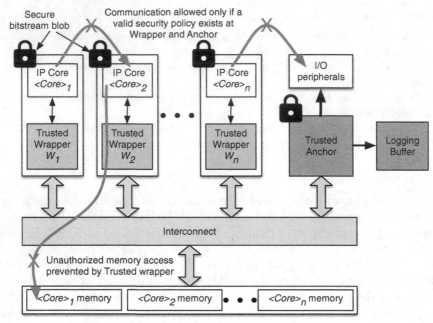

Fig. 1. FIDES Architecture

**Decentralized Information Flow Model.** FIDES uses tag-based information flow control methodology to achieve decentralized and safe flow of information between various elements in the system [19]. In order to do so, during the initialization phase, each Trusted Wrapper $W_i$ will be assigned a *tag* $(\tau_i)$ that reflects the characteristics $(\alpha)$ of the information handled by the ¡Core¿$i$ and also the identity $(i)$ of the participating entity (e.g., IP Core identity).

$$\text{Initialization phase: } W_i \Leftarrow \tau_i; \; \tau_i =< \alpha, i >$$

Where $\alpha = (\mathcal{S}, \mathcal{N}, \mathcal{E})$. Here $\mathcal{S}, \mathcal{N}$ and $\mathcal{E}$ denotes sensitive, non-sensitive and empty tokens respectively. The value of $\alpha$ will be assigned based on the following policies:

- $< Core >^s_j | W_j \Leftarrow < \mathcal{S}, \text{j} >$, $< Core >^{ns}_j | W_j \Leftarrow < \mathcal{N}, \text{j} >$: The IP cores $< Core >^s_i$ and $< Core >^{ns}_i$ will be labeled with $\mathcal{S}$ and $\mathcal{N}$ tokens, respectively, depending on the characteristics of the information handled. In cases where an IP Core processes both sensitive and non sensitive information, the wrapper will be assigned a $\mathcal{S}$ token.
- Tagged physical memory: The physical memory regions $\mathcal{M}$ will be partitioned into sensitive and non-sensitive regions by tagging with $\mathcal{S}$ and $\mathcal{N}$ tokens denoted by $\mathcal{M}^{\mathcal{S}}$ and $\mathcal{M}^{\mathcal{N}}$, respectively. The memory regions can be also tagged with the identity $i$ of the owner to enable horizontal access control protection, if needed. Alternatively speaking, under horizontal access

control protection $< Core >_i^s$ will be prevented from accessing the memory space belonging to $< Core >_j^s$, though both cores are tagged with $\mathcal{S}$.

- $\mathbb{P} \Leftarrow < \mathcal{E} >$: The I/O peripherals (external world), denoted by $\mathbb{P}$, will be labeled with empty tokens ($\mathcal{E}$). This approach of assigning empty tokens will prevent the IP cores from releasing the sensitive information to the external world as tagging based information flow rule requires an IP core to hold an $\mathcal{E}$ token to release the information to the peripherals.

Since the system is distributed and each entity is not aware of the tag of others, the messages exchanged between the entities is labeled appropriately by the Trusted Wrappers. Then the receiving wrappers will use the tagging based information flow rules to determine whether to accept or reject the messages. Enforcing tags on the messages also ensures that the information will be always prefixed with a tag when stored in temporary or permanent memory locations and only components that follows the tagging-based information flow rules can access the information.

**Tagging-Based Information Flow Rule Aka 'DIFC'.** The information labeled with the tag of $\tau_j =< \alpha_j, j >$ can flow to $\tau_k =< \alpha_k, k >$, only if the tags of $\tau_j$ is included in $\tau_k$. We define the partial order $\preceq$ (pronounced can flow to) for two tags $\tau_j$ and $\tau_k$ as

$$\tau_j \preceq \tau_k; \text{ if } \alpha_j = \alpha_k \text{ and } (j, k) \in \Pi_k$$

Where $\Pi_k$ is the security policy defined at the IP core $k$. The security policy $\Pi_i$ essentially captures the authorized set of communications for each IP core $i$ based on the design specifications. The above equation mainly states that core $k$ can accept the data from core $j$ only if the security policy defined at $k$ ($\Pi_k$) allows the communication from core $j$ and the characteristics token $\alpha$ at both $j$ and $k$ matches. Under this rule the following communication will be prevented.

$$\tau_j = (< \mathcal{S}, j >) \npreceq \tau_k = (< \mathcal{N}, k >)$$
$$\tau_j = (< \mathcal{N}, j >) \npreceq \tau_k = (< \mathcal{S}, k >)$$
$$\tau_j = (< \mathcal{S}, j >) \npreceq \mathbb{P} =< \mathcal{E} >$$
$$\tau_j = (< \mathcal{N}, j >) \npreceq \mathbb{P} =< \mathcal{E} >$$

While the above rules prevent the contaminated cores from communicating with other cores or releasing the information, it would also make it implausible for any legal communication activities or any sensitive data to get out of the system. Therefore, DIFC supports *tag declassification* capability (denoted by $\downarrow$) which enables the higher tags to declassify to lower tag to receive information; especially, we consider the following two scenarios:

(a) *IP cores that process both sensitive and non-sensitive information labeled with tag $\mathcal{S}$* - We provide an ability for $W_{i; \forall i \in \mathbb{S}}$ to declassify its tag from $\mathcal{S}$ to $\mathcal{N}$ such that $\mathcal{S} \downarrow \mathcal{N}$. To up the privilege back to $\mathcal{S}$, the $< Core >_i^s | W_i$ will communicate with $\mathcal{TA}$ initially and $\mathcal{TA}$ will set the privilege of $W_i$ back to $\mathcal{S}$, only if security policy at $\mathcal{TA}$ allows. If $W_i$ is allowed to up its privilege without contacting $\mathcal{TA}$, it can be leveraged by a non-sensitive compromised IP core to defeat the system. As an example, consider the attack where a $< Core >_i^{ns}$ uses $< Core >_j^s$ as a conduit (a Man-in-the-middle) to access sensitive memory areas and export the information to the outside world. If in the absence of $\mathcal{TA}$ , the $< Core >_j^s$ will declassify to $\mathcal{N}$ to receive data from the $< Core >_j^{ns}$ and up its privilege back to $\mathcal{S}$ token to access the sensitive regions; once accessed, the IP core will declassify its privilege to $\mathcal{N}$ to export the information to $< Core >_j^{ns}$. To avoid such attack scenarios, we impose the following constraint: a $W_i$ can declassify only after receiving an explicit request from $\mathcal{TA}$;

(b) *IP core that exports the data to the external world (I/O peripherals)* - To export the data, declassification privileges are assigned to $\mathcal{TA}$ (declassify the label from $\mathcal{S}/\mathcal{N}$ to $\mathcal{E}$) based on the pre-defined security policies, $\Psi$ at $\mathcal{TA}$. The $\Psi$ essentially captures the authorized set of peripherals for each IP core based on the design specifications.

**Remark #1:** This paper does not consider the presence of Trojans on interconnect. Existing efforts can be leveraged to build secure and trustworthy interconnects such as the time based techniques in [7] to detect malicious interconnect operations or the use of secure checksums, e.g., Message Authentication Codes (MACs) [8], to prevent the Trojans within the interconnect modifying or spoofing the messages.

**Remark #2:** The security of the proposed FIDES design depends on the policies defined by the user, $\Pi$ and $\Psi$. This paper assumes that the policies are generated by the end consumer based on the design specifications and requirements.

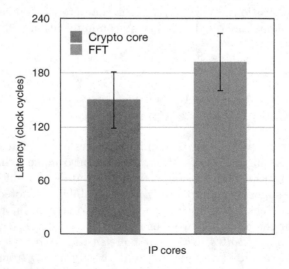

**Fig. 2.** IP cores with distinct latency profiles

**Behavior Monitoring.** Besides labeling and monitoring the communication activities, to boost the trust in an FPGA application, the characteristics of the underlying tagged IP cores and peripherals ($\mathbb{P}$) will be also observed and used by the Trusted Wrappers for identifying malicious behaviors and decision making (e.g., forward/drop the message, report to $\mathcal{TA}$). This technique allows to identify the malicious IP cores that conforms to the access control policies but deviates from the normal execution behavior; e.g., a malicious IP core that performs erroneous computations on the input data. As each IP core exhibit different statistical properties on execution (e.g., power consumption, number of clock cycles, and timing variations), Trusted Wrappers will use these properties to determine the normal functional execution behavior of IP cores defined as *conformant core behavior* ($\mathcal{CCB}$). In Figure 2, we show that each IP core exhibits distinct behavior such as *number of clock cycles* during its execution. Therefore in the FPGA application integration and testing stage, for each $< Core >_i$, we compute a signature, denoted by $\sigma_i$, that captures these statistical properties. Together with the *tag* ($\tau_i$), during the learning phase each wrapper $W_i$ will be assigned $\sigma_i$ as follows:

$$\text{Learning phase: } W_i \Leftarrow \sigma_i$$

In the run-time phase, $W_i$ will monitor the statistical properties produced by $< Core >_i$ and compares with the already learned signature $\sigma_i$. If the difference between the expected and observed behavior exceeds a user-defined threshold, $W_i$ flags the observation as "anomalous" and informs $\mathcal{TA}$ for further actions. Similar to Trusted Wrapper, $\mathcal{TA}$ will also monitor the behavior of external peripherals to detect any anomalous leaking of information. The intuition behind using statistical properties for malicious behavior/anomaly detection comes from [20], [18] where a combination of several statistical properties such as power consumption, clock cycles, called the Hardware Trojan Detection Metric (HDM), can be used to detect malicious IP core operations.

**Remark #3:** In this paper, we do not address heat or power-based Trojans. However, we can easily extend our work with metrics that can detect these Trojans.

**Security Proofs.** We here show with proofs on how FIDES can detect and prevent the attack scenarios presented in [A1]- [A4].

A1. $< Core >_i^s$ accesses the critical and sensitive information and export the information to the outside world using either of the two approaches: (a) covert channel (secret and unnoticeable) and (b) obfuscate (mixing the data with random noise) the information and transport via normal channels:

*Proof.* (a) $< Core >_i^s$ accesses the critical and sensitive information from the memory( $\mathcal{M}^\mathcal{S}$) and forward the information to the $\mathcal{TA}$. Since the covert channel is not an authorized peripheral for $< Core >_i^s$, $\mathcal{TA}$ will reject the information according to the pre-defined policies $\Psi$. (b) As obfuscation leads to noticeable changes from the learned signature $\sigma_i$, wrapper $W_i$ will flag $< Core >_i^s$ as anomalous and informs $\mathcal{TA}$ about the observation.

A2. $< Core >_i^{ns}$ accesses the critical and sensitive information and export the information to the outside world

*Proof.* This attack will fail as tagging based information flow rule restricts $< Core >_i^{ns}$ tagged with $\mathcal{N}$ tag from accessing the sensitive memory regions such that $\mathcal{M}^S \npreceq \tau_i = < \mathcal{N}, i >$

A3. $< Core >_i^{ns}$ uses trusted $< Core >_j^s$ as a conduit (a Man-in-the-middle) to access sensitive regions and export the information to the outside world

*Proof.* As tagging based information flow rule either prevents $< Core >_i^{ns}$ tagged with $\mathcal{N}$ tag from accessing the sensitive IP cores ($\tau_i = (< \mathcal{N}, i >) \npreceq \tau_j = (< \mathcal{S}, j >)$) or forces $< Core >_j^s$ to declassify its tag from $\mathcal{S}$ to $\mathcal{N}$, this attack fails.

A4. Malicious IP core spoof as a legitimate core and access application resources

*Proof.* As each IP core $< Core >_i$ is integrated with $W_i$, all the communications originating from $< Core >_i$ will be appropriately labeled with the tag $\tau_i = ¡\alpha, i¿$ which will prevent a malicious IP core from impersonating as a valid IP core.

## 3    Hardware Implementation of FIDES

The communication framework in FPGA-based systems plays a critical role in supporting the hardware Trojan attacks and hence it is necessary to understand the existing bus-based protocols in the FPGA platform. FPGA-based systems with soft core processors consisted of interconnects such as Avalon in case of Altera and the processor local bus (PLB) in case of Xilinx. With the introduction of hard fused ARM cores in FPGA devices, AXI interconnect serves as the primary protocol for communication between the ARM core and the different IP cores [24]. The AXI protocol is a subset of the ARM Advanced Microcontroller Bus Architecture (AMBA) and the different AXI4 interfaces are compared in Table 2. The selection of AXI protocol allows a designer to focus only on the IP behavior and not the IP interconnect, when targeting different FPGA-ARM platforms. The AXI4-Lite interface is the most area efficient and best suited for control logic data transfer.

**Table 2.** AXI4 interfaces

| Features | AXI4 | AXI4-Lite | AXI4-Stream |
|---|---|---|---|
| Type | High-performance and memory mapped interface | Register-style interface | Non-address based high speed streaming interface |
| Data transfer | 256 cycles | 1 cycle | unlimited cycles |
| Data width | 32-1024 bits | 32-64 bits | unlimited bytes |
| Application | Embedded, memory | Control logic | DSP, video |

In case of Xilinx systems, the ARM core is referred to as the processing system (PS), while the FPGA fabric consisting of reconfigurable gates is called the programmable logic (PL). The IP cores are bundled with the AXI4-Lite interface by the IP Packager tool in Xilinx's Vivado Design suite. Each IP core is wrapped with a AXI wrapper, which configures the data transfer into the IP core using custom register interfaces. These memory mapped registers are configured as write registers for input ports and read registers for the output ports of the IP core. The AXI wrapper initializes these registers to a default size of 32 bits. By default, the AXI wrapper is configured to initialize write registers for the IP core's inputs and the IP core's outputs are routed to external I/O peripherals.

The Trusted Wrapper $W_1$ shown in Figure 3 is the top-level interface to the IP core ¡Core¿$_1$. Each of the IP core's I/O port is assigned a tag $\tau_i$, which is mapped to a register from the AXI4 wrapper. Since the IP core's output is also monitored by $W_1$, the AXI wrapper is modified to incorporate read registers for the output ports. If the output port is directly connected to an external peripheral, the additional read registers for the output port preserves a copy of the data and its tag. Thus the $\mathcal{TA}$ supervises the data being transferred through the external I/O peripherals and is able to provide behavioral monitoring. In summary, the Trusted Wrapper $W_1$ consists of the following register configurations:

- **Write** registers for the input ports of the IP core,
- **Write** registers for tagging the input ports,
- **Read** registers for monitoring the IP core's output ports,
- **Read** registers for tagging the IP core's output ports,
- **Read** register for declassification of data transfer depending on the security policy framed for the IP core,
- **Write** register for providing the modified output label based on the temporary downgrade of the security policy access of the IP core.

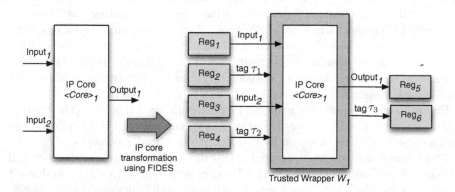

**Fig. 3.** Trusted Wrapper mechanism for an IP Core

The Trusted Wrapper is embedded into the IP core during the Xilinx Vivado tool's IP Packaging and Configuration step. This ensures that the IP core's

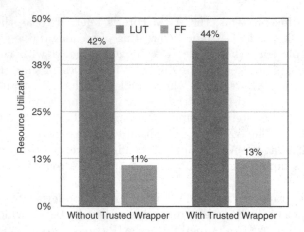

**Fig. 4.** Resource utilization for an IP core with and without a Trusted Wrapper

tagging functionality is available when instantiating the IP core in other designs. The trusted anchor $\mathcal{TA}$ is implemented on the ARM core, as it can easily monitor the data transfer through the AXI interconnect to the I/O peripherals, thus enabling communication and behavioral monitoring of peripherals.

## 4    Results

The FIDES algorithm is prototyped on the MicroZed Xilinx Zynq-based Z7020 FPGA development board. The Zynq 7020 consists of a dual core ARM processor and a Xilinx Artix FPGA with 85K logic cells. Both the baseline and the FIDES implementations are synthesized and implemented using Xilinx Vivado tool. The Vivado tool provides the logic resource utilization of the complete design and also provides a definition file. The definition file is mapped using Xilinx SDK to execute the software algorithm implementation. Figure 4 shows the resource utilization obtained from Xilinx Vivado after embedding the IP core in the Trusted Wrapper. The Trusted Wrapper does not consume much resources and only increases the logic resource (LUTs and FF) utilization by about 1-2% as compared to the baseline implementation. The ARM core is also embedded with timers to measure latency between the IP cores. The timers provide 1 $ns$ (nanosecond) resolution as the ARM core is clocked at 1 GHz.

Figure 5 shows the latency incurred by incorporating FIDES into the existing system. To clearly understand the latency overhead of our FIDES scheme, we implemented two cases, as given by the algorithms 1 and 2 below.

The latency measurement taken for two different IP cores crypto core and (64-point) Fast Fourier Transform (FFT) core, with regard to the Procedures 1 (denoted by 'no declassification' legend in figure) and 2 (denoted by 'declassification' legend in figure). In case of Procedure 1, as the communication is between two non-sensitive IP cores, no declassification messages were sent to $\mathcal{TA}$; the $\mathcal{TA}$ is contacted only once to export the data outside. Since the message passing through the AXI interconnect between the Trusted Wrapper and the $\mathcal{TA}$ contributes to the

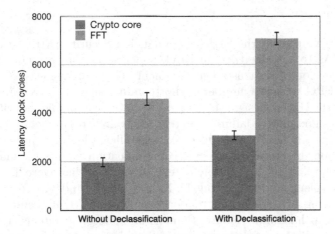

**Fig. 5.** Latency measurement with the Trusted Wrapper

---

**Algorithm 1.** Communication flow between non-critical IP cores

1: $< Core >_i^{ns}$ → Trusted Wrapper $W_i$
2: Trusted Wrapper $W_i$ → Trusted Wrapper $W_j$
3: Trusted Wrapper $W_j$ → $< Core >_j^{ns}$
4: No declassification/classification messages sent from $W_i$ and $W_j$ → to $\mathcal{TA}$

---

latency more as compared to the tag verification, we observed minimal latency for scenarios related to Procedure 1. On the other hand, in case of communication between non-sensitive and sensitive IP cores (or mismatched tags), depicted by Procedure 2, $\mathcal{TA}$ is contacted multiple times for declassification and classification of privileges which in turn led to an increase in latency ($\approx 1.5X$ clock cycles). From the results, we also note that the existing centralized communication framework for policy checking and verification can incur a larger overhead as opposed to the proposed distributed wrapper scheme since the data communication through the AXI Interconnect incurs a significant latency.

---

**Algorithm 2.** Communication flow between critical and non-critical IP cores

1: $< Core >_i^{ns}$ → Trusted Wrapper $W_i$
2: Trusted Wrapper $W_i$ ↛ Trusted Wrapper $W_j$
3: Request for declassification sent to $\mathcal{TA}$ by $W_j$
4: $\mathcal{TA}$ changes the privileges of $W_j$ from $\mathcal{S} \downarrow \mathcal{N}$, if policy allows
5: Trusted Wrapper $W_i$ → Trusted Wrapper $W_j$
6: Trusted Wrapper $W_j$ → $< Core >_j^s$
7: $\mathcal{TA}$ up the privileges of $W_j$ from $\mathcal{N} \uparrow \mathcal{S}$, on completion

---

# 5   Conclusions

In this paper, we present the FIDelity Enhancing Security (FIDES) methodology for FPGAs to enhance trust in FPGA operations that are not completely designed or developed in a trusted environment. The security measures currently available for FPGAs have a number of shortcomings such as (a) require low level knowledge of the IP core design; (b) vulnerable to bus communication attacks; (c) centralized design; and (d) failure to detect hardware Trojans that deviate from normal functional behavior. We addressed a significant loophole present in these existing solutions by proposing a secure communication framework and behavior monitoring module that can reliably detect and prevent hardware Trojan based attacks. We implemented FIDES on the Xilinx Zynq 7020 device for a red-black system consisting of critical and non-critical IP cores. Our results yielded a 1-2% increase in hardware resources and 1.5X increase in latency (worst case scenario where all the communications happen between the Trusted Wrapper and Trusted Anchor) as compared to the baseline implementation. We observe that the resource utilization and latency results can be further optimized by clustering the IP cores into groups that share same characteristics, which will be addressed in future work.

**Acknowledgments.** We would like to thank Prof. Marten van Dijk and his team for fruitful discussions and their helpful feedback.

# References

1. Abramovici, M., Bradley, P.: Integrated circuit security: new threats and solutions. In: Proceedings of the 5th Annual Workshop on Cyber Security and Information Intelligence Research: Cyber Security and Information Intelligence Challenges and Strategies, p. 55. ACM (2009)
2. Adee, S.: The Hunt For The Kill Switch. IEEE Spectrum **45**(5), 34–39 (2008)
3. Bilzor, M., Huffmire, T., Irvine, C., Levin, T.: Security checkers: detecting processor malicious inclusions at runtime. In: 2011 IEEE International Symposium on Hardware-Oriented Security and Trust (HOST), pp. 34–39. IEEE (2011)
4. Chakraborty, R., Bhunia, S.: Security against hardware Trojan through a novel application of design obfuscation. In: IEEE/ACM International Conference on Computer-Aided Design - Digest of Technical Papers, ICCAD 2009, pp. 113–116 (2009)
5. Chakraborty, R., Saha, I., Palchaudhuri, A., Naik, G.: Hardware Trojan Insertion by Direct Modification of FPGA Configuration Bitstream. IEEE Design Test **30**(2), 45–54 (2013)
6. Defense Advanced Research Projects Agency (DARPA), Microsystems Technology Office/MTO Broad Agency Announcement,: Supply chain hardware integrity for electronics defense (SHIELD) (2014)
7. Farag, M.M., Lerner, L.W., Patterson, C.D.: Interacting with hardware Trojans over a network. In: 2012 IEEE International Symposium on Hardware-Oriented Security and Trust (HOST), pp. 69–74. IEEE (2012)
8. Gebotys, C.H.: Security in embedded devices. Springer Science & Business Media (2009)

9. Haider, S.K., Jin, C., Ahmad, M., Shila, D.M., Khan, O., van Dijk, M.: HaTCh: Hardware Trojan Catcher. Cryptology ePrint Archive, Report 2014/943 (2014). http://eprint.iacr.org

10. Hicks, M., Finnicum, M., King, S.T., Martin, M., Smith, J.M.: Overcoming an untrusted computing base: detecting and removing malicious hardware automatically. In: 2010 IEEE Symposium on Security and Privacy (SP), pp. 159–172. IEEE (2010)

11. Huffmire, T., Brotherton, B., Wang, G., Sherwood, T., Kastner, R., Levin, T., Nguyen, T., Irvine, C.: Moats and drawbridges: an isolation primitive for reconfigurable hardware based systems. In: IEEE Symposium on Security and Privacy, SP 2007, pp. 281–295, May 2007

12. Huffmire, T., Levin, T., Nguyen, T., Irvine, C., Brotherton, B., Wang, G., Sherwood, T., Kastner, R.: Security primitives for reconfigurable hardware-based systems. ACM Transactions on Reconfigurable Technology and Systems (TRETS) **3**(2), 10 (2010)

13. Huffmire, T., Prasad, S., Sherwood, T., Kastner, R.: Policy-driven memory protection for reconfigurable hardware. In: Gollmann, D., Meier, J., Sabelfeld, A. (eds.) ESORICS 2006. LNCS, vol. 4189, pp. 461–478. Springer, Heidelberg (2006)

14. Huffmire, T., Sherwood, T., Kastner, R., Levin, T.: Enforcing memory policy specifications in reconfigurable hardware. Computers & Security **27**(5), 197–215 (2008)

15. Intelligence Advanced Research Projects Activity (IARPA): Trusted Integrated Chips (TIC) Program Broad Agency Announcement 11–09 (2011)

16. Jin, Y., Makris, Y.: Hardware Trojans in Wireless Cryptographic ICs. IEEE Design Test of Computers **27**(1), 26–35 (2010)

17. King, S.T., Tucek, J., Cozzie, A., Grier, C., Jiang, W., Zhou, Y.: Designing and implementing malicious hardware. LEET **8**, 1–8 (2008)

18. Lamberti, J., Manikantan Shila, D., Venugopal, V.: xDEFENSE: an extended DEFENSE for mitigating next generation intrusions (abstract only). In: Proceedings of the 2014 ACM/SIGDA International Symposium on Field-programmable Gate Arrays, FPGA 2014, pp. 253–253. ACM, New York (2014)

19. Myers, A.C., Liskov, B.: A decentralized model for information flow control, vol. 31. ACM (1997)

20. Shila, D.M., Venugopal, V.: Design, implementation and security analysis of hardware Trojan threats in FPGA. In: 2014 IEEE International Conference on Communications (ICC), pp. 719–724, June 2014

21. Skorobogatov, S., Woods, C.: Breakthrough silicon scanning discovers backdoor in military chip. In: Prouff, E., Schaumont, P. (eds.) CHES 2012. LNCS, vol. 7428, pp. 23–40. Springer, Heidelberg (2012)

22. Tehranipoor, M., Koushanfar, F.: A survey of hardware trojan taxonomy and detection. IEEE Design Test of Computers **27**(1), 10–25 (2010)

23. Waksman, A., Suozzo, M., Sethumadhavan, S.: FANCI: identification of stealthy malicious logic using boolean functional analysis. In: Proceedings of the 2013 ACM SIGSAC Conference on Computer & Communications Security, pp. 697–708. ACM (2013)

24. Xilinx Inc.: LogiCORE IP AXI Interconnect v2.1 Product Guide (2014)

25. Zhang, J., Yuan, F., Wei, L., Sun, Z., Xu, Q.: VeriTrust: verification for hardware trust. In: Proceedings of the 50th Annual Design Automation Conference, p. 61. ACM (2013)

# DisARM: Mitigating Buffer Overflow Attacks on Embedded Devices

Javid Habibi[✉], Ajay Panicker, Aditi Gupta, and Elisa Bertino

Purdue University, West Lafayette, IN 47907, USA
{jhabibi,apanicke,aditi,bertino}@purdue.edu

**Abstract.** Security of embedded devices today is a critical requirement for the Internet of Things (IoT) as these devices will access sensitive information such as social security numbers and health records. This makes these devices a lucrative target for attacks exploiting vulnerabilities to inject malicious code or reuse existing code to alter the execution of their software. Existing defense techniques have major drawbacks such as requiring source code or symbolic debugging information, and high overhead, limiting their applicability. In this paper we propose a novel defense technique, DisARM, that protects against both code-injection and code-reuse based buffer overflow attacks by breaking the ability for attackers to manipulate the return address of a function. Our approach operates on arbitrary executable binaries and thus does not require compiler support. In addition it does not require user interactions and can thus be automatically applied. Our experimental results show that our approach incurs low overhead and significantly increases the level of security against both code-injection and code-reuse based attacks.

**Keywords:** Internet of Things · Return oriented programming · Control flow integrity · Security · Malware · Embedded systems

## 1 Introduction

Recently, everything from refrigerators to sprinkler systems has evolved into smart devices that are pervasively connected to the Internet and powered by embedded processors. These devices are known collectively as the Internet of Things (IoT). Due to their positioning they have the potential to become more prominent in everyday lives than mobile phones. Cisco's Internet Business Solutions Group estimated 12.5 billion connected devices in existence globally as of 2010 with that number doubling to 25 billion by 2015 [15]. However, whereas on one side of the IoT will make possible many novel applications, such as in smart and connected health, on the other side IoT may increase the risk of data privacy breaches and cyber security attacks. A recent study by HP about the most popular devices in some of the most common IoT niches reveal an alarmingly high average number of vulnerabilities per device [14]. On average, 25 vulnerabilities were found per device. For example 80% of devices failed to require passwords

© Springer International Publishing Switzerland 2015
M. Qiu et al. (Eds.): NSS 2015, LNCS 9408, pp. 112–129, 2015.
DOI: 10.1007/978-3-319-25645-0_8

of sufficient complexity and length, 70% did not encrypt communications to the Internet and local networks, and 60% contained vulnerable user interfaces and/or vulnerable firmware [14]. Several attacks have already been reported in the past on several other embedded systems such as the ones deployed in cars [10,42,45] and sensor networks [31]. We can expect similar attacks to be carried out against IoT embedded devices. Securing embedded devices is thus a critical fundamental step in securing the IoT.

In this paper, we focus on two forms of attacks that exploit buffer overflows on IoT embedded devices, namely code-injection and code reuse attacks. These attacks form a substantial portion of all security attacks due to the fact that buffer overflow vulnerabilities are so common and easy to exploit. Original buffer overflow exploits involved the injection of malicious code [2]. This allows the attacker to subvert the execution of the target program and take control. However, the wide adoption of the $W \oplus X$ protection technique by which all writable addresses are non-executable and vice-versa has rendered code injection attacks ineffective. By contrast, recent code-reuse attacks, such as return-oriented programming (ROP) [36], do not require code injection. These attacks allow an attacker to easily modify the execution path of the target program by reusing existing executable code that primarily exists in the application binary and shared libraries such as libc. In code-reuse, the attacker identifies small sequences of instructions, called gadgets, that end in a ret instruction. By carefully placing a sequence of return addresses on the stack, the attacker can use these gadgets to perform arbitrary computation. ROP attacks have continued to evolve to utilize gadgets that end in both jmp or call instructions [9].

Since code-reuse based attacks rely on detailed knowledge about the location of code in the executable and libraries, the intuitive solution is to randomize process memory images. Address obfuscation [4] and ASLR [34] are two well-known randomization techniques against such attacks. However, they suffer from the major drawback of small randomization spaces and have been shown to be vulnerable on 32-bit architectures [39,41]. In considering a new protection technique, we start with two observations. First, the main shortcoming of earlier randomization-based approaches is insufficient entropy, thus making brute-force attacks feasible. Second, the critical step of a buffer overflow attack is to overwrite the return address in order to manipulate the value of the program counter ( PC).

Our protection technique, referred to as DisARM, introduces a validation technique upon any interaction with the PC, (i.e. ret, call, or jmp instruction). Our validation technique consists of inserting a static check statement before any critical instruction to verify that the program is in the correct state. This invalidates the ability for an attacker to redirect the execution of the target program. By utilizing a hashmap of target addresses XORed with the correct PC values a constant time look up is performed upon our constructed hashmap to validate that the program is in the correct state. Upon a failed validation attempt we force the program to exit, thus stopping an attack. Our protection technique has several advantages. First it stops both forms of buffer overflow attacks with minimal overhead. Second it can be applied to any ELF binary without requiring the source code of an application. Finally it offers an alternative to approaches that dynamically monitor critical data sections such as return addresses.

We are not the only researchers to investigate binary modifications for buffer overflow attack mitigation. As discussed in section 2.3, the other approaches suffer from one or more of the following limitations. First, none of the proposed defense techniques is able to mitigate both code injection and ROP based attacks. Second, some of the existing defenses require source code access or other additional information that is generally not available. Third, the overhead of DisARM is constant when compared to the dynamic techniques that incur overhead throughout the execution of the target application. DisARM addresses these limitations and provides a strong and efficient defense techniques against buffer overflow attacks.

As with any defense technique, there are always costs that must be considered. In our proposed defense technique, there is a one time overhead when applying DisARM to the target binary and a runtime overhead during the process execution. We have evaluated the time to apply DisARM to compiled binaries on a selection of commonly used applications and Linux `coreutils`, showing that the performance penalty for DisARM is reasonable in the average case. Our work demonstrates that, although DisARM imposes certain performance costs, its success in thwarting buffer overflow attacks makes DisARM a feasible approach for embedded systems that prioritize execution integrity over optimal performance.

The remainder of this paper is structured as follows. We start by surveying buffer overflow attack and proposed defenses in Section 2. In Section 3, we introduce the target platform for DisARM and describe our approach in more detail. Section 4 discusses the implementation details of DisARM. Section 5 shows the results from various experiments performed to evaluate our approach. Finally we conclude in Section 6.

## 2   Background and Related Work

In this section we start with a brief summary of attacks based on buffer overflows and existing defense techniques, and then introduce our target platform.

### 2.1   Code Injection

Code injection attacks are one of the first publicized exploits utilizing a vulnerable buffer. This form of exploit allows the execution of arbitrary code under the attacker's control, potentially allowing the attacker to seize control of an entire program or even an entire system (through exploitation of vulnerable targets with elevated privileges). In order to accomplish this, an attacker injects malicious code into a vulnerable target and then redirects the execution to the injected code [2]. In order to perform such form of attack, several prerequisites must be met. First, the targeted program must have a memory corruption vulnerability. Second, there must be a writable and executable region of memory. Third there must be a way to redirect the processor to execute the injected code. The first and third requirements are generally met through a buffer overflow that allows the attacker to push arbitrary code onto the stack and then overwrite the stack return address to redirect to control the attack payload. The second requirement requires finding an area of memory that can both be written to and executed. The processor then begins to execute the attack payload, granting the attacker control of the current thread.

## 2.2 Code Reuse

Return oriented programming (ROP) is a technique that evolved from buffer overflow attacks. As discussed in Section 2.1 previous attacks depended on the presence of an executable stack. However the adoption of $W \oplus X$ (also known as Data Execution Prevention – DEP) under which a memory page is either writable or executable, but not both at the same time, has made such attacks ineffective. Code reuse attacks [36] bypass DEP protection. Instead of executing injected code, attackers identify small sequences of instructions, called gadgets, that end in a `ret` instruction. By carefully constructing a sequence of addresses on the software stack, an attacker can manipulate the `ret` instruction to jump to any gadget to perform arbitrary computations. Code reuse techniques work in both word-aligned architectures like RISC [8] and unaligned CISC architectures [36]. These techniques have been shown to be able to perform privilege escalation in Android [17], create rootkits [28], and even inject code into Harvard architectures [22]. Additionally the same technique has been used to manipulate other instructions, such as `jmp`, and their variants [6,9,13].

## 2.3 Defense Techniques

Several defense techniques for mitigating buffer overflow attacks have been proposed. As mentioned before, DEP is the most widely used. However there are a lot of ARM based microcontrollers that do not support DEP as this protection technique was only introduced in ARMv6 and newer architectures [3].

Address obfuscation [4] and ASLR [34] are two well-known defense techniques against ROP attacks. However, they suffer from small randomization and have been shown to be vulnerable on 32-bit architectures [37,39]. Instruction set randomization (ISR) [29], another well known defense technique, has also been shown to have similar limitations [41]. Several fine grained randomization techniques have been proposed as a defense against code-reuse attacks such as ILR [26], In-place randomization [33], STIR [43], Marlin [25], XIFER [20], Librando [27], Code Shredding [40], ASR [24], Genesis [44], nop-insertion [23] and Bhatkar et al. [5]. Though these defenses have low overhead, they are considerably more invasive in that they require extensive program restructuring which often lead to instability in larger binaries. Also those techniques are not able to account for different optimization levels of binaries and are unable to protect against code-injection based attacks.

Compiler based solutions that create code without return instructions have also been proposed [30,32]. However those solutions are unable to handle ROP variants such as jump oriented programming [6] attacks. Another mitigation tactic for code reuse attacks is to detect and terminate the attack as it occurs. Examples of these include DROP [11], DynIMA [18], CCFIR [47], CFL [7], ROPdefender [19], [12] and [48]. The dynamic monitoring approach used by these techniques make them unsuitable for our target platform where the processor is limited in comparison to its x86 variants.

Lastly there have been techniques proposed to reinforce the control flow on ARM. Two most notable utilities are MoCFI [16] and control-flow restrictor [35]. However these techniques are both unsuitable for our application. While they are able to reinforce the control flow integrity of a target application, the overhead incurred by the verification is far too great. Within MoCFI, the CPU overhead of the verification grows in relation to the number of jumps as it must traverse the binary graph that is included within the binary after MoCFI has been applied [16]. Pewny takes a different approach by integrating itself within the compiler eliminating the need for disassembly and construction of a control flow graph but the verification process is very long [35]. For each valid target of 1 to n, a comparison is made at the end of the function before the final jump instruction. This incurs a large CPU overhead within recursive functions or loops making at worst up to n function calls. As discussed later DisARM, addresses these issues through the usage of a hashmap.

## 2.4  Challenges in Securing Embedded Devices

In most x86 based defenses it is acceptable to introduce performance overhead of a factor of 2x [11,18,19]. This however is not the case with embedded devices since these devices have low power and very limited resources available. These limited resources include CPU cycles, memory and code size. These were the factors considered in the design of DisARM.

With respect to the limited cycles available, the modifications done to the target binary cannot require too much computation. The reason is that different embedded systems have strict deadlines that must be met and typically operate at very high CPU and memory usage already. Therefore any defense implementation cannot have a large performance impact due to possible interrupts or deadlines that must be met in the protected applications.

**x86 vs ARM.** The x86 architecture's calling convention is set up to mainly use two instructions, one to call a function and one to return from it. The **call** and **ret** assembly instructions are the instructions that control the flow for an application. In addition, there are jump instructions that allow the execution to jump to an address stored in a register. The ARM architecture has many differences in the way in which the flow is controlled. The ARM architecture does not have `call` or `ret` instructions but it has something similar. The ARM assembly includes the use of a linking register, `lr`, that is updated when a function is called with the branch and link instruction `bl`. This works exactly like a `call` instruction, with the difference that the return address is stored into the `lr` register, instead of being pushed onto the stack as in x86. It is thus up to the programmer or compiler to make sure that the value is not lost.

Within the strategy that the ARM architecture utilizes there is a special case to highlight. If the function being utilized does not have any further function calls, it will not ever have an `lr` register update. In order then for these functions to 'return', they branch on the value stored in `lr` by executing the instruction `bx lr`. This implies that the value in `lr` has not changed since the beginning of the function. Due to this, even if there were a vulnerability within such a function, the attacker would not be able to redirect the control since the `lr` register is never pushed onto the stack. However this is not the case for extended nested function calling for which the compiler has to push `lr` onto the stack in order to preserve the return address. Through the combination of pushing `lr` onto the stack and branching, we get the same effect as a `call` in x86.

In order to return from a function, the ARM processor pops the value of the `lr` register that is on the stack into either the `lr` register or the `PC`. Once such action is executed, the program will start to execute the instruction at the address referenced by the old value of the `lr` register which is the address from where the function was called from. By contrast in x86 the `ret` instruction both pops off the stack the address to which the execution has to jump and jumps to such address. Such characteristic of ARM simplifies our defense techniques. Within DisARM we only need to look for and verify any instruction that pops values into the `lr` register or the `PC` as these are the entry points into the execution flow of the program.

## 3   DisARM Defense Technique

We now describe our DisARM defense technique to mitigate buffer overflow based attacks targeting the Raspberry Pi platform. DisARM uses a fine-grained analysis of the binary to find all critical interactions that manipulate the hardware PC and verifies any change to the PC before the change is applied. For each such critical instruction, we insert a verification block immediately before the critical instruction in order to evaluate whether the target address is valid with respect to the current instruction the program is executing. If the target address fails the verification, the program is forced to exit (see Figure 2). Our technique prevents the attacker from successfully utilizing an overwritten return address to begin a buffer overflow attack. We now introduce our basic assumptions for a buffer overflow attack scenario and then present the details of DisARM.

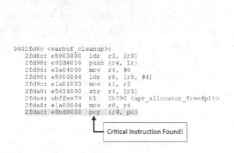

```
0002fd8c <varbuf_cleanup>:
  2fd8c: e5903000   ldr   r3, [r0]
  2fd90: e92d4010   push  {r4, lr}
  2fd94: e3a04000   mov   r4, #0
  2fd98: e5900004   ldr   r0, [r0, #4]
  2fd9c: e1a01003   mov   r1, r3
  2fda0: e5834000   str   r4, [r3]
  2fda4: ebffee79   bl    2b790 <apr_allocator_free@plt>
  2fda8: e1a00004   mov   r0, r4
  2fdac: e8bd8010   pop   {r4, pc}
```

Critical Instruction Found!

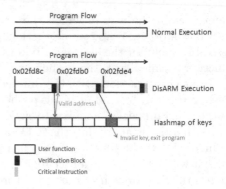

**Fig. 1.** Example of a critical instruction

**Fig. 2.** Example execution of a DisARM'd binary

## 3.1   Enabling Factors and Attack Assumptions

Based on our survey of buffer overflow based attacks and defenses, we have identified distinct characteristics and requirements for a successful exploit. The fundamental assumption and enabling factor such attacks is as follows:

*The attacker is able to modify the return address of the exploited function. That is, if an attacker overflows a buffer, the attacker is able to force the execution to return to a different address than intended and either inject or reuse existing code.*

Given this we assume that the vulnerable application must have a buffer overflow or heap overflow vulnerability that can be leveraged by the attacker to inject an exploit payload. Such payload may either contain native machine code to be executed or a string of gadget addresses previously identified by the attacker. The attacker is assumed to have access to the target binary that has undergone DisARM processing. The attacker is also assumed to be aware of the functionality of DisARM. Our approach protects against both remote and local exploits as long as the attacker is not able to modify the target binary while being executed.

## 3.2   Target Platform

The platform targeted in these attacks is the single board computer Raspberry Pi. This is a popular example of an embedded platform and a prime example of the hardware used in IoT devices. Raspberry Pi is based on an ARM11 32-bit RISC processor clocked at 700 MHz which implements the ARMv6k architecture. The ARM11 microprocessor is a Von Neumann Architecture processor. In this architecture, a processor has one physical signal and storage for instructions and data. This allows the processor to load instructions or read/write values from the same section of memory. This is a critical factor in allowing code injection based attacks. In addition, the program space in ARM is 32-bit word aligned with fixed instruction length. Thus, within DisARM we do not have to handle unintended instruction sets from jumping amidst of a variable length instruction. For the purpose of DisARM we look at the ARM instruction set and not the Thumb or Thumb2 instruction set that ARM processors are also compatible with.

### 3.3   Critical Instructions

Since DisARM reinforces the execution path of a given binary by inserting a verification block before a critical instruction, we must first define what is a critical instruction. A critical instruction is one that takes input from the stack and leads to an update to the `PC`. In the ARM architecture critical instructions are all the instructions of the form  `pop {...,pc}` or `pop {...,lr}`, which are instructions that remove the next X values off the top of the stack and immediately set the `PC` to the last of these values (in the pop pc case) or later set the `PC` to the value popped `bx lr`. No other instructions need to be monitored as discussed in Section 2.4 because of the fact that the ARM architecture is a RISC architecture. An example of a piece of code containing a critical instruction is shown in Figure 1. The code in figure 1 is a code snippet from Apache with a `pop` instruction that updates the values of both registers `r4` and `pc` before the conclusion of the `varbuf_cleanup` function.

### 3.4   Preprocessing Phase

As mentioned above, DisARM operates at the instruction granularity to reinforce the control flow of the target application. This requires us to identify the critical instructions, within the user defined functions, that require verification. In the preprocessing phase, the ELF binary is thus parsed to extract the critical instructions and their location.

### 3.5   Hashmap Construction Phase

Once the instructions and their locations have been identified, a key is calculated from the `target address` $\oplus$ `PC` value. Since the number of keys per binary is static, the most efficient solution is to use a hash function that minimizes the number of collisions. The straight-forward solution would be to use a cryptographic hash function but as discussed in section 2.4, CPU cycles are limited. This would not allow for the calculation of a cryptographic hash within every verification block. Instead, due to the nature of the data set, we utilize a minimum perfect hash function (MPHF). The algorithm we use in the generation of a minimum perfect hash is as follows:

1. Given key `K` and square array `S` of dimension `t`, place each key in `S` at location (x,y), where `x = K / t`, `y = K mod t`.
2. Sort each row in `S` in descending order according to the number of elements it contains.

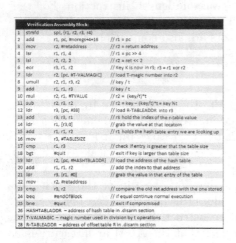

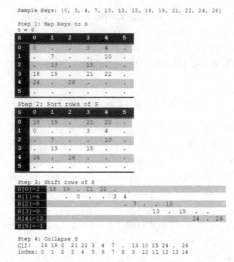

**Fig. 3.** Verification Block Assembly

**Fig. 4.** Example of MPHF construction process over a sample set of keys

3. Slide each row within S of an amount A such that no column has more than one entry. Record the shift amount in an array R.
4. Collapse S into a linear array C.

Thus the hash function uses t and the displacement A calculated in step 3 to locate K such that **index = R[x] + y** and **H(K) = C[index]**. For example, if we were to validate the key 15, x = 2 (15 / 6 by integer division) and y = 3 (15 mod 6). Then the index of the key would be at location index = 8 + 3 = 11 (R[2] + 3). As it stands C[11] does in fact equal the key value of 15.

By using the MPHF we can construct a hashmap resulting in the minimum number of collisions over the set of keys storing the target addresses to be validated within the verification blocks. Upon completion of the hashmap generation, the offset array R and hashmap array C are then appended to the binary in the .disarm section.

### 3.6   PC Lock Phase

After constructing the hashmap, we must lock down each instruction that updates the PC from the stack. To do this we insert our verification block before each critical instruction. By doing this, the relative offsets between instructions are changed and this may affect branch instructions. The reason is that the original destination address for branch instructions is a relative address. Thus, when verification blocks are inserted during the PC lock phase, the targets of these branch instructions are no longer valid and must be corrected to point to the desired location. This is achieved by performing offset patching as discussed next.

## 3.7    Patching Phase

Upon completion of the PC lock phase, the target binary needs to be patched in multiple areas. Due to the additions made in the  .text section for the verification blocks and the addition of data for the hashmap in the  .disarm section, the ELF header needs to patched in addition to all branch and load instructions within the  .text section that have been shifted during the PC Lock Phase. Within the ELF header, both the program header and the section header table need to be patched to account for their new locations.

After completing the ELF patching, each relative load and branch instruction offset by the modifications needs to be patched to point to the proper location. This is achieved by performing patching as the DisARMed binary is generated. During this process, we utilize the information gathered earlier during the Preprocessing Phase such as the original target location of load and branch. With this information and the number of verification blocks installed, we can calculate the new relative offsets for each branch/load instruction to properly patch the binary. This is discussed in more detail in section 4.4

## 4    Implementation Details

We have implemented a DisARM prototype that can operate on any C based ELF binary without requiring its source code. The implementation was done for 32-bit ARMv6 architecture on a system running the Raspbian operating system [21]. The implementation of DisARM involved two major components. The first component consists of preprocessing and constructing the hashmap. The second component deals with applying the verification blocks to the PC and patching the binary. We discuss the details of DisARM implementation below.

### 4.1    Preprocessing

Before we can reinforce the binary, we need to identify the critical instructions and every instruction that will be affected by the installation of the verification blocks. This includes locating all load, relative jump branches, function calls, returns and relative load instructions as these will all needed to be patched. In addition, while parsing the binary, to find these instructions we track the number and location of each critical instruction. To accomplish this we utilized a java based elf parsing library  [46]. This library allows us to read in the entire ELF binary and represent it objectually, thus allowing us to easily update the right sections of the file. However this library does not have all the functionality that we were looking for. In its stock form it treated the  .text section as a block of bytes. We extended this library to also parse each individual instruction byte by byte in order to identify all the information needed for the patching phase.

## 4.2   Hashmap Construction Phase

In this stage, the hashmap to be utilized in the verification blocks is constructed. The first step is to take each PC value and target address of a critical instruction found, XOR their values to generate a key for that pair, and add them to the key list. After generating all keys that will be used in the hashmap, we can construct the MPHF as described by the algorithm in section 3.5. Once both the MPHF and the hashmap are generated, the two arrays (offset array R and flattened hashmap C) are appended to the binary within their own section.

## 4.3   PC Lock Phase

Upon completion of the hashmap construction phase, we must install the verification blocks at the critical instructions to reinforce the program flow of the target binary. Each critical instruction is read in ascending order and wrapped in the verification block, as shown in figure 3. Each verification block utilizes multiple constants that are used during its execution. These include the MPHF t value, the location of the offset table, and the location of the hashmap. During this phase we also track how many verification blocks there were previous to the currently installed block as this information is utilized in the patching phase.

The challenge in this phase was designing and constructing a verification block that does not depend on any external resources aside from the global hashmap and offset table in order to perform that validation. To accomplish this, we followed the same methodology that GCC compiler uses during compilation. Each constant used within the verification block is appended to the end of the verification block after the final branch. This way they are available as immediate values that can be loaded into registers during the execution of a verification block. In addition since each verification block is going to be the primary source of runtime overhead, it had to be minimized. To accomplish this we replaced the expensive division operations with multiplications using magic number constants that provided the same functionality while also hand-optimizing the entire verification process. This reduced the verification block size down to 25 instructions for a combined total of 34 cycles of execution.

## 4.4   Patching Phase

In this stage all patching is performed in the same pass when the DisARMed binary is written. This is done by using the information available from the pre-processing stage. As we process the new binary, whenever a load, relative jump branches, function calls, return or relative load instruction is encountered, we compare the instruction's location within the new binary to the previous binary. If there is a difference due to the installation of a verification block, we generate a patch that will then point the specified instruction to the correct location. However there is a special case with relative load as a relative load instruction and an instruction loading a constant into a register have the exact same signature. To distinguish between these instructions, we analyze the value being 'loaded' into the specified register. If the value is within the program space then the instruction is a relative load and it needs to be patched.

Upon completing the patching for all instructions identified by the preprocessing stage, we must patch the ELF header. The reason is that due to the installation of the verification blocks, the `.text` section has grown which offsets all subsequent sections ( `.fini`, `.data`, `.rodata` etc etc...). In addition, we need to insert an additional entry in the program header of the ELF file to recognize the new `.disarm` section we include. This section contains the hashmap and offset table, generated by the hashmap construction phase (see section 4.2). Finally, a patch is applied within the ELF header to the location of `_start` as its location may have shifted during the installation of verification blocks in the `.text` section.

# 5   Evaluation

We now describe various experiments that we performed to evaluate the DisARM technique. These experiments test the effectiveness of DisARM and also the performance overhead incurred due to the PC verification. These experiments were performed on a Raspberry Pi Model B+ with 512MB of RAM. This Raspberry Pi Model had $W \oplus X$ and ASLR enabled during our experiments. We used `coreutils` binaries, some commonly used application binaries (see figure 5) and byte-unixbench [1] benchmarks to conduct various experiments. In addition to measuring the overhead of instrumenting binaries to apply the DisARM technique, we utilized a Windows 8.1 Machine with an i7 processor and 8GB of RAM. To launch attacks against DisARM-protected binaries, we use ROPgadget (v5.3) [38], an attack tool that automatically creates exploit payload for ROP attacks by searching for gadgets in an application's executable section.

## 5.1   Effectiveness

First, we tested the effectiveness of DisARM using a test application that has a buffer overflow vulnerability. The application, `elf-ARM-ls` is a test binary as part of the ROPgagdet test binaries. We used ROPgadget on this target application and found 1392 unique gadgets. These were sufficient to craft a code exploit payload. When this exploit payload was provided as an input to the unprotected binary, and we were able to redirect the execution. Next, we applied DisARM to this application to lock down the PC and ran the ROPgadget again to find the new locations of the gadgets. We then executed the DisARM-binary with the new payload and it failed. This highlights the crucial factor of buffer overflow attacks that require them to successfully manipulate the PC by overwriting return addresses.

| Application | Version |
|-------------|---------|
| Apache | 2.4.10 |
| Bash | 4.3 |
| Coreutils | 8.23 |
| Git | 2.2.0 |
| Gzip | 1.6 |
| Make | 4.1 |
| Openssh | 6.4 |
| Nano | 2.0.6 |
| Tar | 1.2.8 |
| Vim | 7.4 |
| MySQL | 5.6.22 |
| Lighttpd | 1.4.35 |
| Perl | 5.20.1 |
| Nginx | 1.7.8 |
| Python | 3.4.2 |
| Monkey | 1.5.4 |

**Fig. 5.** Target Applications used in the evaluation of DisARM

## 5.2  DisARM Utility Overhead

When an application is being deployed to an IoT device, DisARM identifies all critical instructions for verification blocks to be installed, and every instruction that will be affected by the installation of the verification blocks that is used later in the patching phase. This computation is unique to each binary. The next phase involves generating the hashmap from all the critical instructions found and the installation of the verification blocks. The last phase involves patching all instructions that were affected by this instrumentation. DisARM processing cost is the combined overhead of all four phases. We measure DisARM processing overhead on the same set of binaries (see figure 5) used throughout the evaluation.

Our first evaluation of DisARM was to measure the execution overhead of applying it to each test application. We noticed that there was a direct correlation to the number of verification blocks being installed within the application and the total runtime of DisARM. Our average runtime was 193.5 seconds over our sample applications. This is due to the fact that we tested on multiple large binaries that had 3000+ verification blocks installed such as Perl, and Python. However the median execution time 5.23 seconds. This is quite reasonable as the larger the target application, the more processing is required for DisARM to reinforce the control flow. Notice that this overhead is incurred only once. Since DisARM modifies the binary so that each critical instruction is secured, it does not need to be run before every execution of the application.

## 5.3  Efficiency

Due to the hashmap that DisARM utilizes in the verification process, as discussed in section 3, DisARMed binaries incur a runtime memory overhead.

**Table 1.** DisARM memory overhead

| Binary | Original Memory Usage | # of Verification Blocks | Additional Memory Usage (KB) | % increase |
|---|---|---|---|---|
| Apache | 3.6 MB | 1287 | 19.11 | 0.518 |
| Bash | 2.7 MB | 2766 | 63.88 | 2.310 |
| sftp | 332 KB | 215 | 7.95 | 2.395 |
| Git | 524 KB | 3983 | 87.04 | 16.611 |
| Gzip | 220 KB | 156 | 7.34 | 3.336 |
| Make | 110 KB | 346 | 10.37 | 9.427 |
| Nano | 852 KB | 817 | 19.05 | 2.236 |
| Tar | 206 KB | 891 | 17.64 | 8.563 |
| Vim | 1.2 MB | 5836 | 148.03 | 12.047 |
| Lighttpd | 1.2 MB | 369 | 17.32 | 1.410 |
| Perl | 2.8 MB | 3509 | 470.41 | 16.407 |
| Nginx | 1.1 MB | 1845 | 46.79 | 4.154 |
| Python | 3.2 MB | 6270 | 368.87 | 11.257 |
| Monkey | 152 KB | 650 | 18.58 | 12.224 |

This overhead is constant per binary due to the fact that each hashmap is unique to the target application. We evaluated the memory efficiency of Dis-ARM by taking 14 common applications (see figure 5), we expect to be widely used in IoT devices, and measured their idle memory usage. Unfortunately for some of the target applications it was not possible to measure the idle memory usage since the memory usage of the application directly correlated to size of its input. Our results, reported in Table 1 show a maximum of 17%, median of 4.1% and an average of 7% increase in memory at runtime. The reason is that, the size of the hashmap directly correlates to how many functions there are within the application and how often they are utilized. We found this overhead to be acceptable as in most tested applications there was less then an average of 10% increase in memory usage.

## 5.4   Code Size

In addition to the memory overhead, we measured the increase in code size of these applications. The increases is due to the modifications we had made to the applications in order to insert the verification blocks and hashmap. We thus wanted to see if there were significant changes in code size. Our results, reported in table 2 show that the code sizes do not significantly increase. As shown in table 2 there is a maximum of 0.21% increase in code size with a median of 0.1% and an average of 0.13%. The reason is that DisARM does not require any special compiler flags to be enabled on target binaries and can operate at any optimization level thus taking advantage of all existing code reduction techniques.

**Table 2.** DisARM Code Size

| Binary | Original Size (MB) | DisARM Size (MB) | % increase |
|--------|--------|--------|--------|
| Apache | 1.5 | 1.66 | 0.10 |
| Bash | 2.5 | 2.86 | 0.14 |
| sftp | 0.30 | 0.34 | 0.10 |
| Git | 5.6 | 6.11 | 0.09 |
| Gzip | 0.261 | 0.28 | 0.09 |
| Make | 0.51 | 0.56 | 0.09 |
| Nano | 0.499 | 0.60 | 0.21 |
| Tar | 1.2 | 1.31 | 0.09 |
| Vim | 5.7 | 6.47 | 0.13 |
| Lighttpd | 0.631 | 0.67 | 0.09 |
| Perl | 1.5 | 1.87 | 0.56 |
| Nginx | 2.8 | 3.00 | 0.09 |
| Python | 6.7 | 7.37 | 0.15 |
| Monkey | 3.9 | 3.97 | 0.02 |

### 5.5    DisARM Runtime Overhead

We measured the runtime overhead of DisARMed binaries to see if the application of DisARM greatly affects the execution time of a binary. For this purpose we use the byte-unixbench binaries. We used the benchmark scores of the stock binaries as a baseline to compare with DisARMed benchmarks. We applied DisARM to each benchmark and took the average of scores from each run. We observed that the benchmark scores were not greatly affected by the application of DisARM to the binaries. The average score generated from the stock Unixbench is 78.4 with a median of 78.8 as opposed to the DisARMed Unixbench which has an average of 76.2 and a median of 76.4. The reason is that each verification block installed consists of only 25 instructions which equates to an additional 34 cycles. This equates to an additional 48 nanoseconds of execution time per function with the processor clocked at 700 MHz. These results support our initial claim of minimal runtime overhead per DisARMed binary.

## 6    Conclusions and Future Work

In this paper, we proposed a verification technique to defend against buffer overflow attacks. This approach installs verification blocks at critical instructions preventing the attacker from manipulating return addresses. We have implemented a prototype of our approach and demonstrated that it is successful in defeating buffer overflow attacks crafted using automated attack tools. We have also evaluated the effectiveness of our approach and showed that the effort to exploit DisARM is significantly high. Based on the results of our analysis and implementation we argue that fine-grained verification is both feasible and practical as a defense against these persistent buffer overflow based attack techniques. Future work will evaluate the effectiveness of this strategy on CISC architectures, such as x86, in addition to exploring techniques that would allow us to apply DisARM to a binary that has been stripped of all symbol information making the deployment of DisARM even more seamless.

**Acknowledgment.** The work reported in this paper has been partially supported by the Purdue Cyber Center and the National Science Foundation under grant CNS-1111512.

# References

1. byte-unixbench: A Unix benchmark suite. http://code.google.com/p/byte-unixbench/
2. Aleph One: Smashing the stack for fun and profit. Phrack Magazine **49**, 14 (November 1996)
3. ARM Holdings plc. ARM Architecture Reference Manual
4. Bhatkar, E., Duvarney, D.C., Sekar, R.: Address obfuscation: an efficient approach to combat a broad range of memory error exploits. In: Proc. of the 12th USENIX Security Symposium, pp. 105–120 (2003)
5. Bhatkar, S., Sekar, R., DuVarney, D.C.: Efficient techniques for comprehensive protection from memory error exploits. In: Proc. of the 14th Conference on USENIX Security Symposium. SSYM 2005, vol. 14, pp. 17–17 (2005)
6. Bletsch, T., Jiang, X., Freeh, V.: Jump-oriented programming: A new class of code-reuse attack. Tech. Rep. TR-2010-8, North Carolina State University (2010)
7. Bletsch, T., Jiang, X., Freeh, V.: Mitigating code-reuse attacks with control-flow locking. In: Proc. of the 27th Annual Computer Security Applications Conference. ACSAC 2011, pp. 353–362. ACM, New York (2011)
8. Buchanan, E., Roemer, R., Shacham, H., Savage, S.: When good instructions go bad: generalizing return-oriented programming to risc. In: Proc. of the 15th ACM Conference on Computer and Communications Security, pp. 27–38 (2008)
9. Checkoway, S., Davi, L., Dmitrienko, A., Sadeghi, A.-R., Shacham, H., Winandy, M.: Return-oriented programming without returns. In: Proc. of the 17th ACM Conference on Computer and Communications Security, pp. 559–572 (2010)
10. Checkoway, S., McCoy, D., Kantor, B., Anderson, D., Shacham, H., Savage, S., Koscher, K., Czeskis, A., Roesner, F., Kohno, T.: Comprehensive experimental analyses of automotive attack surfaces. In: Proc. of the 20th USENIX Conference on Security. SEC 2011, p. 6. USENIX Association, Berkeley (2011)
11. Chen, P., Xiao, H., Shen, X., Yin, X., Mao, B., Xie, L.: DROP: detecting return-oriented programming malicious code. In: Prakash, A., Sen Gupta, I. (eds.) ICISS 2009. LNCS, vol. 5905, pp. 163–177. Springer, Heidelberg (2009)
12. Chen, P., Xing, X., Han, H., Mao, B., Xie, L.: Efficient detection of the return-oriented programming malicious code. In: Jha, S., Mathuria, A. (eds.) ICISS 2010. LNCS, vol. 6503, pp. 140–155. Springer, Heidelberg (2010)
13. Chen, P., Xing, X., Mao, B., Xie, L.: Return-oriented rootkit without returns (on the x86). In: Soriano, M., Qing, S., López, J. (eds.) ICICS 2010. LNCS, vol. 6476, pp. 340–354. Springer, Heidelberg (2010)
14. Miessler, D.: HP Study Reveals 70 Percent of Internet of Things Devices Vulnerable to Attack (July 2014). http://h30499.www3.hp.com/t5/Fortify-Application-Security/HP-Study-Reveals-70-Percent-of-Internet-of-Things-Devices/ba-p/6556284#.VH4faTHF9Zg

15. Evans, D.: The Internet of Things How the Next Evolution of the Internet is Changing Everything (April 2011). http://www.cisco.com/web/about/ac79/docs/innov/IoT_IBSG_0411FINAL.pdf
16. Davi, L., Dmitrienko, A., Egele, M., Fischer, T., Holz, T., Hund, R., Nürnberger, S., Sadeghi, A.-R.: Mocfi: a framework to mitigate control-flow attacks on smartphones. In: NDSS (2012)
17. Davi, L., Dmitrienko, A., Sadeghi, A.-R., Winandy, M.: Privilege escalation attacks on android. In: Proc. of the 13th International Conference on Information Security, pp. 346–360 (2011)
18. Davi, L., Sadeghi, A.-R., Winandy, M.: Dynamic integrity measurement and attestation: towards defense against return-oriented programming attacks. In: Proc. of the 2009 ACM workshop on Scalable trusted computing, pp. 49–54 (2009)
19. Davi, L., Sadeghi, A.-R., Winandy, M.: ROPdefender: a detection tool to defend against return-oriented programming attacks. In: Proc. of the 6th ACM Symposium on Information, Computer and Communications Security, pp. 40–51 (2011)
20. Davi, L.V., Dmitrienko, A., Nürnberger, S., Sadeghi, A.-R.: Gadge me if you can: secure and efficient ad-hoc instruction-level randomization for x86 and arm. In: Proc. of the 8th ACM SIGSAC Symposium on Information, Computer and Communications Security. ASIA CCS 2013, pp. 299–310. ACM, New York (2013)
21. Debian Foundation. Raspbian. http://www.raspbian.org/
22. Francillon, A., Castelluccia, C.: Code injection attacks on harvard-architecture devices. In: Proc. of the 15th ACM Conference on Computer and Communications Security, pp. 15–26 (2008)
23. Franz, M., Brunthaler, S., Larsen, P., Homescu, A., Neisius, S.: Profile-guided automated software diversity. In: Proc. of the 2013 IEEE/ACM International Symposium on Code Generation and Optimization (CGO). CGO 2013, pp. 1–11. IEEE Computer Society, Washington (2013)
24. Giuffrida, C., Kuijsten, A., Tanenbaum, A.S.: Enhanced operating system security through efficient and fine-grained address space randomization. In: Proc. of the 21st USENIX Conference on Security Symposium. Security 2012, pp. 40–40. USENIX Association, Berkeley (2012)
25. Gupta, A., Habibi, J., Kirkpatrick, M., Bertino, E.: Marlin: Mitigating code reuse attacks using code randomization. IEEE Transactions on Dependable and Secure Computing **PP**(99), 1–1 (2014)
26. Hiser, J., Nguyen-Tuong, A., Co, M., Hall, M., Davidson, J.W.: Ilr: where'd my gadgets go? In: Proc. of the 2012 IEEE Symposium on Security and Privacy, pp. 571–585 (2012)
27. Homescu, A., Brunthaler, S., Larsen, P., Franz, M.: Librando: transparent code randomization for just-in-time compilers. In: Proc. of the 2013 ACM SIGSAC Conference on Computer & Communications Security. CCS 2013, pp. 993–1004. ACM, New York (2013)
28. Hund, R., Holz, T., Freiling, F.C.: Return-oriented rootkits: bypassing kernel code integrity protection mechanisms. In: Proc. of the 18th Conference on USENIX Security Symposium. SSYM 2009, pp. 383–398 (2009)
29. Kc, G.S., Keromytis, A.D., Prevelakis, V.: Countering code-injection attacks with instruction-set randomization. In: Proc. of the 10th ACM Conference on Computer and Communications Security. CCS 2003, pp. 272–280. ACM, New York (2003)
30. Li, J., Wang, Z., Jiang, X., Grace, M., Bahram, S.: Defeating return-oriented rootkits with "return-less" kernels. In: Proc. of the 5th European Conference on Computer Systems, pp. 195–208 (2010)

31. Newsome, J., Shi, E., Song, D., Perrig, A.: The sybil attack in sensor networks: analysis & defenses. In: Proc. of the 3rd International Symposium on Information Processing in Sensor Networks. IPSN 2004, pp. 259–268. ACM, New York (2004)
32. Onarlioglu, K., Bilge, L., Lanzi, A., Balzarotti, D., Kirda, E.: G-free: defeating return-oriented programming through gadget-less binaries. In: Proc. of the 26th Annual Computer Security Applications Conference, pp. 49–58 (2010)
33. Pappas, V., Polychronakis, M., Keromytis, A.D.: Smashing the gadgets: hindering return-oriented programming using in-place code randomization. In: Proc. of the 2012 IEEE Symposium on Security and Privacy. SP 2012, pp. 601–615. IEEE Computer Society, Washington (2012)
34. PaX Team. PaX. http://pax.grsecurity.net/
35. Pewny, J., Holz, T.: Control-flow restrictor: compiler-based CFI for IOS. In: Proc. of the 29th Annual Computer Security Applications Conference, pp. 309–318. ACM (2013)
36. Roemer, R., Buchanan, E., Shacham, H., Savage, S.: Return-oriented programming: Systems, languages, and applications. ACM Trans. Inf. Syst. Secur. **15**(1), 2:1–2:34 (2012)
37. Roglia, G., Martignoni, L., Paleari, R., Bruschi, D.: Surgically returning to randomized lib(c). In: Annual Computer Security Applications Conference. ACSAC 2009, pp. 60–69, December 2009
38. Salwan, J.: ROPgadget tool. http://shell-storm.org/project/ROPgadget/
39. Shacham, H., Page, M., Pfaff, B., Goh, E.-J., Modadugu, N., Boneh, D.: On the effectiveness of address-space randomization. In: Proc. of the 11th ACM Conference on Computer and Communications Security, pp. 298–307 (2004)
40. Shioji, E., Kawakoya, Y., Iwamura, M., Hariu, T.: Code shredding: byte-granular randomization of program layout for detecting code-reuse attacks. In: Proc. of the 28th Annual Computer Security Applications Conference. ACSAC 2012, pp. 309–318. ACM, New York (2012)
41. Sovarel, A.N., Evans, D., Paul, N.: Where's the feeb? The effectiveness of instruction set randomization. In: Proc. of the 14th Conference on USENIX Security Symposium, vol. 14, pp. 10–10 (2005)
42. Verdult, R., Garcia, F.D., Balasch, J.: Gone in 360 seconds: hijacking with hitag2. In: Proc. of the 21st USENIX Conference on Security Symposium. Security 2012, pp. 37–37. USENIX Association, Berkeley (2012)
43. Wartell, R., Mohan, V., Hamlen, K.W., Lin, Z.: Binary stirring: self-randomizing instruction addresses of legacy x86 binary code. In: Proc. of the 2012 ACM Conference on Computer and Communications Security. CCS 2012, pp. 157–168. ACM, New York (2012)
44. Williams, D., Hu, W., Davidson, J., Hiser, J., Knight, J., Nguyen-Tuong, A.: Security through diversity: leveraging virtual machine technology. IEEE Security Privacy **7**(1), 26–33 (2009)
45. Wright, A.: Hacking cars. Commun. ACM **54**(11), 18–19 (2011)
46. Li, X.-F.: ELF Parser. http://people.apache.org/xli/
47. Zhang, C., Wei, T., Chen, Z., Duan, L., Szekeres, L., McCamant, S., Song, D., Zou, W.: Practical control flow integrity and randomization for binary executables. In: IEEE Symposium on Security and Privacy. IEEE Computer Society, pp. 559–573 (2013)
48. Zhang, M., Sekar, R.: Control flow integrity for cots binaries. In: Proc. of the 22Nd USENIX Conference on Security. SEC 2013, pp. 337–352. USENIX Association, Berkeley (2013)

# Service in Denial – Clouds Going with the Winds

Vit Bukac[(✉)], Vlasta Stavova, Lukas Nemec, Zdenek Riha, and Vashek Matyas

Faculty of Informatics, Masaryk University, Brno, Czech Republic
{bukac,vlasta.stavova,lukas.nemec,zriha,matyas}@mail.muni.cz

**Abstract.** We analyze the threat of DDoS-for-hire services to low and medium power cloud-based servers or home users. We aim to investigate popularity and availability of such services, their payment models, subscription pricing, complexity of the generated attack traffic and performance.

## 1 Introduction and DDoS-as-a-Service Description

Our research aims to provide a comprehensive analysis of the Distributed Denial of Service as a Service (DDoSaaS) phenomenon. We evaluate the threat that DDoSaaS poses to low to medium power cloud-based servers or home users. Our goal is to measure the performance of generated attacks and properties of attack traffic, investigate financial aspect of the services, evaluate service popularity and compare their source codes. The information we collected allows us to conduct a grounded assessment of DDoSaaS risks for cloud providers and common users.

DDoSaaSs often present themselves as stress testing services (often called booters or stressers), willing to test the resistance of a chosen target to Distributed Denial of Service (DDoS) attacks. The services are accessed via websites that require prior registration. Common features of a DDoSaaS website are: it is in English, lists prices in US dollars and is easily retrievable through mainstream search engines. According to [1], the websites are frequently accessed through aggregated booter lists (e.g., top10stressers.com, thebestbooters.com), hacker sites (e.g., hackforums.net, hackbulletin.com) or Skype resolvers that translate Skype nicknames to latest IP addresses (e.g., iskyperesolve.com, skypegrab.net).

The websites frequently contain a Terms Of Service page, where service operators disclaim any responsibility for damages caused by users of the service. However, service operators do not check whether a customer is ordering attacks on targets under her supervision. Most common DDoSaaS customers are online gamers who seek to gain a competitive advantage over their opponents [2].

When ordering an attack, the customer has to specify a target URL or an IP address, length of the attack (limited by paid subscription, see Section 6.2) and an attack type. These values are inserted into a web form on the stresser webpage and submitted to a back-end server. The server evaluates the request and orders attack servers to initiate an attack.

Most services are very customer friendly. The main webpage contains dashboards with news for customers, such as newly available attack types or bandwidth increases and basic service statistics. A ticketing system is usually prepared for customers to report bugs and any issues. Many services even claim 24/7 support via

© Springer International Publishing Switzerland 2015
M. Qiu et al. (Eds.): NSS 2015, LNCS 9408, pp. 130–143, 2015.
DOI: 10.1007/978-3-319-25645-0_9

instant messaging channels and offer occasional promo actions, such as subscription discounts or free trials.

The bandwidth available for attacks is usually advertised in the order of several gigabits per second or more (e.g., Anonymous Stresser 5 Gbit/s, Quantum Booter 15 Gbit/s). DDoSaaS employs a limited number of powerful servers that send attack traffic. The traffic is usually subsequently amplified by unsuspecting poorly configured intermediaries. DDoSaaSs also quickly adopt newly discovered attack methods. We have encountered sites offering attacks that were amplified through recently discovered vulnerabilities in Joomla content management system, Microsoft SQL Server or SSDP protocol.

The current modus operandi of DDoSaaS provides a good level of anonymity for both providers and technically knowledgeable users. Payments can be sent by anonymous cryptocurrencies (see Section 6.1), attack traffic has spoofed source IP addresses and webpages can be accessed through anonymization proxies.

Section 2 outlines the details of our dataset. Section 3 analyzes the properties of recorded attack traffic. Section 4 provides analyses of aggregated leaked databases of DDoSaaSs. Section 5 investigates DDoSaaS source code. Section 6 discusses the economic aspects of DDoSaaS. Summary of relevant previous work is provided in Section 7. Section 8 concludes our paper.

## 2    Dataset Description

The list of domains that we investigated with respect to DDoSaaS contains 542 records. This list was constructed from searches for keywords such as booter, stresser, ddos-for-hire or ddosaas. These searches were run at Google search engine, YouTube and Hackforums.net site. In order to confirm that a particular domain is hosting a DDoSaaS website, at least one of the following conditions must have been fulfilled:

- The website behind the domain name is still accessible and belongs to a DDoSaaS service.
- A snapshot of the index webpage exists at a third party store (e.g., Google cache, CloudFlare cache, web.archive.org, etc.). The snapshot shows that the index webpage belonged to a DDoSaaS service.
- The domain name was mentioned on a hacker forum in a discussion about DDoSaaS services to be running and serving customers.

We confirmed 423 websites to be associated with DDoSaaS, 84 of which were accessible at some point during our investigation. We were able to create user accounts on 71 of them, to list supported payment methods from 82 and to list available subscription offers from 62 of them.

Most detailed information about the popularity of DDoSaaS can be extracted from leaked databases. Similarly, the internal working of DDoSaaS websites is best evaluated from the website source code. We have collected 53 archives of DDoSaaS website source code and separate 31 database files that have been released to sites such as pastebin.com or leakforums.org.

Database files contain records about user accounts, attacks and payments. We aggregated attack records and user records from multiple databases in order to build a comprehensive view which is not specific to any given DDoSaaS service. Unfortunately, only one payment database file was available for quantitative analysis. An aggregated summary of the databases is provided in Table 1.

The source code archives contain a total of 23,443 files with 13,983 unique MD5 hashes. Aggregated statistics of source code is listed in Table 2. Each archive has an associated name of a stresser whose files it supposedly contains. However, in most cases we were unable to verify that the archive is indeed related to the announced stresser, except for trivial checks such as verifying the logo image.

**Table 1.** Database files summary.

| Database | Booters | Records |
|---|---|---|
| Attack logs | 17 | 153,578 |
| User logs | 31 | 90,962 |
| Payment logs | Quantum | 16,990 |

**Table 2.** Source code files summary.

| File extension | Files | MD5s |
|---|---|---|
| png/gif/jpg | 14,676 | 8,770 |
| php | 4,094 | 2,285 |
| js | 1,832 | 1,227 |
| html/htm | 431 | 316 |
| other/no ext | 2,410 | 1,385 |
| Total | 23,443 | 13,983 |

In order to analyze the properties of attack traffic, we created a high performance virtual server on Amazon Elastic Compute Cloud (EC2). The virtual machine was configured with 4 virtual CPUs running on Intel Xeon core, 15 GB RAM and SSD storage. The server was connected with at least 1 Gbit/s line. Operating system was Ubuntu Trusty 14.04. The server was hosting a dummy webpage that imitated a webpage of a gaming clan. Attack traces were recorded with tcpdump command-line packet analyzer. Traffic records were collected for 300 seconds starting just prior to an attack launch, while the attack itself was executed for 30 s.

A total of 272 attacks were recorded from 16 DDoSaaSs. Attacks were launched against the server between December 2014 and April 2015. Attacks were directed either to the server IP address or to the hosted dummy webpage. Every attack method was tested twice in order to increase the chance of succesful attack traffic recording (see Section 3.1). All attack traces along with supporting documents are available at DDoS-Vault repository [3].

Detailed listing of tested services, global rank of their web pages [1], estimated monthly visits, numbers of created accounts and number of performed attacks can be found in Table 3. We focused on highly popular, extensively used DDoSaaSs with many users. Statistics show that DDoSaaSs are used by tens of thousands of users and are responsible for a staggering number of DDoS attacks. Our 272 recorded attacks are listed by attack classes and source DDoSaaSs in Table 4.

# 3   Traffic Analysis

## 3.1   Attack Success Rate

An attack was considered succesful if its power exceeded predefined bitrate and packet rate limits (see below) and if the real attack type corresponded to the attack type requested by the customer. Power is a key metric of a flooding denial-of-service attack. It is expressed by a bitrate or a packet rate. Bitrate determines the capability to flood network links towards the victim network with an undesired traffic. A high packet rate can cause failures at network devices between attack sources and the victim (e.g., firewall, proxy, office router).

Since DDoSaaSs are primarily used against home connections and small servers, the limits were set in accordance with average Internet connection speeds as listed in Q4 2014 report from Akamai [4]. An attack power was deemed sufficient if the average bandwidth exceeded 25 Mbit/s or if the average packet rate exceeded 20,000 packets per second during the 30 s attack period.

Columns Bit and Packet in Table 4 show the percentage of recorded attacks of a chosen booter that surpass respective attack power limits. Approximately 51% of all attacks, regardless of source booter, *failed to exceed either power limit*. Approximately 43% did not even reach 1 Mbit/s. Such attacks can be considered ineffective against any target.

We also observe significant differences in attack power success rate of different booters. There are numerous potential reasons why a DDoSaaS attack strength is low: underprovision of resources, scams, malfunction of backend stressing infrastructure, DDoS-prevention measures at ISP network and/or cloud infrastructure.

We could not identify any time relations between attacks that fail to reach the desired power. We compared attack bitrates and packet rates between each two attacks with the same attack method on the same booter. Out of 135 pairs of such attacks, both attacks failed to exceed the bitrate/packet rate limits at 60 pairs and one attack failed to exceed the limits at 18 pairs. For example, two DNS amplification attacks were executed at hornystress.me in the span of three hours. The first attack failed to generate any harmful traffic while the second attack reached up to 380 Mbit/s of incoming traffic.

Differences between attack launch times in these 18 pairs oscillate between one hour and three days. Other attacks were also succesfully executed in the meantime at the same booter. Therefore, we believe that a combination of factors is behind power drops. Issues at the side of DDoSaaS are not solely responsible. As a consequence, the success rate of attacks against home connections or cloud providers without a DDoS protection may be significantly higher. Further research will be needed to evaluate the conditions that affect the attack power.

A customer specifies the requested attack type. However, *collected traffic records did not always correspond to the requested type*. Potential reasons include: maintaining public image (booters claim to have capabilities that they actually lack), malfunction of backend stressing infrastructure or unwillingness to use non-spoofed attacks. The column Type in Table 4 shows the percentage of attacks whose dominant portion of traffic corresponds to the customer request.

**Table 3.** Booter statistics for February 2015. Global ranks and monthly visit estimates were collected from [1]. Total user account and executed attack statistics were collected directly from dashboards at stresser web pages where available.

| Booter | Global rank | Est. visits | Accounts | Attacks |
|---|---|---|---|---|
| anonymous-stresser.com | 571,894 | 25,000 | | |
| booter.in | 258,375 | 55,000 | 6,324 | 22,635 |
| booter.io | 464,756 | 35,000 | 9,336 | 45,073 |
| connectionstresser.com | 319,831 | 40,000 | 17,444 | 180,751 |
| destressbooter.com | 659,154 | 25,000 | | |
| hornystress.me | 297,124 | 70,000 | | 16,310 |
| ipstresser.com | 45,082 | 420,000 | | |
| legion.cm | 1,254,496 | 10,000 | 10,393 | |
| networkstresser.com | 215,904 | 100,000 | | 28,523 |
| networkstresser.net | | | | 20,417 |
| powerstresser.com | 169,402 | 130,000 | 10,197 | 44,273 |
| quantumbooter.net | 323,716 | 55,000 | | |
| ragebooter.com | 314,984 | 50,000 | 14,022 | 12,148 |
| restricted-stresser.info | 1,821,164 | 5,000 | | |
| titaniumstresser.net | 79,299 | 310,000 | | 305,494 |
| vdos-s.com | 689,739 | 20,000 | 17,452 | |

**Table 4.** Recorded attacks.

| DDoSaaS | Attack class | | | Booter success (%) | | |
|---|---|---|---|---|---|---|
| | UDP | TCP | HTTP | Bit | Packet | Type |
| anonymous-stresser.com | 8 | 2 | 16 | 15 | 19 | 100 |
| booter.in | 10 | 6 | 0 | 50 | 56 | 63 |
| booter.io | 8 | 4 | 0 | 50 | 67 | 83 |
| connectionstresser.com | 10 | 2 | 0 | 67 | 50 | 100 |
| destressbooter.com | 20 | 0 | 2 | 5 | 0 | 73 |
| hornystress.me | 18 | 14 | 2 | 32 | 44 | 76 |
| ipstresser.com | 14 | 2 | 6 | 59 | 82 | 100 |
| legion.cm | 2 | 0 | 8 | 0 | 0 | 80 |
| networkstresser.com | 12 | 2 | 0 | 86 | 86 | 21 |
| networkstresser.net | 10 | 5 | 0 | 0 | 0 | 100 |
| powerstresser.com | 4 | 4 | 0 | 0 | 0 | 100 |
| quantumbooter.net | 5 | 4 | 0 | 56 | 78 | 100 |
| ragebooter.com | 10 | 6 | 0 | 31 | 6 | 75 |
| restricted-stresser.info | 8 | 4 | 18 | 21 | 29 | 100 |
| titaniumstresser.net | 4 | 2 | 4 | 100 | 50 | 100 |
| vdos-s.com | 4 | 12 | 0 | 63 | 88 | 88 |
| Total attacks | 147 | 69 | 56 | | | |
| Class success (%) Bit | 57 | 17 | 7 | | | |
| Packet | 42 | 55 | 18 | | | |
| Type | 72 | 100 | 100 | | | |

An aspect of DDoSaaS quality is the speed with which an attack is launched after it is requested by the customer. We measured the time between an attack order and the timestamp of first incoming attack traffic packet. Average time to start an attack was 7 seconds and 80% of the attacks started in 10 seconds or less. Such a rapid response is especially important for gamers, who represent a large portion of DDoSaaS customers.

## 3.2   Attack Power

A histogram of measured bitrates of attacks in our dataset is shown in Table 5. Bitrate only rarely exceeds 1 Gbit/s. The attack types most likely to reach a high bitrate are CHARGEN and DNS. TCP-based and HTTP-based attacks showed a poor bitrate performance. Succesful NTP and SSDP attacks have the clearest power boundaries around 400 Mbit/s and 300 Mbit/s respectively.

**Table 5.** Recorded attack bitrate histogram.

| Class | Type | Bitrate (Mbit/s) | | | | | | | Total |
|-------|------|----|-----|-----|-----|-----|------|-------|-------|
| | | 25 | 200 | 400 | 600 | 800 | 1000 | >1000 | |
| HTTP | HTTP | 52 | 0 | 0 | 4 | 0 | 0 | 0 | 56 |
| TCP | SYN | 42 | 3 | 1 | 1 | 0 | 0 | 0 | 47 |
| TCP | TCP | 15 | 7 | 0 | 0 | 0 | 0 | 0 | 22 |
| UDP | CHARGEN | 9 | 2 | 7 | 6 | 3 | 0 | 2 | 29 |
| UDP | DNS | 8 | 6 | 6 | 3 | 2 | 2 | 2 | 29 |
| UDP | NTP | 16 | 1 | 6 | 7 | 0 | 0 | 0 | 30 |
| UDP | Other | 16 | 1 | 3 | 0 | 0 | 0 | 0 | 20 |
| UDP | SSDP | 14 | 5 | 15 | 5 | 0 | 0 | 0 | 39 |

An attack packet rate histogram is given in Table 6. Attack types associated with the high packet rate are SYN, TCP, SSDP and NTP. TCP SYN attacks exhibit below-average values both for bitrate and packet rate, because this attack is based on the exhaustion of victim connection state table buffer.

**Table 6.** Recorded attack packet rate histogram.

| Class | Type | Packet rate (packets per second) | | | | | | | Total |
|-------|------|-----|-----|-----|-----|------|------|-------|-------|
| | | 20k | 40k | 60k | 80k | 100k | 120k | >120k | |
| HTTP | HTTP | 46 | 7 | 3 | 0 | 0 | 0 | 0 | 56 |
| TCP | SYN | 21 | 7 | 10 | 5 | 3 | 0 | 1 | 47 |
| TCP | TCP | 10 | 3 | 2 | 0 | 2 | 1 | 4 | 22 |
| UDP | CHARGEN | 19 | 8 | 2 | 0 | 0 | 0 | 0 | 29 |
| UDP | DNS | 18 | 6 | 2 | 0 | 1 | 0 | 2 | 29 |
| UDP | NTP | 17 | 0 | 0 | 2 | 2 | 3 | 6 | 30 |
| UDP | Other | 16 | 2 | 2 | 0 | 0 | 0 | 0 | 20 |
| UDP | SSDP | 15 | 2 | 2 | 2 | 4 | 8 | 6 | 39 |

Overall, even succesful DDoSaaS attacks were *not powerful enough* to cause a denial-of-service effect against a cloud-based server with high resources. However, the attack power of succesful attacks may be sufficient to saturate uplinks of low- to mid-range servers or at least cause a degradation of service if the traffic reaches the server itself. Conversely, more than 40% of all attacks would fail to overwhelm even home connections with 1 Mbit/s or less download speed.

### 3.3   Attack Traffic Properties

Tables 7 and 8 show values of most common attack traffic source ports and packet lengths. The booters column specifies how many booters contained the listed feature values in their attack traffic. The traffic column indicates the percentage of all traffic in an appropriate attack class that has the respective property. Source ports clearly show that UDP-based attack employ amplifiers, hence the traffic is incoming from well-known ports. Conversely, TCP-based attacks rely on simple IP spoofing and their traffic source ports are evenly distributed. Due to a low number of useable HTTP attack traffic samples, this attack type has been excluded from further research.

**Table 7.** Most frequent packet lengths.

| Attack type | Length (B) | Booters | % traffic |
|---|---|---|---|
| CHARGEN | 57 | 7/9 | 5% |
| DNS | 4044 | 4/10 | 9% |
| NTP | 468 | 9/11 | 99% |
| SSDP | 296 | 10/11 | 6% |
| SYN | 40 | 14/14 | 93% |
| TCP | 40 | 3/4 | 99% |

**Table 8.** Most frequent source ports.

| Attack type | Port | Booters | % traffic |
|---|---|---|---|
| CHARGEN | 19 | 7/9 | 92% |
| DNS | 53 | 10/10 | 54% |
| NTP | 123 | 9/11 | 99% |
| SSDP | 1900 | 10/11 | 90% |
| SYN | 80 | 11/14 | 22% |
| TCP | 80 | 3/4 | <1% |

Table 9 lists some of the manually chosen key unique identifiers that distinguish the attack traffic from the benign traffic. Interesting are similar domain names in DNS amplification attacks. Since a domain name is not inherent to an attack type, we assume that DDoSaaS operators either rent their back-end infrastructure from other providers or buy attack scripts on an open market. Both of these approaches have been known to be used for other service types [5].

**Table 9.** Application-layer artifacts.

| Class | Type | Artifact type | Values | Booters |
|---|---|---|---|---|
| UDP | DNS | Query domain name | fkfkfkfz.guru | 2/10 |
| UDP | DNS | Query domain name | doleta.gov | 2/10 |
| UDP | SSDP | HTTP Location | IGD.xml | 8/11 |
| UDP | SSDP | HTTP Location | rootDesc.xml | 8/11 |
| UDP | NTP | Request code | MON_GETLIST | 9/11 |

NTP traffic in our dataset shows to be extremely homogenous. All attack packets come from port 123/UDP, carry NTP payload with request code 42 (MON_GETLIST) and IP length 468 bytes. These signs are consistent with a well-documented NTP vulnerability CVE-2013-5211. NTP amplification attacks based on MON_GETLIST command were analysed by Czyz et al. in [6].

Predominant SSDP attack variant is fairly new, first observed in July 2014 [7]. The attack is amplified by unpatched home routers and smart appliances.

SYN attacks have a standard well-understood form. Incoming attack traffic has spoofed source IP addresses, packet length 40 B and SYN flag set. Anomalous were TCP window sizes where in 86% of cases values were set to 0.

We can see that *attack traffic even from different DDoSaaS shows remarkable similarities*, such as packet lengths or application-layer artifacts. The traffic is simple, constructed for maximum attack effectiveness rather than for stealthiness. By using attack reflectors, the DDoSaaS operators sacrifice the capability to randomize attack traffic properties (e.g., packet lengths, source ports, header field values) and circumvent advanced victim DDoS protection solutions. DDoSaaS operators have no control over reflectors, therefore the final attack traffic exhibits a high degree of uniformity, because reflectors are configured to respond with standard, non-randomized responses. It is fairly easy to configure rules for packet filters to drop or throttle most of the attack traffic. Since the primary DDoSaaS targets are home connections or low-end servers without trained security teams who would react to evolving attacks, we do not expect any sudden increase in the use of detection avoidance techniques in the future.

## 4    Database Analysis

We have collected records from leaked databases of 31 services. The statistics presented are based on aggregated records of databases as specified in Table 1.

Table 10 shows more than 75% of attacks performed by stressers are at most 10 minutes long. Our aggregated records therefore support the results of Karami and McCoy [2]. Unsurprisingly, most common lengths of actual boots are equivalent to subscription maximum booter lengths (Table 11). Therefore, we can assume that DDoSaaS customers execute attacks for the maximum boot length available to them.

Table 12 shows that *UDP-based flooding attacks have a significantly higher popularity* than TCP-based or HTTP-based attacks. This is likely to be caused, at least partially, by DDoSaaS operators who set UDP attacks as the default option. UDP is also preferable due to its amplification factor. Protocols such as CHARGEN, NTP, SSDP or DNS are frequently exploited by DDoSaaS operators to increase the impact on victims without having to increase the attacker's available bandwidth. TCP-based attacks are almost exclusively variations of SYN flooding. Somewhat surprising is popularity of RUDY and Slowloris attacks compared to generic HTTP GET/POST/HEAD flooding.

In 84% of attacks, the target port of the attack was 80 (HTTP), followed by ports 3074 (Xbox LIVE), 6005 (BMC Software), 25565 (Minecraft/MySQL),

**Table 10.** Boot lengths histogram.

| Interval (s) | Attacks |
|---|---|
| 0 – 100 | 40,836 |
| 101 – 200 | 27,971 |
| 201 – 400 | 31,940 |
| 401 – 600 | 2,649 |
| 601 – 800 | 2,753 |
| 801 – 1000 | 6,650 |
| 1001 – 1200 | 4,076 |
| >1201 | 19,671 |
| Total | 136,546 |

**Table 11.** Boot lengths popularity.

| Length (s) | Attacks | Booters |
|---|---|---|
| 300 | 20,866 | 16 |
| 120 | 18,414 | 16 |
| 60 | 12,570 | 17 |
| 600 | 12,557 | 16 |
| 250 | 6,843 | 11 |
| 100 | 5,749 | 16 |
| 1800 | 5,280 | 10 |
| 90 | 5,205 | 11 |
| 500 | 5,093 | 14 |

53 (DNS) and 27015 (GoldSrc game engine). Port 80 is often used by DDoSaaS as a default value, probably because it is rarely filtered by firewalls. Conversely, several representatives of gaming services in the list of most popular target ports confirm *the prominent role of gamers* among DDoSaaS customers [2].

**Table 12.** Attack types popularity.

| Type | Category | Attacks | Booters |
|---|---|---|---|
| UDP | UDP | 69,635 | 11 |
| ESSYN | TCP | 19,744 | 3 |
| NTP | UDP | 19,416 | 2 |
| SSYN | TCP | 13,714 | 10 |
| RUDY | HTTP | 6,310 | 8 |
| TCP | TCP | 4,648 | 5 |
| Slowloris | HTTP | 2,958 | 8 |
| UDPLAG | UDP | 2,929 | 7 |
| DRDOS | unknown | 2,816 | 4 |

**Table 13.** Victim IP geolocation.

| Country | Attacks |
|---|---|
| US | 53,509 |
| FR | 15,811 |
| UK | 9,239 |
| CA | 6,901 |
| DE | 6,317 |
| NL | 4,962 |
| AU | 4,465 |
| SE | 2,622 |
| Other | 34,861 |

Geographic location of victim IP addresses suggests that DDoSaaSs are used primarily against North American and European targets (Table 13). Almost 39% of attacks are aimed at the US IP space, FR accounts for 11% and UK for 7%.

We analyzed the payment database records of the Quantum booter from September 2012 to March 2014. The database contains records related to 10,269 paying customers out of 20,695 registered. Mean payment was approximately 21 USD, with median and mode both 8 USD. Total income during the period exceeds 220,000 USD, while monthly income averages at 12,000 USD. That is a significantly higher income than the income reported from the twBooter analysis [2] (see 7). We expect that the prospect of such future income, coupled with few barriers to entry (see Section 5) will lead to an increasing number of DDoSaaS sites in the future.

# 5    Website Source Code Analysis

DDoSaaS webpages are built with PHP and common frameworks, such as Bootstrap, jQuery, jQuery UI, jQuery Sparklines, Modernizr, prettyPhoto or Raphael according to our screening of 65 unique live websites.

We collected code from 53 DDoSaaS websites and analyzed them for similarities. All sites used PHP scripts, usually supported by the MySQL database. Each site consisted of 105 PHP source code files on average. We calculated the MD5 hashes of all PHP files and found 94 PHP files that were shared/reused (each) by at least 3 sites. We manually analyzed all the 94 shared files to understand their role and divided them into 7 categories. Table 14 summarizes our findings. Most shared source codes are files handling *user management and CAPTCHA*.

Table 14. Shared source codes categories.

| Category | Files | Category description |
|---|---|---|
| user management | 39 | Managing user accounts and passwords, user logins |
| CAPTCHA | 11 | CAPTCHA |
| index pages | 10 | Index/home page + news/messages |
| lib | 10 | CCS, JavaScript, ... |
| attack management | 7 | Attack management + statistics... |
| PayPal | 6 | PayPal payments |
| misc | 11 | IP geolocation, IP logging, database access etc. |

Finding similarities in source code files is not always trivial. The cryptographic hash algorithm MD5 can only find perfectly identical files. Even a slight change, such as rewriting an email address in a support ticket submission form, makes MD5 matching impossible. Therefore, we decided to also use the spamsum algorithm implemented in the ssdeep program [8]. The spamsum algorithm calculates context triggered piecewise hashes based on the FNV (Fowler/Noll/Vo) hash algorithm. The algorithm was used to find similarities in the source code of the 53 previously mentioned websites. We calculated how many source files across various sites have their ssdeep hash similarity score higher than 95. On average, each site shares at least one ssdeep hash with 7.45 other sites and has 46.5 ssdeep (>95) similarity relationships (i.e., shared similar files).

We have identified 9 similarity clusters. All websites in a cluster share 10 or more files with ssdeep similarity higher than 95. These 9 clusters were formed by 25 websites. Another 20 sites shared some of their files with others, but without distinctive partners. The remaining 9 sites did not share any similarities.

Such similarity might indicate that the same, or similar, teams are behind multiple services. Another reason might be simple code reuse. As the functionality required by most of the websites for a DDoS services is very similar, and as the source code of many web sites has leaked to the public, the coders of the web sites will be tempted to reuse the existing code. Availability of source code will lead to *an easier establishment of new DDoSaaSs*.

# 6    Economics

## 6.1    Payment Methods

Desired properties of payment methods supported by DDoSaaS are user friend-liness for technically unskilled users, anonymity for both seller and buyer and low fees, because exchanged payments are usually fairly small. Service providers also prefer payment methods that do not support payment revocation.

In December 2014, we analyzed payment methods supported by 82 DDoSaaS providers and found 19 different payment systems. The most popular system was PayPal, which was supported by 63 DDoS services, followed by Bitcoin (42) and Google Wallet (21). Contrary to findings in [5], WebMoney was not among supported payment systems of any DDoSaaS.

We have noticed *a distinct move towards the support of cryptocurrencies* dur-ing our research. Cryptocurrencies are anonymous, decentralized, gaining pop-ularity among the general population, subjected to only limited regulation and payments cannot be revoked as soon as they are included in the blockchain. Bitcoin is now a widely accepted payment method among DDoSaaSs, but we also encountered support for Omnicoin, Litecoin and Dogecoin, mostly thanks to aggregating payment gateways such as GoCoin or CoinPayments.

Direct use of credit cards is very rare, supported by only 3 services. However, online payment services that allow the user to transfer money from his credit card or bank account to the service account are still common. Paypal, Skrill, Starpass, 4Virtuals, Okpay and Dwolla all fit into this category. With the exception of PayPal, at least one of these services was supported by 11 DDoSaaSs.

## 6.2    Subscriptions

DDoSaaS services provide a variety of subscriptions for different prices. Subscrip-tions are characterized by price, currency, subscription length, maximal boot time, attack concurrency and available attack bandwidth. Surprisingly, available attack bandwidth is rarely advertised. Some DDoSaaS services employ client-based botnets as their attack infrastructure. Limited knowledge about band-width and availability of particular hosts makes it difficult for service providers to estimate real available bandwidth at any given moment. Attack concurrency is similarly obscured by most services, although generally only one attack is permitted at a time if not otherwise stated.

Subscriptions are time-bound. During the subscription, a customer may ini-tiate an arbitrary number of attacks. Monthly subscriptions are most popular, with more than 95% services offering these, followed by lifetime subscriptions offered by 66%. Price for monthly subscription varies between 1.99 and 35 USD for the cheapest and from 7.5 to 289 USD for the most expensive subscription.

Figure 1 shows samples of monthly subscriptions in USD. We can see that *the boot length/price ratio does not converge to a common value*. Monthly subscrip-tion with the same boot length can be ordered for considerably different prices at different services. Oppositely, increasing attack concurrency clearly increases the

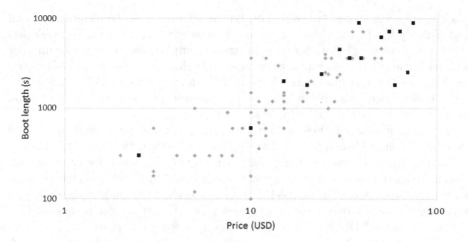

**Fig. 1.** Monthly subscriptions. Light rhombuses mark subscriptions with one concurrent attack. Dark squares mark subscriptions with two or more concurrent attacks. Graph scale is logarithmic.

price of subscription. A combination of low subscription prices with unlimited attacks during the duration of subscription makes the per-attack price potentially extremely low.

In the case of payments via cryptocurrencies, subscriptions are activated automatically. When purchasing a subscription, the customer is offered several payment methods. Once the payment is successfully finished, the customer's requested subscription is activated without any further intervention from an operator. In the case of cryptocurrencies, automated subscriptions decrease the initial time for the customer to be able to launch attacks to a couple of hours at most. Elimination of a direct contact channel between the customer and the DDoSaaS operator also results in increased privacy for both parties.

## 7   Related Work

The first academic paper that focused solely on DDoSaaS services was published by Karami and McCoy in 2013 [2]. The authors analyze the leaked database of the twBooter service and execute several simple attacks against their server. Key revelations are that the attack traffic is generated by servers, attack strength is sufficient to disrupt low to medium-sized web sites, primary service customers are gamers who prefer short attack lengths and most frequent targets are either game servers or game forums.

Yu et al. discuss the threat of DDoS attacks against cloud-based servers as a resource competition problem [9]. They observe that even though the cloud has enough resources to overcome DDoS attacks, the resources are not distributed as needed by customers. Specifically, virtual machine instances are usually reserved with fixed computational, memory and bandwidth limits. A DDoS attack may cause that these limits are exceeded, overwhelming the target instance.

The crimeware-as-a-service (CaaS) business model was investigated by Sood and Enbody [5]. In the CaaS model, roles for service creators and service operators are divided. The authors emphasize the importance of crime forums for advertising and e-currencies for exchange. Web Money is cited as an online payment system that is used extensively in the underground market. DoS attack order is described as a process when key communication between the seller and buyer takes place on an IRC channel.

Investigation into DDoS-for-hire services was highly publicized by articles that have been published by a well known computer security expert Brian Krebs (e.g., [10,11]), who was also fairly successful in tracking several service owners. Krebs argues that most stresser services are operated by US citizens who possess a limited knowledge, rely on PayPal payment system and hide their webpages behind the CloudFlare content delivery network. The author also points out that the source code of DDoSaaS web pages may be frequently reused.

Shortly before submission of our paper, Santanna et al. published two studies about DDoSaaS [12,13]. Our and their studies are complementary. In [12], authors analyze properties of 7 DNS-based and 2 CHARGEN-based DDoSaaS-generated attacks directed against a university network. Compared to their study: (1) We analyze the attacks from the perspective of a cloud-based server. (2) Our scope includes many more independent attacks with a greater variety of attack types. (3) We estimate the attack success rate and evaluate also the application layer traffic properties. Oppositely, [12] complements our paper with the investigation into the geolocation of reflectors and the discussion of a competition between various DDoSaaSs.

Second paper by Santanna et al. focuses on the analysis of booter databases [13]. The paper provides an extensive overview of DDoSaaS user/customer behavior, which fits in with our analysis of economical aspect of DDoSaaS, as well as information about the user location. Our aggregated database with more sources and more records also confirms observations of Santanna et al. that most attacks are shorter than 10 minutes and UDP-based attacks are the most popular.

## 8   Conclusions

Over the years, DDoS-for-hire services have matured into user friendly services with a wide customer base that extends beyond technically savvy users. Main advancements are automated subscription activation, automated attack execution and support for anonymous payment methods such as Bitcoin. The three key findings of our research are as follows:

- Attacks generated by DDoSaaSs are not overly powerful with bitrates only sporadically exceeding 1 Gbit/s.
- Attack traffic has a low complexity, does not employ randomization and shares similarities even between various DDoSaaSs.
- More than a third of attacks were not fully blocked by a cloud provider.

We believe that the threat of DDoSaaS will increase in time, mainly due to a low price, open advertisement, achievable anonymity and a service model that makes these services quickly and widely accessible to many potential customers. In the same time, the number of DDoSaaS services will grow, due to freely available source code and low initial entry costs when compared to potential earnings.

All collected attack traces are available at DDoS-Vault project webpage [3].

**Acknowledgments.** Authors would like to thank to Geraint Price for his comments and valuable suggestions. Vashek Matyas was supported by the Czech Science Foundation project GBP202/12/G061.

# References

1. SimilarWeb. http://www.similarweb.com (accessed June 26, 2015)
2. Karami, M., McCoy, D.: Understanding the emerging threat of DDoS-as-a-Service. In: 6th USENIX Workshop on Large-Scale Exploits and Emergent Threats (2013)
3. Bukac, V.: DDoS-Vault project (2015). https://github.com/crocs-muni/ddos-vault/wiki (accessed August 16, 2015)
4. Akamai. The State of the Internet Report Q4 2014. Technical report (2015)
5. Sood, A.K., Enbody, R.J.: Crimeware-as-a-service - A survey of commoditized crimeware in the underground market. International Journal of Critical Infrastructure Protection **6**(1), 28–38 (2013)
6. Czyz, J., Kallitsis, M., Gharaibeh, M., Papadopoulos, C., Bailey, M., Karir, M.: Taming the 800 Pound Gorilla: the rise and decline of NTP DDoS attacks. In: Proceedings of the 2014 Conference on Internet Measurement. ACM (2014)
7. PLXsert. SSDP Reflection DDoS Attacks. PLXsert Threat Advisory, September 2014
8. Kornblum, J.: Identifying almost identical files using context triggered piecewise hashing. Digital Investigation **3** (2006)
9. Yu, S., Tian, Y., Guo, S., Wu, D.: Can We Beat DDoS Attacks in Clouds?. IEEE Transactions on Parallel and Distributed Systems **25**(9) (2014)
10. Krebs, B.: DDoS Services Advertise Openly, Take PayPal, May 2013. http://krebsonsecurity.com/2013/05/ddos-services-advertise-openly-take-paypal/ (accessed August 16, 2015)
11. Krebs, B.: Lizard Kids: A Long Trail of Fail, December 2014. http://krebsonsecurity.com/2014/12/lizard-kids-a-long-trail-of-fail (accessed August 16, 2015)
12. Santanna, J.J., van Rijswijk-Deij, R., Sperotto, A., Hofstede, R., Wierbosch, M., Zambenedetti Granville, L., Pras, A.: Booters - an analysis of DDoS-as-a-service attacks. In: Proceedings of the 14th IFIP/IEEE Symposium on Integrated Network and Service Management (2015)
13. Santanna, J.J., Durban, R., Sperotto, A., Pras, A.: Inside booters: an analysis on operational databases. In: Proceedings of the 14th IFIP/IEEE Symposium on Integrated Network and Service Management (2015)

# Application Security

# RouteMap: A Route and Map Based Graphical Password Scheme for Better Multiple Password Memory

Weizhi Meng[1,2](✉)

[1] Infocomm Security Department,
Institute for Infocomm Research, Singapore, Singapore
yuxin.meng@my.cityu.edu.hk
[2] Department of Computer Science,
City University of Hong Kong, Hong Kong, Hong Kong (SAR)

**Abstract.** Graphical passwords (GPs) are considered as one promising solution to replace traditional text-based passwords. Many GP schemes have been proposed in the literature such as PassPoints, DAS, Cued Click Points, GeoPass and so on. These schemes reported promising performance in their studies in the aspects of security and usability, however, we notice that these GP schemes may suffer from the issue of multiple password memory. In our first user study, it is identified that this issue has indeed become a big challenge. In real-world applications, users usually have to remember and maintain more than one password in different scenarios, thus, it is very essential to develop a better GP scheme to solve this issue. In this paper, we focus on map-based GPs and propose a scheme of RouteMap for better multiple password memory, which allows users to draw a route on a map as their secrets. In our second user study with 60 participants, it is found that users can achieve better performance using RouteMap in terms of multiple password memory, as compared with two similar schemes. Our effort attempts to complement existing studies and stimulate more research on this issue.

**Keywords:** User authentication · Multiple password memory · Graphical passwords · Map passwords · Security and usability

## 1 Introduction

For user authentication, text-based passwords should be the most commonly used method over the past few decades, where users have to input correct textual strings for registration and authentication. However, it has long been recognized that traditional text-based passwords are suffered from many issues associated with their security and usability [24,25]. For instance, users are hard to remember their passwords for a long time, especially complex and random passwords. Due to the long-term memory (LTM) limitations, users are likely to choose simple

---

W. Meng—The author is previously known as Yuxin Meng.

M. Qiu et al. (Eds.): NSS 2015, LNCS 9408, pp. 147–161, 2015.
DOI: 10.1007/978-3-319-25645-0_10

strings, which would significantly degrade the level of authentication security. The recent study shows that this situation would be even worse than previously believed (i.e., little variation in guessing difficulty) [1].

In this case, graphical passwords (GPs) have been proposed as a promising alternative to text-based passwords. It is known that people generally have better memory and recognition for images than textual strings [15,17]. This observation has motivated a large number of graphical password schemes, which involve users recognizing images or reproducing a drawing on images. For example, Jermyn *et al.* [11] designed *DAS*, a graphical password that allowed users to draw their own passwords on a 2D grid. Wiedenbeck *et al.* [23] then proposed *PassPoints*, a system that allowed users to click on any place on an image in creating their passwords. Later, Chiasson *et al.* [2] proposed a click-based graphical password scheme called Cued Click Points (CCP), which consists of one click-point per image for a sequence of images. The next image displayed is based on the previous click-point so that users could receive immediate implicit feedback and decide whether they are on the correct path.

***Motivations.*** In real-world scenarios, people often have more than one password in hand, as they have to manage different accounts such as email accounts, commercial used accounts, social networking accounts, etc. Due to this, a good GP scheme should be easy for users to remember multiple passwords. However, we notice that multiple password memory has become an issue for current GP schemes, in which users are hard to remember all created GPs after some time. In this work, we focus on this issue and have two targets as follows.

- ***T1.*** The first target is to investigate whether users can remember multiple graphical passwords based on existing GP schemes.
- ***T2.*** The second target is to design a graphical password scheme for better multiple password memory.

***Contributions.*** In order to achieve these two goals, we mainly conduct two user studies in this work. The first one evaluates two popular GP schemes: *DAS* and *PassPoints*. We then design a map- and route-based graphical password scheme called *RouteMap*, which allows users to draw a route on a map as their passwords. Afterwards, the second user study is conducted to investigate the performance of *RouteMap*, as compared to the state-of-the-art schemes. The contributions of this work can be summarized as follows.

- We first conduct a user study to explore whether users are able to remember multiple graphical passwords using *DAS* and *PassPoints*. These two schemes are selected due to their popularity and simplicity. It is found that multiple password memory has become an issue that cannot be ignored.
- We then focus on map-based GPs and design *RouteMap*, a map- and route-based GP scheme that allows to draw a route on a world map. This scheme aims to provide better multiple password memory and is different from previous schemes as we apply distinct rules of password creation.

– We further conduct another user study with 60 participants to investigate the performance of *RouteMap* as compared with two other similar schemes. Experimental results indicate that our scheme can achieve better performance in the aspect of multiple password memory.

The remaining parts of this paper are organized as follows. In Section 2, we review related work regarding graphical passwords, especially map-based graphical passwords. Section 3 describes our first user study relating to multiple password memory based on *DAS* and *PassPoints*. In Section 4, we introduce our proposed *RouteMap* in detail and conduct another user study to explore its performance. Finally, we conclude our work with future directions in Section 5.

## 2  Related Work

### 2.1  GP Classification

Graphical password schemes can be classified into three folders [3,19]: recognition-based scheme (i.e., recognizing images), pure recall-based scheme (i.e., reproducing a drawing without a hint) and cued recall-based scheme (i.e., reproducing a drawing with hints).

– *Recognition-Based GPs.* The recognition-based schemes require users to select one or more images from a large set. For instance, the application of *PassFaces* [16] requires users to recognize a set of human faces during authentication. The scheme of *Story* [5] requires users to recognize a set of images such as people and food from a large image pool.
– *Pure Recall-Based GPs.* The pure recall-based GPs usually ask users to draw something on an image as their passwords. A typical example of these GPs is *DAS* [11], which requires users to draw on a grid. Similarly, the scheme of *Pass-Go* [21] requests users to select intersections on a grid as a way to input a password. Based on *Pass-Go*, Android unlock patterns have been developed on Android phones, which are a tuned application requiring users to unlock their phones by inputting correct patterns.[1] Several similar schemes can be referred to [7,12].
– *Cued Recall-Based GPs.* This kind of graphical passwords demands users to click on a sequence of points to construct their secrets. The system of *PassPoints* belongs to this category where users have to recall a sequence of five selected points. As another example, Chiasson *et al.* [4] designed Persuasive Cued Click-Points (PCCP), which requires users to click a point on each of a sequence of background images.

The current GP schemes are mainly based on the actions of choice, click and draw, so that some combined schemes have also been developed like [13]. Several analyses and studies on GPs can be referred to [6,10,14]

---

[1] https://www.berkeleychurchill.com/software/android-pwgen/pwgen.php.

## 2.2   Map-Based Graphical Passwords

The initial idea of using digital map as a graphical password first appeared in [8], but not much details were given. Then, Spitzer *et al.* [18] developed an implementation of *CCP* that combined the graphical approach with user's familiarity with navigating through Google maps. In their work, users are presented with an image of the United States and simply click to where the key destination is located, using an approach of zooming levels. Their results with over 50 participants indicated that 60% of the users rated the system as easier to remember than text in terms of memorability.

Later, several map-based graphical passwords appeared in 2012. Georgakakis *et al.* [9] proposed a GP scheme called *NAVI*, where the credentials of a user are his username and a password formulated by drawing a route on a pre-defined map. They provided an analysis regarding the strength of the password, but no any user study was provided. Sun *et al.* [20] proposed a map-based GP authentication system called *PassMap*, in which a password consists of a sequence of 2 click-points selected on a world map. Their user study showed that *PassMap* passwords are easy to memorize in practice. Thorpe *et al.* [22] later designed *GeoPass*, a digital map-based authentication scheme, where a user chooses a place as his or her password. In the user study, they found that 97% of the users were able to remember their location password over the span of 8-9 days and most without any failed login attempts. It is worth noting that *PassMap* and *GeoPass* are very similar in that secrets are constructed by clicking one or two places on a world map (e.g., Google map).

In this work, we focus on map-based GPs and show how to handle the issue of multiple password memory. Our designed *RouteMap* is more similar to *NAVI* [9], since both schemes require users to draw a route on a map. However, *RouteMap* is different from *NAVI*, because we apply distinct rules of password creation. More specifically, the creation of a route is different (i.e., the route in *RouteMap* is drawn using straight lines). In addition, we evaluate the performance of *RouteMap* in a user study while there are no any results reported in [9]. Our results aim to complement the existing literature regarding this topic.

## 3   Multiple Graphical Password Memory

In this section, we conduct a user study with 50 participants to explore the issue of multiple password memory. According to the popularity and simplicity, we choose two existing GP schemes: *DAS* and *PassPoints*. The former is a pure recall-based GP, where users can draw their secrets on a grid. The latter is a cued recall-based GP, where users have to remember a sequence of several clicks. All participants are volunteers and have no background of information security (i.e., no participant has taken any courses related to information security before). The information of participants is shown in Table 1.

***Methodology.*** Both schemes are implemented on the same computer settings and we introduced our objectives to all participants in advance. Two examples

**Table 1.** Detailed information of participants in the user study.

| Age Range | Male | Female | Occupation | Male | Female |
|-----------|------|--------|------------|------|--------|
| 18-25 | 8 | 9 | Senior people | 3 | 2 |
| 25-35 | 8 | 8 | Students | 16 | 12 |
| 35-45 | 4 | 3 | Researchers | 3 | 3 |
| 45-55 | 2 | 3 | Engineers | 3 | 3 |
| 55-60 | 3 | 2 | Business people | 2 | 3 |

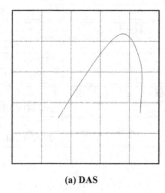

(a) DAS

(b) PassPoints

**Fig. 1.** Two graphical password schemes: (a) DAS and (b) PassPoints.

of these systems are depicted in Figure 1 (a) and Figure 1 (b), and the scheme details can be referred to [11, 23]. To avoid bias, we set a file including all steps in the lab study and gave a detailed description to participants based on the same steps (i.e., how to use these two example systems).

Before the study, every participant can have 3 trails to get familiar with the example systems. In the study, we require all participants to create 5 passwords for each scheme and each password corresponds to a scenario as follows: the first password is created for an email account (personal use), the second one is created for a bank account, the third one is created for another email account (commercial use), the fourth one is created for a forum account and the last one is created for a social networking account. The detailed steps in each experiment are shown as below:

- *Experiment1.* This experiment requires each participant to create 5 *DAS* passwords.
  - Step 1. Creation: creating a password following the rules of *DAS*.
  - Step 2. Confirmation: confirming the password by drawing the same secrets in the correct place. If users incorrectly confirm their password, they can retry the confirmation or return to Step 1.
  - Step 3. Login: logging in the system with the created passwords. Users can cancel an attempt if they noticed an error.
  - Step 4. Feedback: All participants are required to complete a *feedback form* about the password creation and confirmation.

**Table 2.** Success rate for login to *DAS* and *PassPoints* after three weeks.

| Experiment1 (DAS) | Successful Login | Experiment2 (PassPoints) | Successful Login |
|---|---|---|---|
| 1st time | 132/250 (52.8%) | 1st time | 123/250 (49.2%) |
| 2nd time | 163/250 (65.2%) | 2nd time | 150/250 (60.0%) |
| 3rd time | 176/250 (70.4%) | 3rd time | 167/250 (66.8%) |
| DAS (Age in [18, 35]) | Successful Login | PassPoints (Age in [18, 35]) | Successful Login |
| 1st time | 98/165 (59.4%) | 1st time | 80/165 (48.5%) |
| 2nd time | 108/165 (65.5%) | 2nd time | 105/165 (63.6%) |
| 3rd time | 115/165 (69.7%) | 3rd time | 114/165 (69.1%) |
| DAS (Age in [35, 45]) | Successful Login | PassPoints (Age in [35, 45]) | Successful Login |
| 1st time | 12/35 (34.3%) | 1st time | 13/35 (37.1%) |
| 2nd time | 22/35 (62.9%) | 2nd time | 20/35 (57.1%) |
| 3rd time | 27/35 (77.1%) | 3rd time | 25/35 (71.4%) |
| DAS (Age in [45, 60]) | Successful Login | PassPoints (Age in [45, 60]) | Successful Login |
| 1st time | 21/50 (42.0%) | 1st time | 20/50 (40.0%) |
| 2nd time | 33/50 (66.0%) | 2nd time | 25/50 (50.0%) |
| 3rd time | 34/50 (68.0%) | 3rd time | 28/50 (56.0%) |

– *Experiment2.* This experiment requires each participant to create 5 *Pass-Points* passwords.

- Step 1. Creation: creating a password following the rules of *PassPoints*.
- Step 2. Confirmation: confirming the password by drawing the same secrets in the correct place. If users incorrectly confirm their password, they can retry the confirmation or return to Step 1.
- Step 3. Login: logging in the example system with the created passwords. Users can cancel an attempted login if they noticed an error.
- Step 4. Feedback: All participants are required to complete a *feedback form* about the password creation and confirmation.

Each participant will finish these two experiments in the same day. After three weeks, we require all participants to return and input all created passwords for these two schemes. Later, we provide another *feedback form* for participants about their password memory.

**Results.** In this user study, our main purpose is to explore whether users are able to remember and manage multiple graphical passwords. Therefore, we mainly describe and analyze users' performance after three weeks. The success rates of login to *DAS* and *PassPoints* within three attempts are described in Table 2. Three trails are determined based on the observation that most hosts or network accounts do not allow an authentication error more than three times. We have several major observations as below:

– *Overall Performance.* It is seen that participants can only achieve a success rate of 52.8% and 49.2% for *DAS* and *PassPoints* at the first attempt, respectively. After three trails, the success rate can be increased to 70.4% and 66.8%, respectively.

**Table 3.** Several main questions and relevant scores in the user study.

| Questions | Score (average) |
|---|---|
| 1. I could easily remember *DAS* passwords after one month | 4.5 |
| 2. I could easily remember *PassPoints* passwords after one month | 4.2 |
| 3. Are you willing to use *DAS* passwords in practice | 3.2 |
| 4. Are you willing to use *PassPoints* passwords in practice | 4.7 |
| 5. I can manage multiple *DAS* passwords | 3.5 |
| 6. I can manage multiple *PassPoints* passwords | 4.3 |

– *Age Impact.* In Table 2, we also presents the results according to three age groups. It is notice that participants who are aged from 35 to 45 can achieve the best performance in the experiments, while the success rate is not higher than 80% after three attempts (where the rate is 77.1% for *DAS* and 71.4% for *PassPoints*). Overall, it is found that younger participants have some advantages in multiple password memory.

Based on the results, it is found that participants did not show satisfied capability in remembering these two GP schemes. To investigate this issue, we collect the feedback forms and present some key questions/feedback in Table 3. Ten-point Likert scales were used in each feedback question where 1-score indicates strong disagreement and 10-score indicates strong agreement.

It is seen that participants cannot remember these two GPs for a long time, where the average scores of the first and the second question are lower than 5. In addition, most participants are not willing to use these GPs in real-world applications. Similarly, most participants feel it is difficult to remember multiple GPs. We informally interviewed most participants and find two major reasons: (1) for *DAS*, it is not easy to link the graphical password to corresponding accounts and (2) for *PassPoints*, it is easily to forget the click-points when creating more than 3 passwords. Up to 80% participants reported that they have more than 5 different textual passwords in use.

***Discussions.*** This is an initial study which can be improved in the aspects of involved users and GP numbers, while the results indeed indicate that multiple password memory has become a challenging issue for current graphical passwords. In this case, we argue that this issue should be given more attention when designing a graphical password scheme and it is crucial to develop GP schemes targeting for better multiple password memory.

## 4    RouteMap for Better Multiple Password Memory

Based on the study and feedback above, we have two other findings: (1) a background image can help users to remember their secrets, and (2) users should be provided with a few guidelines for creating their GPs. In this section, we describe our proposed *RouteMap* in detail and conduct a user study to investigate its performance, as compared with two similar schemes.

(a) RouteMap with sight

(b) RouteMap without sight

**Fig. 2.** *RouteMap*: (a) a pattern with sight and (b) a pattern without sight.

## 4.1   RouteMap

Our designed *RouteMap* is a kind of map-based graphical passwords, which allows users to draw a route on a map. There are three main reasons why we choose a map to build a GP scheme for better password memory.

- Map-based graphical passwords such as *PassMap* and *GeoPass* can provide large password space (e.g., $2^{36.9} for GeoPass$).
- Map can be easily zoom in or zoom out, so that users can choose a background image which they feel suitable.
- Previous studies show that map-based GPs have good usability (i.e., *GeoPass* shows that 97% participants can remember their passwords over a span of 8-9 days).

***Our Scheme.*** As described earlier, *RouteMap* allows users to draw a route on a map (e.g., Google map). To enhance the memory, *RouteMap* allows users to choose a road-based map or a satellite map to draw their passwords. This because different people may have their own preference in background. In this work, we call it as *sight*. In Figure 2, we present two examples of *RouteMap* patterns with and without sight.

Taking Figure 2 (b) as an example, for this pattern, a user needs to click on the playground first, then move and click on a park and another playground, and finally click and stop at a sport center. Thus, a *RouteMap* pattern will include sight information, first click-point and the whole moved places. To summarize, our scheme is different from other similar schemes in the following aspects.

– *RouteMap* allows users to choose whether to use sight or not, which aims to improve users' memory by placing them in a preferred environment. This selection will be included in the final pattern stored in the system.
– *RouteMap* only allows users to draw straight lines between different places. This aims to improve the usability, as it is noted that drawing curves is not easy for authentication using mouse input (i.e., consuming more time).
– *RouteMap* provides a simple guideline for users, which recommends users to create a route based on their existing memory such as tours and visits. It is found that tour-route or visit-route is private for users, but may enhance the memory of various clicks in a pattern.

***Implementation.*** We built a prototype system of *RouteMap* in our lab environment, which is similar to the design of *PassMap* and *GeoPass*. To fetch a real world map, we utilize Java scripts and Google Maps API, and our system can provide move (drag), zoom in, zoom out and search functions. When users zoom in or zoom out the map, *RouteMap* will report the zoom levels. For the search function, users can use it to shift to a specific area quickly and use zoom in or zoom out to locate a proper area. Afterwards, users can create a password by clicking a place and moving the mouse to click on the next places. Based on the prior work [14], we set the error tolerance to a $21 \times 21$ pixel box around the place they clicked. For the other similar schemes, the error tolerance of *GeoPass* was set to the same $21 \times 21$ pixel while *PassMap* was set to $20 \times 20$ pixel.

In this case, our system is able to record users' inputs and construct a pattern like {Sight, zoom level, the sequence of clicked places}. The value of *sight* is either 0 (not selected) or 1 (selected). The initial zoom level is set to 2 and the maximum level is 18. After clicking on a place, our system will record its coordinate information. It is worth noting that in order to enhance memory, a *red arrow* will be shown in *RouteMap* when users move mouse from one clicked place to another (see Figure 2).

## 4.2   User Study

To explore the performance of *RouteMap* in the aspect of multiple password memory, we further conduct a user study with 60 participants, among which 50 of them are from the former study. The time gap between the first study and this study is one month. The newly joined 10 participants are also volunteers and have no any background in information security. The detailed information of participants is described in Table 4.

**Table 4.** Detailed information of participants in the second user study.

| Age Range | Male | Female | Occupation | Male | Female |
|-----------|------|--------|------------|------|--------|
| 18-25 | 10 | 11 | Senior people | 4 | 2 |
| 25-35 | 8 | 9 | Students | 17 | 15 |
| 35-45 | 5 | 4 | Researchers | 5 | 4 |
| 45-55 | 4 | 3 | Engineers | 3 | 3 |
| 55-60 | 4 | 2 | Business people | 4 | 3 |

In the study, we randomly divided 60 participants into two groups, named *Group1* and *Group2*, and compare *RouteMap* with *PassMap* and *GeoPass*, respectively. More specifically, *Group1* will focus on *RouteMap* and *PassMap*, while *Group2* will focus on *RouteMap* and *GeoPass*. The implementation details of *PassMap* and *GeoPass* can be referred to [20,22]. Similar to our study above, to avoid bias, we train all the participants based on the same steps on how to use these example systems.

Before the study, every participant has 3 trails to get familiar with the example systems. For example, participants in *Group1* will create passwords for *RouteMap* and *PassMap*. In the user study, we require all participants to create 5 passwords for each scheme in their group and each password corresponds to an account: the first password is created for an email account (personal use), the second one is created for a bank account, the third one is created for another email account (commercial use), the fourth one is created for a forum account and the last one is created for a social networking account. The detailed steps in each experiment are shown as below:

- *Experiment G1.* *Group1* conducts this experiment, in which each participant is required to firstly create 5 passwords for *PassMap* and then create 5 passwords for *RouteMap* after one hour rest.
- *Experiment G2.* *Group2* conducts this experiment, in which each participant is required to firstly create 5 passwords for *GeoPass* and then create 5 passwords for *RouteMap* after one hour rest.

Both experiments follow the same steps, which are described as below:

- Step 1. Creation: creating a password following the related rules.
- Step 2. Confirmation: confirming the password by drawing the same secrets in the correct place. If users incorrectly confirm their password, they can retry the confirmation or return to Step 1.
- Step 3. Login: logging in the example system with all created passwords. Users can cancel an attempted login if they noticed an error.
- Step 4. Feedback: All participants are required to complete a *feedback form* about the password creation and confirmation.

All participants have to finish the experiments in the same day. To compare the results with the previous study, after three weeks, we later invite all participants to return and input all created passwords based on their own groups.

**Table 5.** Login success rate for *Group1* and *Group2* after three weeks.

| Experiment G1 (PassMap) | Successful Login | Experiment G1 (RouteMap) | Successful Login |
|---|---|---|---|
| 1st time | 113/150 (75.3%) | 1st time | 133/150 (88.7%) |
| 2nd time | 125/150 (83.3%) | 2nd time | 137/150 (91.3%) |
| 3rd time | 128/150 (85.3%) | 3rd time | 140/150 (93.3%) |
| Experiment G2 (GeoPass) | Successful Login | Experiment G2 (RouteMap) | Successful Login |
| 1st time | 122/150 (81.3%) | 1st time | 134/150 (89.3%) |
| 2nd time | 128/150 (85.3%) | 2nd time | 136/150 (90.7%) |
| 3rd time | 133/150 (88.7%) | 3rd time | 141/150 (94.0%) |

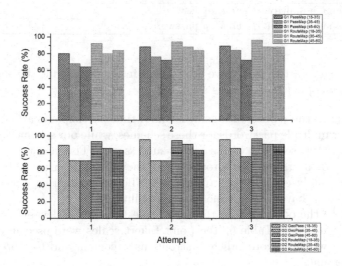

**Fig. 3.** Success rates for each age groups in the study.

After finishing this session, we give a *feedback form* to each participant regarding their password memory.

***Results.*** In this study, our target is to investigate the multiple password memory of *RouteMap* by comparing it with similar schemes. The login success rates for *Group1* and *Group2* within three attempts are presented in Table 5. Our key observations are reported as below:

– *Overall Performance.* As compared with the results in Table 2, it is seen that participants perform much better in this study. *Group1* can achieve a success rate of 75.3% and 88.7% for *PassMap* and *RouteMap* at the first attempt, respectively. After three attempts, the success rate can be increased to 85.3% and 93.3%. On the other hand, *Group2* can achieve a success rate of 81.3% and 89.3% for *GeoPass* and *RouteMap* at the first attempt, respectively. Then, the success rate can be elevated to 88.7% and 94% after three attempts.
– *Age Impact.* It is easily imagine that the results for each age group would be improved, since the overall login success rate increases. Figure 3 indicates

**Table 6.** Several main questions and relevant scores in the user study.

| Questions | Score (average) |
|---|---|
| 1. I could easily remember *PassMap* passwords after one month | 7.3 |
| 2. I could easily remember *GeoPass* passwords after one month | 8.1 |
| 3. I could easily remember *RouteMap* passwords after one month | 9.0 |
| 4. Are you willing to use *PassMap* passwords in practice | 7.8 |
| 5. Are you willing to use *GeoPass* passwords in practice | 8.5 |
| 6. Are you willing to use *RouteMap* passwords in practice | 8.9 |
| 7. I can manage multiple *PassMap* passwords | 7.1 |
| 8. I can manage multiple *GeoPass* passwords | 7.8 |
| 9. I can manage multiple *RouteMap* passwords | 8.7 |

that younger participants have advantages in memory while the success rate of senior people also increases a lot.

According to these observations, it is found that participants are able to better remember multiple passwords for these schemes, while our scheme can outperform the other two schemes with a higher success rate. The major reason is that *RouteMap* leads users to draw a route where they have experienced before. The experience actually enhances the relationship between different clicked places, so that users can have a better memory capability.

To validate the observations, the major questions and relevant scores (feedback) are presented in Table 6. Ten-point Likert scales were used in each feedback question where 1-score indicates strong disagreement and 10-score indicates strong agreement.

It is visible that most participants gave positive feedback for remembering these map-based passwords, in which *RouteMap* receives the highest score of 9.0 among them. Most participants report that the route defined in *RouteMap* can improve their memory of created passwords, due to the correlation between these clicked places. Based on this, participants are also willing to use the map-based passwords in practice such as their email accounts and social networking accounts, where *RouteMap* obtains the highest score of 8.9. Moreover, it is seen that most participants believe that they can manage multiple *RouteMap* passwords with the highest score of 8.7, as compared with the other two schemes (with a score of 7.1 and 7.8, respectively). On the whole, it is considered that *RouteMap* can provide better multiple password memory for users.

### 4.3  Further Discussions

This work mainly focuses on the two defined targets, so that we leave some aspects such as security analysis in our future studies. In this part, we briefly analyze *RouteMap* in the aspects of security and usability.

– *Security Aspect.* As mentioned above, *RouteMap* is a kind of map-based passwords and allows users to click several places on a map in constructing a route as passwords. Intuitively, the password space is generally not lower than *GeoPass* (one clicked place on a map), but due to the relationship between different clicked places, there is not a direct increase by clicking more places. We will provide a full security analysis in our future work.

- *Usability Aspect.* Based on our studies and participant feedback, *RouteMap* obtains higher scores than the other two schemes, so we consider it has good usability. We also informally interviewed most participants and most participants prefer *RouteMap* instead of the other schemes. It is worth noting that the other two map-based schemes also obtain good feedback, when comparing the scores between Table 3 and Table 6.
- *Multiple Password Memory.* Our study results indicate that users have better performance in multiple password memory using *RouteMap*. It is noted that users memory can be enhanced by correlating the clicked places. To explore this issue, an even larger study will be performed in our future work.

## 5   Conclusion

In this paper, our first purpose is to explore whether users can remember multiple graphical passwords for two existing and popular GP schemes. Based on the study results, it is identified that multiple password memory has become a big challenge. To solve this issue, we design *RouteMap*, a map- and route-based graphical password scheme, in which users can draw a route on a Google map as their secrets. To investigate its performance, we further conduct another user study with 60 participants and find that *RouteMap* can enhance multiple password memory for users, as compared with two similar schemes. Our effort aims to complement existing studies and stimulate more research in this area.

There are lots of future directions including providing a more specific analysis on password space and involving more participants in the future evaluation. Future work could also include conducting a thorough security analysis and evaluate the scheme in an adverse environment (i.e., an attacker has some knowledge about the user and build a map password dictionary).

**Acknowledgments.** We first would like to thank Wenjuan Li, Lijun Jiang and Ying Meng for the great support in this work and all participants for their hard work and cooperation in the user study. In addition, we would like to thank all anonymous reviewers for their helpful comments in improving the paper.

## References

1. Bonneau, J.: The science of guessing: analyzing an anonymized corpus of 70 million passwords. In: Proceedings of the 2012 IEEE Symposium on Security and Privacy, pp. 538–552 (2012)
2. Chiasson, S., van Oorschot, P.C., Biddle, R.: Graphical password authentication using cued click points. In: Biskup, J., López, J. (eds.) ESORICS 2007. LNCS, vol. 4734, pp. 359–374. Springer, Heidelberg (2007)

3. Chiasson, S., Biddle, R., van Oorschot, P.C.: A second look at the usability of click-based graphical passwords. In: Proceedings of the 3rd Symposium on Usable Privacy and Security (SOUPS), pp. 1–12. ACM, New York (2007)
4. Chiasson, S., Stobert, E., Forget, A., Biddle, R.: Persuasive Cued Click-Points: Design, Implementation, and Evaluation of a Knowledge-Based Authentication Mechanism. IEEE Transactions on Dependable and Secure Computing **9**(2), 222–235 (2012)
5. Davis, D., Monrose, F., Reiter, M.K.: On user choice in graphical password schemes. In: Proceedings of the 13th Conference on USENIX Security Symposium (SSYM), pp. 151–164. USENIX Association, Berkeley (2004)
6. Dirik, A.E., Memon, N., Birget, J.C.: Modeling user choice in the passpoints graphical password scheme. In: Proceedings of the 3rd Symposium on Usable privacy and security (SOUPS). ACM, New York, pp. 20–28 (2007)
7. Dunphy, P., Yan, J.: Do background images improve "draw a secret" graphical passwords? In: Proceedings of the 14th ACM Conference on Computer and Communications Security (CCS), pp. 36–47 (2007)
8. Fox, S.: Future Online Password Could be a Map (2010). http://www.livescience.com/8622-future-online-password-map.html
9. Georgakakis, E., Komninos, N., Douligeris, C.: NAVI: novel authentication with visual information. In: Proceedings of the 2012 IEEE Symposium on Computers and Communications (ISCC), pp. 588–595 (2012)
10. Gołofit, K.: Click passwords under investigation. In: Biskup, J., López, J. (eds.) ESORICS 2007. LNCS, vol. 4734, pp. 343–358. Springer, Heidelberg (2007)
11. Jermyn, I., Mayer, A., Monrose, F., Reiter, M.K., Rubin, A.D.: The design and analysis of graphical passwords. In: Proceedings of the 8th Conference on USENIX Security Symposium, pp. 1–14. USENIX Association, Berkeley (1999)
12. Lin, D., Dunphy, P., Olivier, P., Yan, J.: Graphical passwords & qualitative spatial relations. In: Proceedings of the 3rd Symposium on Usable Privacy and Security (SOUPS), pp. 161–162 (2007)
13. Meng, Y.: Designing click-draw based graphical password scheme for better authentication. In: Proceedings of the 7th IEEE International Conference on Networking, Architecture, and Storage (NAS), pp. 39–48 (2012)
14. Meng, Y., Li, W.: Evaluating the effect of tolerance on click-draw based graphical password scheme. In: Chim, T.W., Yuen, T.H. (eds.) ICICS 2012. LNCS, vol. 7618, pp. 349–356. Springer, Heidelberg (2012)
15. Nelson, D.L., Reed, V.S., Walling, J.R.: Pictorial superiority effect. Journal of Experimental Psychology: Human Learning and Memory **2**(5), 523–528 (1976)
16. Passfaces. http://www.realuser.com/
17. Shepard, R.N.: Recognition memory for words, sentences, and pictures. Journal of Verbal Learning and Verbal Behavior **6**(1), 156–163 (1967)
18. Spitzer, J., Singh, C., Schweitzer, D.: A Security Class Project in Graphical Passwords. Journal of Computing Sciences in Colleges **26**(2), 7–13 (2010)
19. Suo, X., Zhu, Y., Owen, G.S.: Graphical passwords: a survey. In: Proceedings of the 21st Annual Computer Security Applications Conference (ACSAC), pp. 463–472. IEEE Computer Society, USA (2005)
20. Sun, H., Chen, Y., Fang, C., Chang, S.: PassMap: a map based graphical-password authentication system. In: Proceedings of ASIACCS, pp. 99–100 (2012)
21. Tao, H., Adams, C.: Pass-Go: A Proposal to Improve the Usability of Graphical Passwords. International Journal of Network Security **2**(7), 273–292 (2008)

22. Thorpe, J., MacRae, B., Salehi-Abari, A.: Usability and security evaluation of geopass: a geographic location-password scheme. In: Proceedings of the 9th Symposium on Usable Privacy and Security (SOUPS), pp. 1–14 (2013)
23. Wiedenbeck, S., Waters, J., Birget, J.-C., Brodskiy, A., Memon, N.: Passpoints: Design and Longitudinal Evaluation of A Graphical Password System. International Journal of Human-Computer Studies **63**(1–2), 102–127 (2005)
24. Weir, M., Aggarwal, S., Collins, M., Stern, H.: Testing metrics for password creation policies by attacking large sets of revealed passwords. In: Proceedings of CCS, pp. 162–175 (2010)
25. Yan, J., Blackwell, A., Anderson, R., Grant, A.: Password memorability and security: Empirical results. IEEE Security and Privacy **2**, pp. 25-31 (2004)

# Indicators of Malicious SSL Connections

Riccardo Bortolameotti[1]([⊠]), Andreas Peter[1], Maarten H. Everts[1,2],
and Damiano Bolzoni[1,3]

[1] University of Twente, Enschede, The Netherlands
{r.bortolameotti,a.peter}@utwente.nl
[2] Netherlands Organisation for Applied Scientific Research (TNO),
Groningen, The Netherlands
maarten.everts@tno.nl
[3] SecurityMatters, Eindhoven, The Netherlands
damiano.bolzoni@secmatters.com

**Abstract.** Internet applications use SSL to provide data confidentiality to communicating entities. The use of encryption in SSL makes it impossible to distinguish between benign and malicious connections as the content cannot be inspected. Therefore, we propose and evaluate a set of indicators for malicious SSL connections, which is based on the unencrypted part of SSL (i.e., the SSL handshake protocol). We provide strong evidence for the strength of our indicators to identify malicious connections by cross-checking on blacklists from professional services. Besides the confirmation of prior research results through our indicators, we also found indications for a potential (not yet blacklisted) botnet on SSL. We consider the analysis of such SSL threats as highly relevant and hope that our findings stimulate the research community to further study this direction.

**Keywords:** SSL · Malicious connection indicators · Handshake analysis

## 1 Introduction

The Transport Layer Security (TLS) and its predecessor the Secure Socket Layer (SSL) are the *de-facto* standard protocols for secure communication over the Internet.[1] They provide end-to-end security that guarantees data confidentiality, integrity and authenticity to the communicating entities. In particular, they provide protection against possible active Man-in-the-Middle (MitM) attacks, where the attacker has the control over the entire network. Most of the services that handle sensitive data use SSL to protect the confidentiality of their users' data. In the past years, many papers have been published on SSL that assess its reliability and identify potential vulnerabilities. Some general analyses on characteristics of SSL traffic have shown several practical problems related to its infrastructure. Holz et al. [1] report issues regarding the usage of X.509 certificates: errors within

---

[1] For the remaining of the paper, we refer to both as SSL.

© Springer International Publishing Switzerland 2015
M. Qiu et al. (Eds.): NSS 2015, LNCS 9408, pp. 162–175, 2015.
DOI: 10.1007/978-3-319-25645-0_11

certificate chains, absence of certificate subjects, common usage of expired certificates, etc. Amman et al. [2] have highlighted the complexity of the entire SSL infrastructure by stating that many specifications are left to interpretation while features aiming to improve weaknesses are still poorly implemented. Other works instead focused more on the security vulnerabilities of SSL. For instance, Amman et al. [3] analyze SSL traffic to understand the trust relationships among Certificate Authorities (CA) and to detect transparent MitM attacks. In such attacks, the attacker tries to compromise CAs with the goal of being able to generate a valid certificate for any domain and to start a MitM attack. The authors conclude their work stating that the certificate structure does not give enough information to be able to distinguish between malicious and benign certificates. Georgiev et al. [4] present a security analysis on SSL library implementations for non-browser software, identifying several vulnerabilities that make many applications vulnerable to MitM attacks. In [5], Fahl et al. introduce MalloDroid, a tool for Android apps used to detect SSL implementation vulnerabilities to MitM attacks, identifying more than 1000 potentially vulnerable apps. Although the SSL protocol (its most recent version, TLS 1.2) is considered to be secure from a theoretical perspective, it still shows several practical issues. In response to such problems, researchers started to propose security enhancements, which are not yet widely implemented in current applications [10]. Conti et al. developed MITHYS [6], a proxy for Android applications that addresses the SSL vulnerabilities examined in [5] and [4], and that guarantees MitM protection against rogue access points. Bates et al. [8] propose CERTSHIM, a lightweight retrofit that patches SSL implementations against several SSL vulnerabilities, including those highlighted in [4]. Holz et al. [9] suggest Crossbear, a system that detects MitM attacks on SSL/TLS over the Internet, collecting data in a centralized system from several online probes, which works on browsers.

In contrast to all existing works, we investigate SSL with a focus on malicious connections. Previous works have analyzed SSL connections assuming the client is benign. We define a connection as malicious when both end points of the communication are controlled by the attacker. A possible scenario is data exfiltration, where a compromised machine communicates with an external server, owned by the attacker, over an SSL channel in order to bypass security measures and to camouflage within normal traffic. Botnets are an example of such a scenario.

Our main contributions are the following: (1) we present an initial study on malicious connections within SSL network traffic, by looking at the SSL handshake protocol, (2) we found good indicators for malicious connections using unencrypted information exchanged during the SSL handshake, (3) we verify prior research findings [1,3,4,10] with our newly found indicators, and (4) we discovered the presence of malicious connections examining our indicators within the network traffic of an international university and of an international financial corporation. Within the IT infrastructure of the university we found 34 connections that show the same communication patterns (e.g., expired certificates), where 10 of the associated IP addresses are blacklisted by a professional service, called ThreatStop [16]. Furthermore, analyzing the network traffic of the financial corporation we found two other malicious connections, also blacklisted. Moreover, we found one of these analyzed malicious connections (i.e., the IP address of the server) way before ThreatStop itself and four of them are marked as potential botnets. We consider this a significant result as it shows the strength of our indicators. We hope that our work stimulates the research community to further study these new findings.

## 2    Our Approach and Assumptions

Our goal is to identify a set of features based on the SSL handshake protocol that could indicate the presence of malicious connections within SSL traffic. In our approach, we first select a set of features to analyze within SSL traffic that we think can help us to indicate connection misbehaviors. After an evaluation of this set of features on real data, we identify those that are more promising as maliciousness indicators. Our approach is based on two assumptions:

1. The encrypted part of the SSL protocol is assumed to be secure, meaning that we cannot inspect it.
2. Malware authors have complete control over the client and server applications, therefore they can easily avoid following the SSL standards, and make their "own rules" creating broken SSL connections (e.g., do not properly authenticate application connections).

The first assumption has two positive side-effects: whatever analysis we do, it will (1) respect data confidentiality, and (2) be lightweight as we only focus on the initialization of the SSL connection (i.e., in the SSL handshake) and because we do not have to use complex algorithm to analyze our features. The negative side-effect of assumption (1) is that it is not possible to examine the content of the payload message in order to verify the maliciousness of a connection. The second assumption implies an enforcement of authentication checks on SSL connections at network level. This is done because browsers do not check the validity of SSL connections generated by applications running on the background. The drawback of the second assumption is that malicious connections would not be identified whenever they follow correctly the specifications of the protocol.

Selecting features from the handshake protocol is not a novel approach. In 2014, Pukkawanna et al. [7] proposed different classifiers to automatically assess the security of SSL servers, analyzing handshake protocol features. However, their work focuses only on the security parameters of the server and not on the parameters of the client. The authors use information from the *Server Hello* and *Certificate* messages of the protocol. To achieve our goal, we consider also characteristics of the *Client Hello* message (e.g., *server name*) and we relate them with those from other messages (e.g., *fourth feature* in Section 2) in order to evaluate the behaviour of both communicating parties.

**Selected Set of Features.** The *first feature* that we have selected is the validity of the X.509 certificates. With this feature, we want to check if the certificate is valid, self-signed, revoked, etc. The validity of the certificate can help us to detect misbehaviors, because for normal benign traffic we do not expect to see expired certificates during the authentication phase, neither we expect to see facebook.com to use a self-signed certificate. This feature is commonly used by researchers when analyzing the security of SSL. For instance, self-signed certificates are used in [6] to identify vulnerable applications to MitM attacks. However, in our case we do not restrict our attention to self-signed certificates, because malicious connections can also be authenticated with expired, valid or revoked certificates.

Our *second feature* is the release date of the certificate, especially for self-signed certificates. This feature is appropriate in the context of malicious software, where the lifetime of web domains is short. Therefore, we assume that criminals could generate new self-signed certificates either for each connection or for a short period of time (e.g., one day). We focus on self-signed certificates because they are easy and cheap (i.e., free) to generate and seem more suitable considering the lifetime of domains, unlike expensive commercial certificates.

Our *third feature* is the existence of mutual-authentication. SSL provides the option for a server to require client authentication (e.g., *CertificateRequest* and *CertificateVerify* messages). This feature can be leveraged by criminals in the context of a peer-to-peer botnet, in order to avoid external peers to infiltrate within their system.

Our *fourth feature* is the relation between the SSL extension *server name*, which is included in the *Client Hello* message, and the subjects (i.e., *Subject* and *subjectAltName* X.509 certificate fields) of the X.509 certificate. This is the typical browser authentication check that verifies whether the certificate is valid for the domain requested by the client or not. Whenever there is a mismatch, the connection should be considered untrusted, and potentially vulnerable to MitM attacks (e.g., in the case of DNS poisoning [4], where the attacker can redirect a user from a website to another).

Our *fifth feature* is the Levenshtein distance between the *server name* and a list of the 100 most visited websites, whenever a self-signed certificate is encountered during the handshake. When a user connects to a server (e.g., www.google.com) he should expect to receive a valid certificate, and not a self-signed certificate valid for a similar domain (e.g., www.gogle.com), otherwise it could be a symptom of a MitM attack.

The *sixth feature* is the structure of the *server name* string. A current trend in botnets is to use Domain Generation Algorithms (DGAs)[11] to generate many random domain names that can be exploited as rendezvous point with botnet servers. Therefore, we want to check whether these strings can be identified as random-looking domains or not. This feature is not new in literature and it has been previously used in the context of HTTP [14].

Finally, our *seventh feature* is the format of the *server name* string, which should have a DNS hostname format as described in the specifications of the

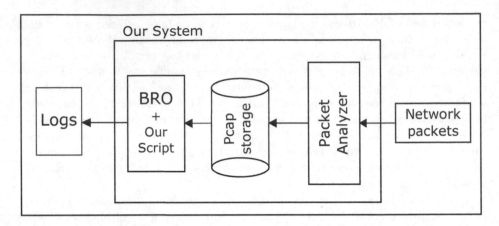

**Fig. 1.** System Architecture

SSL extensions [15]. This protocol field represents the domain the client wants to connect to, therefore we do not expect to see weird values or strings that could represent an exchange of messages, perhaps used by criminals as commands.

A summarized description of the features is shown in Table 1.

## 3   Architecture and Implementation

The architecture of our system is shown in Figure 1. The system takes as input the network traffic and first filters it through a packet analyzer module that recognizes the SSL traffic and stores it on the disk as pcap (packet capture) files. Those files are then given as input to Bro [12], an open source network analysis framework that we use to analyze the traffic. This analysis on SSL connections is based on our own Bro scripts that implement the aforementioned set of features. Once Bro has analyzed the whole traffic, it outputs a set of log containing the connections that, according to our features, might indicate the presence of malicious behavior.

In our implementation we use *tcpdump* [17] as packet analyzer. We filter the traffic on port 443 (i.e., we analyze on HTTPS in our implementation). Once the data is stored on the disk, we run an offline analysis over captured data using Bro. The first feature (see Table 1) uses an already existing script for the Bro's framework, called *validate-certs.bro* [2], which uses the Mozilla root store as trusted base. All the other features are implemented by us through Bro's scripting language, except for the sixth feature related to DGA domains, which uses an *n-gram* technique [13] to determine the level of randomness of a string.

## 4   Analysis of Selected Features

The selection of features is based on our assumptions (see Section 2), therefore we analyze them to see whether they can be useful as indicators of malicious connections or not. In a second step, we discuss the findings of our analyzed features on the SSL network traffic. We ran two different analysis. The first is done on 300 GB of SSL traffic. The goal of this analysis is to define which of the proposed features are helpful to determine the presence of malicious connections. The second evaluation is tailored to the outcomes of the previous analysis and is applied to a different dataset of 1 TB of SSL traffic. The set of features in the second evaluation is smaller as it only includes those features that we have identified as good indicators. In both analyses, our implementation examines only SSL connections that successfully completed the handshake protocol (i.e., the *Finished* message is sent [18]). A connection represents a unique instance of a successful handshake. Therefore, connections are not unique for each pair of hosts.

**Datasets.** We ran our first analysis on the network traffic of an international university[2]. This analysis is done by mirroring the whole traffic of the gateway of the university network to our own server. The traffic is then filtered and analyzed by our system. Our analyzed dataset is collected at the end of May 2014 (from 26th to 29th of May) and consists of 300 GB of SSL traffic. The second dataset, of 1 TB of traffic has been collected between the 8th and the 28th of July 2014. The goal of this second analysis is to further investigate the malicious connections previously identified.

## 4.1   Insignificant Features

Our first analysis on 300 GB of SSL traffic has shown that the release date of the certificate (F2), the existence of mutual authentication (F3) and the Levensthein distance for self-signed certificates (F5) do not seem to indicate the presence of malicious connections. Feature F2 has not shown any evidence of malicious connections. We have identified several certificates with a release date close to the establishment of the connections (e.g., less than 10 minutes), but they were all related to TOR connections, because the certificate subjects matches a typical pattern for TOR certificates (see Section 4.3), therefore they cannot be considered malicious. We found 262 certificates generated 10 minutes before the connection was established, 276 released within 1 day before the connection and 6589 generated more than 1 day before the connection. We found 198 connections, unrelated to TOR, that provided certificates with a release date of less than 1 day, however none of these connections had further indications that they could be considered malicious. Therefore, we consider this feature not relevant for our purposes. Mutual authentication (F3) is not commonly used within SSL communications. Analyzing our dataset of 891110 SSL connections, just 0.38% (i.e., 3386 connections) use *CertificateRequest* and *CertificateVerify* messages during the SSL handshake. 78.8% of such connections are authenticated with a valid certificate and the large majority of them are generated by the Apple Push

---

[2] The university has approximately 12.000 students and employees (combined).

Notification Service. None of these connections that are using mutual authentication are malicious, therefore we mark also this feature as insignificant. Lastly, we did not find any connection authenticated with a self-signed certificate where the Levensthein distance between the subject and the 100 most visited websites indicate a similar domains. Thus, we consider the Levensthein distance as an insignificant feature as well.

## 4.2    Indicating Features

In our analysis, we have found that the certificate chain validation (F1), the relation between server name and certificate subject (F4), the structure of the server name string (F6) and its format (F7) seem to be indicators for malicious connections. During our first analysis we have found 5 different malicious connections, and all these features can be potential indicators. In addition, we found one of these IP addresses before the professional service ThreatStop [16] marked it as malicious. This fact shows the strength of our identified indicators of malicious connections. The certificate chain validation (F1) has shown that 71% of the certificates in our dataset is properly verified as a valid certificate. 21.5% of the certificates instead do not provide their issuer. The amount of self-signed certificates (including those having self-signed certificates in chain) is equivalent to 0.8%. The amount of expired certificates we have encountered is 0.01%, while the rest 6.7% of the certificates was not validated by the Bro script (i.e., *validate-certs.bro* [2]). We consider this feature to be a possible indicator because in the malicious connections we have found, none of them use a properly validated certificate, as shown in Figure 2. In particular, 3 of these connections use an expired certificate from Amazon. Considering the small amount of expired certificates we have found in all our dataset, and the patterns of these malicious communications, we think this feature could be a helpful indicator.

The second indicating feature is the relation between server name and certificate subject (F4). If it is not properly enforced it can lead to a connection vulnerable to MitM attacks. In our entire dataset, 83.2% of the connections use the TLS Server name extension. 98% of these connections provide a proper certificate for the requested domain by the client. This is never true for TOR connections, where the server name never matches (100% of the cases) the certificate subject. Nonetheless, we consider this feature as a potential maliciousness indicator because, as shown in Figure 2, all the malicious connections we found present a mismatch between server name and certificate subject.

The third indicator is the structure of the server name string. TOR connections have shown a clear pattern of random second level domain (SLD), also confirmed by [2]. Two of the malicious connections we analyzed have a random server name (see Figure 2). These are outgoing connections from a TOR node within the university network. We think this feature can be helpful as an indicator.

Lastly, the fourth indicator is the format of the server name string. 0.02% of SSL connections in our dataset have a server name with a format different from the DNS hostname, which is the standard defined by the RFC6066 [15].

156 connections have the IP address of the server, as a server name value. While 111 connections have random values (e.g., 01cf645e.32fa6d90). Considering that 3 malicious connections out of 5 have a server name string that does not follow the standard (e.g., they have IP addresses as server name), we include this feature in our set of indicators (see Figure 2).

We give to our features a different level of strength, which depends on how many times they are encountered within the set of malicious connections. As shown in Table 1, F1 and F4 have a value 5/5, which means that in all the 5 malicious connections these features were present. F6 and F7 have a lower level of strength since they are present just in 2 and 3 cases ,respectively, within the malicious connections. A more detailed representation is depicted in Figure 2.

**Table 1.** Descriptive summary of the selected features. The features used as malicious indicators and their level of strength are identified.

| F# | Feature | Description | Malic. Indic. | Indicator Strength |
|----|---------|-------------|---------------|--------------------|
| F1 | Certificate chain validation | Typical validation chain of X.509 certificates | X | 5/5 |
| F2 | Certificate time generation | Check the time from certificate generation and connection | - | 0/5 |
| F3 | Certificate request & Certificate verify | Check if mutual authentication has been requested | - | 0/5 |
| F4 | Server name belong to certificate subject | Check if the certificate is correct for the requested server name | X | 5/5 |
| F5 | Levensthein distance for self-signed certificate | Check if famous domains provide self signed certificates | - | 0/5 |
| F6 | Random generated server name domain | Check whether the server domain is random or not | X | 2/5 |
| F7 | Format of server name domain | Check whether the server domain follow the DNS hostname standard | X | 3/5 |

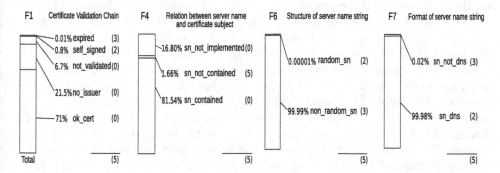

**Fig. 2.** Detailed representation of the analyzed indicating features with format: [% of dataset], [feature value], ([found in x-many malicious connections]).

## 4.3   Application

**Malicious Connections.** We identified 5 malicious connections within the SSL traffic. We verified their maliciousness using the public blacklist service offered by ThreatStop [16], a professional service that provides a blacklist of known criminal addresses. If the IP addresses are not blacklisted, we do not consider the connection as malicious. The connections have been analyzed using ThreatStop few days after the traffic has been captured, and this verification process has been done only once. Therefore, it is possible that our indicators would have identified more malicious connections, whose IP addresses were not yet blacklisted. We have chosen ThreatStop for two main reasons: (1) it is a professional service, meaning that the blacklist is always updated and properly maintained and (2) it focuses on threats that match our scenario such as criminal malware or botnets, which can be used for data exfiltration.

Two of these connections have IP addresses linked to SPAM activities (TOR connection), but do not share any pattern. The other three connections instead show exactly the same patterns: the servers use an expired certificate of Amazon to authenticate themselves (valid for the following domains www.amazon. com, uedata.amazon.com, amazon.com, amzn.com, www.amzn.com), and they have their destination IP address as server name field. Additionally, in the same dataset 3 other connections have been found using these same communication patterns. However, the IP addresses are not blacklisted, thus we cannot consider them to be malicious, although they seem very likely to be malicious due to the exact same characteristics.

We have ran a second analysis with a new dataset of 1TB of SSL traffic to investigate the malicious connections that we have found. In this analysis, we found another 28 connections that have the same patterns, but different IPs. In total, we have observed 34 connections over 14 different countries, where 10 of them have IPs labeled as malicious by ThreatStop [16] and all connections with the same source (i.e., a host inside the university network). Additionally, all these IP addresses, few weeks after being identified, were not reachable anymore on their port 443, as if the service was shutdown. Considering the following facts: (1) an expired certificate of Amazon.com has been used by several blacklisted IPs, (2) the location of these servers was spread all over Europe, and (3) the short lifetime of their services, we believe that what we have found can be considered a (not yet blacklisted) botnet. Another fact is that two of these IP addresses are also marked by ThreatStop as potential botnet. It is interesting to note that only 10 out of 34 IPs are blacklisted, although they share the same traffic characteristics. These connections have been identified due to the presence of features F1, F4 and F7. F1 identified that the certificate used by the server was expired. F7 showed that the format of the server name field was not following the DNS standard but was using an IP address. Finally, F4 showed that the server name and subject were not matching.

Looking at the features, it seems that the server name field plays an important role in identifying malicious connections. Not only the format of the domain, but also its relation with the subject of the certificate, which we believe is the main part of authentication of the server because it shows whether the answer of the server (i.e. certificate) matches the request of the client (i.e., server name). The randomness of the domain name seems also to be useful. Perhaps, using a more sophisticated technique to detect random domains could improve its impact as an indicator. Not surprisingly, also the validity of the certificate seems to be relevant. Malicious connections use certificates that are either expired or self-signed. Therefore, identifying connections that are not identified by proper validated certificates, can be an indicator.

Therefore, we believe our indicators analyze malicious traffic from a new and different perspective. During this second analysis, we have also found three other malicious connections (i.e., blacklisted by ThreatStop [16]) coming from the TOR exit node. Therefore, considering the two TOR malicious connections identified in the 300 GB of SSL traffic, we found a total of 5 malicious connections within TOR network traffic. The features present in these connections were F1, F4 and F6. In these cases the certificates were self-signed, therefore F1 was triggered. F6 identified them as malicious connections due to their "random looking" SLD. Lastly, F4 showed that the provided certificate was not valid to authenticate the requested server name.

**Connections Vulnerable to MitM Attacks.** Although our analysis focuses on malicious connections, the selected features allowed us to identify other mis-behaviours, which weaken the security of SSL connections. We identified 5326 connections (0.6% of the entire dataset) that are potentially vulnerable to MitM attacks, due to a bad implementation of the authentication mechanism (i.e., the requested domain is not contained in the list of subjects of the certificate). 1251 of these connections are authenticated with valid certificates. Several of these misconfigurations are related to Akamai, a well known Content Distribution Network that provides its customers a single SSL certificate valid for different domains (e.g., *.akamaihd.net [3]). Also the Google Project SDPY, an open networking protocol for transporting web content, does not follow the specifications of SSL correctly, using hash values (e.g., 01cf645e.32fa6d90) as the server name in the *ClientHello* request. With this outcome we confirm, as discussed in [4], that there are still several web applications using SSL in a wrong way. However, we apply a further analysis on these connections, and determined we can group the misconfiguration into two sets: *light* and *heavy*. A *light* misconfiguration is when the SLD of the server name matches with the SLD of the certificate subject, but there is a mismatch between subdomains (e.g., example.website.com and fake.website.com). We called them *light* because for an attacker it is hard to create a MitM attack, since he should generate or "steal" a certificate with the same SLD and a different subdomain, or he should compromise a CA and release a certificate with same SLD and different subdomain. A *heavy* misconfiguration is when the SLD of the server name is different from the SLD domain of the certificate subject (e.g., www.example.com and www.malicious.com). In this case the connection can be easily attacked by a MitM, because the certificate is not verified to match with the requested domain.

**TOR.** Analyzing the randomness of domains we encountered several TOR connections within the HTTPS traffic. We identified a simple pattern to distinguish it from normal HTTPS traffic: ServerName= www.[randomstring].com AND Subject=www.[randomSLD].net AND certificate_validation="Unable to get Certificate Issuer". This is a constant pattern in all TOR communications over port 443. All the TOR connections (i.e., 7127) have this pattern. Moreover, we were able to identify an exit node which was generating a lot of TOR traffic within the University network. Amman et al. [2] in their work, arrived at the same conclusions, with a very similar pattern: where Issuer and Subject match the pattern CN=www.[randomstring].[tld]. Both patterns successfully identify connections among TOR nodes. The TOR exit node presents within the university network is responsible for two of the malicious connections that we have found in our analysis. The server name is a random string, typical characteristic of TOR traffic. In these two cases, the connections were exiting the onion network, therefore the certificate provided by the real destination was not respecting the pattern of TOR nodes.

**Financial Corporation.** We analyzed the indicating features (see Section 4.2) in a further scenario. The dataset in this case is approximately 2 TB of network traffic, which has been captured over a period of two weeks, from the 23rd of March to the 9th of April 2015, within the infrastructure of an international financial corporation. Figure 3 shows a simplified architecture of our approach for data collection. The network traffic of client networks is mirrored to our solution, deployed on one of their machines. The traffic seen by our system is previously filtered by state-of-the-art security solutions deployed by the company that prevent clients to communicate with malicious domains. Moreover, the gateway firewall is a state-of-the-art solution capable of inspecting the SSL traffic. It does this decrypting the traffic, analyzing it and re-encrypting it and finally forwarding it towards its destination. However, the inspection is based on certain criteria, therefore not all the traffic is inspected. This firewall highly limits the number of connections analyzed by our system, because it uses self-signed certificates to re-encrypt the traffic, therefore the handshake that our system analyzes is not the original and features like F1 and F4 can be altered. For this reason, we filter these connections: we analyze the handshake of those connections that were not inspected by the firewall.

The analysis of the financial corporation network has also revealed vulnerable connections to MitM (i.e., heavy misconfiguration). We have identified 129 connections, where 118 provide an expired certificate (115 are connections to the same website). The remaining 11 connections have a self signed certificate in chain. We were also able to identify 14 TOR connections, despite the fact that the network traffic was filtered through a blacklisting mechanism to block TOR traffic. This result remarks how blacklisting solutions are not perfect. Lastly, we have identified two malicious connections. They share the same IP address, which is blacklisted by ThreatStop [16] as a potential botnet. Considering the well-protected infrastructure where the malicious connections have been identified, we believe this result underlines the strength of our indicators for the identification of malicious connections over SSL.

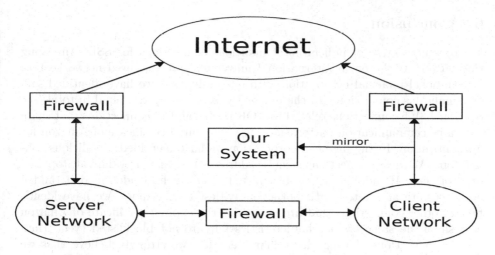

**Fig. 3.** High-Level representation of the data capturing within the Financial Corporation network

## 5   Limitations and Future Works

As we mentioned in the introduction, our work is an initial analysis of SSL malicious connections and it still has its limitations. First of all, the weight of our features has been computed from a small number of observation during the analysis of the first dataset. Although it can give an intuition about the effectiveness, because during the second analysis we found more malicious connections having such indicators, a more extensive validation should be done. This can be realized through an analysis of additional traffic. Another limitation of this work is that the set of features might be under fitting. There could be more handshake features that could be helpful in identifying malicious connection. Moreover, it is possible that more malicious connections have not been identified due to a limited set of indicators. Indeed, in the first analysis we ran ThreatStop against the subset of connections containing at least one of our indicators. This was a design decision, because it does not seem sensible to evaluate our indicators over connections that were not including them. As future work, extending the set of features is a necessary step. The features proposed by Pukkawanna et al. [7] could be used as helpful reference. The usage of machine learning techniques could also be useful in the analysis. Our judgement on the maliciousness of a connection heavily relies on the ThreatStop service. Therefore, it is possible that more connections were malicious and we did not consider them because they were not blacklisted by ThreatStop. This is a typical drawback of using blacklisting. This might be improved using additional sources to verify the maliciousness of IP addresses. Lastly, the design and implementation of an intrusion detection system based on an extension of our work (e.g. with additional indicators) can be considered as interesting future work.

# 6    Conclusion

We presented a set of indicators of malicious connections for SSL. Analyzing the network traffic of an international university and a secured network of an international financial corporation with our indicators, we have identified several malicious connections. In the university setting we have found in total (see Section 4.3): 5 connections related to TOR traffic, and 10 connections that share the same communication patterns and use an expired certificate of Amazon for authentication. In the financial corporation we have identified 2 malicious connections. All these connections have IP addresses blacklisted by ThreatStop [16]. One of these IP addresses was blacklisted after we have identified it, and 4 addresses are associated with botnet activities. Furthermore, we have identified 24 other connections that are also using the expired certificate of Amazon and share the same traffic characteristics but are not blacklisted (yet). Having 34 connections sharing these characteristics, we strongly believe that we have found a potential botnet on SSL. Nonetheless, we have also verified several results of prior research on the identification of many vulnerable SSL connections to MitM attacks, but by using a different method. This work is not intended as an intrusion detection system, although our indicators, through further validation, could potentially be part of such a system. A deeper understanding and further research is needed to turn our work into an intrusion detection system. We consider this as future work. The goal of this work is to identify features that could indicate malicious behaviors. We believe this set of indicators is a good starting point. Further extensions are still needed, as we suggested in Section 5.

**Acknowledgments.** This work was partially supported by the AVATAR project (funded by the Ministry of Security and Justice of the Kingdom of the Netherlands) and the INAETICS project (funded by the European Regional Development Fund). Furthermore, Riccardo Bortolameotti carried out much of his work as part of his final master thesis within the EIT Digital Master program on Security and Privacy. Andreas Peter's and Maarten H. Everts' contributions to this paper were supported by the THeCS project as part of the Dutch national program COMMIT/.

# References

1. Holz, R., Braun, L., Kammenhuber, N., Carle, G.: The SSL landscape: a thorough analysis of the X.509 PKI using active and passive measurements. In: SIGCOMM IMC 2011, pp. 427–444. ACM (2011)
2. Amann, B., Vallentin, M., Hall, S., Sommer, R.: Revisiting SSL: A Large-Scale Study of the Internets Most Trusted Protocol. Technical Report 2012, ICSI (2012)
3. Amann, B., Sommer, R., Vallentin, M., Hall, S.: No attack necessary: the surprising dynamics of SSL trust relationships. In: ACSAC 2013, pp. 179–188. ACM (2013)
4. Georgiev, M., Iyengar, S., Jana, S., Anubhai, R., Boneh, D., Shmatikov, V.: The most dangerous code in the world: validating SSL certificates in non-browser software. In: CCS 2012, pp. 38–49. ACM (2012)
5. Fahl, S., Harbach, M., Muders, T., Baumgrtner, L., Freisleben, B., Smith, M.: Why eve and mallory love android: an analysis of android SSL (in) security. In: CCS 2012, pp. 50–61. ACM (2012)

6. Conti, M., Dragoni, N., Gottardo, S.: MITHYS: mind the hand you shake - protecting mobile devices from SSL usage vulnerabilities. In: Accorsi, R., Ranise, S. (eds.) STM 2013. LNCS, vol. 8203, pp. 65–81. Springer, Heidelberg (2013)
7. Pukkawanna, S., Kadobayashi, Y., Blanc, G., Garcia-Alfaro, J., Debar, H.: Classification of SSL servers based on their SSL handshake for automated security assessment. In: BADGERS 2014 (to appear 2014)
8. Bates, A., Pletcher, J., Nichols, T., Hollembaek, B., Tian, D., Butler, K.R., Alkhelaifi, A.: Securing SSL certificate verification through dynamic linking. In: CCS 2014, pp. 394–405. ACM (2014)
9. Holz, R., Riedmaier, T., Kammenhuber, N., Carle, G.: X.509 forensics: detecting and localising the SSL/TLS men-in-the-middle. In: Foresti, S., Yung, M., Martinelli, F. (eds.) ESORICS 2012. LNCS, vol. 7459, pp. 217–234. Springer, Heidelberg (2012)
10. Clark, J., van Oorschot, P.C.: SoK: SSL and HTTPS: revisiting past challenges and evaluating certificate trust model enhancements. In: Symposium on Security and Privacy (SP) 2013, pp. 511–525. IEEE (2013)
11. Antonakakis, M., Perdisci, R., Nadji, Y., Vasiloglou II, N., Abu-Nimeh, S., Lee, W., Dagon, D.: From throw-away traffic to bots: detecting the rise of DGA-based malware. In: USENIX Security Symposium, pp. 491–506. USENIX
12. Paxson, V.: Bro: a system for detecting network intruders in real-time. In: USENIX Security. USENIX (1998)
13. Wang, K., Parekh, J.J., Stolfo, S.J.: Anagram: a content anomaly detector resistant to mimicry attack. In: Zamboni, D., Kruegel, C. (eds.) RAID 2006. LNCS, vol. 4219, pp. 226–248. Springer, Heidelberg (2006)
14. Schiavoni, S., Maggi, F., Cavallaro, L., Zanero, S.: Phoenix: DGA-based botnet tracking and intelligence. In: Dietrich, S. (ed.) DIMVA 2014. LNCS, vol. 8550, pp. 192–211. Springer, Heidelberg (2014)
15. RFC6066. Internet Engineering Task Force (IETF). Transport Layer Security (TLS) Extensions: Extension Definitions. https://tools.ietf.org/html/rfc6066
16. ThreatStop Check IP service. http://www.threatstop.com/checkip
17. Tcpdump & Libpcap. http://www.tcpdump.org/
18. RFC5246. Internet Engineering Task Force (IETF). The Transport Layer Security (TLS) Protocol Version 1.2 - The TLS Handshaking Protocols. https://tools.ietf.org/html/rfc5246#section-7

# Multi-constrained Orientation Field Modeling and Its Application for Fingerprint Indexing

Jinwei Xu and Jiankun Hu[✉]

School of Engineering and Information Technology,
The University of New South Wales, Canberra, ACT 2600, Australia
jinwei.xu@student.adfa.edu.au, {x.jia,j.hu}@adfa.edu.au

**Abstract.** Fingerprint orientation field, representing the fingerprint ridge-valley structure direction, plays an essential role in fingerprint preprocessing tasks. Orientation field is able to be reconstructed by either non-parameterized or parameterized methods. In this paper, we propose a new parameterized approach for orientation field modeling. The proposed algorithm minimizes a composite model including three constraints corresponding to a least square data fitting term, a total variation regularization and a $L_1$ sparse regularization. This model has been shown to be very effective for fingerprint orientation field reconstruction. Furthermore, its effectiveness has been proven by several experiments. First, the experiments on poor-quality fingerprint images are conducted. Visual comparisons demonstrate the robustness of the proposed method when processing noisy fingerprint images. Then, as another application of the proposed model, its resultant sparse representation is employed for fingerprint indexing. The experiments on FVC 2000 DB2a and FVC 2002 DB1a datasets show the superior performance of the proposed model for fingerprint indexing.

## 1 Introduction

Fingerprint has been broadly used as an unique characteristic for personal recognition in security and forensic community. In fingerprint image, orientation field (OF) is an important feature to represent the direction of ridge-valley structures. For example, OF is applied to tune Gabor filter directional parameters for enhancement of ridge-valley structures. Accordingly, detailed features such as minutiae can be accurately extracted based on the well enhanced ridge-valley segments. However, numerous fingerprint images in real world are more or less contaminated by structural noise. Therefore, the incomplete and corrupted ridge-valley structures of these noisy fingerprint images are unsatisfactory for subsequent processing tasks. To recover the disconnected ridge-valley patterns, OF-driven contextual filtering is a preprocessing step prior to following feature extraction. Consequently, OF has to be estimated as perfectly as possible.

OF estimation methods can be generally categorized into two groups: (i) non-parameterized methods; and (ii) parameterized models. The non-parameterized techniques have been intensively studied during the past decades. For example, a

© Springer International Publishing Switzerland 2015
M. Qiu et al. (Eds.): NSS 2015, LNCS 9408, pp. 176–187, 2015.
DOI: 10.1007/978-3-319-25645-0_12

directional filtering scheme was proposed for ridge-valley structure enhancement [1]. Therein, partial derivatives along $x-$ and $y-$ directions were calculated for ridge-valley orientation estimation. Such method can work well for high-quality fingerprint images (e.g. rolled and plain fingerprints), however, for poor-quality prints (e.g. latent fingerprints), this method is not capable to yield reliable orientation information. To strengthen the robustness resisting structural noise, the orientation estimation was conducted by short time Fourier transform (STFT) [2]. The local Fourier analysis is able to capture the frequency response of the ridge-valley patterns. Therefore, the dominant frequency components in Fourier magnitude spectrum offers a powerful tool for ridge-valley orientation estimation. However, this technique can only work under the following assumption: even the structural noise corruption could be severe, the ridge-valley structures would still be salient to guarantee the capture of the dominant frequency components. However, such assumption is difficult to be satisfied for poor-quality fingerprint images. For further improvement of the noise robustness, an OF template matching and correction approach was developed recently [6]. Such technique applies dictionary learning strategy to construct a large-scale OF template library. Then, using the learned OF templates for the replacement of the incorrect OF fragments depending on context similarity is conducted. However, the context similarity computation is unreliable since the initially estimated OF information could be incorrect.

In contrast to the non-parameterized approaches, the parameterized models have the following advantages:

– **Noisy OF Purification:** A modeling process can be regarded as a denoising process, which means the noisy OF obtained at the initial step can be purified through the modeling procedure;
– **OF Decomposition and Reconstruction:** A modeling process can be regarded as a signal decomposition and composition process, which means the OF can be projected on a set of basis functions and then reconstructed based on a linear combination of appropriate coefficients and selected basis functions.

Using the parameterized model to depict the fingerprint OF can be traced back to [3]. Therein, the fingerprint OF was modeled by a set of 2D Fourier basis functions (namely classical FOMFE model). After FOMFE modeling process, the initially estimated noisy OF can be adaptively corrected and fitted to the ridge-valley structure directions. Later, a smooth extension approach based on FOMFE model was developed to interpolate the orientation information for partial fingerprint images [4] [5]. Motivated by FOMFE model, furthermore, more basis functions were developed for fingerprint OF modeling [7] [8] [9]. For example, instead of the utilization of 2D Fourier basis functions, Legendre polynomial basis functions are employed for OF modeling [7]. Then, 2D discrete cosine basis functions are also adopted [8] [9]. Although the currently developed parameterized models have achieved fairly good performance for fingerprint OF modeling, the exploitation of the OF representation over predefined basis functions is still an open problem. Also, such OF representation, as an useful tool for fingerprint indexing, can be further investigated. In this paper, we propose a new parameterized model for OF modeling by means of sparse representation. As the outcome of the proposed model, the sparse OF representation is then used for fingerprint indexing. Due to the sparse nature of the resultant OF representation, the intrinsic patterns of noisy OF can be captured. In contrast to the dense OF representation (e.g. obtained from the classical FOMFE), the sparse OF representation has the following advantages:

- **Better Anti-noise Property:** A sparse modeling has been proven to be a very powerful strategy to cancel noise effect in image denoising tasks;
- **Intrinsic OF Patterns Capture:** A sparse modeling process can be regarded as a pattern retrieval process, which means the OF can be decomposed into a few essential patterns. These decomposed essential patterns corresponds to some basis functions;
- **Less Storage Needed:** A sparse representation is able to save more storage space, since the most coefficients in the sparse representation vector are zeros.

In this paper, we propose a new OF reconstruction method based on the combination of three constraints, which incorporates a least square data fitting term, a total variation regularization and a $L_1$ sparse regularization. For solving this multi-constrained model, a Composite Splitting Algorithm (CSA) is introduced. The rest of this paper is organized as follows: in Section 2, the multi-constrained model and its numerical solution are introduced; in Section 3, the experiments for poor-quality fingerprint images' OF modeling are conducted and visual comparisons with the classical FOMFE model are demonstrated. Later, the experiments for fingerprint indexing by exploiting the sparse representation are conducted; in Section 4, the conclusion and future research directions are given.

## 2    Proposed Model and Numerical Solution

### 2.1    Proposed Multi-constrained Model

OF is represented by a 2D matrix containing local ridge-valley directions estimated at each block-wise locations of a given fingerprint image. In modeling process, initial estimation of OF is performed as the first step. The initial OF information is expected to be obtained as accurately as possible. However, the initially estimated OF is more or less noisy in real applications, since the initial estimation (or say initial measurement) is usually contaminated by the noise. To be explicit, the initially estimated OF can be decomposed into the following two components:

$$O = \hat{O} + N \tag{1}$$

where $O$ is observed noisy fingerprint OF, $\hat{O}$ is noise-free OF and $N$ is noise.

For the noise-free OF reconstruction, we formulate the following optimization problem as the proposed multi-constrained model:

$$\hat{O} = \arg\min_{O} \left\{ \tfrac{1}{2}\|O - \Phi\gamma\|^2 + \alpha\|O\|_{TV} + \beta\|\gamma\|_1 \right\} \qquad (2)$$

where $\Phi$ is a set of predefined basis functions, $\gamma$ is a sparse representation vector, $\alpha$ and $\beta$ are two positive parameters to balance the total variation regularization $\|\cdot\|_{TV}$ and the $L_1$ sparse regularization $\|\cdot\|_1$.

The motivation to involve TV term $\|\cdot\|_{TV}$ is based on the fact that the piecewise smooth OF of fingerprint image should have small total variations. The TV term is defined as follows:

$$\|O\|_{TV} = \sum_i \sum_j \left( (\nabla_1 O_{ij})^2 + (\nabla_2 O_{ij})^2 \right) \qquad (3)$$

where $\nabla_1$ and $\nabla_2$ denote the forward finite difference operators on $x-$ and $y-$ directions, respectively.

Also, the generally smooth fingerprint OF can be sparsely represented by the basis functions. That is, $L_1$ term $\|\cdot\|_1$ should be as sparse as possible. The relationship between the orientation field $O$ and the sparse representation $\gamma$ is denoted as follows:

$$\gamma = HO \qquad (4)$$

where $H = \left( \Phi^T \Phi \right)^{-1} \Phi^T$.

## 2.2   Proposed Numerical Solution

Both TV regularization and $L_1$ regularization in the proposed model are nonsmooth. Therefore, the formulated minimization problem in Equation (2) is very difficult to solve. The conjugate gradient descent method and partial derivative technique are used to solve it. However, they are very inefficient and impractical for fast fingerprint OF modeling. In this case, the computation becomes the bottleneck to prevent the proposed model from being applied to efficient and effective fingerprint OF reconstruction.

Based on the CSA technique, in this paper, we propose an efficient numerical algorithm to address the minimization problem in Equation (2) by using the combination of variable and operator splitting techniques. We decouple the composite problem in Equation (2) into two subproblems by: (i) firstly separating variable $O$ into two variables $\{O_1, O_2\}$; (ii) then performing operator splitting to minimize TV regularization and $L_1$ regularization subproblems over $\{O_1, O_2\}$ respectively; and (iii) finally yielding the solution $O$ by linear combination of $\{O_1, O_2\}$. This computational procedure follows a standard CSA framework, which has been developed and tested in [15].

To be explicit, the proposed CSA-based numerical algorithm is outlined in Algorithm 1. In Step 2, $O_{ini}$ stands for the initially estimated OF, which can be computed by the gradient-based method [1] [10]. $t$ and $r$ are intermediate variables during the proposed iterative optimization process. $[l, u]$ is the range of $O$. In the case of fingerprint OF modeling, $O = [O_{cos}, O_{sin}]^T$ where $O_{cos} =$

$cos(2\Theta)$ and $O_{sin} = sin(2\Theta)$, respectively ($\Theta$ denotes the ridge-valley direction angle). In Step 4, $O_g$ is updated by gradient descent technique as follows:

$$O_g = r^k - \rho \nabla f(r^k) = r^k - \rho(r^k - \Phi\gamma^k) \tag{5}$$

where $f(r^k) = \frac{1}{2}\|r^k - \Phi\gamma^k\|^2$ and $\gamma^k = Hr^k$. To compute $\gamma^k$, Orthogonal Matching Pursuit (OMP) method is adopted [11].

In Step 5 and 6, the computation of $O_1 = prox_\rho(2\alpha\|O_g\|_{TV})$ and $O_2 = prox_\rho(2\beta\|HO_g\|_1)$ can be efficiently implemented by Fast Iterative Shrinkage Threshold Algorithm (FISTA) [16]. In Step 8, the function $O_{new}^k = proj(O_{old}^k, [l, u])$ is defined as follows:

$$O_{new}^k = \begin{cases} O_{old}^k, & l \leq O_{old}^k \leq u \\ l, & O_{old}^k < l \\ u, & O_{old}^k > u \end{cases} \tag{6}$$

Due to the efficiency and effectiveness of the CSA framework, the fingerprint OF modeling problem in Equation (2) can be properly addressed in terms of the reconstruction accuracy and computation complexity. The experimental results in the following section demonstrate its superior performance compared with the state-of-the-art method for fingerprint OF modeling and fingerprint indexing.

---

**Algorithm 1.** CSA-Based Numerical Solution for The Proposed Model in Equation (2)

---

1: **Inputs:**
   $\rho = 1/L$, $\alpha$, $\beta$, $t^1$, $r^1$, $l$, $u$

2: **Initialize:**
   $L = 1$, $\alpha = 0.001$, $\beta = 0.005$, $t^1 = 1$, $r^1 = O_{ini}$, $l = -1$, $u = 1$

3: **for** $k = 1$ to $K$ **do**
4:    $O_g \leftarrow r^k - \rho(r^k - \Phi\gamma^k)$
5:    $O_1 \leftarrow prox_\rho(2\alpha\|O_g\|_{TV})$
6:    $O_2 \leftarrow prox_\rho(2\beta\|HO_g\|_1)$
7:    $O^k \leftarrow (O_1 + O_2)/2$
8:    $O^k \leftarrow proj(O^k, [l, u])$
9:    $t^{k+1} \leftarrow \left(1 + \sqrt{1 + 4(t^k)^2}\right)\Big/2$
10:   $r^{k+1} \leftarrow O^k + ((t^k - 1)/t^{k+1})(O^k - O^{k-1})$
11: **end for**

---

# 3   Experiments

## 3.1   Fingerprint OF Reconstruction Experiment

The fingerprint images used in this experiment are collected from FVC 2000 DB2a, FVC 2002 DB1a and NIST SD14, respectively. Some fingerprint images are illustrated in Figure 1.

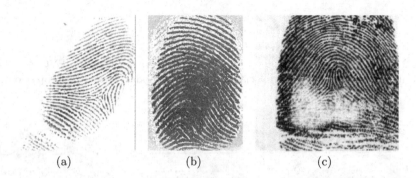

(a)                         (b)                         (c)

**Fig. 1.** Some fingerprint images for OF modeling experiment: (a) FVC 2000 DB2a; (b) FVC 2002 DB1a; and (c) NIST SD14.

In this experiment, the classical FOMFE model and our proposed multi-constrained model are used for fingerprint OF reconstruction. The parameters of the classical FOMFE model are tuned as follows: block size $w = 8$ and basis function order $h = 5$. For the proposed model, the predefined basis functions $\Phi$, block size $w = 8$, and basis function order $h = 5$ are maintained the same as the classical FOMFE model's. The sparse regularization controller $sr = 20\%$ is tuned. That is, the length of the sparse representation vector $\gamma$ is $(2h+1)^2 = 121$, therefore $sr = 20\%$ means that 24 out of 121 coefficients are nonzeros while the remaining coefficients are zeros.

Since no ground truth exists for the evaluation of the reconstructed fingerprint OF, the objective error measurement cannot be easily yielded and it is difficult to assess the quality of the reconstructed OF in a quantitative way [12] [13]. Instead, the quality of the reconstructed OF has to be assessed by means of visual inspection. The reconstructed OF obtained from the classical FOMFE model and the proposed multi-constrained model are shown in Figures 2, 3 and 4. The dense representation and the sparse representation obtained by the classical FOMFE model and the proposed model are shown in Figure 5, respectively. Figures 2, 3 and 4 demonstrate that the proposed model is able to generate more reliable and less noisy OF than the classical FOMFE model, especially when the fingerprint images being processed are in poor quality. Figure 5 shows that the proposed model is more effective to capture prominent OF patterns based on limited basis functions and associated projective coefficients.

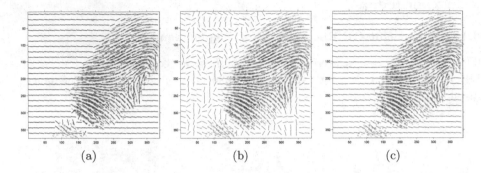

(a)          (b)          (c)

**Fig. 2.** The reconstructed OF for a high-quality fingerprint image in FVC 2000 DB2a: (a) initially estimated OF [1]; (b) classical FOMFE model [3]; and (c) proposed model.

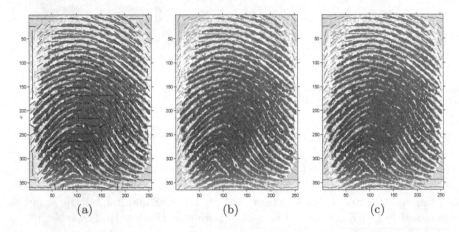

(a)          (b)          (c)

**Fig. 3.** The reconstructed OF for a poor-quality fingerprint image in FVC 2002 DB1a: (a) initially estimated OF [1]; (b) classical FOMFE model [3]; and (c) proposed model.

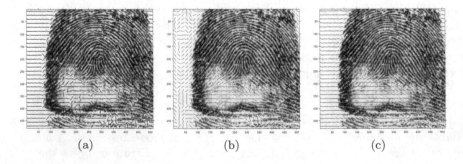

(a)          (b)          (c)

**Fig. 4.** The reconstructed OF for a poor-quality fingerprint image in NIST SD14: (a) initially estimated OF [1]; (b) classical FOMFE model [3]; and (c) proposed model.

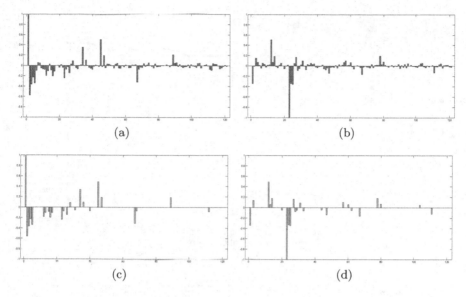

**Fig. 5.** The dense and sparse representations for fingerprint OF in Figure 4: (a) dense coefficient vector obtained by the classical FOMFE model (*cos*); (b) dense coefficient vector obtained by the classical FOMFE model (*sin*); (c) sparse coefficient vector obtained by the proposed model (*cos*); and (d) sparse coefficient vector obtained by the proposed model (*sin*).

## 3.2   Fingerprint Indexing Experiment

Fingerprint indexing experiments are conducted on FVC 2000 DB2a and FVC 2002 DB1a, since both datasets are broadly used for the performance evaluation of the fingerprint indexing [14]. FVC 2000 DB2a consists of 800 fingerprint images collected from 100 fingers by using a capacitive fingerprint scanner (each finger contains 8 different impressions). Also, FVC 2002 DB1a includes 800 fingerprint images captured from 100 fingers by using an optical fingerprint scanner (each finger contains 8 different impressions). In this experiment, the first impressions are chosen as the query samples, while the remaining seven impressions are gathered as a background library. Therefore, 100 images of first impressions are selected as the query samples meanwhile 700 images of other impressions are assembled to form the background database. For both FVC 2000 DB2a and FVC 2002 DB1a, the same data preparation procedure is applied.

To evaluate the fingerprint indexing performance, a Cumulative Match Characteristic (CMC) plot is adopted. The CMC plot indicates the Identification Rate (IR) against the Penetration Rate (PR). For example, given a query fingerprint, it is compared against the whole background database. Accordingly, its one-to-one similarities are computed and queued in descending order. $pr = 10\%$ means that the mated fingerprint corresponding to the query fingerprint appears at

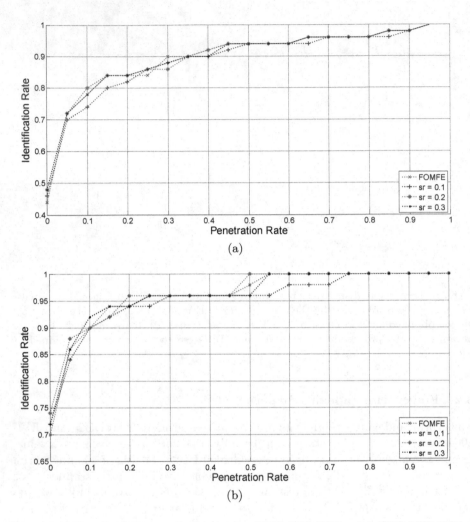

**Fig. 6.** Indexing Performance Evaluation on FVC 2000 DB2a and FVC 2002 DB1a (Average CMC: $\overline{CMC}$): (a) FVC 2000 DB2a; and (b) FVC 2002 DB1a.

**Table 1.** Indexing Performance Evaluation on FVC 2000 DB2a and FVC 2002 DB1a (Average PR: $\overline{pr}$)

|  | FOMFE [3] | Proposed Model | | |
|---|---|---|---|---|
|  |  | $sr = 10\%$ | $sr = 20\%$ | $sr = 30\%$ |
| FVC 2000 DB2a | 14.36% | 15.00% | **13.72%** | 13.84% |
| FVC 2002 DB1a | 6.80% | 7.68% | **6.28%** | 6.56% |

**Table 2.** The Comparison with Other Minutiae-based Indexing Methods (Average PR: $\overline{pr}$)

| | Minutiae Quadruplets [18] | Minutiae Triplets [17] | Proposed Model |
|---|---|---|---|
| FVC 2000 DB2a | 26% | 22% | **13.72%** |
| FVC 2002 DB1a | 11.8% | 9.9% | **6.28%** |

$70^{th}$ in the similarity queue, since the length of the similarity queue equals to the size of the background database ($10\% \times 700 = 70$).

This experiment assesses the indexing performance between two different OF models: the classical FOMFE model [3] and the proposed model. Therein, the representation coefficient vectors of the two models are employed as the features for fingerprint indexing. For the classical FOMFE model, its parameters are tuned as follows: block size $w = 8$ and basis function order $h = 5$. For the proposed model, the predefined basis functions $\Phi$, block size $w = 8$, and basis function order $h = 5$ are maintained the same as the classical FOMFE model's. To further investigate the effect of the sparse regularization controller $sr$, three different values $sr = 10\%$, $sr = 20\%$ and $sr = 30\%$ are tested. The statistics of the indexing performance, such as the average CMC ($\overline{CMC}$) plots and the average PR ($\overline{pr}$) values, are obtained on both FVC 2000 DB2a and FVC 2002 DB1a datasets. These results are demonstrated in Figure 6 and Table 1, respectively.

Figure 6 and Table 1 show that the proposed model performs better than the classical FOMFE model in terms of $\overline{CMC}$ and $\overline{pr}$. That is, the better performance is achieved, since the proposed model's CMC curves are closer to the left upper corner and its PR values keep lower. This evidences the superiority of the proposed model when it is exploited for fingerprint indexing. The variation of the parameter $sr$ can not significantly influence the experimental results. Compared with the effects of $sr = 10\%$ and $sr = 30\%$, the selection of $sr = 20\%$ can yield better results.

Table 2 exhibits the indexing results when the proposed model is compared with minutiae-based techniques on both FVC 2000 DB2a and FVC 2002 DB1a datasets [17] [18]. The proposed model can achieve much better performance by using the same criterion: average PR $\overline{pr}$.

## 4    Conclusion

In this paper, a new OF modeling technique is developed by the minimization of a multi-constrained optimization problem. The proposed model integrates a least square data fitting term, a total variation regularization and a $L_1$ sparse regularization. Such composite optimization problem, due to its nonsmooth nature, is difficult to be solved. According to the CSA framework, we propose an efficient and effective numerical solution to address this challenging problem. The experimental results demonstrate the superiority of the proposed model when it copes with the noisy fingerprint OF. The visual comparison of the reconstructed OF shows that the proposed model performs better than the classical FOMFE model when handling the poor-quality fingerprint images. Furthermore, the sparse representation, obtained by the proposed modeling process, is exploited for fingerprint indexing. The indexing experiment demonstrates the superior performance of the proposed model. Future work can be proceeded in following two directions: (i) developing new basis functions, or even directly learning the basis functions from a given noisy OF; and (ii) involving new constraints to formulate new models and then developing new numerical solvers for new models.

**Acknowledgment.** The first author Jinwei Xu would like to thank Wei Zhou at The University of New South Wales, Canberra Campus, Australia, for her experimental database sharing and helpful discussion.

# References

1. Hong, L., Wan, Y., Jain, A.K.: Fingerprint image enhancement algorithm and performance evaluation. IEEE Transactions on Pattern Analysis and Machine Intelligence **20**(8), 777–789 (1998)
2. Chikkerur, S., Cartwright, A.N., Govindaraju, V.: Fingerprint enhancement using STFT analysis. Pattern Recognition **40**(1), 198–211 (2007)
3. Wang, Y., Hu, J., Phillips, D.: A fingerprint orientation model based on 2D fourier expansion (FOMFE) and its application to singular point detection and fingerprint indexing. IEEE Transactions on Pattern Analysis and Machine Intelligence **29**(4), 573–585 (2007)
4. Wang, Y., Hu, J.: Global ridge orientation modelling for partial fingerprint identification. IEEE Transactions on Pattern Analysis and Machine Intelligence **33**(1), 72–87 (2011)
5. Zhou, W., Hu, J., Petersen, I., Bennamoun, M.: Partial fingerprint reconstruction with improved smooth extension. In: Lopez, J., Huang, X., Sandhu, R. (eds.) NSS 2013. LNCS, vol. 7873, pp. 756–762. Springer, Heidelberg (2013)
6. Feng, J., Zhou, J., Jain, A.K.: Orientation field estimation for latent fingerprint enhancement. IEEE Transactions on Pattern Analysis and Machine Intelligence **35**(4), 925–940 (2013)
7. Ram, S., Bischof, H., Birchbauer, J.: Modeling fingerprint ridge orientation using Legendre polynomials. Pattern Recognition **43**(1), 342–357 (2010)
8. Liu, M., Yap, P.T.: Invariant representation of orientation fields for fingerprint indexing. Pattern Recognition **45**(7), 2532–2542 (2012)
9. Liu, M., Liu, S., Zhao, Q.: Fingerprint orientation field reconstruction by weighted discrete cosine transform. Information Sciences **268**, 65–77 (2014)
10. Maltoni, D., Maio, D., Jain, A.K., Prabhakar, S.: Hand book of fingerprint recognition. Springer Verlag (2009)
11. Tropp, J.: Greed is good: Algorithmic results for sparse approximation. IEEE Transactions on Information Theory **50**(10), 2231–2242 (2004)
12. Zhou, J., Gu, J.: A model-based method for the computation of fingerprints' orientation field. IEEE Transactions on Image Processing **13**(6), 821–835 (2004)
13. Wang, Y., Hu, J., Han, F.: Enhanced gradient-based algorithm for the estimation of fingerprint orientation fields. Applied Mathematics and Computation **185**, 823–833 (2007)

14. Zhou, W., Hu, J., Wang, S., Petersen, I., Bennamoun, M.: Fingerprint indexing based on combination of novel minutiae triplet features. In: Au, M.H., Carminati, B., Kuo, C.-C.J. (eds.) NSS 2014. LNCS, vol. 8792, pp. 377–388. Springer, Heidelberg (2014)
15. Huang, J., Zhang, S., Metaxas, D.: Efficient MR image reconstruction for compressed MR images. Medical Image Analysis **15**, 670–679 (2011)
16. Amir, B., Marc, T.: Fast gradient-based algorithms for constrained total variation image denoising and deblurring problems. IEEE Transactions on Image Processing **18**(11), 2419–2434 (2009)
17. Yuan, B., Su, F., Cai, A.: Fingerprint retrieval approach based on novel minutiae triplet features. In: IEEE International Conference on Biometrics: Theory, Applications and Systems, pp. 170–175 (2012)
18. Iloanusi, O., Gyaourova, A., Ross, A.: Indexing fingerprints using minutiae quadruplets. In: IEEE International Conference on Computer Vision and Pattern Recognition Workshops, pp. 127–133 (2011)

# Security Management

# A Framework for Policy Similarity Evaluation and Migration Based on Change Detection

Jaideep Vaidya[1]([✉]), Basit Shafiq[2], Vijayalakshmi Atluri[1], and David Lorenzi[1]

[1] Rutgers University, Newark, NJ 07102, USA
{jsvaidya,atluri,dlorenzi}@rutgers.edu
[2] Lahore University of Management Sciences, Lahore, Pakistan
basit@lums.edu.pk

**Abstract.** Access control facilitates controlled sharing and protection of resources in an enterprise. However, given the ubiquity of collaborative applications and scenarios, enterprises no longer function in isolation. Being able to measure policy similarity and integrate heterogeneous policies appropriately is an essential step towards secure interoperation. Existing approaches for measuring policy similarity are based on computing similarity between different components of the access control policy. However, this does not provide a pathway for integrating policies, and may not sufficiently take the security context into account. In this paper, we propose a holistic change detection approach that enables policy similarity evaluation and policy migration. Our approach more comprehensively takes into account different access control semantics to compute policy similarity and finds the common organizational policy with the least cost.

**Keywords:** Access control · Policy similarity · Policy migration · Change detection

## 1 Introduction

Today, access control is critical to any enterprise. Essentially, any resource of value needs to be protected from inappropriate access. These protection requirements are typically stated as access control policies, which faciliate the protection as well as controlled sharing of all resources. Indeed, all modern enterprises have effective access control policies specified and enforced. While individual access control policies serve to protect organizational resources in isolation, this does not address the challenges raised by collaboration. With collaborative platforms such as cloud computing, service oriented architectures, and the like, sharing of resources (e.g., data, knowledge, services, etc.), is often necessary to carry out the tasks at hand. Even if organizations are inclined to such sharing to meet a common objective, they would still like to ensure that their own access control policies are enforced while sharing resources. Indeed, having a common access control policy is often a prerequisite to resource sharing. Alternatively, an organization A may be willing to share a resource with another organization B only if their corresponding policies are somewhat *similar*.

© Springer International Publishing Switzerland 2015
M. Qiu et al. (Eds.): NSS 2015, LNCS 9408, pp. 191–205, 2015.
DOI: 10.1007/978-3-319-25645-0_13

This requires having the ability to identify (and quantify) the similarity between policies, and reconcile the differences in an appropriate fashion. Since every organization may have its own perspective in terms of the sensitivity of different resources (as one organization may value a certain resource more than another), different constraints and authorizations may have varying degrees of importance to different organizations. The need for measuring similarity may also arise within a single organization. Specifically, when an access control policy changes, the security administrators as well as the owners of the resources may want to know how similar is the new policy with respect to the earlier one. Whether it is within an organization or across organizations, a policy similarity measure can give the sense of security risk involved in moving to the new state.

In general, it is quite complex to determine if two policies are similar, and to identify and resolve their differences. Lin et al. [10] have proposed a policy similarity metric based on computing the structural similarity between different components of the access control policies by making a one-to-one comparison. While this enables similarity computation and serves as an initial filtering step, it is not effective from the perspective of multi-policy management, including merging and composition of policies. Security semantics such as the sensitivity of resources from an organizational perspective also need to be taken into account. In this paper, we identify key requirements for similarity evaluation from an access control perspective, and propose a formal framework based on change detection that enables policy similarity computation, and other multi-policy management operations such as policy migration.

Our similarity measurement is based on computing the security impact in transitioning from one policy to the other. In effect, this is directly correlated to the number of common accesses between two policies. The smaller the number of common accesses, the larger the transition (and associated cost). Therefore, this well represents the notion of similarity as the extent to which the policies are in agreement over the set of possible accesses. Additionally, it provides a pathway for transitioning from one organizational policy to another.

The rest of the paper is organized as follows. Section 2 discusses the requirements for effective policy similarity evaluation and shows the limitations of existing work with concrete examples. Sections 3 and 4 present our approach to policy similarity measurement and policy migration. Section 5 reviews the related work. Section 6 concludes the paper and discusses future work.

## 2    Problem Motivation and Requirements

We aim to address a family of related problems in the multi-policy environment. Before developing an appropriate solution, we would like to identify the contextual parameters and factors, along with the requirements for an effective solution. Essentially, our goal is to enable policy similarity evaluation and policy migration. Here, policy similarity evaluation gives a single scalar value that defines how similar the group of underlying policies are. A value of 0 indicates that none of the policies have anything in common, while a value of 1 indicates, that all of the underlying policies express the exactly same authorization set.

In policy migration, out of all of the given policies, we would like to identify the policy with the lowest cost of migration – i.e., the policy to which all of the other policies can be transformed with least cost. This is useful in the cases where one of the existing policies must be chosen as the common operating policy.

For the rest of this section, we will assume the following notation: policies are composed of permit and deny rules. Each rule states the set of subjects, $s$, that are allowed (or denied) access to the set of resources, $r$, for the set of actions, $a$, when satisfying any one of the set of conditions, $c$. Thus, $R1 : Permit, \{S_1 - S_5\}, \{R_1 - R_3, R_7 - R_{10}\}, \{A_1\}, \{C1\}$ indicates that the subjects $S_1$ to $S_5$ should be permitted access to the resources $R_1 - R_3$ and the resources $R_7 - R_{10}$, for action $A_1$ when condition $C_1$ is satisfied.

## 2.1  Lin et al. Policy Similarity Scoring Metric

Before going into the detailed problem requirements and motivatory example, we first give a brief overview of the work of Lin et. al[10,18], which is very closely related to the work in this paper. They propose a policy similarity measure for measuring the similarity between two policies. The similarity measure takes into account the policy structure typical of XACML. Given two policies, the similarity score computation algorithm first categorizes the rules based on their effects, which results in a set of Permit Rules (denoted as PR) and a set of Deny Rules (denoted as DR). Each single rule in the first policy is then compared with a rule in the second policy that has the same effect, and a similarity score of two rules is obtained. The similarity score is computed using hierarchy distance and numerical distance, and used to find one-to-many $\Phi$ mappings that determine for each permit/deny rule in one policy which of the rules in the other policy are very similar. Weights are used to allow emphasis on the importance of a target or condition similarity. The $\Phi$ mappings are used to calculate the rule set similarity scores, which are based on categorical and numerical predicates (in essence, the similarity between the rule elements – subjects, resources, actions, and conditions). Finally, the scores obtained for the different components of the policies are aggregated according to a weighted combination in order to produce an overall similarity score. We now look at why this work does not fully capture the semantics of policy comparison.

## 2.2  Transition Cost

Typically, the process of policy comparison is initiated due to some underlying motive, such as the security administrator wishing to merge two policies into one, or trying to figure out what is the transition cost of replacing one security policy with another. For all such cases, a policy similarity metric that is well correlated with the transition cost is essential. While the metric for policy similarity in [10] gives a notion of the difference between the policies (and, as such is useful to figure out if two policies are widely varying or very similar), it is not very effective from the perspective of transitioning between policies. Measuring the similarity between two policies simply on the basis of element level comparison gives us no way to judge the degree of effort required to resolve the two policies into a coherent whole.

Instead, we measure the similarity of two policies $P1$ and $P2$ as the cost of transitioning from one policy to the other. Note that this cost is organization-dependent, i.e., it varies depending on how the organization rates the different subjects, objects, etc. Clearly, the lower the transitioning cost, the more similar are the policies. The intuition behind this is that, such a similarity computation would actually reflect the effort needed to resolve and come up with a coherent policy. In effect, the transition cost is directly correlated to the number of common accesses between two policies. Therefore, this well represents the notion of similarity as the extent to which the policies are in agreement over the set of possible accesses.

With this as a premise, in this section, we first point out that one should take the following three conditions into consideration when computing the similarity: (1) the cost of transitioning from one rule to the other by taking into consideration the cardinality of an element in the rule, the sensitivity of the element and its location in the hierarchy. (2) distinguishing between the different operations in the transition cost, such as deletion, insertion and moving an element. (3) Finally, when multiple policies are present, we need to have the ability to migrate to a single existing policy with least migration cost.

Apart from transition cost, similarity can also be judged from another perspective. Indeed, Lin et al.[10] state another intuitive notion of policy similarity – "if the similarity score of policies P1 and P2 is higher than that of policies P1 and P3, it implies that P1 and P2 may yield the same decisions to a larger common request set than P1 and P3 will do". This is also a very appealing notion of similarity. However, the specific metric proposed in [10] does not always satisfy this. Consider the following example which illustrates this point:

| |
|---|
| P1: R11: Permit,$\{S_1\}\{R_1\}\{A_1\}\{C_1\}$; R12: Permit,$\{S_5\}\{R_1 - R_{100}\}\{A_2\}\{C_2\}$ |
| P2: R21: Permit,$\{S_1 - S_3\}\{R_1\}\{A_1\}\{C_1\}$; R22: Permit,$\{S_5\}\{R_1 - R_{100}\}\{A_2\}\{C_2\}$ |
| P3: R31: Permit,$\{S_1\}\{R_1\}\{A_1\}\{C_1\}$; R32: Permit,$\{S_5 - S_6\}\{R_1 - R_{100}\}\{A_2\}\{C_2\}$ |

Further, assume that for the above example, all of the subjects are hierarchically unrelated (and the same for resources, actions, and conditions). Now, if we compute the similarity according to [10], the similarity between P1 and P2 is determined by the similarity between rules R11 and R21 (since rules R12 and R22 are exactly the same). This is equal to $1/3$ ($|\{S_1\}|/|\{S_1 - S_3\}|$). On the other hand, the similarity between P1 and P3 is determined by the similarity between rules R12 and R32 (since rules R11 and R31 are identical). This is equal to $1/2$ ($|\{S_5\}|/|\{S_5 - S_6\}|$). Clearly, $similarity(P1, P3) > similarity(P1, P2)$. However, if we consider in terms of common access decisions, for P1 and P2, 101 out of the 103 accesses result in exactly the same decisions, where as for Policies P1 and Policy P3, only 101 accesses out of 201 result in the same decision. By the intuitive notion of similarity, the similarity between P1 and P3 should have been lower than the similarity between P1 and P2, which however, is not the case. While this problem exists irrespective of security semantics, this is further exacerbated when we take into account the nature of security.

**Cascading (or effect of operations).** As discussed above, the similarity metric of [10] does not take into account any changes that are to be made to the policies after they have found to be similar. Assuming there is an environment where collaboration is the critical reason for finding two similar policies, the distance metric needs to accurately model the security costs of adding or deleting subjects, resources, actions, or conditions in a particular policy. This leads to a problem we call "cascading" – i.e., what are the policy-wide effects of adding or deleting a subject / resource / action / condition, and the security cost associated with the change. The following example shows that this cost can be significantly different between two policies, even within the same organizational system.

$P1$: R11: Permit,$\{S_1, S_2\}\{R_1, R_2\}\{A_1\}\{C_1\}$
$P1'$: R11: Permit,$\{S_0, S_1, S_2\}\{R_1, R_2\}\{A_1\}\{C_1\}$
$P2$; R21: Permit,$\{S_1 - S_3\}\{R_1 - R_3\}\{A_1, A_2\}\{C_1\}$
$P2'$: R21: Permit,$\{S_0 - S_3\}\{R_1 - R_3\}\{A_1, A_2\}\{C_1\}$

The only difference between $P1$ and $P1'$ is the addition of $S_0$. Similarly, the only difference between $P2$ and $P2'$ is also the addition of $S_0$. However, the cost of $P1$ to $P1'$ is proportional to $2 * 1 * 1 = 2$, where as the cost of $P2$ to $P2'$ is proportional to $3 * 2 * 1 = 6$. Thus, when an element is added into (or deleted from) a rule, the security effect is different based on the context such as:

- cardinality – i.e., the number of other elements in the rule (i.e., the total effect is $|S| \times |R| \times |A| \times |C|$) (as shown in the above example).
- sensitivity of the element (i.e., adding subject $s_i$ could be much worse from the security standpoint than adding subject $s_j$).
- location in the hierarchy – if a hierarchy exists, the location of the element in the hierarchy makes a difference (an element at a higher level ends up affecting much more than an element at a lower level)

**Security Effect of Element Insertion v/s Deletion.** Typically, the security impact of element insertion versus that of element deletion is quite different depending on the context. An element insertion in a *permit* rule typically broadens the scope of possible accesses (thus making the system state more insecure), while an element deletion reduces the scope of possible accesses. The situation is the reverse for *deny* rules. Thus, an element insertion in a deny rule reduces the scope of access as against an element deletion which increases the scope of possible accesses. The net security effect also varies based on what entities are involved. Thus adding access to a sensitive resource will lead to higher security cost than adding access to a less sensitive resource.

This cost is further exacerbated in the case when element moves between rules. For example, if an element moves from a permit to a deny rule or vice versa, the net security effect is significantly higher, since there is a direct conflict between the two policies. To see this, consider the following 3 policies:

$P1$: R11:Permit,$\{S_1\}\{R_1, R_2\}\{A_1\}\{C_1\}$
$P2$: R21:Permit,$\{S_1\}\{R_1\}\{A_1\}\{C_1\}$
$P3$: R31:Permit,$\{S_1\}\{R_1\}\{A_1\}\{C_1\}$; R32:Deny,$\{S_1\}\{R_2\}\{A_1\}\{C_1\}$

Compare $P1$ with $P2$. The only difference between rules R11 and R21 is that resource $R_2$ is dropped. In contrast, when looking at $P1$ and $P3$, the difference is that resource $R_2$ is dropped from the permit rule and actually is in an identical deny rule. If all elements are atomic (i.e., $R_2$ cannot be further subdivided), both of these situations are actually exactly the same, since the access decision on $R_2$ with respect to $S_1$, $A_1$, and $C_1$ is exactly the same. However, assume that $R_1$ and $R_2$ denote two composite resources with overlapping privilege sets (for example, $R_1 = \{p_1, p_2, p_3\}$, and $R_2 = \{p_3, p_4, p_5\}$). In this case, while the situation for $p_1, p_2, p_4, p_5$ is actually the same, the situation for $p_3$ is actually different. When $P1$ is replaced by $P2$, access by $S_1$ to $p_3$ for action $A_1$ in condition $C_1$ is still permitted (since $R_1$ is in the permit rule). However, when $P1$ is replaced by $P3$, access by $S_1$ to $p_3$ for action $A_1$ in condition $C_1$ is *denied* (since $R_2$ is in the deny rule, and assuming that deny overrides permit). Clearly, the similarity between $P1$ and $P3$ should be lower than the similarity between $P1$ and $P2$. However, [10] does not take this into consideration.

## 2.3    Composing Multiple Policies into a Coherent Whole

When multiple organizational systems are required to evaluate and agree on a single global policy in order to enable collaboration, a simple similarity metric that only gives the distance between two policies is not sufficient. In this case, it is necessary to evaluate the rules from all of the policies and compose them into a set that satisfies the requirements for each and every system, such that the resulting policy is the optimum in terms of security costs and ensuring ability to access the requested information.

Indeed, when composing the global policy from the local policies, we may choose to migrate to one of the local policies. Assuming that each side weighs subjects / resources / actions / conditions differently, and adds / deletes differently, the cost for moving from one policy to another is not symmetric. Therefore, when migrating to one of the local policies, the policy that incurs the lowest migration cost overall should be chosen.

# 3    Policy Similarity Evaluation

A similarity metric should be able to evaluate the similarity between two policies based on the access control environment. Essentially, the goal of the metric is to evaluate how similar two policies are in terms of access decisions (whether permit or deny). Our similarity evaluation metric is based on change detection, which is discussed below, followed by a presentation of the actual approach.

## 3.1   Change Detection Using XyDiff

Change detection is the procedure of detecting the changes between two documents. This can be useful for version control tools, merging different documents, mobile synchronization, etc. While most of the original work in change detection has focused only on computing differences between flat files or images, there has been follow on work that looks at change detection for structured data such as trees and XML documents[16]. Since access control policies can be naturally expressed in XACML, which is essentially XML, we can use change detection tools written specifically for XML to identify policy differences.

In our approach, we use a tool called *XyDiff*[5], developed at INRIA, which is a very efficient and scalable diff program developed specifically for XML that provides output very close to optimal in terms of quality (since the actual problem is NP-hard, it is infeasible to efficiently obtain the optimal solution).XyDiff takes two XML documents as input and produces a "delta" file that describes the modifications between two XML documents in terms of a sequence of operations for transforming one document into another. These operations include insert node operation and delete node operations. A node is identified by its position in the XML tree. In the context of XACML policies, a node in the insert/delete operation can be a rule or an element in the rule. An element can be a subject element, resource element, action element or condition element. Table 1 depicts a formal grammar for the delta output provided by XyDiff.

**Table 1.** Grammar for the delta output

| |
|---|
| *change → operation [rule \| element] NodeIndex* |
| *operation → Insert \| Delete* |
| *rule → effect [elemS]$^+$ [elemR]$^+$ [elemA]$^+$ [elemC]$^*$* |
| *effect → Permit \| Deny* |
| *element → Subject \| Resource \| Action \| Condition* |

As an example, consider the following two policies along with their associated XML trees shown in Figure 1.

| |
|---|
| P1: R11: Permit,$\{S_1\}\{R_1, R_2\}\{A_1\}\{C_1\}$; R12: Deny,$\{S_5\}\{R_5\}\{A_2\}\{C_2\}$ |
| P2: R21: Permit,$\{S_1, S_2\}\{R_1\}\{A_1\}\{C_1\}$ |

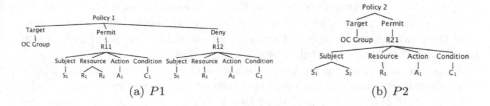

(a) P1                                                    (b) P2

**Fig. 1.** XML representation of the two policies

XyDiff returns the following $\delta$ from $P1$ to $P2$: 1) Insert $S_2$ $NodeIdx_1$, 2) Delete $R_2$ $NodeIdx_2$, and 3) Delete $R12$ $NodeIdx_3$, where $NodeIdx_i$ lists the position in the tree where change $i$ should occur.

## 3.2   Approach

While XyDiff strives to generate the delta output with minimum number of operations, it does not take into account the security costs of the operations. Thus, while it effectively minimizes the transition cost (in terms of operations), it does not directly take into account the security impact. Therefore, to model the security impact, we have to assign a security cost to every change detected, as well as assign security penalties when special cases occur. Once the costs for all of the changes are computed, the absolute distance between the two policies can be computed. Note that when computing the distance between two policies $P_1$ and $P_2$, even though the number of delta operations is the same regardless of whether we compute it from $P_1$ to $P_2$ or vice versa, the weighted distance between them can be different based on each organization's perspective (since they may weigh different subjects, resources, etc. differently). We ensure that our similarity measure is symmetric by averaging the costs from both directions. However, it is still necessary to normalize the measure to enable comparison across policies. The main question is what factor to normalize by? Ideally, we should be normalizing by the number of unique access evaluations in the universe – i.e., if we assume that every policy (either implicitly or explicitly) specifies the access decision for every combination of subject, resource, actions, and conditions, then the size of the access control matrix is given by $(|S| \times |R| \times |A| \times |C|)$, and this can be used as the normalization factor. Unfortunately, this is generally infeasible to calculate (you cannot explicitly lay out all conditions unless they are explicitly stated in the policy). Therefore, instead, we simply consider the universe to be composed of all of the unique subjects, resources, actions, and conditions enumerated across all of the policies to be evaluated. Note that when counting conditions, we simply count all unique conditions without worrying about how they may be related or impact each other (for example, even though one may consider a condition such as ⟨Time in between 6:00 AM - 9:00 AM⟩ to be closer to the condition ⟨Time in between 9:00 AM - 12:00 PM⟩ versus the condition ⟨Time in between 12:00 PM - 6:00 PM⟩, we simply assume that the distance is the same). The alternative would be to create a complete hierarchy of conditions, along with specifying granularities by which they should be considered (i.e., time in increments of a second, filesize in increments of 1k, etc). This would simply make the process more complex. Therefore, for the sake of simplicity, we ignore this, though it can easily be taken into consideration.

Thus, the procedure to calculate similarity is as follows: First, we simply enumerate all unique subjects, resources, actions, and conditions across all the policies to calculate the normalization factor. Then for all pairs of policies, we call the subprocedure *Costs* to calculate the cost of transforming from one policy to the other. The *Costs* algorithm (given in Algorithm 2) simply uses the XyDiff algorithm to calculate the delta to transform from one policy to the other. Each

---

**Algorithm 1.** Policy Similarity Evaluation

---

**Require:** $n$ Organizations $Org_1, \ldots, Org_n$ each with respective policy $P_1, \ldots, P_n$
**Require:** $w_i$, $Org_i$'s set of weights
1: $totalDistance \leftarrow 0$
2: $numSubjects \leftarrow |Subject(P_1) \cup \cdots \cup Subject(P_n)|$
3: $numObjects \leftarrow |Object(P_1) \cup \cdots \cup Object(P_n)|$
4: $numActions \leftarrow |Actions(P_1) \cup \cdots \cup Actions(P_n)|$
5: $numConds \leftarrow |Conditions(P_1) \cup \cdots \cup Conditions(P_n)|$
6: $normalizationFactor \leftarrow numSubjects \times numObjects \times numActions \times numConds$

7: **for** $i = 1 \ldots n$ **do**
8:     **for** $\forall j \in [1,n], s.t. j \neq i$ **do**
9:         $totalDistance \leftarrow totalDistance + \frac{costs(P_i, P_j, w_i)}{normalizationFactor}$
10:     **end for**
11: **end for**
12: $avgdistance \leftarrow \frac{totaldistance}{n(n-1)}$
13: $avgsimilarity \leftarrow 1 - avgdistance$

---

**Algorithm 2.** $Costs(P_x, P_y, w)$ {Return the cost of transforming from $P_x$ to $P_y$ assuming the entity weights $w$}

---

**Require:** Two policies $P_x$, $P_y$
**Require:** Weights $w$ on all entities
1: $tcost \leftarrow 0$
2: $\delta \leftarrow XyDiff(P_x, P_y)$
3: **for** each change operation $e$ in $\delta$ **do**
4:     Security cost $c_e \leftarrow \omega_e \in w$
5:     $CascadePenalty \leftarrow ComputeCascadePenalty(e)$
6:     $MovePenalty \leftarrow DetectConflictingMove(e)$
7:     $c_e \leftarrow c_e \times (CascadePenalty + MovePenalty)$
8:     $tcost \leftarrow tcost + c_e$
9: **end for**
10: **return** tcost

---

change operation is then weighted as per the organization's weighting. After this, the cascade penalty is calculated to compute the total number of accesses that are impacted by this change. Following this, a move penalty gets added if an explicit permit has been replaced by an explicit deny or vice versa. The costs for all change operations are added together to give the total cost. When this cost is returned, it is then normalized and added to the total distance. Finally, since $n(n-1)$ total distances are calculated, we divide by $n(n-1)$ to give the average distance. The average similarity is then simply $1 - avgdistance$. If we would only like to compute the similarity of a pair of policies based on one organization's perspective, then their distance is directly given by the normalized transition costs based on that organizations entity weightage, from which the similarity can be directly computed. There is no need to calculate the average similarity/distance. Algorithm 1 gives the details.

*Example 1.* We now go through an example to illustrate this process. Consider three organizations $Org_1, Org_2, Org_3$, each with a policy $P_1, P_2, P_3$ respectively, as given below:

$P_1$: R11: Permit,$\{S_1\}\{R_1, R_2\}\{A_1\}\{C_1\}$; R12: Deny,$\{S_5\}\{R_5\}\{A_2\}\{C_2\}$

$P_2$: R21: Permit,$\{S_1, S_2, S_4\}\{R_1\}\{A_1\}\{C_1\}$; R22: Deny,$\{S_5, S_6\}\{R_5\}\{A_2\}\{C_2\}$

$P_3$: R31: Permit,$\{S_2, S_3\}\{R_2\}\{A_1\}\{C_1\}$; R32: Deny,$\{S_5\}\{R_4, R_5\}\{A_2\}\{C_2\}$

Now assume, that the weights each organization places on subjects, resources, actions, and conditions are as follows: Assume that $Org_1$ places equal importance on all subjects. Since there are six subjects, the weight of each subject is $1/6 = 0.167$. For $Org_2$ and $Org_3$, assume that while the weights of subjects, $S_1, S_3, S_4, S_5$ and $S_6$ are the same, but for $S_2$, the weight is triple that of the others. Since the total weight should be one, the corresponding weights for $S_1, S_3, S_4, S_5$ and $S_6$ is 0.125 and that of $S_2$ is 0.375. All organizations weigh all resources, actions, and conditions equally. Therefore, since there are only four resources, the weight of each resource is $1/4 = 0.25$. Finally, since there are two actions and two conditions, therefore the weight of each is $1/2 = 0.5$.

Now, consider the similarity computation process in Algorithm 1. The normalizationFactor is $6 \times 4 \times 2 \times 2 = 96$. Supposing we want to calculate only the similarity between $P_1$ and $P_2$ from $Org_1$'s perspective. This can be done as follows: First $\delta(P_1, P_2)$ is computed, which results in the following four change operations: $e_1$: delete $R_2$ from R11; $e_2$: insert $S_2$ into R11; $e_3$: insert $S_4$ into R11; $e_4$: insert $S_6$ into R12. Now, the security cost of $S_2, S_4$, and $S6$ from $Org_1$'s perspective is 0.16, while the cost of $R_2$ is 0.25. There is no move penalty for any of the four change operations. The cascade factor for $e_1$ is $1 \times 1 \times 1 = 1$. Similarly, the effective cascade factor for $e_2, e_3$, and $e_4$ is also 1. Therefore, the total cost for performing the delta is $0.25 + 0.16 + 0.16 + 0.16 = 0.73$. Thus, the normalized distance from $Org_1$'s perspective is $0.73/96 = 0.0076$ and the normalized similarity is $1 - 0.0076 = 0.9924$.

Similarly, the similarity between $P_1$ and $P_3$ from $Org_1$'s perspective can be calculated as follows: $\delta(P_1, P_3)$ consists of the following: $e_1$: delete $R_1$ from R11; $e_2$: delete $S_1$ from R11; $e_3$: insert $S_2$ into R11; $e_4$: insert $S_3$ into R11; $e_5$: insert $R_4$ into R12. The security cost of $S_1, S_2, S_3$ is 0.16 and that of $R_1$ and $R_4$ is 0.25. The cascade factor for $e_1, e_2, e_3, e_4$, and $e_5$ is 1. Therefore, the total cost for performing the delta is $0.25 + 0.16 + 0.16 + 0.16 + 0.25 = 0.98$. Thus, the normalized distance from $Org_1$'s perspective is $0.98/96 = 0.0102$ and the normalized similarity is $1 - 0.0102 = 0.9898$. Clearly, $P_1$ and $P_2$ are closer than $P_1$ and $P_3$ from $Org_1$'s perspective.

We can similarly, compute the similarity of $P_1$ and $P_2$ from $Org_2$'s perspective. All of the calculations remain as above, except for the different weightage of the subjects (and inversion of the operations – insert becomes delete and vice versa, which does not affect the similarity computation). Therefore, the total cost for performing the delta between $P_1$ and $P_2$ from $Org_2$'s perspective is $0.25 + 0.375 + 0.125 + 0.125 = 0.875$. Thus, the normalized distance from $Org_2$'s perspective is $0.875/96 = 0.0091$ and the normalized similarity is $1 - 0.0091 = 0.9908$.

Similarly, the total costs for all of the other deltas can be calculated and are summarized below: The cost of transitioning between $P_2$ and $P_3$ from $Org_2$'s perspective: $0.125+0.125+0.25+0.25+0.125+0.125+0.25 = 1.25$. Since $Org_2$'s weights and $Org_3$'s weights are the same, the cost of transitioning between $P_3$ and $P_2$ from $Org_3$'s perspective is also 1.25, giving a normalized distance of 0.0130 and a normalized similarity of 0.9870. Finally, the cost of transitioning between $P_3$ and $P_1$ from $Org_3$'s perspective is: $0.25+0.125+0.375+0.125+0.25 = 1.125$, giving a normalized distance of 0.0117 and a normalized similarity of 0.9883.

Thus, the overall average distance is $0.0076 + 0.0102 + 0.0091 + 0.0130 + 0.0117 + 0.0130 = 0.0108$, with an average similarity of 0.9892.

## 3.3 Metric Property

Note that the *avgdistance* computed by Algorithm 2 is a metric, since it satisfies all of the axioms required:

- *avgdistance* is non-negative, assuming that all of the weights and penalties are non-negative.
- $avgdistance(P_i, P_j) = avgdistance(P_j, P_i)$, since we take the average of the cost in both directions.
- $avgdistance(P_i, P_i) = 0$, since the $\delta$ will be 0
- $avgdist(P_i, P_j) \le avgdist(P_i, P_k) + avgdist(P_k, P_j)$, as per theorem 1.

**Theorem 1.** $avgdistance(P_i, P_j) \le avgdistance(P_i, P_k) + avgdistance(P_k, P_j)$.

*Proof.* Assume that the $\delta$ between $P_i$ and $P_j$ is given by $\delta_{ij}$, the $\delta$ between $P_i$ and $P_k$ is given by $\delta_{ik}$, and the $\delta$ between $P_k$ and $P_j$ is given by $\delta_{kj}$. Now, for every operation $e \in \delta_{ij}$, $e$ must be in either $\delta_{ik}$ ($P_k$ is identical to $P_j$ for the combination of subject, resource, action, and condition enclosed in $c$) or in $\delta_{kj}$ ($P_k$ is identical to $P_i$ for the combination of subject, resource, action, and condition enclosed in $e$). Thus, assume we separate $\delta_{ij}$ into $\delta^1_{ij}$ and $\delta^2_{ij}$, where $\delta^1_{ij}$ is composed of all operations of $\delta_{ij}$ included in $\delta_{ik}$, while $\delta^2_{ij}$ is composed of all operations of $\delta_{ij}$ included in $\delta_{kj}$. Now,

$$avgdist(P_i, P_j) = \sum_{\forall e \in \delta_{ij}} costs(e) = \sum_{\forall e \in \delta^1_{ij}} costs(e) + \sum_{\forall e \in \delta^2_{ij}} costs(e) \quad (1)$$

$$avgdist(P_i, P_k) = \sum_{\forall e \in \delta_{ik}} costs(e) = \sum_{\forall e \in \delta_{ik} \cap \delta^1_{ij}} costs(e) + \sum_{\forall e \in \delta_{ik} - \delta^1_{ij}} costs(e) \quad (2)$$

$$avgdist(P_k, P_j) = \sum_{\forall e \in \delta_{kj}} costs(e) = \sum_{\forall e \in \delta_{kj} \cap \delta^2_{ij}} costs(e) + \sum_{\forall e \in \delta_{kj} - \delta^2_{ij}} costs(e) \quad (3)$$

From eqns (1), (2) and (3), we can see that $avgdist(P_i, P_k) + avgdist(P_k, P_j) = avgdist(P_i, P_j) + \sum_{\forall e \in \delta_{ik} - \delta^1_{ij}} costs(e) + \sum_{\forall e \in \delta_{kj} - \delta^2_{ij}} costs(e) \ge avgdist(P_i, P_j)$ $\qquad \square$

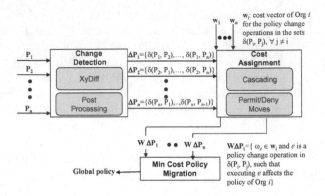

**Fig. 2.** Policy Migration Process

---

**Algorithm 3.** Policy Migration

---

**Require:** $n$ Organizations $Org_1, \ldots, Org_n$ each with respective policy $P_1, \ldots, P_n$
**Require:** $w_i$, $Org_i$'s set of weights
1: $\forall_{i,j \in [1,n], s.t. i \neq j} cost_{i,j} \leftarrow Costs(P_i, P_j, w_i)$
2: **for** $i = 1 \ldots n$ **do**
3:     $TotalCost_i \leftarrow 0$
4:     **for** $j = 1 \ldots n, j \neq i$ **do**
5:         $TotalCost_i \leftarrow TotalCost_i + cost_{j,i}$
6:     **end for**
7: **end for**
8: $GlobalPolicyIndex \leftarrow i$, where $\forall j, j \neq i, TotalCost_i \leq TotalCost_j$
9: $\forall j \neq GlobalPolicyIndex, Result \leftarrow \delta(P_j, P_{GlobalPolicyIndex})$

---

## 4    Policy Migration

In this section, we will now look at the problem of policy migration. Given a set of policies, the key aim of migration is to find the one policy that has the minimum transition cost across all of the policies. We want to find a global policy in a given set of $n$ policies such that the cost of migrating all policies in the set to the global policy is the minimum. In formal notation, given a set of policies $\{P_1, .., P_n\}$ and the set of policy change operations $\{\delta(P_i, P_j)\}$ ($\forall 1 \leq i, j \leq n, i \neq j$). For any policy transition operation $e$, let $c_e$ be the corresponding cost. Then the cost of migrating all policies to $P_j$ is the sum of the cost $c_e$ of each operation $e$ in the set $\cup_{i=1, i \neq j}^{n} \delta(P_i, P_j)$. If this cost is minimum, $P_j$ is the required global policy to which each policy is migrated.

The key idea is similar to the case of similarity evaluation. We again use the XyDiff tool[5] to detect the changes between the policies. As before, while XyDiff strives to generate the delta output with minimum number of operations, it does not take into account the security costs of the operations. Therefore, similar to earlier, we have to assign a security cost to every change detected, as well as assign security penalties when special cases occur. Once the costs for all of the changes are computed, the policy composition algorithm then computes the appropriate composite policy with minimum cost. The key question is how this is done? For this, consider a simple case where we have two policies ($P_1$ and $P_2$) owned by two different organizations ($Org_1$ and $Org_2$ respectively). Assume that the only difference between the two policies is that of a single rule – i.e., the two policies are identical except for the presence of one rule (say, $R_1$) in one of the policies (say, $P_1$). When migrating to a joint policy, if $P_2$ is chosen to be the joint policy, then $R_1$ must be deleted from $P_1$. Alternatively, if $P_1$ is chosen to be the joint policy, then $R_1$ must be added to $P_2$. The critical point is to realize that the cost of this can be different based on each organization's perspective. Thus, to find the optimum policy, it is necessary to compare the cost of deleting $R_1$ from $P_1$'s perspective versus the cost of adding $R_2$ from $P_2$'s perspective. Whichever cost is lower guides the choice of the global migration policy. Generalizing this to multiple changes, the cost of migrating to a policy is given by the sum of the costs of performing each change (add or delete) from the migrating organization's perspective. Generalizing this to multiple organizations and policies, whenever there are multiple policies, the cost of migrating to a policy is given by the sum of the costs of performing each change (add or delete) for all of the migrating organizations. Based on this, the overall procedure is as depicted in Figure 2. For every pair of policies, the Costs subprocedure (Algorithm 2) is used to get the transition cost from one policy to the other. Now, the cost of migrating to each policy is calculated based on the delta from all of the other policies as well as those organizational weights. Finally, the policy with the minimum transition cost is chosen as the global migration policy. The corresponding delta gives the transition path. Algorithm 3 gives the details.

*Example 2.* We now reexamine Example 1 to illustrate the process of policy migration. As before, all of the transition costs are calculated. Now, the cost of migrating to Policy $P_1$ is given by sum of the cost of transitioning from $P_2$ and $P_3$. Thus, $TotalCost_1 = 0.875 + 1.125 = 2$. Similarly, $TotalCost_2 = 0.73 + 1.25 = 1.98$. Finally, $TotalCost_3 = 0.98 + 1.25 = 2.23$. Since $TotalCost_2$ is the lowest, policy $P_2$ is the optimal policy for migration and $\delta(P_1, P_2)$ and $\delta(P_3, P_2)$ give the migration paths.

## 5 Related Work

There exists significant research in the area of policy composition [2–4,13]. However, little work exists on policy similarity. Koch et al. [9] propose a graph transformation based approach for comparing different policy models. While they present detailed examples, no specific algorithm has been presented. While this work remained at a conceptual level, on the other hand, Fisler et al. [7] developed a software tool for analyzing RBAC policies specified in XACML. This tool can verify policy properties and analyze differences between versions of policies. Backes et al. [2] propose an approach for checking refinement of privacy policies, which can be considered relevant to policy similarity because it checks if one policy is a subset of another.

Other relevant related research is in the area of policy conflict detection [11,14]. More recent work by Agrawal et al. [1] proposes an approach to determine satisfiability of boolean expressions corresponding to different policies, and develops a tool to check if a new policy can be added to a set of policies. Mazzoleni et al. [12] proposed a policy integration approach, in which they considered the policy similarity problem, but is limited to identifying policies specified on the same attribute. The most recent work by Lin et al. [10,18] is the most closely related work to this paper, which has been discussed in Section 2. This work does not fully capture the necessary semantics for policy comparison, and also cannot be directly used for policy migration.

There is also significant work done on policy reconciliation in the context of secure interoperation in a multiorganizational environment [6,8,11,17]. However, this is not directly relevant to this paper and also does not consider policy similarity.

# 6    Conclusions and Future Work

The primary contribution of this paper is to propose a holistic change detection approach to policy similarity evaluation and policy migration. Compared to the state of the art, our approach more comprehensively takes into account different access control semantics in computing policy similarity. In the future, we plan to extend our work to also provide a reconciliation strategy for organizations to transition their local policy to an optimal collaborative policy. We also plan to take into account more advanced constraints such as static and dynamic separation of duties.

# References

1. Agrawal, D., Giles, J., Lee, K.-W., Lobo, J.: Policy ratification. In: POLICY 2005, pp. 223–232. IEEE Computer Society, Washington, DC (2005)
2. Backes, M., Dürmuth, M., Steinwandt, R.: An algebra for composing enterprise privacy policies. In: Samarati, P., Ryan, P., Gollmann, D., Molva, R. (eds.) ESORICS 2004. LNCS, vol. 3193, pp. 33–52. Springer, Heidelberg (2004)
3. Bonatti, P., De Capitani di Vimercati, S., Samarati, P.: An algebra for composing access control policies. ACM Transactions on Information and System Security 5(1), 1–35 (2002)
4. Bruns, G., Dantas, D.S., Huth, M.: A simple and expressive semantic framework for policy composition in access control. In: Proceedings of the 5th ACM Workshop on Formal Methods in Security Engineering (2007)
5. Cobena, G., Abiteboul, S., Marian, A.: Detecting changes in xml documents. In: ICDE (2002)
6. Dawson, S., Qian, S., Samarati, P.: Providing security and interoperation of heterogeneous systems. Distributed and Parallel Databases 8, 119–145 (2000)
7. Fisler, K., Krishnamurthi, S., Meyerovich, L.A., Tschantz, M.C.: Verification and change-impact analysis of access-control policies. In: ICSE, pp. 196–205 (2005)
8. Gong, L., Qian, X.: Computational issues in secure interoperation. IEEE TSE 22(1), 43–52 (1996)

9. Koch, M., Mancini, L.V., Parisi-Presicce, F.: On the specification and evolution of access control policies. In: SACMAT 2001, pp. 121–130 (2001)
10. Lin, D., Rao, P., Bertino, E., Lobo, J.: An approach to evaluate policy similarity. In: SACMAT 2007, pp. 1–10. ACM, New York (2007)
11. Lupu, E., Sloman, M.: Conflicts in policy-based distributed systems management. IEEE TSE **25**(6), 852–869 (1999)
12. Mazzoleni, P., Bertino, E., Crispo, B., Sivasubramanian, S.: Xacml policy integration algorithms: not to be confused with xacml policy combination algorithms! In: SACMAT 2006, New York, NY, USA, pp. 219–227 (2006)
13. McDaniel, P., Prakash, A.: Methods and limitations of security policy reconciliation. ACM Transactions on Information and System Security **9**(3) (2006)
14. Moffett, J.D., Sloman, M.S.: Policy conflict analysis in distributed system management. Journal of Organizational Computing (1993)
15. Moses, T.: Extensible access control markup language (XACML) version 1.0. Technical report, OASIS (2003)
16. Peters, L.: Change detection in XML trees: a survey. In: 3rd Twente Student Conference on IT. University of Twente, June 2005
17. Shafiq, B., Joshi, J., Bertino, E., Ghafoor, A.: Secure interoperation in a multidomain environment employing rbac policies. IEEE Trans. Knowl. Data Eng. **17**(11), 1557–1577 (2005)
18. Lin, D., Rao, P., Ferrini, R., Bertino, E., Lobo, J.: A similarity measure for comparing XACML policies. IEEE Trans. Knowl. Data Eng. **25**(9), 1946–1959 (2013)

# MT-ABAC: A Multi-Tenant Attribute-Based Access Control Model with Tenant Trust

Navid Pustchi$^{(\boxtimes)}$ and Ravi Sandhu

Institute for Cyber Security, Department of Computer Science,
University of Texas San Antonio, One UTSA Circle, San Antonio, TX 78249, USA
tam498@my.utsa.edu, ravi.sandhu@utsa.edu

**Abstract.** A major barrier to the adoption of cloud Infrastructure-as-a-Service (IaaS) is collaboration, where multiple tenants engage in collaborative tasks requiring resources to be shared across tenant boundaries. Currently, cloud IaaS providers focus on multi-tenant isolation, and offer limited or no cross-tenant access capabilities in their IaaS APIs. In this paper, we present a novel attribute-based access control (ABAC) model to enable collaboration between tenants in a cloud IaaS, as well as more generally. Our approach allows cross-tenant attribute assignment to provide access to shared resources across tenants. Particularly, our tenant-trust authorizes a trustee tenant to assign its attributes to users from a trustor tenant, enabling access to the trustee tenant's resources. We designate our multi-tenant attribute-based access control model as MT-ABAC. Previously, a multi-tenant role-based access control (MT-RBAC) model has been defined in the literature wherein a trustee tenant can assign its roles to users from a trustor tenant. We demonstrate that MT-ABAC can be configured to enforce MT-RBAC thus subsuming it as a special case.

**Keywords:** Attribute-based access control · Distributed access control · Multi-tenant · Authorization federation · Security

## 1 Introduction

Cloud computing has dramatically altered the delivery of IT infrastructure and resources to organizations. Characteristics such as on-demand self service and resource pooling, provide flexibility and dynamicity at scale for cloud service consumers [16]. The benefits of cloud computing have been well documented in the literature and proven in the marketplace.

Cloud service providers (CSPs) segregate the resources and customer's data into tenants to protect data privacy and integrity. Tenants are isolated containers with tenant-specific virtual computing environments. Each tenant corresponds to an organization, a department of an organization, or an individual who uses cloud services. In this scenario, each tenant is considered as a cloud customer with resources whose integrity and privacy must be protected. The focus on tenant isolation diminishes the scope for collaboration across tenants.

© Springer International Publishing Switzerland 2015
M. Qiu et al. (Eds.): NSS 2015, LNCS 9408, pp. 206–220, 2015.
DOI: 10.1007/978-3-319-25645-0_14

At the dawn of cloud systems, the multi-tenancy concern was resource seg-regation, whereas recent enterprise cloud adoption has raised the issue of multi-tenancy resource sharing. The drive for multi-tenant collaboration arises from at least two distinct directions. First, a large organization may utilize multiple ten-ants for security and reliability, where each tenant can represent a department. For example, an organization's financial department processes sensitive financial data while its marketing department publishes open information to the public, so they need to be isolated but yet may need controlled collaboration. Second, distinct enterprises may have collaborative tasks across their corresponding ten-ants. Current cloud Infrastructure-as-a-service (IaaS) providers such as Amazon EC2 [1] or OpenStack [2] offer limited or no cross-tenant access [14].

In this paper we present a novel attribute-based access control model to enable collaboration between tenants in cloud systems. Our scope is limited to cross-tenant collaboration in a single cloud. This allows us to focus more on collaborative access control models, and defer consideration of cross-cloud integration issues.

To motivate the problem, consider the example illustrated in Figure 1, which depicts an organization with multiple tenants in a cloud service provider. We use HP as an organization with multiple locations and departments. In such organizations it is not feasible to locate all data and users into one tenant due to different security and reliability levels required as well as management barriers. Also, adding accounts for users across each collaborating tenant is impractical.

A practical approach for the cloud service provider is to support collabo-ration mechanisms across trusted ten-ants. Users in one tenant can access resources in another tenant consis-tent with cross-tenant trust relation-ships. It is natural for software devel-opment, testing, and support teams to collaborate. Software developers such as Alice can access cross-tenant resources in Software Testing and Software Support tenants to per-form their assigned tasks. Enabling seamless collaboration across tenants is essential for the overall organiza-tion. Similar scenarios arise for cross-organization collaboration.

Current cloud IaaS providers such as Amazon or Rackspace provide intra-tenant access control using vari-ations of the well-known role-based

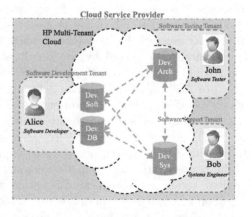

**Fig. 1.** A Multi-Tenant Collaboration Example

access control (RBAC) [6,20] approach. In RBAC access to a resource is based upon role-membership of the requesting user and resource-permission.

The notion of multi-tenant RBAC has been proposed to support multi-tenant collaboration in single cloud [24,26] or multi-cloud [17] environments.

RBAC has been the dominant access-control paradigm for over two decades. Nevertheless, various limitations of RBAC have been recognized over this period and increasingly there is a push to move towards attribute-based access control [9,10,18] in general. ABAC advantages over RBAC specifically in cloud computing have been discussed in the literature [5]. A user's access to a resource in ABAC depends on the relative values of the user and resource attributes. An attribute is simply a name:value pair. Attributes are used to represent security-relevant properties of users and resources. We anticipate that CSPs will incorporate ABAC features in addition to their currently implemented RBAC.

Our contribution in this paper is to develop a multi-tenant ABAC model with cross-tenant trust. To our knowledge this is the first work to consider cross-tenant attribute assignment in ABAC in a multi-tenant context.

The remainder of this paper is organized as follows. Section 2 introduces our core ABAC model entities and attribute functions in a single tenant model. In Section 3, our multi-tenant ABAC (MT-ABAC) model is proposed and specified. In section 4, we review the multi-tenant RBAC model from the literature and demonstrate how it can be configured in MT-ABAC. Section 5 discusses related work and section 6 gives our conclusions.

## 2    $ABAC_0$ Model

In this section, we present our core ABAC model which we designate as $ABAC_0$. This model is designed to be sufficient for our purpose in developing MT-ABAC and is not intended to be a comprehensive ABAC model. ABAC has been defined in various ways in the literature, usually for some specific purpose. Our model is specifically motivated by the previously defined $ABAC_\alpha$ model [11] and is compatible with the recently defined NIST ABAC framework [9].

Core $ABAC_0$ model element sets and functions are illustrated in Figure 2, which includes three basic components: users $(U)$, objects $(O)$, and actions $(A)$. Attributes are properties associated with users and objects which we represent by $UATT$ and $OATT$ respectively. Users and objects are collectively called entities. Authorization predicates $(Auth)$ express access rules in the system which evaluate user attributes against object attributes and render a decision to permit or deny access to the requested resource with respect to the specific action.

Each *attribute* is a function which takes users or objects as input and returns a value from the attribute's range (we use the terms range and scope interchangeably). For example, a user attribute function such as $Role \in UATT$ maps $u_1 \in U$ to a value *cloud_admin*. Depending upon attribute type each attribute function will return a single value or a set of values. An atomic-valued attribute will return one value while a set-valued attribute will return a subset of values within its defined scope.

A user can be a human or non-person
entity, such as an application, making
requests to perform actions on an object.
We consider a user $(u \in U)$ to be a person for simplicity. Each user is represented
by a finite set of user attributes $(UATT)$
such as name, salary, clearance, role, etc.
User attribute function values are specified
by security architects at system creation or
modification time.

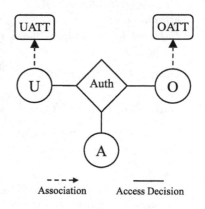

Objects are system resources for which
access should be protected such as files,
applications, virtual machines (VMs), etc.
Objects are associated with attribute functions $(OATT)$ representing resource properties such as risk level, location, and classification. At creation or modification time
object attributes might be constrained by the
attributes of creating user in the system, for

**Fig. 2.** Core ABAC$_0$ Model Structure.

example, a new VM object can inherit attributes such as VM owner from corresponding user attributes such as user id. The details of such constraints are not
material for our purpose in this paper, hence we do not explicitly model them.
The approach of ABAC$_\alpha$ [11] in this regard could be adapted to ABAC$_0$.

Actions are allowed operations in the system. These operations typically
include create, read, update and delete. We use the terms actions and operations
interchangeably. An action is applied to an object by a user. The term action is
more commonly used in ABAC whereas operation is more common in the RBAC
literature. An RBAC permission is defined to be an object, operation pair, which
terminology we also use in this paper.

Actions are evaluated by authorization policy to enable access of a user to
an object. Authorization policy is expressed as a propositional logic predicate
for each action in the system, which takes as input a user and an object. Based
on the values of the user and object attributes the authorization predicate for a
given action returns true or false.

We formalize the above in the following definition, specifying sets, functions
and authorization policy language.

**Definition 1.** *Core ABAC$_0$ is defined by the basic component sets, functions
and authorization policy language given below.*

- *$U$ and $O$ represent finite sets of existing users and objects respectively.*
- *$A$ represents a finite set of actions available on objects. Typically $A = \{create, read, update, delete\}$.*
- *$UATT$ and $OATT$ represent finite sets of user and object attribute functions
  respectively.*
- *For each att in $UATT \cup OATT$, Scope(att) represents the attribute's scope,
  a finite set of atomic values.*

- $attType : UATT \cup OATT \rightarrow \{set, atomic\}$, *specifies attributes as set or atomic valued.*
- *Each attribute function maps elements in $U$ and $O$ to atomic or set values as follows.*

$$\forall uatt \in UATT.uatt : U \rightarrow \begin{cases} Scope(uatt) \; if \; attType(uatt) = atomic \\ 2^{Scope(uatt)} \; if \; attType(uatt) = set \end{cases}$$

$$\forall oatt \in OATT.oatt : O \rightarrow \begin{cases} Scope(oatt) \; if \; attType(oatt) = atomic \\ 2^{Scope(oatt)} \; if \; attType(oatt) = set \end{cases}$$

- *For each $a \in A$, $Authorization_a(u : U, o : O)$ is a propositional logic predicate, defined using the following language:*
  - $\varphi ::= \varphi \wedge \varphi \mid \varphi \vee \varphi \mid (\varphi) \mid \neg \varphi \mid \exists x \in set.\varphi \mid \forall x \in set.\varphi \mid set \; \triangle \; set \mid atomic \in set \mid atomic \; \nabla \; atomic$
  - $set ::= setuatt(u) \mid setoatt(o)$
  - $atomic ::= atomicuatt(u) \mid atomicoatt(o)$
  - $\triangle ::= \subset \mid = \mid \subseteq \mid \nsubseteq$
  - $\nabla ::= < \mid = \mid \leq$
  - $setuatt \in \{uatt \mid uatt \in UATT \wedge attType(uatt) = set\}$
  - $setoatt \in \{oatt \mid oatt \in OATT \wedge attType(oatt) = set\}$
  - $atomicoatt \in \{oatt \mid oatt \in OATT \wedge attType(oatt) = atomic\}$
  - $atomicuatt \in \{uatt \mid uatt \in UATT \wedge attType(uatt) = atomic\}$

Core $ABAC_0$ is a simplified version of $ABAC_\alpha$ [11], suitable for our purpose in this paper. In particular it eliminates subjects as being distinct from users as is in $ABAC_\alpha$, and simply treats them to be equivalent.

## 3   Multi-Tenant $ABAC_0$ Model

In this section we build upon $ABAC_0$ to formulate a multi-tenant attribute-based access control model enabling cross-tenant collaboration which we designate as MT-$ABAC_0$. The model structure is depicted in Figure 3, adding the tenant $(T)$ entity in addition to the users and objects of core $ABAC_0$. *Tenants* are isolated operation domains leased by cloud service consumers.

Each user and each object is uniquely owned by a single tenant. For this purpose the model requires each user to have a system defined attribute *userOwner* which is a many-to-one atomic-valued function from users $U$ to tenants $T$. Note that the arrowhead indicate the many side of the function while the absence of an arrowhead represents the one side. Likewise the model requires each object to have a system defined attribute *objOwner* which similarly is a many-to-one atomic-valued function from objects $O$ to tenants $T$.

Further, each user attribute and each object attribute is also uniquely owned by a single tenant, depicted respectively by the many-to-one atomic-valued functions *uattOwner* and *oattOwner* in Figure 3. The crucial concept is that each tenant is responsible for assigning values to attributes that it owns. With isolated tenants, a user can have assigned values only for those attributes owned

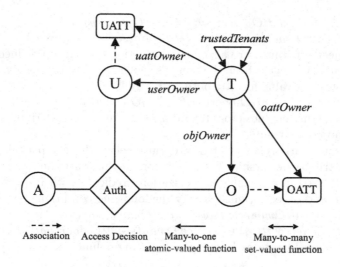

**Fig. 3.** Multi-Tenant $ABAC_0$ Model Structure.

by the user's owning tenant. We will see that, with appropriate trust relationship between tenants, users belonging to one tenant can be assigned values for attributes belonging to a different tenant. In our model for objects, we require that an object can have assigned values only for those attributes owned by the object's owning tenant. It is not possible for an object to be assigned values for attributes that belong to a tenant that does not own that object, regardless of tenant trust relationships. In summary cross-tenant attributes can be assigned to users under appropriate trust relationships but not to objects.

We define trust as a required attribute function *trustedTenants* mapping trustor tenant to trustee tenants which we refer to as tenant-trust. This is a many-to-many set-valued function. We use "$\trianglelefteq$" to represent the tenant-trust relation where $T_A \trianglelefteq T_B$ signifies that $T_B \in trustedTenants(T_A)$, i.e., $T_B$ is trusted by $T_A$. In such cases we say $T_A$ is the trustor tenant and $T_B$ the trustee tenant. We have the following definition for tenant-trust.[1]

**Definition 2.** *If $T_A \trianglelefteq T_B$, Tenant $T_B$ is authorized to assign values for $T_B$'s user attributes to Tenant $T_A$'s users. Tenant $T_A$ controls tenant-trust existence while $T_B$ controls cross-tenant attribute assignments.*

In general $\trianglelefteq$ is required to be a reflexive relation but is not required to be symmetric, anti-symmetric or transitive.

In light of the above definitions, we need to clarify the validity of attributes for users and objects. User attribute functions now become partial functions, because valid attribute values for a given user can only be assigned to certain user attributes. Specifically, a user $u$ can be assigned a value for attribute *uatt* only if

---

[1] More generally different kinds of trust could be considered as discussed in Section 3.1.

$$uattOwner(uatt) = userOwner(u) \lor$$
$$uattOwner(uatt) \in trustedTenants(userOwner(u))$$

Similarly object attributes are also partial functions which are defined only for object attributes which are from the object's owner tenant. Specifically, an object $o$ can be assigned a value for attribute $oatt$ only if

$$oattOwner(oatt) = objOwner(o)$$

In other words trust enables cross-tenant assignment of user attributes but does not impact object attributes.

Finally, each authorization predicate must verify the compatibility of user and object attribute ownership. For this reason, any user attribute $uatt$ or object attribute $oatt$ used in a action's authorization predicate with respect to a particular user $u$ and object $o$, must satisfy the following condition.

$$uattOwner(uatt(u)) = oattOwner(oatt(o)) \lor$$
$$oattOwner(oatt(o)) \in trustedTenants(uattOwner(uatt(u)))$$

The above considerations lead to the following definition.

**Definition 3.** *Multi-tenant $ABAC_0$ is defined by the following enhancement and modifications to core $ABAC_0$.*

- *$U$, $O$, and $A$ are defined as in core $ABAC_0$.*
- *$T$ represents a finite set of existing tenants.*
- *$UATT$, $OATT$, Scope, and attType are defined as in core $ABAC_0$.*
- *userOwner : $(u : U) \rightarrow T$, required attribute function mapping user $u$ to owner tenant $t$.*
- *objOwner : $(o : O) \rightarrow T$, required attribute function mapping object $o$ to owner tenant $t$.*
- *$MATT = \{uattOwner, oattOwner\}$, required meta-attribute functions.*

  - *uattOwner : $(uatt : UATT) \rightarrow T$, meta attribute function, mapping user attribute $uatt$ to attribute owner tenant $t$.*
  - *oattOwner : $(oatt : OATT) \rightarrow T$, meta attribute function, mapping object attribute $oatt$ to attribute owner tenant $t$.*

- *trustedTenants : $(t : T) \rightarrow 2^T$, required attribute function, mapping tenant $t$ to powerset of trusted $T$, called tenant-trust, written as $\trianglelefteq$ where $t_1 \trianglelefteq t_2$ iff $t_2 \in trustedTenants(t_1)$ (i.e., trustor tenant $t_1$ trusts trustee tenant $t_2$). Trustee tenant $t_2$ can assign its attribute values $uatt_{t_2}$ to users $u_{t_1}$ from trustor tenant $t_1$ where $t_2 \in trustedTenants(userOwner(u))$.*
- *Each attribute function $uatt \in UATT$ is modified to be a partial function.*
$$\forall uatt \in UATT.uatt : U \hookrightarrow \begin{cases} Scope(uatt) \ if \ attType(uatt) = atomic \\ 2^{Scope(uatt)} \ if \ attType(uatt) = set \end{cases}$$
*$uatt(u : U)$ is defined only if $(uattOwner(uatt) = userOwner(u)) \lor (uattOwner(uatt) \in trustedTenants(userOwner(u)))$.*
- *Each attribute function $oatt \in OATT$ is modified to be a partial function.*
$$\forall oatt \in OATT.oatt : O \hookrightarrow \begin{cases} Scope(oatt) \ if \ attType(oatt) = atomic \\ 2^{Scope(oatt)} \ if \ attType(oatt) = set \end{cases}$$
*$OATT(o : O)$ is defined only if $oattOwner(oatt) = objOwner(o)$.*

- $\forall a \in A$, $Authorization_a(u : U, o : O)$ is a propositional logic predicate (using language defined in $ABAC_0$), with the additional required condition that $uattOwner(uatt(u)) = oattOwner(oatt(o)) \lor oattOwner(oatt(o)) \in trusted\text{-}Tenants(uattOwner(uatt(u)))$ which must always be included in conjunction with all other requirements.

## 3.1 Concept of Tenant Trust

In a tenant trust relation, in general there are two issues: (i) who controls trust relation's existence, and (ii) who has the authority to issue cross-tenant assignments. Together these characterize the trust type. In this paper, for simplicity, we adopted a specific definition of trust where trustee tenant is authorized to assign its attribute values to trustor tenant's user attributes which is analogous to the type-$\beta$ tenant-trust of [24–26]. In this section, we briefly discuss trust types analogous to the type-$\alpha$ and type-$\gamma$ tenant-trust types of [24–26].

In type-$\alpha$ trust, the trustor is responsible to establish the trust relationship with the trustee, as well as assigns the trustor's attributes to the trustee's users. We use $\unlhd_\alpha$ to show this trust type where $T_A \unlhd_\alpha T_B$ indicates that $T_B \in trustedTenants(T_A)$. With this notation, type-$\alpha$ tenant-trust is defined as follows.

**Definition 4.** If $T_A \unlhd_\alpha T_B$, Tenant $T_A$ is authorized to assign values for $T_A$'s user attributes to Tenant $T_B$'s users. Tenant $T_A$ controls tenant-trust existence and cross-tenant attribute assignments.

In type-$\alpha$ trust, valid attribute values for given users are from owner tenants and trustor tenants. A user is assigned a value for an attribute $uatt$ only if

$$uattOwner(uatt) = userOwner(u) \lor$$
$$userOwner(u) \in trustedTenants(uattOwner(uatt))$$

Each authorization predicate in type-$\alpha$ must satisfy following user and object attribute ownership condition.

$$uattOwner(uatt(u)) = oattOwner(oatt(o)) \lor$$
$$uattOwner(uatt(u)) \in trustedTenants(oattOwner(oatt(o)))$$

In type-$\gamma$ trust, by trusting a tenant, trustor authorizes trustee to assign its attribute values to trustee tenant user attributes. We use $\unlhd_\gamma$ to represent type-$\gamma$ tenant-trust where $T_A \unlhd_\gamma T_B$ signifies that $T_B \in trustedTenants(T_A)$. We define type-$\gamma$ trust as follows.

**Definition 5.** If $T_A \unlhd_\gamma T_B$, Tenant $T_B$ is authorized to assign values for $T_A$'s user attributes to Tenant $T_B$'s users. Tenant $T_A$ controls tenant-trust existence while $T_B$ controls cross-tenant attribute assignments.

Type-$\gamma$ user attribute assignment and authorization predicate conditions are similar to above mentioned conditions in type-$\alpha$. Type-$\gamma$ differs from type-$\alpha$, in which participating tenant has cross-tenant attribute assignment authority.

In relation to figure 1, when software development (SD) tenant trusts software testing (ST) tenant with type-$\beta$, it authorizes ST tenant to assign its attribute values to software developers such as Alice to access resources in ST tenant. In type-$\alpha$ and Type-$\gamma$ tenant-trust enables ST users such as John to access resources in SD tenant, where in type-$\alpha$ SD tenant assigns its attributes to John and in type-$\gamma$ ST tenant assigns SD attribute values to its user John.

# 4    MT-ABAC$_0$ Model Covering MT-RBAC$_0$

In this section we first give a definition of multi-tenant RBAC (MT-RBAC$_0$) adapted from various slightly different but related models given in [24–26]. We then show how MT-RBAC$_0$ can be configured in MT-ABAC$_0$.

## 4.1    Multi-Tenant RBAC$_0$ Model

MT-RBAC$_0$ model element sets and relations are illustrated in Figure 4, showing the six components: tenants $(T)$, users $(U)$, roles $(R)$, operations $(OPS)$, objects $(OBS)$, and permissions $(PRMS)$. A *user* is an individual which is associated with a single tenant via $UO$ relation. We recognize *role* as a job function associated with a single tenant while a tenant has multiple roles. *Objects* are tenant resources in the system (each object has a single owner tenant) which are coupled with *operations*. In RBAC, *permissions* are operation, object pairs indicating operations on objects.

MT-RBAC$_0$ model is defined in terms of users, roles, and objects owned by tenants. These ownership relations are many-to-one representing tenant ownership which is depicted as user-ownership $(UO)$, role-ownership $(RO)$, and object-ownership $(OO)$ in figure 4.

As core to RBAC, user assignment $(UA)$ and permission assignment $(PA)$ relations enable assignment of users and permissions to roles. Tenant-trust $(TT)$

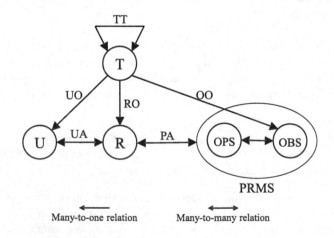

**Fig. 4.** Multi-Tenant RBAC$_0$ Model Structure.

identifies a many-to-many trust relation between tenants. Similar to MT-ABAC$_0$ we use $\trianglelefteq$ to show trust between two tenants such $T_A$ and $T_B$ as $T_A \trianglelefteq T_B$ means trustor tenant $T_A$ trusts, trustee tenant $T_B$. With this specification, we define tenant-trust relation as follows.

**Definition 6.** *If $T_A \trianglelefteq T_B$, Tenant $T_B$ is authorized to assign Tenant $T_A$'s users to $T_B$'s roles.*

In such trust relation, trusting a tenant enables trustee to assign trustor's users to its set of roles. This type of trust is intuitive in a sense that resource owners control access to their shared resources while user domains control their users' access by granted authority over trust relation continuation.

With existence of trust between tenants, user assignment is defined as many-to-many user relation mapping users to roles, if and only if users and roles owned by the same tenant or user owner tenant trusts object owner tenant. We express user assignment condition as $owner\_user(u) = owner\_role(r)$ (where $owner\_user$ returns owner tenant of user $u$ and $owner\_role$ returns role $r$ owner tenant) or $owner\_user(u) \trianglelefteq owner\_role(r)$. Permission assignment is a many-to-many relation which maps permissions to roles requiring both elements owned by the same tenant.

Each user is assigned to one or many roles within their resident tenants or trusted tenants. The function $assigned\_user\_roles$ returns the roles assigned to a user. The permissions available to a user, are permissions assigned to roles (permissions available to a role are expressed by function $assigned\_permissions$) that are available to a user which are given by function $authorized\_user\_permissions$. Function $authorized\_user\_permissions$ designates set of permissions available to each user in the system. We formally define MT-RBAC$_0$ as follows.

**Definition 7.** *Multi-tenant RBAC$_0$.*

- *TENANTS, USERS, ROLES, OPS, and OBS (tenants, users, roles, operations, and objects respectively).*
- *$t \in TENANTS$, $u \in USERS$, $r \in ROLES$, $op \in OPS$, and $ob \in OBS$.*
- *$PRMS = OPS \times OBS$ , the set of permissions.[2]*
- *$UO \subseteq USERS \times TENANTS$, a many-to-one user-to-tenant owner relation.*
- *$RO \subseteq ROLES \times TENANTS$, a many-to-one role-to-tenant owner relation.*
- *$OO \subseteq OBS \times TENANTS$, a many-to-one object-to-tenant owner relation.*
- *$owner\_user : (u : USERS) \rightarrow TENANTS$, the mapping of user $u$ into its owner tenant. Formally: $owner\_user(u) = t$ where $(u,t) \in UO$.*
- *$owner\_role : (r : ROLE) \rightarrow TENANTS$, the mapping of role $r$ into its owner tenant. Formally: $owner\_role(r) = t$ where $(r,t) \in RO$.*
- *$owner\_object : (ob : OBS) \rightarrow TENANTS$, the mapping of object $ob$ into its owner tenant. Formally: $owner\_object(ob) = t$ where $(o,t) \in OO$.*

---

[2] This is slightly different from NIST standard model where $PRMS = 2^{(OPS \times OBS)}$, and more appropriate for our purpose.

- $TT \subseteq TENANTS \times TENANTS$, is a many-to-many reflexive relation on TENANTS called tenant trust relation, written as $\trianglelefteq$ where $t_1 \trianglelefteq t_2$ (trustor tenant $t_1$ trusts trustee tenant $t_2$) only if all users of $t_1$ can be assigned to roles of $t_2$.
- $trustee\_tenants : (t : TENANTS) \rightarrow 2^{TENANTS}$, the mapping of tenant $t$ into a set of trusted tenants. Formally: $trustee\_tenant(t) = \{t' \in TENANTS \mid t \trianglelefteq t'\}$.
- $UA \subseteq USERS \times ROLES$, a many-to-many mapping user-to-role assignment relation requiring that $(u,r) \in UA \Rightarrow owner\_user(u) = owner\_role(r) \vee owner\_user(u) \trianglelefteq owner\_role(r)$.
- $PA \subseteq PRMS \times ROLES$, a many-to-many mapping permission-to-role assignment relation requiring that $((op, ob), r) \in PA \Rightarrow owner\_object(ob) = owner\_role(r)$.
- $assigned\_roles : (op : OPS, ob : OBS) \rightarrow 2^{ROLES}$, the mapping of object operation pair $(op, ob)$ into a set of roles. Formally: $assigned\_roles(op, ob) = \{r \in ROLES \mid ((op, ob), r) \in PA\}$.
- $assigned\_user\_roles : (u : USERS) \rightarrow 2^{ROLES}$, the mapping of user $u$ into a set of roles. Formally: $assigned\_user\_roles(u) = \{r \in ROLES \mid (u, r) \in UA\}$.
- $assigned\_permissions : (r : ROLES) \rightarrow 2^{PRMS}$, the mapping of role $r$ into a set of permissions. Formally: $assigned\_permissions(r) = \{p \in PRMS \mid (p, r) \in PA\}$.
- $authorized\_user\_permissions : (u : USER) \rightarrow 2^{PRMS}$, the mapping of user $u$ into a set of permissions. $authorized\_user\_permissions(u) =$
$$\bigcup_{r \in assigned\_user\_roles(u)} assigned\_permissions(r).$$

## 4.2   Configuring MT-RBAC$_0$ to MT-ABAC$_0$

We show configuring MT-RBAC$_0$ in MT-ABAC$_0$ by adding role as an attribute function. Once roles become attributes, the consideration that roles are collections of permissions no longer applies since they are merely attribute values. Consequently, we must define appropriate object attributes and authorization predicates in MT-ABAC$_0$. To represent user assigned roles in MT-RBAC$_0$ ($assigned\_user\_roles$ function), we use a set-valued attribute function $userRole$. However users may be assigned roles owned by distinct tenants, for this purpose we identified user attributes as $userRole_j$ where $j$ represents tenants.

In order to represent permission assignment, we define attribute function $objRole$ as a set-valued attribute function. Attribute $objRole$ captures roles related to each object in RBAC (permissions assigned to roles represented by $assigned\_roles$ function). In RBAC each object is owned by a tenant and coupled with a set of operations, for this reason we designate object attributes as $objRole_{i,k}$ where $i$ is an operation in RBAC and $k$ is owner tenant. The scope of both $userRole$ and $objRole$ attributes are the same as defined set of role names $ROLES$. We represent role ownership ($RO$) in RBAC by atomic-valued meta-attributes, $uattOwner$ and $oattOwner$ respectively mapping user and object role attributes (*userRole* and *objRole*) to owner tenants. In the presence of roles attributes, authorization policy evaluates user and object respective role name attributes to be equal as well as user and object attributes ownership.

The summary of above is formalized as follows.

**Definition 8.** *A given MT-RBAC$_0$ instance is configured in MT-ABAC$_0$ as follows.*

- $U = USERS$, $O = OBS$, $A = OPS = \{a_1, ..., a_n\}$ *where* $n = |A|$, *and* $T = TENANTS = \{t_1, ..., t_m\}$ *where* $m = |T|$.
- $UATT = \{userRole_j \mid j = 1, ..., |T|\}$.
- $OATT = \{objRole_{i,k} \mid i = 1, ..., |A|, k = 1, ..., |T|\}$.
- $userOwner : (u : U) \rightarrow T$, *required attribute function, mapping user* $u$ *to owner tenant* $t$. *Formally:* $userOwner(u) = owner\_user(u)$.
- $objOwner : (o : O) \rightarrow T$, *required attribute function, mapping object* $o$ *to owner tenant* $t$. *Formally:* $objOwner(o) = owner\_object(o)$.
- $userRole_j : (u : U) \rightarrow 2^{ROLES}$ *where* $t_j \in T$, *attribute function, mapping user* $u$ *to powerset of ROLES. Formally:* $userRole_j(u) = \{r \in ROLES \mid r \in assigned\_user\_roles(u) \land owner\_role(r) = t_j\}$.
- $objRole_{i,k} : (o : O) \rightarrow 2^{ROLES}$ *where* $a_i \in A$ *and* $t_k \in T$, *attribute function, mapping object* $o$ *for operation* $a_i$ *to powerset of ROLES. Formally:* $objRole_{i,k}(o) = \{r \in ROLES \mid r \in assigned\_roles(a_i, o) \land owner\_role(r) = t_k\}$.
- $MATT = \{uattOwner, oattOwner\}$.
  - $uattOwner : (userRole_j : UATT) \rightarrow T$, *meta attribute function, mapping user role attribute* $userRole_j$ *to attribute owner tenant* $t_j$. *Formally:* $uattOwner(userRole_j) - t_j$.
  - $oattOwner : (objRole_{i,k} : OATT) \rightarrow T$, *meta attribute function, mapping object role attribute* $objRole_{i,k}$ *for operation* $a_i$ *to attribute owner tenant* $t_k$. *Formally:* $oattOwner(objRole_{i,k}) = t_k$.
- $trustedTenants : (t : T) \rightarrow 2^T$, *attribute function, mapping tenant* $t$ *to powerset of trusted T. Formally:* $trustedTenants(t) = trustee\_tenants(t)$.
- $Authorization_i$ $(u : U, o : O) = \bigvee_{k=1,...,|T|} [userRole_k(u) \cap objRole_{i,k}(o) \neq \emptyset \land (t_k = userOwner(u) \lor t_k \in trustedTenants(userOwner(u)))]$.

## 5   Related Work

Several attribute-based access control models and systems have been proposed. In [9,10], ABAC and its functional components, implementation, and operation considerations are illustrated. This serves as an overview of components rather than considering modeling issues. Jin et al. [11] proposed ABAC$_\alpha$ model, designed to cover simple forms of DAC [21], MAC [19], and RBAC [6,20]. While this provides a realistic family of attribute-based models within single tenant environments, it does not consider collaboration and multi-tenancy issues. Smari et al. [22] investigated trust and privacy in collaborative management systems.

They extend attributes associated with objects and subjects to address trust and privacy issues. Although collaboration is considered, multi-tenancy has not been addressed.

Other approaches extending RBAC with combination of attributes and roles have been studied widely. Kuhn et al. [13] presented a spectrum of possible methods to combine RBAC and ABAC, specifically a policy-enhanced RBAC to accommodate attribute based features. However, the attributes are limited to user-centered attributes. In RABAC [12], authors integrate roles and attributes using a role centric approach. Parameterized role [3], object sensitive role [7], and attributed role [27] have also been proposed in this context.

Recent work on multi-tenancy collaboration such as CTTM [24] and OSAC-DT [25] extends RBAC to inherit its benefits towards collaboration. CTTM enables trust between tenants in a single cloud and OSAC-DT which is closely related to CTTM further extends it towards compatibility with OpenStack [2] platform. Tang [23] specifies a multi-tenant attribute based access control enabling cross-tenant access for subjects. Our model differs in structure and cross-tenant access where attribute value assignment enables such collaboration.

In order to benefit the RBAC capabilities in multiple organizations, prior extensions such as ROBAC [29] and GB-RBAC [15] have been proposed. ROBAC manages authorization in multiple organizations which is comparable to multi-tenancy, however organization collaboration is not considered in this context. In GB-RBAC collaboration is allowed among groups, yet it lacks the administration management since the administrator can not manage users in the groups. Role-based delegation [4,8,28] models have been proposed to permit collaboration, however chained delegation relations are not dynamic and flexible enough to be deployed in multi-tenant collaborative environments since trust relations in such collaborations are dynamic.

## 6    Conclusion

We presented a multi-tenant attribute-based access control model for resource sharing, where collaboration is enabled through cross-tenant attribute value assignments supported by the cloud service provider. In our proposed approach, we identified trust as a required attribute for tenants where trustee tenants are authorized to assign attribute values to trustor tenants' user attributes. In our approach, we eliminated attribute conflicts in presence of attribute assignments by isolating attributes to tenants. We believe our approach is applicable to other types of trust beyond presented trust types. A potential future work is to extend this model to address various types of trust. Another future research is extending our model to multi-cloud environments. Finally, our vision is to develop an implementation within current cloud platforms.

**Acknowledgement.** This research is supported by NSF Grant CNS-1111925 and CNS-1423481.

# References

1. Amazon AWS. http://aws.amazon.com/es/ec2
2. OpenStack. http://www.openstack.org/
3. Abdallah, A.E., Khayat, E.J.: A formal model for parameterized role-based access control. In: Dimitrakos, T., Martinelli, F. (eds.) FAST 2005. IFIP, vol. 173, pp. 233–246. Springer, Heidelberg (2005)
4. Barka, E., Sandhu, R.: Framework for role-based delegation models. In: Proc. of Annual Conf. on Comp. Sec. Applications (ACSAC), pp. 168–176. IEEE (2000)
5. Coyne, E., Weil, T.R.: ABAC and RBAC: Scalable, flexible, and auditable access management. IT Professional **3**, 14–16 (2013)
6. Ferraiolo, D.F., Sandhu, R., Gavrila, S., Kuhn, D.R., Chandramouli, R.: Proposed NIST standard for role-based access control. TISSEC **4**(3), 224–274 (2001)
7. Fischer, J., Marino, D., Majumdar, R., Millstein, T.: Fine-grained access control with object-sensitive roles. In: Drossopoulou, S. (ed.) ECOOP 2009. LNCS, vol. 5653, pp. 173–194. Springer, Heidelberg (2009)
8. Freudenthal, E., Pesin, T., et al.: dRBAC: distributed role-based access control for dynamic coalition environments. In: Proc. of ICDCS, pp. 411–420. IEEE (2002)
9. Hu, V.C., Ferraiolo, D., et al.: Guide to attribute based access control (ABAC) definition and considerations. NIST Special Publication **800**, 162 (2014)
10. Hu, V.C., Kuhn, D.R., Ferraiolo, D.F.: Attribute-based access control. Computer **2**, 85–88 (2015)
11. Jin, X., Krishnan, R., Sandhu, R.S.: A unified attribute-based access control model covering DAC, MAC and RBAC. DBSec **12**, 41–55 (2012)
12. Jin, X., Sandhu, R., Krishnan, R.: RABAC: role-centric attribute-based access control. In: Kotenko, I., Skormin, V. (eds.) MMM-ACNS 2012. LNCS, vol. 7531, pp. 84–96. Springer, Heidelberg (2012)
13. Kuhn, D.R., Coyne, E.J., Weil, T.R.: Adding attributes to role-based access control. Computer **6**, 79–81 (2010)
14. Kurmus, A., Gupta, M., Pletka, R., Cachin, C., Haas, R.: A comparison of secure multi-tenancy architectures for filesystem storage clouds. In: Kon, F., Kermarrec, A.-M. (eds.) Middleware 2011. LNCS, vol. 7049, pp. 471–490. Springer, Heidelberg (2011)
15. Li, Q., Zhang, X., Xu, M., Wu, J.: Towards secure dynamic collaborations with group-based RBAC model. Computers & Security **28**(5), 260–275 (2009)
16. Mell, P., Grance, T.: The NIST definition of cloud computing (2011)
17. Pustchi, N., Krishnan, R., Sandhu, R.: Authorization federation in IaaS multi cloud. In: Proc. of Security in Cloud Computing, pp. 63–71. ACM (2015)
18. Sandhu, R.: The authorization leap from rights to attributes: maturation or chaos? In: Proc. of SACMAT, pp. 69–70. ACM (2012)
19. Sandhu, R.S.: Lattice-based access control models. Computer **26**(11), 9–19 (1993)
20. Sandhu, R.S., Coyne, E.J., Feinstein, H.L., Youman, C.E.: Role-based access control models. Computer **29**(2), 38–47 (1996)
21. Sandhu, R.S., Samarati, P.: Access control: principle and practice. IEEE Communications Magazine **32**(9), 40–48 (1994)
22. Smari, W.W., Clemente, P., Lalande, J.-F.: An extended attribute based access control model with trust and privacy: Application to a collaborative crisis management system. Future Generation Computer Systems **31**, 147–168 (2014)
23. Tang, B.: Multi-Tenant Access Control for Cloud Services. PhD thesis, University of Texas at San Antonio (2014)

24. Tang, B., Sandhu, R.: Cross-tenant trust models in cloud computing. In: Proc. of Int. Conf. IRI, pp. 129–136. IEEE (2013)
25. Tang, B., Sandhu, R.: Extending openstack access control with domain trust. In: Au, M.H., Carminati, B., Kuo, C.-C.J. (eds.) NSS 2014. LNCS, vol. 8792, pp. 54–69. Springer, Heidelberg (2014)
26. Tang, B., Sandhu, R., Li, Q.: Multi-tenancy authorization models for collaborative cloud services. In: Proc. of CTS, pp. 132–138. IEEE (2013)
27. Yong, J., Bertino, E., Roberts, M.T.D.: Extended RBAC with role attributes. In: Proc. of PACIS, pages 457–469 (2006)
28. Zhang, X., Oh, S., Sandhu, R.: PBDM: a flexible delegation model in RBAC. In: Proc. of SACMAT, pp. 149–157. ACM (2003)
29. Zhang, Z., Zhang, X., Sandhu, R.: ROBAC: Scalable role and organization based access control models. In: Proc. of CollaborateCom, pp. 1–9. IEEE (2006)

# Managing Multi-dimensional Multi-granular Security Policies Using Data Warehousing

Mahendra Pratap Singh[1], Shamik Sural[1], Vijayalakshmi Atluri[2],
Jaideep Vaidya[2(✉)], and Ussama Yakub[2]

[1] School of Information Technology, IIT Kharagpur, Kharagpur, India
{mp_singh,shamik}@sit.iitkgp.ernet.in
[2] MSIS Department, Rutgers University, Newark, NJ, USA
{ussama.yaqub,atluri,jsvaidya}@rutgers.edu

**Abstract.** Over the last several years, sophisticated access control models have been proposed to take into account different dimensions such as time, space, role, context, attribute, etc. These enable specification of fine grained access control policies that can better express evolving organizational needs. However, there is no comprehensive solution that can uniformly specify, evaluate, maintain and analyze this multitude of policies in a consistent fashion. In this paper, we show that specifying and enforcing access control policies of multiple granularities and dimensions can be transformed into the problem of storing and querying data at multiple granularities and dimensions. Specifically, we develop a unified schema to represent several standard access control policies and show how they can be automatically evaluated. We have implemented the system in Oracle, and evaluated its scalability.

## 1 Introduction

Owing to the growing application needs and changing environment, access control research has evolved significantly in the past few decades. This has led to broadening of the set of access control parameters by including novel attributes based on mobility, context, location, time, role, etc. Several models and research prototypes exist today that embody these concepts. In some cases, the more complicated models expand upon and enhance earlier ones, while others represent a rethinking of the fundamental manner in which access control should be done. These different access control models often attempt to enhance the expressive power by enabling specification of fine grained access control policies [20]. As a result, organizations can more precisely specify any high level abstract policy they wish to enforce or accurately comply with regulations such as HIPAA, FERPA, SOX and PCI. While it seems desirable to have highly granular access control from this perspective, the cost of managing, evaluating and maintaining the same could be prohibitively high. In a recent panel discussion [19], one of the specific questions discussed was "at what cost should we strive for a perfect, fine-grained policy?"

© Springer International Publishing Switzerland 2015
M. Qiu et al. (Eds.): NSS 2015, LNCS 9408, pp. 221–235, 2015.
DOI: 10.1007/978-3-319-25645-0_15

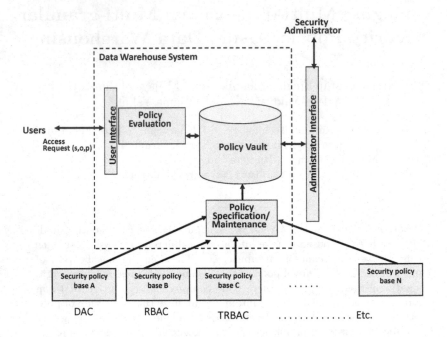

**Fig. 1.** System Architecture

Despite the number of highly granular access control models that exist in research literature, very few have found deployment in real life. This is due to the difficulty in specifying, enforcing and maintaining policies at different granularities in a usable fashion. Currently, access control is implemented through a careful examination of the stated policies and then choosing the most suitable tool available and configuring it manually. Suppose, certain resources are protected under one policy (say, Discretionary Access Control) and other resources are protected under a different policy (say, Role Based Access Control), one either has to have two separate security systems in place, or need to transform one policy into the other so that it can be enforced with the chosen tool. Moreover, it is also possible that some resources are protected under more than one security policy. Additionally, there could be certain policies that are specific to an organization and cannot be specified using a standard model. Such policies are often implemented as application code. All these factors make specification, management and enforcement of security policies difficult.

Ferraiolo and Atluri [11] first discussed the need for a meta-model. Following this, Barker [4] proposed an access control meta-model along with a logic language for describing the same. While Barker's work is a step in the direction of resolving the issue of multitude of access control models, it is limited to addressing the problem of specification alone. It does not take into account the policy evaluation and enforcement aspects. Flexibility is a key desirable feature, wherein applications can pick and choose the access control policy and its level of granularity, as necessary for different situations, users and resources. Therefore, what is needed is a comprehensive and flexible modeling methodology that allows for specification and evaluation at different granularity and dimensions. In this paper, we propose a comprehensive solution that provides all of these features.

Our key insight is that, while the multiple granularities, models and application domains make effective access control complex when viewed from a security perspective, the challenge of multi-resolution data has been effectively tackled by the database community, through the notion of a *data warehouse*. In this paper, we map the access control problem to the data warehouse environment, thus enabling specification and evaluation of flexible access control policies through data warehousing technology. Specifically, we demonstrate this with a commercially available data warehouse product, namely, Oracle. In particular, we show how Discretionary Access Control (DAC) [14,17], Mandatory Access Control (MAC) [7], Role Based Access Control (RBAC) [13] and Temporal Role Based Access Control (TRBAC) [5] policies can be specified in a unified manner and evaluated using the query processing ability of Oracle. Since Oracle is a general purpose software product that was not developed with modeling of access control systems in mind, we expect to face some performance issues. Hence, an extensive performance analysis using simulated data sets has been done, and we present these results in the paper.

The rest of the paper is organized as follows. Section 2 presents the overall data warehouse framework for specifying and enforcing access control policies. Section 3 shows how DAC, MAC, RBAC and TRBAC policies can be specified in this framework, while Section 4 describes how access requests are evaluated. Section 5 discusses our implementation in Oracle and presents the results of experimental evaluation. Related work is surveyed in Section 6 and finally, Section 7 concludes the paper, providing directions towards future research.

## 2   Framework

Figure 1 depicts the overall architecture of our proposed access control system that embeds data warehousing technology. The different policy bases at the bottom represent the different types of access control policies of each unit within an organization. These may be multi-granular and multi-dimensional in nature. While the specification module allows these policies to be specified in the data warehouse, the maintenance module ensures that changes to the local policies be reflected at the warehouse level. When users submit access requests, these are verified by the evaluation module. The administrator interface is meant to help the administrator specify and visualize the policies as well as visualize the results of making changes in the policies. Before going into the detailed discussion of how multi-granular and multi-dimensional access control policies can be specified and evaluated using data warehouse technologies, we first present a brief overview of data warehouses.

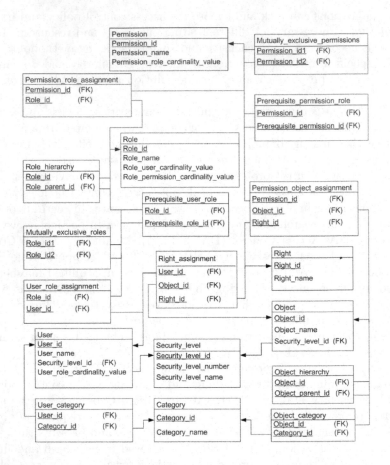

**Fig. 2.** Unified Schema for representing DAC, MAC and RBAC Access Control Policies

A data warehouse is a collection of integrated, subject-oriented databases, where each unit of data is relevant to some moment in time [9]. It is a repository of information that was extracted, integrated, summarized, and stored from multiple sources in order to support analysis queries of users. To facilitate complex analysis and visualization, a data warehouse employs a multi-dimensional model to capture all the dimensions of interest. These dimensions together uniquely form a set of numeric measures that are the objects of analysis. They may also be hierarchical.

The typical data models employed to specify a schema using which multi-dimensional data is stored are: *star schema, snowflake schema,* and the *fact constellation schema.* While star schema is the simplest among the three, the other two schemas are normalized, meaning that data can be stored in a less redundant fashion. Under the star schema, the database consists of a single fact table and one table for each dimension. The dimension tables are usu-

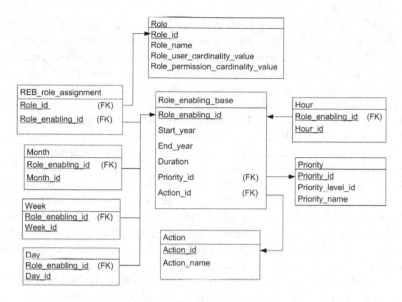

**Fig. 3.** Schema for representing Temporal RBAC Policies

ally de-normalized to provide symmetric access to the fact table. On the other hand, in snowflake schema, dimension tables are normalized, especially since de-normalization introduces scope for inconsistency, which will have a negative impact on the system integrity. It may, however, be noted that many of the data warehouse extensions/toolkits of commercial database management systems like Oracle, support multi-dimensional visualization of data from star schema only with a well-defined fact table. In order to meet both these requirements, in this paper, we have developed a suitable schema for supporting various access control models, which we discuss in the following section.

## 3    Policy Specification

Since DAC, MAC and RBAC along with its temporal extension TRBAC are some of the basic access control models, in this section, we present a unified schema for specifying policies supported by these models. Note that while our discussion below is limited to the four above-mentioned models only, in principle, more complex access control systems such as GTRBAC [16], STARBAC [2], etc., can also be modeled in the same framework.

Figures 2 and 3 present the unified schema that we have developed to specify DAC, MAC, RBAC and TRBAC policies in a consistent and integrated fashion. For the sake of clarity, the TRBAC scheme is shown separately in Figure 3. To enable unification of the four access control models, we use a common set of notations. For example, we use the term *user* to denote a subject (DAC and MAC terminology) as well as a user (RBAC and TRBAC terminology). Similarly, in RBAC and TRBAC, permissions are defined as *operations* on objects, whereas DAC and MAC use the term *right* to denote possible modes of accessing an object. In the unified models shown in Figures 2 and 3, we represent permissions as rights on objects. Thus, for representing the DAC policies, the relations *User*, *Object*, *Right* and *Right_assignment* are used. Of these, the relation *Right* contains all the different generic rights supported by a particular system. The relation *Right_assignment* acts as the fact table, while the other three relations serve as the dimension tables in the data warehousing terminology.

MAC models like the Bell-LaPadula model make use of security *levels* and *categories* for both users and objects. Each user belongs to only one security level and so does each object. However, each user or each object could belong to multiple categories. Owing to this, the security level is directly captured in the relations *User* and *Object*, whereas their categories are captured in the relations *User_category* and *Object_category*, respectively. In order to ensure normalization for avoiding potential inconsistencies, the descriptions for security levels and categories are stored in the relations *Security_level* and *Category*, respectively. It may be noted that, had we wanted to use strictly a star schema design, we would have de-normalized the *User* and *Object* relations to store the categories in them as well. Since, in MAC, there is no direct assignment of rights on objects to users, rather, they get appropriate read and write rights by virtue of their respective security levels and categories, there is no explicit fact table for modeling MAC.

The rest of the relations in the schema shown in Figure 2 are used to specify RBAC policies. The proposed schema supports the basic RBAC model (RBAC0 as mentioned in [23]) as well as role hierarchy and various types of constraints (respectively RBAC1 and RBAC2 of [23]). The primary relations used to model RBAC0 are *User*, *Role*, *Permission*, *User_role_assignment*, *Permission_role_Assignment* and *Permission_object_assignment*. Of these, the *User_role_assignment* and *Permission_role_assignment* relations respectively capture the user assignment (UA) and permission assignment (PA) relations of RBAC, while *Permission_object_assignment* maintains the definitions of the various permissions in terms of the operations (rights) on different objects. Each user can belong to one or more roles and each role can have one or more permissions associated with it. A single permission can represent one or more operations on objects. The fact tables relevant for RBAC, thus, are *User_role_assignment*, *Permission_role_assignment* and *Permission_object_assignment*. The role hierarchy is maintained in the relation named *Role_hierarchy*.

RBAC supports a variety of constraints, which can be used to specify different types of access control policies. One of the most important policies supported by RBAC is Separation of Duty (SoD), which is enforced through mutually exclusive roles. Our schema captures the SoD requirements in the relation named *Mutually_exclusive_roles*. At a more granular level, SoD can be provided by specifying mutually exclusive permissions in the *Mutually_exclusive_permissions* relation. RBAC also supports pre-requisite constraints and cardinality constraints [23]. Four types of cardinality constraints are supported in the proposed schema. These are: maximum number of users that can be assigned to each role (column *Role_user_cardinality_value* of the *Role* relation), maximum number of permissions that can be assigned to each role (column *Role_permission_cardinality_value* of the *Role* relation), maximum number of roles that can be assigned to each user (column *User_role_cardinality_value* of the *User* relation) and maximum number of roles that can be assigned to each permission (column *Permission_role_cardinality_value* of the *Permission* relation). Finally, the relations *Prerequisite_user_role* and *Prerequisite_permission_role* are used to define policies on pre-requisite roles for users and permissions, respectively.

TRBAC [5], an extension of the RBAC model, imposes temporal constraints on each role by restricting the set of time intervals during which the role can be enabled. It is specified in a Role Enabling Base (REB) and is expressed as $\langle[begin, end], P\rangle$, where $P$ is a periodic expression denoting an infinite set of periodic time intervals, while *begin* and *end* are date expressions respectively imposing lower and upper bounds on the set of time intervals represented by $P$. Each periodic expression is written in terms of a set of *Calendars*. Enabling or disabling of a role $r$ is captured using an event expression of the form *enable r* or *disable r* along with the corresponding periodic expression. In Figure 3, the relation *REB_role_assignment* serves as the fact table linking each role with its REB entry. The various periodic events are specified in the relation *Role_enabling_base*, which when joined with the other relations shown in the figure, returns the various time intervals during which any given role is enabled or disabled and the corresponding priority.

As in the case of DAC and MAC, for RBAC and TRBAC also, we normalize the dimension tables to ensure protection against possible inconsistencies that might otherwise creep in, if a pure star schema design is used. To support multi-granular access control, we use a relation named *Object_hierarchy* for representing hierarchy among objects like file-folder-drive-disk, etc.

## 4 Policy Evaluation

Once the policies have been appropriately specified, the next related issue is that of policy evaluation and aggregation. Some examples of how different access control requests using DAC, RBAC and TRBAC can be expressed in the form of queries are given below. Similar queries can be framed for MAC as well.

First, consider the case where the administrator wants to know the complete set of DAC privileges (rights) various users have on different objects. The corresponding query can be written as follows:

```
Query: Q1
SELECT DISTINCT ra.user_id, user_name, ra.object_id, object_name,
ra.right_id, right_name
FROM user, object, right, right_assignment ra
WHERE ra.user_id = user.user_id AND ra.object_id = object.object_id
AND ra.right_id = right.right_id;
```

If a particular user (denoted by #u) requests an access that exercises a particular right (denoted by #r) on a particular object (denoted by #o), the following query needs to be executed. If it returns zero, the access is denied; otherwise, the access is granted.

```
Query: Q2
SELECT COUNT(*) FROM right_assignment ra WHERE ra.user_id = #u
AND ra.object_id = #o AND ra.right_id = #r;
```

Next, we consider RBAC related queries. In an RBAC system employing the schema shown in Figure 2, consider that the administrator wants to retrieve the complete role hierarchy of the organization. The following query can be used to get the result.

```
Query: Q3
WITH recursive_rh (rk, rpk) AS
(SELECT role_id, role_parent_id FROM role_hierarchy
WHERE role_parent_id IS NULL UNION ALL
SELECT rh.role_id, rh.role_parent_id
FROM role_hierarchy rh, recursive_rh rrh
WHERE rh.role_parent_id = rrh.rk)
SELECT DISTINCT rk, rpk FROM recursive_rh ORDER BY rk;
```

In the above recursive query Q3, the complete role hierarchy is traversed using the relation *role_hierarchy*, which is joined with itself through the attributes *role_id* and *role_parent_id*. While this form of the query returns the role hierarchy in terms of the ids of various roles and their parents, these ids could be further joined with the *role* relation to obtain the corresponding role names as well.

For enforcing access control in RBAC, consider the situation in which a user #u requests an access that exercises a right #r on an object #o (and hence the corresponding permission is *r on o*), the following query needs to be executed. If it returns zero, the access is denied; otherwise, the access is granted.

```
Query: Q4
WITH recursive_rh (rk, rpk) AS
(SELECT rh.role_id, rh.role_parent_id
FROM role_hierarchy rh, user_role_assignment ura
WHERE rh.role_parent_id = ura.role_id
AND ura.user_id = #u UNION ALL
SELECT rh.role_id, rh.role_parent_id
FROM role_hierarchy rh, recursive_rh rrh
WHERE rh.role_parent_id = rrh.rk)
SELECT COUNT(*) FROM (SELECT poa.object_id, poa.right_id
FROM permission_object_assignment poa
WHERE poa.permission_id IN (SELECT  pra.permission_id
FROM permission_role_assignment pra WHERE pra.role_id IN
(SELECT rk from recursive_rh UNION
SELECT role_id FROM user_role_assignment WHERE user_id = #u)))
WHERE object_id = #o AND right_id = #r;
```

Similar to the way the role hierarchy has been used recursively in the above two queries to find all the roles assigned to a user (directly or indirectly), the object hierarchy can also be used to determine the objects that can be accessed by a user (either the user directly has the requisite right on the object or has the requisite right on another object higher up in the object hierarchy). This can be done using the query shown below, thus depicting the ability of the proposed framework to handle multi-granular access control policies.

```
Query: Q5
WITH recursive_oh (ok, opk) AS
(SELECT object_id, object_parent_id FROM object_hierarchy
WHERE object_parent_id IS NULL UNION ALL
SELECT oh.object_id,oh.object_parent_id FROM object_hierarchy oh,
recursive_oh roh WHERE oh.object_parent_id = roh.ok)
SELECT COUNT(*) FROM
(SELECT object_id, right_id FROM permission_object_assignment poa,
recursive_oh roh WHERE roh.ok = poa.object_id AND permission_id IN
(SELECT permission_id FROM permission_role_assignment pra,
user_role_assignment ura
WHERE ura.user_id = #u AND ura.role_id = pra.role_id))
WHERE object_id = #o AND right_id = #r;
```

In contrast to the above five queries, for TRBAC queries, we not only need to check whether the user has the requisite rights on an object, the current time of access should also satisfy the conditions during which the corresponding roles are enabled. If we denote the current system time as SYSDATE, the corresponding year, month, week, day and hour can be easily extracted by using built-in functions in the database management system providing data warehousing support including Oracle.

```
Query: Q6
Augment Query Q4 with:
AND EXISTS
(SELECT * FROM recursive_rh rrh, reb_role_assignment rra,
role_enabling_base reb WHERE rrh.rk = rra.role_id
AND rra.role_enabling_id = reb.role_enabling_id
AND (SYSDATE BETWEEN start_year AND end_year))
AND (SELECT EXTRACT (MONTH FROM SYSDATE) FROM dual) IN
(SELECT month_id FROM recursive_rh rrh, reb_role_assignment rra,
month WHERE rrh.rk = rra.role_id
AND rra.role_enabling_id = month.role_enabling_id)
AND (SELECT TO_CHAR(SYSDATE, 'W') FROM dual) IN
(SELECT week_id FROM recursive_rh rrh, reb_role_assignment rra,
week WHERE rrh.rk = rra.role_id
AND rra.role_enabling_id = week.role_enabling_id)
AND (SELECT TO_CHAR(SYSDATE, 'D') FROM dual) IN
(SELECT day_id FROM recursive_rh rrh, reb_role_assignment rra,
day WHERE rrh.rk = rra.role_id
AND rra.role_enabling_id = day.role_enabling_id)
AND EXISTS
(SELECT * FROM recursive_rh rrh, reb_role_assignment rra,
```

```
role_enabling_base reb, hour WHERE rrh.rk = rra.role_id
AND rra.role_enabling_id = reb.role_enabling_id
AND rra.role_enabling_id = hour.role_enabling_id
AND TO_CHAR(SYSDATE,'HH24')>= hour_id
AND TO_CHAR(SYSDATE,'HH24')<=(hour_id+duration));
```

The above query first finds the roles associated with the given user either directly or through the role hierarchy and then checks if any of those roles allows the requested access, and finally, whether those roles are currently enabled as specified in the REB (relation *Role_enabling_base* and its other associated relations in Figure 3). It effectively utilizes Query Q4 as a sub-query and additionally checks for the role enabling conditions.

**Table 1.** Data Set Details showing the Number of Rows in various Relations

| Data Sets | #Users | #Objects | #Rights | #Roles | #Permissions | #Perm Role Assignments | #User Role Assignments |
|-----------|--------|----------|---------|--------|--------------|------------------------|------------------------|
| Data Set 1 | 100 | 100 | 5 | 10 | 150 | 150 | 200 |
| Data Set 2 | 500 | 500 | 10 | 50 | 750 | 750 | 1000 |
| Data Set 3 | 500 | 1000 | 10 | 50 | 1500 | 1500 | 1000 |
| Data Set 4 | 1000 | 5000 | 10 | 100 | 7500 | 7500 | 2000 |
| Data Set 5 | 5000 | 25000 | 10 | 100 | 40000 | 40000 | 10000 |

As mentioned before, the goal of this work is to provide a unified framework for specifying and enforcing different kinds of access control policies. Assume that the different units of an organization have already implemented DAC, MAC, RBAC or TRBAC policies independently. The data needs to be suitably populated from the various units in the schema shown in Figures 2 and 3. If a unified access is to be given when a user #u makes an access request in a certain mode (i.e., he wants to exercise right #r) on a certain object (say #o), the individual policies will be evaluated. The final decision whether to actually provide the requested access or not will depend on a meta policy about how to combine the existing ones. For example, if the meta policy is that a user would be given access if at least one of DAC, MAC, RBAC and TRBAC allows him access, then we have to evaluate the DAC query Q2, the RBAC query Q4 or Q5 depending on the granularity of access, the TRBAC query Q6 and the applicable MAC query (not shown here for brevity, can be built in a similar manner). If any of the queries allows access, the request will be granted. Implementation of other policy combination mechanisms like "Allow access if all the policies allow access", "Allow access if majority of the policies allow access", etc., would be a simple extension of this concept.

While we have primarily focused on evaluation of administrative and user queries, other queries to check for violation of Separation of Duty, Cardinality constraint and Pre-requisite constraint can be easily developed on the schema of Figures 2 and 3.

# 5    Experimental Evaluation

In this section, we present implementation details along with results of experiments on the scalability of the proposed approach. The schemas shown in Figures 2 and 3 of Section 3 were instantiated as database tables in Oracle 12c on a 3.10 GHz Intel i5 machine having 4 GB RAM running 64 bit Windows 7 operating system. Oracle Analytic Workspace Manager is used for defining, maintaining and visualizing the data cubes.

In Table 1, we show the details of five synthetic data sets with different feature sizes that we have created. From Data Set 1 to Data Set 5, sizes of various relations in terms of their number of rows increase. In the table, we show the main relations that affect the query execution time. The other relations are populated based on the data included in the ones shown here. In Data Set 1, the relations *User*, *Object* and *Right* have respectively 100, 100 and 5 rows. The number of rows in the relation *Right_assignment* is such that each subject at least has one right on an object and each object is accessible to at least one subject in some mode. It may be noted that, the number of possible generic rights has not been varied to a large extent across the data sets since there is usually a limited number of such operations possible in a system. For example, for access control in an operating system, the possible rights could be *read*, *write*, *own*, *execute* and *append*, while there would be rights like *select*, *insert*, *update*, *delete*, *grant* and *revoke* in a database system, irrespective of the number of users.

In order to emulate real-world situations, we have considered up to four levels in the role hierarchy for each of the data sets. Further, every role has been considered to be included in at least one role hierarchy. The choice for the sizes of the various parameters shown in Table 1 was made as follows. The number of users was varied from 100 to 5000 representing small to large organizations. The number of permissions was chosen in a way that every object was included in at least one permission for access in one of the valid number of ways specified in the form of rights. The number of roles was kept at 10% of the number of users for Data sets 1 to 4. For Data set 5 (with 5000 users), we have the same number of roles as Data set 4 (with 1000 users) since, beyond a certain point, the number of roles in an organization does not increase even if there are more number of users. On an average, two roles were considered per user for all the data sets. However, while assigning roles to users, it was ensured that every user belongs to at least one role and some of the users are assigned to more than two roles. Assignment of permissions to roles was also done in a similar manner.

For every data set, each of the six queries Q1-Q6 was executed 30 times with different inputs (Queries 1 and 3 do not need any input parameter, but were still run for 30 times to average out the effect of other system processes). Table 2 shows the results of executing the six queries. The average execution time in seconds over the 30 samples is reported in the table. It is observed that, even for a 50 fold increase in the number of users, 250 fold increase in the number of objects and more than 250 fold increase in the number of permissions, the execution time of the queries does not increase significantly. Query 1, which is the most expensive, returning all the rights of all the users on all the objects, also runs in

**Table 2.** Query Execution Time (seconds)

| Data Sets | Query 1 | Query 2 | Query 3 | Query 4 | Query 5 | Query 6 |
|---|---|---|---|---|---|---|
| Data Set 1 | 0.05 | 0.01 | 0.01 | 0.02 | 0.03 | 0.06 |
| Data Set 2 | 0.09 | 0.01 | 0.01 | 0.02 | 0.03 | 0.06 |
| Data Set 3 | 0.13 | 0.02 | 0.01 | 0.03 | 0.03 | 0.07 |
| Data Set 4 | 0.23 | 0.03 | 0.02 | 0.05 | 0.04 | 0.08 |
| Data Set 5 | 0.47 | 0.04 | 0.03 | 0.06 | 0.05 | 0.09 |

less than 0.5 second for data set 5. The actual enforcement queries (Q2, Q4, Q5 and Q6) run in less than 0.15 second. It may be noted that, Q2 (DAC enforcement query) takes less time than Q4 and Q5 (RBAC enforcement query) as well as TRBAC enforcement query Q6, since the RBAC and TRBAC queries consider the entire role/object hierarchy to determine whether the requested access may be given to the user or not. On the other hand, DAC directly checks for the availability of the requisite right in a single relation. It may, thus, be concluded that the proposed framework is quite scalable from small to large organizations employing DAC, RBAC or TRBAC. We have not separately reported the results for MAC, which are also of the same order as the other two.

## 6   Related Work

To cater to today's new applications and environments, traditional access control models have been incorporated with a number of attributes including those based on the mobility, context, location, time, role, etc., resulting in a spectrum of access control models including: Discretionary Access Control (DAC) [14,17], Mandatory Access Control (MAC) [7], Role Based Access Control (RBAC) [13], and temporal, geospatial and mobile data authorization models. In addition, several variants of RBAC have been proposed that extend RBAC in temporal, spatial and spatio-temporal dimensions, thereby providing access control at higher levels of granularity. These include temporal RBAC (e.g., TRBAC [5] and GTRBAC [16]), spatial RBAC (e.g., Geo-RBAC [8] and LRBAC [21]) and spatio-temporal RBAC models [1,26] (e.g., STRBAC [22] and STARBAC [2]).

There are attempts to develop unified policy languages to specify different types of policies. For example, the OASIS standard eXtensible Access Control Markup Language (XACML) [24] and the Ponder policy specification language [10] provide partial solution to meet general policy specification needs. XACML is both a policy language as well as an access control decision request/response language (both encoded in XML). The former describes general access control requirements, while the latter can be used to address queries like whether a given action should be allowed, and also to interpret the result. XACML suffers from the drawback that its Policy Decision Point (PDP) is stateless, thus limiting the kind of policies that can be meaningfully specified and enforced. On the other hand, Ponder is a declarative object oriented language used to specify security and management policies for distributed object systems. Policies are expressed in its specification language and enforcement is done by mapping into the chosen access control mechanisms. This, effectively, separates a policy from its implementation.

In response to questions raised by Ferraiolo and Atluri in a panel discussion at SACMAT 2008 [11] about an access control meta model to unify the large variety of existing access control policies, Barker proposed a meta model for access control and demonstrated that several access control models can be instantiated as special cases of this meta model [4]. Barker advocates that existing access control models are essentially based on a small number of primitive notions, and states that the degree of overlap among existing access control models is significant. He demonstrates that multiple access control models can be expressed in terms of these primitive notions, and states that new access control models can be developed by simple combination of the access control primitives in novel ways. Several competing proposals have been made for defining a general, declarative framework that can specify a variety of access control policies. This includes the RT family of role-trust models [18], FAF language [15] and SecPAL [6]. Beyond providing a unifying model as these proposals do, the policy machine [12] also presents a meta-model for specifying generic access control policies, and offers a mechanism for implementing the unifying model.

However, all these attempts are limited only to the specification of different types of access control and to some extent their enforcement. They do not address the issue of multiple granularities as well as configuring, implementing and maintaining these variety of policies that are highly granular and multi dimensional in nature. Note that while there has been some work in securing the data in a warehouse [3,25], our paper employs the warehouse to maintain the access control data.

## 7 Conclusions and Future Work

In this paper, we have presented a novel approach towards unifying different access control models using data warehousing design concepts and shown how off-the-shelf data analysis tools like Oracle Analytic Workspace Manager can be used to specify and evaluate various access control policies. In particular, we have proposed a common schema for representing DAC, MAC, RBAC and TRBAC policies. Separation of duty, pre-requisite constraints and cardinality constraints are also supported by the proposed model. Relations for capturing role and object hierarchies included in the schema facilitate specification of policies at different levels of granularity. Experimental results show that the proposed schema when implemented in a commercial database environment like Oracle running even on standard desktop PCs is quite scalable for a 50 fold increase in the number of users and 250 fold increase in the number of objects. Our proposed framework is extensible to other access control models and can easily support policies with multiple granularities and dimensions. It also provides other features required of an access control system like policy combination and policy analysis. In the future, we plan to develop these extensions.

# References

1. Abdunabi, R., Al-Lail, M., Ray, I., France, R.B.: Specification, validation, and enforcement of a generalized spatio-temporal role-based access control model. IEEE Systems Journal **7**(3), 501–515 (2013)
2. Aich, S., Sural, S., Majumdar, A.K.: STARBAC: Spatiotemporal Role Based Access Control. In: Meersman, R., Tari, Z. (eds.) OTM 2007, Part II. LNCS, vol. 4804, pp. 1567–1582. Springer, Heidelberg (2007)
3. Ali, S., Rauf, A., Khusro, S., Zubair, M., Farman, H., Ullah, S.: An authorization model to access the summarized data of data warehouse. Life Sciences Journal **11**(6s) (2014)
4. Barker, S.: The next 700 access control models or a unifying meta-model? In: ACM Symposium on Access Control Models and technologies, pp. 187–196 (2009)
5. Bertino, E., Bonatti, P.A., Ferrari, E.: TRBAC: A temporal role-based access control model. ACM Trans. on Information and System Security **4**(3), 191–233 (2001)
6. Becker, M., Fournet, C., Gordon, A.: Design and semantics of a decentralized authorization language. In: IEEE Computer Security Foundations Symposium, pp. 3–15 (2007)
7. Bell, D., LaPadula, L.: Secure computer systems: Unified exposition and multics interpretation. Technical Report MTR-2997, The Mitre Corporation, March 1976
8. Bertino, E., Catania, B., Damiani, M.L., Perlasca, P.: GEO-RBAC: a spatially aware RBAC. In: ACM Symposium on Access Control Models and Technologies, pp. 29–37. ACM, June 2005
9. Chaudhuri, S., Dayal, U.: An overview of data warehousing and OLAP technology. SIGMOD Record **26**(1), 65–74 (1997)
10. Damianou, N., Dulay, N., Lupu, E.C., Sloman, M.: The ponder policy specification language. In: Sloman, M., Lobo, J., Lupu, E.C. (eds.) POLICY 2001. LNCS, vol. 1995, pp. 18–38. Springer, Heidelberg (2001)
11. Ferraiolo, D., Atluri, V.: A meta model for access control: why is it needed and is it even possible to achieve? In: ACM Symposium on Access Control Models and Technologies, pp. 153–154 (2008)
12. Ferraiolo, D.F., Atluri, V., Gavrila, S.I.: The policy machine: A novel architecture and framework for access control policy specification and enforcement. Journal of Systems Architecture - Embedded Systems Design **57**(4), 412–424 (2011)
13. Ferraiolo, D.F., Sandhu, R., Gavrila, S., Kuhn, D.R., Chandramouli, R.: Proposed NIST standard for role-based access control. ACM Trans. on Information and System Security **4**(3), 224–274 (2001)
14. Graham, G., Denning, P.: Protection principles and practice. In: AFIPS Spring Joint Computer Conference, pp. 417–429 (1972)
15. Jajodia, S., Samarati, P., et al.: Flexible support for multiple access control policies. ACM Tran. on Database Systems **26**(2), 214–260 (2001)
16. Joshi, J., Bertino, E., Latif, U., Ghafoor, A.: A generalized temporal role-based access control model. IEEE Trans. Knowl. Data Eng. **17**(1), 4–23 (2005)
17. Lampson, B.: Protection. In: 5th Princeton Symposium on Information Science and Systems, pp. 437–443 (1971)
18. Li, N., Mitchell, J., Winsborough, W.: Design of a role-based trust-management framework. In: IEEE Symposium on Security and Privacy, p. 114 (2002)
19. Molloy, I., Tripunitara, M.V., et al.: Panel on granularity in access control. In: ACM Symposium on Access Control Models and Technologies, pp. 85–86 (2013)

20. National Institute of Standards and Technology, and National Security Agency. A survey of access control methods. Technical report (2009)
21. Ray, I., Kumar, M., Yu, L.: LRBAC: a location-aware role-based access control model. In: Bagchi, A., Atluri, V. (eds.) ICISS 2006. LNCS, vol. 4332, pp. 147–161. Springer, Heidelberg (2006)
22. Ray, I., Toahchoodee, M.: A spatio temporal role based access control model. In: IFIP WG 11.3 Working Conference on Data and Applications Security, pp. 211–226 (2007)
23. Sandhu, R., et al.: Role-based Access Control Models. IEEE Computer, 38–47 (1996)
24. OASIS XACML Technical Committee. OASIS extensible access control markup language (XACML) version 2.0
25. Thuraisingham, B., Kantarcioglu, M., et al.: Extended rbac-based design and implementation for a secure data warehouse. International Journal of Business Intelligence and Data Mining $2(1)$, 367–382 (2007)
26. Toahchoodee, M., Ray, I.: On the formalization and analysis of a spatio-temporal role-based access control model. Journal of Computer Security $19(3)$, 399–452 (2011)

# Applied Cryptography

# CLKS: Certificateless Keyword Search on Encrypted Data

Qingji Zheng[1]([✉]), Xiangxue Li[2], and Aytac Azgin[1]

[1] Huawei Research Center, Santa Clara, CA 95050, USA
{qingji.zheng,aytac.azgin}@huawei.com
[2] Department of Computer Science & Technology,
East China Normal University, Shanghai, China
xxli@cs.ecnu.edu.cn

**Abstract.** Keyword search on encrypted data enables one to search keyword ciphertexts without compromising keyword security. We further investigate this problem and propose a novel variant, dubbed *certificateless keyword search on encrypted data* (CLKS). CLKS not only supports keyword search on encrypted data, but also brings promising features due to the certificateless cryptography. In contrast to the certificated-based keyword search, CLKS requires no validation on the trustworthy of the public key before encrypting keywords; in contrast to the identity-based keyword search, CLKS prevents the key issuer (e.g., key generator center) from penetrating any information on keyword ciphertexts by leveraging the capability of accessing all data users' (partial) private keys. Specifically, we rigorously define the syntax and security definitions for CLKS, and present the construction that is provably secure in the standard model under the Decisional Linear assumption. We implemented the proposed CLKS scheme and evaluated its performance. To the best of our knowledge, this is the *first* attempt to integrate certificateless cryptography with keyword search on encrypted data.

**Keywords:** Keyword search · Certificateless cryptography

## 1 Introduction

Cloud computing enables data owners to outsource their data to the cloud at affordable price and access/share the outsourced data with other users. The outsourcing, however, separates the data ownership and its (physical) storage ownership and brings the security concern [18, 20, 33] such as data privacy. Though it is natural for data owners to encrypt their own data before outsourcing, the encryption operation makes some useful functions, such as keyword search, become infeasible. Fortunately, the subject of keyword search on encrypted data has been extensively studied and a large number of solutions have been proposed. Roughly speaking, keyword search on encrypted data can be divided into three categories according to the key distribution/generation setting: symmetric

© Springer International Publishing Switzerland 2015
M. Qiu et al. (Eds.): NSS 2015, LNCS 9408, pp. 239–253, 2015.
DOI: 10.1007/978-3-319-25645-0_16

key based keyword search, certificate-based keyword search[1] and identity-based (or attribute-based) keyword search[2]. Comparing with symmetric key based keyword search, the last two kinds of keyword search are more flexible and promising because they do not require any key sharing between the data owner and the target user who the data will be shared with.

For certificate-based keyword search, when the data owner wants to share the data with a target user, he will encrypt the data with the target user's public key. Note that before this operation, the data owner needs to validate the certificate which binds the target user's identity and the corresponding public key in order to assure that the public key is really associated with the target user, which needs to rely on some trust/certificate management system such as PKI. In addition, the data owner might need to conduct costly certificate chain verification (until finding a certificate authority he trusts) for certificate validation. In order to mitigate this downside, identity-based (attribute-based) keyword search [28,31,34] is introduced where the public key is exactly the same as the target user's identity (attributes) and therefore there is no need to validate the correctness of the public key. Despite its benefits, identity-based (attribute-based) keyword search suffers from the key escrow problem that the key generation authority has full access to all data users' private keys.

**Contribution.** We propose *certificateless keyword search on encrypted data* (CLKS), which preserves the merits of identity-based keyword search (e.g., no certificate management and validation) without inherent key escrow problem. To be specific, we follow the basic principle underlying the certificateless cryptography: treating the user's identity as part of the public key and letting the user' private key consisting of two components, one generated by the key generation center and the other chosen by the user. Thus, CLKS allows users to put less trust on the key generation center. We summarize our contribution as follows and compare three kinds of keyword search solutions in Table 1:

- We first integrate the certificateless cryptography with keyword search on encrypted data. We formalize the notion for CLKS, and rigorously define its security properties.
- We present a CLKS scheme that is provably secure in the standard model under the Decisional Linear assumption. Similar to other certificateless primitives, the proposed certificateless keyword search scheme leverages the identity as user's partial public key and eliminates the key escrow problem. We implemented the proposed scheme and conducted the performance evaluation on real data to show its feasibility.

---

[1] Certificate-based keyword search means keyword search on encrypted data in traditional public key setting, where users generate the public/private by themselves and the certificate is used to bind the user identity and the public key.

[2] Attribute-based keyword search can be treated as the generalized version of identity-based keyword search. We put them together because of the same key generation manner.

**Table 1.** Comparison of three kinds of keyword search primitives that are involved with the public/private keys.

| Type of keyword search | Who generates user's private key | Required trust Model/Infrastructure |
|---|---|---|
| Certificate-based | User | Certificate binds the user identity and public key |
| Identity(attribute)-based | Third party authority | Fully trusted third party authority |
| Certificateless (our paper) | User and third party authority | Honest-but-curious third party authority |

**Organization.** Section 2 describes the related work. Section 3 presents cryptographic assumptions and primitives. Section 4 presents the system and threat model, and Section 5 formalizes the syntax and security definitions. Section 6 presents the main construction Section 7 presents the performance.

## 2   Related Work

We briefly review the relevant techniques on keyword search on encrypted data, which are separated into three categories as follows:

**Symmetric Key Based Keyword Search.** It allows the data owner to encrypt keywords and the corresponding data, and outsource keyword ciphertexts and data ciphertexts to the remote server. Only the data owner, or someone with the symmetric key, can generate the search token in order to ask the cloud to conduct search on keyword ciphertexts. [27] proposed the first symmetric key based keyword search scheme. Many variants, e.g., [8,11,12,14,17,22,23] have been proposed with various features, for example, improved security [14], dynamic support [22], UC security [23], verifiability [11] and multi-user sharing [21]. The main advantage of the symmetric key based keyword search is its high efficiency since it does not involve any costly public key operations (e.g. exponentiation, pairing). In the data sharing scenario, however, the technique requires the data owner and the target user (or remote server) sharing some common secret [21].

**Certificate-Based Keyword Search.** For certificate-based keyword search, the data owner encrypts keywords and data with the public key of the target user, so that the target user can use his own private key to generate the search token and then conduct the search on keyword ciphertexts. Many solutions, e.g., [1,4,5,7,9,10,26,29,30], have been proposed after [6] initiated the first study. While certificate-based keyword search is more flexible compared with symmetric key based keyword search, it requires the data owner validating the target user's public key before encrypting keywords. The trust and certificate management infrastructure, e.g., PKI, has been introduced to facilitate the validation process.

**Identity-Based (attribute-based) Keyword Search.** For identity-based (attribute- based) keyword search, the data owner encrypts the keyword and data with the target user's identity (or attributes in attribute-based keyword search). The target user, after acquiring the private key from the key generation authority, can generate the search token and then conduct search on keyword ciphertexts. [31] presented the first identity-based keyword search scheme and

[28,34] independently introduced the attribute-based keyword search. In this setting, data owner does not need to validate whether the used public key is associated with the target user or not, since the public key is exactly the same as the user's identity or attributes. While it mitigates the certificate management issue, it indeed introduces another issue – key escrow problem, since the key generation authority can access all users' private keys.

## 3    Preliminaries

Let $x \xleftarrow{R} X$ denote selecting an element $x$ from the set $X$ uniformly at random. Let $\mathcal{I}$ be the user universe where each user is associated to a unique identity id.

Let $(e, p, g, G, G_T) \leftarrow \mathsf{BMP}(1^\ell)$ be the function that generates a bilinear map $e : G \times G \to G_T$ by taking as input a security parameter $\ell$, such that $p$ is an $\ell$-bit prime, $G$ and $G_T$ are two cyclic groups of prime order $p$ and $g$ is a random generator of group $G$. The bilinear map $e$ should satisfy (i) $\forall a, b \in \mathbb{Z}_p$, $e(g^a, g^b) = e(g, g)^{ab}$; (ii) $e(g, g) \neq 1$ and (iii) $e$ can be computed efficiently.

We assume that the identities are distinct $n$-bit numbers. Let $H_1 : \{0,1\}^n \to G$, $H_2 : \{0,1\}^* \to \mathbb{Z}_p^*$, where $H_1$ is a function mapping id to an element in $G$ (defined as in section 6) and $H_2$ is modeled as a collision-resistant hash function.

**Decisional Linear (DL) Assumption** Let $(e, p, g, G, G_T) \leftarrow \mathsf{BMP}(1^\ell)$. Given $g, h, f, Q \xleftarrow{R} G$ and $g^{r_2}, h^{r_1}$, where $r_1, r_2 \xleftarrow{R} \mathbb{Z}_p^*$ are unknown, the DL assumption states that any probabilistic polynomial-time algorithm $\mathcal{A}$ can determine whether $Q = f^{r_1 + r_2}$ or not at most with a negligible advantage with respect to the security parameter $\ell$, where the "advantage" is defined as

$$\mathsf{Adv}_{DL}(\ell) = |\Pr[\mathcal{A}(g, h, f, g^{r_2}, h^{r_1}, f^{r_1+r_2}) = 1] - \Pr[\mathcal{A}(g, h, f, g^{r_2}, h^{r_1}, Q) = 1]|.$$

## 4    System and Threat Model

**System Model.** We consider the system model as shown in Figure 1, consisting of three entities: the key generation center KGC issuing partial private keys to data users, the cloud server providing storage and search services, and data users (i.e., data owner and target users). The data owner encrypts his data (data files and keywords that index the data files) with the target user's public key (note that the target user can be either himself or the user who the data will be shared with). The data owner outsources to the cloud keyword ciphertexts, data file ciphertexts and the mappings between the keyword ciphertexts and data file ciphertexts (given a keyword ciphertext, the mapping can be used to find the relevant data file ciphertexts). With his own private key, the target user can generate a search token, which is sent to the cloud, so that the cloud can conduct keyword search on the keyword ciphertexts and return the corresponding data file ciphertexts. Since the data files can be encrypted by with hybrid encryption with various public key encryption, e.g., certificateless encryption [2] and certificateless proxy re-encryption [32], for simplicity, in the rest of paper we only consider how to encrypt keywords in the certificateless setting. We also assume that there exists a proper authentication protocol allowing KGC to authenticate the users' identities when issuing the partial private keys.

**Application Example.** For illustrating the model visually, we consider the application of sharing Electronic Health Record (EHRs): The health service vendor (e.g., software infrastructure) acts as key generation center, and patients can be the data owners of EHRs, and will share EHRs with professionals for treatment purpose. When the user (either patients or professionals) registers the system, he will be assigned with a partial private key with respect to his unique identity and can generate the private/public key. To share EHRs with a professional, the patient can use that professional's public key (requiring no validation of the public key) to encrypt the indexed keywords (e.g. age, name, DOB etc.) and store the encrypted keywords and the associated encrypted EHRs in the storage system. The professional then generates the tokens based on keywords together with his own private key, and asks the storage system to return the encrypted EHRs having matched keywords. We can see that the benefit is that the vendor cannot leverage its knowledge on partial private keys to learn extra information from the encrypted index, and the patients require no validation on public key.

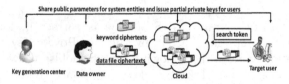

**Fig. 1.** The system model where the certificateless keyword search scheme can operate.

**Threat Model.** Similar to the threat model in the certificateless setting, we assume that the KGC cannot be fully trusted. That is, the KGC follows the protocol specification honestly but might attempt to use the information he obtained to penetrate more information. We assume that the users might be malicious, meaning that the users might pretend to be some target user and distribute the fake public key (i.e., the public key is different from that published by the target user) on behalf of the target user in order to learn information about the target user's ciphertexts. We assume that the cloud server is honest-but-curious, meaning that it will honestly execute the pre-defined protocols, but attempt to learn as much private information as possible. In addition, we assume that the KGC and the users cannot collude together.

## 5    Definitions

**Definition 1.** *A* CLKS *scheme is associated with the keyword space* $\mathcal{M}$ *and the identity space* $\mathcal{I}$ *and defined by seven algorithms as follows:*

- Setup($1^\ell$): *This algorithm, run by the KGC, takes as input a security parameter $\ell$ and returns the system parameter* param *and master key* mk. *The* param *is made publicly known and* mk *is kept private. For simplicity, we implicitly assume the following algorithms take* param *as part of inputs.*
- Gen-Partial-Private-Key(mk, id): *This algorithm, run by the KGC, takes as input* mk *and the user* id, *and generates a partial private key* $psk_{id}$, *which is sent to the user via a secure channel.*
- Gen-Private-Key($psk_{id}$): *This algorithm, run by the user, takes as input* $psk_{id}$, *and returns a complete private key* $sk_{id}$, *which is kept private.*
- Gen-Public-Key($sk_{id}$, $psk_{id}$): *This algorithm, run by the user, takes as input the* $sk_{id}$ *and* $psk_{id}$, *and returns a public key* $pk_{id}$.
- Enc($pk_{id}$, id, kw): *This algorithm, run by any user, takes as input the the target user's public key* $pk_{id}$, *identity* id *and the keyword* kw, *and returns a ciphertext* cph.
- Gen-Token($sk_{id}$, kw): *This algorithm, run by the user* id, *takes as input the* $sk_{id}$ *and the keyword* kw, *and returns a search token* token.
- Match(token, cph): *This algorithm, run by the cloud server (or entities holding keyword ciphertexts), takes as input the search token* token *and a ciphertext* cph, *and returns 1 if* token *and* cph *correspond to the same identity* id *and the same keyword. Otherwise, it returns 0.*

**Correctness.** We say that a CLKS scheme is correct if, for all id $\in \mathcal{I}$, mk output by the Setup, $sk_{id}$ output by the Gen-Private-Key, and $pk_{id}$ output by the Gen-Public-Key, the following always holds: $\forall$ kw $\in \mathcal{M}$, cph $\leftarrow$ Enc($pk_{id}$, id, kw), token $\leftarrow$ Gen-Token($sk_{id}$, kw) : 1 $\leftarrow$ Match(token, cph)

**Security.** Intuitively, the adversary model against CLKS consists of two kinds of adversaries similar to that of certificateless encryptions [13]: Type 1 adversary models the outsider, who is allowed to manipulate users' public key without accessing the KGC's master key mk; and Type 2 adversary models the insider, who can acquire the KGC's master key mk without manipulating users' public keys.

To be specific, we capture the two security requirements against the two adversaries via the following games. Let $\mathcal{A}$ be Type 1 adversary (Game A) or Type 2 adversary (Game B). The security games are played between $\mathcal{A}$ and the challenger, who maintains two lists:

- TokenList: It stores the tuple [id, kw], meaning that the search token with respect to the keyword kw for the user id has been queried by $\mathcal{A}$.
- UserInfoList: It stores the tuple [id, $psk_{id}$, $sk_{id}$, $pk_{id}$, $P_1$, $P_2$, $P_3$], where the boolean value $P_1 = 1$ means that $\mathcal{A}$ has acquired $psk_{id}$ and $P_1 = 0$ not, the boolean value $P_2 = 1$ means that $\mathcal{A}$ has acquired $sk_{id}$ and $P_2 = 0$ not, and the boolean value $P_3 = 1$ means that $\mathcal{A}$ has replaced id's public key $pk_{id}$ and $P_3 = 0$ not.

## Game A

**Setup:** The challenger runs Setup($1^\ell$) to initialize the system parameter param and the master key mk. The challenger sends param to $\mathcal{A}$, and sets two lists TokenList and UserInfoList empty.

**Phase 1:** $\mathcal{A}$ is allowed to query the following oracles in polynomial many times. We use the bracket $[\cdot]$ to indicate the input to the oracle from $\mathcal{A}$.

- Gen-Partial-Private-Key[id]: Given the user id from $\mathcal{A}$, if $\mathsf{psk}_{id}$ in UserInfoList is not null, then the challenger returns $\mathsf{psk}_{id}$. Otherwise, the challenger runs Gen-Partial-Private-Key(mk, id) to get $\mathsf{psk}_{id}$, adds $[id, \mathsf{psk}_{id}, \star, \star, 1, 0, 0]$ to UserInfoList where $\star$ means null, and returns $\mathsf{psk}_{id}$ to $\mathcal{A}$.
- Gen-Private-Key[id]: Given the user id from $\mathcal{A}$, the oracle works as follows:
  - If $\mathsf{sk}_{id}$ in UserInfoList is not null, then the challenger retrieves $\mathsf{sk}_{id}$.
  - Else if $\mathsf{psk}_{id}$ in UserInfoList is not null, then the challenger retrieves $\mathsf{psk}_{id}$, runs $\mathsf{sk}_{id} \leftarrow$ Gen-Private-Key($\mathsf{psk}_{id}$) and adds $\mathsf{sk}_{id}$ to the UserInfoList.
  - Otherwise, the challenger runs $\mathsf{psk}_{id} \leftarrow$ Gen-Partial-Private-Key(mk, id) and $\mathsf{sk}_{id} \leftarrow$ Gen-Private-Key($\mathsf{psk}_{id}$), and adds $(id, \mathsf{psk}_{id}, \mathsf{sk}_{id})$ to UserInfoList.

  The challenger updates $P_1 = 1$ and $P_2 = 1$ in UserInfoList with respect to id and returns $\mathsf{sk}_{id}$ to $\mathcal{A}$.
- Gen-Public-Key[id]: Given the user id from $\mathcal{A}$, the oracle works as follows:
  - If $\mathsf{pk}_{id}$ in UserInfoList is not null, then the challenger retrieves $\mathsf{pk}_{id}$.
  - Else if $\mathsf{sk}_{id}$ in UserInfoList is not null, then retrieve $\mathsf{sk}_{id}$, the challenger runs $\mathsf{pk}_{id} \leftarrow$ Gen-Public-Key($\mathsf{sk}_{id}$) and adds $\mathsf{pk}_{id}$ to the UserInfoList with respect to id.
  - Else if $\mathsf{psk}_{id}$ in UserInfoList is not null , then the challenger retrieves $\mathsf{psk}_{id}$, runs $\mathsf{sk}_{id} \leftarrow$ Gen-Private-Key($\mathsf{psk}_{id}$) and $\mathsf{pk}_{id} \leftarrow$ Gen-Public-Key($\mathsf{sk}_{id}, \mathsf{psk}_{id}$) and adds $\mathsf{sk}_{id}, \mathsf{pk}_{id}$ to the UserInfoList with respect to id.
  - Otherwise, the challenger runs $\mathsf{psk}_{id} \leftarrow$ Gen-Partial-Private-Key(mk, id), $\mathsf{sk}_{id} \leftarrow$ Gen-Private-Key($\mathsf{psk}_{id}$) and $\mathsf{pk}_{id} \leftarrow$ Gen-Public-Key($\mathsf{sk}_{id}, \mathsf{psk}_{id}$), and adds $(id, \mathsf{psk}_{id}, \mathsf{sk}_{id}, \mathsf{pk}_{id}, 0, 0, 0)$ to UserInfoList.

  The challenger returns $\mathsf{pk}_{id}$ to $\mathcal{A}$.
- Replace-Public-Key[id, pk] : Given the user id and the replaced public key pk from $\mathcal{A}$ (assume that $\mathsf{pk}_{id}$ has been generated before), the challenger updates $\mathsf{pk}_{id}$ in UserInfoList with pk, and sets $P_3 = 1$ with respect to id.
- Gen-Token[id, kw] : Given the user id and the keyword kw from $\mathcal{A}$, the challenger retrieves $\mathsf{sk}_{id}$ from UserInfoList, runs Gen-Token($\mathsf{sk}_{id}$, kw) to get token. The challenger adds $[id, kw]$ to the TokenList and returns token to $\mathcal{A}$.

**Challenge Phase:** $\mathcal{A}$ presents two keywords of the same length, $kw_0$ and $kw_1$, and the user $id^*$. Let $[id^*, \mathsf{psk}_{id^*}, \mathsf{sk}_{id^*}, \mathsf{pk}_{id^*}, P_1, P_2, P_3]$ be the tuple stored in UserInfoList, we require that

- $P_1 = 0$ and $P_2 = 0$, meaning that $\mathsf{psk}_{id^*}$ and $\mathsf{sk}_{id^*}$ are not acquired by $\mathcal{A}$.
- Both $(id^*, kw_0)$ and $(id^*, kw_1)$ are not stored in TokenList.

Note that $P_3$ can be either 0 or 1, meaning that $id^*$'s public key can be replaced or not. The challenger picks $\lambda \xleftarrow{R} \{0, 1\}$, runs $cph^* \leftarrow \mathsf{Enc}(pk_{id^*}, id^*, kw_\lambda)$, and returns $cph^*$ to $\mathcal{A}$.

**Phase 2:** $\mathcal{A}$ continues to query the oracles as in Phase 1, while following these restrictions:

- $\mathcal{A}$ cannot query Gen-Partial-Private-Key[$id^*$] or Gen-Private-Key[$id^*$].
- $\mathcal{A}$ cannot query Gen-Token[$id^*$, $kw_0$] or Gen-Token[$id^*$, $kw_1$].

**Guess:** $\mathcal{A}$ outputs a bit $\lambda^*$. We say $\mathcal{A}$ wins the game if $\lambda^* = \lambda$.

**Definition 2.** *A CLKS scheme achieves ciphertext indistinguishability against Type 1 adversary if for any probabilistic polynomial time algorithm $\mathcal{A}$, it wins the above security game with a negligible advantage at most with respect to the security parameter $\ell$, where the "advantage" is defined as $|\Pr[\lambda = \lambda^*] - \frac{1}{2}|$.*

## Game B

**Setup:** The challenger runs $\mathsf{Setup}(1^\ell)$ to initialize the system parameter param and the master key mk. The challenger sends param and mk to $\mathcal{A}$, and initializes the empty lists TokenList and UserInfoList.

**Phase 1:** $\mathcal{A}$ is allowed to query the following oracles in polynomial many times. We use the bracket $[\cdot]$ to indicate the input to the oracle from $\mathcal{A}$.

- Gen-Partial-Private-Key[id]: Given the user id from $\mathcal{A}$, if $psk_{id}$ in UserInfoList is not null, then the challenger returns $psk_{id}$. Otherwise, the challenger runs Gen-Partial-Private-Key(mk, id) to get $psk_{id}$, adds $[id, psk_{id}, \star, \star, 1, 0, 0]$ to UserInfoList where $\star$ means null, and returns $psk_{id}$ to $\mathcal{A}$.
- Gen-Private-Key[id]: Given the user id from $\mathcal{A}$, the oracle works as follows:
  - If $sk_{id}$ in UserInfoList is not null with respect to id, then retrieve $sk_{id}$.
  - Otherwise, run $psk_{id} \leftarrow$ Gen-Partial-Private-Key(mk, id) and $sk_{id} \leftarrow$ Gen-Private-Key($psk_{id}$), and add $(id, psk_{id}, sk_{id})$ to UserInfoList.
  
  The challenger updates $P_1 = 1$ and $P_2 = 1$ in UserInfoList with respect to id and returns $psk_{id}$, $sk_{id}$ to $\mathcal{A}$.
- Gen-Public-Key[id]: Given the user id from $\mathcal{A}$, the oracle works as follows:
  - If $pk_{id}$ in UserInfoList is not null with respect to id, then retrieve $pk_{id}$.
  - Else, the challenger runs $psk_{id} \leftarrow$ Gen-Partial-Private-Key(mk, id), $sk_{id} \leftarrow$ Gen-Private-Key($psk_{id}$) and $pk_{id} \leftarrow$ Gen-Public-Key($sk_{id}$, $psk_{id}$), and add $(id, psk_{id}, sk_{id}, pk_{id})$ to UserInfoList.
  
  The challenger updates $P_1 = 1$ in UserInfoList and returns $psk_{id}$, $pk_{id}$ to $\mathcal{A}$.
- Gen-Token[id, kw] : Given the user id and the keyword kw from $\mathcal{A}$, the challenger retrieves $sk_{id}$ from UserInfoList, runs Gen-Token($sk_{id}$, kw) to get token. The challenger adds $[id, kw]$ to the TokenList and returns token to $\mathcal{A}$.

**Challenge Phase:** $\mathcal{A}$ presents two keywords of the same length, $kw_0$ and $kw_1$, and the user $id^*$. Let $[id^*, psk_{id^*}, sk_{id^*}, pk_{id^*}, P_1, P_2, P_3]$ be the tuple stored in UserInfoList, we require that

– $P_2 = 0$, meaning that $\mathsf{sk}_{\mathsf{id}^*}$ is not acquired by $\mathcal{A}$.
– Both $(\mathsf{id}^*, \mathsf{kw}_0)$ and $(\mathsf{id}^*, \mathsf{kw}_1)$ are not stored in TokenList.

The challenger picks $\lambda \overset{R}{\leftarrow} \{0,1\}$, runs $\mathsf{cph}^* \leftarrow \mathsf{Enc}(\mathsf{pk}_{\mathsf{id}^*}, \mathsf{id}^*, \mathsf{kw}_\lambda)$, and returns $\mathsf{cph}^*$ to $\mathcal{A}$.

**Phase 2:** $\mathcal{A}$ continues to query the oracles as in Phase 1, while following the below restrictions:

– $\mathcal{A}$ cannot query Gen-Private-Key[$\mathsf{id}^*$].
– $\mathcal{A}$ cannot query Gen-Token[$\mathsf{id}^*, \mathsf{kw}_0$] or Gen-Token[$\mathsf{id}^*, \mathsf{kw}_1$].

**Guess:** $\mathcal{A}$ outputs a bit $\lambda^*$. We say $\mathcal{A}$ wins the game if $\lambda^* = \lambda$.

**Definition 3.** *A CLKS scheme achieves ciphertext indistinguishability against Type 2 adversary if for any probabilistic polynomial time algorithm $\mathcal{A}$, it wins the above security game with a negligible advantage at most with respect to the security parameter $\ell$, where the "advantage" is defined as $|\Pr[\lambda = \lambda^*] - \frac{1}{2}|$.*

# 6  Main construction

**High Level Idea.** Motivated by the DL assumption, we encrypt the keyword kw as follows: Let $a, b, c$ be the private key $(a, b, c \overset{R}{\leftarrow} \mathbb{Z}_p^*)$ and $g^a, g^b, g^c$ be the public key, and set the keyword ciphertext as

$$W_1 = g^{cr_1}, \qquad W_2 = g^{a(r_1+r_2)}g^{bH_2(\mathsf{kw})r_1}, \qquad W_3 = g^{r_2},$$

where $H_2 : \{0,1\}^* \to \mathbb{Z}_p^*$ is a collision resistant hash function. According to the DL assumption, the keyword kw is perfectly hidden. Note that $g^b$ in the term $g^{bH_2(\mathsf{kw})r_1}$ is to facilitate the security proof.

If one knows the term $g^{ac}$, then he can generate the search token with respect to any keyword kw′: Select $s \overset{R}{\leftarrow} \mathbb{Z}_p^*$ ($s$ is to preserve the secrecy of $g^{ac}$) and set

$$V_1 = g^{acs}, \qquad V_2 = g^{cs}, \qquad V_3 = g^{as}g^{bH_2(\mathsf{kw}')s}.$$

If $\mathsf{kw} = \mathsf{kw}'$, then the respective keyword ciphertext and search token should match:

$$e(W_2, V_2) = e(W_1, V_3)e(W_3, V_1).$$

This is because

$$e(W_2, V_2) = e(g,g)^{acs(r_1+r_2)}e(g,g)^{bcsr_1H_2(\mathsf{kw})},$$
$$e(W_1, V_3) = e(g,g)^{acsr_1}e(g,g)^{bcsr_1H_2(\mathsf{kw}')}$$
$$e(W_3, V_1) = e(g,g)^{acsr_2},$$

On the other hand, we observe that the adversary can only acquire either KGC's master key (w.r.t Type 1 adversary) or the user's secret values (w.r.t Type 2 adversary with replaced public key), rather than both. This observation motivates use to expand the private key setting, such that KGC has the private key $a, b, c$ and public key $g^a, g^b, g^c$, and the user has the private key $a', c'$ ($a', c' \xleftarrow{R} \mathbb{Z}_p^*$) and public key $g^{a'}, g^{c'}$. Therefore, the keyword ciphertext is constructed:

$$W_1 = g^{(c+c')r_1}, \quad W_2 = g^{(a+a')(r_1+r_2)}g^{bH_2(\text{kw})r_1}, \quad W_3 = g^{r_2}, \quad W_4 = H_1(\text{id})^{r_2},$$

where $H_1$ is a hash function converting id to an element of $G$. Noting that we implicitly let the user id as part of the public key (cf. $W_4$), so that the ciphertext is associated to the user id. To this end, only knowing either $a, c$ or $a', c'$ cannot infer any information about the ciphertext.

In order to generate search token, the user id, holding $a', c'$, needs to acquire the term $g^{ac}$. We achieve it based on the idea how the secret key was distributed in attribute-based encryption, where user id is treated as an attribute. That is, KGC generates the partial private key for the user id as

$$\text{sk}_1 = g^{t_1} \quad \text{and} \quad \text{sk}_2 = g^{ac}H_1(\text{id})^{t_1} \quad \text{where } t_1 \xleftarrow{R} \mathbb{Z}_p^*.$$

**Our Construction** We now show the CLKS construction as follows.

- Setup($1^\ell$): The KGC runs $(e, p, g, G, G_T) \leftarrow \text{BMP}(1^\ell)$ to generate the bilinear map $e : G \times G \to G_T$. Let $a, b, c \xleftarrow{R} \mathbb{Z}_p^*$ so that it has $g^a, g^b, g^c$. Let id be an $n$-bit number such that $\text{id} = \text{id}_1\text{id}_2\ldots\text{id}_n$. It selects vectors $(u, u_1, \ldots, u_n) \xleftarrow{R} G^{n+1}$ and defines the hash function $H_1(\text{id}) = u\prod_{j=1}^n u_j^{\text{id}_j}$. Let $H_2 : \{0,1\}^* \to \mathbb{Z}_p^*$ be a collision-resistant hash function and set the system parameter $\text{param} = (e, G, G_T, p, g, g^a, g^b, g^c, u, u_1, \ldots, u_n, H_1, H_2)$.
- Gen-Partial-Private-Key($\text{mk}, \text{id}$): Given the user id, KGC proceeds as follows:
  - It selects $t_1 \xleftarrow{R} \mathbb{Z}_p^*$ and sets $\text{sk}_1 = g^{t_1}, \text{sk}_2 = g^{ac}H_1(\text{id})^{t_1}$.
  - The partial private key is set to $\text{psk}_{\text{id}} = (\text{sk}_1, \text{sk}_2)$, which is sent to the user id via a secure channel.
- Gen-Private-Key($\text{psk}_{\text{id}}$): Given $\text{psk}_{\text{id}}$, the user selects $a', c' \xleftarrow{R} \mathbb{Z}_p^*$ and sets $\text{sk}_{\text{id}} = (a', c', \text{sk}_1, \text{sk}_2)$.
- Gen-Public-Key($\text{sk}_{\text{id}}$): Given $\text{sk}_{\text{id}}$, the user sets its public key as $\text{pk} = (\text{pk}_1, \text{pk}_2) = (g^{a'}, g^{c'})$.
- Enc($\text{pk}_{\text{id}}, \text{id}, \text{kw}$): The user encrypts the keyword kw and returns a ciphertext cph by selecting $r_1, r_2 \xleftarrow{R} \mathbb{Z}_p^*$ and setting $\text{cph} = (W_1, W_2, W_3, W_4)$ where

$$W_1 = g^{(c+c')r_1}, \quad W_2 = g^{(a+a')(r_1+r_2)}g^{bH_2(\text{kw})r_1}, \quad W_3 = g^{r_2}, \quad W_4 = H_1(\text{id})^{r_2}.$$

- Gen-Token($\text{sk}_{\text{id}}, \text{kw}$): The user id generates a search token token by selecting $s \xleftarrow{R} \mathbb{Z}_p^*$ and setting $\text{token} = (V_1, V_2, V_3, V_4)$ where

$$V_1 = \text{sk}_1^s = g^{t_1 s}, \quad V_2 = (g^{ac'}g^{a'c}g^{a'c'})^s \text{sk}_2^s = g^{(a+a')(c+c')s}H_1(\text{id})^{t_1 s},$$
$$V_3 = g^{(c+c')s}, \quad V_4 = g^{(a+a')s}g^{bH_2(\text{kw})s}.$$

- Match(token, cph): This algorithm returns 1 if $e(W_2, V_3) = \frac{e(W_3, V_2)}{e(W_4, V_1)} e(W_1, V_4)$. Otherwise, return 0.

**Correctness.** The correctness can be verified as follows:

Because $\quad \dfrac{e(W_3, V_2)}{e(W_4, V_1)} = \dfrac{e(g^{r_2}, g^{(a+a')(c+c')s} H_1(\mathrm{id})^{t_1 s})}{e(H_1(\mathrm{id})^{r_2}, g^{t_1 s})} = e(g, g)^{(a+a')(c+c')s r_2},$

and $\quad e(W_1, V_4) = e(g^{(c+c')r_1}, g^{(a+a')s} g^{b H_2(\mathrm{kw})s}) = e(g, g)^{(c+c')r_1 s(a+a'+b H_2(\mathrm{kw}))},$

then $\quad \dfrac{e(W_3, V_2)}{e(W_4, V_1)} e(W_1, V_4) = e(g, g)^{(a+a')(c+c')s(r_1+r_2)} e(g, g)^{b^2 H_2(\mathrm{kw})r_1 s}.$

$e(W_2, V_3) = e(g^{(a+a')(r_1+r_2)} g^{b H_2(\mathrm{kw})r_1}, g^{(c+c')s}) = e(g, g)^{(a+a')(c+c')(r_1+r_2)s} e(g, g)^{b^2 H_2(\mathrm{kw})r_1 s}$

**Remark.** Given a search token, the attacker can launch the off-line keyword guessing attack (aka. predicate privacy [25]) because he can utilize the public information (e.g., public key) to test whether the given search token corresponds to some keyword. Such attack is inherent for certificate-based keyword search, identity-based (attribute-based) keyword search and our proposed CLKS. Some research efforts has been made to prevent such attack. For example, [19,24,31] considered the approaches where the search token can be transmitted over the public channel (i.e., search token indistinguishability) but the user needs to share some secret with the remote server, which cannot completely solve the off-line keyword guessing attack because the remote server can still launch this attack.

The security of our proposed scheme can be assured by the following theorems, which proofs are shown in the Appendix of the full version [35].

**Theorem 1.** *Suppose $\mathcal{A}$ is the Type 1 adversary making at most $\xi_{eppk}$ queries to oracle* Gen-Partial-Private-Key *and $\xi_{prk}$ queries to oracle* Gen-Private-Key*. Let* $\mathrm{Adv}_{H_2}$ *be the advantage of $\mathcal{A}$ breaking the collision-resistant hash function $H_2$ (i.e., $\mathrm{Adv}_{H_2} = \Pr[(H_2(\mathrm{kw}_1) = H_2(\mathrm{kw}_2)) \cap (\mathrm{kw}_1 \neq \mathrm{kw}_2)|\mathrm{kw}_1, \mathrm{kw}_2 \in \{0,1\}^*])$ and $\mathrm{Adv}_{DL}(\ell)$ be the advantage of $\mathcal{A}$ breaking the DL assumption. Then the advantage of Type 1 adversary breaking the ciphertext indistinguishability is*

$$\mathrm{Adv}_{Type\ 1} \leq \mathrm{Adv}_{H_2} + 2(\xi_{prk} + \xi_{eppk})(n+1)\mathrm{Adv}_{DL}(\ell)$$

**Theorem 2.** *Suppose $\mathcal{A}$ is the Type 2 adversary making at most $\xi_{prk}$ queries to oracle* Gen-Private-Key *and $\xi_{tk}$ queries to oracle* Gen-Token*. Let $\mathrm{Adv}_{H_2}$ be the advantage of $\mathcal{A}$ breaking the collision-resistant hash function $H_2$ and $\mathrm{Adv}_{DL}(\ell)$ be the advantage of $\mathcal{A}$ breaking the DL assumption. Then the advantage of Type 2 adversary breaking the ciphertext indistinguishability is*

$$\mathrm{Adv}_{Type\ 2} \leq \mathrm{Adv}_{H_2} + 2\xi_{prk}\xi_{tk}(n+1)\mathrm{Adv}_{DL}(\ell)$$

# 7  Performance Evaluation

We implemented the CLKS scheme in Java with JPBC Library [15], by instantiating the bilinear map with Type A pairing ($\ell = 512$) offering a level of security
equivalent to 1024-bit Discrete Logarithm security. We used the SHA-1 to hash
keywords and identities (both are strings) into the 128-bit data, which are then
transformed to the elements in $\mathbb{Z}_p^*$ and $G$ respectively.

To evaluate the feasibility of the CLKS in practice, we conducted the experiments with the real data, which is composed of 6,000 distinct keywords extracted
from the ACM Digital Library. We ran the experiments on two machines: The
user machine is a Windows 7 running laptop with Intel i5 2.60GHz CPU and
8GB RAM to simulate the user that runs the algorithm Enc; the server machine
is a Linux running desktop with Intel Core i7-2600 3.4GHz CPU and 4GB RAM
to simulate the cloud server that runs the algorithm Match.

We ran six experiments using different number of keywords varying from 1000
to 6000 with step 1000. We repeated each experiment 5 times to determine the
average execution time. Figure 2(a) compares the execution time for encrypting
all keywords (on the user machine) and for finding the matched keyword ciphertexts with a given search token (on the server machine). From Figure 2(a) we see
that encrypting entire keywords are more costly than finding matched keyword
ciphertexts. Fortunately, encrypting entire keywords will be executed only once,
while finding matched ciphertext needs to be executed once per search request.
Figure 2(b) shows the size of keyword ciphertexts that are serialized to the disk,
showing that the size of keyword ciphertexts is linear to the number of keywords.

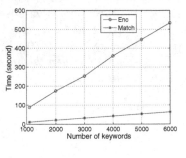
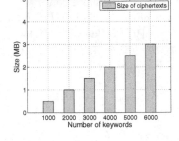

(a) Execution time          (b) Size of keyword ciphertexts

**Fig. 2.** Performance of CLKS. Note that we set that it needs to run Match algorithm
on half of the entire keyword ciphertexts to find a matched keyword ciphertext.

# 8  Conclusion

We have proposed a novel variant of keyword search – certificateless keyword
search(CLKS), supporting keyword search on encrypted data while enjoying the
benefits from certificateless cryptography. We presented a concrete construction,
and proved its security under the DL assumption in the standard model.

**Acknowledgments.** Q. Zheng is supported in part by NSFC under Grant No.61472472. X. Li is supported by NSFC under Grant No. 61572192 and 61272536, and Science and Technology Commission of Shanghai Municipality under Grant No.13JC1403500.

# References

1. Abdalla, M., Bellare, M., Catalano, D., Kiltz, E., Kohno, T., Lange, T., Malone-Lee, J., Neven, G., Paillier, P., Shi, H.: Searchable encryption revisited: Consistency properties, relation to anonymous ibe, and extensions. J. Cryptol. **21**(3), 350–391 (2008)
2. Al-Riyami, S.S., Paterson, K.G.: Certificateless public key cryptography. In: Laih, C.-S. (ed.) ASIACRYPT 2003. LNCS, vol. 2894, pp. 452–473. Springer, Heidelberg (2003)
3. Baek, J., Safavi-Naini, R., Susilo, W.: Certificateless public key encryption without pairing. In: Zhou, J., López, J., Deng, R.H., Bao, F. (eds.) ISC 2005. LNCS, vol. 3650, pp. 134–148. Springer, Heidelberg (2005)
4. Baek, J., Safavi-Naini, R., Susilo, W.: Public key encryption with keyword search revisited. In: Gervasi, O., Murgante, B., Laganà, A., Taniar, D., Mun, Y., Gavrilova, M.L. (eds.) ICCSA 2008, Part I. LNCS, vol. 5072, pp. 1249–1259. Springer, Heidelberg (2008)
5. Bao, F., Deng, R.H., Ding, X., Yang, Y.: Private query on encrypted data in multi-user settings. In: Chen, L., Mu, Y., Susilo, W. (eds.) ISPEC 2008. LNCS, vol. 4991, pp. 71–85. Springer, Heidelberg (2008)
6. Boneh, D., Di Crescenzo, G., Ostrovsky, R., Persiano, G.: Public key encryption with keyword search. In: Cachin, C., Camenisch, J.L. (eds.) EUROCRYPT 2004. LNCS, vol. 3027, pp. 506–522. Springer, Heidelberg (2004)
7. Boneh, D., Waters, B.: Conjunctive, subset, and range queries on encrypted data. In: Vadhan, S.P. (ed.) TCC 2007. LNCS, vol. 4392, pp. 535–554. Springer, Heidelberg (2007)
8. Bösch, C., Peter, A., Leenders, B., Lim, H.W., Tang, Q., Wang, H., Hartel, P.H., Jonker, W.: Distributed searchable symmetric encryption. In: 2014 Twelfth Annual International Conference on Privacy, Security and Trust, Toronto, ON, Canada, 2014, pp. 330–337 (2014)
9. Camenisch, J., Kohlweiss, M., Rial, A., Sheedy, C.: Blind and anonymous identity-based encryption and authorised private searches on public key encrypted data. In: Jarecki, S., Tsudik, G. (eds.) PKC 2009. LNCS, vol. 5443, pp. 196–214. Springer, Heidelberg (2009)
10. Cao, N., Wang, C., Li, M., Ren, K., Lou, W.: Privacy-preserving multi-keyword ranked search over encrypted cloud data. IEEE Trans. Parallel Distrib. Syst. **25**(1), 222–233 (2014)
11. Chai, Q., Gong, G.: Verifiable symmetric searchable encryption for semi-honest-but-curious cloud servers. In: ICC 2012, Ottawa, ON, Canada, pp. 917–922 (2012)
12. Chang, Y.-C., Mitzenmacher, M.: Privacy preserving keyword searches on remote encrypted data. In: Ioannidis, J., Keromytis, A.D., Yung, M. (eds.) ACNS 2005. LNCS, vol. 3531, pp. 442–455. Springer, Heidelberg (2005)
13. Chen, Y.-C., Tso, R., Susilo, W., Huang, X., Horng, G.: Certificateless signatures: Structural extensions of security models and new provably secure schemes. Cryptology ePrint Archive, Report 2013/193 (2013). http://eprint.iacr.org/

14. Curtmola, R., Garay, J.A., Kamara, S., Ostrovsky, R.: Searchable symmetric encryption: improved definitions and efficient constructions. In: CCS 2006, Alexandria, VA, USA, pp. 79–88 (2006)
15. De Caro, A., Iovino, V.: jpbc: Java pairing based cryptography. In: Proceedings of the 16th IEEE Symposium on Computers and Communications, ISCC 2011, Kerkyra, Corfu, Greece, pp. 850–855 (2011)
16. Dent, A.W.: A note on game-hopping proofs. Cryptology ePrint Archive, Report 2006/260 (2006). http://eprint.iacr.org/
17. Goh, E.: Secure indexes. IACR Cryptology ePrint Archive, 2003:216 (2003)
18. Homer, J., Zhang, S., Ou, X., Schmidt, D., Du, Y., Rajagopalan, S.R., Singhal, A.: Aggregating vulnerability metrics in enterprise networks using attack graphs. Journal of Computer Security **21**(4), 561–597 (2013)
19. Hu, C., Liu, P.: An enhanced searchable public key encryption scheme with a designated tester and its extensions. JCP **7**(3), 716–723 (2012)
20. Huang, H., Zhang, S., Ou, X., Prakash, A., Sakallah, K.A.: Distilling critical attack graph surface iteratively through minimum-cost SAT solving. In: ACSAC 2011, Orlando, FL, USA, pp. 31–40 (2011)
21. Jarecki, S., Jutla, C.S., Krawczyk, H., Rosu, M., Steiner, M.: Outsourced symmetric private information retrieval. In: CCS 2013, Berlin, Germany, pp. 875–888 (2013)
22. Kamara, S., Papamanthou, C., Roeder, T.: Dynamic searchable symmetric encryption. In: CCS 2012, Raleigh, NC, USA, pp. 965–976 (2012)
23. Kurosawa, K., Ohtaki, Y.: UC-secure searchable symmetric encryption. In: Keromytis, A.D. (ed.) FC 2012. LNCS, vol. 7397, pp. 285–298. Springer, Heidelberg (2012)
24. Rhee, H.S., Park, J.H., Susilo, W., Lee, D.H.: Trapdoor security in a searchable public-key encryption scheme with a designated tester. Journal of Systems and Software **83**(5), 763–771 (2010)
25. Shen, E., Shi, E., Waters, B.: Predicate privacy in encryption systems. In: Reingold, O. (ed.) TCC 2009. LNCS, vol. 5444, pp. 457–473. Springer, Heidelberg (2009)
26. Shi, J., Lai, J., Li, Y., Deng, R.H., Weng, J.: Authorized keyword search on encrypted data. In: Kutyłowski, M., Vaidya, J. (eds.) ICAIS 2014, Part I. LNCS, vol. 8712, pp. 419–435. Springer, Heidelberg (2014)
27. Song, D.X., Wagner, D., Perrig. A.: Practical techniques for searches on encrypted data. In: 2000 IEEE Symposium on Security and Privacy, Berkeley, California, USA, pp. 44–55 (2000)
28. Sun, W., Yu, S., Lou, W., Hou, Y.T., Li, H.: Protecting your right: attribute-based keyword search with fine-grained owner-enforced search authorization in the cloud. In: 2014 IEEE Conference on Computer Communikations, INFOCOM 2014, Toronto, Canada, pp. 226–234 (2014)
29. Tang, Q., Chen, X.: Towards asymmetric searchable encryption with message recovery and flexible search authorization. In: 8th ACM Symposium on Information, Computer and Communications Security, ASIA CCS 2013, Hangzhou, China, pp. 253–264 (2013)
30. Wang, C., Cao, N., Ren, K., Lou, W.: Enabling secure and efficient ranked keyword search over outsourced cloud data. IEEE Trans. Parallel Distrib. Syst. **23**(8), 1467–1479 (2012)
31. Wu, T.-Y., Tsai, T.-T., Tseng, Y.-M.: Efficient searchable id-based encryption with a designated server, vol. 69, pp. 391–402. Springer Paris (2014)
32. Xu, L., Wu, X., Zhang, X.: CL-PRE: a certificateless proxy re-encryption scheme for secure data sharing with public cloud. In: ASIACCS 2012, Seoul, Korea, pp. 87–88 (2012)

33. Zhang, S., Zhang, X., Ou, X.: After we knew it: empirical study and modeling of cost-effectiveness of exploiting prevalent known vulnerabilities across iaas cloud. In: ASIA CCS 2014, Kyoto, Japan - June 03–06, 2014, pp. 317–328 (2014)
34. Zheng, Q., Xu, S., Ateniese, G.: VABKS: verifiable attribute-based keyword search over outsourced encrypted data. In: 2014 IEEE Conference on Computer Communikations, INFOCOM 2014, Toronto, Canada, April 27 – May 2, 2014, pp. 522–530 (2014)
35. Zheng, Q., Li, X., Azgin, A.: Clks: Certificateless keyword search on encrypted data. Cryptology ePrint Archive, Report 2015/814 (2015). http://eprint.iacr.org/
36. Zhu, B., Zhu B., Ren, K.: Peksrand: providing predicate privacy in public-key encryption with keyword search. In: Proceedings of IEEE International Conference on Communications, ICC 2011, Kyoto, Japan, June 5–9, 2011, pp. 1–6 (2011)

# Secure Cloud Storage for Dynamic Group: How to Achieve Identity Privacy-Preserving and Privilege Control

Hui Ma[1,2] and Rui Zhang[1(✉)]

[1] State Key Laboratory of Information Security, Institute of Information
Engineering, Chinese Academy of Sciences, Beijing 100093, China
{mahui,r-zhang}@iie.ac.cn
[2] University of Chinese Academy of Sciences, Beijing 100049, China

**Abstract.** We propose the first secure cloud storage system with public audit for dynamic group, which achieves identity privacy-preserving and privilege control among mobile users. We utilize multi-key ciphertext policy attribute-based key encapsulation mechanisms (MCP-AB-KEMs) to achieve privileges of operations on the cloud data and the anonymity among the mobile users, and we utilize proxy re-signatures to update tags efficiently. In addition, a third party auditor (TPA) helps to check data integrity without the knowledge of users' identities. We also give a security model and present the security analysis within the model.

**Keywords:** Secure cloud storage · Dynamic group · Privilege control · Identity privacy-preserving

## 1 Introduction

**The Problem.** Consider the following scenario: in a sports club, a group of members share photos, videos and training materials. The members care much about their privacy, i.e., they do sports but do not want others to know more than this. However, the issues become very complicated when the group consists of mobile users. Even a new member joins the group or a member leaves will cause a refresh of the group key, otherwise, forward/backward security cannot be retained. Besides, due to the limited storage of smart phones, they may want to store the data in the cloud. Since the actual data is under the control of the cloud storage and the users do not have a copy themselves, users should adopt an integrity verification protocol to guarantee the data integrity, and a third party auditor (TPA) will also be involved. Actually, this was recently considered in [24], where Yu et al. came up with a (partial) solution.

We argue that two practical issues were not considered in the previous work: 1) According to the users' different characters in the group, the users should own different privileges of operations on the cloud data. 2) The users in the group only want to share the data but do not want extra connections with other users. In this paper, we investigate this problem, namely secure cloud storage scheme for dynamic group with public audit mechanisms that achieve both user identity privacy and privilege control.

© Springer International Publishing Switzerland 2015
M. Qiu et al. (Eds.): NSS 2015, LNCS 9408, pp. 254–267, 2015.
DOI: 10.1007/978-3-319-25645-0_17

Table 1. Comparison with Existing Mechanisms

| Functionality | [18] | [16] | [19] | [24] | Ours |
|---|---|---|---|---|---|
| Dynamic Group | × | ✓ | ✓ | ✓ | ✓ |
| Public Audit | ✓ | × | ✓ | ✓ | ✓ |
| Identity Privacy to TPA | ✓ | ✓ | ✓ | ✓ | ✓ |
| Privilege Control | × | × | × | × | ✓ |
| Identity Privacy among Users | × | ✓ | × | × | ✓ |

**Related Work.** To guarantee the cloud data integrity, Deswarte, Quisquater and Saïdane [7], Filho and Barreto [9], Naor and Rothblum [12], and Schwarz and Miller [13] were among the first to consider the problem of remotely checking data integrity. Later research focused designing schemes with formal security models, e.g., authenticators [12], PDP [1,3,8,26], proof of retrievability (PoR) [10,14,22] and secure cloud storage [5,6,20,23]. In particular, they not only care about the integrity of the user data, but also focus on extractability of the data during the verification phase. The above schemes are all designed for traditional cloud storage and not suitable for a group of mobile users.

To protect the user identity privacy from public auditors, several works [16–19] proposed their solutions. However, [16] imposed a heavy burden on generating tags; [18] was not suitable for dynamic group; [17,19] cannot afford the tolerance against the collusion attack launched by a revoked user and the cloud server. Recently, Yu et al. [24] proposed a secure mobile cloud storage protocol for dynamic group that supports identity privacy-preserving and public audit. They utilized the dynamic asymmetric group key agreement scheme in [25] to negotiate the group key, thus [24] offered the user anonymity to a third party auditor (TPA). However, the users must communicate with others in the group during the negotiation, thus [24] does not offer the anonymity among users. Moreover, [24] does not offer the privilege control on the cloud data, and the computation cost on the user side is heavy. Thus it is still much work to do towards the user anonymity and the privilege control in the group data sharing.

**Our Contributions.** In this paper, we propose the first secure cloud storage scheme for dynamic group with public audit that achieves identity privacy-preserving and privilege control. First, we discuss the potential threats and formalize the security model. Second, we propose a concrete scheme that provides anonymity among users, user anonymity to TPA, privilege control and tag-updating. Finally, we discuss the tolerance against collusion attacks and give the security proof. Table 1 shows a comparison between our scheme and existing mechanisms. To our best knowledge, this paper first combines secure cloud storage for dynamic group with privilege control.

## 2    Preliminary

**Notations.** Let $A(a, b, ...) \rightarrow z$ denote the operation of running an algorithm $A$ with inputs $a, b, ...$ and output $z$. If $d$ is a string, $|d|$ denotes its length. Let $x||y$ denote the concatenation of two strings $x$ and $y$.

**Definition 1 (Bilinear Groups).** *Let* $\mathbf{G}$ *be an algorithm that takes as input a security parameter* $\lambda$ *and outputs a tuple* $(p, \mathbb{G}_0, \mathbb{G}_1, e)$, *where* $\mathbb{G}_0$ *and* $\mathbb{G}_1$ *are multiplicative cyclic groups of prime order* $p$, *and* $e : \mathbb{G}_0 \times \mathbb{G}_0 \rightarrow \mathbb{G}_1$ *is a bilinear map such that: 1) Bilinearity: for all* $g, h \in \mathbb{G}_0$ *and* $a, b \in \mathbb{Z}_p^*$, *we have* $e(g^a, h^b) = e(g, h)^{ab}$. *2) Nondegeneracy:* $e(g, h) \neq 1$ *whenever* $g, h \neq 1_{\mathbb{G}_0}$.

**Definition 2 (Access Tree $\mathcal{T}$).** *Let* $\mathcal{T}$ *be a tree representing an access structure. If* $num_x$ *is the number of children of a node* $x$ *and* $k_x$ *is its threshold value, then* $0 < k_x \leq num_x$. *When* $k_x = 1$, *it is an OR gate and when* $k_x = num_x$, *it is an AND gate. Each leaf node* $x$ *of the tree is described by an attribute and a threshold value* $k_x = 1$. *We denote the parent of the node* $x$ *by* parent(x). *The function* att(x) *is defined only if* $x$ *is a leaf node and denotes the attribute associated with the leaf node* $x$. *And the children of a node are numbered from 1 to num. The* index(x) *returns such a number associated the node* $x$.

## 3    The Security Model

In this section, we present the system model and the security model.

### 3.1    The System Model

**System Model.** A dynamic group of mobile users want to share data and they care much about the identity privacy. Due to the limited resources, they store the data in public cloud storage. Since the actual data is under the control of the cloud, users adopt a data auditing protocol and a TPA is involved. According to users' different characters, they own different privileges of operations on the cloud data and a local server manages the privileges. Specifically, the lowest privilege is reading data, every user owns this; the higher privilege is reading and creating data; the topmost privilege is reading, creating and deleting data. There are 4 entities in our system (Fig. 1):

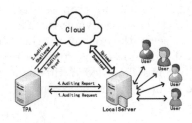

**Fig. 1.** The System Model

- Mobile users do not have enough storage space to store large amount of data.
- Local server is trusted by the users, there is a secure channel between each user and the local server, and the local server's functionality includes: managing privilege control, connecting every user and the cloud, and helping users generate and update tags (users can also generate and update tags by themselves if they like).
- TPA is a third party auditor that offers the auditing service.
- Public cloud that has tremendous resources, providing storage service.

**Threat Model.** Users are curious about others' identities and try to obtain higher privileges that are not theirs. TPA follows the protocol honestly but is curious about users' identities as in [16–19]. The cloud server will follow the protocol honestly but may be self-interested, such as when the file is totally or partially missing, it may try to convince the TPA that it possesses the file to maintain its reputation.

**Poblem Setting.** In this paper, we not only achieve *user anonymity to TPA*, *group dynamic* and *efficient tag-updating* as in [24], but also focus on *anonymity among users* and *privilege control*. Besides, the system should offer *lightweight operations on user side* and *tolerance against users' collusion attacks*.

## 3.2   System Components

Our system includes 3 main components: A privilege control scheme, a data auditing protocol and a system manage module.

**The Privilege Control Scheme** consists of the following 4 algorithms:

MCP-AB-KEM.Setup. Taking a security parameter $\lambda$ as input, this algorithm outputs a public key $PK$ and a master key $MSK$.

MCP-AB-KEM.KeyGen. Taking the $MSK$ and a set of attributes $S$ as input, this algorithm generates a private key $sk$ that identifies with that set.

MCP-AB-KEM.Enc. Taking the $PK$ and an access tree $T$ as input, this algorithm outputs a privilege control ciphertext $PCT$ and a set of privilege keys $\{key_i\}_{i=1}^{l}$.

MCP-AB-KEM.Dec. Taking a $PCT$, which contains an access tree $T$, and a $sk$, which contains a set of attributes as input, if the set of attributes satisfies the access policy, this algorithm will decrypt the $PCT$ and return the privilege keys $\{key_j\}_{j=1}^{n}$, where $1 \leq n \leq l$.

**The Data Auditing Protocol** consists of the following 4 algorithms:

TagGen. Taking a group pair $(Gpk, Gsk)$ and a data block $F_i$ of the file $F$ as input, this algorithm generates a tag $Tag_i$ for the block.

Audit. Taking a request from the server as input, this algorithm generates a challenge $Chal$ to query the integrity of the data file.

Prove. Taking the $Gpk$, data blocks $\{F_i\}$, tags $\{Tag_i\}$ and the challenge $Chal$ as input, this algorithm responds a proof $P$ for the challenged blocks.

Verify. Taking the $Gpk$ and a proof $P$ as input, this algorithm outputs the verification result of the proof $P$.

**The System Manage Module** consists of the following 4 algorithms:

GKeyGen. Taking the $PK$, the $MSK$, all the $N$ users' attribute sets $\{S_i\}_{i=1,...,N}$ (an attribute of Token is in each $S_i$) and an access tree $T$ (a necessary leaf node is Token, such as "Token $\wedge$ ...") as input, the local server first runs MCP-AB-KEM.KeyGen($MSK, S_i$) to generate every user's private key $sk_i$ and sends it to the user $u_i$ privately. Then it runs MCP-AB-KEM.Enc($PK, T$) to generate a $PCT$ and a set of privilege keys $\{key_{\text{type}}\}_{\text{type} \in \{\text{"read"}, \text{"create"}, \text{"delete"}\}}$ for reading, creating and deleting data and computes $Gsk$ and $Gpk$ with $key_{\text{create}}$. At last, it broadcasts the $PCT$ to all the users publicly.

Operation. Taking a $sk_i$ and a $PCT$ as input, a user $u_i$ first runs MCP-AB-KEM.Dec($PCT, sk_i$) to obtain the privilege keys $\{key'_{\text{type}}\}$. Then the user does as follows.

- type = "read": The privilege of the operation is reading the cloud data. The user sends the read instruction to the local server. Then the local server downloads the data and sends it to the user $u_i$.
- type = "create": The privilege of the operation is creating the cloud data. The users first computes $Gsk$ and $Gpk$, then sends the create instruction to the local server. Then the local server optionally runs TagGen($Gpk, Gsk, \{F_i\}$) to generate $Tag_i$ for each data block $F_i$, and uploads the data ($\{F_i\}, \{Tag_i\}$) to the cloud. At last, it sends feedback to the user $u_i$. Alternatively, users can also generate tags by themselves if they like.
- type = "delete": The privilege of the operation is deleting the cloud data. The user sends the delete instruction to the local server. Then the local server deletes the data and its tags. At last, it sends feedback to the user $u_i$.

Join. The local server runs GKeyGen again except that the number of the users is $N + 1$ and $Token$ is updated. And it updates all the tags.

Leave. The local server runs GKeyGen again except that the number of the users is $N - 1$ and $Token$ is updated. And it updates all the tags.

### 3.3   The Security Model

The proposed system includes MCP-AB-KEM and the data auditing protocol. Similar to the hybrid encryption, the group key is encapsulated in the ciphertext of MCP-AB-KEM. Thus, we consider the two security models separately.

The security model of the data auditing protocols should ensure that if any cheating prover that convinces the verification algorithm that it is storing a file $F$ is actually storing that file. Shacham and waters [14] define that it yields up the file $F$ to an extractor algorithm that interacts with it using the proof-of-retrievability protocol. We expend this model by adding the *update* oracle. Consider the following game between an adversary $\mathcal{A}$ and an environment $\mathcal{E}$:

1. $\mathcal{E}$ generates $(Gpk, Gsk)$ by running GKeyGen, and provides $Gpk$ to $\mathcal{A}$.
2. $\mathcal{A}$ can now interact with $\mathcal{E}$. It can make queries to a store oracle, providing, for each query, some file F. $\mathcal{E}$ computes TagGen($Gpk, Gsk, F$) $\rightarrow T$ and returns $(F, T)$ to $\mathcal{A}$. When the group changes, it should make queries to an

update oracle, providing, for each query, some file $F$ and the tags. $\mathcal{E}$ updates the tags and returns the updated tags and the new public key to $\mathcal{A}$.

3. For any $F$ on which it previously made a store query or an update query, $\mathcal{A}$ can undertake executions of the proof-of-retrievability protocol, by specifying the corresponding tag $T$. In these protocol executions, $\mathcal{E}$ plays the part of the verifier and $\mathcal{A}$ plays the part of the prover. When a protocol execution completes, $\mathcal{A}$ is provided with the output of $\mathcal{E}$. These protocol executions can be arbitrarily interleaved with each other and with the store and update queries described above.

4. Finally, $\mathcal{A}$ outputs a challenge tag $T$ returned from some store and update queries, and the description of a prover $P'$.

The cheating prover $P'$ is $\epsilon$-admissible if it convincingly answers an $\epsilon$ fraction of verification challenges, i.e., if $\Pr[((\text{Verifier} \leftrightharpoons P') = 1)] \geq \epsilon$. Here the probability is over the coins of the verifier and the prover. Let $F$ be the message input to the store and update query that returned the challenge tag $T$.

**Definition 3.** *A proof-of-retrievability scheme is $\epsilon$-sound if there exists an efficient extraction algorithm such that, for every adversary $\mathcal{A}$, whenever $\mathcal{A}$, playing the security game, outputs an $\epsilon$-admissible cheating prover $P'$ for a file $F$, the extraction algorithm recovers $F$ from $P'$, except with negligible probability.*

The system model of the privilege control is based on CP-ABE proposed by Bethencourt, Sahai and Waters [4]. Consider the following security game between an adversary $\mathcal{A}$ and a challenger $\mathcal{C}$:

- **Setup.** $\mathcal{C}$ runs MCP-AB-KEM.Setup and gives the public parameters to $\mathcal{A}$.
- **Phase 1.** $\mathcal{A}$ makes private keys corresponding to sets of attributes $S_1, ..., S_{q_1}$.
- **Challenge.** $\mathcal{A}$ gives a challenge access structure $\mathbb{A}^*$ and the topmost encapsulated key (The key is encapsulated by the whole tree) with the restriction that none of the sets $S_1, ..., S_{q_1}$ from Phase 1 satisfies the access structure (the whole tree). $\mathcal{C}$ runs MCP-AB-KEM.Enc to obtain $(key^*, PCT^*)$ and flips a random coin $b \in \{0, 1\}$. If $b = 0$, it returns $(key^*, PCT^*)$. If $b = 1$, it picks a random key $R^*$ in the encapsulated key space and returns $(R^*, PCT^*)$.
- **Phase 2.** Phase 1 is repeated with the restriction that none of the sets of attributes $S_{q_1+1}, ..., S_q$ satisfy the challenge access structure.
- **Guess.** $\mathcal{A}$ outputs a guess $b'$ of b.

The advantage of an adversary $\mathcal{A}$ in the above game is defined as $\Pr[b' = b] - \frac{1}{2}$. We note that the model can easily be extended to describe MCP-AB-KEM: In the Challenge, the topmost encapsulated key is replaced to the target encapsulated key. And in the Phase 1 and Phase 2, none of the sets of attribute $S_1, ..., S_q$ satisfies the subtree whose root node encapsulates the target key.

**Definition 4.** *A Multi-key Ciphertext Policy Attributed-Based Key Encapsulation Mechanism (MCP-AB-KEM) scheme is CPA-secure if all polynomial time adversaries have at most a negligible advantage in the above game.*

# 4   Our Construction

In this section, we present our concrete construction and give an illustration.

## 4.1   The Concrete Construction

**Intuition.** To achieve privilege control and user anonymity among users, we modify CP-ABE in [4] to Multi-key CP-AB-KEM, which is similar to [21]. Naturally, a private key of the public verification scheme in [14] is encapsulated in the PCT. To achieve tag-updating, we utilize the idea of proxy re-signature [2]. Moreover, a secure channel between every user and the local server can protect user's instructions and some entries (identity, time, session ID etc.) can prevent some known attacks, such as the replay attack [15] etc.

Let $\mathbb{G}_0$ be a bilinear group of prime order $p$, and let $g, g'$ be two generators of $\mathbb{G}_0$. And let $e : \mathbb{G}_0 \times \mathbb{G}_0 \to \mathbb{G}_1$ denote the bilinear map. A security parameter $\lambda$ determines the size of the groups. We also define the Lagrange coefficient $\triangle_{i,S}$ for $i \in \mathbb{Z}_p$ and a set $S$, of elements in $\mathbb{Z}_p$ : $\triangle_{i,S}(x) = \prod_{j \in S, j \neq i} \frac{x-j}{i-j}$. Let $H : \{0,1\}^* \to \mathbb{G}_0$, $H' : \{0,1\}^* \to \mathbb{Z}_p^*$ represent two hash functions and KDF represent the key derivation function [11] with the output length $l$. Our construction is as follows.

**MCP-AB-KEM.Setup.** The setup algorithm will choose a bilinear group $\mathbb{G}_0$ of prime order $p$ with generator $g$. Next it will choose two random exponents $\alpha, \beta \in \mathbb{Z}_p$. The public key is published as: $PK = \{\mathbb{G}_0, g, h = g^\beta, e(g,g)^\alpha\}$ and the master key $MSK$ is $(\beta, g^\alpha)$.

**MCP-AB-KEM.KeyGen.** Taking a $MSK$ and a set of attributes $S$ as input, this algorithm generates a private key $sk$ that identifies with $S$. It first chooses a random $r \in \mathbb{Z}_p$, and random $r_j \in \mathbb{Z}_p$ for each attribute $j \in S$. Then it computes the private key as $sk = (PK, D = g^{(a+r)/\beta}, \forall j \in S : D_j = g^r \cdot H(j)^{r_j}, D'_j = g^{r_j})$.

**MCP-AB-KEM.Enc.** Taking a $PK$ and an access tree $T$ as input, this algorithm outputs a privilege control ciphertext $PCT$ and a set of privilege keys $\{key_i\}_{i=1}^l$. It first chooses a polynomial $q_x$ for each node $x$ in the tree $T$. These polynomials are chosen in the following way in a top-down manner, starting from the root node $R$. For each node $x$ in the tree, set the degree $d_x$ of the polynomial $q_x$ to be one less than the threshold value $k_x$ of that node, that is $d_x = k_x - 1$.

The access tree $T$ has $l$ privilege nodes $N_1, N_2, ..., N_l$. Every such node $N_i$ that is the root of a subtree that is mapped to a privilege level $p_i$, where $i = 1, 2, ..., l$. Starting with the root node $R$, it chooses a random $s \in \mathbb{Z}_p$ and sets $q_1(0) = s$. Then it chooses $d_1$ other points of the polynomial $q_1$ randomly to define it completely. For any other node $x$, it sets $q_x(0) = q_{parent(x)}(index(x))$ and chooses $d_x$ other points randomly to completely define $q_x$. At last, it chooses $l$ random privilege keys $\{key_i\}_{i=1}^l$. Let $Y$ be the set of the leaf nodes in $T$. The PCT is then constructed by giving the tree access structure $T$ and computing

$$PCT = (T, \{\widetilde{C_i} = key_i \cdot e(g,g)^{\alpha q_i(0)}\}_{i=1}^l, \{\overline{C_i} = h^{q_i(0)}\}_{i=1}^l,$$

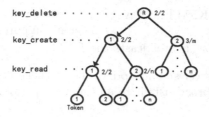

**Fig. 2.** Privilege Tree

$$\forall y \in Y : \ C_y = g^{q_y(0)}, \ C'_y = H(att(y))^{q_y(0)}).$$

MCP-AB-KEM.Dec. Taking a $PCT$, which contains an access policy $T$, and a $sk$, which contains a set of attributes as input, if the set of attributes satisfies the access policy, this algorithm will decrypt the $PCT$ and return the privilege keys $\{key_j\}_{j=1}^{n}$, where $1 \leq n \leq l$. If the node $x$ is a leaf node then we let $i = att(x)$ and define as follows: If $i \in S$, then

$$\mathrm{DecryptNode}(PCT, sk, x) = \frac{e(D_i, C_x)}{e(D'_i, C'_x)} = \frac{e(g^r \cdot H(i)^{r_i}, g^{q_x(0)})}{e(g^{r_i}, H(i)^{q_x(0)})} = e(g,g)^{rq_x(0)}.$$

If $i \notin S$, then we define $\mathrm{DecryptNode}(PCT, sk, x) = \bot$.

We now consider the recursive case when $x$ is a non-leaf node. The algorithm $\mathrm{DecryptNode}(PCT, sk, x)$ then proceeds as follows: For all nodes $z$ that are children of $x$, it calls $\mathrm{DecryptNode}(PCT, sk, z)$ and stores the output as $F_z$. Let $S_x$ be an arbitrary $k_x$-sized set of child nodes $z$ such that $F_z \neq \bot$. If no such set exists then the node was not satisfied and the function returns $\bot$. Otherwise, we compute

$$F_x = \prod_{z \in S_x} F_z^{\triangle_{i,S'_x}(0)} = \prod_{z \in S_x} (e(g,g)^{r \cdot q_z(0)})^{\triangle_{i,S'_x}(0)} = \prod_{z \in S_x} (e(g,g)^{r \cdot q_{parent(z)}(index(z))})^{\triangle_{i,S'_x}(0)}$$

$$= \prod_{z \in S_x} (e(g,g)^{r \cdot q_x(i) \cdot \triangle_{i,S'_x}(0)} = e(g,g)^{r \cdot q_x(0)}, \quad where \ i = index(x), S'_x = \{index(z) : z \in S_x\},$$

and return the result. Next, the algorithm begins by simply calling the function on the privilege node $Node_i, i \in \{1,2,..,l\}$ of the tree $T$. If the subtree whose root node is $Node_i$ is satisfied by $S$, we set A=$\mathrm{DecryptNode}(PCT, sk, Node_i) = e(g,g)^{rq_i(0)}$. The algorithm now decrypts by computing

$$\widetilde{C_i}/(e(\overline{C_i}, D)/A) = \widetilde{C_i}/(e(h^{q_i(0)}, g^{(\alpha+r)/\beta})/e(g,g)^{rq_i(0)}) = key_i, \ i \in \{1,2,...,l\}.$$

GKeyGen. Taking a $PK$, a $MSK$, all the $N$ users' attribute sets $\{S_i\}_{i=1,...,N}$ (an attribute of Token must be included in each $S_i$, the Token of each user in the group is the same. When a user joins or leaves the group, the Token is updated.) and an access tree $T$ (a necessary leaf node is Token, as shown in Fig. 2) as input, the local server first runs MCP-AB-KEM.KeyGen($MSK, S_i$) to generate every user's private key $sk_i$ and sends it to each user privately.

Then it runs MCP-AB-KEM.Enc$(PK, T)$ to generate a $PCT$ and a set of privilege keys $\{key_{type}\}_{type \in \{\text{"read", "create", "delete"}\}}$. Then it computes $Gsk = H'(key_{create})$ and $Gpk = g'^{Gsk}$. At last, it broadcasts the $PCT$.

*Remark 1.* The local server should update the privilege keys on time by generating a new $PCT$ and broadcasts it to all the users periodically.

TagGen. Taking a group pair $(Gpk, Gsk)$ and a file $F = \{m_1, ..., m_t\}$ as input, this algorithm splits $m_j$ into $s$ sectors $m_j = \{m_{j1}, ..., m_{js}\}$ and chooses $s$ random values $u_1, ..., u_s \in \mathbb{G}$. Then, for each block $m_j$ ($j \in [1, t]$), compute a tag $Tag_j$ as

$$Tag_j = (H(F_{id}||j) \cdot \prod_{l=1}^{s} u_l^{m_{jl}})^{Gsk},$$

where $F_{id}$ is the unique identifier of the file $F$ and $j$ denotes the block number of $F_j$. It outputs the set of data tags $T = \{Tag_j\}_{j \in [1, t]}$.

Audit. Taking a request from the local server as input, TPA selects some data blocks to construct a challenge set $Q$ and picks a random $v_j \in \mathbb{Z}_p^*$ for each $F_j$ ($j \in Q$), and then sends the challenge $Chal = \{j, v_j\}_{j \in Q}$ to the cloud server.

Prove. Taking a $Gpk$, data blocks $\{F_i\}$, tags $\{Tag_i\}$ and a challenge $Chal$ as input, the cloud server computes

$$\mu_l = \sum_{j \in Q} v_j m_{jl} \in \mathbb{Z}_p \; for \; 1 \le l \le s, \; and \; \sigma = \prod_{j \in Q} Tag_j^{v_j} \in \mathbb{G}_0.$$

The cloud server responds a proof $P = \{\mu_1, ..., \mu_s, \sigma\}$ to TPA.

Verify. Taking the $Gpk$ and a proof $P$ as input, TPA checks whether

$$e(\sigma, g') \stackrel{?}{=} e(\prod_{j \in Q} H(F_{id}||j)^{v_j} \cdot \prod_{l=1}^{s} u_l^{\mu_l}, \; Gpk).$$

If so, output 1; otherwise, output 0 (to the local server).

Operation. Taking a $sk_i$ and a $PCT$ as input, a user $u_i$ first runs MCP-AB-KEM.Dec$(PCT, sk_i)$ to obtain a set of privilege keys $\{key'_{type}\}$. Then the user can do as follows.

- type = "read": The privilege of the operation is reading the cloud data. The user sends $m = key_{read}||ID||time||sid||dataname$ to the local server, where $key_{create}$ identifies the operation, $ID$ is the user's identity, $time$ is the current time, $sid$ is the session ID and $dataname$ labels the targeted data. Then the local server downloads the data $dataname$ and sends it to the user.

- type = "create": The privilege of the operation is creating the cloud data. The users first computes $Gsk = H'(key_{\text{create}})$ and $Gpk = g'^{Gsk}$, then sends $m = key_{\text{create}}||ID||time||sid||dataname||\{F_i\}$ to the local server. The local server runs $\text{TagGen}(Gpk, Gsk, \{F_i\})$ to generate $Tag_i$ for each block $F_i$ and uploads $(\{F_i\}, \{Tag_i\})$ to the cloud. At last, it sends an "Ack" to the user. Alternatively, users can also generate tags by themselves and add tags into $m$ if they like.
- type = "delete": The privilege of the operation is deleting the cloud data. The user sends $m = key_{\text{delete}}||ID||time||sid||dataname$ to the local server. The local server deletes $dataname$ and its tags. Then send an "Ack" to the user.

*Remark 2.* We assume that a user and local server have authenticated each other before the above communication.

**Join.** The local server runs GKeyGen again except that the number of the users is $N + 1$ and $Token$ is updated. After generating a new pair $(Gpk', Gsk')$, the local server generates a proxy re-signature key $ReGsk = Gsk'/Gsk$, downloads all the tags and computes $Tag'_j = Tag_j^{ReGsk}$ for each $Tag_j$. Finally, it updates all the new tags to the cloud and sends $Gpk'$ to TPA.

**Leave.** The local server runs GKeyGen again except that the number of the users is $N - 1$ and $Token$ is updated. After generating a new pair $(Gpk', Gsk')$, the local server generates a proxy re-signature key $ReGsk = Gsk'/Gsk$, downloads all the tags and computes $Tag'_j = Tag_j^{ReGsk}$ for each $Tag_j$. Finally, it updates all the new tags to the cloud and sends $Gpk'$ to TPA.

*Correctness.* The correctness of our construction is obvious, so we just omit the correctness due to the limit of the space.

## 4.2   The Example

We use an example to further illustrate how the proposed system works. The local server first generates the private key $sk_i$ and sends it to the user $u_i$ privately. Then it periodically generates and broadcasts $PCT$, so privilege keys can be updated on time. A $PCT$ encapsulates a privilege key chain ($k3 \rightarrow k2 \rightarrow k1$):

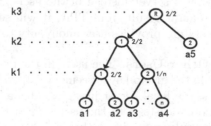

**Fig. 3.** Privilege Tree for the Example

Reading data (k1) is the lowest privilege that every user owns; the higher privilege (k2) is reading and creating data; the topmost privilege (k3) is reading, creating and deleting data. And an access tree is shown in Fig. 3. The user can decrypt the $PCT$ with his private key to obtain his privilege keys.

**Table 2.** Some Attribute Sets for the Example

| User | Attribute set | Privilege keys | Granted operations |
|------|---------------|----------------|--------------------|
| User 1 | a1, a2 | $k1$ | Read |
| User 2 | a1, a2, a3 | $k1, k2$ | Read, Create |
| User 3 | a1, a2, a4 | $k1, k2$ | Read, Create |
| User 4 | a1, a2, a5 | $k1$ | Read |
| User 5 | a1, a2, a3, a5 | $k1, k2, k3$ | Read, Create, Delete |

Table 2 shows a portion of the attribute sets for the example. User 1 who has attributes (a1, a2) and User 4 who has attributes (a1, a2, a5) can only recover $k1$, hence they only can read the cloud data. User 2 and User 3 have the attributes that can recover $k1$ and $k2$, hence they can read and create the cloud data. Because of the attributes that can satisfy the whole tree $T$, User 5 can recover all the keys $(k1, k2, k3)$ and have the access to read, create and delete the cloud data. When the user wants to do the granted privilege operation, he just sends the corresponding instruction to the local server, and the local server will help the user finish the operation.

### 4.3   Practicality

In [24], mobile users should negotiate the group keys and generate/update tags. In our system, a local server helps users generate/update tags, so mobile users only do the decryption periodically when the privilege keys need to be updated.

## 5   Security Analysis

**User Anonymity to TPA.** The public-secret key pair for the data auditing protocol corresponds to the whole group, not any specific user. Besides, TPA communicates with the local server instead of the users. Specifically, after the local server receives the audit result from TPA, it will send the result to the users. In summary, the system provides user anonymity to TPA.

**User Anonymity to Other Users.** The users in the group do not communicate with each other to do the group key agreement [24]. When the system needs to update privilege keys, the local server just generates a new privilege control ciphertext ($PCT$) and broadcasts it to the users. Then the users just decrypt the $PCT$ with their private keys to obtain their privilege keys. In summary, the identity of the user will not leakage to other users.

**Tolerance Against Users' Collusion Attack.** In order to access higher privileges that are not theirs, the corrupted users may collude with each other, and have enough attributes to satisfy the subtree that encapsulates the privilege key. However, in MCP-AB-KEM, when two different private keys' components are combined, the combined private key cannot go through the polynomial interpolation in the decryption algorithm due to the different random numbers in each key. Therefore, our system is secure under users' collusion attack.

**Tolerance Against a Revoked User and the Cloud Storage' Collusion Attack.** In our system, once a user is revoked, all the users' private and privilege keys must be updated immediately. Thus, the cloud storage cannot obtain valid group private key from any revoked user to forge a valid proof. .

**Theorem 1.** *The privilege keys that encapsulated in the privilege control ciphertext (PCT) have privacy with respect to the joining or leaving mobile users as long as the MCP-AB-KEM scheme is CPA-secure.*

*Proof.* The privacy of privilege keys indicates that any probabilistic polynomial time (PPT) adversary cannot obtain privilege keys. First, we consider the case of no users' joining or leaving the group. The proof is obvious. All the privilege keys are encrypted by $PCT$, and the MCP-AB-KEM scheme is proved to be CPA-secure in the random oracle model in [4]. So any PPT adversary cannot distinguish the random key and the real encapsulated privilege key based on the $PCT$. Definitely, any adversary cannot obtain the privilege keys without the private key that satisfies the access structure. Next, we consider mobile users' joining or leaving the group. If there is no further protection, the system is not secure, e.g., a user, who has left the group but holds his own private key, once accesses a $PCT$ in the new group, the user can easily obtain the current privilege keys by decrypting the $PCT$. Our solution is adding a same attribute Token to each user's private key and modifying the access tree by adding a necessary leaf node Token, such as "Token ∧ ...". The Token of each user in the current group is the same. When a user joins or leaves the group, the Token should be updated, then the old private key is invalid.

**Theorem 2.** *All the probabilistic polynomial time adversaries cannot forge a proof that can be accepted by the TPA in the data auditing protocol within nonnegligible probability.*

*Proof.* In the security game of the data auditing protocol, the only difference from [14] is that we add an update oracle. The update oracle works when a user joins or leaves the group. The environment $\mathcal{E}$ only generates a new key pair $(Gpk', Gsk')$, updates tags by using a proxy re-signature key $ReGsk$ and gives new tags and $Gpk'$ to the adversary $\mathcal{A}$. The capability of $\mathcal{A}$ is the same as [14]. Thus, following the proof of the public scheme in [14], the unforgeability of an auditing proof can be reduced to the Computational Diffie-Hellman (CDH) assumption.

# 6   Conclusion

In this paper, we proposed the first secure cloud storage system with public audit for dynamic group, which achieves identity privacy-preserving and privilege control among mobile users. By designing the MCP-AB-KEM, mobile users own different privileges of operations on the cloud data and the anonymity among mobile users. Since the mobile users share a group key pair for the data auditing protocol, a TPA can check the data integrity without the knowledge of mobile users' identities. Utilizing the proxy re-signature, it is easy to update tags.

**Acknowledgment.** We would like to thank the anonymous reviewers for helpful comments. This work was partially supported by the Foundation of Science and Technology on Information Assurance Laboratory (No. KJ-14-002), Strategic Priority Research Program of the Chinese Academy of Sciences (No. XDA06010703), and One Hundred Talents Project of the Chinese Academy of Sciences.

# References

1. Ateniese, G., Burns, R.C., Curtmola, R., Herring, J., Kissner, L., Peterson, Z.N.J., Song, D.X.: Provable data possession at untrusted stores. In: ACM Conference on Computer and Communications Security, pp. 598–609 (2007)
2. Ateniese, G., Hohenberger, S.: Proxy re-signatures: new definitions, algorithms, and applications. In: Proceedings of the 12th ACM Conference on Computer and Communications Security, CCS 2005, Alexandria, USA, pp. 310–319 (2005)
3. Ateniese, G., Pietro, R.D., Mancini, L.V., Tsudik, G.: Scalable and efficient provable data possession. In: 4th International ICST Conference on Security and Privacy in Communication Networks, SECURECOMM 2008, Istanbul, Turkey, September 22–25, 2008, p. 9 (2008)
4. Bethencourt, J., Sahai, A., Waters, B.: Ciphertext-policy attribute-based encryption. In: IEEE Symposium on Security and Privacy, 2007, pp. 321–334 (2007)
5. Bowers, K.D., Juels, A., Oprea, A.: HAIL: a high-availability and integrity layer for cloud storage. In: Proceedings of the 2009 ACM Conference on Computer and Communications Security, CCS 2009, Chicago, Illinois, USA, pp. 187–198 (2009)
6. Chen, F., Xiang, T., Yang, Y., Chow, S.S.: Secure cloud storage meets with secure network coding. In: Proceeding of INFOCOM 2014, pp. 673–681. IEEE (2014)
7. Deswarte, Y., Quisquater, J.-J., Saïdane, A.: Remote integrity checking. In: Jajodia, S., Strous, L. (eds.) IICIS 2003. IFIP, vol. 140, pp. 1–11. Springer, Heidelberg (2004)
8. Erway, C., Küpçü, A., Papamanthou, C., Tamassia, R.: Dynamic provable data possession. In: Proceedings of the 16th ACM Conference on Computer and Communications Security, pp. 213–222. ACM (2009)
9. Filho, D.L.G., Barreto, P.S.L.M.: Demonstrating data possession and uncheatable data transfer. Cryptology ePrint Archive, Report 2006/150 (2006)
10. Juels, A., Kaliski Jr., B.S.: Pors: proofs of retrievability for large files. In: The 14th ACM Conference on Computer and Communications Security, 2007, pp. 584–597 (2007)
11. Krawczyk, H.: Cryptographic extraction and key derivation: the HKDF scheme. In: Rabin, T. (ed.) CRYPTO 2010. LNCS, vol. 6223, pp. 631–648. Springer, Heidelberg (2010)

12. Naor, M., Rothblum, G.N.: The complexity of online memory checking. In: IEEE 54th Annual Symposium on FOCS 2005, pp. 573–584 (2005)
13. Schwarz, T., Miller, E.L.: Store, forget, and check: using algebraic signatures to check remotely administered storage. In: Proceedings of the IEEE Int'l Conference on Distributed Computing Systems (ICDCS 2006) (2006)
14. Shacham, H., Waters, B.: Compact proofs of retrievability. In: Pieprzyk, J. (ed.) ASIACRYPT 2008. LNCS, vol. 5350, pp. 90–107. Springer, Heidelberg (2008)
15. Syverson, P.F.: A taxonomy of replay attacks. In: Proceedings of Seventh IEEE Computer Security Foundations Workshop - CSFW 1994, Franconia, New Hampshire, USA, June 14–16, 1994, pp. 187–191 (1994)
16. Wang, B., Li, B., Li, H.: Knox: privacy-preserving auditing for shared data with large groups in the cloud. In: Bao, F., Samarati, P., Zhou, J. (eds.) ACNS 2012. LNCS, vol. 7341, pp. 507–525. Springer, Heidelberg (2012)
17. Wang, B., Li, B., Li, H.: Public auditing for shared data with efficient user revocation in the cloud. In: Proceedings of the IEEE INFOCOM 2013, Turin, Italy, April 14–19, 2013, pp. 2904–2912 (2013)
18. Wang, B., Li, B., Li, H.: Oruta: Privacy-preserving public auditingfor shared data in the cloud. IEEE T. Cloud Computing 2(1), 43–56 (2014)
19. Wang, B., Li, H., Li, M.: Privacy-preserving public auditing for shared cloud data supporting group dynamics. In: Proceedings of IEEE International Conference on Communications, ICC 2013, Budapest, Hungary, June 9–13, 2013, pp. 1946–1950 (2013)
20. Wang, C., Wang, Q., Ren, K., Cao, N., Lou, W.: Toward secure and dependable storage services in cloud computing. IEEE T. Services Computing 5(2), 220–232
21. Wu, Y., Wei, Z., Deng, R.H.: Attribute-based access to scalable media in cloud-assisted content sharing networks. IEEE Transactions on Multimedia 15(4), 778–788 (2013)
22. Xu, J., Chang, E.C.: Towards efficient proofs of retrievability. In: Proceedings of the 7th ACM Symposium on Information, Computer and Communications Security, pp. 79–80. ACM (2012)
23. Yang, K., Jia, X.: An efficient and secure dynamic auditing protocol for data storage in cloud computing. IEEE Trans. Parallel Distrib. Syst. 24(9), 1717–1726 (2013)
24. Yu, Y., Mu, Y., Ni, J., Deng, J., Huang, K.: Identity privacy-preserving public auditing with dynamic group for secure mobile cloud storage. In: Au, M.H., Carminati, B., Kuo, C.-C.J. (eds.) NSS 2014. LNCS, vol. 8792, pp. 28–40. Springer, Heidelberg (2014)
25. Zhao, X., Zhang, F., Tian, H.: Dynamic asymmetric group key agreement for ad hoc networks. Ad Hoc Networks 9(5), 928–939 (2011)
26. Zhu, Y., Wang, H., Hu, Z., Ahn, G.J., Hu, H., Yau, S.S.: Efficient provable data possession for hybrid clouds. In: Proceedings of the 17th ACM Conference on Computer and Communications Security, pp. 756–758. ACM (2010)

# GP-ORAM: A Generalized Partition ORAM

Jinsheng Zhang$^{(\boxtimes)}$, Wensheng Zhang, and Daji Qiao

Iowa State University, Ames, IA 50010, USA
{alexzjs,wzhang,daji}@iastate.edu

**Abstract.** Oblivious RAM (ORAM) is a provable technique to protect a user's access pattern to outsourced data. Recently, many ORAM constructions have been proposed, but most of them are impractical due to high communication and user-side storage costs. Motivated by Partition ORAM (P-ORAM) [15], a state-of-the-art communication-efficient ORAM construction, this paper proposes GP-ORAM (Generalized Partition ORAM) as a new framework to assemble multiple ORAM partitions together while overcoming the limitations of the P-ORAM construction. GP-ORAM allows smaller and adjustable number of partitions, fully utilizes the available user-side storage to reduce communication cost, and can efficiently export the index table to the server. As a result, GP-ORAM incurs low bandwidth cost (i.e., $O(\log N)$ data blocks per query in practice) and has significantly less user-side storage cost than P-ORAM. We demonstrate the security and practicality of GP-ORAM through extensive performance analysis.

## 1 Introduction

Oblivious RAM (ORAM) [3], which was originally proposed by Goldreich and Ostrovsky, has been a provable approach to preserving a user's access pattern to data outsourced to a remote storage server. The past decades have witnessed numerous ORAM constructions [2,4–8,11–15,17,18] developed for various purposes. Although many neat asymptotical results have been reported, the practicality of these constructions is still not satisfactory. Particularly, the designs either demand for large user-side storage or incur high communication cost.

Partition ORAM (P-ORAM) [15] is one recent effort in developing practical ORAMs. The P-ORAM construction was designed to achieve a low and thus practically acceptable communication cost. Specifically, the server-side storage of P-ORAM is organized as $\sqrt{N}$ partitions, assuming $N$ is the number of exported data blocks, and each partition is an ORAM. The user-side storage includes an index table recording the location of each block, a shuffling buffer that can store and shuffle all data blocks of any ORAM partition, and $\sqrt{N}$ stash slots. With such a storage arrangement, it has been shown that the communication cost for data query and shuffling is as low as $\log N$ data blocks per query. Compared to other state-of-the-art ORAM constructions[9,16,19], P-ORAM achieves higher communication efficiency.

© Springer International Publishing Switzerland 2015
M. Qiu et al. (Eds.): NSS 2015, LNCS 9408, pp. 268–282, 2015.
DOI: 10.1007/978-3-319-25645-0_18

However, P-ORAM design has its limitations. First of all, it requires a large and fixed local storage to store the index table and facilitate shuffling. For example, when $N = 2^{32}$ and block size is 64 KB, 31 GB local storage is needed. Second, the index table cannot be efficiently exported to the server. According to our evaluation, if the index structure is exported to the server, in order to query just a single block, more than 1000 data blocks on average have to be retrieved. In addition, the user's accesses to data blocks have to be entirely sequential in order to compress the index table.

To address the above limitations of P-ORAM, while inheriting its nice feature of low communication cost, this paper proposes a generalized version of P-ORAM, called GP-ORAM. There are a few key improvements of GP-ORAM over P-ORAM. First, the number of partitions is adjustable in GP-ORAM. This way, even with a smaller local storage than what P-ORAM requires, GP-ORAM may still achieve a low communication overhead via properly adjusting the number of partitions. Second, each ORAM partition in GP-ORAM is redesigned (different from that in P-ORAM) to enable efficient query and shuffling. Finally, the index structure in GP-ORAM is also redesigned to enable efficient exportation of it and accommodate the above changes.

Rigorous security analysis has been conducted to prove that the proposed GP-ORAM construction can preserve a user's access pattern and the construction fails with only a probability of $O(N^{-\log\log N})$. Extensive cost analysis has also been conducted to show that GP-ORAM is a more practical construction than P-ORAM. Particularly, the local storage demanded by the recursive version of our proposed GP-ORAM scheme is only 2.5%~0.14% of that by the non-recursive version of the P-ORAM scheme (note: as shown in Section 6, the recursive version of the P-ORAM scheme is impractical due to its extremely high communication cost, and therefore is not considered), while GP-ORAM only yields 1 to 3 times higher communication cost than P-ORAM.

In the rest of the paper, Section 2 formalizes the problem. Section 3 describes the intuitions behind the proposed GP-ORAM design, and Section 4 elaborates the details of the GP-ORAM construction. Sections 5 and 6 present the security and cost analyses of GP-ORAM, respectively. Section 7 briefly reviews the existing ORAM constructions. Finally, Section 8 concludes the work.

## 2    Problem Statement

We consider a system composed of a user and a remote storage server. The user exports a large set of data to the server, and wishes to access these data without exposing the access pattern to the storage server. Data is assumed to be stored and accessed in the unit of block, and typically a block is no less than 64 KB [15]. Let $N$ and $B$ denote the total number of blocks exported and the size of a block (in bits), respectively.

Server and user may have different storage capabilities. The cloud server could hold terabytes to petabytes of data in its storage cluster. The user may use thin devices such as tablets and smartphones, and thus may have only gigabytes of RAM and local storage available. Moreover, in practice, bandwidth is usually more expensive than computation and storage. Thus, we aim to design an ORAM scheme that can utilize the given user-side storage efficiently so that the bandwidth cost can be minimized.

In an ORAM system, each data request from the user, which the user wishes to keep private, can be one of the following types: *(1) read a data block $D_i$ of unique ID i from the storage, denoted as a 3-tuple $(read, i, D_i)$; (2) write/modify a data block $D_i$ of unique ID i to the storage, denoted as a 3-tuple $(write, i, D_i)$.* To accomplish a data request, the user may need to access the remote storage multiple times. Each access to the remote storage, which is observable by the server, can be one of the following types: *(1) retrieve (read) a data block $D_i$ from a location loc at the remote storage, denoted as $(read, loc, D_i)$; (2) upload (write) a data block $D_i$ to a location loc at the remote storage, denoted as $(write, loc, D_i)$.*

**Security Definition.** We assume that the server is honest but curious. That is, it behaves faithfully according to the ORAM design to store data and serve users' read or write requests, but it may attempt to figure out the user's data access pattern. The network connection between the user and the server is assumed to be secure; in practice, this can be achieved using well-known techniques such as SSL [1].

We inherit the standard security definition of ORAM in [15] to define the security of our proposed ORAM. Intuitively, an ORAM system is considered secure if the server learns nothing about user's access pattern. More precisely, it is defined as follows:

**Definition 1.** *Let $x = \langle (op_1, i_1, D_1), (op_2, i_2, D_2), \cdots \rangle$ denote a private sequence of user's intended data requests, where each op is either a read or write operation, and $A(x) = \langle (op'_1, loc_1, D'_1), (op'_2, loc_2, D'_2), \cdots \rangle$ denote the sequence of user's accesses to the remote storage (observable by the server) to accomplish the intended data requests. An ORAM system is said to be secure if (i) for any two equal-length private sequences $x$ and $y$ of intended data requests, their corresponding observable access sequences $A(x)$ and $A(y)$ are computationally indistinguishable; and (ii) the probability that the ORAM system fails to operate is small, i.e., $O(N^{-\log \log N})$.*

## 3   Intuition

As GP-ORAM is generalized from P-ORAM, we first review the key ideas and limitations of P-ORAM. As shown in Figure 1, the server-side storage of P-ORAM is organized as $\sqrt{N}$ ORAM partitions, while the user-side storage includes an index table recording the location (i.e., partition ID, layer number and layer offset) of each block, a shuffling buffer that can store and shuffle $O(\sqrt{N})$ data blocks and $\sqrt{N}$ stash slots each corresponding to one partition. To query one data block, it needs to retrieve one data block from each layer of an ORAM partition on the server, which results in $O(\log N)$ data blocks of communication cost, and the query target block is relocated to a randomly selected

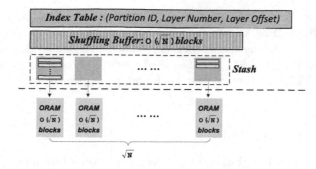

**Fig. 1.** P-ORAM Storage Organization.

stash slot. Each query is followed by a background eviction, in which some data blocks are evicted from stash slots into their corresponding ORAM partitions; the evictions cause the ORAM partitions to be gradually reshuffled, and shuffling causes $O(\log N)$ data blocks of communication cost per query, on average. To summarize, as bandwidth is usually more expensive than storage, P-ORAM was designed to achieve a low communication overhead at the cost of increased local storage.

However, P-ORAM has the following limitations. First, P-ORAM requires a large local storage ($O(\sqrt{N}B)$ bits), due to $\sqrt{N}$ stash slots and a shuffling buffer with a capacity of $O(\sqrt{N})$ blocks. This limits P-ORAM's practical applicability as it is impossible to implement P-ORAM if the user has less local storage than required. Second, the index table cannot be efficiently outsourced to the server. Each entry of the table has three fields: partition ID, layer number, and layer offset. The layer number and layer offset need to be updated during both query and shuffling processes. If the index table is outsourced to the server, the query and shuffling processes need to frequently query and update the index table, which leads to impractically high communication cost. Third, the user's data accesses have to be entirely sequential in order to compress the index table.

Motivated by P-ORAM and also to overcome its limitations, we present GP-ORAM as a new framework to assemble multiple ORAM partitions together. It has the following key ideas. First, the number of partitions is not fixed so that the user can adjust the number of partitions according to the available local storage. Second, the index table is re-designed so that it can be outsourced to the server efficiently. Third, to make full use the available local storage, each ORAM partition is based on a revised S-ORAM [19] construction. As a result, GP-ORAM inherits the security property and the communication efficiency of P-ORAM while being able to work with and fully utilize a wide range of available local storage.

## 4   The Proposed GP-ORAM Construction

We elaborate the design of GP-ORAM in terms of storage organization, system initialization, query process, and background eviction process. To simplify the presentation, we assume the user stores index entries of all outsourced data blocks locally. In practice, to save the user's local storage, the index entries can be recursively exported to the storage server, following the same ideas used in tree ORAM [13] and Path-ORAM [16]. Detailed description of the recursive version of the GP-ORAM construction can be found in Appendix I of our technical report [20].

## 4.1 Storage Organization

GP-ORAM stores both real blocks (i.e., user's $N$ actual data blocks outsourced to the server) and dummy blocks (i.e., faked data blocks with random padding). When a block is in plain-text, it can be split into *pieces* and the size of each piece is $b = \log N$ bits. For each real block, the block ID $i$ is contained in its first piece, denoted as $d_{i,1}$, while the first piece of each dummy block is set to $-1$. The remaining pieces store the content of that block, denoted as $d_{i,2}$, $d_{i,3}$, $\cdots$, $d_{i,\eta-1}$.

Before being exported to the remote storage server, the plain-text block is encrypted using CTR encryption mode (counter encryption mode) [10] piece by piece with a secret key $k$. Specifically, the ciphertext of each block $D_i$ contains $\eta$ pieces, denoted as $c_{i,0}, \cdots, c_{i,\eta-1}$, where

$c_{i,0} = E_k(ctr)$, where $ctr$ is a nounce generated by a pseudo-random function;

$c_{i,1} = E_k(ctr + 1) \oplus d_{i,1}$;

$\cdots$ ;

$c_{i,\eta-1} = E_k(ctr + \eta - 1) \oplus d_{i,\eta-1}.$

$$(1)$$

Thus, the encrypted block (denoted as $D_i$) is $D_i = (c_{i,0}, c_{i,1}, c_{i,2}, \cdots, c_{i,\eta-1})$.

**Server Storage.** The server-side storage is divided into $P$ smaller fully-functional ORAM partitions, where $P$ is a system parameter. Each partition can hold $1.1N/P$ real blocks. As shown in Lemma 1 (Section 5), given that $\log N \log \log N \leq P \leq \sqrt{N}$, the number of real blocks in each partition is upper bounded by $1.1N/P$ with a probability of $1 - O(N^{-\log \log N})$.

In GP-ORAM, each ORAM partition is a revised version of the S-ORAM [19] construction. Specifically, each partition is organized as a pyramidical structure shown in Figure 2, where the total number of layers is denoted as $L_2 = \lceil \log(N/P) \rceil$. The top layer, i.e., layer 1, is an array containing up to four blocks. Each of the rest layers is organized as one or multiple segments. These layers are further divided into single-segment layers (i.e., T1-layers, including layers 2 to $L_1 = \lfloor \log(3 \log^2 N) \rfloor - 1$) and multi-segment layers (i.e., T2-layers, including layers $L_1 + 1$ to $L_2$).

Each T1-layer $l$ has a single segment. The segment stores $2^{l+1}$ blocks, at most half of which are real blocks, and one encrypted index block $I_l$ with $2^{l+1}$ entries. Each entry of $I_l$ corresponds to a block in the segment and consists

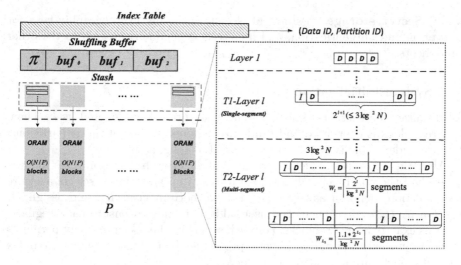

**Fig. 2.** Organization of the server-side storage.

of three fields: *ID of the block, location of the block in the segment*, and *access bit* indicating whether the block has been accessed since it was placed to the segment.

For each T2-layer $l < L_2$, it is composed of $W_l = \lceil 2^l / \log^2 N \rceil$ segments, while the bottom layer (i.e., layer $L_2$) contains $W_{L_2} = \lceil 1.1 * 2^{L_2} / \log^2 N \rceil$ segments. The bottom layer has slightly more segments, because it should be able to accommodate $1.1N/P$ real data blocks. A T2-layer segment has the same format as a T1-layer segment except that it needs to contain exactly $3 \log^2 N$ data blocks. Having $3 \log^2 N$ data blocks per segment is to ensure the security property of the design and it has been proved in [19].

Inside each segment, there is an index block with at most $3 \log^2 N$ entries and each entry contains three fields: *ID of the block* (needing $\log N$ bits), *location of the block in the segment* (needing $\log(3 \log^2(1.1N/P))$ bits), and *access bit* (needing 1 bit). Thus, an index block needs at most $3 \log^2 N[\log N + \log(3 \log^2(1.1N/P)) + 1]$ bits. In practice, with $N \leq 2^{32}$ which is considered large enough to accommodate most practical applications, the size of an index block is less than 32 KB, which can fit into a typical block assumed in P-ORAM [15].

In addition, each ORAM partition $p$ maintains a counter $C_p$ to keep track of the times that the partition has been queried.

**User Storage.** The user-side storage consists of the following components. (i) **Stash with P slots:** each stash slot corresponds to one of the ORAM partitions; that is, it buffers the blocks that should be written to the corresponding partition later. (ii) **Shuffling buffer:** the shuffling buffer (with the capacity of $S$ blocks) is used for data shuffling process. (iii) **Index table:** the index table records the information of each block. Specifically, it has $N$ entries and each entry $(p_i, l_i)$ has two fields; the block is in partition $p_i$ and the block is latest stored on layer

$l_i$. (iv) **Secret storage:** it stores all secrets including cryptographic keys for encryption and authentication, and its size is negligible compared to the other components.

### 4.2    System Initialization

To initialize, the user first selects a data encryption key, denoted as $k$. Then, each real block is encrypted and randomly assigned to one of the $P$ partitions; the local index table is initialized to reflect the assignment.

After the above assignment, the user initializes each partition $p_i$ as follows. For each of the real blocks $D_j$ assigned to partition $p_i$, the user selects a secure hash function, denoted as $H_{p_i,L_2}(*)$, for the bottom layer $L_2$, and assign $D_j$ to segment $H_{p_i,L_2}(j)$. Then, the user adds dummies to ensure each segment contains exactly $3 \log^2 N$ blocks. For each segment, the user randomly permutes all blocks inside it and builds an encrypted index block for it. Finally, the index and data blocks are uploaded to the server.

### 4.3    Data Query

To query a data block $D_t$, the user first searches the index table to get partition ID $p_t$ and layer number $l_t$ for $D_t$. Then, the user searches the stash slot of $p_t$. If $D_t$ is not found, the user will launch a query for $D_t$ in partition $p_t$; otherwise, a dummy query to $p_t$ will be launched.

---

**Algorithm 1.** $Query(D_t, p_t)$

---

1: $\mathcal{L} \leftarrow$ the set of non-empty layers of partition $p_t$
2: Retrieve $C_p$ from partition $p_t$
3: **if** ($D_t$ is a dummy block) **then**
4:     $\mathcal{S} \leftarrow \{seg_l | \forall\, l \in \mathcal{L}, seg_l$ is a randomly-selected segment of layer $l\}$
5:     Retrieve the index block of each segment in $\mathcal{S}$
6:     From each segment in $\mathcal{S}$, retrieve a dummy block that has not been accessed
7:     Update, re-encrypt & upload the retrieved index block
8: **else**
9:     Find layer $\hat{l}_t$ where $D_t$ is located; $seg_{\hat{l}_t} \leftarrow H_{p_t, \hat{l}_t}(t)$
       //Secure hash function $H_{p_t, \hat{l}_t}(t)$ decides which segment of layer $\hat{l}_t$ in partition $p_t$ stores $D_t$
10:     $\mathcal{S} \leftarrow \{seg_l | \forall\, l \in \mathcal{L} \setminus \{\hat{l}_t\}, seg_l$ is a randomly-selected segment of layer $l\}$
11:     Retrieve the index blocks of segments in $\mathcal{S} \cup \{seg_{\hat{l}_t}\}$
12:     From each segment $s \in \mathcal{S} \cup \{seg_{\hat{l}_t}\}$, retrieve a dummy block that has not been accessed if $s \in \mathcal{S}$, or $D_t$ otherwise
13:     Update, re-encrypt & upload the retrieved index block
14: **end if**

---

The algorithm for querying $D_t$ in partition $p_t$, i.e., $Query(D_t, p_t)$, is revised from the query algorithm in S-ORAM [19] and formally presented in Algorithm 1.

In the algorithm, the layer $\hat{l}_t$ where $D_t$ is located is found as follows: First, based on the query counter $C_{p_t}$, the most recently shuffled layer $l'$ can be inferred. Then, $\hat{l}_t \leftarrow l'$ if $l' \geq l_t$ because $D_t$ must have been shuffled to $l'$ during the most recent shuffling process; otherwise, $\hat{l}_t \leftarrow l_t$.

## 4.4   Background Eviction

After each data query, a background eviction process as described in Algorithm 2 should be launched to avoid stash overflowing. Similar to P-ORAM, this process could be sequential or random. For simplicity, we adopt the sequential approach. Suppose $\psi$ records the last evicted stash slot and $\lambda$ denotes the eviction rate (i.e., the number of stash slots that should be evicted after each data query). The eviction operation essentially pushes one data block from its stash slot to layer 1 of its corresponding partition. As the capacity of layer 1 is limited, every four eviction operations performed on a partition could result in layer 1 overflow and thus should trigger a data shuffling of that partition.

---

**Algorithm 2.** Sequential Background Eviction $(\lambda)$

---

1: **for** $k = 1$ to $\lambda$ **do**
2:     $\psi \leftarrow (\psi + 1) \mod P$
3:     **if** (stash slot$[\psi]$ does not contain real block) **then** write a dummy to layer 1 of $p_\psi$
4:     **else** remove a real block from stash slot$[\psi]$ and write it to layer 1 of $p_\psi$
5:     **end if**
6:     $C_{p_\psi} \leftarrow C_{p_\psi} + 1$
7:     **if** $(C_{p_\psi} \mod 4 = 0)$ **then**
8:         Shuffle partition $p_\psi$
9:     **end if**
10: **end for**

---

Different from P-ORAM, GP-ORAM shuffles data in *pieces* instead of *blocks*, as in S-ORAM [19]. To shuffle a certain $x$ number of blocks in the unit of piece, only $bx$ bits of local storage is needed, while $Bx$ bits of local storage would be needed if shuffling these blocks in the unit of block. Hence, GP-ORAM can utilize the shuffling buffer more efficiently than P-ORAM. To facilitate fine-grained shuffling, the shuffling buffer is split into the following two components (as shown in Figure 2): (i) $\pi$, which is a buffer to store a *permutation* of up to $2m^2$ inputs and thus needs $2m^2 \log(2m^2)$ bits, where $m$ is a system parameter; (ii) $buf_0$, which is used to temporarily store up to $2m^2$ data pieces. Recall that each data piece has $b$ bits and the capacity of the shuffling buffer is $S$ bits. In GP-ORAM, we set the shuffling buffer size to

$$S = 4.4 \cdot \frac{N}{P} \cdot (\log(4.4 \cdot \frac{N}{P}) + b). \tag{2}$$

The purpose is to ensure that, for any layer of each partition, each block is downloaded and uploaded for only once during a shuffling process. The shuffling process is the same as in S-ORAM [19], and thus is skipped here due to space limitation.

## 5  Security Analysis

To show that GP-ORAM is secure according to Definition 1 in Section 2, we develop a proof in two parts: (1) GP-ORAM generates a random access pattern independent of user's actual access pattern, and (2) GP-ORAM fails with a probability of $O(N^{-\log\log N})$. For the second part, there are three aspects to be proved in detail: (i) the stash overflows with a probability of $O(N^{-\log\log N})$, (ii) any partition overflows with a probability of $O(N^{-\log\log N})$, and (iii) any layer of any partition overflows during data shuffling with a probability of $O(N^{-\log N})$.

**Lemma 1.** *Given that $P \geq \log N \log\log N$, the total number of real blocks in the stash at any time during data queries is upper bounded by $2P(1 - 2/P)$ with a probability of $1 - O(N^{-\log\log N})$.*

**Lemma 2.** *Given that $\log N \log\log N \leq P \leq \sqrt{N}$, the total number of real blocks for any partition at any time during data queries is upper bounded by $\Phi = 1.1N/P$ with a probability of $1 - O(N^{-\log\log N})$.*

**Theorem 1.** *GP-ORAM is secure under the security definition in Section 2.*

Due to space limitation, please refer to Appendices II, III, and IV of our technical report [20] for the proofs of the above lemmas and theorem.

## 6  Cost Analysis

In this section, we analyze the costs of non-recursive and recursive GP-ORAM constructions, and compare them to P-ORAM [15], Path-ORAM [16] and S-ORAM [19], which are the most communication-efficient state-of-the-art ORAM constructions.

**Cost Analysis for Non-recursive GP-ORAM.** The communication cost includes query and background eviction costs. Each data query retrieves two blocks (i.e., one index block and one data block) from and uploads only the index block to each non-empty layer of the server. As there are $L_2 = \lceil \log(N/P) \rceil$ layers, query cost on average is: $C_{\text{query}} < 1.5 \cdot \log(\frac{N}{P}) \cdot B$.

As for the background eviction cost, after each query, $\lambda$ blocks are written to $\lambda$ consecutive partitions at the server. Thus, $P/\lambda$ queries result in all $P$ partitions being accessed once. Therefore, for each partition, layer $l$ ($1 < l < L_2$) is involved in a shuffling process every $2 \cdot 2^l \cdot P/\lambda$ queries, while layer $L_2$ is shuffled every $2^{L_2} \cdot P/\lambda$ queries. Recall that shuffling a T1-layer $l$ involves $2 \cdot 2^l$ blocks, shuffling a T2-layer $l$ involves $4 \cdot 2^l$ blocks, and shuffling layer $L_2$ involves $5.3 \cdot 2^{L_2}$ blocks. Hence, the amortized shuffling cost is $C_{\text{shuffle}} = (\sum_{l=2}^{L_1} \frac{2 \cdot 2^l \cdot P}{2 \cdot 2^l \cdot P/\lambda} + \sum_{l=L_1+1}^{L_2-1} \frac{4 \cdot 2^l \cdot P}{2 \cdot 2^l \cdot P/\lambda} +$

$\frac{4.4 \cdot 2^{L_2} \cdot P}{2^{L_2} \cdot P / \lambda})B$, Therefore, the communication cost for non-recursive GP-ORAM is

$C_{\text{GP-ORAM(NR)}} = C_{\text{query}} + C_{\text{shuffle}} = (1.5 + 2\lambda) \log \frac{N}{P} \cdot B - \lambda (\log \log N - 2.8) \cdot B$.

For storage cost, as stated in Lemmas 1 and 2, the user needs to maintain the following amount of storage space: $2P(1 - \frac{2}{P})B + S + N \cdot (\log N + \log \log \frac{1.1N}{P})$, where $P \geq \log N \log \log N$. The size of the stash is $2P(1 - 2/P)B$, the size of the shuffling buffer is $S$, and the size of the index table is $N \cdot (\log N + \log \log \frac{1.1N}{P})$, respectively. Note that, the shuffling buffer storage is temporary, while the stash and index table spaces are permanently needed. For server storage, each partition contains at most $5.3N/P$ blocks. Thus, the server storage is less than $5.3NB$.

**Cost Analysis for Recursive GP-ORAM.** Suppose there are $\phi$ levels of recursion in the recursive construction, and the $i^{\text{th}}$ level of recursion is implemented by GP-ORAM$_i$. Thus, GP-ORAM$_1$, which is used to store the user's data blocks, requires a stash of size $2P(1 - 2/P)B$ and a shuffling buffer of size $S$ in the user's local storage, while the index table is exported to the server as GP-ORAM$_2$. The compression rate for GP-ORAM$_2$ can be smaller than $2^{-13}$ (i.e., the size of GP-ORAM$_2$ can be less than $\frac{1}{2^{13}}$ of that of GP-ORAM$_1$) when $N \leq 2^{44}$ and $B \geq 64\,KB$, which covers the practical scenarios considered in [15]. Therefore, parameter $\phi$ is no more than 4; that is, no more than 4 levels of recursion are needed in practice.

Since GP-ORAM$_1$ has much larger capacity than other GP-ORAMs, the extra communication cost introduced by recursion can be computed as $O(\sum_{i=1}^{\phi} \log(\alpha^{-i}N) \cdot B)$ in practice. For the extra local storage cost, it mainly comes from the stashes for extra GP-ORAMs (note that the shuffling buffer for GP-ORAM$_1$ can be reused for other smaller GP-ORAMs), and the total size of these stashes is much less than that for GP-ORAM$_1$. Specifically, a stash of size $3P(1 - 2/P)B$ is enough for recursive constructions. At last, the extra cost on server storage is $O(\sum_{i=1}^{\phi} \alpha^{-i}N \cdot B)$.

**Tradeoff Between Local Storage Capacity and Communication Cost in GP-ORAM.** Suppose a user exports $N$ data blocks each of $B$ bits, and the local storage capacity is $S_l$. The user could find an optimal $P$ (i.e., number of partitions) for GP-ORAM to minimize the communication cost.

According to $C_{\text{GP-ORAM(NR)}}$ in the non-recursive GP-ORAM cost analysis, the larger is $P$, the smaller is the communication cost. Hence, the optimal $P$ should be the largest $P$ without incurring a local storage cost higher than $S_l$. Formally:

Maximize $P$,

subject to $2P(1 - \frac{2}{P})B + S + \frac{NB}{\alpha} \leq S_l$ for non-recursive GP-ORAM,

subject to $3P(1 - \frac{2}{P})B + S \leq S_l$ for recursive GP-ORAM.

The example plotted in Figure 3(a) shows the relation between $P$ and local storage consumption in the recursive GP-ORAM. Recall that, the local storage includes shuffling buffer and stash. As we can see from Figure 3(a), when $P$

is small, local storage consumption decreases as $P$ increases; when $P$ becomes large, local storage consumption increases as $P$ increases. This phenomenon can be explained as follows.

- When $P$ is small, the size of each partition is large; hence, the shuffling buffer dominates the local storage. As $P$ increases, shuffling buffer decreases which causes the local storage to decrease as well.
- When $P$ is large, the number of partitions gets large and so the stashes dominates the local storage. As $P$ increases, the size of stashes increases which causes the local storage to increase too.

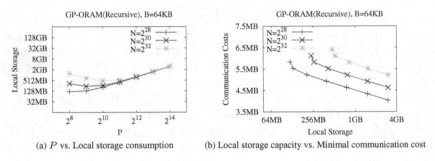

(a) $P$ vs. Local storage consumption      (b) Local storage capacity vs. Minimal communication cost

**Fig. 3.** Examples illustrating the relation between $P$, local storage, and minimal communication cost.

Based on the relation plotted in Figure 3(a), the user can find a range of $P$, with which the required local storage does not exceed $S_l$. Because the communication cost decreases as $P$ increases, the maximum $P$ within the range becomes the optimal $P$ that minimizes the communication cost. This way, for any given $S_l$, the communication cost corresponding to the optimal $P$ can be found. Figure 3(b) plots an example to illustrate the relation between local storage capacity and minimal communication cost in the recursive GP-ORAM.

**GP-ORAM VS. P-ORAM.** Table 1 compares GP-ORAM with P-ORAM in terms of asymptotical performance. From the table, we have the following observations: (i) When $P$ is set to $N^c$ ($c < 0.5$) and $S$ is set as in Equation (2), the communication costs for both non-recursive and recursive GP-ORAM can be re-written as $O(\log N \cdot B)$, which is comparable to the cost for non-recursive P-ORAM and much lower than that for recursive P-ORAM. (ii) The local storage costs for non-recursive P-ORAM and GP-ORAM are both $O(NB)$, as the costs are dominated by the index table. The local storage cost for recursive GP-ORAM is $O(PB + S)$, which is asymptotically smaller than $O(\sqrt{N}B)$ as $P < \sqrt{N}$.

Figures 4 and 5 compare the performance of GP-ORAM with P-ORAM under the practical system settings used in [15] (i.e., block size ranging from 64 KB to 1 MB; the number of blocks ranging from $2^{24}$ to $2^{32}$). From the figures, we have the following observations: (i) The local storage demanded by recursive GP-ORAM is only 2.5%~0.14% of that by non-recursive P-ORAM, while GP-ORAM only yields about 1 to 3 times higher communication cost than P-ORAM.

Table 1. Asymptotical Performance Comparison.

| Scheme | Bandwidth Cost | User Storage | Server Storage | Failure Prob. |
|---|---|---|---|---|
| P-ORAM (NR) | $O(\log N \cdot B)$ | $O(NB)$ | $< 4NB$ | $O(\frac{1}{N^c})$ |
| P-ORAM (R) | $O(\log^2 N \cdot B)$ | $O(\sqrt{N}B)$ | $< 8NB$ | $O(\frac{1}{N^c})$ |
| GP-ORAM (NR) | $O(\frac{\log^3(N/P)}{\log^2 S} \cdot B)$ | $O(NB)$ | $< 5.3NB$ | $O(N^{-\log\log N})$ |
| GP-ORAM (R) | $O(\frac{\log^3(N/P)}{\log^2 S} \cdot B)$ | $O(PB + S)$ | $< 5.3NB$ | $O(N^{-\log\log N})$ |

(ii) Recursive P-ORAM is impractical due to its extremely high communication cost.

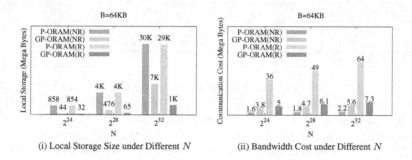

(i) Local Storage Size under Different $N$          (ii) Bandwidth Cost under Different $N$

**Fig. 4.** Comparing local storage and communication cost when $B = 64$ KB.

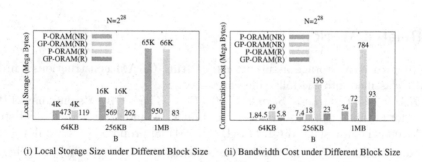

(i) Local Storage Size under Different Block Size     (ii) Bandwidth Cost under Different Block Size

**Fig. 5.** Comparing local storage and communication cost when $N = 2^{28}$.

**Comparing GP-ORAM, Path-ORAM and S-ORAM.** Table 2 shows the asymptotical performance comparisons between GP-ORAM, Path-ORAM and S-ORAM. Compared to S-ORAM and Path-ORAM, GP-ORAM introduces one adjustable system parameter $P$, which makes it more tunable.

The performance comparison between GP-ORAM and Path-ORAM under practical scenarios [15] is shown in Table 3. From the table, it can be seen that GP-ORAM can fully utilize the local storage to achieve better communication efficiency, and it incurs lower server-side storage cost.

**Table 2.** Asymptotical Performance Comparison.

| Scheme | Bandwidth Cost | User Storage | Server Storage | Failure Prob. |
|---|---|---|---|---|
| S-ORAM | $O(\frac{\log^3 N}{\log^2 S} \cdot B)$ | $O(S)$ | $< 6NB$ | $O(N^{-\log N})$ |
| Path-ORAM (NR) | $O(\log N \cdot B)$ | $O(NB)$ | $10NB$ | $N^{-\omega(1)}$ |
| Path-ORAM (R) | $O(\log^2 N \cdot B)$ | $O(\log N \cdot B) \cdot \omega(1)$ | $> 10NB$ | $N^{-\omega(1)}$ |
| GP-ORAM (NR) | $O(\frac{\log^3(N/P)}{\log^2 S} \cdot B)$ | $O(NB)$ | $< 5.3NB$ | $O(N^{-\log\log N})$ |
| GP-ORAM (R) | $O(\frac{\log^3(N/P)}{\log^2 S} \cdot B)$ | $O(PB + S)$ | $< 5.3NB$ | $O(N^{-\log\log N})$ |

**Table 3.** Practical Performance Comparison.

| Scheme | Bandwidth Cost | User Storage | Server Storage |
|---|---|---|---|
| Path-ORAM (NR) | $10\log N \cdot B$ | $N\log N + \log N \cdot B \cdot \omega(1)$ | $10NB$ |
| Path-ORAM (R) | $10\log^2 N \cdot B$ | $\log N \cdot B \cdot \omega(1)$ | $20NB$ |
| GP-ORAM (NR) | $< 4\log N \cdot B$ | $N\log N + PB + S$ | $< 5.3NB$ |
| GP-ORAM (R) | $< 6\log N \cdot B$ | $PB + S$ | $< 5.3NB$ |

Figure 6 shows the performance comparison between GP-ORAM and S-ORAM under practical scenarios [15]. From the figure, we can see that S-ORAM is not fully tunable as local storage increases. Especially when the local storage is large enough, the communication cost cannot be further reduced. For example, when $N = 2^{32}$, $B = 64$KB and the local storage size has exceeded 1.2 GB, the communication remains the same regardless of the increase in local storage size, while GP-ORAM can achieve 50%-60% savings in communication cost as the local storage gets larger.

## 7   Related Work

According to local storage assumptions, existing ORAM constructions can be roughly classified into the following categories.

*ORAMs with $O(1)$ Local Storage [2–9, 11, 13].* These ORAMs only have little state information, such as secret keys and query counters, stored in local storage. Among them, Balanced ORAM (B-ORAM) [8] proposed by Kushilevitz et. al. incurs the lowest asymptotical communication cost $O(\frac{\log^2 N}{\log\log N})$. In general, these constructions are impractical as the hidden constants behind the big-O notation are quite large due to the heavy data shuffling and background eviction processes. Recently, S-ORAM [19] with constant local storage was proposed to incur $O(\log^2 N)$ communication cost but with practically small constants behind the big-O notation. It leverages the fact that block size is usually large and introduced segmentation-based design of query and shuffling. However, the local storage was not fully utilized as in GP-ORAM.

*ORAMs with $O(\log^c N)$ Local Storage [4, 12, 16, 18].* Among these constructions, Path-ORAM [16] re-designed the tree structure ORAM [13] and reduced the bucket size by adding an additional stash to local storage, which resulted in only $O(\log^2 N)$ communication cost. PrivateFS [18] modified and improved

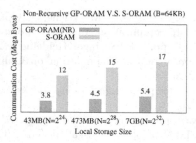
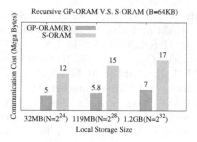

**Fig. 6.** GP-ORAM vs. S-ORAM with same given local storage.

a Bloom filter based ORAM solution [17] to approach practicality and concurrency, and resulted in $O(\log^2 N \log\log N)$ communication cost. These ORAMs still have high communication costs, needing to retrieve more than 1000 data blocks per query.

*ORAMs with $O(N^c)$ Local Storage [3,4,15–17].* The first ORAM with square-root local storage appeared in [3]. Though the actual communication cost is higher than $\sqrt{N}$ data blocks per query, it is still an inspiring solution that opens the door for subsequent research. Since then, a novel Bloom filter ORAM [17] was proposed which integrates a more efficient shuffling method to achieve better performance. ORAMs with $O(N^c)$ $(c > 0)$ local storage were also studied in [4]. Recently, P-ORAM, with sublinear local storage [15] (square-root local storage in practice) and efficient implementation [16], has achieved much lower communication cost of $O(\log N)$. However, as discussed in Section 6, the user-side storage cost could be too high to be acceptable, especially when the number of outsourced data blocks is large.

## 8 Conclusion

This paper proposed a new ORAM construction, called Generalized Partition ORAM (GP-ORAM). GP-ORAM utilizes a new shuffling method, adjusts the number of partitions according to the available user-side local storage, and outsources the index table to the server. Through these techniques, it achieves low bandwidth cost ($O(\log N)$) and has significantly less user-side storage cost than P-ORAM. We demonstrate the effectiveness of GP-ORAM via extensive security and cost analysis.

**Acknowledgement.** This work was partly supported by NSF under grant CNS-1422402.

## References

1. Freier, A.O., Karlton, P., Kocher, P.C.: The secure sockets layer (SSL) protocol version 3.0. In: RFC 6101 (2011)

2. Gentry, C., Goldman, K.A., Halevi, S., Julta, C., Raykova, M., Wichs, D.: Optimizing ORAM and using it efficiently for secure computation. In: De Cristofaro, E., Wright, M. (eds.) PETS 2013. LNCS, vol. 7981, pp. 1–18. Springer, Heidelberg (2013)

3. Goldreich, O., Ostrovsky, R.: Software protection and simulation on Oblivious RAM. Journal of the ACM **43**(3), May 1996

4. Goodrich, M.T., Mitzenmacher, M.: Mapreduce parallel cuckoo hashing and oblivious RAM simulations. In: Proc. CoRR (2010)

5. Goodrich, M.T., Mitzenmacher, M.: Privacy-preserving access of outsourced data via oblivious RAM simulation. In: Aceto, L., Henzinger, M., Sgall, J. (eds.) ICALP 2011, Part II. LNCS, vol. 6756, pp. 576–587. Springer, Heidelberg (2011)

6. Goodrich, M.T., Mitzenmacher, M., Ohrimenko, O., Tamassia, R.: Oblivious RAM simulation with efficient worst-case access overhead. In: Proc. CCSW (2011)

7. Goodrich, M.T., Mitzenmacher, M., Ohrimenko, O., Tamassia, R.: Privacy-preserving group data access via stateless oblivious RAM simulation. In: Proc. SODA (2012)

8. Kushilevitz, E., Lu, S., Ostrovsky, R.: On the (in)security of hash-based oblivious RAM and a new balancing scheme. In: Proc. SODA (2012)

9. Mayberry, T., Blass, E.-O., Chan, A.H.: Efficient private file retrieval by combining ORAM and PIR. In: Proc. NDSS (2014)

10. NIST. Block cipher modes. http://csrc.nist.gov/groups/ST/toolkit/BCM/index.html

11. Pinkas, B., Reinman, T.: Oblivious RAM revisited. In: Rabin, T. (ed.) CRYPTO 2010. LNCS, vol. 6223, pp. 502–519. Springer, Heidelberg (2010)

12. Ren, L., Yu, X., Fletcher, C.W., van Dijk, M., Devadas, S.: Design space exploration and optimization of path oblivious RAM in secure processors. In: Proc. ISCA (2006)

13. Shi, E., Chan, T.-H.H., Stefanov, E., Li, M.: Oblivious RAM with $O((\log N)^3)$ worst-case cost. In: Lee, D.H., Wang, X. (eds.) ASIACRYPT 2011. LNCS, vol. 7073, pp. 197–214. Springer, Heidelberg (2011)

14. Stefanov, E., Shi, E.: ObliviStore: high performance oblivious cloud storage. In: Proc. S&P (2013)

15. Stefanov, E., Shi, E., Song, D.: Towards practical oblivious RAM. In: Proc. NDSS (2011)

16. Stefanov, E., van Dijk, M., Shi, E., Fletcher, C., Ren, L., Yu, X., Devadas, S.: Path ORAM: an extremely simple oblivious RAM protocol. In: Proc. CCS (2013)

17. Williams, P., Sion, R.: Building castles out of mud: practical access pattern privacy and correctness on untrusted storage. In: Proc. CCS (2008)

18. Williams, P., Sion, R., Tomescu, A.: PrivateFS: a parallel oblivious file system. In: Proc. CCS (2012)

19. Zhang, J., Zhang, W., Qiao, D.: S-ORAM: a segmentation-based oblivious RAM. In: Proc. ASIACCS (2014)

20. Zhang, J., Zhang, W., Qiao, D.: GP-ORAM: A Generalized Partition ORAM. In ISU digital repository Computer Science Technical Report #378 (2015). http://lib.dr.iastate.edu/cs_techreports/378

# Anonymous Evaluation System

Kamil Kluczniak$^{(\boxtimes)}$, Lucjan Hanzlik, Przemysław Kubiak,
and Mirosław Kutyłowski

Faculty of Fundamental Problems of Technology,
Wrocław University of Technology, Wrocław, Poland
{kamil.kluczniak,lucjan.hanzlik,przemyslaw.kubiak,
miroslaw.kutylowski}@pwr.edu.pl

**Abstract.** We present a pragmatic evaluation system, where privacy of
each evaluator is guaranteed in a cryptographic way. Each evaluation
report is signed with a *domain signature* that is related to the anonymous signer and to the evaluation subject in the way that (a) a given user
cannot appear under different pseudonym for a given evaluation subject
(no Sybil attack possible), (b) it is infeasible to decide whether the signatures for different subjects have been created by the same evaluator,
(c) each evaluator holds a single private key.

Unlike available anonymous credential systems and domain signatures
proposed so far, our scheme is based on standard operations available on
most cryptographic smart cards and easy to implement in the scenarios
where the set of evaluators is determined. We describe one application
scenario – a university evaluation system with courses feedback from the
students.

**Keywords:** Anonymity · Authentication · Domain specific pseudonym ·
Digital signature · Unlinkability · White list

# 1 Introduction

## 1.1 Anonymity in IT Systems

We are facing a dynamic growth of electronic data processing. More and more frequently processing sensitive data takes place, where confidentiality requirements
cannot be limited to data contents but also to who is creating or processing the
data.

There are many areas where we urgently need anonymity. This concerns e.g.
whistleblowers, witness protection in criminal prosecutions, protection of children in court trials, certain health care areas, and many democratic processes.
The general rule is that only those data should be processed/available, which are
necessary for the process. Identity of actors of the process are frequently unnec-
essary. On the other hand, identity has been widely used in the non-electronic
era for the sheer reason that it was hard and costly to gather these identity data

---

work done under support of Wrocław University of Technology

M. Qiu et al. (Eds.): NSS 2015, LNCS 9408, pp. 283–299, 2015.
DOI: 10.1007/978-3-319-25645-0_19

and reuse them for malicious purposes. In the meantime the price for data intelligence has declined by order of magnitude, while on the other hand the level of data protection has not increased accordingly.

**Current Situation.** A typical approach is to use pseudonyms, erase explicit identification data and make sure that anonymity set is big enough (anonymity set is the set of identities that match a given data set). None of these techniques is effective in practice. The users are forced to trust the system administrators, the only other option is to opt-out from IT systems. As long as the data administrators are not caught to process sensitive data in an illegal way, the user cannot do anything. Illegal data trade of this kind might be very intensive.

The current legal concepts for data protection are not effective as well. The European directive [1] puts responsibility for unauthorized disclosure of personal data. However, practical implementation is not a success story. The data can emerge on a server where there are no rules of data protection, and once published it can be processed without limitations. A proposed regulation on personal data protection in Europe goes far beyond that, but still it seems that legal means alone cannot solve the problem.

**Available Technologies.** There are a few techniques aimed to protect anonymity of a user of IT systems. A basic solution is what we will call **domain separation**. According to this approach each domain is a separate islet with separate domain identities - pseudonyms, and independent authentication methods. However, this approach is problematic due to scalability problems, burden for the user and, frequently, insecure behavior of the users (e.g. reusing the same pseudonyms, keys, passwords, ...).

**Federated identity management**, and **single log-on** systems are aimed to be a solution for scalability problems. However the price is high: they require a single point of trust receiving data about all users' activities. The eIDAS concept [2] is similar: a national authentication center participates in authentication of their citizens abroad.

**Anonymous credential** [3–5] systems enable a user to prove his chosen attributes. The proof is based on cryptographic data provided by the credentials issuer. However, neither the user's identity nor credentials are revealed. By design, a verifier must not be able to learn any attributes that not revealed by the user or to link multiple presentations of the same user. On the other hand, a user must not be able to prove possession of attributes not confirmed by the issuer. Lost, expired or stolen credentials have to be revoked. The problem is that we cannot just blacklist a credential since the main idea is to protect anonymity. Therefore other techniques such as cryptographic accumulators are used [6, 7].

Anonymous credential concept is quite close to real world needs. E.g. for age verification (obligatory in some countries during purchase of alcohol) it should be sufficient to prove possession of an ID card issued for adults and matching face image from the ID card with the face of the document holder. Other attributes should be hidden.

A **group signature** scheme [8,9] allows to set up a group of users which then may sign data as group members. There are many versions of group signatures, however the main point is that the signature reveals nothing except for the group membership of the signer. Namely, it is infeasible to decide whether two signatures come from the same person (unless the scheme contains an opening procedure that enables to deanonimize the author of a signature).

**Ring signatures** [10] provide a similar functionality as group signatures. However, they do not require a join procedure and the group, called a ring, can be created ad hoc by a signer using public keys of other users. In contrary to group signatures, anonymity within the group is unconditional while the group is explicitly presented. In particular, the signatures of the same person are not linkable.

**Domain signature** schemes [11,12] enable a user to sign messages as a group member and referring to his pseudonym – a domain specific identity. Each user holds a single secret key, and using this key may derive exactly one pseudonym for a given domain and create his signatures under this pseudonym. The domain pseudonyms must not be linkable across multiple domains: a verifier holding domain pseudonyms and corresponding signatures from distinct domains must not be able to check which of them come from the same user.

**Restricted identification** [13] scheme enables a user to identify himself as a group member and derive a domain specific pseudonym. The main difference between restricted identification and domain signatures is that the first one is a pure identification scheme. It is simultable, i.e. any verifier holding the global public parameters may produce an properly distributed transcript of a protocol execution with any user of the system. So, it cannot be used for authenticating digital data stored in a system.

## 1.2 Anonymous Evaluation Systems

In this paper we focus on anonymous evaluation systems – a very specific application area where a strong anonymity protection is necessary, while on the other hand reliable and unbiased feedback is the main value.

A representative example for such evaluation systems is the feedback from the students about university courses. Such an evaluation is becoming a standard approach in many countries as part of quality control. A pilot of such a system has been implemented by the ABC4Trust project (https://abc4trust.eu/).

University course evaluation system is an interesting application case with high level of requirements. First, there is a problem of scale. Typically there are thousands of students enrolled to many courses. This yields a huge number of reports ($\approx 300K$ per year in our university – infeasible for paper based reporting). Moreover, without anonymity guarantees the students might fear to speak openly – especially in IT related departments where the students might be well aware of the threats of naive solutions (a web questionnaire with authentication via the University IT system). Last not least, some students might be eager to hack the system.

## 2    Requirements for Anonymous Evaluation

**Soundness Requirements.** In order to get sound evaluation results we have to guarantee fulfilling the following conditions:

**Resilience to Sybil Attacks:** A single (physical) person must not be able to appear under different identities in a given domain. Otherwise, it would be possible to heavily bias the evaluation results (both in a negative and a positive way). On the other hand, it makes sense to enable an evaluator to submit more than one opinion in the course of time as new issues may emerge. However, these opinions have to be linked to originate from the same person. Thereby, one can compare correctly the number of positive and negative voices.

**Domain Membership:** it must be guaranteed that only entitled evaluators provide their opinions. So for each domain there is an explicit or implicit set of domain members, and only the members may issue valid opinions. An explicit set of domain members may be defined via a set of certificates with public keys to be used for signature verification. An implicit set can be defined by possession of some cryptographic data – an entitled evaluator may use this data to create a proof of being a group member.
This property included in particular *seclusiveness*: nobody, including a coalition of legitimate group members, may authenticate himself as a member of a domain under a fake anonymous identity, not related to any legitimate member.

**Unforgeability:** It should be infeasible to impersonate a legitimate user within a domain. Impersonation means submitting an opinion that would be accepted and linked with a legitimate domain member.

**Unlinkability:** the authentication process should not create data that would provide <u>additional</u> knowledge regarding "who-is-who". That is, while the same opinions of the same domain member can be linked, it should be (computationally) infeasible to find any relationship between the opinions from different domains. In particular, it must be infeasible to link opinions of the same domain member with a real identity of the author.

**Implementation and Infrastructure Requirements.** As we are focusing on real world systems, we have to take into account additional limitations:

**Key Protection:** the keys used for signing evaluation reports should be protected just as other signing keys. This points to cryptographic smart cards as the only secure technology available on the market. Solutions such as software keys in smartphone apps are out of question due to possible key selling.

**Constant Number of Keys:** there is a constant number of long term private keys per user, while the number of domains is potentially unlimited. Moreover, for a given person it is a priori unpredictable for which domains this person will create opinions. "A constant number of keys" means here really a few keys: preferably just one.

The number of ephemeral secrets per authentication should be also limited to just a few values, which may be stored in a severely limited memory of devices such as smart cards. The same concerns storage for public keys, certificates, etc.

**Cryptographic Algorithms:** the operations involving secret keys of a signatory should be limited to cryptographic operations that are implemented on standard cryptographic devices. This means in practice that there are only a few signature algorithms at hand.

**Limited Infrastructure:** the system should not require building a complicated and large scale infrastructure, even such as X.509 PKI infrastructure.

**Existing Anonymity Techniques Versus the Requirements.** Let us discuss the standard anonymity tools and explain why they are not suited for anonymous evaluation systems:

**Domain Separation:** this solution might be perfect regarding unlinkability, however in practice a user (or his device) can hold only a few secrets.

**Federated Identity Management:** there is a single point of trust and its misbehavior may lead to identity disclosure. Therefore the evaluators would have to take into account that their identities will be forwarded to third parties, e.g. to the evaluated persons.

**Anonymous Credentials:** many schemes offer unlinkability of the actions of the same user in a domain, therefore the aimed application area is completely different. Moreover, so far all anonymous credential systems are pretty heavy regarding computation and storage.

**Restricted Identification:** this is a pure identification system. So we have to trust the administration of evaluation results repository and depend on their declarations. This concerns in particular linking the reports of the same evaluator.

**Group Signatures:** the main problem with standard group signatures is that we cannot link the reports of the same evaluator. Complicated procedures for joining the group and specially tailored signature schemes is also an implementation problem. Group signatures typically define procedures to reveal identity of a signer (either by the group manager or by the group members) – and this undermines their utility for evaluation systems.

**Ring Signatures:** ring signatures do not enable linking opinions of the same person. As this is a fundamental feature of ring signatures, the ring signatures are not suited for anonymous evaluation systems.

**Domain Signatures:** so far the proposed domain signature schemes assume that each user is by default a member of each domain. Creating a system of domain signatures was focused on the issue how to avoid e.g. necessity of issuing a certificate separately for each domain. The main issue however is low maturity of these schemes. E.g. the solution from [13] requires unconditional security of smart card devices.

# 3    Solution Framework

In this section we describe our proposal for anonymous evaluation. The presented instantiation uses the DSA signature scheme and a multiplicative group of a prime order. However, our framework can be instantiated with other groups and signatures schemes, e.g. ECDSA or Schnorr signatures. According to already used terminology each evaluation questionnaire concerns some domain and each evaluator has the right to submit reports within some specific set of domains.

The scenario presented here is closely related to a former paper [14]. However, the present solution is not based on an ad hoc designed signature scheme; it is a general framework where most signatures based on discrete logarithm problem can be used.

In our framework there are the following actors:

**Evaluators** – users which register their public keys and finally may submit evaluation questionnaires.

**Registration Server** – an authority responsible for user registration and assigning them rights to submit evaluation questionnaires in certain domains. It initiates creation of the white lists for each domain.

**Questionnaire Server** – a server receiving questionnaires submitted by evaluators, checking their validity based on white lists received from the Registration Server and archiving them.

**Mix Servers** – servers forming a chain between the registration and the questionnaire servers. They transform the list obtained from the registration server and finally output a white list for a given domain. The chain may consist of a single server.

**Inspection System** – a party that may challenge and control the output of mix servers.

## 3.1    Idea

In order to join the system, an evaluator has to register his public key at the registration server. The public key is a standard DSA public key, i.e. $g^x$, where $g$ is the generator of a prime order group and the exponent $x$ is the private key. The registration server stores the list of all public keys of the registered evaluators.

As the evaluation reports must be anonymous, the questionnaire server cannot just use the registered public keys for verification of submitted questionnaires. Instead, the questionnaire server receives a list that contains public keys corresponding to generator $g^r$. Namely, for an evaluator holding a private key $x$ the list has to contain the key $(g^r)^x$. The exponent $r$ is shared between the registration and mix servers, i.e. each server holds a random exponent $r_i$ and their product equals $r$. The list of public keys for the questionnaire server is created by raising the original list of public keys for a domain to all powers $r_i$. The process is sequential: after raising to power $r_i$ the list is given to the next server in the chain where it is raised to power $r_{i+1}$.

To protect against malicious mix servers we use an idea similar to [15]. (One could try to appply a more efficient solution from [16], but the problem would be to hide the links.) Apart from the standard list that is sent to the next mix server, the current one computes $N$ virtual lists that are computed using the exponent $r_i \cdot b_{i,j}$ (for $0 < j \leq N$). The number $N$ is a system parameter and it could be just 1. During an inspection the mix server is challenged by the inspection system to return, for each virtual list, either $r_i \cdot b_{i,j}$ or $b_{i,j}$. The first exponent can be used to verify that the virtual list corresponds to the input list of the mix server. The second exponent can be used to verify that the virtual list corresponds to the output list. With probability $1 - 2^{-N}$ the inspection system would detect an attempt to cheat by a mix server.

## 3.2  Detailed Description

**Registration Server Setup.** On input a security parameter $\lambda$, the registration server chooses a safe prime modulus $2^{\lambda-1} < p = 2q + 1 < 2^{\lambda}$. Then the registration server chooses a group generator $g \in \mathbb{GF}(p)$ of prime order $q$ at random, a secure hash function $H$, and a deterministic pseudorandom number generator DRNG which outputs pseudorandom numbers in $\mathbb{Z}_q$. The registration server chooses at random a secret seed $x_D$, $0 \leq x_D < 2^{\lambda}$, for the DRNG. It also sets parameter the parameter $N \geq 1$. Finally, the registration server sets the public parameters $pp = (\lambda, N, q, G, H, DRNG)$ and outputs $pp$. The secret seed $x_D$ is given securely to the questionnaire server.

**Evaluator Setup.** On input the public parameters $pp$, evaluator $U$ chooses a secret exponent $x_U \in \mathbb{Z}_q$ at random, and computes his public key $X_U := g^{x_U}$.

**Mix Server Setup.** Each mix server $S$, takes as input the public parameters $pp$ and chooses a secret seed $0 \leq x_S < 2^{\lambda}$ at random.

**Evaluator Registration.** In order to register an evaluator $U$ holding a secret/public key pair $(X_U, x_U)$, the following steps are executed:

1. The user $U$ interacts with the registration server and proves that he has the right to become an evaluator.
2. $U$ creates a DSA signature of his public key $X_U$, that is, he performs the following steps: choose $k \in \mathbb{Z}_q$ at random, compute $r := (g^k \mod p) \mod q$, and $s := (k^{-1}(H(X_U) + xr)) \mod q$.
3. $U$ sends the signature $\sigma = (r, s)$ and the public key $X_U$ to the registration server.
4. The registration server verifies the signature. That is, it computes $w := s^{-1} \mod q$, $u_1 := H(m) \cdot w \mod q$, $u_2 := r \cdot w \mod q$, and checks whether $r = ((g^{u_1} \cdot X_U^{u_2}) \mod p) \mod q$. If, the equality holds, then the registration server stores $(U, X_U)$ in its database.

**White List Generation.** It is initiated by the registration server and involves the chain of $l$ mix servers.

## Registration Server

On input the public parameters $pp$, a set of $n$ public keys $B = (X_1, \ldots, X_n)$ of evaluators and other auxiliary data such as a white list identifier wlID (e.g. the domain name) the following steps are executed by the registration server:

1. compute a secret key $r_0 := \mathsf{DRNG}(x_D, \mathtt{wlID})$, unique for the white list wlID,
2. compute $B_0[j] := (B[j])^{r_0}$, for $0 < j \le n$,
3. sort the list $B_0$,
4. compute $P_0 := g^{r_0}$ and send $L = (B_0, \mathtt{wlID}, P_0)$ to the first mix server.

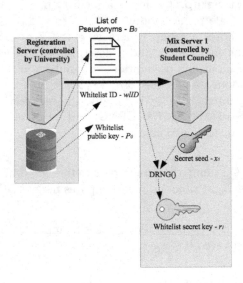

**Fig. 1.** The first part of the Whitelist generation procedure

## Mix Servers

The $i$th mix server obtains the following batch of data:

$$L = (B_0, \mathtt{wlID}, P_0, \ldots, (P_{i-1}, B_{i-1}, \{V_{i-1,1}, \ldots, V_{i-1,N}\})),$$

Then using the public parameters $pp$ and its secret seed $x_S$ the mix server executes the following steps:

1. compute a secret key $r_i := \mathsf{DRNG}(x_S, \mathtt{wlID})$ unique for the white list wlID,
2. for $0 < j \le N$ compute $b_{i,j} := \mathsf{DRNG}(x_S, \mathtt{wlID}, j)$,

3. for $0 < j \leq n$ compute $B_i[j] := (B_{i-1}[j])^{r_i}$,
4. for $0 < j \leq N$ and $0 < k \leq n$ compute $V_{i,j}[k] := (B_{i-1}[k])^{r_i \cdot b_{i,j}}$,
5. sort each of the following lists: $B_i, V_{i,1}, \ldots, V_{i,N}$,
6. compute $P_i := P_{i-1}^{r_i}$,
7. append $(P_i, B_i, \{V_{i,1}, \ldots, V_{i,N}\})$ to the list $L$,
8. if $i = l$, then send $L$ to the questionnaire server, else send $L$ to the mix server $i + 1$.

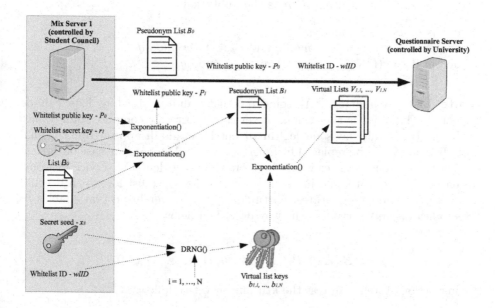

**Fig. 2.** The second part of the Whitelist generation procedure

**White List Finalization.** The questionnaire server obtains a list

$$L = (B_0, \mathtt{wlID}, P_0, \ldots, (P_l, B_l, \{V_{l,1}, \ldots, V_{l,N}\}))$$

and takes as input the public parameters $pp$. The server sets $W_{\mathtt{wlID}} = B_l$, the white list public key $PK_{\mathtt{wlID}} = P_l$ and outputs $(W_{\mathtt{wlID}}, \mathtt{wlID}, PK_{\mathtt{wlID}})$.

**Submitting an Opinion.** An evaluator $U$ holding a private key $x_U$ may fill in a questionnaire and submit it to the questionnaire server. First, the questionnaire server publishes the white list identifier $\mathtt{wlID}$ and the white list public key $PK_{\mathtt{wlID}}$. Let $m$ be a filled questionnaire prepared by the evaluator $U$. Now, he executes the following steps:

1. compute the pseudonym $nym := (PK_{\mathtt{wlID}})^{x_U} \mod p$ of $U$ in the domain $\mathtt{wlID}$,

2. compute a signature of $m$ related to the generator $PK_{\texttt{wlID}}$, the private key $x_U$ and the public key $nym$:
   - choose $k \in \mathbb{Z}_q$ at random,
   - compute $r := ((PK_{\texttt{wlID}})^k \mod p) \mod q$ ,
   - compute $s := k^{-1}(\mathsf{H}(m) + xr) \mod q$ ,
3. send the filled questionnaire $m$, the signature $\sigma = (r, s)$ of $m$, the white list identifier $\texttt{wlID}$, and the pseudonym $nym$ to the questionnaire server.

Now the questionnaire server checks whether $nym$ is on the white list and verifies the signature $\sigma$ using $nym$ as the public key:

1. compute $w := s^{-1} \mod q$,
2. compute $u_1 := \mathsf{H}(m) \cdot w \mod q$ and $u_2 := r \cdot w \mod q$,
3. accept if $r = ((PK_{\texttt{wlID}}^{u_1} \cdot nym^{u_2}) \mod p) \mod q$.

**White List Inspection.** At some moment validity of white lists can be inspected. The point is that a mix server can incorrectly compute some values on the list $B_i$. In this way some legitimate entries would disappear from the final white list and would be replaced by incorrect values. Moreover, in case of the last mix server the consequences would be more than just denial of service for some evaluators. Namely, it could insert an entry on the white list for which it could create corresponding signatures. Fortunately, mix server inspection enables to detect cheating mix servers in the way described below.

Given the batch

$$L = (B, \texttt{wlID}, P_0, \dots, (P_l, B_l, \{V_{l,1}, \dots, V_{l,N}\}))$$

the inspection system can test the $k$th mix server as follows:

1. For each $0 < j \leq N$ the inspection system flips a coin in order to determine a bit $t_j$. Then it challenges the $k$th mix server for the value $b_{k,j}$ if $t_j = 0$ or for the value of $b_{k,j} \cdot r_k$ if $t_j = 1$.
2. The inspected mix server recomputes the values $b_{k,j}$ and $r_k$ and returns the requested value.
   Let $e_{k,j}$ stand for the value returned by the mix server.
3. For $0 < j \leq N$ and $0 < t \leq n$ the inspection system computes

$$V'_{k,j}[t] := (V_{k,j}[t])^{e_{k,j}^{-1}} .$$

4. For each $0 < j \leq N$ the inspection system verifies that $V'_{k,j}$ contains the same elements as $B_k$ if $t_j = 0$ or the same elements as $B_{k-1}$ if $t_j = 1$.

The above procedure is interactive, i.e. the mix server must answer the challenge created by the inspection system. However, using Fiat-Shamir heuristic we may transform this procedure into a non-interactive one. Note that we only require that the challenges are not known to the mix server a priori.

# 4   Security Overview

We give some non-formalized discussion on the security of our solution. In particular, we focus on three key properties of an evaluation system, namely unforgeability, seclusiveness and domain unlinkability.

**Unforgeability.** In our scheme unforgeability is based on the unforgeability of the underlying signature scheme (DSA according to our description). Note that we exactly follow the DSA signature scheme, except for substituting the underlying base. To be more specific, let $g \in \mathbb{G}$ be the generator of the multiplicative group $\mathbb{G}$ on which we run DSA. Furthermore, let us focus on an evaluator $U$ with the public key $X_U = g^{x_U}$. While processing a white list, the registration server chooses a random $r_0 \in \mathbb{Z}_q$ and each mix server chooses a random $r_i \in \mathbb{Z}_q$, and exponentiates all the public keys present in a batch. Thus, at the end of the white list generation procedure the public key of the white list equals $PK_{\text{wlID}} = (g^{\Pi_{0 \leq i \leq l} r_i})$ and the pseudonym of the user $U$ takes the form $nym = (X_U)^{\Pi_{0 \leq i \leq l} r_i} = (g^{\Pi_{0 \leq i \leq l} r_i})^{x_U} = (PK_{\text{wlID}})^{x_U}$. Then, the DSA signature is made using $PK_{\text{wlID}}$ instead of the generator $g$ and $nym$ instead of the user public key $X_U$.

Note that if we could forge a signature for such a modified base, we could forge the original signature. Indeed, having a signature $(r, s)$ for $PK_{\text{wlID}} = g^{\Pi_{0 \leq i \leq l} r_i}$, we could create a signature for the base element $g$ defined as $(r, s')$ where $s' = s/(\Pi_{0 \leq i \leq l} r_i)$. Indeed, as $r = PK_{\text{wlID}}^k$, we can treat it as $r = g^{k \cdot \Pi_{0 \leq i \leq l} r_i}$ and modify $s$ accordingly.

**Seclusiveness.** Obviously, if the mix servers act according to the protocol description, then the adversary would have to produce a signature corresponding to a public key which is on the white list. In this case, the forgery would point to a real user public key, and the adversary would actually break the unforgeability property.

Another way to break seclusiveness, would be due to a misbehavior of some mix servers. In order to ensure that a mix server executes the protocol according to the specification, we use the inspection system and require the mix servers to process $N$ additional white lists. The additional white lists are computed using the exponent $r_i \cdot b_{i,j}$, instead of $r_i$, for $0 < j \leq N$. In case of an inspection, the inspection system tosses a coin $t_j$ and the mix server needs to publish $b_{i,j}$ if $t_j = 0$ or $r_i \cdot b_{i,j}$ if $t_j = 1$. In the first case, the inspection system might check whether the outgoing white list corresponds to the additional white list. In the second case, the inspection system might check whether the outgoing additional white list corresponds to the previous white list (the white list sent by the previous mix server). Hence, in case a mix server would induce any changes to the public keys being processed, he would need to change each additional white lists and, in order to not get caught by the inspection system, guess the choice of each $t_j$ in advance. The probability of any undetected misconduct by a mix server is $1/2^N$. Of course, the challenges $t_j$ must be inpredictable. In order to prevent a collusion between the inspection server and the mix servers these numbers could be determined based, e.g., on a hash of stock exchange data. The whole data computed by the inspection server must be published in order to enable recomputation by interested parties.

**Domain Unlinkability.** By domain unlinkability we mean the inability to correlate a pseudonym with the user's real identity. However, a formal definition of unlinkability is a challenging issue. One direction followed by some authors is to reduce the task of the adversary to a simplest case: just a single pair of users and two domains and then ask which pseudonyms in these domains correspond to the same user. The situation is then described by a left-or-right game and the scheme satisfies unlinkability property, if the advantage of an adversary is negligible. Such a game is defined in [11] (it contains a mistake pointed to in [12] – no domain signature scheme may satisfy this definition).

Another problem with unlinkability proofs is taking into account active adversaries. Such an adversary may corrupt any user and ask for the owner of every pseudonym (except for the pseudonyms and users involved in the left-or-right query). Moreover, the decision about the corruption target can be made based on the outcome of the previous interaction. [12] attempts to provide a proof in this dynamic case, however due to hidden assumptions the adversary is not fully dynamic. Moreover, the reduction tightness depends on the number of users.

In practice, there are many factors that may deanonimize a user regardless of the cryptographic scheme used. For instance, if a user submits all questionnaires at the same time, then the time corellation reveals the link between different pseudonyms. Therefore we propose to say that a scheme provides unlinkability if it does not matter which of the following two options is used by the user:

1. the user chooses a pair of keys for creating a signature within a given domain at random, independently of the choices for the other domains,
2. the pair of keys for this domain are chosen according to the scheme proposed.

Note that the first option corresponds to the most optimistic case: the user cannot do more to hide his identity in a system. We say that the scheme satisfies unlinkability property if an adversary cannot distinguish with a non-negligible advantage which of these two options has been chosen by the user.

In case of the proposed scheme, unlinkability follows from hardness of the decisional Diffie-Hellman problem. Let $X_U = g^{x_U}$, $PK_{\text{wlID}} = g^r$ and $nym = g^{x_U \cdot r}$, where $r \in \mathbb{Z}_q$ is a random element. So if DDH holds, then distinguishing the distributions

$$(X_U, PK_{\text{wlID}}, nym) \quad \text{and} \quad (X_U, PK_{\text{wlID}}, Z),$$

where $Z$ is chosen uniformly from $\mathbb{Z}_q$, is hard. Moreover, if we denote $r = r_0 \cdot r_1 \cdot \ldots \cdot r_l \mod q$, where $r_i$ is the secret exponent of a mix server $i$, it is easy to see that at least one honest server is necessary to provide unlinkability of pseudonyms. Given a case for DDH problem it is straightforward to build a scenario for the unlinkability question for our scheme.

# 5    Implementation Issues and Details

The critical point of any cryptographic anonymity system is implementation of the user's secret keys. Theoretically, smart cards and similar devices may serve as secure cryptographic suite, but there is a long way between protocol design and an affordable implementation. The best way is to reuse already available ID cards of the users (in our case, the student electronic ID cards), and adjust to the existing technical limitations.

Most smart cards used in practice today are closed architectures which do not allow any modifications. On the other hand, developing a new or modified card is costly, especially if card certification is required. A good option is to use Java Card (JC) technology that aims to preserve security features while allowing to install independently developed software on the card. However, we have to be aware that for Java Cards there are severe limitations and we cannot be sure in advance that the aimed protocol can be implemented successfully. JC technology is distributed by Oracle in a form of free standards. If defines, among others, the Java Card Virtual Machine (JCVM) and the Application Programming Interface (API). Programmers can use this API in their applets, written usually in the Java Card language. It is a subset of the standard Java programming language, e.g. it supports only data types up to **short** (16 bits). Moreover, one can only use the Java Card API and no standard Java library is supported.

Fortunately, we have succeeded with a test implementation on the Gemalto smart cards compatible with student IDs. A part of the source code for the cards is given on Fig. 3. Below we explain some crucial details.

Our protocol defines two operations to be implemented on a smart card: the pseudonym generation and creating a signature over a filled questionnaire (or its hash value).

The second part is fairly standard as signing is the main use case for smart cards. However, for efficiency reasons we are forced to use the signatures that are defined by the JC API and supported by the card's cryptographic coprocessor. Therefore we have to focus on DSA or ECDSA. In our implementation we first create the **Signature** object (line 32) with support for ECDSA. Then (line 55) we initialize this object with an ephemeral private key. This key holds the same secret value as the long term key of the user (set in line 54), but takes the public key of a course as the group generator (set in line 52). Finally (line 56), the data contained in the array **dataToSign** is signed.

Deriving the pseudonyms is more tricky, as it requires the exponentiation operation, which is not a standard cryptographic algorithm supported by the JC (with the cryptographic coprocessor). Moreover, we cannot use software implementation due to its inefficiency. Fortunately, we can abuse some algorithms implemented on the cryptographic coprocessor to do the job (compare [17]). In case of DSA we can use the **Cipher** class and the RSA algorithm without padding. For elliptic curves we can use the **KeyAgreement** class, implementing the elliptic curve Diffie-Hellman algorithm, as instantiated in line 31 in Fig. 3. This object is then initialized with the user's private key (line 34). Finally, the pseudonym for the particular course is computed using the public key of the course (line 48).

Note that some Java Cards only support a version of the ECDH algorithm which returns the hash value of the x-coordinate of the resulting point (as per IEEE P1363). However, in such a case we can just use this value as the user's pseudonym. In the implementation in Fig. 3 we require the plain version of the ECDH algorithm. This is defined by the 0x03 argument for the .getInstance method in line 31.

**Evaluation of the Implementation.** We evaluated efficiency of the user side implementation. To provide some reference data we have chosen smart card implementations of anonymous credential (AC) systems. This is one of the main use cases for AC and such implementation was also the deliverable of the European ABC4Trust project (https://abc4trust.eu/). Of course, AC have more features than our evaluation protocol. Thus, to provide realistic reference data we consider the case when users have only two attributes, i.e. the right to evaluate the course and the master secret key. Note that this is the best case scenario for AC (more attributes in credentials increase the time of presentation) and the users will have to create a different credential for each course they participate. We use the data from [19] regarding efficiency of the major AC systems, namely U-Prove and Idemix, on less constrained smart cards.

**Table 1.** Running times comparison

| protocol | average running time | security level (according to [19]) |
|---|---|---|
| our protocol | 549 ms | 128 (brainpool 256 bit curve) |
| U-Prove | 487 ms | 80 (1024 bit group) |
| Idemix | 997 ms | 80 (1024 bit group) |

The particular timings are presented in Table 1. In case of our solution this is the time required to generate the users pseudonym, send 64 bytes to the smart card and sign them. In case of AC the timings refer to the creation of a presentation token of 1 of 2 attributes. Note that presentation tokens require a nonce which may be the signed message.

An important disadvantage for AC based solutions is that the number of attributes is not just two – a student normally attends many courses at the time and use one credential for all courses. This increases memory usage while the memory size is a serious bottleneck for smart cards. Our solution would work for an unlimited number of courses with the same memory usage.

```
 1 /*
 2 * @author Lucjan Hanzlik
 3 * copyright: Wroclaw University of Technology
 4 */
 5 public class questionnaireJCApplet extends Applet {
 6
 7 ...
 8
 9 ECPublicKey pub;
10 ECPrivateKey priv;
11 ECPrivateKey ephPriv;
12 KeyAgreement ka;
13 KeyPair kp;
14 Signature sign;
15 byte[] pseudonym;
16 byte[] base;
17 short lenOfDataToSign;
18 byte[] dataToSign;
19 byte[] signature;
20 byte[] s;
21
22 private questionnaireJCApplet() {
23     register();
24     pub = (ECPublicKey)KeyBuilder.buildKey(
25        KeyBuilder.TYPE_EC_FP_PUBLIC,(short)(FIELDLen*8),false);
26     priv = (ECPrivateKey)KeyBuilder.buildKey(
27        KeyBuilder.TYPE_EC_FP_PRIVATE,(short)(FIELDLen*8),false);
28     ...
29     kp = new KeyPair(pub,priv);
30     kp.genKeyPair();
31     ka = KeyAgreement.getInstance((byte)0x03,false); //ECDH
32     sign = Signature.getInstance((byte)0x11,false); //ECDSA
33     ...
34     ka.init(priv);
35 }
36
37 ...
38
39 // Main function
40 public void process(APDU apdu){
41     byte[] buffer = apdu.getBuffer();
42     byte INS = buffer[ISO7816.OFFSET_INS];
43     short LC = (short)buffer[ISO7816.OFFSET_LC];
44     switch (INS) {
45        ...
46        case (byte)0x03: // sign
47           Util.arrayCopy(buffer,(short)ISO7816.OFFSET_CDATA,base,(short)0,LC);
48           ka.generateSecret(base,(short)0,(short)base.length,pseudonym,(short)0);
49           priv.getS(s,(short)0);
50           ephPriv = (ECPrivateKey)KeyBuilder.buildKey(
51              KeyBuilder.TYPE_EC_FP_PRIVATE,(short)(FIELDLen*8),false);
52           ephPriv.setG(base,(short)0,(short)base.length);
53           ...
54           ephPriv.setS(s,(short)0,(short)s.length);
55           sign.init(ephPriv,Signature.MODE_SIGN);
56           sign.sign(dataToSign,(short)0,lenOfDataToSign,signature,(short)0);
57           ...
58           break;
59        ...
60     }
61     ...
62 }
63 }
```

Fig. 3. Java Card implementation source code - main parts

## 6    Conclusions

We have shown that there is a fairly practical way to create a system fulfilling privacy-by-design principle in one of the key application areas requiring strong anonymization – namely, authentication of anonymous evaluation reports. While anonymous credentials technology can be used for these purposes as well, its complexity and requirements on user's hardware make them less suitable for practical applications, especially when we concern the general purpose smart cards available today. Moreover, we apply widely used and standard cryptographic methods that are relatively safe regarding patent violation claims and other threats regarding intelectual property rights.

## References

1. European Parliament and of the Council: Directive 95/46/EC of 24 October 1995 on the protection of individuals with regard to the processing of personal data and on the free movement of such data. Official Journal of the European Communities L(281) (23/11/1995)
2. European Commision: Proposal for a regulation of the European Parliament and of the Council on electronic identification and trust services for electronic transactions in the internal market (June 4, 2012). http://eur-lex.europa.eu/LexUriServ/LexUriServ.do?uri=COM:2012:0238:FIN:EN:PDF
3. Camenisch, J.L., Lysyanskaya, A.: A signature scheme with efficient protocols. In: Cimato, S., Galdi, C., Persiano, G. (eds.) SCN 2002. LNCS, vol. 2576, pp. 268–289. Springer, Heidelberg (2003)
4. Brands, S.: Untraceable off-line cash in wallets with observers. In: Stinson, D.R. (ed.) CRYPTO 1993. LNCS, vol. 773, pp. 302–318. Springer, Heidelberg (1994)
5. Baldimtsi, F., Lysyanskaya, A.: Anonymous credentials light. In: Proc. ACM SIGSAC Computer & Communications Security (CCS 2013), pp. 1087–1098. ACM (2013)
6. Acar, T., Chow, S.S.M., Nguyen, L.: Accumulators and U-prove revocation. In: Sadeghi, A.-R. (ed.) FC 2013. LNCS, vol. 7859, pp. 189–196. Springer, Heidelberg (2013)
7. Nguyen, L., Paquin, C.: U-Prove designated-verifier accumulator revocation extension. MSR-TR-2015-40, May 2015. http://research.microsoft.com/apps/pubs/default.aspx?id=219671
8. Bellare, M., Micciancio, D., Warinschi, B.: Foundations of group signatures: formal definitions, simplified requirements, and a construction based on general assumptions. In: Biham, E. (ed.) EUROCRYPT 2003. LNCS, vol. 2656, pp. 614–629. Springer, Heidelberg (2003)
9. Bellare, M., Shi, H., Zhang, C.: Foundations of group signatures: the case of dynamic groups. In: Menezes, A. (ed.) CT-RSA 2005. LNCS, vol. 3376, pp. 136–153. Springer, Heidelberg (2005)
10. Herranz, J., Sáez, G.: Forking lemmas for ring signature schemes. In: Johansson, T., Maitra, S. (eds.) INDOCRYPT 2003. LNCS, vol. 2904, pp. 266–279. Springer, Heidelberg (2003)
11. Bender, J., Dagdelen, Ö., Fischlin, M., Kügler, D.: Domain-specific pseudonymous signatures for the german identity card. In: Gollmann, D., Freiling, F.C. (eds.) ISC 2012. LNCS, vol. 7483, pp. 104–119. Springer, Heidelberg (2012)

12. Bringer, J., Chabanne, H., Lescuyer, R., Patey, A.: Efficient and strongly secure dynamic domain-specific pseudonymous signatures for ID documents. In: Christin, N., Safavi-Naini, R. (eds.) FC 2014. LNCS, vol. 8437, pp. 252–269. Springer, Heidelberg (2014)
13. BSI: Advanced Security Mechanisms for Machine Readable Travel Documents and eIDAS Token 2.20. Technical Guideline TR-03110-2 (2015). https://www.bsi. bund.de/EN/Publications/TechnicalGuidelines/TR03110/BSITR03110-eIDAS_ Token_Specification.html
14. Kutyłowski, M., Shao, J.: Signing with multiple ID's and a single key. In: IEEE Consumer Communications and Networking Conference (CCNC), pp. 519–520 (2011)
15. Choi, J.Y., Golle, P., Jakobsson, M.: Auditable privacy: on tamper-evident mix networks. In: Di Crescenzo, G., Rubin, A. (eds.) FC 2006. LNCS, vol. 4107, pp. 126–141. Springer, Heidelberg (2006)
16. Ateniese, G., Camenisch, J.L., Joye, M., Tsudik, G.: A practical and provably secure coalition-resistant group signature scheme. In: Bellare, M. (ed.) CRYPTO 2000. LNCS, vol. 1880, p. 255. Springer, Heidelberg (2000)
17. Bichsel, P., Camenisch, J., Groß, T., Shoup, V.: Anonymous credentials on a standard java card. In: ACM Computer and Communications Security (CCS), pp. 600–610 (2009)
18. Vullers, P.: Efficient Implementations of Attribute-based Credentials on Smart Cards (2014). http://www.cs.ru.nl/~pim/publications/2014_phd_thesis.pdf
19. Barker, E., Roginsky, A.: NIST Special Publication 800–131A - Transitioning the Use of Cryptographic Algorithms and Key Lengths. Technical report, July 2015. http://csrc.nist.gov/publications/drafts/800-131A/sp800-131a_r1_draft.pdf

# Cryptosystems

# An Efficient Leveled Identity-Based FHE

Fuqun Wang[1,2,3]($\boxtimes$), Kunpeng Wang[1,2], and Bao Li[1,2]

[1] State Key Laboratory of Information Security, Institute of Information
Engineering, Chinese Academy of Sciences, Beijing, China
{fqwang,kpwang,lb}@is.ac.cn
[2] Data Assurance and Communication Security Research Center,
Chinese Academy of Sciences, Beijing, China
[3] University of Chinese Academy of Sciences, Beijing, China

**Abstract.** Gentry, Sahai and Waters constructed the first identity-based fully homomorphic encryption schemes from identity-based encryption schemes in CRYPTO 2013. In this work, we focus on improving their IBFHE schemes, using Micciancio and Peikert's novel and powerful trapdoor in conjunction with Alperin-Sheriff and Peikert's simple and tight noise analysis technique when performing homomorphic evaluation.

**Keywords:** Fully homomorphic encryption · Identity-based encryption · Identity-based fully homomorphic encryption · Learning with errors

## 1 Introduction

Fully homomorphic encryption (FHE) is a special variant of public-key encryption (PKE) [15]. In an FHE system, anyone can compute any computable function over encrypted data without decrypting them first. These schemes with fully homomorphic property have extensive applications especially in cloud computing setting. The first realization of FHE is based on ideal lattices [15]. And several FHE schemes are built upon lattices [4,8,9,17,26,27] or integers [23].

Identity-based encryption (IBE) is also a special variant of PKE [22]. In an IBE system, the encrypter can produce a ciphertext masking $\mu$ to an identity $id$ only using the master public key of the system and the target identity $id$. Therefore, there is no need to issue a user-specific public key for each user in an IBE system. The first constructions of IBE are based on Bilinear Diffie-Hellman [5] or Quadratic Residues [14]. Since then, a multitude of IBE schemes are proposed over pairing [6,25] or lattices [1,2,10,16].

As a matter of course, identity-based fully homomorphic encryption (IBFHE) captures researchers' attention as it aggregates the advantages of both FHE and

This work is supported in part by the National Basic Research Program of China (973 project) (Grant No. 2013CB338001) and in part by the National Nature Science Foundation of China (Grant No. 61272040 and No. 61379137).

© Springer International Publishing Switzerland 2015
M. Qiu et al. (Eds.): NSS 2015, LNCS 9408, pp. 303–315, 2015.
DOI: 10.1007/978-3-319-25645-0_20

IBE. However, there are few results. In CRYPTO 2013, Gentry, Sahai and Waters [17] built a compiler that can *compile* all lattices-based IBE schemes [1,2,10,16] and obtained the first IBFHE schemes. Based on Gentry-Sahai-Waters' technique, Clear and McGoldrick [12] designed the first multi-identity IBFHE from GPV-IBE [16] in the random oracle model in CRYPTO 2015. All IBFHEs above are leveled homomorphic, meaning that they only can compute homomorphically a priori polynomial-depth circuits, but no more. Recently, Clear and McGoldrick [13] built the first non-leveled IBFHE assuming that indistinguishable obfuscator exists.

**Contribution.** We improve the ABB-IBE [1] to a new one with shorter public parameters, using Micciancio-Peikert's new trapdoor for lattices [18] (called MP12-trapdoor). We note that Micciancio and Peikert [18] had pointed out that their new trapdoor can be used to optimize all lattices-based cryptography with trapdoor containing ABB-IBE scheme (outlined in [20]). But, there are no details for IBE schemes. We observe that how to release the energy of MP12-trapdoor in the identity-based setting is nontrivial, as we have to choose subtly the noise used in encryption to show its security. In fact, if we choose noise as that in [1], we do not know how the simulator simulates the attack context and reduces the hardness of learning with errors (LWE) to the IBE scheme. In other words, the idea of security proof follows that in [1] in high level, but the details in technical level are very different. We note also that it can be extended to hierarchical IBE as that in [1,17], and to ring setting for less storage space and higher efficiency.

Our main result is an efficient leveled IBFHE *compiling* the new IBE above. We use the *approximate eigenvector* method first proposed by Gentry, Sahai and Waters [17] to eliminate the user-specific keys (i.e., evaluation key). In addition, to slow the noise growth under homomorphic evaluation, we perfectly randomize the noise under homomorphic operations and utilize subgaussianity to measure the noise level. Both of them are first employed by Alperin-Sheriff and Peikert [4] to lower the parameters meanwhile maintaining equal security level.

**Paper Organization.** In Sect. 2, we give some background on lattices and related tools used in this paper. We describe formally an optimized IBE scheme in Sect. 3. In Sect. 4, we present the leveled IBFHE compiling the IBE proposed in last section. Finally, we conclude in Sect. 5.

## 2 Preliminaries

The following notations will be used throughout. The bold upper-case letters (e.g. $\mathbf{A}, \mathbf{B}$) represent matrices and bold lower-case letters (e.g. $\mathbf{a}, \mathbf{b}$) represent column vectors. We use $a_i$ to denote the $i$-entry of $\mathbf{a}$ and $||\mathbf{a}||_2 = \sqrt{\sum a_i^2}$ to denote the Euclidean norm. We write $[\mathbf{A}||\mathbf{B}]$ to denote the concatenation of two matrices and $(\mathbf{a}, \mathbf{b})$ to denote the concatenation of two column vectors. Let $n$ denote the *security parameter* throughout. Let $[n] = \{1, 2, \ldots, n\}$ and negl($n$) denote a negligible function that grows slower than $n^{-c}$ for any constant $c > 0$

and any large enough value of $n$. An event occurs with overwhelming probability meaning that it occurs with probability at least $1 - \text{negl}(n)$.

## 2.1 IBE and IBFHE

IBE consists of the following four PPT algorithms: (Setup, Extract, Enc, Dec) with syntax: The Setup algorithm outputs a master public-key $mpk$ and a master secret-key $msk$. The Extract algorithm takes $msk$ and an identity $id$ as input and produces a private key $sk_{id}$ for identity $id$. The Enc algorithm encrypts a message to identity $id$ using $mpk$ and $id$, and the Dec algorithm decrypts ciphertext using the knowledge of $sk_{id}$ corresponding to identity $id$.

Identity-based fully homomorphic encryption, as a special variant of IBE, has the fifth algorithm Eval. For some function $f$, given $t$ ciphertexts: $c_i \leftarrow$ Enc$(mpk, id, \mu_i)$ for $i = 1, 2, \ldots, t$, anyone can compute a new ciphertext $c \leftarrow$ Eval$(f, mpk, id, c_1, c_2, \ldots, c_t)$ encrypting $f(\mu_1, \mu_2, \ldots, \mu_t)$. Generally speaking, the depth of the function $f$ combined by NAND-gates is constrained by L for some L, because it is considerably expensive to perform homomorphically high-depth circuit. We called it leveled IBFHE. In this work, we will mainly focus on the leveled IBFHE schemes, and thus we will omit "leveled" for simplicity.

**Security.** An IBE system should be semantically secure under chosen-identity-attack and chosen-plaintext-attack (IND-ID-CPA). A weaker security model of IBE constricts that the adversary has to make the identity it plans to attack public prior to receiving the master public-key (IND-sID-CPA). A stronger security model of IBE is also considered, in which the ciphertext is indistinguishable from a random member in the ciphertext space (INDr-ID-CPA), and which implies both semantic security and recipient anonymity. The security model of IBFHE is same as that of IBE without reference to the evaluation algorithm, as the evaluation algorithm is public and does not impact the security.

In this work, we will mainly focus on the INDr-sID-CPA security game for IBE (or IBFHE) defined as follows. Consider a security game between two parties with a challenger and a PPT adversary. After receiving the target identity $id^*$ which the adversary plans to attack, the challenger runs Setup algorithm to gain $(mpk, msk)$ and sends $mpk$ back to the adversary. Moreover, the challenger has to return the secret-key $sk_{id_j}$ corresponding to $id_j$ that is chosen adaptively by the adversary for polynomial many identities conditioning on $id_j \neq id^*$. Then, once the challenger receives a message $\mu^*$ chosen randomly by the adversary, it picks a random bit $b \in \{0, 1\}$ and a random ciphertext $\mathbf{c}$ from ciphertext space. If $b = 0$, it sets the challenge ciphertext to $\mathbf{c}^* = $ Enc$(mpk, id^*, \mu^*)$. Otherwise, it sets the challenge ciphertext to $\mathbf{c}^* = \mathbf{c}$. After that, it returns the $\mathbf{c}^*$ as the IBE (or IBFHE) challenge to the adversary. Finally, the adversary outputs a guess $b'$ and wins if $b' = b$. We say that an IBE (or IBFHE) scheme is INDr-sID-CPA secure if $\Pr[b' = b] \leq \frac{1}{2} + \text{negl}(\lambda)$.

## 2.2    Hashing and Subgaussianity

In this section, we will recall some facts about hash function and subgaussianity.

**Hashing.** Let $\mathcal{A}$ and $\mathcal{B}$ be two finite sets, a family $\mathcal{H}$ of functions mapping $\mathcal{A}$ to $\mathcal{B}$ is 2-universal if for all $a, a' \in \mathcal{A}, a \neq a'$, $\Pr_{h \xleftarrow{s} \mathcal{H}}[h(a) = h(a')] = 1/|\mathcal{B}|$.

Let $\mathcal{D}$ be a distribution over $\{-1, 0, 1\}$ that outputs 0 with probability 0.5, -1 with probability 0.25 and 1 with probability 0.25 (We use $\mathcal{D}$ to denote this distribution throughout). A version of leftover hash lemma holds as follows.

**Lemma 1 ([3]).** *Let $\mathcal{B} = \mathbb{Z}_q$ be a finite abelian group and $k \geq 1$ be an integer. For $\mathbf{b} \in \mathcal{B}^k$, define $h_{\mathbf{b}} : \mathcal{D}^k \to \mathcal{B}$ as $h_{\mathbf{b}}(\mathbf{a}) = \sum_{i=1}^k a_i b_i$. Then the family $\mathcal{H} = \{h_{\mathbf{b}}\}_{\mathbf{b} \in \mathcal{B}^k}$ is 2-universal. It follows that $(h_{\mathbf{b}}, h_{\mathbf{b}}(\mathbf{a}))$ is $\frac{1}{2}\sqrt{q/2^k}$-uniform.*

**Subgaussian Random Variable.** In this work, it is conducive to manipulate the noise growth using subgaussian random variable. A real random variable $X$ is subgaussian with parameter $s \geq 0$ if for all $t \geq 0$, it holds that $\Pr[|X| > t] \leq 2\exp(-\pi t^2/s^2)$. Gaussian tails then imply subgaussianity if $\mathbb{E}[X] = 0$. Any $B$-bounded 0-mean random variable $X$ is subgaussian with parameter $B\sqrt{2\pi}$. A detailed introduction of subgaussianity can be found in [24]. The following lemma is useful to analyze the change of noise under homomorphic evaluation.

**Lemma 2 ([7]).** *Let $X_1, X_2, \ldots, X_k$ be independent, 0-mean, real subgaussian random variables with parameter $s$ and $\mathbf{a} = (a_1, a_2, \ldots, a_k) \in \mathbb{R}^k$. Then $\sum_i (a_i X_i)$ is a subgaussian random variable with parameter $s \cdot ||\mathbf{a}||_2$.*

Subgaussianity can be generalized to vectors: a random real vector $\mathbf{x}$ is subgaussian with parameter $s$ if for all unit vector $\mathbf{u}$, the marginal $\langle \mathbf{x}, \mathbf{u} \rangle \in \mathbb{R}$ is subgaussian with parameter $s$. It follows that the concatenation of independent subgaussian random variables with equal $s$ is also subgaussian with parameter $s$. In addition, it can be extended to subgaussian random matrix in direct manner.

A standard result of subgaussianity [24] follows.

**Lemma 3 ([24]).** *Let $\mathbf{X} \in \mathbb{R}^{n \times m}$ be a subgaussian random matrix with parameter $s$. There then exists a constant $c > 0$ such that, with overwhelming probability, $||\mathbf{X}||_2 \leq c \cdot s \cdot (\sqrt{m} + \sqrt{n})$ where $||\mathbf{X}||_2 \triangleq \max(||\mathbf{X}\mathbf{u}||_2)$ for all unit vector $\mathbf{u}$.*

## 2.3    Background on Lattices and Hard Problems

**Lattices.** For a matrix $\mathbf{A} \in \mathbb{Z}_q^{n \times m}$ we define the following $q$-ary integer lattice:

$$\Lambda^{\perp}(\mathbf{A}) = \{\mathbf{x} \in \mathbb{Z}^m : \mathbf{A}\mathbf{x} = \mathbf{0} \mod q\}.$$

For a vector $\mathbf{u} \in \mathbb{Z}_q^n$, we define the coset (or "shifted" lattice):

$$\Lambda_{\mathbf{u}}^{\perp}(\mathbf{A}) = \{\mathbf{x} \in \mathbb{Z}^m : \mathbf{A}\mathbf{x} = \mathbf{u} \mod q\}.$$

**LWE.** We give a variant of learning with errors problem used extensively in fully homomorphic cryptography. For two positive integers $n$ and $q \geq 2$, an arbitrary vector $\mathbf{s} \in \mathbb{Z}_q^n$ and a probability distribution $\chi$ over $\mathbb{Z}$, let $A_{\mathbf{s},\chi}$ be the distribution obtained by choosing a vector $\mathbf{a} \xleftarrow{\$} \mathbb{Z}_q^n$ and an error term $e \leftarrow \chi$, and outputting $(\mathbf{a}, [\langle \mathbf{a}, \mathbf{s} \rangle - 2e]_q) \in \mathbb{Z}_q^n \times \mathbb{Z}_q$. The search learning with errors (LWE$_{n,m,q,\chi}$) problem is, given $m = \text{poly}(n)$ independent samples from $A_{\mathbf{s},\chi}$, to find $\mathbf{s}$ for some random $\mathbf{s} \in \mathbb{Z}_q^n$. The decisional learning with errors (DLWE$_{n,m,q,\chi}$) problem is, given $m$ independent samples, to decide that, with non-negligible advantage, they are sampled from $A_{\mathbf{s},\chi}$ for a uniformly random and secret $\mathbf{s} \in \mathbb{Z}_q^n$, or from the uniform distribution over $\mathbb{Z}_q^n \times \mathbb{Z}_q$. We often write DLWE$_{n,m,q,\alpha}$ to denote DLWE$_{n,m,q,\chi}$ and $A_{\mathbf{s},\alpha}$ to denote $A_{\mathbf{s},\chi}$ for $\chi = \mathcal{D}_{\mathbb{Z},\alpha q}$.

For certain parameters, solving the DLWE problem in the average-case is known to be as hard as approximation lattices problems, such as decisional shortest vector problem (GapSVP) and shortest independent vector problem (SIVP), in the worst-case. In particular, for $\alpha q \geq 2\sqrt{n}$, solving DLWE$_{n,m,q,\alpha}$ is as hard as solving above worst-case lattices problems with approximation factors of $\widetilde{O}(n/\alpha)$, using a quantum or classical reduction [19,21].

**Lattices Trapdoor.** Here we recall the MP12-trapdoor generation algorithm, subgaussian sampling algorithm and Gaussian sampling algorithm [18]. We ignore all details of implementation which are not strictly necessary in this work.

For an odd integer $q$ and $\ell = \lceil \log q \rceil$, let $\mathbf{G} = \mathbf{I}_n \otimes \mathbf{g}^T \in \mathbb{Z}_q^{n \times n\ell}$, where $\mathbf{g}^T = (1, 2, 2^2, \ldots, 2^{\ell-1})$ and $\mathbf{I}_n$ denotes the $n$-dimensional identity matrix.

**Lemma 4 ([18]).** *Let $n, m_0, m_1, m, q, \ell$ be positive integers such that $q = q(n), \ell = \lceil \log q \rceil, m_0 = n\ell + O(n), m_1 = n\ell$ and $m = m_0 + m_1$. For $\mathbf{A}_0 \xleftarrow{\$} \mathbb{Z}_q^{n \times m_0}$, invertible $\mathbf{H} \in \mathbb{Z}_q^{n \times n}$ and $\mathbf{R} \leftarrow \mathcal{D}^{m_0 \times m_1}$ where $\mathcal{D}$ is defined in section 2.2, there exists an efficiently randomized algorithm $\mathsf{GenTrap}(\mathbf{A}_0, \mathbf{H})$ to generate a matrix $\mathbf{A} (= [\mathbf{A}_0 || \mathbf{H}\mathbf{G} - \mathbf{A}_0\mathbf{R}]) \in \mathbb{Z}_q^{n \times m}$ with trapdoor $\mathbf{R}$ and tag $\mathbf{H}$ such that $\mathbf{A}$ is $\text{negl}(n)$-far from uniform. $\mathbf{R}$ is called an MP12-trapdoor of $\mathbf{A}$ with tag $\mathbf{H}$.*

**Lemma 5 ([4,18]).** *Given the gadget matrix $\mathbf{G}$ defined above, for any matrix $\mathbf{A} \in \mathbb{Z}_q^{n \times m_0}$ there exists efficiently randomized algorithm to sample a subgaussian matrix $\mathbf{X} \in \mathbb{Z}_q^{m_1 \times m_0}$ with parameter $O(1)$ such that $\mathbf{X} = \mathbf{G}^{-1}(\mathbf{A})$.*

**Lemma 6 ([18]).** *Given parameters in Lemma 4 and a uniformly random vector $\mathbf{u} \in \mathbb{Z}_q^n$, for some $s \in \mathbb{R}$ and a fixed function $\omega(\sqrt{\log n})$ growing asymptotically faster than $\sqrt{\log n}$, there exists an efficient algorithm $\mathsf{SampleD}(\mathbf{R}, \mathbf{A}_0, \mathbf{H}, \mathbf{u}, s)$ that samples a vector $\mathbf{t}$ from $\mathcal{D}^m_{\mathbb{Z}, s \cdot \omega(\sqrt{\log n})}$ such that $\mathbf{A} \cdot \mathbf{t} = \mathbf{u}$.*

## 3  Identity Based Encryption

In this section, we first propose an IBE with smaller parameters which is an improvement of ABB-IBE [1], using MP12-trapdoor. We then show that the proposed IBE is INDr-sID-CPA secure under the DLWE assumption. We note that Micciancio and Peikert [18] already pointed out that their new trapdoor could be used to optimize lattices-based IBE schemes. But, they did not give much details. In fact, we must choose and manage noise subtly for security proof. So, it is necessary to particularly describe it and prepare for the next section.

## 3.1   The Basic Identity-Based Encryption

Recall that $n$ is the security parameter. In order to describe the IBE scheme succinctly, we give some public parameters as follows.

- The modulus $q$ is a sufficiently large prime $q = \text{poly}(n)$. Let $\ell = \lceil \log q \rceil$, $m_0 = n(\ell + O(1))$, $m_1 = n\ell$ and $m = m_0 + m_1$.
- $\mathbf{G} = \mathbf{I}_n \otimes \mathbf{g}^T \in \mathbb{Z}_q^{n \times n\ell}$ for $\mathbf{g}^T = (1, 2, 2^2, \ldots, 2^{\ell-1})$ is the gadget matrix.
- Let $\mathcal{D}$ be the distribution over $\{-1, 0, 1\}$ as defined in Sect. 2.2, such that $(\mathbf{A}_0, \mathbf{A}_0\mathbf{R})$ is $\text{negl}(n)$-far from $(\mathbf{U}_0, \mathbf{U}_1) \xleftarrow{\$} \mathbb{Z}_q^{n \times m_0} \times \mathbb{Z}_q^{n \times m_1}$ for $\mathbf{A}_0 \xleftarrow{\$} \mathbb{Z}_q^{n \times m_0}$ and $\mathbf{R} \leftarrow \mathcal{D}^{m_0 \times m_1}$. Note that this regularity is yet discussed in [18] and we also can sample $\mathbf{R} \leftarrow \mathcal{D}_{\mathbb{Z}, \omega(\sqrt{\log n})}^{m_0 \times m_1}$ resulting mildly larger parameters.
- We assume that identities are elements in $\text{GF}(q^n)$, and say $\mathbf{H} : \text{GF}(q^n) \to \mathbb{Z}_q^{n \times n}$ is an invertible difference, if $\mathbf{H}(id_1) - \mathbf{H}(id_2)$ is invertible for any two different identities $id_1, id_2$ and $\mathbf{H}$ is computable in polynomial time in $n\ell$ (see an example in [1]).
- The LWE error rate $\alpha$ for IBE should be large enough such that $\alpha q \geq 2\sqrt{n}$.

Now we describe the proposed scheme IBE.

- IBE.Setup($1^n$): Choose $\mathbf{A}_0 \xleftarrow{\$} \mathbb{Z}_q^{n \times m_0}$, $\mathbf{u} \xleftarrow{\$} \mathbb{Z}_q^n$ and $\mathbf{R} \leftarrow \mathcal{D}^{m_0 \times m_1}$. Let $\mathbf{A} = [\mathbf{A}_0 || \mathbf{A}_1] = [\mathbf{A}_0 || -\mathbf{A}_0\mathbf{R}] \in \mathbb{Z}_q^{n \times m}$ as Lemma 4 and set master public key as $mpk = [\mathbf{u} || \mathbf{A}]$ and master secret key as $msk = \mathbf{R}$. Note that $\mathbf{A} \cdot \begin{bmatrix} \mathbf{R} \\ \mathbf{I}_{m_1} \end{bmatrix} = \mathbf{0}$.
- IBE.Extract($\mathbf{R}, id$): Compute $\mathbf{H}(id)$ for $id \in \mathbb{Z}_q^n$ and let $\mathbf{A}_{id} = [\mathbf{A}_0 || \mathbf{A}_1 + \mathbf{H}(id) \cdot \mathbf{G}]$ (Remark that $\mathbf{R}$ is an MP12-trapdoor of $\mathbf{A}_{id}$ with tag $\mathbf{H}(id)$). Run SampleD($\mathbf{R}, \mathbf{A}_0, \mathbf{H}(id), \mathbf{u}, \|\mathbf{R}\|_2$) to generate a short vector $\mathbf{t} \in \mathbb{Z}^m$ such that $\mathbf{A}_{id} \cdot \mathbf{t} = \mathbf{u}$. Set user-specific public key $pk_{id} = \mathbf{P} = [\mathbf{u} || \mathbf{A}_{id}]$ and secret key $sk_{id} = \mathbf{s} = (1, -\mathbf{t})$ with small entries. Note that $\mathbf{P} \cdot \mathbf{s} = \mathbf{0}$.
- IBE.Enc($mpk, id, \mu \in \{0, 1\}$): To encrypt a bit $\mu \in \{0, 1\}$, choose two vectors $\mathbf{y} \xleftarrow{\$} \mathbb{Z}_q^n$ and $\mathbf{e} = (-e, -\mathbf{e}_0, \mathbf{e}_1) \in \mathbb{Z}^{m+1}$, where $e \leftarrow \mathcal{D}_{\mathbb{Z}, \alpha q}$, $\mathbf{e}_0 \leftarrow \mathcal{D}_{\mathbb{Z}, \alpha q}^{m_0}$ and $\mathbf{e}_1 \leftarrow \mathcal{D}_{\mathbb{Z}, s}^{m_1}$ for $s^2 = (\|\mathbf{e}_0\|_2^2 + m_0\alpha^2 q^2) \cdot \omega(\sqrt{\log n})^2$. Output a ciphertext vecor

$$\mathbf{c} = \mu\mathbf{v} + \mathbf{P}^T\mathbf{y} + 2\mathbf{e} \in \mathbb{Z}_q^{m+1},$$

where $\mathbf{v} = (1, 0, \ldots, 0)^T$ is the first $(m+1)$-length standard unit vector.
- IBE.Dec($\mathbf{c}, sk_{id}$): Output $\mu' = \langle \mathbf{c}, \mathbf{s} \rangle \bmod q \bmod 2$.

*Remark.* The noise $\mathbf{e}_1$ sampled from a slight wider (than $\mathbf{e}_0$) discrete Gaussian distribution $\mathcal{D}_{\mathbb{Z}, s}^{m_1}$ for $s^2 = (\|\mathbf{e}_0\|_2^2 + m_0\alpha^2 q^2) \cdot \omega(\sqrt{\log n})^2$ plays a vital role in the security proof.

**Table 1.** Parameters comparison with ABB-IBE [1]

| IBE | $m_0$ | $m_1$ | $q$ | $\alpha$ | |
|---|---|---|---|---|---|
| ABB-IBE [1] | $6n \log q$ | $6n \log q$ | $m_0^{2.5} \cdot \omega(\sqrt{\log n})$ | $(m_0^2 \cdot \omega(\sqrt{\log n}))^{-1}$ | a |
| This work | $n(\log q + O(1))$ | $n \log q$ | $m_0^2 \cdot \omega(\sqrt{\log n})^3$ | $(m_0^{1.5} \cdot \omega(\sqrt{\log n})^3)^{-1}$ | |

a Note that $m = m_0 = m_1$ in [1] while we use them to denote different integers. Given parameters above, the lengths of $mpk, msk, sk_{id}$ and ciphertext can be compared too, e.g., the bit-length of $mpk$ of the proposed IBE is around $\frac{4}{15}$ of that of ABB-IBE.

### 3.2 Parameters

**Lemma 7.** *Let* $q = m_0^2 \cdot \omega(\sqrt{\log n})^3, \alpha = (m_0^{1.5} \cdot \omega(\sqrt{\log n})^3)^{-1}$ *and other parameters set in Sect. 3.1. The decryption algorithm in basic* IBE *scheme above then works with overwhelming probability.*

*Proof.* It is very easy to see that, by decryption,

$$\langle \mathbf{c}, \mathbf{s} \rangle = \mu \cdot \langle \mathbf{v}, \mathbf{s} \rangle + 2\langle \mathbf{e}, \mathbf{s} \rangle = \mu + 2\langle \mathbf{e}, \mathbf{s} \rangle = \mu - 2e + 2\langle \mathbf{e}_0, \mathbf{t}_0 \rangle - 2\langle \mathbf{e}_1, \mathbf{t}_1 \rangle,$$

where short vector $\mathbf{t} = (\mathbf{t}_0, \mathbf{t}_1) \in \mathbb{Z}^{m_0} \times \mathbb{Z}^{m_1}$. We now bound $|\langle \mathbf{e}_1, \mathbf{t}_1 \rangle|$.

By Lemma 3, we have $\|\mathbf{e}_1\|_2 \le c \cdot O(\sqrt{m_0}\alpha q \cdot \omega(\sqrt{\log n})) \cdot \sqrt{m_1} \le m_0 \alpha q \cdot \omega(\sqrt{\log n})$ with overwhelming probability. So, by Lemma 12 in [1], we get

$$|\langle \mathbf{e}_1, \mathbf{t}_1 \rangle| \le \|\mathbf{e}_1\|_2 \cdot (O(\sqrt{m_0}) \cdot \omega(\sqrt{\log m_0}) \cdot \omega(\sqrt{\log m_1}) + \frac{1}{2}\sqrt{m_1}) \le m_0^{1.5}\alpha q \cdot \omega(\sqrt{\log n})^3.$$

By our parameter setting, we then have $|\langle \mathbf{e}_1, \mathbf{t}_1 \rangle| \le m_0^2 \cdot \omega(\sqrt{\log n})^3$ with overwhelming probability. Similarly, $|\langle \mathbf{e}_0, \mathbf{t}_0 \rangle| \le m_0^2 \cdot \omega(\log n)$ with overwhelming probability. It is easy to see that $|e| \le \alpha q \sqrt{n}$ and thus $|\langle \mathbf{c}, \mathbf{s} \rangle| \le m_0^2 \cdot \omega(\sqrt{\log n})^3$. The correctness of decryption follows. $\square$

We compare the parameters of the proposed IBE above with ABB-IBE [1] in Table 1, from which we can see that all parameters are optimized.

### 3.3 Security

We prove that the basic scheme IBE constructed above is INDr-sID-CPA secure. In other words, a valid cipertext is indistinguishable from a random membership in ciphertext space under a selective chosen-identity and chosen-plaintext attack. The proof follows from the security proof of ABB-IBE in [1] in the high level and the security proof of CCA-secure PKE in [18] in the technical level.

**Theorem 1.** *The basic scheme* IBE *constructed in Sect. 3.1 is* INDr-sID-CPA *secure assuming that the* $DLWE_{n,m_0+1,q,\alpha}$ *assumption holds.*

*Proof.* We now reduce the DLWE to INDr-sID-CPA security of the IBE scheme.

After seeing the DLWE challenge $\{(\mathbf{a}_i, b_i)\}_{i \in [m_0+1]}$ to decide them from $A_{\mathbf{y},\alpha}$ or random and the challenge identity $id^*$ which a PPT adversary wants to attack, the challenger will interact with the adversary as follows.

In the **setup** phase, the challenger first constructs $\mathbf{A}_0 = (\mathbf{a}_1, \mathbf{a}_2, \ldots, \mathbf{a}_{m_0})$ and $\mathbf{u} = \mathbf{a}_0$. It then picks $\mathbf{R} \leftarrow \mathcal{D}^{m_0 \times m_1}$ and computes $\mathbf{A}_1 = -\mathbf{A}_0\mathbf{R} - \mathbf{H}(id^*)\mathbf{G}$. It finally lets the master secret key $msk = \mathbf{R}$ being MP12-trapdoor for $[\mathbf{A}_0\|\mathbf{A}_1]$ with tag $-\mathbf{H}(id^*)$ and the master public key $mpk = \{\mathbf{A}_0, \mathbf{A}_1, \mathbf{u}\}$, and sends $mpk$ to the adversary. Note that by hypothesis on $m_0$ and $\mathcal{D}$ and Lemma 1, the master public-key $mpk$ is $\mathrm{negl}(n)$-far from uniform in statistical distance.

In the **identity-secret-key query** phase, for $id_j$ queried by adversary, the challenger constructs $\mathbf{A}_{id_j} = [\mathbf{A}_0\| - \mathbf{A}_0\mathbf{R} + (\mathbf{H}(id_j) - \mathbf{H}(id^*)) \cdot \mathbf{G}]$. If $id_j \neq id^*$, the challenger can use MP12-trapdoor $\mathbf{R}$ (in the help of $\mathbf{G}$) to sample a short vector $\mathbf{t}$ from $\Lambda_{\mathbf{u}}^{\perp}(\mathbf{A}_{id_j}) = \Lambda_{\mathbf{u}}^{\perp}([\mathbf{A}_0\| - \mathbf{A}_0\mathbf{R} + (\mathbf{H}(id_j) - \mathbf{H}(id^*)) \cdot \mathbf{G}])$ by Lemma 6 and sends $\mathbf{t}$ back to the adversary. But, if $id_j = id^*$, the challenger can not sample a short vector from $\Lambda_{\mathbf{u}}^{\perp}(\mathbf{A}_{id_j})$, as the trapdoor-functionality disappears. This means that the challenger can answer all identity-secret-key queries other than $id^*$. So, the challenger can perfectly simulate the identity-secret-key query.

In the **challenge** phase, after seeing a message bit $\mu^*$ chosen by the adversary, the challenger prepares a challenge ciphertext to the target identity $id^*$ as follows:

1. Let $b_0, b_1, \ldots, b_{m_0}$ be entries of the DLWE challenge. Mask the message bit via setting $c_0^* = b_0 + \mu^* \in \mathbb{Z}_q$.

2. Set $\mathbf{b}^* = (b_1, \ldots, b_{m_0})^T$ and $\mathbf{c}_1^* = \begin{bmatrix} \mathbf{b}^* \\ -\mathbf{R}^T\mathbf{b}^* + 2\hat{\mathbf{e}} \end{bmatrix} \in \mathbb{Z}_q^m$, where $\mathbf{R}$ is the master secret key and $\hat{\mathbf{e}} \leftarrow \mathcal{D}_{\mathbb{Z}, \alpha q \sqrt{m_0} \cdot \omega(\sqrt{\log n})}^{m_1}$.

3. Send challenge ciphertext $\mathbf{c}^* = (c_0^*, \mathbf{c}_1^*)$ to the adversary.

We argue that if the DLWE challenge comes from $A_{\mathbf{y}, \alpha}$, then $\mathbf{c}^*$ looks like a valid ciphertext (i.e., indistinguishable from fresh ciphertext) of $\mu^*$ under the identity $id^*$. Recall that $b_0 = \mathbf{a}_0^T\mathbf{y} - 2e$ for some $e$ sampled from $\mathcal{D}_{\mathbb{Z}, \alpha q}$, and thus $c_0^*$ in step 1 fits $c_0^* = \mathbf{a}_0^T\mathbf{y} - 2e + \mu^*$, just as the first part of a valid challenge ciphertext. Also recall that $\mathbf{A}_{id^*} = [\mathbf{A}_0\| - \mathbf{A}_0\mathbf{R}]$ and $\mathbf{b}^* = \mathbf{A}_0^T\mathbf{y} - 2\mathbf{e}_0$ for some $\mathbf{e}_0$ sampled from $\mathcal{D}_{\mathbb{Z}, \alpha q}^{m_0}$. For $\mathbf{c}_1^*$ defined in step 2 above, it then holds that

$$\mathbf{c}_1^* = \begin{bmatrix} \mathbf{A}_0^T\mathbf{y} - 2\mathbf{e}_0 \\ -\mathbf{R}^T(\mathbf{A}_0^T\mathbf{y} - 2\mathbf{e}_0) + 2\hat{\mathbf{e}} \end{bmatrix} = \mathbf{A}_{id^*}^T\mathbf{y} + \begin{bmatrix} -2\mathbf{e}_0 \\ 2(\mathbf{R}^T\mathbf{e}_0 + \hat{\mathbf{e}}) \end{bmatrix}.$$

Therefore, it is sufficient to show that for settled $\mathbf{e}_0$, every $\mathbf{r}_i^T \cdot \mathbf{e}_0 + \hat{e}_i$ is $\mathrm{negl}(n)$-far from $\mathcal{D}_{\mathbb{Z}, s}$, where $s^2 = (\|\mathbf{e}_0\|_2^2 + m_0\alpha^2 q^2) \cdot \omega(\sqrt{\log n})^2$, over the randomness of $\mathbf{r}_i$ and of $\hat{e}_i$. As every $\mathbf{r}_i$ is indepentent discrete subgaussian, the claim follows by the security proof of CCA-PKE in [18], but adapted from discrete Gaussian variable to discrete subgaussian variable.

If the DLWE challenge comes from uniform, we have that both $b_0$ and $\mathbf{b}^*$ are uniform. So, $-\mathbf{R}^T\mathbf{b}^*$ is uniform and independent over $\mathbb{Z}_q^{m_1}$ by a version of leftover hash lemma (lemma 1), where the hash function is defined via the matrix $[-\mathbf{A}_0^T\| - \mathbf{b}^*]$ and guarantees that both $-\mathbf{A}_0\mathbf{R}$ and $-\mathbf{R}^T\mathbf{b}^*$ are uniform and independent. Therefore, $-\mathbf{R}^T\mathbf{b}^* + 2\hat{\mathbf{e}}$ is also uniform. This means that the challenge ciphertext $\mathbf{c}^*$ constructed by the challenger is uniform over $\mathbb{Z}_q^{m+1}$.

Finally, once receiving a guess $b'$ from the adversary, the challenger can solve DLWE challenge only by outputting the guess $b'$. This finishes the proof.  $\square$

# 4    Identity-Based Fully Homomorphic Encryption

We now present a leveled IBFHE scheme from the proposed IBE scheme in last section. The new IBFHE scheme is more efficient than GSW-IBFHE [17].

## 4.1    The Identity-Based FHE Scheme

Recall that $n$ is the security parameter. Our scheme needs some public parameters as follows.

- Let $L$ be the maximum multiplication depth of circuit the scheme can evaluate homomorphically and $q$ is a sufficiently large prime $q = q(n, L)$. Let $\ell = \lceil \log q \rceil$, $m_0 = n(\ell + O(1))$, $m_1 = n\ell$ and $m = m_0 + m_1$.
- $\mathbf{G}, \mathcal{D}, \mathbf{H}$ are defined as in last section.
- $\mathbf{M} = \mathbf{I}_{m+1} \otimes \mathbf{g}^T \in \mathbb{Z}_q^{(m+1)\times(m+1)\ell}$ for $\mathbf{g}^T = (1, 2, 2^2, \ldots, 2^{\ell-1})$ is another gadget matrix. By Lemma 5, for any matrix $\mathbf{A} \in \mathbb{Z}_q^{(m+1)\times(m+1)\ell}$, we can sample a subgaussian matrix $\mathbf{X} \in \mathbb{Z}^{(m+1)\ell \times (m+1)\ell}$ with parameter $O(1)$ such that $\mathbf{X} = \mathbf{M}^{-1}(\mathbf{A})$.

Now we describe the proposed scheme IBFHE.

- IBFHE.Setup$(1^n, 1^L)$: This algorithm is identical to IBE.Setup. Recall that $\mathbf{A} = [\mathbf{A}_0||\mathbf{A}_1] = [\mathbf{A}_0|| - \mathbf{A}_0\mathbf{R}] \in \mathbb{Z}_q^{n\times m}$, $mpk = [\mathbf{u}||\mathbf{A}]$ and $msk = \mathbf{R}$.
- IBFHE.Extract$(\mathbf{R}, id)$: This algorithm is identical to IBE.Extract. Recall that $pk_{id} = \mathbf{P} = [\mathbf{u}||\mathbf{A}_{id}]$ and $sk_{id} = \mathbf{s} = (1, -\mathbf{t})$.
- IBFHE.Enc$(mpk, id, \mu \in \{0,1\})$: To encrypt a bit $\mu \in \{0,1\}$, choose two matrices $\mathbf{Y} \xleftarrow{\$} \mathbb{Z}_q^{n\times(m+1)\ell}$ and $\mathbf{E} = [-\mathbf{e}|| - \mathbf{E}_0||\mathbf{E}_1]^T \in \mathbb{Z}^{(m+1)\times(m+1)\ell}$, where $\mathbf{e} \leftarrow \mathcal{D}_{\mathbb{Z},\alpha q}^{(m+1)\ell}$, $\mathbf{E}_0 = [\mathbf{e}_{0,1}||\mathbf{e}_{0,2}|| \cdots ||\mathbf{e}_{0,(m+1)\ell}]^T \leftarrow \mathcal{D}_{\mathbb{Z},\alpha q}^{(m+1)\ell \times m_0}$ and $\mathbf{E}_1 = [\mathbf{e}_{1,1}||\mathbf{e}_{1,2}|| \cdots ||\mathbf{e}_{1,(m+1)\ell}]^T$ where $\mathbf{e}_{1,i} \leftarrow \mathcal{D}_{\mathbb{Z},s_i}^{m_1}$ for $s_i^2 = (||\mathbf{e}_{0,i}||_2^2 + m_0(\alpha q)^2) \cdot \omega(\sqrt{\log n})^2$. Output the ciphertext matrix

$$\mathbf{C} = \mu\mathbf{M} + \mathbf{P}^T\mathbf{Y} + 2\mathbf{E} \in \mathbb{Z}_q^{(m+1)\times(m+1)\ell}.$$

- IBFHE.Dec$(\mathbf{C}, sk_{id})$: Let $\mathbf{c}$ be the first column of $\mathbf{C}$. Output $\mu' = \langle \mathbf{c}, \mathbf{s} \rangle \bmod q \bmod 2$.
- IBFHE.NAND$(\mathbf{C}_1, \mathbf{C}_2)$: Given two ciphertext matrices $\mathbf{C}_1, \mathbf{C}_2$ under identical identity for two plaintexts $\mu_1, \mu_2$, output

$$\mathbf{C}_{\text{NAND}} = \mathbf{M} - \mathbf{C}_1 \odot \mathbf{C}_2 \odot \mathbf{M} \overset{\triangle}{=} \mathbf{M} - \mathbf{C}_1 \cdot \mathbf{M}^{-1}(\mathbf{C}_2 \cdot \mathbf{M}^{-1}(\mathbf{M})).$$

Note that this algorithm is randomized, as $\mathbf{M}^{-1}$ is randomized.
- IBFHE.Eval$(f, \mathbf{C}_1, \mathbf{C}_2, \ldots, \mathbf{C}_t)$: Apply a NAND-circuit $f : \{0,1\}^t \to \{0,1\}$ to $t$ ciphertexts $\mathbf{C}_1, \mathbf{C}_2, \ldots, \mathbf{C}_t$, and output a ciphertext $\mathbf{C}_f$.

## 4.2  Analysis

We discuss the correctness, security and homomorphic property in this section.

**Correctness.** Correctness of IBFHE follows because:

$$\mathbf{C}^T \cdot \mathbf{s} = \mu \mathbf{M}^T \mathbf{s} + \mathbf{Y}^T \mathbf{P} \mathbf{s} + 2\mathbf{E}^T \mathbf{s} = \mu \mathbf{M}^T \mathbf{s} + 2\mathbf{E}^T \mathbf{s}.$$

So, let $\mathbf{c}$ be the first column of $\mathbf{C}$, we obtain $\langle \mathbf{c}, \mathbf{s} \rangle = \mu + 2 \cdot \langle (-e_1, -\mathbf{e}_{0,1}, \mathbf{e}_{1,1}), \mathbf{s} \rangle$. The decryption will be correct if setting the same parameters as last section.

**Security.** The security follows from the security of the IBE in previous section using a standard hybrid analysis, because a ciphertext $\mathbf{C}$ of message 0 of IBFHE is just the concatenation of $(m+1)\ell$ ciphertexts of message 0 of IBE and $\mathbf{C}$ is indistinguishable from $\mathbf{C} + \mathbf{M}$ that is a ciphertext of message 1.

## Homomorphic Property

**Lemma 8.** *Let two fresh ciphertexts be* $\mathbf{C}_1, \mathbf{C}_2$ *such that* $\mathbf{C}_i^T \cdot \mathbf{s} = \mu_i \mathbf{M}^T \mathbf{s} + 2\mathbf{E}_{(i)}^T \mathbf{s}, i = 1, 2.$ *We then have with overwhelming probability that*

$$\mathbf{C}_{\mathrm{NAND}}^T \cdot \mathbf{s} = (1 - \mu_1\mu_2)\mathbf{M}^T \mathbf{s} - 2\mu_1 \mathbf{X}_2^T \mathbf{E}_{(2)}^T \mathbf{s} + 2\mathbf{X}_1^T \mathbf{E}_{(1)}^T \mathbf{s} \overset{\Delta}{=} (1 - \mu_1\mu_2)\mathbf{M}^T \mathbf{s} + 2\mathbf{e}^*,$$

*where* $\mathbf{X}_i$ *is some subgaussian matrix and the entries of* $\mathbf{e}^*$ *are mutually independent and subgaussian with parameter* $O(m_0^{2.5} \cdot \sqrt{\ell}) \cdot \omega(\sqrt{\log n})^3).$

*In particular, we can decrypt correctly after one-time homomorphic NAND computation if* $q/4 \geq O(m_0^3 \cdot \sqrt{\ell}) \cdot \omega(\sqrt{\log n})^3.$

*Proof.* For any two fresh cipertexts $\mathbf{C}_1, \mathbf{C}_2$, we have

$$
\begin{aligned}
\mathbf{C}_{\mathrm{NAND}}^T \cdot \mathbf{s} &= (\mathbf{M} - \mathbf{C}_1 \odot \mathbf{C}_2 \odot \mathbf{M})^T \cdot \mathbf{s} \\
&= \mathbf{M}^T \mathbf{s} - (\mathbf{C}_1 \cdot \mathbf{X}_1)^T \cdot \mathbf{s} \\
&= \mathbf{M}^T \mathbf{s} - \mathbf{X}_1^T (\mu_1 \mathbf{M}^T \mathbf{s} + 2\mathbf{E}_{(1)}^T \mathbf{s}) \\
&= \mathbf{M}^T \mathbf{s} - \mu_1 \mathbf{X}_1^T \mathbf{M}^T \mathbf{s} + 2\mathbf{X}_1^T \mathbf{E}_{(1)}^T \mathbf{s} \\
&= \mathbf{M}^T \mathbf{s} - \mu_1 (\mathbf{C}_2 \cdot \mathbf{M}^{-1}(\mathbf{M}))^T \mathbf{s} + 2\mathbf{X}_1^T \mathbf{E}_{(1)}^T \mathbf{s} \\
&= \mathbf{M}^T \mathbf{s} - \mu_1 \cdot (\mathbf{M}^{-1}(\mathbf{M}))^T (\mathbf{C}_2^T \mathbf{s}) + 2\mathbf{X}_1^T \mathbf{E}_{(1)}^T \mathbf{s} \\
&= \mathbf{M}^T \mathbf{s} - \mu_1 \cdot \mathbf{X}_2^T (\mu_2 \mathbf{M}^T \mathbf{s} + 2\mathbf{E}_{(2)}^T \mathbf{s}) + 2\mathbf{X}_1^T \mathbf{E}_{(1)}^T \mathbf{s} \\
&= (1 - \mu_1\mu_2)\mathbf{M}^T \mathbf{s} - 2\mu_1 \mathbf{X}_2^T \mathbf{E}_{(2)}^T \mathbf{s} + 2\mathbf{X}_1^T \mathbf{E}_{(1)}^T \mathbf{s}
\end{aligned}
$$

where $\mathbf{X}_1, \mathbf{X}_2$ are two subgaussian random matrix with parameters $O(1)$. By Lemma 7, it holds that $\|\mathbf{E}_{(i)}^T \mathbf{s}\|_\infty \leq m_0^2 \cdot \omega(\sqrt{\log n})^3$, $i = 1, 2$. Thus, by Lemma 2, it holds that $\mathbf{X}_i^T \mathbf{E}_{(i)}^T \mathbf{s}$ is subgaussian with parameter

$$O(1) \cdot \|\mathbf{E}_{(i)}^T \mathbf{s}\|_2 \leq O(1) \cdot \sqrt{(m+1)\ell} \cdot m_0^2 \cdot \omega(\sqrt{\log n})^3 < O(m_0^{2.5} \cdot \sqrt{\ell}) \cdot \omega(\sqrt{\log n})^3.$$

Therefore, the decryption correctness follows by Lemma 3. The mutually independence of the entries of $\mathbf{e}^*$ comes from the independence of $\mathbf{X}_i$. This finishes the proof. $\qquad\square$

Using above lemma successively, we can gain the main theorem represents that the IBFHE scheme is an $L$-leveled IBFHE scheme. The proof follows the observation that after one-time homomorphic NAND computation, the level of noise roughly grows from $O(m_0^2) \cdot \omega(\sqrt{\log n})^3$ to $O(m_0^3 \cdot \sqrt{\ell}) \cdot \omega(\sqrt{\log n})^3$.

**Theorem 2.** *Given a depth-$L$ NAND-circuit $f$, if its input are fresh ciphertext and $q/4 \geq O(m_0 \cdot \sqrt{\ell})^L \cdot O(m_0^2) \cdot \omega(\sqrt{\log n})^3$, it then holds that the decryption algorithm of* IBFHE *works correctly with overwhelming probability.*

*Remark.* We note that one can use techniques in [4] to further reduce the parameters as the noise growth is asymmetric under homomorphic computation. However, the proposed IBFHE can not be bootstrapped, as bootstrapping needs user-specific parameters (i.e., encrypted identity-secret-key) to bootstrap which destroys both anonymity and indistinguishability.

## 5 Conclusion and Open Problem

In this work, we improved the ABB-IBE [1] to a new one taking advantages of MP12-trapdoor and gained an efficient IBFHE scheme from it utilizing Alperin-Sheriff and Peikert's novel noise-manage technique. The proposed IBFHE scheme with shorter parameters is more efficient without lowering the security. However, it is still a leveled homomorphic scheme as GSW-IBFHE. Therefore it remains open to build a non-leveled IBFHE without using indistinguishable obfuscator.

**Acknowledgments.** We are very grateful to the anonymous reviewers for their helpful comments and suggestions.

## References

1. Agrawal, S., Boneh, D., Boyen, X.: Efficient lattice (H)IBE in the standard model. In: Gilbert, H. (ed.) EUROCRYPT 2010. LNCS, vol. 6110, pp. 553–572. Springer, Heidelberg (2010)
2. Agrawal, S., Boneh, D., Boyen, X.: Lattice basis delegation in fixed dimension and shorter-ciphertext hierarchical IBE. In: Rabin, T. (ed.) CRYPTO 2010. LNCS, vol. 6223, pp. 98–115. Springer, Heidelberg (2010)
3. Alwen, J., Peikert, C.: Generating shorter bases for hard random lattices. Theory of Computing Systems **48**(3), 535–553 (2011)
4. Alperin-Sheriff, J., Peikert, C.: Faster bootstrapping with polynomial error. In: Garay, J.A., Gennaro, R. (eds.) CRYPTO 2014, Part I. LNCS, vol. 8616, pp. 297–314. Springer, Heidelberg (2014)
5. Boneh, D., Franklin, M.: Identity-based encryption from the weil pairing. In: Kilian, J. (ed.) CRYPTO 2001. LNCS, vol. 2139, pp. 213–229. Springer, Heidelberg (2001)

6. Boneh, D., Boyen, X.: Secure identity based encryption without random oracles. In: Franklin, M. (ed.) CRYPTO 2004. LNCS, vol. 3152, pp. 443–459. Springer, Heidelberg (2004)

7. Banerjee, A., Peikert, C.: New and improved key-homomorphic pseudorandom functions. In: Garay, J.A., Gennaro, R. (eds.) CRYPTO 2014, Part I. LNCS, vol. 8616, pp. 353–370. Springer, Heidelberg (2014)

8. Brakerski, Z.: Fully homomorphic encryption without modulus switching from classical gapSVP. In: Safavi-Naini, R., Canetti, R. (eds.) CRYPTO 2012. LNCS, vol. 7417, pp. 868–886. Springer, Heidelberg (2012)

9. Brakerski, Z., Vaikuntanathan, V.: Efficient fully homomorphic encryption from (standard) LWE. In: FOCS 2011, pp. 97–106. IEEE Computer Society (2011)

10. Cash, D., Hofheinz, D., Kiltz, E., Peikert, C.: Bonsai trees, or how to delegate a lattice basis. In: Gilbert, H. (ed.) EUROCRYPT 2010. LNCS, vol. 6110, pp. 523–552. Springer, Heidelberg (2010)

11. Cheon, J.H., Coron, J.-S., Kim, J., Lee, M.S., Lepoint, T., Tibouchi, M., Yun, A.: Batch fully homomorphic encryption over the integers. In: Johansson, T., Nguyen, P.Q. (eds.) EUROCRYPT 2013. LNCS, vol. 7881, pp. 315–335. Springer, Heidelberg (2013)

12. Clear, M., McGoldrick, C.: Multi-identity and multi-key leveled FHE from learning with errors. In: Gennaro, R., Robshaw, M. (eds.) CRYPTO 2015. LNCS, vol. 9216, pp. 630–656. Springer, Heidelberg (2015)

13. Clear, M., McGoldrick, C.: Bootstrappable identity-based fully homomorphic encryption. In: Gritzalis, D., Kiayias, A., Askoxylakis, I. (eds.) CANS 2014. LNCS, vol. 8813, pp. 1–19. Springer, Heidelberg (2014)

14. Cocks, C.: An identity based encryption scheme based on quadratic residues. In: Honary, B. (ed.) Cryptography and Coding 2001. LNCS, vol. 2260, pp. 360–363. Springer, Heidelberg (2001)

15. Gentry, C.: Fully homomorphic encryption using ideal lattices. In: STOC 2009, pp. 169–178. ACM (2009)

16. Gentry, C., Peikert, C., Vaikuntanathan, V.: Trapdoors for hard lattices and new cryptographic constructions. In: STOC 2008, pp. 197–206. ACM (2008)

17. Gentry, C., Sahai, A., Waters, B.: Homomorphic encryption from learning with errors: conceptually-simpler, asymptotically-faster, attribute-based. In: Canetti, R., Garay, J.A. (eds.) CRYPTO 2013, Part I. LNCS, vol. 8042, pp. 75–92. Springer, Heidelberg (2013)

18. Micciancio, D., Peikert, C.: Trapdoors for lattices: simpler, tighter, faster, smaller. In: Pointcheval, D., Johansson, T. (eds.) EUROCRYPT 2012. LNCS, vol. 7237, pp. 700–718. Springer, Heidelberg (2012)

19. Peikert, C.: Public key cryptosystems from the worst-case shortest vector problem. In: STOC 2009, pp. 333–32. ACM (2009)

20. Peikert, C.: Lattice-based cryptography: constructing trapdoors and more applications. Tutorials from crypt@b-it 2013 summer school at Bonn University. http://www.cc.gatech.edu/cpeikert/pubs/slides-abit4.pdf

21. Regev, O.: On lattices, learning with errors, random linear codes, and cryptography. In: STOC 2005, pp. 84–93. ACM (2005)

22. Shamir, A.: Identity-based cryptosystems and signature schemes. In: Blakely, G.R., Chaum, D. (eds.) CRYPTO 1984. LNCS, vol. 196, pp. 47–53. Springer, Heidelberg (1985)

23. van Dijk, M., Gentry, C., Halevi, S., Vaikuntanathan, V.: Fully homomorphic encryption over the integers. In: Gilbert, H. (ed.) EUROCRYPT 2010. LNCS, vol. 6110, pp. 24–43. Springer, Heidelberg (2010)

24. Vershynin, R.: Compressed Sensing, Theory and Applications, chapter 5, pp. 210–268. Cambridge University Press (2012). http://www-personal.umich.edu/~romanv/papers/non-asymptotic-rmt-plain.pdf
25. Waters, B.: Dual system encryption: realizing fully secure IBE and HIBE under simple assumptions. In: Halevi, S. (ed.) CRYPTO 2009. LNCS, vol. 5677, pp. 619–636. Springer, Heidelberg (2009)
26. Wang, F., Wang, K.: Fully homomorphic encryption with auxiliary inputs. In: Lin, D., Yung, M., Zhou, J. (eds.) Inscrypt 2014. LNCS, vol. 8957, pp. 220–238. Springer, Heidelberg (2015)
27. Wang, F., Wang, K., Li, B.: LWE-based FHE with better parameters. In: Tanaka, K., Suga, Y. (eds.) IWSEC 2015. LNCS, vol. 9241, pp. 175–192. Springer, Heidelberg (2015)

# Evolving Highly Nonlinear Balanced Boolean Functions with Improved Resistance to DPA Attacks

Ashish Jain[1](✉) and Narendra S. Chaudhari[1,2]

[1] Discipline of Computer Science and Engineering,
Indian Institute of Technology (IIT), Indore, India
phd11120101@iiti.ac.in
[2] Visvesvaraya National Institute of Technology (VNIT), Nagpur, India
nsc0183@gmail.com

**Abstract.** Recent years have witnessed significant increase in number of side-channel attacks on the cryptographic algorithms and hence the attempts to defend them. Note that Differential Power Analysis (DPA) is the most powerful attack which belongs to the class of side channel attacks. In order to defend against DPA attacks, there is a growing demand for the construction of Boolean functions and S-boxes. In this regard, we develop three effective algorithms that are based on evolutionary computing techniques. As a result, three 8-bit highly nonlinear balanced Boolean functions have been evolved in this work that have higher DPA resistance than others published previously.

**Keywords:** Cryptographic boolean functions · Security and privacy · Side-channel attacks · Evolutionary computing

## 1 Introduction

Cryptographic algorithms have two divisions: symmetric key algorithms and asymmetric (public) key algorithms. Symmetric key algorithms are further categorized into two areas: stream ciphers and block ciphers. In these types of ciphers, the nonlinear elements often play the key role [1]. Usually, Boolean functions and S-boxes (or vectorial Boolean functions) are used as nonlinear elements, most notably in stream ciphers and block ciphers, respectively [2]. In literature, a prior attempt that concerns the resistance of S-boxes to side channel attacks (i.e. good transparency order) has been vaguely explored [3]. Furthermore, the study of evolving balanced Boolean functions with high nonlinearity level and good transparency order is investigated by Picek et al. [4] alone.

Finding Boolean functions with all optimal cryptographic properties is an NP-hard problem, since for $n$ inputs there can exist $2^{2^n}$ possible Boolean functions. For example, if $n=8$ ("this input size is appropriate for current need of security") this gives $2^{256}$ possible Boolean functions. Note that for $n$ greater than or equals to 5, determining Boolean functions with all desirable properties is impractical through an exhaustive computer search. Therefore, over the years there has been numerous works on constructing Boolean functions and S-boxes. Random search [5], algebraic constructions [6] and optimization heuristics [7] are few approaches to construct these nonlinear elements. Main benefits of optimization heuristics are in a relatively easy addition of cryptographic properties to the evaluation functions and in results comparable with algebraic constructions. Hence, this paper presents the effective use of few optimization heuristics of evolutionary family for construction of DPA-resistant Boolean functions.

## 2   Related Work and Our Contributions

This paper contributes towards evolution (via optimization heuristics) of better Boolean functions that have higher resistance to unintentional output channels often called as side channels, typically, made available to attackers in small embedded devices e.g. smart cards[1]. In our work, we use three computational intelligence techniques: Cartesian Genetic Programming (CGP), Genetic Algorithm (GA) and Binary Particle Swarm Optimization (BPSO) where the best performance was shown by CGP. Moreover, we have evolved three Boolean functions with better transparency order values than previously reported by Picek et al. [4]. To the best of our knowledge, only this work and the work proposed by Picek et al. consider the transparency order property that concerns the resistance of Boolean function to DPA attacks. Accordingly, this paper gives a fair comparison between Boolean functions computed by Picek et al. and determined in this research. Additionally, we compare some of the recently reported Boolean functions that have been determined by McLaughlin and Clark [9], and Cid et al. [6] via simulated annealing and algebraic method, respectively.

## 3   Preliminaries: Boolean Functions

The area of Boolean functions is extensive and therefore we do not promise to present here an exhaustive theory of Boolean functions. Rather, in this section we present a comprehensive study of Boolean functions that is required by the reader to completely understand the research reported in this paper.

Let $F_2^n$ be the $n$-dimensional vector space over the finite field that contains all the binary vectors of length $n$. An $n$-variable Boolean function $f$ may be viewed as a mapping from $F_2^n$ to $F_2$. Note that the Hamming weight denoted by $wt(f)$ is a useful measure of $f$ that represents the number of 1's in its binary vector (or truth table) [10], where truth tables are one of the unique representation of Boolean functions. The function $f$ with $n$-input variables denoted by $x$ has a truth table with $2^n$ elements, where each element $x \in \{0, 1\}$.

---

[1] *The small computing devices releases some physical leakage that relates to the operations and/or even data being processed, there are several side channels possible when considering unleashed physical information, such as power consumption or electromagnetic emanation* [4]. *For more details on power analysis attacks we refer interested readers to* [8].

For the cryptographic use, the strict property of Boolean functions is balancedness. A balanced Boolean function $f$ with $n$ inputs has equal number of $0's$ and $1's$ in its truth table i.e. $wt(f) = 2^{n-1}$ [10]. Two other useful representations of a Boolean function are its Algebraic Normal Form and Walsh Hadamard Transformation. Walsh Hadamard Transformation is also known as Walsh transform that can be denoted as $-W_f$. Here, we discuss only the Walsh transform due to its significant efficiency in directly computing certain characteristics and properties of a Boolean function that we require in this research.

The Walsh transform of a Boolean function $f$ measures the relation between $f(\mathbf{x})$ and $\mathbf{x}.\mathbf{y}$, where $\mathbf{x}$ and $\mathbf{y}$ are two vectors in $F_2^n$ [10].

The Walsh transformation of $f$ can be easily computed via its Fourier transformation as [5]:

$$W_f(\mathbf{y}) = 2^n \delta(\mathbf{y}) - 2F_f(\mathbf{y}), \tag{1}$$

where $\delta(\mathbf{y})=1$ or $\delta(\mathbf{y})=0$ in case of $\mathbf{y}=\mathbf{0}$ and $\mathbf{y} \neq \mathbf{0}$, respectively. The Fourier transform of $f$ can be computed as [5]:

$$F_f(\mathbf{y}) = \sum_{\mathbf{x} \in F_2^n} f(\mathbf{x}) \times (-1)^{\mathbf{x}.\mathbf{y}}, \tag{2}$$

where $\mathbf{x}.\mathbf{y}$ is the dot product of vectors $\mathbf{x}$ and $\mathbf{y}$. In the next paragraph, we discuss two important properties (nonlinearity and transparency) of Boolean functions that we have considered to optimize in this research.

The nonlinearity of a Boolean function $NL_f$ can be defined as its minimum Hamming distance to any affine function and it can be computed as [11]:

$$NL_f = 2^{n-1} - max(|W_f(\mathbf{y})|), \tag{3}$$

where $max(-W_f(\mathbf{y})-)$ is a largest absolute output value contained in the Walsh spectrum of the investigated Boolean function $f$ corresponding to the $n$-input vector $\mathbf{y}$.

Transparency order is a new cryptographic property of vectorial Boolean functions that has been introduced by Prouff [12]. Transparency order of Boolean functions with $n$-inputs and $m$-outputs can be formally defined as [12]:

$$T_f = max_{\alpha \in F_2^m}(|m - 2wt(\alpha)| - \frac{1}{2^n(2^n - 1)}$$
$$\sum_{\mathbf{y} \in F_2^{n*}} | \sum_{\beta \in F_2^m, wt(\beta)=1} (-1)^{\alpha\beta} W_{D_{\mathbf{y}}f}(\mathbf{0}, \beta)|), \tag{4}$$

where $W_{D_{\mathbf{y}}f}$ corresponds to Walsh transform of the derivative of Boolean function $f$ with respect to a vector $\mathbf{y} \in F_2^{n*}$ that can be computed as:

$$W_{D_{\mathbf{y}}f}(\mathbf{0}, \beta) = \sum_{\mathbf{x} \in F_2^n} (-1)^{\beta(f(\mathbf{x}) \oplus f(\mathbf{x} \oplus \mathbf{y}))}. \tag{5}$$

Prouff [12] examined that the transparency level of S-boxes should be as low as possible in order to make them high resistance against DPA attacks.

Since we are interested in evolving DPA-resistant Boolean functions with one output variable, i.e. $m$ equals one in Eq. (4) and therefore the worst possible value of transparency of a Boolean function equals one. On the other end the best transparency value can equal zero [12], but it is possible with linear or affine functions that are not appropriate for cryptographic applications. A Boolean function is appropriate for use in cryptography when it is balanced, highly nonlinear and also satisfies other important properties that are required by the cryptographic applications. For details about the structure of linear and/or affine functions and for several important cryptographic properties of Boolean functions, we refer the interested reader to [13].

Since our aim of the research is to determine balanced Boolean functions with high nonlinearity (for instance, an even value in 112–118 for 8-bit Boolean function) and low transparency than that achieved by Picek et al. [4]. In this regard, we emphasize that the results reported by Picek et al. [4] are benchmarks for our study. Therefore, we focus on evolving balanced Boolean functions that have at least that level of nonlinearity (which is shown in Table 2), but with improved (low) transparency level values. This paper utilizes the following optimization heuristics for achieving the goal.

# 4    Optimization Heuristics

In the following subsections, we describe in brief a generic overview of evolutionary computation methods GA, BPSO and CGP that are used in this paper for evolving DPA-resistant Boolean functions.

## 4.1    Genetic Algorithms

Genetic Algorithms (GAs) have emerged based on the concept of imitating the evolution of a species. In GA, an initial population of individuals (or chromosomes) is generated using an intelligent method or typically random. Each of these individuals is encoded as a binary string that represents a possible candidate solution to the problem at hand. At each generation, the survival strength of each candidate solution is measured by the fitness function. Afterwards, the evolutionary process is constrained by three genetic operators: selection, crossover (or recombination) and mutation. An appropriate selection procedure chooses two or more individuals from the parent population. A crossover operator recombines these individuals and generates one or more offspring. A probabilistic crossover rate is usually used to generate offspring. Mutation operators produce one child from one parent by flipping a bit/bits of the parent. A probabilistic mutation rate is usually used that determines whether a particular change is to occur within an individual or not. For detailed information about genetic algorithms and their applications in optimization problems, we refer the interested reader to [14, 15].

## 4.2    Particle Swarm Optimization

Particle swarm optimization is a nature-inspired heuristic originated from the simulation studies of birds flocking. It has two divisions: real-PSO and binary-PSO (or BPSO). In these types of methods, a swarm is initialized as population of particles. Afterwards, all particles move in a search space to find an optimal solution. A position vector $X_i = (x_{i1}, x_{i2}, ..., x_{in})$ and a velocity vector $V_i = (v_{i1}, v_{i2}, ..., v_{in})$ are associated with each particle for guiding their movements. The best previous position of the $i^{th}$ particle and the global best position of the swarm is represented by $Lbest_i(t) = (lbest_{i1}, lbest_{i2}, ..., lbest_{in})$ and $Gbest(t) = (gbest_1(t), gbest_2(t), ..., gbest_n(t))$, respectively. Here, a "cost" function is used to assess $Lbest_i(t)$ and $Gbest(t)$. Now we focus on the BPSO methods, since the problem being considered is of discrete type. In BPSO methods, $x_{ij} \in (0,1)$ represents the $j^{th}$ positional coordinate of the $i^{th}$ particle and $v_{ij} \in (0,1)$ represents the velocity of $j^{th}$ positional coordinates of the $i^{th}$ particle constrained by $V_{max}$, where $i = 1, 2, ..., m$ and $j = 1, 2, ..., n$. Here, $m$ is the number of particles and $n$ means a potential solution in the $n$-dimensional space. In this research, we utilize a Novel BPSO method that can be described as follows.

*Novel BPSO.* In 2007, Khanesar et al. [16] have proposed a Novel BPSO method. In this method, the interpretation of velocity is different than the conventional BPSO [17]. In Novel BPSO, two velocity vectors $v_{ij}^0$ and $v_{ij}^1$ are associated with each of the particles that are updated using Eq. (6) and Eq. (7), respectively. However, the final selection of one between these two is decided by using corresponding existing value of particle's positional coordinates (see Eq. (8). Furthermore, Eq. (9) is used to update the particle's positions, where $x_{i\bar{j}}(t)$ is the complement of $x_{ij}(t)$.

$$v_{ij}^0(t+1) = w \times v_{ij}^0(t) + d_{ij,1}^0(t) + d_{ij,2}^0(t) \tag{6}$$

$$v_{ij}^1(t+1) = w \times v_{ij}^1(t) + d_{ij,1}^1(t) + d_{ij,2}^1(t) \tag{7}$$

$$v_{ij}'(t+1) = \begin{cases} v_{ij}^1(t+1), & \text{if } x_{ij}(t) = 0 \\ v_{ij}^0(t+1), & \text{if } x_{ij}(t) = 1 \end{cases} \tag{8}$$

$$x_{ij}(t+1) = \begin{cases} x_{ij}^-(t), & \text{if } Sig(v_{ij}'(t+1)) > U(0,1) \\ x_{ij}(t), & \text{otherwise} \end{cases} \tag{9}$$

Here, $w$ is the inertia weight that was introduced by Shi and Eberhart [18] to control the exploration and exploitation abilities of the swarm, and $c_1$ and $c_2$ are the acceleration constants. $Sig(v_{ij}(t+1)$ is a sigmoid function which is used to transform velocity in the interval (0,1). The terms $d_{ij}^0(t)$ and $d_{ij}^1(t)$ used in the Eq. (6) and Eq. (7) can be calculated using the following rules [16]:

If $lbest_{ij}(t) = 0$ Then $d_{ij,1}^0(t) = c_1 r_1$ and $d_{ij,1}^1(t) = -c_1 r_1$
If $lbest_{ij}(t) = 1$ Then $d_{ij,1}^1(t) = c_1 r_1$ and $d_{ij,1}^0(t) = -c_1 r_1$
If $gbest_j(t) = 0$ Then $d_{ij,2}^0(t) = c_2 r_2$ and $d_{ij,2}^1(t) = -c_2 r_2$
If $gbest_j(t) = 1$ Then $d_{ij,2}^1(t) = c_2 r_2$ and $d_{ij,2}^0(t) = -c_2 r_2$

where, $r_1$ and $r_2$ are two random variables in the range of (0,1). The main concept behind the above rules is as follows: let $j^{th}$ bit of $i^{th}$ local best particle is '1' (see rule number second). Then for guiding the particle to its best position, velocity $v_{ij}^0$ for that particle decreases (since $d_{ij,1}^0(t) = -c_1 r_1$), while velocity $v_{ij}^1$ increases (since $d_{ij,1}^1(t) = c_1 r_1$). For more details about Novel BPSO interested readers can refer to [16].

### 4.3   Cartesian Genetic Programming

Cartesian genetic programming is a general form of genetic programming where a program is modeled as two dimensional grid of $n_r$ rows and $n_c$ columns that forms a directed acyclic graph [19]. Nodes of the graph are used as programmable elements and therefore referred as computational nodes, where at a time maximum $n_r \times n_c$ nodes can actively participate in the computation [19]. An example program is helpful here (see Fig. 1). The number of program inputs $n_i$ and the number of program outputs $n_o$ are defined by the user to perform a particular task. For example, in the Fig. 1, $n_i=2$ and $n_o=2$. Each node input can be connected to one of the program inputs or output of a node located in the previous $l$ columns [19], where $l$ is referred to as levels-back parameter.

Each node is programmed to compute one of "$n_p$-input function" listed in the function table $\Gamma$ [19]. The function table $\Gamma$ is decided by the user according to the problem domain. In the example, $\Gamma=\{+, *, -\}$, where code of functions are $\{0, 1, 2\}$, respectively. Formally, each node is encoded by $n_p+1$ genes. In example, upper top left most node encodes as (0 1 0), where the first two (since $n_p=2$) genes are indexes of input connections and the last gene is the code of node function. In this way, encoding of the program is represented by the chromosome: (0 1 0; 1 1 1; 2 3 2; 0 3 1; 3 4 0; 5 5 2; 6 7). Here, the last two genes represent the code of output indexes. Even though the results of such encoding have fix sized chromosomes; advantage is variable sized phenotype, that is achievable by disabling few computational nodes.

In CGP, an initial population is generated either randomly or by an intelligent procedure. The initial population may be seeded by an existing solution for improvement [19]. CGP usually uses small population sizes and has no crossover operator [20]. Every new population consists of the best individual of the previous generation and its $\lambda$ offspring and as a search mechanism a variant of a simple $(1 + \lambda)$ evolutionary algorithm is used [21]. In most of CGP implementations, a point mutation operator is used to generate offspring [21]. Mutation modifies $h$ randomly selected genes to another randomly generated (but valid) values. Details on CGP and their applications is extensively treated by Miller and Thomson [19] and Miller [21].

## 5   Proposed Methods with Experimental Details

Heuristics based on GA and BPSO for evolving DPA-resistant Boolean functions are shown in Algorithm 1 and Algorithm 2, respectively. In the subsequent

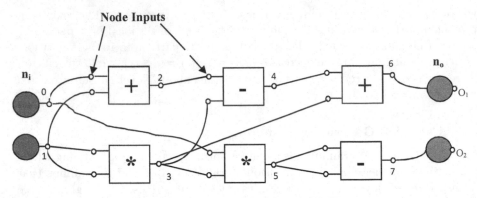

**Fig. 1.** An example program of CGP

sections, we discuss the important aspects of each algorithm precisely along with a discussion on heuristic based on the CGP.

### 5.1    Heuristic Based on GA

First of all, every individual of the population is initialized randomly, where each individual is represented as a binary vector of size $2^n$ (i.e. size of the truth table). Since the first objective of the research is to find $n$-bit (more specifically, 8-bit) balanced Boolean functions with nonlinearity at least as the level that has been achieved by Picek et al. [4]. In this context, *Cost* of a Boolean function in its truth table representation can be simple to define as $Cost = B_f + Nl_f$.

*Description (Algorithm 3).* In the above mentioned formula, the term $B_f$ gets a value 'zero', if the corresponding truth table is balanced, otherwise $B_f$ gets a *Penalty (-ve)* value equal to the 'amount of bits need to be inverted for balancing the truth table multiplied by a fixed value $X$'. In the experiment, we fixed the value of $X$ (=5) which is chosen as per the literature [4].

As shown in Algorithm 1, for generating a new population from the old population, we used a simple one-point crossover operator, where at each call this operator generates an offspring from two best individuals among three. Here, each time a simple tournament selection procedure is called that returns three individuals of the parent population by the uniform random selection procedure. In the experiment, we fixed $N$=112, since Picek et al. have achieved the highest nonlinearity of 112 in case of 8-bit Boolean function via genetic algorithm. Now, we focus on the second objective, where the key driving force is to achieve better (lower than existing) transparency level for those individuals that are balanced and have the nonlinearity level of at least $N$ (see step 15). For this purpose, we include the transparency order term $T_f$ in the *Cost* function as: $Cost+(1-T_f)$ ('1-$T_f$', since we are interested in minimizing $T_f$ i.e. maximizing '1-$T_f$') and then apply a specific mutation operator (see Mutation-I). However, individuals that are unbalanced and/or have nonlinearity less than $N$, we apply an another mutation operator (see Mutation-II).

*Mutation-I (Balanced Mutation).* This operator preserves the balancedness property of the function by changing two bits of the corresponding individual (if balanced). During the experiment, we applied this mutation to those individuals that are balanced and have the nonlinearity level of at least 112. This mutation operator speeds up the search for better transparency level Boolean functions.

*Mutation-II.* For balanced or unbalanced Boolean function with nonlinearity less than $N$, we design an effective mutation operator that maintains the population diversity form one generation to the next. We divide the operator into three sub mutation operators: Mutation-1: for each individual, one-third times (of the size of the population) a single bit is inverted. Mutation-2: another one-third times, the order of a small subset of bits is inverted. Mutation-3: the remaining one-third times a small subset of bits is shuffled. The small subset is chosen between two random points of an individual. In experiment, we limited the size of subset to 10% of the size of the individual and the probability of mutation for each individual was fixed to 0.3.

## 5.2   Heuristic Based on the Novel BPSO and Hybrid Novel BPSO

First of all, we initialize the velocity and position (binary vectors of size $2^n$) of all particles randomly, where particle position vectors are truth tables of Boolean functions. Unlike GA, in BPSO we include the transparency order in the *Cost* function along with nonlinearity and balancedness, and the reason is as follows: in case of GA, we update the *Cost* function by introducing transparency order property in between crossover and mutation operator, while these operators have not been defined in case of standard BPSO algorithms. However, like GA, each BPSO variant calls Algorithm 3 in order to check the balancedness level of investigating truth table (see Section 5.1, Paragraph-2). For details about terminology such as local and global best particle position and for thier use, see section 4.1.

As shown in Table 1, the maximum nonlinearity level that we have achieved through standard Novel BPSO algorithms is 110 which is not better than 112 that has been achieved using GA approach. Thus our next step is to develop a heuristic based on the Novel BPSO that can perform at least comparably to GA. In this regard, hybrids of PSO methods can be developed by incorporating evolutionary operators such as mutation [22] and selection [23]. Furthermore, Ratnaweera et al. stated that the lack of population diversity in PSO algorithms is understood to be a factor in their convergence on local optima. Therefore, the addition of a mutation operator to PSO should enhance its global search capacity and thus improve its performance [24]. Hence, this paper investigates the influence of addition of a mutation operator in BPSO methods.

We tested various combinations of mutation operators that were discussed in the Algorithm 1 and then decided the inclusion of Mutation-III (see Algorithm 2, step-19). Novel BPSO algorithms along with proposed mutation operator (Mutation-III) can be termed as Hybrid Novel BPSO.

**Common Parameters (Algorithm 1 and Algorithm 2).** Population size= 400, size of Boolean function=8, size of truth table=256. With these settings, we have obtained the best results in 50 individual runs of each algorithm separately.

## 5.3    Heuristic Based on CGP

In 1999, Miller [25] recognized CGP as a suitable option for generating Boolean functions. Moreover, the recent results reported by Picek et al. [26] motivate us to evolve DPA resistance Boolean functions by using CGP strategy.

*Solution Representation and Implementation.* The size of individual (particle) in case of GA (BPSO) is simple to define and is equal to the size of the truth table of the investigating Boolean function. In fact, the individuals themselves are the truth tables of Boolean functions. Consequently, GA and BPSO approaches can directly evolve the truth table and therefore the complexity of implementation of the truth table is not involved. However, in case of CGP, individuals (i.e. chromosomes or genotypes) are implemented as directed graph of Boolean primitives and therefore its size cannot be directly related to the size of the truth table. In the context of evolving DPA-resistant Boolean functions, we decided to include AND, NAND, OR, XOR, XNOR as Boolean primitives that form a digital circuit (or directed graph). When the circuit is evolved effectively by CGP, we determine its truth table to examine whether the function has desired characteristics (for instance, balancedness, nonlinearity and transparency).

*Parameters Choice and Experimental Setup.* For evolving 8-bit Boolean functions, we conducted experiments with the following choice of parameters: $n_i=8$, $n_o=1$ and $n_r=1$ along with different sized $n_c$ that results in different sized chromosomes abbreviated as $c_{size}$, here $c_{size}=n_c$, since $n_r=1$. Note that setting the number of rows to be one and levels-back parameter equal to the number of columns is regarded as the best and most general choice. In this research, we use this choice since no specialist knowledge about the problem is known. Here, the levels-back parameter controls the connectivity of the graph, i.e. it determines which columns a node can get its input from. Finally, the chromosome is mapped to the directed graph that is executed as a program. Experimental setup for evolving cryptographic Boolean functions is prepared as per the guidelines reported in [26] and can be summarized as follows.

1. Each node has two inputs and one function, where, the function is taken from $\Gamma=$\{AND, NAND, OR, XOR, XNOR\} as \{0, 1, 2, 3, 4\}, respectively.
2. Population size is equal to five and number of offspring are limited to four (i.e. $\lambda=4$). However, the offspring are favored over parents when they have a fitness less than the fitness of the parent.
3. One-point mutation operator is used with a fixed probability, where, number of genes that are altered by mutation operator is defined as a fixed percentage of the total number of genes. The genes chosen for mutation might be a node input connection or a function. Note, the single output gene, which is placed at the last position of the chromosome is not mutated.

Determining the best combination of chromosome sizes (i.e. number of gates in this case) and the mutation rate is an important step in hitting the parameter sweet spot for CGP. Indeed, it has been shown that generally very large sized chromosomes and small mutation rates perform very well [27]. In order to investigate the influence of chromosome sizes ($c_{size}$) and mutation rates ($p_m$) on the ability of CGP to find good solutions, we performed some experiments with several combinations of $c_{size}$ and $p_m$. The best results were obtained with $c_{size}=900$ and $p_m=5$ (see Table 1), where the different choices of $c_{size}$ and $p_m$ were taken according to the benchmark guidelines reported in literature [26]. In case of CGP, the stopping condition for number of evaluations was set to 3,00,000.

---

**Algorithm 1.** Pseudocode for Genetic Algorithm

1: **Output:** a best Boolean function.
2: **Initialization:** a population of $m$-individuals is generated randomly, where individuals are truth tables of $n$-variable Boolean functions.
3: **repeat**
4:     **for** each individual i=1, 2, ..., $m$ **do**
5:         $B_f$=call Algorithm 3;
6:         $Cost=B_f+NL_f$, here, evaluate $NL_f$ using Eq. (1).
7:     **end for**
8:     Load the best individual of current population in next generation population.
9:     **for** generating new individuals i=1, 2, ..., $m$ **do**
10:         Select three individuals of old population using tournament selection.
11:         Generate the offspring by applying one point crossover between two best individuals among three that are selected in the previous step.
12:     **end for**
13:     **for** each individual i=1, 2, ..., $m$ **do**
14:         Apply Mutation-II to individuals that have $Cost_i N$.
15:         Evaluate transparency order value of those individuals that are balanced and have $Cost \geq N$. Then update $Cost=Cost+1-T_f$ and then apply Mutation-I.
16:     **end for**
17:     Load the next generation population in the evolution process.
18: **until** "termination condition of 70 generations are satisfied"

---

# 6    Results and Discussion

In this section, we present the best results obtained in this work and also compare them with some of the recent results where the main goal was to determine Boolean functions for cryptographic use (for example, [4], [6] and [9]). For accurate comparison, we have taken the best results reported by Picek et al.[4] (see Table 2, #{1 to 4}), and McLaughlin and Clark [9] (see Table 2, #5). Also, we compare the results reported by Cid et al.[6] (see Table 2, #6). Note that the Boolean function used in modern state-of-the-art Rakaposhi stream cipher is termed as Rakaposhi Boolean function [6].

---

**Algorithm 2.** Pseudocode for Novel BPSO and Hybrid Novel BPSO

---

1: **Output:** a best Boolean function
2: **Initialization of $m$ particles swarm:** the binary vectors $X_i$ and $V_i$ are initialized randomly, where the position vectors $X_1, X_2, ..., X_m$ represent the truth tables of $n$-variable Boolean functions.
3: **Initialize $m$ local best particle positions and their cost as:** $Lbest_i \leftarrow 0$ and $Cost_{Lbest_i} \leftarrow 0$
4: **Initialize the global best particle position and its cost as:** $Gbest \leftarrow 0$ and $Cost_{Gbest} \leftarrow 0$
5: **repeat**
6:     **for** each particle i = 1, 2, ..., $m$ **do**
7:         $B_f$=call Algorithm 3;
8:         $Cost = B_f + NL_f + (1 - T_f)$, where $NL_f$ and $T_f$ are evaluated using Eq. (1).
9:     **end for**
        Update local best particle positions and their associated cost as follows:
10:     **for** each particle i = 1, 2, ..., $m$ **do**
11:         **if** the cost of $i^{th}$ particle is better than the cost of $Lbest_i$ (best fitness value in the history corresponding to the $i^{th}$ particle) **then**
12:             $Cost_{Lbest_i} \leftarrow Cost_i$
13:         **end if**
14:     **end for**
15:     Update the global best particle position $Gbest \leftarrow best(X_i)$ i.e. $X_i$ that has the best fitness value in the swarm.
16:     **for** each particle i = 1, 2, ..., $m$ **do**
17:         **Update** particle velocity using Eq. (8)
            **Update** particle position using Eq. (9)
18:     **end for**
        **Perform following step in case of Hybrid Novel BPSO.**
19:     Mutation-III: Half of the time a single bit of the position vector is flipped and another half of the time a small subset of bits is shuffled. In both cases the probability of mutation is fixed to 0.2.
20: **until** "termination condition of 100 iterations are satisfied"

---

---

**Algorithm 3.** Pseudocode for determining balancedness value of a truth table

---

1: **Input:** Truth table
2: **Output:** This subroutine return balancedness value $B_f$ of investigating truth table

3: **if** the truth table is balanced i.e. $wt$(truth-table)=$2^{n-1}$ **then**
4:     $B_f$=0
5: **else**
6:     Compute the difference of balancedness as follows
7:     $Difference = -2^{n-1} - wt(\text{truth-table}) -$
8:     Penalty=$Difference \times X$
9:     $B_f$=-Penalty
10: **end if**

---

The best results that we have obtained in this research are shown in Table 1. Based on the existing best results, the nonlinearity levels of 112 and 116 are most interesting ones. These nonlinearity levels along with transparency levels are marked in bold and underlined (see Table 1). The best result corresponding to nonlinearity level 112 has been achieved by Hybrid Novel BPSO where we can clearly see that this Boolean function has better transparency level than the GP and Rakaposhi Boolean function. On the other hand, the best result corresponding to nonlinearity level 116 has been achieved by CGP. In this case, we emphasize that this Boolean function has better transparency level than the GP and Simulated Annealing.

The previous studies show it is possible to use evolutionary computing methods to generate high-quality Boolean functions that even beat those generated by algebraic constructions. However, till now, there was a single work (e.g., [26]) that investigate the use of CGP for producing Boolean functions appropriate for cryptography. Thus, we have investigated CGP and compared its performance with few popular evolutionary computing methods (i.e., GA and BPSO) to find out that which option is better suited for evolving DPA-resistant Boolean functions. As evident from the results, CGP method performs much better than GA and BPSO when the objective is obtaining as high as possible nonlinearity. Our results indicate that CGP should be further explored with different fitness objectives in order to check the boundaries of its performance.

It is noticeable from the results that the improvements in transparency level are quite small. However, as shown by Mazumdar et al. that 0.1 decrease in transparency value over the AES (an example of $8 \times 8$ S-boxes), is significant. Hence, we cannot expect a big difference with Boolean functions (maximum $\frac{1}{8}=0.0125$ can be expected), since analogy with S-boxes is valid. Furthermore, side-channel attacks of stream ciphers are more difficult and thus even small improvements are relevant.

**Table 1.** Improved DPA-resistant balanced Boolean functions reported in this paper.

| #| Developed Heuristics | Nonlinearity Level | Transparency Level |
|---|---|---|---|
| 1. | CGP (C_size=900, P_m=5) | **116** | **0.958** |
| 2. | Hybrid Novel BPSO | **112** | **0.917** |
| 3. | CGP (C_size=300, P_m=3) | 116 | 0.966 |
| 4. | Genetic Algorithm | 112 | 0.930 |
| 5. | Novel BPSO | 110 | 0.913 |

## 7   Conclusion

This paper demonstrates several new heuristics for evolving DPA-resistant cryptographic Boolean functions. In this research, we had two objectives, first was to evolve balanced Boolean functions with nonlinearity level at least as reported in literature with improved transparency order. Second was to investigate the

**Table 2.** DPA-resistant balanced Boolean functions reported by other authors.

| # | Developed Heuristics | Nonlinearity Level | Transparency Level |
|---|---|---|---|
| 1. | GP with simple mutation | **116** | **0.962** |
| 2. | GP with variable mutation | **112** | **0.919** |
| 3. | GA (variable & balanced mutation) | **112** | **0.931** |
| 4. | Random search | 110 | 0.934 |
| 5. | Simulated Annealing | 116 | 0.969 |
| 6. | Rakaposhi | 112 | 0.946 |

application of CGP and BPSO, whose efficiency has not been explored previously for determining DPA-resistant Boolean functions. We found that GA generates better results than Novel BPSO, while Novel BPSO method along with efficient mutation operator generates better results than GA. It is noteworthy that CGP produces the results that are clearly better than other approaches proposed in literature and other heuristics presented in this paper. Hence, we infer that CGP is a valid option for this kind of problem. Moreover, from the cryptographic perspective, the new Boolean functions evolved in this research present practical choice for future implementations because they are offering improvement in the properties while not bringing additional memory or speed drawbacks.

# References

1. Menezes, A.J., Van Oorschot, P.C., Vanstone, S.A.: Handbook of applied cryptography. CRC Press (1996)
2. Carlet, C.: Boolean functions for cryptography and error correcting codes. Boolean Models and Methods in Mathematics, Computer Science, and Engineering **134**, 257 (2010)
3. Mazumdar, B., Mukhopadhyay, D., Sengupta, I.: Constrained search for a class of good bijective-boxes with improved DPA resistivity. IEEE Transactions on Information Forensics and Security **8**(12), 2154–2163 (2013)
4. Picek, S., Batina, L., Jakobovic, D.: Evolving DPA-resistant boolean functions. In: Bartz-Beielstein, T., Branke, J., Filipič, B., Smith, J. (eds.) PPSN 2014. LNCS, vol. 8672, pp. 812–821. Springer, Heidelberg (2014)
5. Burnett, L.D.: Heuristic Optimization of Boolean Functions and Substitution Boxes for Cryptography. Ph.D. thesis (2005)
6. Cid, C., Kiyomoto, S., Kurihara, J.: The RAKAPOSHI stream cipher. In: Qing, S., Mitchell, C.J., Wang, G. (eds.) ICICS 2009. LNCS, vol. 5927, pp. 32–46. Springer, Heidelberg (2009)
7. Millan, W.L., Clark, A.J., Dawson, E.: Heuristic design of cryptographically strong balanced boolean functions. In: Nyberg, K. (ed.) EUROCRYPT 1998. LNCS, vol. 1403, pp. 489–499. Springer, Heidelberg (1998)
8. Mangard, S., Oswald, E., Popp, T.: Power analysis attacks: Revealing the secrets of smart cards, vol. 31. Springer Science & Business Media (2008)
9. McLaughlin, J., Clark, J.A.: Evolving balanced boolean functions with optimal resistance to algebraic and fast algebraic attacks, maximal algebraic degree, and very high nonlinearity. IACR Cryptology ePrint Archive **2013**, 11 (2013)

10. Sarkar, P., Maitra, S.: Construction of nonlinear boolean functions with important cryptographic properties. In: Preneel, B. (ed.) EUROCRYPT 2000. LNCS, vol. 1807, pp. 485–506. Springer, Heidelberg (2000)
11. Filiol, É., Fontaine, C.: Highly nonlinear balanced boolean functions with a good correlation-immunity. In: Nyberg, K. (ed.) EUROCRYPT 1998. LNCS, vol. 1403, pp. 475–488. Springer, Heidelberg (1998)
12. Prouff, E.: DPA attacks and S-boxes. In: Gilbert, H., Handschuh, H. (eds.) FSE 2005. LNCS, vol. 3557, pp. 424–441. Springer, Heidelberg (2005)
13. Braeken, A.: Cryptographic properties of Boolean functions and S-boxes. Ph.D. thesis (2006)
14. Goldberg, D.: Genetic Algorithms in Search, Optimization and Machine Learning. Addison-Wesly (1989)
15. Srinivas, M., Patnaik, L.M.: Genetic algorithms: A survey. Computer **27**(6), 17–26 (1994)
16. Khanesar, M.A., Teshnehlab, M., Shoorehdeli, M.A.: A novel binary particle swarm optimization. In: Mediterranean Conference on Control & Automation, pp. 1–6. IEEE (2007)
17. Kennedy, J., Eberhart, R.C.: A discrete binary version of the particle swarm algorithm. In: IEEE International Conference on Systems, Man, and Cybernetics. Computational Cybernetics and Simulation, vol. 5, pp. 4104–4108. IEEE (1997)
18. Shi, Y., Eberhart, R.: A modified particle swarm optimizer. In: Evolutionary Computation Proceedings. IEEE World Congress on Computational Intelligence, pp. 69–73. IEEE (1998)
19. Miller, J.F., Thomson, P.: Cartesian genetic programming. In: Poli, R., Banzhaf, W., Langdon, W.B., Miller, J., Nordin, P., Fogarty, T.C. (eds.) EuroGP 2000. LNCS, vol. 1802, pp. 121–132. Springer, Heidelberg (2000)
20. Harding, S.L., Miller, J.F., Banzhaf, W.: Self-modifying cartesian genetic programming. In: Cartesian Genetic Programming, pp. 101–124. Springer (2011)
21. Miller, J.F.: Cartesian genetic programming. Natural Computing Series. Springer (2011)
22. Andrews, P.S.: An investigation into mutation operators for particle swarm optimization. In: IEEE Congress on Evolutionary Computation. CEC 2006, pp. 1044–1051. IEEE (2006)
23. Angeline, P.J.: Using selection to improve particle swarm optimization. In: Proceedings of IEEE International Conference on Evolutionary Computation, vol. 89 (1998)
24. Ratnaweera, A., Halgamuge, S., Watson, H.C.: Self-organizing hierarchical particle swarm optimizer with time-varying acceleration coefficients. IEEE Transactions on Evolutionary Computation **8**(3), 240–255 (2004)
25. Miller, J.F.: An empirical study of the efficiency of learning boolean functions using a cartesian genetic programming approach. In: Proceedings of the Genetic and Evolutionary Computation Conference, vol. 2, pp. 1135–1142 (1999)
26. Picek, S., Jakobovic, D., Miller, J.F., Marchiori, E., Batina, L.: Evolutionary methods for the construction of cryptographic boolean functions. In: Genetic Programming, pp. 192–204. Springer (2015)
27. Miller, J.F., Smith, S.L.: Redundancy and computational efficiency in cartesian genetic programming. IEEE Transactions on Evolutionary Computation **10**(2), 167–174 (2006)

## APPENDICES

Any researchers who would like the full set of truth tables of determined Boolean functions that are shown in Table 1 are welcome to contact the authors directly (phd11120101@iiti.ac.in). Here, we present the truth tables (in hexadecimal format) of two best evolved Boolean functions along with their nonlinearity and transparency level.

$NL_f$=116, $T_f$=0.958

AFFA AFFA 39C6 C639 FA50 00A6

C635 A635 50EA CO7A C6C6

3939 0450 FDA5 3939 3939

$NL_f$=112, $T_f$=0.917

2F0D 7998 FFC3 C33C 13CF 8997

F0F0 00C3 DF02 8997 3CFF

0000 E3C1 7998 33CC C3FF

# Related-Key Rectangle Attack
# on Round-reduced *Khudra* Block Cipher

Xiaoshuang Ma[1,2] and Kexin Qiao[1,2(✉)]

[1] State Key Laboratory of Information Security, Institute of Information
Engineering, Chinese Academy of Sciences, Beijing 100093, China
{xshma13,kxqiao13}@is.ac.cn
[2] Data Assurance and Communication Security Research Center,
Chinese Academy of Sciences, Beijing 100093, China

**Abstract.** *Khudra* is a block cipher proposed in the SPACE'2014 conference, whose main design goal is to achieve suitability for the increasingly popular Field Programmable Gate Array (FPGA) implementation.
It is an 18-round lightweight cipher based on recursive Feistel structure,
with a 64-bit block size and 80-bit key size. In this paper, we compute
the minimum number of active $F$-functions in differential characteristics
in the related-key setting, and give a more accurate measurement of the
resistance of *Khudra* against related-key differential cryptanalysis. We
construct a related-key boomerang quartet with probability $2^{-48}$ for the
14-round *Khudra*, which is better than the highest probability related-
key boomerang quartet of the 14-round *Khudra* of probability at most
$2^{-72}$ claimed by the designers. Then we propose a related-key rectangle
attack on the 16-round *Khudra* without whitening key by constructing a
related-key rectangle distinguisher for 12-round *Khudra* with a probability of $2^{-23.82}$. The attack has time complexity of $2^{78.68}$ memory accesses
and data complexity of $2^{57.82}$ chosen plaintexts, and requires only four
related keys. This is the best known attack on the round-reduced *Khudra*.

**Keywords:** *Khudra* block cipher · Rectangle attack · Related-key
attack

# 1 Introduction

Differential cryptanalysis was first proposed by Biham and Shamir in [5] and
is one of the most powerful attacks on block ciphers. Differential cryptanalysis analyzes differential propagation patterns of a cipher to discover its non-
random behaviors, and uses these behaviors to build a distinguisher or recover
the key. Under the model of related-key attack [1], which considers the information extracted from the two encryptions under two related keys, related-key
differential attack [11] allows the attacker to operate differences not only in the
plaintexts, but also in keys, though the key values are initially unknown.

For differential attacks, finding out differential characteristics with high probabilities is of great importance, and there are several ways to try a good searching

© Springer International Publishing Switzerland 2015
M. Qiu et al. (Eds.): NSS 2015, LNCS 9408, pp. 331–344, 2015.
DOI: 10.1007/978-3-319-25645-0_22

for such differential characteristics. After the Mixed-Integer Linear Programming (MILP) technique was used to analyze ciphers [6], Mouha *et al.* [15] and Wu *et al.* [21] proposed MILP based techniques to find automatically a lower bound of the number of differentially active S-boxes of word-oriented symmetric ciphers. Later, Sun *et al.* [17,19] and Qiao *et al.* [16] improved Mouha *et al.*'s method to make it capable of searching for the actual differential characteristics. In this paper, we will apply the methods in [16,17,19] and some other techniques to find related-key differential characteristics of the new cipher *Khudra*.

The rectangle-boomerang style attacks [2,10,20] are clever extensions of differential cryptanalysis. In a rectangle-boomerang style attack, the cipher is treated as a cascade of two sub-ciphers, where differential with high probability is used in each of these sub-ciphers. The aim of the attack is to benefit from the slow mixing in reduced round versions of the cipher attacked. The rectangle attack [2] is transited from the boomerang attack [20], and the amplified boomerang attack [10] considers all possible intermediate differences and significantly increases the probability of a right quartet, easing the requirements to a chosen plaintext attack instead of adaptive chosen plaintext and ciphertext attack.

To improve the results of the rectangle attack, Biham *et al.* [3] proposed a new algorithm and a generic way for launching key recovery attacks and calculating the time and data complexity with boomerang or rectangle distinguishers. In this paper, we will combine the rectangle attack with related-key differentials we found to give an analysis on the 16-round *Khudra* block cipher.

The *Khudra* block cipher [13] was proposed by Kolay *et al.* in the SPACE'2014 conference. It is a lightweight cipher suitable for Field Programmable Gate Array (FPGA) implementation. *Khudra* is an 18-round block cipher based on the recursive generalized Feistel structure, and has a 64-bit block size and 80-bit key size. In this paper, we will firstly compute the minimum number of active $F$-functions in the related-key differential characteristics of *Khudra*, and give a more accurate measurement of the resistance of *Khudra* against differential cryptanalysis. We will construct a related-key boomerang quartet of probability of $2^{-48}$ for the 14-round *Khudra*, while the designers of *Khudra* claimed that the highest probability related-key boomerang quartets of 14-round *Khudra* have the probability at most $2^{-72}$. Then we will propose a related-key rectangle attack on the 16-round *Khudra* without whitening key by constructing a related-key rectangle distinguisher for 12-round *Khudra* with a probability of $2^{-23.82}$. The attack has time complexity of $2^{78.68}$ memory accesses, $2^{59.77}$ encryptions, and $2^{57.72}$ decryptions, and data complexity of $2^{57.82}$ chosen plaintexts. It requires only four related keys. This is the best known attack on the round-reduced *Khudra*.

**Organization of the Paper.** We give a brief introduction of *Khudra* in Section 2, and present our analysis result on *Khudra* against related-key differencial attack in Section 3. In Section 4, we firstly describe the construction of the related-key rectangle distinguishers, and then introduce our related-key rectangle attack on round-reduced *Khudra*. Finally we conclude the paper in Section 5.

## 2    Description of *Khudra*

In this section, we briefly recall the design of the block cipher *Khudra* and we refer the readers to [13] for more details.

*Khudra* is a lightweight block cipher suitable for resource-constrained devices. The designers of *Khudra* have shown that the strategies for designing lightweight block cipher on Application Specific Integrated Circuits (ASICs) are not suitable for Field Programmable Gate Arrays (FPGAs). They have identified new methods and design criteria for designing lightweight block ciphers on FPGAs. *Khudra* is an actual practice of these guidelines.

*Khudra* is an 18-round block cipher based on the recursive Feistel structure, which has a 64-bit block size and 80-bit key size. To encrypt a 64-bit plaintext block using a 80-bit key, *Khudra* employs a generalized type-2 transformation (GFS) [7] of a classical Feistel structure, with four branches in one round. The output of the $F$-function then XORs with the next branch and the round key, then passes through the Feistel permutation. The structure of the encryption algorithm is demonstrated in the left part of Fig. 1, which is called the Outer Structure of the cipher.

**The Inner Structure.** The inner structure of 4-branch type-2 generalized Feistel structure of *Khudra* is also used for the construction for the $F$-function, see the right part of Fig. 1. The structure of the $F$-function is called the Inner Structure of the cipher. It is implemented with a two-level recursive structure. In the inner structure, half of the state is updated by $4 \times 4$ S-boxes to achieve nonlinear operations.

Let the input block of the $i$-th round be $(P_0(i-1), P_1(i-1), P_2(i-1), P_3(i-1)) \in \{0,1\}^{16} \times \{0,1\}^{16} \times \{0,1\}^{16} \times \{0,1\}^{16}$, and $RK_i$ denote the round key. The data processing procedure can be described as follows:

$$
\begin{aligned}
P_0(i) &= P_1(i-1) \oplus F(P_0(i-1)) \oplus RK_{2(i-1)}, \\
P_1(i) &= P_2(i-1), \\
P_2(i) &= P_3(i-1) \oplus F(P_2(i-1)) \oplus RK_{2(i-1)+1}, \\
P_3(i) &= P_0(i-1)
\end{aligned}
\tag{1}
$$

for $i = 1, \cdots, 18$.

**The S-box.** *Khudra* uses the S-box in the PRESENT block cipher as its substitution box. The S-box is shown in Table 1. The difference distribution table of the S-box is given in Appendix A. Note that throughout this paper we write bit-strings in their hexadecimal format, *e.g.*, the binary string 1100 is written as a hexadecimal symbol $C$.

**The Key Schedule.** The key schedule algorithm of the cipher generates 36 round keys $RK_i$ ($0 \le i < 36$) and 4 whitening keys $WK_i$ ($0 \le i < 4$), all of 16 bits. Represent the 80-bit master key as $(K_0, K_1, K_2, K_3, K_4)$, each $K_i$ is of 16 bits. The whitening keys $WK_i$ and the round keys $RK_i$ are generated as follows:

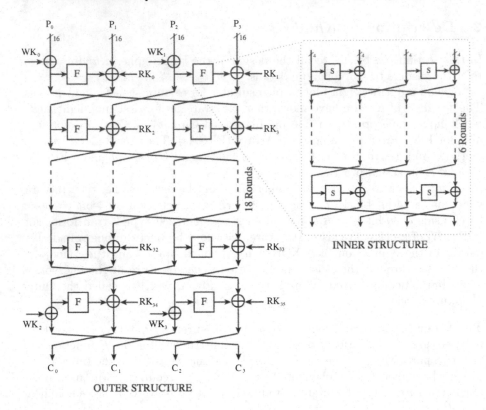

**Fig. 1.** The Structure of *Khudra* [13]

**Table 1.** The S-box of *Khudra*

| $x$ | 0 | 1 | 2 | 3 | 4 | 5 | 6 | 7 | 8 | 9 | A | B | C | D | E | F |
|---|---|---|---|---|---|---|---|---|---|---|---|---|---|---|---|---|
| $S(x)$ | C | 5 | 6 | B | 9 | 0 | A | D | 3 | E | F | 8 | 4 | 7 | 1 | 2 |

$$WK_0 = K_0, WK_1 = K_1, WK_2 = K_3, WK_3 = K_4,$$
$$RC_i = \{0||i_{(6)}||00||i_{(6)}||0\}, \tag{2}$$
$$RK_i = K_{i \bmod 5} \oplus RC_i$$

for $i = 0, \cdots, 35$, where $i_{(6)}$ is the 6 bit representation of the round counter $i$.

## 3    Security Analysis of *Khudra* against Related-key Differential Attack

In this section, we apply the MILP based methods presented in [14,16,17,19] to *Khudra* in the related-key model.

We develop a Python program to generate the MILP instances for *Khudra* in the "lp" format [9]. In order to find the characteristic with the maximal probability, we implement the technique proposed by Sun *et al.* [19] in our Python framework for automatic cryptanalysis. We have computed the minimum number of active $F$-functions in differential characteristics for related-key model, which gives a more accurate measurement of the resistance of *Khudra* against related-key differential cryptanalysis.

**Table 2.** Minimum number of active $F$-functions in related-key model

| No. of Rounds | | 1 | 2 | 3 | 4 | 5 | 6 | 7 | 8 | 9 |
|---|---|---|---|---|---|---|---|---|---|---|
| Min. # Act. | Related-key ([13]) | 0 | 0 | 0 | 1 | 2 | 3 | 3 | 3 | 4 |
| $F$-functions | Related-key (this paper) | 0 | 0 | 0 | 0 | 1 | 1 | 2 | 3 | - |

In Table 2 we list our results and that of the designers. Clearly, we can see that we found related-key differential characteristics with fewer active $F$-functions compared with that of the designers. Particularly, we give in Table 3 a related-key differential characteristic for the 4-round *Khudra* without whitening key, which is a characteristic with no active $F$-function.

**Table 3.** A related-key differential characteristic for 4-round *Khudra*

| r | $\Delta I$ | $\Delta RK_{2(r-1)}$ | $\Delta RK_{2(r-1)+1}$ | NAS | Prob. |
|---|---|---|---|---|---|
| 1 | 0000000000000004 | 0000 | 0004 | 0 | 1 |
| 2 | 0000000000000000 | 0000 | 0000 | 0 | 1 |
| 3 | 0000000000000000 | 0000 | 0000 | 0 | 1 |
| 4 | 0000000000000000 | 0004 | 0000 | 0 | 1 |
| 5 | 0004000000000000 | | | | |

Table 2 shows that *Khudra* is not as secure as the designers claimed in [13]. We can construct a boomerang quartet of probablity of $2^{-48}$ for the 14-round *Khudra* as a cascade of two 7-round sub-ciphers, while the designers [13] claimed that the highest probability boomerang quartet of 14-round *Khudra* have a probability at most $2^{-72}$.

## 4 Related-Key Rectangle Attacks on *Khudra*

In this section, we firstly give a brief introduction to the construction of the related-key rectangle distinguisher for block ciphers. Then we introduce an analysis on the 16-round *Khudra* without whitening key. The related-key differential characteristics presented here are derived from an application of the MILP based method of Sun *et al.* [18].

### 4.1   Related-Key Rectangle Distinguisher

The related-key rectangle attack [4,8,12] is a combination of the related-key and rectangle attack. Let $E$ denote the encryption function of a block cipher. The related-key differential is a quadruple of a plaintext difference $\Delta P$, a ciphertext difference $\Delta C$, a key difference $\Delta K$, and the corresponding probability $\Pr[E_K(P) \oplus E_{K \oplus \Delta K}(P \oplus \Delta P) = \Delta C]$.

The rectangle attack treats $E$ as a cascade of four sub-ciphers as $E = E_f \circ E_1 \circ E_0 \circ E_b$, where $E$ is composed of a core $E' = E_1 \circ E_0$ covered by additional rounds $E_b$ and $E_f$. Assume that for $E_0$ we have a differential $\alpha \to \beta$ under a key difference $\Delta K^0$ with probability $p$, and for $E_1$ there exists a differential $\gamma \to \delta$ under key difference $\Delta K^1$ with probability $q$, where $(\alpha, \beta)$ and $(\gamma, \delta)$ stand for the input-output differences for $E_0$ and $E_1$ respectively. The rectangle attack can be mounted for all possible differences $\beta$ at the end of $E_0$ and $\gamma$ at the beginning of $E_1$. Thus we define $\hat{p}_\alpha$ and $\hat{q}_\delta$ as the probabilities related to $\alpha$ and $\delta$ respectively as follows:

$$\hat{p}_\alpha = \sqrt{\sum_\beta \Pr^2[\alpha \to \beta]}, \quad \hat{q}_\delta = \sqrt{\sum_\gamma \Pr^2[\gamma \to \delta]}. \tag{3}$$

The related-key rectangle attack involves four different unknown but related keys – $K^a, K^b = K^a \oplus \Delta K^0, K^c = K^a \oplus \Delta K^1, K^d = K^a \oplus \Delta K^0 \oplus \Delta K^1$, where the key differences $\Delta K^0$ and $\Delta K^1$ are the respective key differences for sub-ciphers $E_0$ and $E_1$. The basic related-key rectangle distinguisher is constructed as follows:

**Step 1.** Choose $N_0$ plaintext pairs $(P^a, P^b)$ satisfying $P^a \oplus P^b = \alpha$ at random and ask for the encryption of $P^a$ under $K^a$ and of $P^b$ under $K^b$, i.e., $C^a = E_{K^a}(P^a)$ and $C^b = E_{K^b}(P^b)$.

**Step 2.** Choose $N_1$ palintext pairs $(P^c, P^d)$ satisfying $P^c \oplus P^d = \alpha$ at random and ask for the encryption of $P^c$ under $K^c$ and of $P^d$ under $K^d$, i.e., $C^c = E_{K^c}(P^c)$ and $C^d = E_{K^d}(P^d)$.

**Step 3.** Search for quartets of cipertexts $(C^a, C^b, C^c, C^d)$ satisfying $C^a \oplus C^c = C^b \oplus C^d = \delta$.

The probability of the rectangle distinguisher is given by $\Pr = 2^{-n} \hat{p}_\alpha^2 \hat{q}_\delta^2$ where $n$ is the block size. The related-key differentials should satisfy the condition $\hat{p}_\alpha^2 \cdot \hat{q}_\delta^2 > 2^{-n}$ to make the distinguisher make sense. As we expect the number of right quartets is taken to be 4 to get at least one right quartet in the data set with probability 0.982, we set the number of plaintext pairs needed as $2^{n/2+1}/\hat{p}_\alpha \hat{q}_\delta$. As in general differential attacks, after the distinguisher has been detected, one or more rounds are attached before and after the distinguisher for key recovery.

### 4.2   The First Differential ($E_0$) and Second Differential ($E_1$)

Our methods apply the methods in [3] in related-key model with improvement on reducing time complexity by exploiting the properties of a right quartet depending on the GFS feature. We treat the 16-round *Khudra* encryption function $E$

as a cascade of four sub-ciphers as $E = E_f \circ E_1 \circ E_0 \circ E_b$, where $E$ is composed of a core $E' = E_1 \circ E_0$ covered by additional rounds $E_b$ and $E_f$. $E_0$ is composed of rounds $3 - 8$, $E_1$ commences with round 9 and stops at the end of round 14. Rounds $1 - 2$ and rounds $15 - 16$ serve as the rounds before and after the distinguisher respectively ($E_b$ and $E_f$).

**Table 4.** The number of characteristics for $E_0$ of different probability

| Prob. | Num. | Prob. | Num. | Prob. | Num. | Prob. | Num. |
|---|---|---|---|---|---|---|---|
| $2^{-12}$ | 1 | $2^{-22}$ | 4 | $2^{-24}$ | 54 | $2^{-26}$ | 130 |
| $2^{-14}$ | 2 | $2^{-23}$ | 21 | $2^{-25}$ | 88 | $2^{-27}$ | 65 |

All the related-key differential characteristics used in sub-cipher $E_0$ have the same input difference $\alpha = 0000000000005C00$ and they all work with the master key difference $\Delta K^0 = 5C00000000005C000000$. We found many such characteristics with varying differences at the end of 8th round by the MILP method [18]. The numbers of characteristics with different probabilities are shown in Table 4. Therefore the overall probability for $E_0$ is

$$\hat{p}_\alpha = \sqrt{1 \cdot (2^{-12})^2 + 2 \cdot (2^{-14})^2 + 4 \cdot (2^{-22})^2 + \cdots + 65 \cdot (2^{-27})^2} \approx 2^{-11.91}$$

according to Equation (3). Table 5 shows one of the characteristics used for $E_0$. The probability of the differential characteristic is $2^{-12}$.

**Table 5.** The related key differential characteristic for sub-cipher $E_0$ of *Khudra*

| r | $\Delta I$ | $\Delta RK_{2(r-1)}$ | $\Delta RK_{2(r-1)+1}$ | NAS | Prob. |
|---|---|---|---|---|---|
| 3 | 0000000000005C00 | 0000 | 5C00 | 0 | 1 |
| 4 | 0000000000000000 | 0000 | 0000 | 0 | 1 |
| 5 | 0000000000000000 | 5C00 | 0000 | 0 | 1 |
| 6 | 5C00000000000000 | 5C00 | 0000 | 6 | $2^{-12}$ |
| 7 | 0000000000005C00 | 0000 | 5C00 | 0 | 1 |
| 8 | 0000000000000000 | 0000 | 5C00 | 0 | 1 |
| 9 | 000000005C000000 | | | | |

All the related-key differential characteristics used in sub-cipher $E_1$ have the same output difference $\delta = 000000005C000000$ and they work with the master key difference $\Delta K^1 = 5C0000005C0000000000$. Due to the symmetry of GFS that *Khudra* applied, we can also find the same number of characteristics of different probability in $E_1$ as in $E_0$. As it can be seen in Table 4, the overall probability for $E_1$ is also $\hat{q}_\delta \approx 2^{-11.91}$. Thus, the probability of the related-key rectangle distinguisher is given by $\Pr = 2^{-64}\hat{p}_\alpha^2\hat{q}_\delta^2 \approx 2^{-111.64}$.

## 4.3    The Construction of Differential in $E_b$ and Differential in $E_f$

Since *Khudra* applies the generalized Feistel structure, we can deduce the relation among the differences. Given the $\alpha$ difference, Fig. 2 shows the differential propagation pattern of $E_b$.

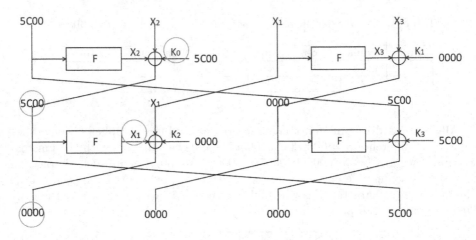

**Fig. 2.** The differential propagation pattern of $E_b$

As is seen in Fig. 2, $X_1$ and $X_2$ are the output differences of the $F$-function when the input difference is $5C00$, and $X_3$ is the output difference of the $F$-function with respect to $X_1$ as the input difference. It turns out that there are $2^{14.52}$ kind of reasonable $X_1$. When the input pair of the $F$-function is fixed with a difference of $5C00(X_1)$, the corresponding output pair of the $F$-function will have a fixed output difference. The sub-keys used in $E_b$ that can affect $\alpha$ difference is $K_0$ (16-bit), and the corresponding related-key difference is $\Delta K_0^0 = 5C00$. The way it influence the difference before round 3 is also shown in Fig. 2 with the circle. Thus we find out the pattern of plaintext differences that can possibly lead to $\alpha$ difference in $E_b$.

Given the $\delta$ difference, we can deduce the relation between the differences after $\delta$. Fig. 3 shows the differential propagation pattern of $E_f$, where $Y_1$ is the output difference of the $F$-function when the input difference is $5C00$, and $Y_2$ is the output difference of the $F$-function with respect to $Y_1$ as the input difference. It turns out that there are $2^{14.52}$ kind of reasonable $Y_1$. When the input pair of the $F$-function is fixed with a difference of $5C00$ ($Y_1$), the corresponding output pair of the $F$-function will have a fixed output difference. Thus we find out the pattern of ciphertext differences that $\delta$ can possibly lead to in $E_f$.

As is seen in Fig. 3, the subkeys used for decryption in $E_f$ that affect $\delta$ difference is $K_0$ (16-bit), and the corresponding related-key difference is $\Delta K_0^1 = 5C00$. The way it influence the difference after round 14 is also shown in Fig. 3 with the circle.

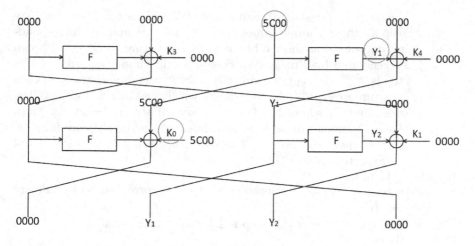

**Fig. 3.** The differential propagation pattern of $E_f$

## 4.4   The Attack

The basic idea of the attack is to try all subkeys which affect the differences before and after the distinguisher (i.e., in $E_b$ and $E_f$). The selection criterion of right subkeys is whether it can lead to an $\alpha$ difference at the beginning of $E_0$, and the $\delta$ difference at the end of $E_1$ can lead to the ciphertext difference.

To attack the 16-round *Khudra*, we request $2^{24.82}$ structures of $2^{32}$ plaintexts each.

The attack works as follows:

1. Data Generation:
   a) Generate $Y = 2^{24.82}$ structures $S_1^a, \cdots, S_Y^a$, each of $2^{32}$ plaintexts. In each structure, fix the left most 32 bits of the plaintexts and enumerate the right most 32 bits. Ask for the encryption of the structures under $K^a$.
   b) For any $i$ ($i = 1, \cdots, Y$), describe any plaintext in structure $S_i^a$ with $P_a = (P_0^a, P_1^a, *, *)$ ($P_0^a$ and $P_1^a$ represent 16 fix bits respectively, and $*$ represents 16 arbitrary bits). According to Fig. 2, the plaintexts in structure $S_b^i$ are generated as follows:

$$P_0^b = P_0^a \oplus 5C00,$$
$$P_1^b = P_1^a \oplus F(P_0^a) \oplus F(P_0^b).$$

   Ask for the encryption of the resulting plaintext $P_b = (P_0^b, P_1^b, *, *)$ under $K^b = K^a \oplus \Delta K^0$ for obtaining $S_1^b, \cdots, S_Y^b$.
   c) Ask for the encryption of plaintexts generated in Step1(a) under $K^c = K^a \oplus \Delta K^1$ (to obtain $S_1^c, \cdots, S_Y^c$).
   d) Ask for the encryption of plaintexts generated in Step1(b) under $K^d = K^a \oplus \Delta K^0 \oplus \Delta K^1$ (to obtain $S_1^d, \cdots, S_Y^d$).

- This step requires data complexity of $2^{57.82}$ chosen plaintexts. We keep all the $2^{16}$ input values of the $F$-function and the corresponding output values in a table and each structure in $S_1^b, \cdots, S_Y^b$ can be generated by 2 memory accesses. So the time complexity of this step is $2^{58.82}$ encryptions, and $2Y = 2^{25.82}$ memory accesses. In each structure we get $2^{64}$ plaintext pairs, which lead to $2^{32}$ kinds of differences after $E_b$, where $2^{32}$ of them satisfy $\alpha$ difference before $E_0$. Thus, the total number of pairs with $\alpha$ difference before the core function is $2^{56.82}$ that produce $2^{113.64}$ quartets of which $2^{113.64} \cdot 2^{-111.64} = 4$ are expected to be *right*.

2. Initializing Counters:

   Initialize an array of $2^{16}$ counters. Each counter corresponds to a different guess of $K_{0[15:0]}^a$.
   - Time complexity of this step is $2^{16}$ memory accesses.

3. Data Analysis:

   a) According to Fig. 3, insert the $N = 2^{58.82}$ ciphertexts of $S^a, S^b, S^c$ and $S^d$ into four hash tables $T^a, T^b, T^c$ and $T^d$ respectively indexed by the left most 16 bits and the right most 16 bits. If a collision occurs in the same bins of $(T^a, T^c)$, denote the ciphertexts as $C^a = (C_0^a, C_1^a, C_2^a, C_3^a)$ and $C^c = (C_0^c, C_1^c, C_2^c, C_3^c)$. For each $C^a$ in each bin of $T^a$, build a hash table indexed by $2^16$ values of $C_1^c$, and insert the corresponding value of $C_2^c$ by the equation $C_2^c \oplus C_2^a = F(C_1^a) \oplus F(C_1^c)$. Check whether the corresponding $2^{m+32+16} = 2^{m+48} = 2^{72.82}$ values of candidate $C^c$ in $T^c$. If this is the case, check whether $\Delta = C_1^a \oplus C_1^c \oplus 5C00$ is one of the $2^{14.52}$ possible output differences may be caused by an input difference $5C00$ to the $F$-function. Do the same for $T_b$ and $T_d$.
      - This step has time complexity of $2^{58.82}$ memory accesses from inserting all the ciphertexts in hash tables. In the hash tables there exist $2^{32}$ bins and in each bin we expect to have $2^{24.82}$ ciphertexts. Therefore, we need $2^{72.82}$ memory accesses to build the hash table for $C^a$, and $2^{72.82}$ memory accesses to check if the candidate $C^c$ is in $T^c$. There are $2^{65.64}$ pairs of $C^a$ and $C^c$ to be checked in the next situation. Out of the $2^{16}$ possible differences for a pair, only $2^{14.52}$ differences can be caused by the $\delta$ difference from the distinguisher and thus about $2^{64.16}$ pairs remain in $T^a$ $(T^b)$ and $T^c$ $(T^d)$. We keep all the $2^{14.52}$ differences that can be caused by $\delta$ in a hash table, and thus the check requires one memory access for each colliding pair. The time complexity of this step is $2^{74.82} + 2^{65.16}$ memory accesses.
   b) For each surviving pairs $(C^a, C^c)$ $((C^b, C^d))$ from the previous step, denote $C^i$'s structure by $S^{C^i}$ and attach to $C^a$ $(C^b)$ the index of $S^{C^c}$ $(S^{C^d})$. After all the remaining pairs are processed, keep a hash table $H^{S_i^a}$ for each structure $S_i^a$ $(i = 1, 2, \cdots, Y)$ and insert the ciphertexts in $S_i^a$ into $H_{S_i^a}$ according to the indexes of the structures that the ciphertext is related to. Similarly, keep the hash tables $H_{S_i^b}$ for $S_i^b$ $(i = 1, 2, \cdots, Y)$.
      - This step requires one memory access for each remaining pair of the previous step and thus needs $2^{65.16}$ memory accesses.

c) For a right quartet $(P^a, P^b, P^c, P^d)$ and the corresponding ciphertexts $(C^a, C^b, C^c, C^d)$, it must be combined by some $P^a \in S_i^a$, $P^b \in S_i^b$ and $P^c \in S_j^c$, $P^d \in S_j^d$ where $S_j^c$ is related to $C^a$ and $S_j^d$ is related to $C^b$ and $i, j \in 1, 2, \cdots, Y$ (not necessarily distinct). In each pair of structures $(S_i^a, S_i^b)$ $(i = 1, \cdots, Y)$, we search for two ciphertexts $C^a$ and $C^b$ from $S_a^i$ and $S_b^i$ respectively which are attach to some other pair of structures $(S_j^c, S_j^d)$. When we found such a pair, check whether the differences of $(P^a, P^b)$ and $(P^c, P^d)$ can cause $\alpha$. Denote the corresponding plaintexts as $P^a = (P_0^a, P_1^a, P_2^a, P_3^a)$ and $P^b = (P_0^b, P_1^b, P_2^b, P_3^b)$. First we check whether the equation $P_3^a \oplus P_3^b = F(P_2^a) \oplus F(P_2^b)$ to be true. With this move, we can reduce the candidate quartets by $2^{-16}$. Then check the same for the plaintexts to which $C^a$ and $C^b$ are related. For the quartets remained after this move, check whether the difference of $P_2^a$ and $P_2^b$ is one of the $2^{14.52}$ possible output differences may be caused by an input difference $5C00$ to the $F$-function, and the same for $P_2^c$ and $P_2^d$.

- There are $2^{64.16}$ attachments (colliding pairs) distributed over $2^{24.82}$ structures, The first filter here can reduce the candidate quartets to $2^{21.86}$ in each structure. Out of the $2^{16}$ possible differences for a pair of plaintexts, only $2^{14.52}$ differences can cause the $\alpha$ difference into the distinguisher. Therefore, out of the $2^{46.68}$ possible quartets only $2^{43.72}$ quartets remain. Since this filtering requires one memory access for each candidate quartet, thus the algorithm requires $2^{78.68} + 2^{62.68} + 2^{46.68} + 2^{45.20}$ memory accesses.

4. Subkey Bits Guess: For each remaining quartet $((P^a, P^b), (P^c, P^d))$, $((C^a, C^b), (C^c, C^d))$ perform:

(a) For each guess of the 16 bits of $K_0^a$, we have

$$K_0^b = K_0^a \oplus \Delta K_0^0,$$
$$K_0^c = K_0^a \oplus \Delta K_0^1, \qquad (4)$$
$$K_0^d = K_0^a \oplus \Delta K_0^0 \oplus \Delta K_0^1.$$

(b) Increment the counter that correspond to $K_0^a$ if

$$E_{b_{K_0^a}}(P^a) \oplus E_{b_{K_0^b}}(P^b) = E_{b_{K_0^c}}(P^c) \oplus E_{b_{K_0^d}}(P^d) = \alpha \qquad (5)$$

and

$$E_{f_{K_0^a}}^{-1}(C^a) \oplus E_{f_{K_0^c}}^{-1}(C^c) = E_{f_{K_0^b}}^{-1}(C^b) \oplus E_{f_{K_0^d}}^{-1}(C^d) = \delta. \qquad (6)$$

- There are $2^{14.52}$ possible input differences that lead to $\alpha$ difference after $E_b$ and totally $2^{16}$ guesses of subkey bits of $K_a$, therefore, $2^{1.48}$ subkeys on average take one of these differences to $\alpha$. As each pair suggests $2^{1.48}$ subkeys, a quartet agrees on $(2^{1.48})^2/2^{16} = 2^{-13.04}$ subkeys for $E_b$. Similarly, a quartet agrees on $2^{-13.04}$ subkeys for $E_f$. In total, we get a candidate list of $2^{-42.08}$ subkeys from each quartet. Thus, for the $2^{43.72}$ remaining quartets, there are total $2^{16}$ possible subkeys and $2^{1.64}$ hits. Averagely, the number of hits for a wrong subkey is $2^{-14.36}$, while the number of expected hits for the right one is 4. Thus, the attack can almost always succeed in recovering subkey bits. This step requires about $2^{57.72}$ encryptions and $2^{57.72}$ decryptions and $2^{59.72}$ memory accesses.

5. Output the subkey with maximal counter.
   - This step requires $2^{16}$ memory accesses.

Thus, the overall attack has data complexity of $2^{57.82}$ chosen plaintexts, time complexity of $2^{78.68}$ memory accesses, $2^{59.77}$ encryptions, and $2^{57.72}$ decryptions. The expected number of right quartets is taken to be 4.

# 5    Conclusion

In this paper, we have launched an related-key rectangle attack on 16-round *Khudra*, with time complexity of $2^{78.68}$ memory accesses, $2^{59.77}$ encryptions and $2^{57.72}$ decryptions, and data complexity of $2^{57.82}$ chosen plaintexts. The attack is a generic related-key rectangle attack with a differential distinguisher deduced from an MILP based search. This is the best known cryptanalysis presented on round-reduced *Khudra*.

**Acknowledgments.** The authors would like to thank the anonymous reviewers for their helpful comments and suggestions. The work of this paper was supported by the National Key Basic Research Program of China (2013CB834203), the National Natural Science Foundation of China (Grants 61472417, 61402469 and 61472415), the Strategic Priority Research Program of Chinese Academy of Sciences under Grant XDA06010702, and the State Key Laboratory of Information Security, Chinese Academy of Sciences.

# References

1. Biham, E.: New types of cryptanalytic attacks using related keys. Journal of Cryptology **7**(4), 229–246 (1994)
2. Biham, E., Dunkelman, O., Keller, N.: The rectangle attack - rectangling the serpent. In: Pfitzmann, B. (ed.) EUROCRYPT 2001. LNCS, vol. 2045, pp. 340–357. Springer, Heidelberg (2001)
3. Biham, E., Dunkelman, O., Keller, N.: New results on boomerang and rectangle attacks. In: Daemen, J., Rijmen, V. (eds.) FSE 2002. LNCS, vol. 2365, pp. 1–16. Springer, Heidelberg (2002)
4. Biham, E., Dunkelman, O., Keller, N.: Related-key boomerang and rectangle attacks. In: Cramer, R. (ed.) EUROCRYPT 2005. LNCS, vol. 3494, pp. 507–525. Springer, Heidelberg (2005)
5. Biham, E., Shamir, A.: Differential cryptanalysis of DES-like cryptosystems. Journal of Cryptology **4**(1), 3–72 (1991)
6. Borghoff, J., Knudsen, L.R., Stolpe, M.: Bivium as a mixed-integer linear programming problem. In: Parker, M.G. (ed.) Cryptography and Coding 2009. LNCS, vol. 5921, pp. 133–152. Springer, Heidelberg (2009)
7. Hoang, V.T., Rogaway, P.: On generalized feistel networks. In: Rabin, T. (ed.) CRYPTO 2010. LNCS, vol. 6223, pp. 613–630. Springer, Heidelberg (2010)

8. Hong, S.H., Kim, J.-S., Lee, S.-J., Preneel, B.: Related-key rectangle attacks on reduced versions of SHACAL-1 and AES-192. In: Gilbert, H., Handschuh, H. (eds.) FSE 2005. LNCS, vol. 3557, pp. 368–383. Springer, Heidelberg (2005)

9. IBMsoftware-group: User-manual cplex 12 (2011). http://www-01.ibm.com

10. Kelsey, J., Kohno, T., Schneier, B.: Amplified boomerang attacks against reduced-round MARS and Serpent. In: Schneier, B. (ed.) FSE 2000. LNCS, vol. 1978, pp. 75–93. Springer, Heidelberg (2001)

11. Kelsey, J., Schneier, B., Wagner, D.: Related-key cryptanalysis of 3-WAY, Biham-DES, CAST, DES-X, NewDES, RC2, and TEA. Information and Communications Security, 233–246 (1997)

12. Kim, J.-S., Kim, G., Hong, S.H., Lee, S.-J., Hong, D.: The related-key rectangle attack – application to SHACAL-1. In: Wang, H., Pieprzyk, J., Varadharajan, V. (eds.) ACISP 2004. LNCS, vol. 3108, pp. 123–136. Springer, Heidelberg (2004)

13. Kolay, S., Mukhopadhyay, D.: Khudra: a new lightweight block cipher for FPGAs. In: Chakraborty, R.S., Matyas, V., Schaumont, P. (eds.) SPACE 2014. LNCS, vol. 8804, pp. 126–145. Springer, Heidelberg (2014)

14. Ma, X., Hu, L., Sun, S., Qiao, K., Shan, J.: Tighter security bound of MIBS block cipher against differential attack. In: Au, M.H., Carminati, B., Kuo, C.-C.J. (eds.) NSS 2014. LNCS, vol. 8792, pp. 518–525. Springer, Heidelberg (2014)

15. Mouha, N., Wang, Q., Gu, D., Preneel, B.: Differential and linear cryptanalysis using mixed-integer linear programming. In: Wu, C.-K., Yung, M., Lin, D. (eds.) Inscrypt 2011. LNCS, vol. 7537, pp. 57–76. Springer, Heidelberg (2012)

16. Qiao, K., Hu, L., Sun, S., Ma, X., Kan, H.: Improved MILP Modeling for Automatic Security Evaluation and Application to FOX. IEICE TRANSACTIONS on Cryptography and Information Security (Special) (to appear)

17. Sun, S., Hu, L., Song, L., Xie, Y., Wang, P.: Automatic security evaluation of block ciphers with S-bP structures against related-key differential attacks. In: Lin, D., Xu, S., Yung, M. (eds.) Inscrypt 2013. LNCS, vol. 8567, pp. 39–51. Springer, Heidelberg (2014)

18. Sun, S., Hu, L., Wang, M., Wang, P., Qiao, K., Ma, X., Shi, D., Song, L., Fu, K.: Towards finding the best characteristics of some bit-oriented block ciphers and automatic enumeration of (related-key) differential and linear characteristics with predefined properties (2014). Cryptology ePrint Archive, Report 2014/747. http://eprint.iacr.org/

19. Sun, S., Hu, L., Wang, P., Qiao, K., Ma, X., Song, L.: Automatic security evaluation and (related-key) differential characteristic search: application to SIMON, PRESENT, LBlock, DES(L) and other bit-oriented block ciphers. In: Sarkar, P., Iwata, T. (eds.) ASIACRYPT 2014. LNCS, vol. 8873, pp. 158–178. Springer, Heidelberg (2014)

20. Wagner, D.: The boomerang attack. In: Knudsen, L.R. (ed.) FSE 1999. LNCS, vol. 1636, pp. 156–170. Springer, Heidelberg (1999)

21. Wu, S., Wang, M.: Security evaluation against differential cryptanalysis for block cipher structures. Tech. rep., Cryptology ePrint Archive, Report 2011/551 (2011)

# A    The Difference Distribution Table (DDT) of the S-box of *Khudra*

|   | 0 | 1 | 2 | 3 | 4 | 5 | 6 | 7 | 8 | 9 | A | B | C | D | E | F |
|---|---|---|---|---|---|---|---|---|---|---|---|---|---|---|---|---|
| 0 | 16 | 0 | 0 | 0 | 0 | 0 | 0 | 0 | 0 | 0 | 0 | 0 | 0 | 0 | 0 | 0 |
| 1 | 0 | 0 | 0 | 4 | 0 | 0 | 0 | 4 | 0 | 4 | 0 | 0 | 0 | 4 | 0 | 0 |
| 2 | 0 | 0 | 0 | 2 | 0 | 4 | 2 | 0 | 0 | 0 | 2 | 0 | 2 | 2 | 2 | 0 |
| 3 | 0 | 2 | 0 | 2 | 2 | 0 | 4 | 2 | 0 | 0 | 2 | 2 | 0 | 0 | 0 | 0 |
| 4 | 0 | 0 | 0 | 0 | 0 | 4 | 2 | 2 | 0 | 2 | 2 | 0 | 2 | 0 | 2 | 0 |
| 5 | 0 | 2 | 0 | 0 | 2 | 0 | 0 | 0 | 0 | 2 | 2 | 2 | 4 | 2 | 0 | 0 |
| 6 | 0 | 0 | 2 | 0 | 0 | 0 | 2 | 0 | 2 | 0 | 0 | 4 | 2 | 0 | 0 | 4 |
| 7 | 0 | 4 | 2 | 0 | 0 | 0 | 2 | 0 | 2 | 0 | 0 | 0 | 2 | 0 | 0 | 4 |
| 8 | 0 | 0 | 0 | 2 | 0 | 0 | 0 | 2 | 0 | 2 | 0 | 4 | 0 | 2 | 0 | 4 |
| 9 | 0 | 0 | 2 | 0 | 4 | 0 | 2 | 0 | 2 | 0 | 0 | 0 | 2 | 0 | 4 | 0 |
| A | 0 | 0 | 2 | 2 | 0 | 4 | 0 | 0 | 2 | 0 | 2 | 0 | 0 | 2 | 2 | 0 |
| B | 0 | 2 | 0 | 0 | 2 | 0 | 0 | 0 | 4 | 2 | 2 | 2 | 0 | 2 | 0 | 0 |
| C | 0 | 0 | 2 | 0 | 0 | 4 | 0 | 2 | 2 | 2 | 2 | 0 | 0 | 0 | 2 | 0 |
| D | 0 | 2 | 4 | 2 | 2 | 0 | 0 | 2 | 0 | 0 | 2 | 2 | 0 | 0 | 0 | 0 |
| E | 0 | 0 | 2 | 2 | 0 | 0 | 2 | 2 | 2 | 2 | 0 | 0 | 2 | 2 | 0 | 0 |
| F | 0 | 4 | 0 | 0 | 4 | 0 | 0 | 0 | 0 | 0 | 0 | 0 | 0 | 0 | 4 | 4 |

# A New Statistical Approach for Integral Attack

Jiageng Chen[1,2]($\boxtimes$), Atsuko Miyaji[2,3,4], Chunhua Su[2], and Liang Zhao[5]

[1] Computer School, Central China Normal University, Wuhan 430079, China
chinkako@gmail.com
[2] School of Information Science, Japan Advanced Institute of Science and Technology, 1-1 Asahidai, Nomi, Ishikawa 923-1292, Japan
{miyaji,chsu}@jaist.ac.jp
[3] CREST, Japan Science and Technology Agency, Kawaguchi Center Building 4-1-8, Honcho, Kawaguchi-shi, Saitama 332-0012, Japan
[4] Osaka University, 1-1 Yamadaoka, Suita, Osaka Prefecture 565-0871, Japan
[5] College of Computer Science, SICHUAN University, Chengdu 610065, China
lzhaoscu@163.com

**Abstract.** Statistical saturation attack is one of the powerful attacks against block ciphers, however, the requirement of identifying the weak permutation somehow restrict its wide applications. Integral attack can be considered as the deterministic version of the statistical saturation attack, which works by tracing the properties of the integral sets after certain rounds of encryption. It aims to build an integral characteristic path for a large number of rounds. By searching within the message space, it expects to find a characteristic path in a deterministic way assuming the random behavior of the cipher. In this paper, we provide the first study on how to take advantage of the integral attack and apply it to cryptanalysis by using statistical approach, and our new approach does not rely on identifying weak permutations. One of our contributions is to firstly apply the internal collision of a set as the evaluated statistics and show how this property can be efficiently propagated in the General Feistel Structure (GFS) with bijective map S-Box. Secondly, we provide a simple statistical framework to evaluate the data complexity. Finally, we evaluate several GFS and find out for some of the designs, our approach provide a better result compared with other statistical attack such as differential and linear attack.

**Keywords:** Integral attack · Internal collisions · Generalized feistel structure (GFS)

J. Chen—This study is partly supported by the National Natural Science Foundation of China under Grant 61302161.
A. Miyaji—This study is partly supported by Grant-in-Aid for Scientific Research (C)(15K00183) and (15K00189).
C. Su—This study is partly supported by JSPS KAKENHI 15K16005.
L. Zhao—This study is partly supported by the National Natural Science Foundation of China under Grant 61302161.

M. Qiu et al. (Eds.): NSS 2015, LNCS 9408, pp. 345–356, 2015.
DOI: 10.1007/978-3-319-25645-0_23

# 1   Introduction

Among the cryptanalysis techniques against block ciphers, besides the classical differential and linear attack, integral attack is one of the most popular method. First it was proposed as the "Square attack" in [6] to attack block cipher Square. Since then, several attacks following the similar technique were applied to analyze different ciphers, and thus different names were given such as saturation attack [9] and multiset attack [3]. Later in [7], Knudsen and Wagen unified all these similar attacks to integral attack. In this paper, we employ statistical approach to revisit the integral attack and we show that our statistical tools aided attack outperforms some existing statistical attacks. Morever, we also present some new properties of the integral attacks to which we should pay our attention.

The idea of the integral attack is to construct an efficient distinguisher based on the integral characteristic path. Generally speaking, for byte-based or nibble-based block ciphers, the attacker first collects a set of plaintexts which contains all possible values for some bytes or nibbles, while assigns constant values for the rest of the parts. Thus in the integral attack, we usually observe the propagation of three properties:

- "C"(constant): elements in the set equal a constant value $c \in \{0, 1\}^n$.
- "P"(permutation): elements in the set are all distinct.
- "B"(xor-balanced): the xor sum of the elements is zero.

The constant parts which are usually assigned to the property "C" will be propagated freely through rounds, while the key point is to study the propagation of the all possible value property "P". Usually, after several rounds, the properties are degraded to property "B" which means that the sum of the set is zero. And finally the property "B" will be propagated to something untraceable anymore.

In recent years, all the previous researches on integral attacks try to build a distinguisher which will end at some round containing one or several observable property "B" such as [14]. Meanwhile, it is known that the probability of this distinguisher is one given the random behavior of the cipher, which is quite different from statistic based attack such as differential and linear attack. Since the distinguisher has property of probability one, it is not difficult to find the best integral path by simple computing. The attacker can start by setting one byte or nibble of the internal state to have property "P" while others are set to be "C". In most cases, setting only one "P" will give the best result. Then trace the propagation of "P" in the forward direction until no properties can be observed. We can further increase the number of rounds by going backwards since we have not used any message space. Assuming everything is randomly distributed, then we go backwards to trace the property until message space is used over. This integral characteristic can be found with computational complexity approximately that is equal to the data complexity and once found, it holds with probability one and can be used to launch the key recovery attack. As a result, most of the researches try to improve the integral attack by putting their focus on the key recovery part instead of how to build a better distinguisher.

Another similar approach is statistical saturation attack [5]. Unlike integral attack, [5] is statistical in essence. However, it relies on weak permutations to some degree. The attack on block cipher PRESENT is by far the most successful example, but it seems difficult to apply to other ciphers.

**Contributions.** Our motivation is to find an attack which is statistical in essence based on the deterministic integral attack. The open problem here is to find out the deterministic propagation rules of the integral attack. If the property "B" goes through S-Box, then we totally lose the property information immediately. Thus the natural question is that whether we can find a way to extend the property propagation in the probabilistic way.

Our contribution can be summarized as follows:

- This paper gives the first attempt by investigating the application of the internal collision of the integral set. The motivation comes from the fact that when we xor two permutations, the distribution of the number of collisions in the set can be distinguished from random distribution given enough plaintexts. More interestingly, our result can be derived for more than two permutations.
- We show that the number of collisions within the integral set will not be changed after applying S-Box transformation assuming it is a bijective map. This problem was first studied in converting **PRP** to **PRF**. And in the recent result [13], the accurate evaluation of the collision probability is provided. In this paper, we show that for byte or nibble-based block ciphers, the permutation will not break the structure of the integral set, and thus the collision property will remain. We can apply the evaluation of $n$ xored permutation to byte or nibble based block cipher. It becomes difficult to distinguish the distributions when $n$ becomes large.
- We also provide a statistic framework based on [1] to distinguish the two collision distributions, and we apply our methods to attack generalized Feistel structure (GFS). We show that for some of the designs, our method can achieve the same or even better result than other statistical attacks such as differential or linear attacks.

**Organization of the Paper.** The rest of the paper is organized as follows. Section 2 introduces the concepts of collisions of the permutations and describe the expect value of the collision number. Then a simple statistic framework is provided to distinguish between two collision distributions in Section 3. In Section 4, we evaluate the security margin of several generalized Feistel structure against our attack. Finally, we conclude our results in Section 5.

## 2   Integral Internal Collisions

The distinguisher of our probabilistic integral attack relies on the fact that we can actually distinguish a pseudorandom function(**PRF**) from $r$ xored pseudorandom permutation(**PRP**) when $r$ is not too large. The related problem was first investigated on how to convert **PRP** to **PRF**. The transformation suffers from security loss where it can be distinguished from **PRF** using birthday attack. The natural question comes in mind is that what is the security level when **PRF** is built by xoring several **PRP**. Several security bounds have been given since then. [8] demonstrated that xoring $k$ **PRP** can build a **PRF** with security in $\mathcal{O}(2^{\frac{k+1}{k}n})$. [2] gave a tight bound for the case of two **PRP**, which is at least $\mathcal{O}(2^{\frac{n}{2}})$ and at most $\mathcal{O}(2^n)$. Also in [12], the security level is proven to be exactly $\mathcal{O}(2^n)$ for the two **PRP** case. Later in [13], accurate evaluation was considered for building **PRF** from $k$ **PRP**, especially, they provided the evaluation when not all the $2^n$ input and output are given. Since if all the $2^n$ input and output are known to the adversary, the xor sum is always zero and thus can be distinguished from a **PRF**. Thus to address the problem excluding this trivial case, [13] considered the situation where not all permutations are available to the adversary. In other words, there are few points that the adversary cannot know. However, when doing the probability evaluation, the result is equivalent to the adversary having full access to the permutations. This quantitative approach is crucial in our analysis, which differs from the traditional integral attack where when a balanced integral property "B" goes through an S-Box, we will not be able to observe the balanced property anymore. Here we summarize the result of [13] into the following theorem.

**Theorem 1 ([13]).** *Assume generator $A = f_1 \oplus f_2 \oplus \cdots \oplus f_k$ where $f_i, i \in [1, k]$ is a permutation chosen uniformly from $D_n$, where $D_n$ denotes the set of all permutations from $\{0, 1\}^n$ to $\{0, 1\}^n$. Also assume generator $H = h \in_R F_n$, where $F_n$ denotes the set of all applications from $\{0, 1\}^n$ to $\{0, 1\}^n$. We want to distinguish $A$ from $H$ with non-negligible advantage given $m \approx 2^n$ input and output.*

*For generator $A$, the expected value and variance for the number of collisions are as follows:*

$$E_{col}(A) = \frac{m(m-1)}{2 \cdot 2^n}[1 + \frac{(-1)^k}{(2^n - 1)^{k-1}}] \tag{1}$$

$$\sigma_{col}(A) = \mathcal{O}(\frac{m}{\sqrt{2^n}}) \tag{2}$$

*For generator $H$, the expected value and variance for the number of collisions are as follows:*

$$E_{col}(H) = \frac{m(m-1)}{2 \cdot 2^n} \tag{3}$$

$$\sigma_{col}(H) = \mathcal{O}(\frac{m}{\sqrt{2^n}}) \tag{4}$$

$\square$

## 2.1   Experimental Analysis of Xor Collisions

From Theorem 1, we know that there is a difference between a pseudorandom function, which should be the ideal case and the xor of pseudorandom permutations regarding the number of collisions within the set. We first provide an

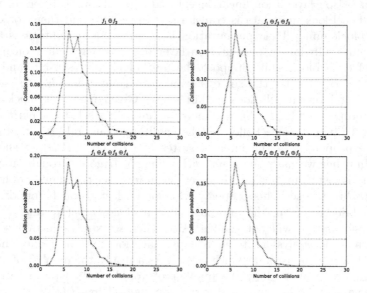

Fig. 1. Experimental result on internal collisions for XORed PRPs

experimental verification of the internal collisions to show correctness and accurateness of the theorem . The experiment is done by counting the probabilities for different collision numbers averaged over $10^9$ trials, in other words, $10^9$ random permutations are generated and then the collisions for different settings are counted. The result of $f_1 \oplus f_2$ to $f_1 \oplus \cdots f_5$ are summarized in Figure 1.

From Figure 1, we can see that as we xor more permutations, the distribution of the internal collisions tends to get stable. It it clear that $f_1 \oplus f_2$ shows a significant difference from other settings, and we can hardly tell the difference from the figure when number of xored permutations gets larger than 4. Also we can observe that the distribution of the number of internal collisions tends to have bell curve shape.

## 2.2   Apply to Real World Block Ciphers

As shown in the subsection above, we have confirmed that there is an observable difference between the distribution of the internal collisions of the xored PRP and the ideal case of PRF. To attack the real world block cipher, we still have to refine this technology. Since we focus on analyzing the generalized Feistel structure in our cryptanalysis in this paper, we address the feasibility by demonstrating the Type-II GFS as follows.

Assume that the non-linear function $F$ is implemented as $S$-Box, which is the most common way of designing a block cipher, one round of Type-II GFS includes an $S$-Box layer (non-linear layer) and a permutation layer. In the $S$-Box layer, two block unit data is transformed by $S$-Box, and then xored with two other block units. Then permutation layer proceeds permutations among the block units. Obviously, permutation layer does not have effect on internal collisions of each block unit. Suppose the unit block size is $n$-bit, and $f^r = \oplus_{i=1}^r f_i$, $f_i \in_R B_n$ denotes the xor of $r$ random permutations. $E_{col}(S)$ denotes the number of internal collisions within set $S$. Given four unit block inputs having the property of $(P, P, P, C)$, namely, we have three sets to be permutation and one set to be constant. Following the traditional integral attack, after two rounds, the properties of the internal states will be $(B, ?, P, B)$ as shown in Figure 2. In other words, when a set with property $B$ goes through an $S$-Box, the property is lost from then on. However, when we trace the number of internal collisions within the set, this property will not be lost through rounds. Since $S$-Box is a bijective map, the internal collision of a set before and after the $S$-Box transformation will not change. Also when we xor a constant set to a permutation, it is equivalent to map a permutation to a new one, thus the internal collision remains same which is zero. As a result, the number of internal collisions can be evaluated by the number of xored random permutations as shown in Figure 2. For example, after two rounds of Type-II GFS, the number of internal collisions will be $(E_{col}(f^2), E_{col}(f^3), E_{col}(f^1), E_{col}(f^2))$.

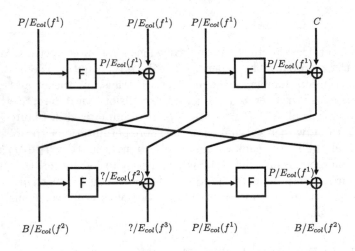

**Fig. 2.** Type-II GFS

## 3    Successful Probability of Statistical Integral Attack

In this section, we apply the framework in [1] to fit our specific requirements here. Suppose we would like to recover the last rounds subkey $k_i, i \in [0, 2^m - 1]$ of $m$-bit length, with which the attacker can compute backwards to get the derived internal state given the ciphertexts. For each of the key candidate, we associate a counter with it to denote the number of internal collisions within the plaintext and ciphertext sets. Denote $k_0$ be the right key and $k_i, i \in [1, 2^m - 1]$ be the wrong keys. Let's denote $X^i$ be the total counter of the number of collisions computed from each subkey candidate $k_i$. It is obvious that the total counter $X^i$ can be derived by $X^i = X_0^i + X_1^i + \cdots X_{N-1}^i/N$, where $N$ is the number of integral plaintext and ciphertext sets, and $X_j^i$ denotes the counter of internal collision for one integral set. Assume that $X_0^i, ..., X_{N-1}^i$ are independent random variable which follows the same distribution with mean $\mu_w$ and variance $\sigma_w^2$ for the wrong key candidates where $w \in [1, 2^m - 1]$, and $\mu_0$ and $\sigma_0^2$ for the right key candidate. Consider that $N$ is very large in the practical setting, by central limit theorem,

$$X^i \sim \mathcal{N}(\mu_w, \frac{\sigma_w^2}{N}), \quad X^0 \sim \mathcal{N}(\mu_0, \frac{\sigma_0^2}{N})$$

Then let's further define the bias for the two categories as follows:

$$Y^i = |X^i - \mu_w|, i \neq 0, \quad Y^0 = X^0 - \mu_w$$

Here we assume $\mu_0 > \mu_w$, and we only reverse the sign of $Y^0$ in the other case. Let's sort the biases of the wrong key candidates and denote them as $W_1, ..., W_{2^m-1}$, where $W_1$ is the smallest bias. According to the previous section, the bias for the correct key candidate can be considered to be the largest one. Thus naturally, to attack successfully, we would like $Y^0 > W_{2^m-1}$. This condition can be loosen a little bit by putting the counter of the right key within the top $r$ candidates. Then the attack provides a complexity reduction by a factor of $2^{m-lg_r}$ over brute force search. Since $X^i - \mu_w$ follows normal distribution $\mathcal{N}(0, \frac{\sigma_w^2}{N})$, the absolute value $Y^i$ follows the folded normal distribution $\mathcal{FN}(0, \frac{\sigma_w^2}{N})$. Let's suppose the advantage of the attack is $a$-bit, in other words, in the sorted sequence $W_1, ..., W_{2^m-1}$, the correct key locates at the $r$th position, and we only need to search the candidates from $W_{2^m-1}$ back to $r$. As a result, the advantage over the brute force search is $a = lg\frac{2^m}{2^m-r}$, thus $r = 2^m - 2^{m-a}$. Then we would like the bias of the correct key to be greater than $W_{2^m-2^{m-a}}$, namely,

$$Y^0 > 0, \quad Y^0 > W_{2^m-2^{m-a}}$$

As we know that $W_{2^m-2^{m-a}}$ follows a normal distribution $\mathcal{N}(\mu_q, \sigma_q^2)$ according to the order statistics, mean and variance can be derived as follows:

$$\mu_q = F_w^{-1}(1 - 2^{-a}) = 0 + \frac{\sigma_w}{\sqrt{N}}\Phi^{-1}(1 - 2^{-a-1}) = \frac{\sigma_w}{\sqrt{N}}\Phi^{-1}(1 - 2^{-a-1})$$

$$\sigma_q = \frac{1}{f_w(\mu_q)}2^{-\frac{m+a}{2}} = \frac{\sigma_w/\sqrt{N}}{2\phi(\Phi^{-1}(1 - 2^{-a-1}))}2^{-\frac{m+a}{2}}$$

Here $F_w$ is the cumulative distribution function of $Y^w$, which is folded normal. Also $Y^0$ follows the normal distribution $\mathcal{N}(\mu_0 - \mu_w, \frac{\sigma_0^2}{N})$. Then the successful probability of the attack can be denoted as:

$$P_{success} = \int_0^\infty \int_{-\infty}^x f_q(y) dy f_0(x) dx$$

where $f_q$ and $f_0$ denote the density functions for $W_{2^m-2^{m-a}}$ and $Y^0$ respectively. Since the probability for $W_{2^m-2^{m-a}} < 0$ is negligible, we could ignore the probability $Y^0 > 0$, as a result, we can simplify the calculation as follows:

$$P_s = P(Y^0 > W_{2^m-2^{m-a}}) = \int_\infty^{\frac{\mu_0 - \mu_w - \mu_q}{\sqrt{\frac{\sigma_0^2}{N} + \sigma_q^2}}} \phi(x) dx$$

Since it was shown that $\sigma_q$ is negligible regarding the final result, we could usually ignore it so the successful probability for the attack could be approximated by:

$$P_s = \Phi(\frac{\mu_0 - \mu_w - \frac{\sigma_w}{\sqrt{N}}\Phi^{-1}(1 - 2^{-a-1})}{\sigma_0/\sqrt{N}})$$

As a result, the number of required integral sets for the attack can be expressed as follows:

$$N = (\frac{\sigma_0\Phi^{-1}(P_s) + \sigma_w\Phi^{-1}(1 - 2^{-a-1})}{\mu_0 - \mu_w})^2$$

Then given the statistical framework, we can answer the question of how many random permutations can be accumulated before we can distinguish it from a pseudorandom function. In other words, we want to reveal the relationship between the data complexity and the number of xored permutations. Here we choose the permutation size to be 4-bit, since this setting is recently widely used in many lightweight block ciphers such as TWINE [17] and LBlock [18], and also the GFS cipher can deploy the unit block setting to be 4-bit as well. Considering the structure of GFS and most recent popular block ciphers, we choose the following block sizes: 32-bit, 48-bit and 64-bit versions. A successful attack requires the data complexity to be lower than the full code block. Another criteria is the advantage setting which we consider the following three versions: 8, 16 and 32. Based on the above settings, we can observe the allowed number of accumulated permutations for different block sizes. We notice that the data complexity will not vary much regarding the different advantage parameters. Thus in the following analysis, we will choose $a = 16$ for the ease of demonstration. Second, to launch a legal attack under the previous statistical framework, the allowed accumulated permutations are 3, 5, 7 for 32-bit, 48-bit and 64-bit versions of block cipher. Note that we have already included the data complexity with in one integral set, namely, $2^4$ in the 4-bit version. The key recovery attack can be performed by the traditional last round attack. In Section 4, we will construct and evaluate the characteristic path of various GFS without the key recovery phase.

## 4    Security Evaluation on Generalized Feistel Structure

In this section, we provide our evaluation on Generalized Feistel Structure (GFS) with bijective S-Box design using statistical integral approach. Our evaluation mainly focus on the number of rounds to distinguish and the corresponding data complexity. Time complexity depends on analyzing the concrete structure of the cipher, and since it is rather straightforward based on the distinguisher, we omit the discussion here.

GFS extends the traditional Feistel ciphers in dividing a message into $k > 2$ sub blocks instead of two. Type-II GFS [19] is one of the most popular form which received much of the attention. Each round, the Type-II GFS applies Feistel transformation $(x, y) \rightarrow (x, F(x) \oplus y)$ for every two blocks and performs a left cyclic shift of the sub blocks. Some of the recent proposed block ciphers are based on the Type-II GFS such as CLEFIA [15]. Although Type-II GFS with large $k$ is believed to be suitable for small-scale implementations, it suffers from low diffusion. [16] investigates the permutation strategy in detail and pointed out that the left cyclic shift is not the optimal permutation which can achieve the best diffusion. They first define the maximum diffusion rounds **DRmax** for a specific permutation $\pi$, and then they exhaustive search for the optimum shuffles that can maximize the **DRmax** value. As a result, they found a shuffle family with good diffusion regarding the impossible differential attack, differential/linear attack and integral attack. The result showed that the security margin against these attacks have been significantly improved compared with Type-II GFS and Nyberg type [11]. Figure 3 shows one generalized structure when $k = 16$ which was applied in block cipher TWINE.

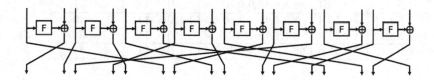

**Fig. 3.** Generalized Feistel Structure of TWINE (k=16)

To demonstrate, we analyze the case for $k = 8$ (32-bit) and $k = 16$ (64-bit) versions with 4-bit S-box. We try to find the path for $k = 8$ where the accumulated permutation is less or equal than 4, and for $k = 16$ where the accumulated permutations is less or equal than 8. In other words, 4 and 8 are the largest number of permutations we will allow in the output of the path. We set only one input to $P$ and all the rest input blocks to 'C'. In our model, we treat the initial 'P' as value '1', and whenever we face the case of $P \oplus P$, we just do plus one counting, and finally we try to find which input will result in an output that is within the bound of legal data complexity. The search is straightforward and can be completed in less a second considering all the cases. The evaluation of the case when $k = 8$ and $k = 16$ regarding different shuffling is given in Tables 1 and 2. Shuffling except Type II and Nyberg were illustrated in [16].

**Table 1.** Security evaluation - data complexity for $k = 8$

| $k = 8$ | block shuffle | rounds | data (in log) |
|---------|---------------|--------|---------------|
| TypeII | {7,0,1,2,3,4,5,6} | 10 | 11.8697 |
| Nyberg | {2,0,4,1,6,3,7,5} | 11 | 19.6835 |
| No.1 | {3,0,1,4,7,2,5,6} | 8 | 19.6835 |
| No.2 | {3,0,7,4,5,6,1,2} | 8 | 19.6835 |

**Table 2.** Security evaluation - data complexity for $k = 16$

| $k = 16$ | block shuffle | rounds | data (in log) |
|----------|---------------|--------|---------------|
| TypeII | {15,0,1,2,3,4,5,6,7,8,9,10,11,12,13,14} | 18 | 11.87 |
| Nyberg | {2,0,4,1,6,3,8,5,10,7,12,9,14,11,15,13} | 19 | 58.75 |
| No.1 | {1,2,9,4,15,6,5,8,13,10,7,14,11,12,3,0} | 11 | 27.49 |
| No.2 | {1,2,11,4,9,6,7,8,15,12,5,10,3,0,13,14} | 11 | 35.31 |
| No.3 | {1,2,11,4,9,6,15,8,5,12,7,10,3,0,13,14} | 11 | 43.13 |
| No.4 | {5,2,9,4,1,6,11,8,15,12,3,10,7,0,13,14} | 11 | 43.13 |
| No.5 | {5,2,9,4,11,6,15,8,3,12,1,10,7,0,13,14} | 11 | 43.13 |
| No.6 | {5,2,11,4,1,6,15,8,3,12,13,10,7,0,9,14} | 11 | 43.13 |
| No.7 | {1,2,11,4,3,6,7,8,15,12,5,14,9,0,13,10} | 11 | 43.13 |
| No.8 | {1,2,11,4,9,6,7,8,15,12,13,14,3,0,5,10} | 11 | 43.13 |
| No.9 | {1,2,11,4,9,6,15,8,5,12,7,14,3,0,13,10} | 12 | 58.75 |
| No.10 | {7,2,13,4,11,8,3,6,15,0,9,10,1,14,5,12} | 11 | 35.31 |
| No.11 | {7,2,13,4,11,8,9,6,15,0,3,10,5,14,1,12} | 11 | 27.49 |
| No.12 | {1,2,11,4,15,8,3,6,7,0,9,12,5,14,13,10} | 11 | 35.31 |
| No.13 | {5,2,11,6,13,8,15,0,3,4,9,12,1,14,7,10} | 11 | 35.31 |

Notice that in paper [16], security evaluation on statistical attacks such as differential and linear attacks are given in the form of active S-boxes. Let's assume we apply the S-Box which is used in PRESENT [4], which is also a 4-bit S-box, thus the best differential probability of the S-box is $2^{-2}$. Then we can easily derive the bound of rounds for the differential or linear attack, which is 11 rounds for Type-II and No.2 for $k = 8$, 17 rounds for Type-II, $k = 16$, and 16 rounds for No.1, $k = 16$. Before the comparison, we need to point out that evaluation using active S-boxes is rather loose. From designer's point of view, it may provide enough security margin, however, on the other hand, the efficiency of the design may suffer due to this kind of evaluation. In the case of Present's S-Box, among 15 input difference, 12 input differences will have only one output difference with the maximum probability $2^{-2}$. So the probability for the single path may be several rounds smaller than the approximated one. The exact value should be derived by using branch and bound algorithm, which was first applied to derive the linear and differential path for DES in [10]. Notice that if we take the clustering effect of the differential or linear paths into consideration, the maximum probability of the single path may grow, but for block size greater than 32-bit and large number of rounds, it is difficult to compute the complete cluster, which is remained as a future work. On the other hand, what we have derived here is the much more accurate data complexity. The direct comparison may not be fair, but still we notice that for $k = 8$, our methods have almost the same effect regarding Type-II permutation. For $k = 64$, surprisingly, we discover that our result is even better in case of Type-II compared with the loosely evaluated version. For most of the optimized shuffling, our proposed methods can not achieve a better result than the integral attack.

Notice from Table 1 and 2 that the data complexity is rather low. It seems that there is a space to go for more rounds. But the case is that other sub blocks will have a rather high number of permutations, and the xor of the two will immediately go out of the legal range. However, we can apply the similar techniques as multilinear or multidifferential attack to consider all the accumulated permutations in all the sub blocks instead of one. This will further reduce the data complexity that is required to distinguish between the distributions, and thus the number of rounds may be further improved.

## 5 Conclusion

In this paper, we investigate and extend a new cryptanalysis method called statistical integral attack. This attack traces the bias of the internal collision of the integral set, and try to construct a distinguisher for many rounds. It is a statistical attack in essence which is similar to differential and linear attack, while we take advantage of the internal collision as the evaluated statistics. This result provides us a new way to evaluate block ciphers with S-box design such as general Feistel structure in a statistical approach other than the traditional differential and linear cryptanalysis. Depending on the cipher's concrete structure, this approach could give a better distinguisher than differential or linear attack as shown in the paper. Also, searching the probabilistic integral path is a rather simple job compared with the differential or linear path. Thus this method provides us with a quick and straightforward approach to evaluate the security margin of the underlined ciphers. Since the output of the distinguisher is restricted to only one sub block, it should be cheap for the key recovery phase. On the other hand, we can also take advantage of other accumulated permutations of the output to reduce the data complexity. In that way, the cost for the key recovery phase may increase, and how to balance the two to get the best data and time complexity is left as a future work.

## References

1. Selçuk, A.A., Biçak, A.: On probability of success in linear and differential cryptanalysis. In: Cimato, S., Galdi, C., Persiano, G. (eds.) SCN 2002. LNCS, vol. 2576, pp. 174–185. Springer, Heidelberg (2003)

2. Bellare, M., Impagliazzo, R.: A tool for obtaining tighter security analyses of pseudorandom function based constructions, with applications to PRP PRF conversion. In: Proceedings of 40th Annual Symposium on Foundations of Computer Science. Citeseer (1999)

3. Biryukov, A., Shamir, A.: Structural cryptanalysis of SASAS. In: Pfitzmann, B. (ed.) EUROCRYPT 2001. LNCS, vol. 2045, pp. 395–405. Springer, Heidelberg (2001)

4. Bogdanov, A.A., Knudsen, L.R., Leander, G., Paar, C., Poschmann, A., Robshaw, M., Seurin, Y., Vikkelsoe, C.: PRESENT: an ultra-lightweight block cipher. In: Paillier, P., Verbauwhede, I. (eds.) CHES 2007. LNCS, vol. 4727, pp. 450–466. Springer, Heidelberg (2007)

5. Collard, B., Standaert, F.-X.: A statistical saturation attack against the block cipher PRESENT. In: Fischlin, M. (ed.) CT-RSA 2009. LNCS, vol. 5473, pp. 195–210. Springer, Heidelberg (2009)

6. Daemen, J., Knudsen, L.R., Rijmen, V.: The block cipher SQUARE. In: Biham, E. (ed.) FSE 1997. LNCS, vol. 1267, pp. 149–165. Springer, Heidelberg (1997)

7. Knudsen, L.R., Wagner, D.: Integral cryptanalysis. In: Daemen, J., Rijmen, V. (eds.) FSE 2002. LNCS, vol. 2365, pp. 112–127. Springer, Heidelberg (2002)

8. Lucks, S.: The sum of PRPs is a secure PRF. In: Preneel, B. (ed.) EUROCRYPT 2000. LNCS, vol. 1807, pp. 470–484. Springer, Heidelberg (2000)

9. Lucks, S., et al.: Attacking seven rounds of rijndael under 192-bit and 256-bit keys. In: AES Candidate Conference, vol. 2000 (2000)

10. Matsui, M.: On correlation between the order of S-boxes and the strength of DES. In: De Santis, A. (ed.) EUROCRYPT 1994. LNCS, vol. 950, pp. 366–375. Springer, Heidelberg (1995)

11. Nyberg, K.: Generalized feistel networks. In: Kim, K., Matsumoto, T. (eds.) Advances in Cryptology — ASIACRYPT 1996. LNCS, vol. 1163, pp. 91–104. Springer, Berlin Heidelberg (1996)

12. Patarin, J.: A proof of security in $\mathcal{O}(2^n)$ for the xor of two random permutations. In: Safavi-Naini, R. (ed.) ICITS 2008. LNCS, vol. 5155, pp. 232–248. Springer, Heidelberg (2008)

13. Patarin, J.: Generic attacks for the xor of $k$ random permutations. In: Jacobson, M., Locasto, M., Mohassel, P., Safavi-Naini, R. (eds.) ACNS 2013. LNCS, vol. 7954, pp. 154–169. Springer, Heidelberg (2013)

14. Sasaki, Y., Wang, L.: Meet-in-the-middle technique for integral attacks against feistel ciphers. In: Knudsen, L.R., Wu, H. (eds.) SAC 2012. LNCS, vol. 7707, pp. 234–251. Springer, Heidelberg (2013)

15. Shirai, T., Shibutani, K., Akishita, T., Moriai, S., Iwata, T.: The 128-bit block-cipher CLEFIA (extended abstract). In: Biryukov, A. (ed.) FSE 2007. LNCS, vol. 4593, pp. 181–195. Springer, Heidelberg (2007)

16. Suzaki, T., Minematsu, K.: Improving the generalized feistel. In: Hong, S., Iwata, T. (eds.) FSE 2010. LNCS, vol. 6147, pp. 19–39. Springer, Heidelberg (2010)

17. Suzaki, T., Minematsu, K., Morioka, S., Kobayashi, E.: TWINE: a lightweight block cipher for multiple platforms. In: Knudsen, L.R., Wu, H. (eds.) SAC 2012. LNCS, vol. 7707, pp. 339–354. Springer, Heidelberg (2013)

18. Wu, W., Zhang, L.: LBlock: a lightweight block cipher. In: Lopez, J., Tsudik, G. (eds.) ACNS 2011. LNCS, vol. 6715, pp. 327–344. Springer, Heidelberg (2011)

19. Zheng, Y., Matsumoto, T., Imai, H.: On the construction of block ciphers provably secure and not relying on any unproved hypotheses. In: Brassard, G. (ed.) CRYPTO 1989. LNCS, vol. 435, pp. 461–480. Springer, Heidelberg (1990)

# Short Papers: Cryptographic Mechanisms

# Foundations of Optical Encryption:
# A Candidate Short-Key Scheme

Giovanni Di Crescenzo[1]([✉]), Ronald Menendez[2], and Shahab Etemad[2]

[1] Applied Communication Sciences, Basking Ridge, NJ, USA
gdicrescenzo@appcomsci.com
[2] Work Done While at Applied Communication Sciences, Basking Ridge, NJ, USA

**Abstract.** We propose an encryption scheme with the following properties:

1. it has an *"all-optical"* implementation, thus preserving ultra-high communication speed of recently deployed optical networks;
2. sender and receiver only share a *short* key; that is, a key of length constant with respect to the message length.

## 1 Introduction

Encryption is a fundamental building block in securing communication and several real-life applications. The one-time pad encryption scheme [13] is provably secure but requires sender and received to share a key at least as long as the encrypted data to be encrypted [11]. Thus, currently used encryption techniques are based on block ciphers which only require sender and receiver to share a short key, and yet are believed to be secure as they have resisted significant attack efforts from researchers. Such techniques are readily overlaid over essentially any type of communication networks.

Motivated by the ultra-high performance in data transfer over certain types of existing optical networks, researchers have recently studied the problem of specializing encryption within such networks (see, e.g., [5,9,10,15] and follow-up research). Because overlaying the mentioned encryption techniques over such optical networks would reduce the performance to that of the encryption technique used, researchers are looking into designing "all-optical" encryption techniques; that is, encryption techniques that can be directly implemented in such optical networks. With this approach, the goal is to transfer encrypted data with ultra-high performance, currently scalable to 100Gb/s, and typically up to one order of magnitude faster than conventional, non-optical, techniques. Known results in this direction include a scheme from [3], which presents an all-optical random shift of the plaintext, and an all-optical xor gate, capable of realizing the one-time pad encryption scheme, as surveyed in [15]. Both schemes are or can be rigorously analyzed in a cryptographic model and provably satisfy perfect secrecy of the encrypted data, assuming sender and receiver share more randomness than the data to be encrypted. A natural open problem has then become constructing an all-optical encryption scheme where the key shared by sender

© Springer International Publishing Switzerland 2015
M. Qiu et al. (Eds.): NSS 2015, LNCS 9408, pp. 359–367, 2015.
DOI: 10.1007/978-3-319-25645-0_24

and receiver is fixed (i.e., not dependent on the data rate); that is, the optical analogue of non-optical encryption schemes based on block ciphers.

In this paper we propose a candidate solution for this problem using an optical code division multiple access (OCDMA) overlay over a wavelength division multiplexed (WDM) optical network. Our proposed encryption scheme satisfies a rigorously formulated notion of decryption correctness, has an 'all-optical" implementation on such networks (a previous attempt of ours [2] seemed to require novel optical component implementations), and only requires short keys to be shared between sender and receiver. Under certain (seemingly reasonable) assumptions about this optical network, we also provide some intuition as to why our scheme might satisfy some form of provable security guarantees (although consistently with the state of the art of short-key non-optical encryption, we do not know if our scheme actually satisfies any form of provable security.) Specifically, we assume that the so-called intercode phase shifts, intrinsic in optical fibers within such networks, exhibit a sufficiently random behavior, which can be frequently updated, an assumption that seems to be reasonably true if the update rates are relatively low. Our scheme requires the sender to use a large amount of (unshared) randomness, proportional to a small constant times the data rate.

## 2 Encryption: Formal Notions and Definitions

We define an *optical encryption scheme* as a triple (Schedule,OpEncrypt, OpDecrypt) with the following syntax and properties. On input a (plaintext) data block from the data stream $M(t)$, a key $k$, and a random block from the random stream $R(t)$, the *optical scheduling function* Schedule returns $n$ pseudo-data bits, each corresponding to a *pseudo-data stream* $D_j(t)$, for $j = 1\ldots, n$. On input $n$ pseudo-data bits $\delta_1, \ldots, \delta_n$, a key $k$, and a random block from the random stream $R(t)$, the *optical encrypting function* OpEncrypt returns a ciphertext block from the *ciphertext signal* $\sigma(t)$. On input a ciphertext block from the optical ciphertext signal $\sigma(t)$, an index $j \in \{1, \ldots, n\}$, and key $k$, the *optical decrypting function* OpDecrypt returns a data block $\rho$ from the data stream $M'(t)$, or a special decoding failure symbol $\perp$. We say that the optical scheme (Schedule,OpEncrypt,OpDecrypt) satisfies *decryption correctness* if with probability 1 the stream $M'(t)$ decrypted by the receiver is equal to the plaintext stream $M(t)$.

We say that the scheme (Schedule,OpEncrypt,OpDecrypt) satisfies *blockwise decryption correctness* if for any $j = 1, \ldots, n$, it holds that with probability 1 the data bit $\rho$ from stream $M'(t)$ decrypted by the receiver using the $e$-bit key $k$, is equal to the $j$-th bit in the $(t, n, \ell)$-data block $m$ from data stream $M(t)$, where, following [3,7,9], $\rho$ is obtained, mathematically speaking, as follows:

1. $(\delta_1, \ldots, \delta_n) = \text{Schedule}(n, w, r, t, \ell, k, m)$
2. $((\chi_{i1}, \ldots, \chi_{in})_{i=1}^n) = \text{OpEncrypt}(n, w, r, e, \ell, t, k, \{\delta_i\}_{i=1}^n)$
3. for $i = 1, \ldots, w$, $f_i = c/\lambda_i$
4. $\sigma = \sum_{j=1}^n \sum_{i=1}^w \cos(f_i \cdot t + \chi_{ij} + \phi_j)$
5. $\rho = \text{OpDecrypt}(n, w, e, \ell, t, j, k, \sigma)$.

Here, $\lambda_i$ is the *i-th wavelength* used, $f_i$ is the *i*-th wavelength's *frequency*, $c$ is the *speed of light*, $\chi_{i1}, \ldots, \chi_{in} \in [0, \pi]^w$ are the $n$ codewords used, $\phi_1, \ldots, \phi_n \in [0, 2\pi]$ are the *intercode phase shifts* associated to these codewords that are due to laser frequency and temperature fluctuations resulting from the aggregation process of the $n$ data streams into a single optical fiber, and we assume that $n \leq w$. The above steps can be described in more detail as follows: step 1 consists of the optical scheduling function associating a data block from a plaintext stream and a key block from a key stream to $n$ pseudo-data blocks being part of "pseudo-data streams"; steps 2-4 consist of the aggregation of the $n$ pseudo-data streams into a single encrypted signal $\sigma(t)$; and step 5 consists of the receiver's decrypting the $j$-th data stream from $\sigma(t)$. The reader interested in details on the optical transforms underlying such steps is referred, for instance, to [5–7,9,15].

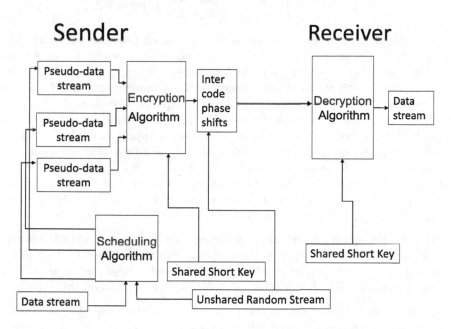

**Fig. 1.** Model for streaming, encrypted, optical communication.

# 3 A Candidate for All-Optical Encryption with Short Keys

Our scheme is obtained as an improved variant of some schemes studied in the optical network literature (see, e.g., [2,5]), for which no security evidence or all-optical implementation was provided, and using a number of all-optical techniques: a 'random phase shifting' technique, an 'unshared randomness usage' technique, a non-trivial 'scheduling' of unshared random bits and 0's as pseudo-data bits, and periodic random updates of the intercode phase shifts. In particular, scheduling of unshared random bits and 0's as pseudo-data bits in our scheme (and absent in all previous ones) is critical to obtain some security evidence for our scheme, which we now describe.

**Communication Over Optical Networks.** Similarly as in many previous proposals (see, e.g., [2,3]), this scheme achieves reliable optical communication by choosing orthogonal codewords to allow encoding and reliable decoding of multiple data streams of elements in $\{0,1\}$. One popular choice for an orthogonal encoding matrix is the Hadamard matrix, defined for all positive integers $u \geq 1$, with the following recursion:

$$H_2 = \begin{pmatrix} 1 & 1 \\ 1 & -1 \end{pmatrix} \quad H_{2u} = \begin{pmatrix} H_u & H_u \\ H_u & -H_u \end{pmatrix}, \text{for } u \geq 1.$$

Rows of this matrix have been used in the mentioned previous works as codewords in the following way: if the $j$-th row is used as a codeword to transmit one data bit, wavelength $i$ is being sent with phase $(1 - h_{ij})\pi/2$, where $h_{ij}$ denotes the entry in the $j$-th row and $i$-th column of the symmetric matrix $H_w$, where $w = 2n$. Then this scheme uses the $j$-th row (resp., $(n + j)$-th row) of $H_{2n}$ as a codeword to transmit/receive the next bit from the $j$-th pseudo-data stream if this bit is $= 0$ (resp., is $= 1$). As using the same approach would not suffice to achieve our secrecy goals, we modify it slightly so to preserve orthogonality, as follows: we use the symmetric matrix $H_w$, where $w = n$ (instead of $w = 2n$), and we use as codewords a different selection of the rows of $H_n$: the $j$-th row (resp., $(j + n/2 \bmod n)$-th row) of $H_n$ as a codeword to transmit/receive the next bit from the $j$-th pseudo-data stream if this bit is $= 0$ (resp., is $= 1$).

**A formal Description of Our Scheme.** To define our optical encryption scheme, we formally specify three optical functions Schedule, OpEncode, OpDecode. In the process, we mention an example all-optical realization of each of these functions. (See, for instance, [5–7,9], for more details on this aspect).

*Function* Schedule. This function takes as input parameter values for the number of pseudo-data streams $n$, the number of wavelengths $w$, and the time interval length $\ell$, such that $n = 4q$, for some integer $q \geq 1$, $w = n$, and $\ell = 2$, the current time $t$, the $e$-bit shared key $k$, the next unused $n/4$-length plaintext data block $m = m_0|\cdots|m_{n/4-1}$, and the next unused $3n/2$-length random stream block $r = r_0|\cdots|r_{3n/2-1}$. Given these inputs, this function schedules $m$ into the lower-indexed $n/4$ pseudo-data streams if $t$ is odd or in the pseudo-data streams indexed as $n/4,\ldots,n/2-1$ if $t$ is even and fills each of the remaining pseudo-data streams either with 0's (this helps towards the desired decryption correctness) or with a random bit from the random stream block $r$ (this helps towards achieving some evidence of secrecy). Furthermore, it randomly shifts the intercode phase shifts by 0 or $\pi$ modulo $2\pi$. More precisely, when $t$ is odd, the function sets:

1. $\delta_j(t) = m_j$, for $j = 0,\ldots,n/4-1$;
2. $\delta_j(t) = r_{j-n/4}$, for $j = n/4,\ldots,n/2-1$;

3. $\delta_j(t) = 0$, for $j = n/2, \ldots, n/2 + n/4 - 1$;
4. $\delta_j(t) = r_{j-n/2}$, for $j = n/2 + n/4, \ldots, n - 1$;
5. $\phi_j(t) = \phi_j(t-2) +_{2\pi} r_{n/2+j} \cdot \pi$, for $j = 0, \ldots, n - 1$,

where $+_{2\pi}$ denotes sum modulo $2\pi$. Here note that when t is even, steps 1 to 4 are executed with the only difference that all indices j of quantities $\delta_j(t)$ are shifted by $n/4$ (modulo $n$), and step 5 is executed by setting $\phi_j(t) = \phi_j(t-1)$, for $j = 0, \ldots, n - 1$. More specifically, when $t$ is even, the function sets:

1. $\delta_j(t) = r_j$, for $j = 0, \ldots, n/4 - 1$;
2. $\delta_j(t) = m_{j-n/4}$, for $j = n/4, \ldots, n/2 - 1$;
3. $\delta_j(t) = r_{j-n/4}$, for $j = n/2, \ldots, n/2 + n/4 - 1$;
4. $\delta_j(t) = 0$, for $j = n/2 + n/4, \ldots, n - 1$;
5. $\phi_j(t) = \phi_j(t-1)$, for $j = 0, \ldots, n - 1$.

We note that while this function has an all-optical realization, the non-optical equivalent realization, using an inverse multiplexer, is just as fast (and, in fact, more practical).

*Function* OpEncrypt. This function, implementable using an array of (optical) phase modulators, takes as input values for parameters $n, w, e$ and the time interval length $\ell$, such that $n \geq 1$, $w = n = e$ and $\ell = 2$, the current time $t$, an the e-bit shared key $k = k_1 | \cdots | k_e$, and pseudo-data bits $\delta_1(t), \ldots, \delta_n(t)$. Given these inputs, this function returns, for $i = 1, \ldots, w$ and $j = 1, \ldots, n$, the value $\chi_{ij}(t) = k_i' +_{2\pi} \delta_{ij}'(t)$. Here, the symbol $+_{2\pi}$ denotes sum modulo $2\pi$, the quantity $k_i'$ is computed as $= \pi \cdot k_i \in \{0, \pi\}$ for $i = 1, \ldots, n$, and the quantity $\delta_{ij}'(t)$ is computed as $(1 - h_{iq})\pi/2$, where $h_{iq}$ is the entry of the Hadamard matrix $H_n$ in the $q$-th row and $i$-th column, $q$ being set as follows: $q = j$ if $\delta_j(t) = 0$ or $q = j + n/2 \bmod n$ if $\delta_j(t) = 1$.

*Function* OpDecrypt. This function takes as input values for parameters $n, w, e$ such that $n \geq 1$, $e = w = n$, the current time $t$, assumed to be odd (the other case being similar), an index $j' \in \{1, \ldots, n\}$, an e-bit shared key $k$ and the signal $\sigma = \sum_{j=1}^{n} \sum_{i=1}^{w} \cos(f_i \cdot t + \chi_{ij}(t) + \phi_j(t))$. Given these inputs, this function returns bit $\rho$, computed as follows. First, this function computes $(\sigma_1(t), \ldots, \sigma_w(t))$, where, for $i = 1, \ldots, w$, it holds that $\sigma_i = \sum_{j=1}^{n} \cos(\chi_{ij}(t) + \phi_j(t))$. Then, the contribution from the key block is removed by computing, for $i = 1, \ldots, w$, the quantities $\sigma_i(t) \cdot \cos(k_i') = \sum_{j=1}^{n} \cos(\delta_{ij}'(t) + \phi_j(t))$. Finally, the next bit sent on the $j'$-th pseudo-data stream, for $j' = 1, \ldots, n/4 - 1$, will be $=0$ (resp., $=1$) if the quantity $\sum_{i=1}^{w} h_{ij'} \cdot (\sigma_i(t) \cdot \cos(k_i'))$, is different from 0 (resp, equal to 0). In practice, where it is more appropriate to assume non-continuous measurements, the latter test can be replaced by a natural approximate version which merely tests if this quantity is significantly different or significantly close to 0, for appropriate distance parameters. Measurement questions are very well studied in the optical network literature and dealt with using conventional digital thresholding techniques. The steps in this function can be implemented using an optical demultiplexer, an optical homodyne, an optical modulator, and an array of optical phase shifters.

**Properties of the Scheme.** The "all-optical" implementability of our scheme was already discussed in the above description. The scalability to ultra-high speed can be argued similarly as for the scheme in [3]. The blockwise decryption correctness of our scheme follows by observing the following: (1) the decoding correctness of an optical communication scheme that uses the Hadamard matrix $H_n$ as an encoding/decoding matrix; (2) the orthogonality of matrix $K \cdot H_n$ is preserved, when $K$ is a diagonal matrix; (3) orthogonal encoding/decoding implies that a value computed by function OpDecrypt is 1 or 0 if $\delta_{ij'}(t)$ is 0 or nonzero, respectively, regardless of the value of the intercode phase shifts $\phi_j(t)$. More formally, we now show that the scheme satisfies blockwise decryption correctness. We detail the proof in the case $t$ is odd, and then mention the minor changes needed to extend this proof to the case when $t$ is even. First of all, we note that on input $n, w, e, t, k, m$, our function Schedule sets $\delta_j(t)$ equal to the $j$-th bit of the $n/4$-bit data block $m$, for $j = 0, \ldots, n/4 - 1$.

Then, we note that on input $n, w, e, t, k, \delta_1(t), \ldots, \delta_n(t)$, our function OpEncrypt returns the tuple $((\chi_{i1}(t), \ldots, \chi_{in}(t))_{i=1,\ldots,n})$ such that $\chi_{ij}(t) = k_i' +_{2\pi} \delta_{ij}'(t)$, where the two quantities $k_i', \delta_{ij}'$ are computed as follows. First, $k_i' = \pi \cdot k_i \in \{0, \pi\}$, where $k_i \in \{0, 1\}$ for $i = 0, \ldots, n - 1$. Second, $\delta_{ij}' = (1 - h_{i,j+(n/2)\cdot\delta_j(t)})\pi/2$, where $h_{i,j+(n/2)\cdot\delta_j(t)}$ is the entry of the Hadamard matrix $H_n$ in the $(j + (n/2) \cdot \delta_j(t))$-th row and $i$-th column. Thus, we can write $\chi_{ij} = (\pi \cdot k_i) + (1 - h_{i,j+(n/2)\cdot\delta_j(t)})\pi/2$.

At this point, values $f_i$ and $\sigma$ are computed as in the decryption correctness experiment in Section 2, and the bit $\rho$ is computed by our function OpDecrypt as follows. On input $n, w, e, t, j', k, \sigma$, the value $\sigma_i = \sum_{j=1}^n \cos(\chi_{ij}(t) + \phi_j(t))$ is computed for $i = 1, \ldots, w$. Note that for $i = 0, \ldots, n/4 - 1$, the value $\sigma_i(t)$ can be written as

$$\sigma_i(t) = \sum_{j=1}^n \cos((\pi \cdot k_i) + (1 - h_{i,j+(n/2)\cdot\delta_j(t)})\pi/2 + \phi_j(t))$$

$$= \cos(\pi \cdot k_i) \cdot \sum_{j=1}^n \cos(1 - h_{i,j+(n/2)\cdot\delta_j(t)})\pi/2 + \phi_j(t))$$

Then, note that our function OpDecrypt computes $\sigma_i \cdot \cos(k_i')$, which can be written as

$$\sum_{j=1}^n \cos((1 - h_{i,j+(n/2)\cdot\delta_j(t)})\pi/2 + \phi_j(t)) = h_{i,j+(n/2)\cdot\delta_j(t)} \cdot \sum_{j=1}^n \cos(\phi_j(t))$$

as for these values of $i$, it holds that $\cos^2(k_i') = 1$. Finally, OpDecrypt computes $\sum_{i=1}^w h_{i,j'} \cdot (\sigma_i(t) \cdot \cos(k_i'))$, which is then equal to

$$\sum_{i=1}^w h_{i,j'} \cdot h_{i,j+(n/2)\cdot\delta_j(t)} \cdot (\sigma_i(t) \cdot \cos(k_i')) = (\sum_{j=1}^n \cos(\phi_j(t))) \cdot (\sum_{i=1}^w h_{i,j'} \cdot h_{i,j+(n/2)\cdot\delta_j(t)}) \cdot$$

By orthogonality of matrix $H_n$, the latter expression is then $= n \cdot \sum_{j=1}^{n} \cos(\phi_j) > 0$ when $\delta_j(t) = 0$ and thus $j' = j$ (and the function returns $\rho = \delta_j = 0$), or equal to 0 when $\delta_j(t) = 1$ and thus $j' = j + n/2$ (and the function returns $\rho - \delta_j = 1$).

The proof is extended to the case when $t$ is even by substituting the data block interval $j = 0, \ldots, n/4-1$ with $j = n/2, \ldots, n/2+n/4-1$, and by replacing all additions $j + n/2$ with $j + n/2 \bmod n$. We obtain the following

**Theorem 1.** The described triple (Schedule, OpEncrypt, OpDecrypt) is an optical encryption scheme with the following two properties:

1. sender and receiver only need to share random keys of length constant with respect to the message length; and
2. it satisfies blockwise decryption correctness.

## 4   Security Considerations

We now provide some considerations in favor of some plausible security of our proposed short-key scheme. Denote as $\rho_1, \ldots, \rho_n$ (resp., $\rho_{n+1}, \ldots, \rho_{2n}$) the per-wavelength decompositions of the ciphertext block at time $t$ (resp., time $t + 1$), and consider the distribution of $\rho_1, \ldots, \rho_{2n}$ over the following random processes: the random choice of the $e$-bit key $k$, the arbitrary distribution $D$ used to generate $(t, n/4, \ell)$-data block $m_1$ (resp., $m_2$) as plaintext, and the randomness used by algorithm OpEncrypt on input $k$ and $m_1$ (resp., $k$ and $m_2$).

Consider first the case of odd time $t$. After performing optical beat detection, the adversary obtains a vector $(\rho_1, \ldots, \rho_w)$, where, for $i = 1, \ldots, w$, each $\rho_i$ is defined as $\sum_{j=1}^{n} \cos(\chi_{i,j} + \phi_j)$ and can be rewritten as:

$$\rho_i = \sum_{j=1}^{n} \cos(\chi_{ij} + \phi_j) = \sum_{j=1}^{n} \cos(k_i' + \delta_{ij}' + \phi_j),$$

the latter equality being obtained by expanding $\chi_{ij}$. When $i = 0, \ldots, n-1$, using $k_i' = \pi \cdot k_i$ with $k_i \in \{0,1\}$, and the derivation of $\delta_{ij}'$ from the Hadamard matrix $H_n$, we further have

$$\rho_i = (\cos(k_i')) \cdot \sum_{j=1}^{n} \cos(\delta_{ij}' + \phi_j) = (\cos(k_i')) \cdot \sum_{j=1}^{n} h_{iq} \cdot \cos(\phi_j),$$

where $h_{iq}$ is the entry of the Hadamard matrix $H_n$ in the $q$-th row and $i$-th column, $q$ being set as follows: $q = j$ if $\delta_j = 0$ or $q = j + n/2 \bmod n$ if $\delta_j = 1$.

We note that in this expression the vector $h_{iq}$ is the only vector dependent on the actual data bits and has components equal to $-1, +1$ according to the value of the data bit. Moreover, this vector is essentially componentwise multiplied with the cosine of the intercode phase shifts vector, also with components having signs in $\{-1, +1\}$, at each $i = 1, \ldots, w$.

A first important observation here is that the inter-code phase shifts are assumed to be random, and thus the signs of the cosine function of the inter-code phase shifts is random too. Then the above equality implies a group operation (in $\{-1, +1\}^n$) between the vector of signs of the inter-code phase shifts and the vector of the cosines of the Hadamard matrix elements due to actual data bits, thus resulting in a perfect randomization of the data bits, in correspondence of the values $j = 0, \ldots, n/4-1$. In other words, there is a 'one-time pad' encryption effect between the data bits and the random signs associated with the cosines of the intercode phase shifts used to encrypt such data bits at time $t$. Because the random bits used to achieve this effect are the sender's unshared random bits, this would seem to hide the plaintext bits up to time $t$.

A second important observation here is that the signs of the cosines of the inter-code phase shifts that are not used to encrypt actual data bits at a given time $t$ but are used for this purpose at the time $t+1$ still remain random at time $t+1$ after being used at time $t$ to encrypt random bits. This follows precisely from the randomness of such bits on the pseudo-data streams, which implies a similar group operation between the vector of signs of the cosines of the inter-code phase shifts and the vector of random pseudo-data bits. In other words, there is a 'one-time pad' encryption effect between the random bits from the random streams and the random signs associated with the cosines of the intercode phase shifts that are unused at time $t$ to encrypt actual data. Thus, the latter random signs can be used to encrypt the next data bits at time $t+1$.

Furthermore, we note that at time $t+1$ the plaintext data is only in the values $\delta_j$, for $j = n/4, \ldots, n/2-1$, and that the corresponding sender's random values $r_{n/2+j}$, although used at time $t$, are independent from $\rho_1(t), \ldots, \rho_n(t)$, as a consequence of fact (2) above. This, together with the previous discussions, might seem to suggest that some form of secrecy might hold on both times $t$ and $t+1$, and then for all $t$.

**Acknowledgments.** This publication is dedicated to the memory of Ronald Menendez, who was a great pleasure and fun to work with, and is very much missed.
Part of this work was supported by DARPA SPAWAR contract N66001-07-2010. Any opinions, findings and conclusions or recommendations expressed in this material are those of the author(s) and do not necessarily reflect the views of DARPA.

# References

1. Bellovin, S., Blaze, M.: Cryptographic modes of operation for the internet. In: 2nd NIST Workshop on Modes of Operation (2001)
2. Di Crescenzo, G., Menendez, R., Etemad, S.: OCDM-based photonic encryption with provable security guarantees. In: Proc. of OFC/NFOEC (2008)
3. Di Crescenzo, G., Menendez, R., Etemad, S., Jackel, J.: Foundations of optical encryption: formal modeling and achieving shannon secrecy. In: Calude, C.S., Costa, J.F., Dershowitz, N., Freire, E., Rozenberg, G. (eds.) UC 2009. LNCS, vol. 5715, pp. 125–142. Springer, Heidelberg (2009)
4. Etemad, S., Agarwal, A., Banwell, T., Di Crescenzo, G., Jackel, J., Menendez, R., Toliver, P.: An Overlay Photonic Layer Security Approach Scalable to 100 Gb/s. IEEE Communications Magazine **46**(8), 32–39 (2008)

5. Etemad, S., Agarwal, A., Banwell, T., Jackel, J., Menendez, R., Toliver, P.: OCDM-Based Photonic Layer "Security" Scalable to 100 Gb/s for Existing WDM Networks. Journal of Optical Networking **6**(7), 948–976 (2007)
6. Goldberg, S., Menendez, R., Prucnal, P.: Towards a cryptanalysis of spectral-phase encoded OCDMA with phase-scrambling. In: Proc. of OFC/NFOEC (2007)
7. Goldberg, S.: Towards a Cryptanalysis of Spectral-Phase Encoded OCDMA with Phase-Scrambling. TR-771-06, Princeton University, November 2006
8. Prucnal, P.: Optical Code Division Multiple Access: Fundamentals and Applications. CRC Press (2005)
9. Shake, T.: Security performance of optical CDMA against eavesdropping. IEEE J. of Lightwave Technology **23**(2), 655–670 (2005)
10. Shake, T.: Confidentiality performance of spectral-phase-encoded optical CDMA. IEEE J. of Lightwave Technology **23**(4), 1652–1666 (2005)
11. Shannon, C.: Communication Theory of Secrecy Systems. Bell System Technical Journal **28**(4), 656–715 (1949)
12. Toliver, T., Agarwal, A., Banwell, T., Menendez, R., Jackel, J., Etemad, S.: Demonstration of high spectral efficiency coherent OCDM using DQPSK, FEC, and integrated ring resonator-based spectral phase encoder/decoders. In: Proc. of OFC/NFOEC (2007)
13. Vernam, G.: Secret Signaling Systems. United States Patent, July 1919
14. Wang, Z., Huang, Y., Deng, Y., Chang, J, Prucnal, P.: Optical Encryption with OCDMA Code Swapping Using All-Optical XOR Logic Gate. IEEE Photonics Technology Letters **21**(7) (2009)
15. Wu, B., Shastri, B., Prucnal, P.: Secure communications in fiber-optic networks. In: Akhgar, B., Arabnia, H.R. (eds.) Emerging Trends in ICT Security. Morgan Kaufman (2014)

# From Pretty Good to Great: Enhancing PGP Using Bitcoin and the Blockchain

Duane Wilson[1]([✉]) and Giuseppe Ateniese[2]

[1] Department of Computer Science, Johns Hopkins University, Baltimore, USA
mr.duanewilson@gmail.com
[2] Department of Computer Science, Sapienza University of Rome, Rome, Italy

**Abstract.** PGP is built upon a Distributed Web of Trust in which a user's trustworthiness is established by others who can vouch through a digital signature for that user's identity. Preventing its wholesale adoption are a number of inherent weaknesses to include (but not limited to) the following: **1)** Trust Relationships are built on a subjective honor system, **2)** Only first degree relationships can be fully trusted, **3)** Levels of trust are difficult to quantify with actual values, and **4)** Issues with the Web of Trust itself (Certification and Endorsement). Although the security that PGP provides is proven to be reliable, it has largely failed to garner large scale adoption. In this paper, we propose several novel contributions to address the aforementioned issues with PGP and associated Web of Trust. To address the subjectivity of the Web of Trust, we provide a new certificate format based on Bitcoin which allows a user to verify a PGP certificate using Bitcoin identity-verification transactions - forming first degree trust relationships that are tied to actual values (i.e., number of Bitcoins transferred during transaction). Secondly, we present the design of a novel Distributed PGP key server that leverages the Bitcoin transaction blockchain to store and retrieve our certificates.

## 1 Introduction

In a recent article, Yahoo announced its intentions to add an extension that will provide its customers with the ability to digitally sign and encrypt messages using Pretty Good Privacy (PGP). Yahoo plans to use a fork of Google's End to End OpenPGP plugin that is currently in development. Yahoo follows the likes of Google, Facebook and Microsoft, who also recently announced they would encrypt internal traffic in response to the Snowden spying revelations [1]. Traditional methods of securely sharing between two or more parties rely on the use of Public-Key Encryption within a Public Key Infrastructure (PKI). In a traditional PKI scheme, a certificate authority or certification authority (CA) is an entity that issues digital certificates. The digital certificate certifies the ownership of a public key by the named subject of the certificate. This allows others (relying parties) to rely upon signatures or assertions made by the private key that corresponds to the public key that is certified. In this model of trust relationships, a CA is a Trusted Third Party (TTP) that is trusted by both the

© Springer International Publishing Switzerland 2015
M. Qiu et al. (Eds.): NSS 2015, LNCS 9408, pp. 368–375, 2015.
DOI: 10.1007/978-3-319-25645-0_25

subject (owner) of the certificate and the party relying upon the certificate. CAs are characteristic of many PKI schemes [2]. Currently, the most viable alternative for Public Key Crytography based on a CA is PGP. PGP is built upon a Distributed Web of Trust in which a user's trustworthiness is established by others who can vouch for that user's identity. Preventing its wholesale adoption are a number of inherent weaknesses to include (but not limited to) the following: **1)** Trust Relationships are built on a subjective honor system, **2)** Only first degree relationships can be fully trusted, **3)** Levels of trust are difficult to quantify with actual values, and **4)** Issues with the Web of Trust itself: **Certification.** It is currently difficult to get certified if the key is new. In general people complain that it is hard to find endorsers to enhance the trustworthiness of a new key - which will limit its use. **Endorsement.** Competence and willingness of endorsers. There is currently no incentive to endorse a key of someone you know - much less someone you indirectly know through a friend or relative.

Bitcoin is a form of digital currency, created and held electronically [3]. According to "Crypto Coin News", the number of active Bitcoin users worldwide will reach 4.7 million by the end of 2019, marking a significant gain over the 1.3 million last year, according to a report from Juniper Research [4]. As a result of its popularity, we introduce a new Bitcoin-Based PGP certificate format, certificate validation methodology, and certificate endorsement model that overcomes the issues we have highlighted above. Issues 1 and 2 with the Web of Trust can be easily solved using our new Bitcoin-Based PGP certificate format and verification system. Issue 4 can be resolved by use of endorsement fee. The amount of the fee can be determined by the user and will vary based on the current value of a Bitcoin - which has been relatively stable of late [5]. In Issue 2, the bitcoin payment ensures that the endorser follows the "authentication" procedure otherwise they risk losing bitcoins - which demonstrates both their competence and willingness to serve as a viable certificate endorser.

There are some interesting properties of our trust establishment protocol that could result in safer use of PGP. Property 1) People have the option of using previous transactions before using a certificate OR directly establishing a trust relationship themselves with a certificate owner (i.e., direct trust). Property 2) As mentioned above, because of the risk of losing bitcoins via the identity-verification process, people will be less likely to leverage our certificates without a direct trust establishment. Property 3) The block chain and associated identity-verification transactions provide transparency into the trustworthiness of others. In addition to these benefits, we also provide the design of a novel PGP Key Server based on the blockchain's ability to store pieces of data since the 0.9.0 release. The 0.9.0 release of Bitcoin Core added a new standard transaction type granting access to a previously disallowed script function, *OP-RETURN* [6]. This function accepts a user-defined sequence of up to 80 bytes. Once realized, this new key server will be completely de-centralized and serve as an appropriate repository for Bitcoin-Based PGP Certificates. Our work specifically provides the following contributions:

- **Bitcoin-Based PGP Certificate:** Contains Bitcoin address for identity verification and certificate revocation.
- **Identity-Verification and Revocation Transactions:** Serves as alternative means of verifying a certificate owner's Public Key contained in a Bitcoin-Based PGP Certificate. Also provides a mechanism for certificate revocation.
- **PGP Trust Levels:** Allows users to specify the amount of Bitcoins they are willing to "risk" in order to verify a particular Bitcoin-Based PGP certificate.
- **Bitcoin-Based PGP Key Server Design:** Demonstrates method of using the Bitcoin Transaction Blockchain for PGP Key Storage and Retrieval

The rest of this paper is organized as follows: Section 2 discusses the work related to this area of research, Section 3 provides an overview of our Bitcoin-Based PGP certificate, Section 4 presents an overview of PGP threats addressed by our contributions, Section 5 discusses the design of our application and new key server, and Section 6 concludes the paper and identifies areas for future work.

## 2   Related Work

According to [7], BitPay has launched a project that leverages bitcoin technology to facilitate a decentralized authentication system. Called BitAuth, the system uses cryptographic signatures in place of server-side password storage. BitAuth is a way to do secure, password-less authentication using the same elliptic-curve cryptography as Bitcoin. Instead of using a shared secret, the client signs each request using a private key and the server checks to make sure the signature is valid and matches the public key. A nonce is used to prevent replay attacks and provide sequence enforcement [8]. Similar to our novel Bitcoin-Based PGP certificate, BitAuth provides "portable" identity in that the same identity can be used with multiple services. BitAuth is a promising new method of authentication, but currently relies heavily on the System Identification Number (SIN). The SIN is a new concept that is similar to a Bitcoin address, however, is not widely adopted. Whereas, our scheme relies on popular Bitcoin primitives - address, transactions, and the block chain - that are widely being used. Additionally, since the focus of BitAuth is on authentication, it cannot be used to protect the confidentiality of information shared between two parties - as is the primary benefit of our Bitcoin-Based PGP Certificate.

Off-the-Record (OTR) Messaging is a protocol designed for private social communications. According to [9,10], the notion of an off-the-record conversation captures the semantics one intuitively wants from private communication - only the two parties involved are privy to the contents of the conversation; after the conversation is over, no one (not even the parties involved) can produce a transcript; and although the participants are assured of each other's identities, neither they nor anyone else can prove this information to a third party. Current versions of the OTR protocol, support mutual authentication of users using a shared secret through the socialist minimalist protocol. This feature makes it possible for users to verify the identity of the remote party and avoid a man-in-the-middle attack without the inconvenience of manually comparing public key fingerprints through an outside channel. OTR's primary weakness lies in the fact that it is primarily applicable in the domain of instant messaging - whereas our Bitcoin-Based PGP certificate can be used in virtually any domain in which secure information sharing is desired. According to the authors of the OTR protocol, "The high latency of email communication makes using our "off-the-record" protocol impractical in the setting of email."

In [11], a secure replacement for CAs is proposed. Rather than employing a traditionally hard-coded list of immutable CAs, Convergence allows one to configure a dynamic set of Notaries which use network perspective to validate user communications. It provides the following guarantees: Trust Agility, Robustness, Backwards Compatibility, Extensibility and Anonymity. This all occurs within a distributed environment in which anyone can serve as a trust notary. Convergence originated from the ideas originally developed by the Perspectives Project at Carnegie Mellon University [12]. Convergence has great promise in the domain of web browser security and other areas where SSL is prominent. However, it suffers from the fact that the number of notaries currently in existence for performing CA functions is limited (due to it being a fairly new effort). As a result, this could lead to potential Denial of Service (DoS) attacks in the event the notaries become overwhelmed with requests. The Bitcoin infrastructure - upon which our certificate primarily relies - has successfully processed nearly 40 million transactions (to date) [13]. This makes it robust against volume-based security attacks such as DoS and DDoS - when applicable.

## 3   Bitcoin-Based PGP Certificates

Our Bitcoin-Based PGP certificate contains all the relevant elements found in a traditional PGP Certificate but also includes a Bitcoin Address for Identity-Verification and one used for Certificate Revocation. A Bitcoin address is an identifier of 27-34 alphanumeric characters, beginning with the number 1 or 3, that represents a possible destination for a Bitcoin payment. A Bitcoin transaction is a signed section of data that is broadcast to the network and collected into blocks. It typically references previous transaction(s) and dedicates a certain number of bitcoins from it to one or more new public key(s) (Bitcoin address) [14]. Because transactions must be verified by miners, Bitcoin users are sometimes forced to wait until they have finished mining. The bitcoin protocol is set so that each block takes roughly 10 minutes to mine. In the case of a purchase, some merchants may make users wait until this block has been confirmed, which will delay the receipt of the digital goods that have been paid for - whereas in other cases (e.g., low value transactions), a merchant will give access to the goods prior to the transaction being verified by the miners [15]. In our case, the delay does not pose a major problem since it will only take place when a trust relationship is being established for the first time - not upon certificate generation.

The value of using Bitcoin in the context of a PGP certificate centers around the fact that because it is built upon a peer-to-peer network, it is able to perform its functions (e.g., money transfers, double-spending prevention) without the aid of a CA - similar to the traditional web of trust. This is advantageous in any context where end-to-end data confidentiality is needed or desired (e.g., email, text message, cloud sharing, or social network communications). Users are more likely to trust an infrastructure that is independent of any CAs, but can still offer the same cryptographic guarantees (i.e., confidentiality and integrity) as an environment that is under their full control or purview.

## 4    PGP Threats and Security Goals

In this section, we expound on the threats we identified in the introduction and describe our security goals. We make the primary assumptions that PGP users are leveraging all of the features of PGP to include the Web of Trust, Levels of Trust, and Validity. Although there are a number of well documented issues with PGP, we primarily focus on threats relating to certificate validation, endorsement, and trust relationship establishment. With our new endorsement process offered via Bitcoin, the threat of assigning invalid levels of trust or valid-ity would be mitigated by the following constructs of our scheme: 1) Certificate Signing MUST precede the incentive fee. A fixed fee of 0.001 BTC is sent to the Bitcoin address provided by the certificate endorser (fee is paid from the certificate owner's bitcoin address - as available - and can change based on the owner's discretion). This fee serves as a small incentive to willing and compe-tent endorsers, 2) Endorsement process is not automated. Our prototype forces users to go through a step by step process in order to sign a certificate stored on our server, and 3) Levels of Trust are established by the certificate endorser, not certificate owner. In our scheme, when performing an identity-verification transaction, any amount of Bitcoins can be sent for verification purposes. These Bitcoins are 'at risk' until the certificate owner returns them. As a result, this serves as a very clear indication of trust between certificate endorser and owner.

A few additional threats to consider with leveraging Bitcoin as an alternative method of certificate verification are those related to rogue certificate owners, wealthy endorsers, and untrustworthy endorsers. In the first case, a certificate owner can generate a PGP key and use it for collecting payments and never return incoming identity-verification transactions to endorsers. To further com-plicate this scenario, a wealthy endorser risks very little by endorsing such users. To address these threats, we still rely on the PGP trust model that allows for out-of-band methods of certificate verification and a web of trust. The inference is that users will not initiate an identity-verification transaction with someone they do not already know and trust from prior interactions. Additionally, in the case of the wealthy endorser, only one verification transaction is considered valid for a particular certificate. Thus, their credibility (over time) will come into ques-tion as they continue to endorse untrustworthy certificates. Lastly, we consider the scenario where endorsers are suspected of being malicious by endorsing 'just for the sake of endorsing'. Since our endorsement scheme does not invalidate - but augments - the endorsement process provided by PGP, over time a malicious endorser would be classified as someone who cannot be trusted - especially if they are endorsing both questionable and legitimate certificates. A legitimate case to consider is someone who is a professional certificate endorser. Someone whose professional responsibility is to endorse new certificates has their job (and reputation) to consider if they are found to be endorsing certificates that are not legitimate - over time.

## 5   Prototype Design

The primary motivations for creating a new certificate server are to 1) Accommodate our new Bitcoin-Based PGP certificates, 2) Enable Identity-Verification and Revocation transactions, and 3) Enable Certificate Signing Endorsements. To facilitate these "features", our certificate server will provide the following functions: Generate, Revoke, Verify, and Sign. Each Bitcoin-Based PGP certificate will contain a set of required parameters prior to generation and items that will be automatically generated by the prototype application. One thing to note is that we do not modify the original PGP certificate format - but leverage the PGP comment field to store Bitcoin addresses. In PGP, users can revoke their certificate if they feel like the certificate has been compromised. PGP also allows a user to designate a certificate revoker. With PGP certificates, the user usually posts the revoked certificate on a certificate server. To enable an easier revocation process for our Bitcoin-Based PGP certificate, we perform a transaction between the 2 addresses within the certificate. With information from the blockchain, one can find out how much value belonged to each address at any point in Bitcoin history [17].

Key revocation is arguably the most important component of any certificate-based identification system. Our implementation deliberately forces the user to make a valid Bitcoin transaction to a legitimate Bitcoin address in his possession. Alternatively, the revocation status could be stored in *OP-RETURN* fields if our decentralized approach is adopted. Our current method, however, has an important technical advantage: It makes verification of a certificate status extremely efficient since revocation transactions will be stored in the Bitcoin Unspent Transaction Outputs (UXTO) database and propagated among all nodes automatically. The UXTO are redeemable transactions and the information on certificate status will be kept in main memory for efficient verification. An identity-verification transaction is the primary mechanism by which a user can verify another user's Public Key in a Bitcoin-Based PGP certificate.

**Blockchain PGP Key Server** Historically, the use of bitcoins blockchain to store data unrelated to bitcoin payments has been a controversial subject. Many developers consider such use abusive and want to discourage it. Others view it as a demonstration of the powerful capabilities of blockchain technology and want to encourage such experimentation. Those who object to the inclusion of non-payment data argue that it causes "blockchain bloat", burdening those running full bitcoin nodes with carrying the cost of disk storage for data that the blockchain was not intended to carry. Moreover, such transactions create UTXO that cannot be spent, using the destination bitcoin address as a free-form 20-byte field. Because the address is used for data, it does not correspond to a private key and the resulting UTXO can never be spent [18]. As a result, these transactions continue to increase the size of the blockchain over time. In version 0.9 of the Bitcoin Core client, a compromise was reached with the introduction of the *OP-RETURN* operator. *OP-RETURN* allows developers to add 40 bytes (now 80 bytes) of nonpayment data to a transaction output. However, unlike the use of "fake" UTXO, the *OP-RETURN* operator creates a (provably) unspendable output, which does not need to be stored in the UTXO set. *OP-RETURN* outputs are recorded on the blockchain, so they consume disk space and contribute to the increase in the blockchains size, but they are not stored in the UTXO set and therefore do not bloat the UTXO memory pool and burden full nodes with the cost of more expensive RAM [18].

**STORAGE:** Depending on the size of PGP key generated, the size could range from 1018 bytes (1024-Bit key) to 3100 bytes (4096-Bit key). PGP supports up to an 8192-Bit key which corresponds to an even larger on-disk or memory capacity for storage purposes. Keeping this in mind, along with the fact that the blockchain only accepts 'data' transactions of up to 80 bytes in size, our storage leverages an innovative certificate fragmentation mechanism to enable both logical storage and efficient retrieval. A message within our PGP Key Server will consist of a 5 Byte Header which will include the PGP Key ID (4 bytes), Fragment ID (4 bits), Total Fragments (4 bits), and the Message Data (75 bytes). **RETRIEVAL:** The Retrieval of a PGP Key from the blockchain is similar to the defragmentation process of an IP datagram. At a high level, the user will request a certificate by either Bitcoin Address or KeyID. Once the transactions associated with the query string is returned, the number of total fragments are computed. If all transactions were retrieved successfully, application will reassemble the Key and return it to user.

## 6    Conclusions and Future Work

In this paper we presented a number of enhancements to PGP and associated Web of Trust - which has suffered from a litany of issues since its inception. Specific issues of certification, endorsement, and ambiguous levels of trust have prevented its wide scale adoption. Future work will consist of examining alternative methods of employing Bitcoin for identity-verification using actual Bitcoin Distributed Contracts or alternative methods that do not require modification of the original PGP certificate format. Keybase.io allows you to get a public key, safely, starting just with someone's social media username(s), but also provides other mechanisms of verifying a particular key (e.g., pgp fingerprint and bitcoin addresses) [19]. A potential area for future work would be to enable verifiers to leverage one or more of the online identifications provided by Keybase.io to strengthen the trust of certificate stored on our server (via their API). Additionally, the integration of Bitcoin-Based PGP Certificates into infrastructures where secure sharing is offered (via text messaging, chat applications, and Secure Cloud Storage servers) would demonstrate their usefulness in actual environments. Lastly, a stronger form of certificate revocation should be explored that builds on the procedure we present. Full version of paper can be found at http://arxiv.org/.

# References

1. Saarinen, J.: Yahoo to Provide PGP Encryption for Mail. ITnews for Australian Business. ITnews, August 08, 2014. Web August 26, 2014
2. Froomkin, A.M.: 1996 A.Michael Froomkin: The Essential Role Of Trusted Third Parties in Electronic Commerce. 1996 A.Michael Froomkin: The Essential Role of Trusted Third Parties in Electronic Commerce. N.p., October 14, 1994. Web February 18, 2014
3. Coindesk. What Is Bitcoin? CoinDesk RSS. Coindesk, March 20, 2015. Web August 13, 2015
4. Maras, E.: Bitcoin Users To Approach 5 Million Mark By 2019, Juniper Research Reports - CCN: Financial Bitcoin/Cryptocurrency News. CCN Financial Bitcoin Cryptocurrency News. CCN.LA, March 17, 2015. Web August 13, 2015
5. Torpey, K.: The Bitcoin Price Has Been Remarkably Stable Lately. The Bitcoin Price Has Been Remarkably Stable Lately. Inside Bitcoins, February 27, 2015. Web August 13, 2015
6. Apodaca, R.: OP-RETURN and the Future of Bitcoin. Bitzuma July 29, 2014. Web April 29, 2015
7. Cawrey, D.: BitPay Seeks to Decentralize Digital Identification with BitAuth. CoinDesk. CoinDesk, July 01, 2014. Web July 06, 2014
8. Bitpay. BitAuth, for Decentralized Authentication. Bitpay, July 01, 2014. Web July 06, 2014
9. Goldberg, I.: Off-the-Record Messaging. OTR Development Team (2012). Web February 25, 2014
10. Goldberg, I., Borisov, N., Brewer, E.: Off-the-Record Communication or, Why Not to use PGP. Zero-Knowlege Systems and U.C. Berkely, (2012). Print
11. Thoughtcrime Labs. Convergence Details. Convergence. Thoughtcrime Labs (2011). Web May 02, 2014
12. Wendlandt, D., Anderson, D.G., Perrig, A.: Perspectives: Improving SSH-style Host Authentication with Multi-Path Probing. Carnegie Mellon University (2011). Print
13. Bitcoin. Bitcoin Charts Various Bitcoin Charts and Currency Statistics. Bitcoin Charts. The Bitcoin Foundation (2009). Web. 02 May 2014
14. Bitcoin.org. Transacations. Bitcoin. Bitcoin.org (2014). Web May 06, 2014
15. CoinDesk. How Do Bitcoin Transactions Work? CoinDesk RSS March 06, 2014. Web July 02, 2014
16. Poor Decision-Making Can Lead to Cybersecurity Breaches Communications of the ACM. (n.d.) Web May 04, 2015. (Retrieved from http://cacm.acm.org/news/183571-poor-decision-making-can-lead-to-cybersecurity-breaches/fulltext)
17. Bitcoin. Block Chain. Bitcoin Wiki. Bitcoin, April 21, 2014. Web July 15, 2014
18. O'Reilly. Transactions. Mastering Bitcoin. O'Reilly (2013). Web May 01, 2015
19. Krohn, M.: Keybase. Keybase. Caroline Hadilaksono, n.d. Web February 10, 2015

# A Scalable Multiparty Private Set Intersection

Atsuko Miyaji[1,2,3]([✉]) and Shohei Nishida[1]

[1] Japan Advanced Institute of Science and Technology, Nomi, Japan
{miyaji,shohei-n}@jaist.ac.jp
[2] Japan Science and Technology Agency (JST) CREST, Tokyo, Japan
[3] Graduate School of Engineering, Osaka University, Suita, Japan

**Abstract.** Both scalability and flexibility become crucial for privacy preserving protocols in the age of Big Data. Private Set Intersection (PSI) is one of important privacy preserving protocols. Usually, PSI is executed by 2-parties, a client and a server, where both a client and a server compute jointly the intersection of their private sets and at the end only the client learns the intersection and the server learns nothing. From the scalable point of view, however, the number of parties are not limited to two. In this paper, we propose a scalable and flexible multiparty PSI (MPSI) for the first time: the data size of each party is independent to each other and the computational complexity is independent to the number of parties. We also propose $d$-and-over MPSI for the first time.

## 1 Introduction

Both scalability and flexibility become crucial for privacy preserving protocols in the age of Big Data. Private Set Intersection (PSI) is one of important privacy preserving protocols. PSI is executed by 2 parties, a client and a server, where both compute jointly the intersection of their private sets and, at the end, only the client learns the intersection and the server learns nothing. From the scalable point of view, however, the number of parties are not limited to two. This is why a multiparty PSI (MPSI) [8,14] becomes important. However, both are far from scalability: the computational complexity depends on the number of parties, and the data size of each party is equal to each other in [14] and [8] computes only the approximate number of intersection.

In this paper, we propose a scalable and flexible MPSI: the data size of each party is independent to each other and the computational complexity is independent to the number of parties. Furthermore we also propose a new notion of $d$-and-over multiparty PSI ($d$-and-over MPSI) for $d \leq n$. A $d$-and-over MPSI means to compute securely $\bigcap^{\geq d} S_j = \bigcup_{n \geq \ell \geq d}(S_{j_1} \cap \cdots \cap S_{j_\ell})$, where $S_i$ is a set of $\mathbf{P_i}$. Let us think the following scenario: There are $n$ shops $\mathbf{P_i}$ in a shopping mall whose customers' list is $S_i$. Shops think to promote number of customers each other and plan to have a promotion campaign. In the promotion campaign, a

This study is partly supported by Grant-in-Aid for Scientific Research (C) (15K00183) and (15K00189).

shop $P_i$ wants to know customers who joins an intersection of 3-and-over shops including $P_i$ without learning any information about customers that are not in the intersection. Such a scalable MPSI has, however, not proposed yet as far as authors know.

This paper is organized as follows. Section 2 summarises security assumption and building blocks used in our proposal. Section 3 explains the previous results. Then, after investigating set operations required in the case of $n$ parties in Section 4, we propose concrete schemes of MPSI and $d$-and-over MPSI in Section 5. Comparison with the previous MPSI [14] is shown in Section 6.

## 2  Preliminary

This section summarises security assumption and building blocks used in our proposal.

### 2.1  Security Assumption

We describe two standard adversary models [10]: semi-honest adversaries and malicious adversaries. In semi-honest adversaries model, all players act according to their prescribed actions in the protocol. If a protocol is secure in a semi-honest model, then no player gains information about other player's private input sets, other than what can be deduced from the result of the protocol. On the other hand, in malicious adversaries model, an adversary player can behave arbitrarily. In particular, we cannot hope to prevent a malicious player from refusing to participate in the protocol, substituting an input with an arbitrary value, and aborting the protocol prematurely.

The security assumptions used in our protocol are defined as follows.

**Definition 1 (DDH Assumption).** *Let $\mathbb{F}_p$ be a finite field, $g \in \mathbb{F}_p$ with prime order $q$ and size of $q$ is $\ell$. The DDH(Decisional Diffie-Hellman) problem is hard in $\mathbb{G}$ if, for any efficient algorithm $A$, there exists $\epsilon > 0$ and the following probability is satisfied: $|\Pr[x, y \leftarrow \{0,1\}^\ell : A(g, g^x, g^y, g^{xy}) = 1] - \Pr[x, y, z \leftarrow \{0,1\}^\ell : A(g, g^x, g^y, g^z) = 1]| < \epsilon$.*

### 2.2  Bloom Filter

A Bloom filter [2], denoted by BF, is a space-efficient probabilistic data structure, that is used to test whether an element $x$ is included in a set $S$. False positive matches are possible, but false negatives are not, thus a Bloom filter has a 100% recall rate. Elements can be added to the set, but not removed. A Bloom filter is an array of $m$ bits that can represent a set $S$ with at most $w$ elements. A Bloom filter uses a set of $k$ independent uniform hash functions $\mathcal{H} = \{H_0, ..., H_{k-1}\}$, where $H_i : \{0,1\}^* \longrightarrow \{0, 1, \cdots, m-1\}(0 \leq \forall i \leq k-1)$. Here after, we denote a Bloom filter parametrised $(m, k)$ by $\mathsf{BF}_{m,k}(S)$ that encodes a set $S$. Let us explain how BF is constructed, which is given by const.BF (see Algorithm 1):

output $BF_{m,k}(S)$ for input of a set $S$. Initially, all bits in the array are set to 0. To insert an element $x \in S$ into the filter, the element is hashed using $k$ hash functions to get $k$ index numbers. Bits at these indexes are set to 1, i.e. set $BF_{m,k}[H_i(x)] = 1$ for $0 \leq i \leq k - 1$. To check if an item $y$ is in $S$, we execute check.BF (see Algorithm 2): $y$ is hashed by $k$ hash functions, and all locations where $y$ is hashed are checked. If any bit at the locations is 0, $y$ is not in $S$, otherwise $y$ is probably in $S$. However, a false positive is possible, i.e. it is possible that $y$ is not in the set $S$, but all $BF[H_i(y)]$ are set to 1. The false positive probability $p$ is [3]: $p = \left\{ 1 - \left(1 - \frac{1}{m}\right)^{kw} \right\}^k \approx \left\{ 1 - e^{-kw/m} \right\}^k$. For a given $m$ and $w$, the value of $k$ that minimizes the false positive probability is: $k = \frac{m}{w} \ln 2$. When $e^{-kw/m} = 1/2$, the false positive probability $p = (1/2)^k \approx (0.6185)^{m/w}$. The number $z$ of 0 bits in a Bloom filter for a set $S$ is strongly concentrated around its expectation $m(1 - 1/m)^{k|S|}$ [3]. Therefore, given $z$, $m$ and $k$, the size of S is given approximately to $|S| = \frac{\ln(z/m)}{k \ln(1 - 1/m)}$.

---

**Algorithm 1.** const.BF($S$)

**Require:** A set $S$
**Ensure:** A Bloom filter $BF_{m,k}(S)$
 1: **for** $i = 0$ to $m - 1$ **do**
 2:　　$BF_{m,k}[i] \leftarrow 0$
 3: **end for**
 4: **for all** $x \in S$ **do**
 5:　　**for** $i = 0$ to $k - 1$ **do**
 6:　　　$j = H_i(x)$
 7:　　　**if** $BF_{m,k}[j] = 0$ **then**
 8:　　　　$BF_{m,k}[j] \leftarrow 1$
 9:　　　**end if**
10:　　**end for**
11: **end for**

---

**Algorithm 2.** check.BF($BF, S_q$)

**Require:** A Bloom filter $BF_{m,k}(S)$, a set $S_q$
**Ensure:** A set $S_\cap (= S \cap S_q)$
 1: generates the empty set $S_\cap = \{\}$
 2: **for all** $x \in S_q$ **do**
 3:　　**for** $i = 0$ to $k - 1$ **do**
 4:　　　$j = H_i(x)$
 5:　　**end for**
 6:　　**if** all $BF_{m,k}[j] = 1$ **then**
 7:　　　add $x$ to the set $S_\cap$
 8:　　**end if**
 9: **end for**

---

## 2.3 Additive Homomorphic Encryption

An additive homomorphic encryption is important tool to deal with encrypted data. One of typical additive homomorphic encryption is Paillier encryption[16]. In our scheme, an additive homomorphic encryption is used for matching, and, thus exponential ElGamal encryption [4] is enough and more efficient than Paillier encryption. In fact, results of decryption in ex-ElGamal can distinguish whether two message $m_1$ and $m_2$ are equal although it can not decrypt a message itself. Furthermore, ex-ElGamal can be extended to decrypt a ciphertext distributedly, where $n$ parties $\mathbf{P}_i (1 \leq i \leq n)$ jointly decrypt, which consists of three functions:

**Key Generation:**
Let $\mathbb{F}_p$ be a finite field, $g \in \mathbb{F}_p$ with prime order $q$. Each party chooses $x_i \in \mathbb{Z}_q$

randomly and computes $y_i = g^{x_i} \pmod{p}$, then $y = \prod_{i=1}^{n} y_i \pmod{p}$ is a public key and each $x_i$ is a share for a party to decrypt a ciphertext.

**Encryption:** $\mathsf{Enc}[m] \to (u, v)$
For a message $m \in \mathbb{Z}_q$ with a public key $y$, choose $r \in \mathbb{Z}_q$ randomly, compute both $u = g^r \pmod{p}$ and $v = g^m y^r \pmod{p}$, then output $(u, v)$ as a ciphertext of $m$.

**Decryption:** $\mathsf{dis.Dec}[(u, v)] \to g^m$
Each party computes $z_i = u^{x_i} \pmod{p}$ and $z = \prod_{i=1}^{n} z_i \pmod{p}$ jointly and decrypt the ciphertext as $g^m = v/z \pmod{p}$.

Both ex-ElGamal encryption and the above distributed version have the following features: (1)an additive homomorphism for messages $m_1, m_2 \in \mathbb{Z}_p$ : $\mathsf{Enc}(m_1)\mathsf{Enc}(m_2) = \mathsf{Enc}(m_1 + m_2)$. (2) a scalar homomorphism for message $m$ and $k \in \mathbb{Z}_q$: $\mathsf{Enc}(m)^k = \mathsf{Enc}(km)$.

# 3   Previous Works

This section overviews prior works on PSI between a server and a client and MPSI among $n$ parties. In PSI, let server and client data sets be $S = \{s_1, ..., s_v\}$ and $C = \{c_1, ..., c_w\}$, where $|S| = v$ and $|C| = w$. In MPSI, we assume that the number of each party's set is equal to each other for simplicity.

**PSI Protocol Based on Polynomial Evaluation:** Main idea is to represent elements in $C$ as roots of a polynomial, and send its encrypted polynomial to a server; evaluate it on elements in $S$, which introduced by Freedman [9] for the first time. This is secure against semi-honest adversaries under a public key encryption. The computational complexity is $O(vw)$ exponentiations, and communicational complexity is $O(v + w)$. The computational complexity is reduced to $O(v \log \log w)$ exponentiations by using balanced allocations technique [1]. Kissner and Song extended protocols to MPSI [14]. The computational complexity is $O(nw^2)$ exponentiations and communicational complexity is $O(nw)$ and it is secure against semi-honest and malicious adversaries (in the random oracle model) using generic zero-knowledge proofs.

**PSI Protocol Based on DDH:** Main idea is to apply DDH assumption [6]: after presenting each data by hash value $\{h(s_i)\}$ and $\{h(c_i)\}$, the client sends a set of $\{h(c_i)^{r_i}\}$ encrypted by a random number $r_i$; the server sends back $\{h(c_i)^{r r_i}\}$ and $\{h(s_i)^r\}$ for a random number $r$, finally the client evaluate $S \cap C$ by decrypting to $\{h(c_i)^r\}$. This is secure against semi-honest adversaries under DDH assumption. The total computational complexity is $O(v + w)$ exponentiations and the total communicational complexity is $O(v + w)$. The security is enhanced to against malicious adversaries in the random oracle model in [5] by using blind signature. Any extension to MPSI based on DDH, however, has not been proposed.

**PSI Protocol Based on Bloom Filter:** PSI based on Bloom filter is proposed in [15] for the first time by just executing AND of Bloom filters of server and client. This protocol, however, is not secure because Bloom filter itself leaks information about other party's set. In [13], the security is enhanced by combining Bloom filters with the Goldwasser Micali encryption [11]. In a semi-honest version, the computational complexity is both $O(kw)$ hash operations and $O(m)$ public key operations and the communicational complexity is $O(m)$, where $(m, k)$ is a parameter of Bloom filter. Another protocol combined Bloom filter, Oblivious transfer extension [12,17], and garbled Bloom filter constructed newly is proposed [7]. The main difference between Bloom filter and garbled Bloom filter is that a Bloom filter is 1-bit array while a garbled Bloom filter is a $\lambda$-bit array. To add an element $x \in S$ to a garbled Bloom filter, $x$ is split into $k$ shares with $\lambda$ bits using the XOR-based secret sharing ($x = x_1 \oplus ... \oplus x_k$) and mapped $x_i$ into an index of $H_i(x)$. To query an element $y$, all bit strings at $H_i(y)$ is XOR them together. If the result is $y$, then $y$ is in $S$, otherwise $y$ is not in $S$. The client uses Bloom filter $\mathsf{BF}(C)$ and the server uses garbled Bloom filter $\mathsf{GBF}(S)$. Then, if an element $x$ is in $C \cap S$, then for every position $i$ it hashes to, $\mathsf{BF}(C)[i]$ must be 1 and $\mathsf{GBF}(S)[i]$ must be $x_i$. Thus, the client evaluates $C \cap S$. The computational complexity is $O(kw)$ hash operations and $O(m)$ public key operations and communicational complexity is $O(m)$, where the number of public key operations can be changed to $O(\lambda)$ by using Oblivious transfer extension. This is secure against semi-honest adversaries under secure Oblivious transfer protocol. Another research computes the approximate number of multiparty set union in [8]. However, MPSI based on Bloom filter has been proposed.

## 4    Multiparty Set Intersection

We investigate what set operations are required in the case of $n$ parties. Let us investigate the following scenarios: There are $n$ medical institutions $\mathbf{P_i}$ whose patient list is $S_i$. Patients often use several medical institutions. Each medical institution $\mathbf{P_i}$ wants to find common patients without learning any information about patients that are not in $S_i$. That is, $\mathbf{P_1}$ wants to know patients who uses 2-and-over medical institutions including $\mathbf{P_i}$ without learning any information about patients that are not in $\mathbf{P_i}$, which is denoted by $\cap^{\geq 2} S_j[1]$.

Let us formalize intersections of $n$ parties. As we have seen the above scenario, intersections of all parities and $d$-and-over parties for $\forall d(\leq n)$ are necessary, which are called MPSI and $d$-and-over MPSI, respectively. Here, $d$-and-over MPSI is denoted by $\bigcap^{\geq d} S_j = \bigcup_{n \geq \ell > d}(S_{j_1} \cap \cdots \cap S_{j_\ell})$. For example, given 4 party-set $S_1 = \{g, h, i, j, f, n, o, k\}$, $S_2 = \{a, h, n, m, b, i, o, \ell\}$, $S_3 = \{f, n, o, k, e, m, l, d\}$, and $S_4 = \{b, i, o, l, c, j, k, d\}$. Then MPSI is $\{o\}$; and 3-and-over MPSI is given by $\bigcap^3 S_i = \{i, k, \ell, n, o\}$. Then, intersection of 3-and-over MPSI given to each $\mathbf{P_i}$ is $\cap^{\geq 3} S_j[1] = \{i, k, n, o\}$, $\cap^{\geq 3} S_j[2] = \{i, \ell, n, o\}$, $\cap^{\geq 3} S_j[3] = \{k, \ell, n, o\}$, and $\cap^{\geq 3} S_j[4] = \{i, k, \ell, o\}$.

Let us discuss how to achieve MPSI and $d$-and-over MPSI. If we apply PSI to achieve MPSI, the computation and communication complexity seems to depend to the number of parties, which exactly happens to [14]. On the other hand, if we apply MPSI to achieve a $d$-and-over MPSI, we would need to execute MPSI in

$_nC_d$ times, which is rather wastefulness. This is why it is necessary to construct MPSI and $d$-and over MPSI directly. On the other hand, privacy issues on MPSI and $d$-and-over MPSI are informally give as follows.

**MPSI Privacy:** An MPSI scheme is party-private if any party $\mathbf{P_i}$ learns no information about elements of other parties' set except elements in $\cap S_j$.

**$d$-and-over MPSI Privacy:** A $d$-and-over MPSI scheme is party-private if any party $\mathbf{P_i}$ learns no information about elements of other parties' set except elements in $\cap^{\geq d} S_j[i]$.

# 5 Scalable Multiparty PSI

Our schemes of MPSI and $d$-and-over MPSI will be presented after describing protocol intuition briefly.

## 5.1 Protocol Intuition

The following notations are used in our two protocols.

- $\mathbf{P_i}$: $i$-th party, where the number of parties is $n$
- $\mathbf{D}$: dealer who does not know anything about inputs or outputs
- $S_i = \{s_{i,1}, s_{i,2}, \cdots, s_{i,w_i}\}$: a set of $\mathbf{P_i}$, where $|S_i| = \omega_i$
- $\cap S_j$ or $\cap^{\geq d} S_j$: intersection of all or $d$-and-over parties out of $n$
- $\cap^{\geq d} S[i]$: intersection of $d$-and-over parties possessed by $\mathbf{P_i}$, $\cap^{\geq d} S \subset S_i$
- Enc/dis.Dec: distributed ex-ElGamal encryption/decryption by all $\mathbf{P_i}$
- $m$: size of Bloom filter
- $\mathcal{H} = \{H_0, ..., H_{k-1}\}$: set of hashes used in Bloom filter, where $k$ is $\#\mathcal{H}$.
- $\boldsymbol{\ell} = [\ell, \cdots, \ell]$ $(1 \leq \ell < n)$: an $m$-dimension array, where all strings in the array are set to $\ell$
- $\mathrm{BF}_{m,k}(S_i) = [\mathrm{BF}_i[0], \cdots, \mathrm{BF}_i[m-1]]$: Bloom filter on a set $S_i$
- $\mathrm{IBF}_{m,k}(\cup S_i) = [\sum_{i=1}^{n} \mathrm{BF}_i[0], \cdots, \sum_{i=1}^{n} \mathrm{BF}_i[m-1]]$: integrated Bloom filter of $n$ sets $\{S_i\}$, where $\sum_{i=1}^{n} \mathrm{BF}_i[j]$ presents the sum of all parties' array.
- $\mathrm{IBF}_{m,k}(\cup S_i) \setminus \boldsymbol{\ell} = [\sum_{i=1}^{\ell} \mathrm{BF}_i[0] - \ell, \cdots, \sum_{i=1}^{n} \mathrm{BF}_i[m-1] - \ell](1 \leq \ell \leq n)$: $\ell$-subtraction from $\mathrm{IBF}_{m,k}(\cup S_i)$.

Our scheme is flexible for the data size of party, and, thus, the data size of each party is independent to each other. We introduce a dealer $\mathbf{D}$ to reduce the computational complexity of parties. $\mathbf{D}$ can be outsourced since it does not know anything about $S_i$ or $|S_i|$. A distributed ex-ElGamal encryption among $n$-party is used to achieve all computation without knowing $S_i$ themselves and at the end decryption is jointly done. In both protocols, each $\mathbf{P_i}$ constructs $\mathrm{BF}_{m,k}(S_i)$ for a set $S_i$ and encrypts each array by Enc. All encrypted Bloom filters are securely added by a dealer $\mathbf{D}$ without decrypting. These procedures are executed in both MPSI and $d$-and-over MPSI. In MPSI, $\mathbf{D}$ encrypts a randomized $n$-*subtraction* of $\mathrm{IBF}_{m,k}(\cup S_i)$, $\boldsymbol{r}(\mathrm{IBF}_{m,k}(\cup S_i) \setminus \boldsymbol{n})$. If $x \in \cap S_i$, the corresponding array locations in an encrypted array where $x$ is mapped by $k$ hashes is an encryption of 0; an encryption of randomized value otherwise. In $d$-and-over MPSI, $\mathbf{D}$ computes a randomized encryption of $\ell$-*subtraction* of $r(\mathsf{IBF}_{m,k}(\cup S_i) \setminus \ell)$ for $d \leq \ell \leq n$. If $x \in \cap^\ell S$ for $d \leq \exists \ell \leq n$, the corresponding array locations in $\mathsf{IBF}_{m,k}(\cup S_i) \setminus j$ for $\ell \leq \exists j \leq n$ where $x$ is mapped by $k$ hashes is an encryption of 0; an encryption of randomized value otherwise. An difference from MPSI is that the corresponding array locations in $\mathsf{IBF}_{m,k}(\cup S_i) \setminus \ell$ is not a necessary encryption of 0 even if $x \in \cap^\ell S$.

## 5.2  MPSI and $d$-and-over MPSI

First, we present MPSI, MPSI consists of 4 phases: initialization, $\mathbf{P}_i$'s Bloom filter construction, $\mathbf{D}$'s Encryption of $n$-subtraction of $\mathsf{IBF}_{m,k}(\cup S_i)$, and, finally, $\mathbf{P}_i$'s MPSI computation. As system parameters, a finite field $\mathbb{F}_p$ and a base-point $g \in \mathbb{F}_p$ with order $q$ for a distributed ex-ElGamal encryption (Enc, dis.Dec), given to $\mathbf{P}_i$ and $\mathbf{D}$, but both const.BF$(S)$ and check.BF$(\mathsf{BF}, S_q)$ are given to only $\mathbf{P}_i$. When we encrypt or randomize a vector such as a Bloom filter $\mathsf{BF}_{m,k} = [a_0, \cdots, a_{m-1}]$, each location is encrypted or randomized independently: $\mathsf{Enc}(\mathsf{BF}_{m,k}) = [\mathsf{Enc}(a_0), \cdots, \mathsf{Enc}(a_{m-1})]$ or $r\mathsf{BF}_{m,k} = [r_0 a_0, \cdots, r_{m-1} a_{m-1}]$ by $r = [r_0, \cdots, r_{m-1}] \in \mathbb{Z}_q^m$, respectively.

**Initialization:** $\mathbf{P}_i$ executes the following:

1. Generate a secret key $x_i \in \mathbb{Z}_q$ and compute a public key $y_i = g^{x_i} \in \mathbb{Z}_q$ and broadcast $y_i$ to other parties.
2. Compute an $n$-party public key $y = \prod_i y_i$ whose secret key is $x = \sum x_i$.

$\mathsf{BF}_{m,k}(S_i)$ **construction:** $\mathbf{P}_i$ executes the following:

1. Do const.$\mathsf{BF}_{m,k}(S_i) \longrightarrow \mathsf{BF}_{m,k}(S_i) = [\mathsf{BF}_i[0], \cdots, \mathsf{BF}_i[m-1]]$ (Algorithm 1).
2. Encrypt each array of $\mathsf{BF}_{m,k}(S_i)$ by using $\mathsf{Enc}_y$ with a public key $y$:
   $\mathsf{Enc}_y(\mathsf{BF}_{m,k}(S_i)) = [\mathsf{Enc}_y(\mathsf{BF}_i[0]), \cdots, \mathsf{Enc}_y(\mathsf{BF}_i[m-1])]$.
3. Send $\mathsf{Enc}_y(\mathsf{BF}_{m,k}(S_i))$ to $\mathbf{D}$.

**Encryption of $n$-subtraction of $\mathsf{IBF}_{m,k}(\cup S_i)$:** $\mathbf{D}$ executes the following:

1. Encrypt $\mathsf{IBF}_{m,k}(\cup S_i)$ by $\mathsf{Enc}_y$ without knowing $\mathsf{IBF}_{m,k}(\cup S_i)$ as follows:
   $\mathsf{Enc}_y(\mathsf{IBF}_{m,k}(\cup S_i)) = \prod_{i=1}^n \mathsf{Enc}_y(\mathsf{BF}_{m,k}(S_i))$.
2. Encrypt $\mathsf{IBF}_{m,k}(\cup S_i) \setminus n$ randomized by $r = [r_0, \cdots, r_{m-1}] \in \mathbb{Z}_q^m$:
   $\mathsf{Enc}_y(r(\mathsf{IBF}_{m,k}(\cup S_i) \setminus n)) = (\mathsf{Enc}_y(\mathsf{IBF}_{m,k}(\cup S_i)) \cdot \mathsf{Enc}_y(-n))^r$,
   where $\mathsf{Enc}_y(-n) = [\mathsf{Enc}_y(-n), \cdots, \mathsf{Enc}_y(-n)]$.
3. Broadcast $\mathsf{Enc}_y(r(\mathsf{IBF}_{m,k}(\cup S_i) \setminus n))$ to $\mathbf{P}_i$.

**MPSI computation:** $\mathbf{P}_i$ executes the following:

1. All $\mathbf{P}_i$ jointly decrypt $\mathsf{Enc}_y(r(\mathsf{IBF}_{m,k}(\cup S_i) \setminus n))$.
2. Execute check.$\mathsf{BF}_{m,k}(r(\mathsf{IBF}_{m,k}(\cup S_i) \setminus n), S_i) \longrightarrow \cap S_i$ and output $\cap S_i$.

Correctness of MPSI follows from the fact that if an element $x$ is included in $\cap S_i$, the corresponding array locations in $\mathsf{Enc}_y(r(\mathsf{IBF}_{m,k}(\cup S_i) \setminus n))$ where $x$ is mapped by $k$ hashes is an encryption of 0, which are decrypted to 1; an encryption of randomized value otherwise.

Next, we present $d$-and-over MPSI. Procedures of $d$-and-over MPSI is the same as that of MPSI until $\mathbf{D}$ computes $\mathsf{Enc}_y(\mathsf{IBF}_{m,k}(\cup S_i))$. So, we describe after $\mathbf{D}$ computes $\mathsf{Enc}_y(\mathsf{IBF}_{m,k}(\cup S_i))$.

**Encryption of $\ell$-subtraction of $\mathsf{IBF}_{m,k}(\cup S_i)$:** $\mathbf{D}$ executes the following:

1. Encrypt $\mathsf{IBF}_{m,k}(\cup S_i) \setminus \ell$ randomized by $\boldsymbol{r} = [r_0, \cdots, r_{m-1}] \in \mathbb{Z}_q^m (d \leq \ell \leq n)$:
   $\mathsf{Enc}_y(\boldsymbol{r}(\mathsf{IBF}_{m,k}(\cup S_i) \setminus \ell)) = (\mathsf{Enc}_y(\mathsf{IBF}_{m,k}(\cup S_i)) \cdot \mathsf{Enc}_y(-\ell))^{\boldsymbol{r}}$.
2. Broadcast $\{\mathsf{Enc}_y(\boldsymbol{r}(\mathsf{IBF}_{m,k}(\cup S_i) \setminus \ell))\}_\ell$ $(d \leq \ell \leq n)$ to $\mathbf{P_i}$.

**$d$-and-over MPSI computation:** $\mathbf{P_i}$ executes the following:

1. All $\mathbf{P_i}$ jointly decrypt $\{\mathsf{Enc}_y(\boldsymbol{r}(\mathsf{IBF}_{m,k}(\cup S_i) \setminus \ell))\}_\ell$.
2. Let $\mathsf{CBF}_\ell$ be an $m$-array for $d \leq \ell \leq n$, where an array is set to 1 if and only if the corresponding array of $\boldsymbol{r}\mathsf{IBF}_{m,k}(\cup S_i) \setminus \ell$ is 1, and others are set to 0.
3. Set $\mathsf{CBF} = \mathsf{CBF}_\ell \vee \cdots \vee \mathsf{CBF}_n$.
4. Execute $\mathsf{check.BF}_{m,k}(\mathsf{CBF}, S_i) \longrightarrow \cap^{\geq d} S[i]$ and output $\cap^{\geq d} S[i]$.

Correctness of $d$-and-over MPSI follows from the fact that if an element $x \in \cap^\ell S$ for $d \leq \exists \ell \leq n$, the corresponding array locations in $\mathsf{IBF}_{m,k}(\cup S_i) \setminus \boldsymbol{j}$ for $\ell \leq \exists j \leq n$ where $x$ is mapped by $k$ hashes is an encryption of 0, which are decrypted to 1; an encryption of randomized value otherwise.

The security of both protocols is given as follows, whose proof will be presented in the final paper.

**Theorem 1.** *If the Decisional Diffie-Hellman assumption holds, then both MPSI and $d$-and-over are secure against semi-honest adversary.*

## 6 Comparison

Table 1 compares the computational and communicational complexity of our protocol with [14]. Each protocol is secure against semi-honest adversaries without the trusted third party under each security assumption of employed public key encryption: [14] uses Paillier encryption (Decisional Composite Residue (DCR)) and our protocols use ex-ElGamal encryption (DDH). Bloom filter parameters $(m, k)$ used in our protocol are set as follows: $k = 80$ and $m = 80\omega/\ln 2$, where $\omega$ is the maximum $|S_i| = \omega_i$. Then, the false positives probability is given by $p = 2^{-80}$. $\mathbf{P_i}$'s dominant computational complexity is Bloom filter construction and MPSI or $d$-and-over MPSI computation, which is $O(\omega_i)$ and doesn't depend on the number of parties unlike [14]. $\mathbf{D}$'s dominant computational complexity is $\boldsymbol{n}$-subtraction of $\mathsf{IBF}_{m,k}(\cup S_i)$, which is $O(n\omega)$ in both MPSI and $d$-and over MPSI. Our scheme is flexible for the data size of party, and, thus, the data size of each party is independent to each other. An approach to compute approximate number of MPSI is proposed in [8] by using features of Bloom Filter. Our protocol can be converted to compute easily approximate number of $|\cap S_j|$ or $|\cap^{\geq d} S[i]|$.

**Table 1.** Comparison of MPSI

| Protocol | [14] | Our protocol |
|---|---|---|
| Computational complexity | $O(n\omega^2)$ | $\mathbf{P}_i : O(\omega_i), \mathbf{D} : O(n\omega)$ |
| Communicational complexity | $O(n\omega)$ | $O(n\omega)$ |
| Number of input data | $|S_1| = ... = |S_n|$ | any |
| Privacy | $S_1, ..., S_n$ | $S_1, ..., S_n, |S_1|, ..., |S_n|$ |

# 7   Conclusion

In this paper, we have proposed a scalable and flexible multiparty PSI (MPSI). We have also proposed a new notion of $d$-and-over MPSI and presented a concrete protocol. Our schemes are flexible: data size of each party is independent to each other. We also introduce a dealer $\mathbf{D}$ to reduce the computational complexity of parties, who acts as opposed to the trusted third party and does not know anything about inputs or outputs (including its size), and, it thus can be outsourced. Thanks to $\mathbf{D}$, $\mathbf{P}_i$'s, computational complexity is $O(\omega_i)$, which doesn't depend on the number of parties unlike [14].

# References

1. Azar, Y., et al.: Balanced allocations. SIAM journal on computing **29**(1), 180–200 (1999)
2. Bloom, B.H.: Space/time trade-offs in hash coding with allowable errors. Communications of the ACM **13**(7), 422–426 (1970)
3. Broder, A., Mitzenmacher, M.: Network applications of bloom filters: A survey. Internet mathematics **1**(4), 485–509 (2004)
4. Cramer, R., et al.: A secure and optimally efficient multi-authority election scheme. European transactions on Telecommunications **8**(5), 481–490 (1997)
5. De Cristofaro, E., Kim, J., Tsudik, G.: Linear-complexity private set intersection protocols secure in malicious model. In: Abe, M. (ed.) ASIACRYPT 2010. LNCS, vol. 6477, pp. 213–231. Springer, Heidelberg (2010)
6. De Cristofaro, E., Tsudik, G.: Practical private set intersection protocols with linear complexity. In: Sion, R. (ed.) FC 2010. LNCS, vol. 6052, pp. 143–159. Springer, Heidelberg (2010)
7. Dong, C., et al.: When private set intersection meets big data: an efficient and scalable protocol. In: ACMCCS 2013, pp. 789–800. ACM (2013)
8. Egert, R., Fischlin, M., Gens, D., Jacob, S., Senker, M., Tillmanns, J.: Privately computing set-union and set-intersection cardinality via bloom filters. In: Foo, E., Stebila, D. (eds.) ACISP 2015. LNCS, vol. 9144, pp. 413–430. Springer, Heidelberg (2015)
9. Freedman, M.J., Nissim, K., Pinkas, B.: Efficient private matching and set intersection. In: Cachin, C., Camenisch, J.L. (eds.) EUROCRYPT 2004. LNCS, vol. 3027, pp. 1–19. Springer, Heidelberg (2004)
10. Goldreich, O.: Secure multi-party computation. Manuscript, Preliminary version (1998)

11. Goldwasser, S., Micali, S.: Probabilistic encryption. Journal of computer and system sciences **28**(2), 270–299 (1984)
12. Ishai, Y., Kilian, J., Nissim, K., Petrank, E.: Extending oblivious transfers efficiently. In: Boneh, D. (ed.) CRYPTO 2003. LNCS, vol. 2729, pp. 145–161. Springer, Heidelberg (2003)
13. Kerschbaum, F.: Outsourced private set intersection using homomorphic encryption. In: ACMCCS 2012, pp. 85–86. ACM (2012)
14. Kissner, L., Song, D.: Privacy-preserving set operations. In: Shoup, V. (ed.) CRYPTO 2005. LNCS, vol. 3621, pp. 241–257. Springer, Heidelberg (2005)
15. Many, D., et al.: Fast private set operations with sepia. Technical Report 345 (2012)
16. Paillier, P.: Public-key cryptosystems based on composite degree residuosity classes. In: Stern, J. (ed.) EUROCRYPT 1999. LNCS, vol. 1592, p. 223. Springer, Heidelberg (1999)
17. Rabin, M.O.: How to exchange secrets with oblivious transfer. Tech. Memo, TR-81 (1981)

# Electronic Contract Signing Without Using Trusted Third Party

Zhiguo Wan[1][(✉)], Robert H. Deng[2], and David Lee[1]

[1] Sim Kim Boon Institute for Financial Economics,
Singapore Management University, Singapore, Singapore
zgwan@smu.edu.sg
[2] School of Information Science, Singapore Management University,
Singapore, Singapore

**Abstract.** Electronic contract signing allows two potentially dis-trustful parties to digitally sign an electronic document "simultaneously" across a network. Existing solutions for electronic contract signing either require the involvement of a trusted third party (TTP), or are complex and expensive in communication and computation. In this paper we propose an electronic contract signing protocol between two parties with the following advantages over existing solutions: 1) it is practical and scalable due to its simplicity and high efficiency; 2) it does not require any trusted third party as the mediator; and 3) it guarantees fairness between the two signing parties. We achieve these properties by employing a trustworthy timestamping service in our protocol, where the timestamping service can be either centralized or decentralized. We also provide a detailed analysis on security and performance of our scheme.

## 1 Introduction

Contract signing is a frequent activity in business as well as in our daily lives, e.g. purchasing real estates and insurance, employment, and financial trading. Almost all important commercial and financial activities require legally signed contracts to guarantee that the involved parties commit to mutually agreed terms and conditions and fulfill their obligations. Most important contracts today, however, are signed physically, e.g., using pen and paper. As a result, signing a contract could be very time consuming and costly, and it may take several days or weeks to complete. As the information technology and digital signature laws are becoming more and more pervasive, it is high time to consider digitally signing electronic contracts across the Internet.

Fairness is a critical requirement for electronic contract signing, which ensures that the two involved parties either obtain each other's signature "simultaneously" or nothing useful. The fairness property implies that a dishonest party who tries to cheat cannot get any advantage over the other party. Achieving fairness is straightforward for physically signing contracts; however, due to lack of simultaneity in computer networks, achieving true fairness in electronic contract signing over Internet has been a challenging problem. Many electronic contract

© Springer International Publishing Switzerland 2015
M. Qiu et al. (Eds.): NSS 2015, LNCS 9408, pp. 386–394, 2015.
DOI: 10.1007/978-3-319-25645-0_27

signing or fair exchange protocols have been proposed in the literature, but none of them have gained widespread adoption. Among these protocols, some require an online or offline trusted third party (TTP) to mediate the exchange, while others are TTP-free but impractical due to high computation and communication overhead.

In this paper, we propose a practical electronic contract signing protocol built on a trustworthy timestamping service, without using any TTP. Our protocol enjoys the following advantages over existing ones. First, it is very practical and scalable due to its simplicity and high efficiency in computation and communication. Unlike TTP-free protocols which need multiple rounds of communication between the two signing parties [1], our protocol only requires three messages to be exchanged. The protocol at the same time does not require complex computations except a few digital signatures, which makes it very efficient in computation. Secondly, our protocol does not require any TTP, thus removing the single point of failure and the bottleneck for scalability. Third, the protocol guarantees fairness between the two signing parties. The two parties negotiate and agree on a deadline before which the contract must be signed by both of them. Failing to fulfill this requirement leads to invalidity of the contract, and this protects the interest of the first party against malicious behaviors of the second party.

## 2    Related Work

Electronic commerce has greatly motivated research in electronic contract signing. According to the extent to which a TTP is involved in the contract signing process, existing protocols can be divided into three groups: 1) TTP-free protocols; 2) protocols with an online TTP; and 3) protocols with an offline TTP.

**TTP-Free Protocols.** TTP-free protocols have the advantage of no need for a specialized TTP, and its design goal is to fulfill the computational fairness [1]. The idea is for two signing parties to exchange their signatures on a contract "bit-by-bit". Whenever any of the two parties terminates prematurely, both of them can still complete the exchange offline by exhaustively searching the remaining bits of the signatures. Although this approach enjoys the great advantage of being TTP-free, it is impractical for most real-world applications. The main reason is due to the high computation and communication cost of such protocols.

**Online-TTP Protocols.** Since a TTP facilitates the execution of the signing process, contract-signing protocols with an online TTP can be much simpler and efficient [2]. Under the online-TTP setting, a TTP acts as a mediator between the two signing parties. The main issue with the online-TTP protocols is that the TTP is likely to become a performance and security bottleneck of the system, especially when there are a huge number of participants in the system.

**Offline-TTP Protocols.** Contract-signing protocols with an offline TTP [3–5] are more appealing and practical because the TTP is not involved during the execution of an exchange unless some problems occur. Fair exchange protocols for digital signatures employed two different cryptographic techniques: verifiable encrypted signatures [5] and verifiable escrows [3].

# 3    The Proposed Protocol

## 3.1    System Model

Our proposed contract signing protocol involves three types of generic entities or roles: a PKI, a timestamping server and signing parties. The design goal is to enable any two parties to sign an electronic contract in a fair manner. We assume that each party has a public key/private key pair in a signature scheme. The PKI is responsible for public key certificate management for all parties. To ensure security and resilience of the PKI, a resilient PKI system in [6] can be used.

The trustworthy timestamping service is crucial to ensure fairness in our contract signing protocol. It is used to produce irrefutable timestamped proofs that digital signatures on a common contract document are submitted by the two parties before a mutually agreed deadline. These proofs are maintained by the timestamping server, and no party can forge or tamper the proofs without being detected.

## 3.2    Threat Model

We assume that both the PKI and the timestamping service are trustworthy. Specifically, the timestamping server does not need to be trusted as a TTP.

The adversary can be a peer with whom a party wants to sign a contract, other uninvolved parties or simply an outsider. The adversary is assumed to have only limited computation capability, and he cannot break the digital signature algorithm used in the proposed protocol. The ultimate goal of the adversary is to trick an honest party into signing a contract he would otherwise not want to sign. The adversary can launch both passive and active attacks against the contract signing protocol, including message eavesdropping, modification, forgery, replaying and so on.

## 3.3    Protocol Description

After two parties, referred to here as $A$ and $B$, have finished negotiating terms and conditions, they agree on a final contract document $C$. Let $Cert_X$ denote the public key certificate of party $X$ and $\mathsf{Sign}_X(M)$ the signature generated by signing message $M$ with the private key of party $X$, where $X$ can be either $A$ or $B$. Let $\mathsf{Ver}_X(M)$ denote verification of a signature on $M$ using $X$'s public key, which outputs true if the verification is successful and false otherwise.

As showed in Fig. 1, the proposed protocol is composed of three phases: signing by the first party, verification and signing by the other party, and timestamping the signed contract. They are described in detail as follows.

**Signing by the First Party.** To sign a contract, $A$ and $B$ negotiate with each other and decide on a future time $T_d$ as the deadline before which the two parties must sign on $C$; otherwise the contract becomes void. How to set this parameter depends on specific applications. It may be in seconds, minutes, hours, or even days. Party $A$, who signs the contract first, needs to make sure that this parameter is not too long to render herself in a disadvantageous situation. For example, if $A$ wants to trade forex with the other party, then $T_d$ should be as short as a few seconds since forex prices fluctuate at seconds.

Party $A$ then creates a message containing a hash of the contract $C$, the deadline $T_d$, $A$'s identity and $B$'s identity, and signs this message with her private key. That is, $A$ generates the signature $Sig_A = \mathsf{Sign}_A(H(C)|T_d|A|B)$, where $|$ denotes concatenation, and $H()$ is a secure one-way hash function. Then $A$ sends the following to $B$:

$$H(C), T_d, Sig_A, Cert_A \qquad (1)$$

**Verification and Signing by the Second Party.** Upon receiving the message from $A$, the second party, $B$, first checks that the $Cert_A$ is valid, the deadline $T_d$ has not expired and there is sufficient time left to finish the contract; otherwise he aborts the protocol. To continue the contract signing protocol, $B$ checks that $H(C)$ is the hash computed over the contract document $C$ he negotiated with $A$, and verifies that $Sig_A$ is $A$'s valid signature on $(H(C)|T_d|A|B)$ . If the verifications fail, $B$ aborts; otherwise, $B$ signs the message $(H(C), T_d, A, B, Sig_A)$ to obtain a signature $Sig_B = \mathsf{Sign}_B(H(C)|T_d|A|B|Sig_A)$, and sends the following message to the timestamping server:

$$H(C), T_d, A, B, Sig_A, Sig_B, Cert_A, Cert_B. \qquad (2)$$

We refer to the above message $(H(C), T_d, A, B, Sig_A, Sig_B, Cert_A, Cert_B)$ as the signed contract and denote it as **CT** in the following.

**Timestamping the Signed Contract.** After receiving **CT** from $B$, the timestamping server **TS** first checks that $Cert_A$ and $Cert_B$ are valid, that $T_d$ has not expired and that the two signatures $Sig_A$ and $Sig_B$ were generated on the same hash value $H(C)$ by parties $A$ and $B$, respectively. Only if all verifications are successful will **TS** proceed to generate a trustworthy timestamp on the signed contract **CT** $= (H(C), T_d, Sig_A, Sig_B, Cert_A, Cert_B)$. The timestamping server then sends the following message to both parties $A$ and $B$ as a proof that the contract has been signed successfully:

$$\mathbf{CT}, \mathsf{ts}(\mathbf{CT}), \qquad (3)$$

where $\mathsf{ts}(\mathbf{CT})$ denotes the timestamp on **CT**. What constitutes the timestamp will be described in the following subsection.

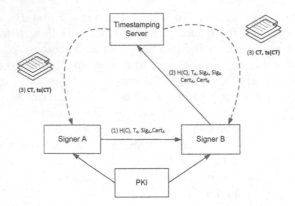

**Fig. 1.** The Contract Signing Protocol.

### 3.4   Timestamping Service

The trustworthy timestamping service referred to above in our protocol description can be implemented with a centralized server as in [7] or a decentralized system based on the blockchain mechanism in Bitcoin [8]. Both implementations adopt a similar approach to trustworthy timestamping as described below.

This timestamping service is built on the Merkle tree structure, a binary tree as showed in 2(a). A node at $(i, j)$ on the Merkle tree has two children: $(i + 1, 2j - 1)$ and $(i + 1, 2j)$. The root node is labeled as $(0, 1)$, meaning it is the first node at layer 0. The value $H(i, j)$ for a leaf node $(i, j)$ is simply the hash of the corresponding contract content, i.e. $H(\mathbf{CT}(i))$. The value of an interior node is calculated from its two children by the formula $H(i, j) = H(H(i+1, 2j-1)|H(i+1, 2j))$. The hash function can be any cryptographically secure hash algorithm, e.g. SHA256. The value calculated at the root is called the Merkle root.

The timestamping service divides time into fixed time intervals and at the end of each interval compresses submitted contracts into a Merkle root. This Merkle root, along with the current time, is taken as an input into a hash chain which is computed and maintained by a server in the centralized system or by a group of nodes in the decentralized system. The output of the hash chain and some auxiliary data corresponding to the specific contract are returned to the parties as the trustworthy timestamp on their contract.

The process of timestamping a Merkle root and hence all the contracts embedded in the root proceeds as illustrated in Fig. 2(b). In each fixed time interval, a Merkle root is calculated as above for all contracts submitted during this interval. The Merkle root, the current time and the previous hash value of the hash chain are fed into the hash function to calculate a new value, and the hash chain is extended by 1. Suppose the current time is $T_i$, the previous hash value of the hash chain is $h_{i-1}$, and the current Merkle root is $root_i$, then the new hash value is computed as $h_i = H(h_{i-1}|T_i|root_i)$.

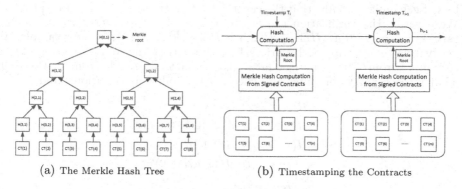

(a) The Merkle Hash Tree

(b) Timestamping the Contracts

**Fig. 2.** The Timestamping Service

The timestamp for a contract, say $\mathbf{CT}(3)$, at time interval $T_i$, is given by

$$\mathbf{ts}(\mathbf{CT}(3)) = (H(0,1), H(1,2), H(2,1), H(3,4), T_i, h_{i-1}, h_i).$$

For a centralized solution, the timestamping server needs to publish all tuples $(h_i, T_i, root_i)$. The latest hash values obtained in this way by a centralized server need to be published on an unalterable public media in a fixed interval (e.g., New York Times every week [7]). Therefore, even the centralized server cannot change the hash chain or the Merkle tree after publishing the last value on the hash chain. Thus the centralized server needs not be a TTP.

A decentralized timestamping service can be realized based on the notion of blockchain in Bitcoin [8], where hash values represent proof-of-work done collectively by a group of entities (e.g., users of the timestamping service). At each time interval $T_i$, the group of entities finds a random value as the input to the hash chain computation formula such that the output of the hash computation is less than a pre-determined public threshold. That is, the hash chain computation formula becomes $h_i = H(h_{i-1}|T_i|root_i|r_i)$, and one has to find an $r_i$ such that $h_i$ is less than the public threshold, which is called proof-of-work.

Finally, all hash values and the proof-of-work $r_i$'s are published on the blockchain so that everyone can check them. Due to the one-wayness of the hash function $H()$, finding a valid $r_i$ such that $h_i$ is less than a threshold could be very difficult. The amount of computation to find $r_i$ can be adjusted by varying the value of the threshold.

Since finding a valid $r_i$ is so difficult and the hash chain is continuously increasing, it is computationally infeasible to change a timestamped contract which is embedded in the hash chain, especially when the chain becomes longer [8]. Hence this decentralized system achieves trustworthy timestamping without relying on any centralized entity or trusted third party.

## 3.5   Timestamp and Contract Verifications

When both parties receive a timestamp on their signed contract from the timestamping server, they proceed to verify the timestamp for correctness. Without loss of generality, assume that the centralized timestamping service in [7] is used. We describe the verification process by taking the aforementioned timestamp $\mathbf{ts}(\mathbf{CT}(3)) = (H(0,1), H(1,2), H(2,1), H(3,4), T_i, h_{i-1}, h_i)$ as an example. To verify this timestamp, both parties first check that the Merkle root is indeed computed from $\mathbf{CT}(3)$ by evaluating the hash tree from bottom to the root. That is, each party computes and checks if the following equations hold:

$$H(3,3) = H(\mathbf{CT}(3));$$
$$H(2,2) = H(H(3,3)|H(3,4));$$
$$H(1,1) = H(H(2,1)|H(2,2));$$
$$root = H(H(1,1)|H(1,2));$$
$$root \overset{?}{=} H(0,1).$$

Then each party verifies if the hash chain value is correctly calculated by testing the following equation: $h_i \overset{?}{=} H(h_{i-1}|T_i|root)$.

Next, both parties retrieve subsequent published tuples $(h_{i+1}, T_{i+1}, root_{i+1})$, $(h_{i+2}, T_{i+2}, root_{i+2})..., (h_m, T_m, root_m)$ from the timestamping server, where $h_m$ is the latest hash value published on the unalterable public media (i.e. newspaper). Then they verify all of the hash values are correctly computed as follows: $h_{i+k} \overset{?}{=} H(h_{i+k-1}|T_{i+k}|root_{i+k})$, where $k = 1, 2, ..., m - i$. If all verifications are successful, then they can be ensured that the timestamped proof is trustworthy.

Whenever a dispute occurs about a contract, either party can present the original contract document $\mathcal{C}^*$, the signed contract $\mathbf{CT} = (H(\mathcal{C}), T_d, A, B, Sig_A, Sig_B, Cert_A, Cert_B)$ and its timestamp to a judge for dispute resolution. To verify that parties $A$ and $B$ had indeed committed to the contract before time $T_i$, the judge first tests if the following equations are true:

$$H(\mathcal{C}^*) \overset{?}{=} H(\mathcal{C});$$
$$Sig_A \overset{?}{=} \mathsf{Sign}_A(H(\mathcal{C})|T_d|A|B);$$
$$Sig_B \overset{?}{=} \mathsf{Sign}_B(H(\mathcal{C})|T_d|A|B|Sig_A).$$

Then the judge verifies the timestamp following the same procedure as discussed earlier in this subsection. The contract is declared valid only if the signed contract and the timestamp both pass verification.

## 4    Discussion and Analysis

**The First Party is Dishonest.** In any contract signing scenario, the party who signs first is always in an unfavorable situation since he is the first to make a commitment. The second party always has two options to choose depending on which one is in his favor. The best choice for the first party $A$ is to set $T_d$ as early as possible so that party $B$ is left with little time to exploit the situation. Nevertheless, $A$ may try to cheat $B$ by modifying content of the contract, delaying to send her signature, or changing the deadline $T_d$. But none of these methods can bring $A$ any advantage over $B$.

**The Second Party is Dishonest.** As the last one to commit to the contract, the second party $B$ can always choose whether or not to commit the contract, and hence possesses obvious advantages over the first committer $A$. Specifically, a dishonest $B$ can launch attacks by modifying the deadline $T_d$, delaying contract signing, or modifying the contract content. But these attacks will be easily detected by the timestamping server.

**Contract Privacy.** Privacy of content of a signed contract is well protected from disclosure by hashing the contract instead of submitting the original contract document. As a result, even the timestamping server does not know the content, but only a hash over the contract. Only when a dispute occurs between the signing parties will the contract document need to be disclosed for dispute resolution.

**Performance.** The proposed scheme is very concise with only three message transmissions. The computation cost for the first party is only one signature generation, while the second party needs to verify the first party's signature and then generate his own signature. For each contract timestamping request, the timestamping server needs to verify two signatures, which is insignificant for a resourceful server. The computation cost of the timestamping server is on the order of $O(n)$ where $n$ is the number of requests for timestamping services, so the proposed protocol scales to the number of requests.

## 5   Conclusion

In this paper, we have proposed a practical fair electronic contract signing protocol which does not require any online or offline TTP. The proposed protocol relies on a trustworthy timestamping service which can be implemented without any trusted third party. The protocol contains only three messages and is very efficient in computation and communication. We have also provided a detailed analysis on its security and performance. Due to its simplicity and efficiency, the proposed protocol is highly practical for many e-commerce applications.

## References

1. Goldreich, O.: A simple protocol for signing contracts. In: Proc. CRYPTO 1983, pp. 133–136. Plenum Press (1983)
2. Ben-Or, M., Goldreich, O., Micali, S., Rivest, R.L.: A Fair Protocol for Signing Contracts. IEEE Trans. Inf. Theory **36**(1), 40–46 (1990)
3. Asokan, N., Shoup, V., Waidner, M.: Optimistic fair exchange of digital signatures. In: Nyberg, K. (ed.) EUROCRYPT 1998. LNCS, vol. 1403, pp. 591–606. Springer, Heidelberg (1998)
4. Ateniese, G.: Efficient verifiable encryption (and Fair Exchange) of digital signature. In: Proc. ACM Conf. CCS 1999, pp. 138–146. ACM Press (1999)
5. Bao, F., Deng, R.H., Mao, W.: Efficient and practical fair exchange protocols with off-line TTP. In: Proc. IEEE Symp. Security and Privacy, pp. 77–85 (1998)

6. Kim, T., Huang, L.-S., Perrig, A., Jackson, C., Gligor, V.: Accountable key infrastructure (AKI): a proposal for a public-key validation infrastructure. In: Proc. of the International World Wide Web Conference (WWW) (2013)
7. Haber, S., Stornetta, W.S.: How to Time-stamp a Digital Document. Journal of Cryptology **3**(2), 99–111 (1991)
8. Nakamoto, S.: Bitcoin: A Peer-to-Peer Electronic Cash System. http://bitcoin.org/bitcoin.pdf (2008)

# New Message Authentication Code
# Based on APN Functions and Stream Ciphers

Teng Wu$^{(\boxtimes)}$ and Guang Gong

Department of Electrical and Computer Engineering,
University of Waterloo, Waterloo, ON N2L 3G1, Canada
teng.wu@uwaterloo.ca

**Abstract.** After the concept of the active wiretapper was proposed, integrity protection became more important than ever before. Therefore, message authentication code, a method that protects the message from being modified in an undetectable way, attracts more attention. In this paper, we propose a new message authentication code based on APN functions and stream ciphers. This new construction has provable security, which proves that the probability of successful substitution forgery attacks against our new message authentication code is upper bounded by a negligible value. We implement our algorithm, and compare its time consumption with the time consumption of EIA1, the message authentication code used in the 4G LTE system. The results show that our algorithm is much faster than EIA1. Moreover, our new construction is resistant to cycling and linear forgery attacks, which can be applied to EIA1.

**Keywords:** MAC · APN · AXU · Efficient · Security

## 1 Introduction

When the active wiretapper was proposed [14], integrity protection attracted more attention. Simmons [11] proposed the first authentication model using Message Authentication Code (MAC). In his paper, Simmons demonstrated two different attacking models against MAC: the impersonation forgery attack and the substitution forgery attack. Impersonation forgery means that the opponent can forge without intercepting any message-tag pairs, and substitution forgery means that the opponent can forge by observing some message-tag pairs. The success rate of these two attacks are denoted by $P_I$ and $P_S$ respectively.

Many MACs are constructed on top of hash functions. There are two branches of constructing MACs by hash functions. The first one is based on the universal hash functions, such as Stinson's work [12]. Another branch uses cryptographic hash functions to construct MAC, such as HMAC [7].

This paper focuses on the constructions based on universal hash functions. Krawczyk demonstrated that any Almost XOR Universal (AXU) hash function is equivalent to a secure message authentication code [6]. The definition of AXU hash function is given below.

© Springer International Publishing Switzerland 2015
M. Qiu et al. (Eds.): NSS 2015, LNCS 9408, pp. 395–402, 2015.
DOI: 10.1007/978-3-319-25645-0_28

**Definition 1.** *Let $\mathcal{H} = \{h|h : \mathcal{A} \to \mathcal{B}\}$. If*

$$\max_{a,a' \in \mathcal{A}, b \in \mathcal{B}} Pr_h[h(a) + h(a') = b] = \epsilon,$$

*the hash function family $\mathcal{H}$ is called $\epsilon$-AXU hash function family.*

The MACs constructed using AXU hash function families are called AXU-MAC, such as GCM [9], EIA1 (UIA2) [1]. GCM is standardized by NIST as an authenticated encryption (AE) scheme, and EIA1 is the integrity protection algorithm deployed in the 4G LTE system. These two MACs are similar, because both of them are based on the evaluation of polynomials. We call such kind of MACs polynomial based MACs in this paper. The security proof of polynomial based MACs is based on AXU property of the underlying hash function families. The difference between these two is that EIA1 uses a method called secure truncation [2] to get a fixed-length output, while GCM just simply truncates the output to a fixed size.

The definition of AXU hash function family is quite similar to the definition of APN function, which is defined as follows.

**Definition 2.** *Let $f(x) : \mathbb{F}_{2^n} \mapsto \mathbb{F}_{2^n}$. For any $a, b \in \mathbb{F}_{2^n}$, we denote*

$$\delta(a, b) = \#\{x \in \mathbb{F}_{2^n}, f(x) + f(x + a) = b\}.$$

*If*

$$\max_{a \neq 0, b \in \mathbb{F}_{2^n}} \delta(a, b) = 2,$$

*the function $f(x)$ is called almost perfect nonlinear (APN) function.*

Thus, it is straightforward that APN functions can be used to construct AXU MACs. Chanson *et al.* [4] proposed MACs based on functions with optimal nonlinearity for the first time. Ding *et al.* [5] and Carlet *et al.* [3] continued the work of Chanson *et al.*, and proposed more constructions. Jian *et al.* [8] showed that the relationship between perfect nonlinearity functions and universal hash functions, and constructed an authentication code based on universal hash function.

## 1.1 Our Contributions

Although our construction is based on APN functions, it is different from the previous work. All the previous constructions can only map from $m$-bit input to $n$-bit output. Compared with CBC-MAC, HMAC, and XOR-MAC, such constructions are very inflexible. The length of the message is fixed, which means to protect an $L$-bit message, we need $\lceil L/m \rceil \times n$-bit tags. Our construction can take any length of input, and output $n$ bits. As the previous work, we can prove the security of our construction by proving our MAC is an AXU MAC, and the probability of a substitution forgery attack is upper bounded by a negligible value.

We implement our algorithm, and compare it with EIA1, which is also an AXU MAC. The experiment results demonstrate that our algorithm is much faster than EIA1. Moreover, our construction is resistant to the cycling attack [10] and the linear forgery attack [13], which can be applied to EIA1.

## 1.2   Organization

This paper is organized as follows. Section 2 demonstrates a new construction of MAC, and gives a theorem that proves the security of the construction. Section 3 discusses the efficiency and implementation issues. The experiment results are presented in this section as well. The last section, Section 4, concludes the whole paper.

## 1.3   Notations

For the purpose of this paper, we list all the notations used in the rest sections.

**Table 1.** Notations

| Notation | Explanation |
|---|---|
| $GF(2^n)$ or $\mathbb{F}_{2^n}$ | The Galois Field with $2^n$ elements. |
| $\mathbb{F}_2^n$ | The $n$ dimensional vector space over $\mathbb{F}_2$. |
| $\mathbf{M} = \{M_0, \cdots, M_{m-1}\}$, $M_i \in GF(2^n)$ for $0 \le i < m$ | The vector over a Galois Field $GF(2^m)$. |
| $a \| b$ | The concatenation of $a$ and $b$. |

# 2   New Construction Based on APN Functions and Security Analysis

In this section, we present a new construction of MAC based on APN functions. To prove the security of the new MAC, we make two assumptions. The first one is that the underlying cipher $\mathcal{C}$ maps an integrity key to a key stream uniformly. Formally, let the integrity key size be $k$ and the length of the key stream generated by $\mathcal{C}$ using key $K$ be $len$. When $len \le k$, there are $2^{k-len}$ different values of $K$, which can generate this key stream. When $len > k$, this key stream is generated by one possible $K$ with probability $2^{k-len}$. The second assumption is that any two $n$-bit tuples generated by $\mathcal{C}$ are independent.

## 2.1   Construction

We use $n$, $k$ and $l$ to denote the length of the output, the key and the number of blocks in the message respectively. Note that the size of one block is the same as the length of the output.

We construct a MAC from $\mathbb{F}_2^* \times \mathbb{F}_2^k$ to $\mathbb{F}_2^n$ using an APN function $f(x)$ : $\mathbb{F}_2^n \to \mathbb{F}_2^n$ and an underlying cipher $\mathcal{C}$. We remark that the underlying cipher $\mathcal{C}$ is a stream cipher or a block cipher (keyed hash function) in counter mode. For a stream cipher or a block cipher in counter mode, there are two stages, the initializing phase and running phase, which are denoted as **Init** and **Gen** in the following pseudo code respectively. **Init**$(K,N,\mathcal{C})$ means initialize the cipher with integrity key and the nonce, and **Gen**$(\mathcal{C}, \mathbf{i})$ means get the $i$-th $n$-bit block from the key stream generated by $\mathcal{C}$. Our construction takes four inputs. The first one is the message, followed by the length of this message in bit. The third input is the integrity key, and the last argument is the nonce.

---

**Algorithm 1.** MAC

---

**Input**: Message ($\overline{\mathbf{M}}$), Length of $\overline{\mathbf{M}}$ ($L$), Key ($K$), Nonce ($N$)
$len \leftarrow L/n$;
$res \leftarrow L \bmod n$;
$ret = 0$;
$\mathtt{Init}(K,N,\mathcal{C})$;
**for** $i \leftarrow 0 \ldots len - 1$ **do**
$\quad \mid \quad H_1 \leftarrow \mathtt{Gen}(\mathcal{C}, \mathtt{i})$;
$\quad \mid \quad ret \leftarrow ret + M_i \cdot H_1$;
**end**
$i \leftarrow len$;
**if** $res \neq 0$ **then**
$\quad \mid \quad H_1 \leftarrow \mathtt{Gen}(\mathcal{C}, \mathtt{i})$;
$\quad \mid \quad ret \leftarrow ret + (M_{len}||\overline{\mathbf{0}}) \cdot H_1$;
$\quad \mid \quad i \leftarrow i + 1$;
**end**
$H_1 \leftarrow \mathtt{Gen}(\mathcal{C}, \mathtt{i})$;
$ret \leftarrow ret + L \cdot H_1$;
$(OTP||H_0) \leftarrow \mathtt{Gen}(\mathcal{C}, \mathtt{i})$;
$ret \leftarrow f(ret + H_0) + OTP$;
**return** $ret$;

---

Algorithm 1 demonstrates the computation of the tag. The message is partitioned into blocks, and each block $M_i$ has $n$ bits. If the length of $\overline{\mathbf{M}}$ is not a multiple of $n$, the last block is padded with zeros to make it a complete block, whose length is $n$. $OTP$, $H_0$ and $H_1 \in \mathbb{F}_2^n$ are three random numbers, which are generated by the underlying cipher $\mathcal{C}$.

**Theorem 1.** *If $f(x) : \mathbb{F}_2^n \to \mathbb{F}_2^n$ is an APN function, then the success probability of the substitution forgery attack against Algorithm 1 is upper bounded by*

$$P_S \leq \frac{1}{2^{n-1}} - \frac{1}{2^{2n}}.$$

Due to the page restriction, the proof of this theorem will be shown in the full version of this paper.

## 2.2 Security Analysis

*Remark 1.* Although the complexity of forgery attacks is $O(2^{n-1})$, we still consider this security level is enough, because this bound is for any length of messages. In other words, the bound will not change when the length of the messages increases. To decrease this bound, we can compute in a larger field and apply secure truncation [2] to the tag, the same as EIA1.

Since the new construction is an AXU MAC, it is resistant against most attacks. However, some AXU MACs are prone to cycling attack [10] and linear forgery attack [13]. We only consider these two attacks in the rest part of this section.

**Cycling Attack.** Cycling attack is a kind of attack that can be applied to all polynomial based MACs. The polynomial based MACs have a polynomial evaluation block, which is addressed as follows.

$$T = \sum_i M_i P^{i+1},$$

where $M_i$ is a message block and $P$ is a random number. It treats message as a polynomial over finite field and evaluates this polynomial at $P$. If the order of $P$ is smaller than the length of the message in block, there exists at least one pair of $P^i = P^j, i \neq j$. Then the adversary can switch $M_i$ and $M_j$ without changing the MAC. EIA1 is vulnerable to this attack.

In our algorithm, the sub-key in each round plays a similar role of $P^i$ in polynomial based MAC. However, since our sub-key is generated by a stream cipher each time, the same sub-key appears twice with negligible probability. Moreover, even the same sub-key appears, it is hard to tell the exact position of this sub-key. Thus, the adversary can hardly conduct cycling attack against out algorithm.

**Linear Forgery Attack.** This attack was proposed by Wu and Gong on Wisec13'. Because of the linear structure, known two pairs of message and tag pair generated by EIA1, the adversary can forge up to $2^{32}$ message and tag pairs. The new construction in this paper is resistant to this attack, because the sub-key is generated by a stream cipher, and the degree of APN function is higher. The structure is no longer linear.

## 3   Implementation and Efficiency

In this section, we present some consideration regarding the implementation. At the end of this section, we compare our algorithm with EIA1, a MAC deployed in the 4G LTE system.

### 3.1   Selection of Fields and APN Function

We want our algorithm to work with both the legacy systems and the modern systems. For this reason, our design has four versions, 32-bit, 64-bit, 128-bit and 256-bit.

**Selection of Finite Fields.** The multiplication over finite filed is a necessary block of our algorithm. Assume the defining polynomial of the finite field $GF(2^n)$ over $GF(2)$ is

$$f(x) = x^n + g(x).$$

To make the multiplication more efficient, we want both the degree and the number of terms of $g(x)$ to be as small as possible. Usually, for a USIM card used in cellphones, there is an 8-bit chip inside, which means it can compute 8-bit XOR simultaneously. The 8-bit platform is currently the smallest platform considered by us. Therefore, we restrict the degree of $g(x)$ to be smaller than eight. By exhaustive search, we find the defining polynomial for each version of our design. The defining polynomials are listed in Table 2. Note that for the field $GF(2^{256})$, we cannot find a polynomial satisfies our criteria. Thus, we loosen our condition, and find a polynomial that the degree of $g(x)$ is ten. It is not efficient on the 8-bit platform, because the XOR is computed in two clock cycles. But it is still efficient on the 16-bit and higher platforms.

**Table 2.** Defining Polynomials

| Version | Field | Defining Polynomial |
|---------|-------|---------------------|
| 32-bit | $GF(2^{32})$ | $x^{32} + x^7 + x^6 + x^2 + 1$ |
| 64-bit | $GF(2^{64})$ | $x^{64} + x^4 + x^3 + x + 1$ |
| 128-bit | $GF(2^{128})$ | $x^{128} + x^7 + x^2 + x + 1$ |
| 256-bit | $GF(2^{256})$ | $x^{256} + x^{10} + x^9 + x^8 + x^7 + x^4 + x^2 + x + 1$ |

**Selection of APN Function.** Another critical block is the underlying APN function. There are several constructions of APN functions. Among all those constructions, we are looking for the one that has the following properties.

 - Work in the field $GF(2^n)$, where $n$ is even;
 - Be efficient to compute.

We choose $x^3$ as our underlying APN function, because the computation is relatively efficient. If the field element is represented under a normal basis, the square is simply shifting one bit. To compute $x^3$, we may first compute $x^2$, and then compute $x^2 \cdot x$.

### 3.2   Experiment Result of Efficiency

Since our MAC is based on APN function, we call it AMAC. We implement AMAC and compared it with EIA1. Figure 1 shows the comparison of EIA1 and our algorithm.

In this test, we choose ZUC as our underlying cipher. The experiment is conducted on a Mac Book Pro laptop, which has a 2.6 GHz Intel Core i5 CPU and 8 GB 1600 MHz DDR3 memory. From the figure we can clearly see that our algorithm is overwhelmingly faster than EIA1.

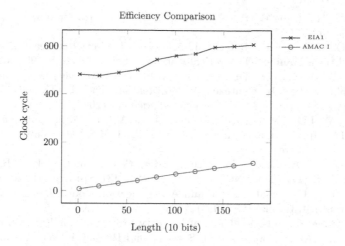

**Fig. 1.** Efficiency comparison among EIA1 and AMAC

## 4   Conclusion

We propose a new MAC construction using APN functions. Compared with previous work based on APN functions, ours can take messages with any length as the input, and output a fixed-length tag as MAC. Such design is more flexible and practical. Like the previous work, we also have security proof for our construction. We compare the security and efficiency of our algorithm with a well known stream ciphers based MAC, EIA1, which is deployed in the 4G LTE system. Our algorithm resists the cycling attack and linear forgery attack, which can be applied to EIA1, and our experiment results show that the speed of our new MAC is faster than EIA1.

## References

1. 3GPP. Specification of The 3GPP Confidentiality and Integrity Algorithms UEA2 & UIA2. Document 1: UEA2 and UIA2 Specification (2006)
2. Bernstein, D.J.: Stronger security bounds for wegman-carter-shoup authenticators. In: Cramer, R. (ed.) EUROCRYPT 2005. LNCS, vol. 3494, pp. 164–180. Springer, Heidelberg (2005)
3. Carlet, C., Ding, C., Niederreiter, H.: Authentication Schemes from Highly Nonlinear Functions. Designs, Codes and Cryptography **40**(1), 71–79 (2006)
4. Chanson, S., Ding, C., Salomaa, A.: Cartesian Authentication Codes from Functions with Optimal Nonlinearity. Theoretical Computer Science **290**(3), 1737–1752 (2003)
5. Ding, C., Niederreiter, H.: Systematic Authentication Codes from Highly Nonlinear Functions. IEEE Transactions on Information Theory **50**(10), 2421–2428 (2004)
6. Krawczyk, H.: LFSR-based hashing and authentication. In: Desmedt, Y.G. (ed.) CRYPTO 1994. LNCS, vol. 839, pp. 129–139. Springer, Heidelberg (1994)

7. Krawczyk, H., Canetti, R., Bellare, M.: HMAC: Keyed-hashing for Message Authentication (1997)
8. Liu, J., Chen, L.: On the Relationships between Perfect Nonlinear Functions and Universal Hash Families. Theoretical Computer Science **513**, 85–95 (2013)
9. McGrew, D.A., Viega, J.: The security and performance of the galois/counter mode (GCM) of operation. In: Canteaut, A., Viswanathan, K. (eds.) INDOCRYPT 2004. LNCS, vol. 3348, pp. 343–355. Springer, Heidelberg (2004)
10. Saarinen, M.-J.O.: Cycling attacks on GCM, GHASH and other polynomial MACs and hashes. In: Canteaut, A. (ed.) FSE 2012. LNCS, vol. 7549, pp. 216–225. Springer, Heidelberg (2012)
11. Simmons, G.J.: Authentication theory/coding theory. In: Blakely, G.R., Chaum, D. (eds.) CRYPTO 1984. LNCS, vol. 196, pp. 411–431. Springer, Heidelberg (1985)
12. Stinson, D.R.: Universal Hashing and Authentication Codes. Designs, Codes and Cryptography **4**(3), 369–380 (1994)
13. Wu, T., Gong, G.: The weakness of integrity protection for lte. In: Proceedings of The Sixth ACM Conference on Security and Privacy in Wireless and Mobile Ntworks, pp. 79–88. ACM (2013)
14. Wyner, A.D.: The Wire-tap Channel. The Bell System Technical Journal **54**(8), 1355–1387 (1975)

# Short Papers: Security Mechanisms

Part E Pest Security Mechanisms

# Assessing Attack Surface with Component-Based Package Dependency

Su Zhang[1]([✉]), Xinwen Zhang[2], Xinming Ou[3],
Liqun Chen[4], Nigel Edwards[4], and Jing Jin[5]

[1] Symantec Corporation, California, USA
westlifezs@gmail.com
[2] Samsung Research America, Mountain View, USA
xinwenzhang@gmail.com
[3] University of South Florida, Tampa, USA
xou@usf.edu
[4] Hewlett-Packard Laboratories, Bristol, UK
{liqun.chen,nigel.edwards}@hp.com
[5] Intuit Inc., California, USA
wendy_jin@intuit.com

**Abstract.** Package dependency has been considered in many vulnerability assessment systems. However, existing approaches are either coarse-grained and do not accurately reveal the influence and severity of vulnerabilities, or do not provide comprehensive (both incoming and outgoing) analysis of attack surface through package dependency. We propose a systematic approach of measuring attack surface exposed by individual vulnerabilities through component level dependency analysis. The metric could potentially extended to calculate attack surfaces at component, package, and system levels. It could also be used to calculate both incoming and outgoing attack surfaces, which enables system administrators to accurately evaluate how much risk that a vulnerability, a component or a package to the complete system, and the risk that is injected to a component or package by packages it depends on in a given system. To our best knowledge, our approach is the first to quantitatively assess attack surfaces of vulnerabilities, components, packages, and systems through component level dependency.

## 1 Introduction

Attack surface usually refers to exploitable resource exposed to attackers [18,19]. The attack surface brought by a vulnerability could be dramatically enlarged when more packages installed depending on the vulnerable application because more resource can be accessed by the attacker to exploit the vulnerability. Therefore the attack surface metric could serve as an effective indicator for vulnerability assessment, which is considered as a critical task for security prioritization. Currently, the well known and de facto standard vulnerability scoring system – common vulnerability scoring system (CVSS) [21] – quantifies the risk

M. Qiu et al. (Eds.): NSS 2015, LNCS 9408, pp. 405–417, 2015.
DOI: 10.1007/978-3-319-25645-0_29

for each known vulnerability. Specifically, CVSS measures exploitability metrics (access vector, access complexity, and authentication) and impact metrics (confidentiality, integrity, and availability loss) of a vulnerability, which are then used to calculate a base score ranging from 0 to 10 indicating the severity of the vulnerability.

Moreover, CVSS does not take into consideration of package dependency, which, based on our analysis in this paper, dramatically affects the exploitability of a vulnerability, especially when it appears in a prevalent package used by many other packages. Therefore current CVSS does not reveal the fact that vulnerabilities on highly depended packages usually bring larger attack surfaces compared to those detected on a client application, even when they have the same CVSS scores. Because packages depended by a number of applications are usually more exposable than "ground" software (with no dependent), attackers have more incentive to intrude a system through each of these dependents (or their dependents). Therefore, the attack surface brought by package dependency should not be ignored, and accurately measuring the attack surface is non-trivial when evaluating vulnerability severity.

Researchers have proposed to measure risk with the consideration of package dependency. Neuhaus et al. [23] study package dependency on Red Hat systems, and infer beauty packages (with low risk) and beast packages (high risk) based on the inter-package dependencies and historical vulnerability information for each package. Their output can be used by developers to choose dependable packages with low risks or historical vulnerabilities. *But they only consider the number of historical vulnerabilities as the risk factor for each package, rather than measuring the attack surface brought by known vulnerabilities on a given system.* Raemaekers et al. [31] study the risk of a package brought by third party libraries. They evaluate potential risks from third party applications by considering if the referenced packages are well scrutinized, the number of referenced packages, and the number of classes with referenced libraries. *However, they only measure incoming risk (risk brought by third party libraries) at package level, and do not consider any finer-grained (component level) or coarser-grained (system level) incoming attack surface.* Moreover, this work *does not evaluate outgoing attack surfaces*, which are brought by individual vulnerabilities, components, and packages to a system, and are important inputs when prioritizing security related plans such as patching and hardening by system administrators, and choosing dependent packages for developers.

With our approach, vulnerability and component level metrics can assist system administrators in prioritizing patching or hardening plans towards the entire system, while the overall package and system level metrics can help developers to choose secure and reliable development images, platforms, and specific systems. Our solution also helps other stakeholders to observe the evolution of package dependency based attack surface for a given system.

## 2   Overview

### 2.1   A Real Motivating Example

To motivate our attack surface analysis with package dependency, we systematically analyze the risk trend of a set of VMware products through VMware Security Advisories (VMSA)[1]. Each VMSA indicates an official notification regarding a set of known security vulnerabilities that affects VMware products, each of which represents a Common Vulnerabilities and Exposures (CVE) record included in the U.S. National Vulnerability Database (NVD[2]). Each VMSA entry includes the origin of the vulnerabilities, vulnerability IDs, affected applications, and proposed solutions to the issue. Based on our analysis of VMSA entries from July 2007 to December 2012, we find out that almost two thirds (56/90) of the VMSAs include vulnerabilities originated from third party applications that affect VMware products, as Table 1 shows. For instance, ESX – the last generation hypervisor – may be exploited by vulnerabilities described in 27 VMSAs detected on the Linux management console, which provides management functions for ESX like executing scripts or installing third party agents for hardware monitoring, backup, and system management [1]. For another instance, Java Runtime Environment (JRE) is required by a number of VMware products including ESX, Server, vMA, vCenter, and vCenter Update Manager, therefore a known vulnerability on JRE could possibly make each of these products exploitable. Other major attack surface carriers include OpenSSL (9 out of 90), Kerberos 5 (8 out of 90), Apache Tomcat (6 out of 90), and libxml (6 out of 90). Note that one VMSA usually mentions multiple risks included in different applications (See Table 1 for details).

**Table 1.** Risks from Third Party Packages to VMware Products

| Third-party Package Name | # of VMSAs | Affected VMware Products |
|---|---|---|
| Console Operating System | 27 | ESX |
| JRE | 11 | ESX, Server, vMA, vCenter, vCenter Update Manager |
| OpenSSL | 9 | ESX, ESXi, vCenter |
| kerberos5 | 8 | ESX, ESXi |
| Apache Tomcat | 6 | ESX, vCenter |
| libxml | 6 | ESX |

Our analysis with VMSA motivates a security metric with the consideration of package dependency, which can help system administrator and software developer to identify vulnerabilities on highly depended programs (e.g., JRE and Linux_console) with larger attack surfaces, compared to others such as client side vulnerabilities (see Figure 1). Consequently, the system administrator may want

---

[1]  http://www.vmware.com/security/advisories/

[2]  http://nvd.nist.gov/

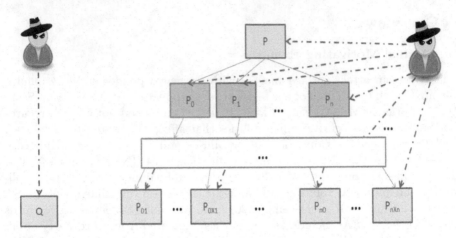

**Fig. 1.** Comparison of attack paths to a vulnerable client side application Q and a highly depended library P.

to patch a JRE vulnerability affecting a number of products earlier than others even they may have the same CVSS score. A system level metric can also help stakeholders in choosing system images with smaller attack surface and monitor how the dependency based attack surfaces evolve over time.

## 2.2   Why Component Level Dependency Analysis?

From the perspective of software engineering, a system can be decomposed into various of packages. One package can usually be further divided into one or more components, each of which is made up from classes with related functions. From above motivating example with VMSA, we have seen attack surfaces from third party packages should not be ignored for risk analysis, and we need to look into package dependencies to know how the attack surface is injected by external packages to a system. When measuring such *dependency based attack surfaces*, we analyze at component level for the following reasons.

*More accurate dependency information than package level:*   Component level dependency is finer-grained than package level, therefore it could locate attack surfaces with higher accuracy. As Figure 2 shows, given two packages with the same dependency map at package level, their attack surfaces could vary significantly if known vulnerabilities on the two packages are on components with different dependency maps. Also, components on the same package should be differentiated as their effects on the attack surface can be significantly different.

*Less complex dependency information than class level:* We keep our dependency analysis at component level rather than go further into class or object level because it is usually difficult to distinguish the sources or causes of vulnerabilities at that level. Each component is a unit to realize a set of related functions. Classes within the same component are usually more integrated and interacted

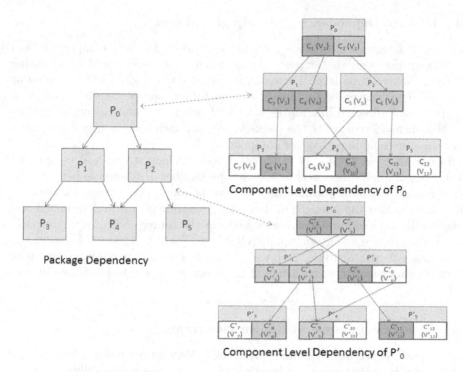

**Fig. 2.** One package level dependency with two different component level dependencies.

compared to those in different components. Therefore for each vulnerability, its exploitability highly depends on its accessibility at the component level. Previous studies also show that a vulnerability becomes significantly more exploitable when attackers know that its component is accessible [25, 26]. Besides, it is usually difficult to construct a map between vulnerabilities and the classes on which they detected. Furthermore, proprietary software vendors usually do not disclose their product information at class level. However security bugs and alerts are usually maintained by database like Bugzilla at component level[3], which makes the vulnerability-component map retrievable [24]. Moreover, the complexity of a class level dependency map is exponentially higher compared to a component level dependency graph. We believe it is infeasible to achieve efficient analysis with class level graph when dealing with a complex system including a large number of software packages.

## 3  Dependency-Based Attack Surface Analysis

This section explains the details of our dependency-based attack surface analysis. Before that we explain the definitions for various attack surface metrics.

---

[3] A vulnerability is usually identified as a security bug in Bugzilla.

### 3.1   Package Dependency at Component Level

In general, a package dependency refers to a code reuse by a component from the library packages that it relies upon. Such code reuse could be at either binary or source code level. For example, third party code could be called as a compiled jar file or be imported as head files in source code. As shown in Figure 2, each directed line represents one dependency relationship, where the destination node represents the package or component that reuses some codes from the source node package or component.

In our analysis, we do not differentiate dependency strength at component level. Even though other metrics such as the number of references between the two components can be obtained and used as the weight, the correlation between these metrics and the strength of dependency is difficult to be determined and judged without a comprehensive analysis over the source code of a target package. Therefore, we assign an equal weight 1 to each dependency between two components in our analysis. But we still keep a weight variable in our algorithms just for future customization of the dependency weight based on different preferences.

### 3.2   Component-Based Attack Surface Analysis

**Vulnerability Attack Surface.** We define VAS as a system wide package dependency based attack surface originated from a given vulnerability. VAS can be used to compare the exploitabilities of different vulnerabilities *within the same system*. The comparison results can be used to prioritize patching or hardening tasks at vulnerability level.

As Algorithm 1 shows, for each vulnerability, we first identify its component. Usually, the vulnerability-component map is provided by software vendors through security advisories, e.g., Oracle Security Advisories[4]. Starting from the component of the target vulnerability, we do a breadth first search until depth $d$, where $d$ is the level of dependency. For example, if package $p_a$ depends on $p_b$ which depends on $p_c$, then when evaluating $p_a$, $p_a$ and $p_b$ are considered but not $p_c$ if $d$ is one. However, all of them are considered when $d$ is larger than one. The depth could be customized based on user preferences. Each component (directly or indirectly) depending on the vulnerable component is considered as part of the attack surface brought by the vulnerability. The impact factor on each component is the attack surface of the target vulnerability exposed through that component. We assign the CVSS score of the vulnerability as the impact factor of the component where it resides (the 'vulnerable component')[5]. For components on multiple depending chains from the vulnerable component, we only consider its closest dependency and ignore the rest. For example, component $c_a$ depends on $c_b$ which depends on $c_c$, and $c_a$ also depends on $c_c$ directly. Under

---

[4] http://www.oracle.com/technetwork/topics/security/
[5] The calculation of impact factors of dependent components will be illustrated in the following paragraph.

this circumstance, we ignore the dependency $c_a \implies c_b \implies c_c$ but only consider $c_a \implies c_c$.

We define a damping factor[6] (ranging from 0 to 1) to represent the residual risk after each level of dependency, which is used to estimate attack surface from/to nested depended packages. The impact factor on a given component equals to the multiplication of the dependency impact value from the component it depends on (the dependency impact value is returned by function depImpact $(c_1, c_2)$ when $c_1$ depends on $c_2$. We assign "1" to all impact values in our experiments because we treat all dependencies equally as mentioned in Section 3.1), the damping factor and the impact factor of the component it depends on. Their impact factor values will be eventually added up to one number, indicating the attack surface of the given vulnerability to the whole system.

In a nutshell, we process a weighted (component-based) dependency graph through breadth first search, we calculate an impact factor for each component (within the dependency graph from the vulnerable component) from the given vulnerability. We then add up all of these impact factors into one number, indicating the attack surface exposed by the target vulnerability.

## 4    Future Work

We propose an attack surface at vulnerability level. The metric could also be aggregated into higher levels. Component level attack surface will let state holders to know how much risk is brought by each individual component and plan hardening accordingly. Package level attack surface can be used to determine which package to depend upon among similar packages. System level attack surface can be used to indicate the health level of individual systems/images. This will help potential users to decide which image to use. Experiments can also be conducted under different environments [5,16,28–30,41,42,46,53,54,56,57] along with other approaches [14,15,32,34–40,44,45,48,51,52]. Moreover, presentation tools like attack graph [10,12,17,47,49,50,55] can be used to visualize risks from software dependencies.

## 5    Related Work

Risks from package dependency have been well researched [2,4,7,13,23,25,31, 43,58]. Neuhaus et al. [23] evaluate risk per Red Hat package based on historical security vulnerabilities and package dependencies. But they do not evaluate attack surface exposed by individual vulnerabilities. Besides, they only measure outgoing risk but not incoming risk for each package. Raemaekers et al. [31] explore the risk from third party applications. Instead of measuring

---

[6] We assign 0.1 as the damping factor for our experiments

[7] We assign "1" to all DIV as mentioned in Section 3.1

[8] The damping factor represents the residual risk after each level of dependency. User can assign a value between 0 and 1 based on their own estimation.

---

**Algorithm 1.** Dependency-based Attack Surface Measurement for Individual Vulnerabilities: **VAS**($v_0, d$)

---

**Input: Parameters:** $v_0$ – the Target vulnerability; $d$ – Depth of assessment.
    **System configurations:**
    A map between the vulnerability $v_0$ and its component component ($v_0$).
    A system wide component dependency map (dependents of component c are depen-
    dOn(c)).
**Output:** The package dependency based attack surface VAS brought by vulnerability
    $v_0$.
    $c_0 \leftarrow$ component($v_0$) {Retrieve the vulnerable component}
    Queue Q $\leftarrow (c_0, 0)$ {Q is a queue of pairs (vulnerableComponent, depth)}
    Table $v_0.t \leftarrow$ *empty table*
    {$v_0.t$ is a table tracking processed components. The key is the affected component
    and the value is its impact factor from vulnerability $v_0$.}
    $v_0.t$.put($c_0, v_0.cvss$) {The impact factor of $c_0$ equals to the CVSS score of $v_0$}
    **while** Q is not empty **do**
        $(c_n, n) \leftarrow$ dequeue(Q)
        **if** $n \geq d$ **then**
            continue {if current component has already reached the pre-defined deepest
            level, then no need to retrieve its dependents}
        **end if**
        **for each** $c_k$ in dependOn(c) **do**
            **if** $v_0.t$.containsKey ($c_k$) **then**
                continue
                {If the component has been previously processed, then we skip it}
            **end if**
            Q.enqueue($c_k, n + 1$) {Update Q in order to process dependents of $c_k$ if within
            our predefined depth}
            $IF_c = v_0.t$.get(c) {retrieve the impact factor of the current component c}
            $DIV = depImpact(c, c_k)$
            { $depImpact(c, c_k)$ returns dependency impact value[7]between c and $c_k$.}
            $IF = DIV \times DF \times IF_c$ {DF means Damping Factor[8]. This is the calculation
            of impact factor (IF) of component $c_k$}
            $VAS+ = IF$ {Cumulatively update attack surface}
            $v_0.t$.put($c_k, IF$) {Update processed element table}
        **end for**
    **end while**
    **return** VAS {Sum up all impact factors of $v_0$ into VAS}

---

attack surface from individual known vulnerabilities, they focus on if a referenced package is well scrutinized and the prevalence of usage per package. A set
of work [2,13,43,58] study the importance of component level dependency when
assessing software quality but no concrete security metric has been proposed.
Chowdhury et al. [4] evaluate risk from source code (class) level of dependency
(e.g. complexity, coupling, and cohesion). However, their work is about inferring
unknown vulnerabilities rather than evaluate attack surface for known vulnerabilities.

A number of work study risks from Java applications [6, 8, 9, 20, 22, 26, 27]. Nasiri et al. [22] evaluate the attack surface from J2EE and .Net platform by quantitatively comparing their CVSS scores directly, but no package dependency is considered during the evaluation. Drake et al. [6] evaluate JRE memory corruption attack surface from engineering point of view, but they do not provide quantitative measurement of the attack surface. Gong et al. [9] retrospect the evolution of security mechanism on Java in the past ten years at high level. Both Pérez et al..[27] and Goichon et al. [8] propose vulnerability detection approaches after scanning Java source code. Marouf [20] classifies vulnerabilities specific to Java and proposes possible countermeasures against these threats. Similarly, Parrend et al.[26] classify Java vulnerability at component level rather than source code level.

Work regarding attack surface evaluation have been conducted by researchers [3, 11, 18, 19, 24, 24, 33]. Neuhaus et al. [24] rank vulnerable components in Firefox based on historical detected vulnerabilities. Similar to us, they evaluate risk at component level. However, they consider these components as independent units rather than inter-depended nodes.

The definition of attack surface is also adapted in industry. Similar to [18], which evaluates attack surface over Linux systems, Microsoft attack surface[9] focuses on Windows by enlisting a number of threats based on the configuration of a given system. However, none of these takes package dependency into consideration while measuring system attack surface.

## 6    Conclusions

We define attack surface exposed through package dependency at vulnerability level. Besides outgoing attack surfaces, we propose algorithms calculating incoming attack surfaces injected through package dependency into individual components and packages. Our approach provides systematic methodology to prioritize security tasks for system administrators, and provides inputs for choosing system images for application developers with multiple dependency options.

## References

1. VMware ESX and VMware ESXi - The Market Leading Production-Proven Hypervisors. VMware Inc. (2009). http://www.vmware.com/files/pdf/VMware-ESX-and-VMware-ESXi-DS-EN.pdf
2. Abate, P., Di Cosmo, R., Boender, J., Zacchiroli, S.: Strong dependencies between software components. In: Proceedings of the 2009 3rd International Symposium on Empirical Software Engineering and Measurement, pp. 89–99. IEEE Computer Society (2009)
3. Cheng, P., Wang, L., Jajodia, S., Singhal, A.: Aggregating cvss base scores for semantics-rich network security metrics. In: Proceedings of the 31st IEEE International Symposium on Reliable Distributed Systems (SRDS 2012). IEEE Computer Society (2012)

---

[9] http://www.microsoft.com/en-us/download/details.aspx?id=24487

4.  Chowdhury, I., Zulkernine, M.: Can complexity, coupling, and cohesion metrics be used as early indicators of vulnerabilities?. In: Proceedings of the 2010 ACM Symposium on Applied Computing, pp. 1963–1969. ACM (2010)
5.  DeLoach, S.A., Ou, X., Zhuang, R., Zhang, S.: Model-driven, moving-target defense for enterprise network security. In: Bencomo, N., France, R., Cheng, B.H.C., Aßmann, U. (eds.) Models@run.time. LNCS, vol. 8378, pp. 137–161. Springer, Heidelberg (2014)
6.  Drake, J.J.: Exploiting memory corruption vulnerabilities in the java runtime (2011)
7.  Ellison, R.J., Goodenough, J.B., Weinstock, C.B., Woody, C.: Evaluating and mitigating software supply chain security risks. Technical report, DTIC Document (2010)
8.  Goichon, F., Salagnac, G., Parrend, P., Frénot, S.: Static vulnerability detection in java service-oriented components. Journal in Computer Virology, 1–12 (2012)
9.  Gong, L.: Java security: a ten year retrospective. In: Annual Computer Security Applications Conference, ACSAC 2009, pp. 395–405. IEEE (2009)
10. Homer, J., Zhang, S., Ou, X., Schmidt, D., Du, Y., Rajagopalan, S.R., Singhal, A.: Aggregating vulnerability metrics in enterprise networks using attack graphs. Journal of Computer Security **21**(4), 561–597 (2013)
11. Howard, M., Pincus, J., Wing, J.: Measuring relative attack surfaces. In: Computer Security in the 21st Century, pp. 109–137 (2005)
12. Huang, H., Zhang, S., Ou, X., Prakash, A., Sakallah, K.: Distilling critical attack graph surface iteratively through minimum-cost sat solving. In: Proceedings of the 27th Annual Computer Security Applications Conference, pp. 31–40. ACM (2011)
13. Khan, M.A., Mahmood, S.: A graph based requirements clustering approach for component selection. Advances in Engineering Software **54**, 1–16 (2012)
14. Li, T., Zhou, X., Brandstatter, K., Raicu, I.: Distributed key-value store on hpc and cloud systems. In: 2nd Greater Chicago Area System Research Workshop (GCASR). Citeseer (2013)
15. Li, T., Zhou, X., Brandstatter, K., Zhao, D., Wang, K., Rajendran, A., Zhang, Z., Raicu, I.: Zht: A light-weight reliable persistent dynamic scalable zero-hop distributed hash table. In: 2013 IEEE 27th International Symposium on Parallel & Distributed Processing (IPDPS), pp. 775–787. IEEE (2013)
16. Liu, X., Edwards, S., Riga, N., Medhi, D.: Design of a software-defined resilient virtualized networking environment. In: 11th International Conference on the Design of Reliable Communication Networks (DRCN), pp. 111–114. IEEE (2015)
17. Lv, Z., Su, T.: 3D seabed modeling and visualization on ubiquitous context. In: SIGGRAPH Asia 2014 Posters, SA 2014, pp. 33:1–33:1. ACM, New York (2014)
18. Manadhata, P., Wing, J.M.: Measuring a system's attack surface. Technical report, DTIC Document (2004)
19. Manadhata, P.K., Wing, J.M.: An attack surface metric. IEEE Transactions on Software Engineering **37**(3), 371–386 (2011)
20. Marouf, S.M.: An Extensive Analysis of the Software Security Vulnerabilities that exist within the Java Software Execution Environment. PhD thesis, University of Wisconsin (2008)
21. Mell, P., Scarfone, K., Romanosky, S.: A complete guide to the common vulnerability scoring system version 2.0. In: Published by FIRST-Forum of Incident Response and Security Teams, pp. 1–23 (2007)
22. Nasiri, S., Azmi, R., Khalaj, R.: Adaptive and quantitative comparison of J2EE vs. net based on attack surface metric. In: 2010 5th International Symposium on Telecommunications (IST), pp. 199–205. IEEE (2010)

23. Neuhaus, S., Zimmermann, T.: The beauty and the beast: vulnerabilities in red hat's packages. In: Proceedings of the 2009 Conference on USENIX Annual Technical Conference, USENIX 2009, p. 30. USENIX Association, Berkeley (2009)
24. Neuhaus, S., Zimmermann, T., Holler, C., Zeller, A.: Predicting vulnerable software components. In: Proceedings of the 14th ACM Conference on Computer and Communications Security, pp. 529–540. ACM (2007)
25. Parrend, P.: Enhancing automated detection of vulnerabilities in java components. In: International Conference on Availability, Reliability and Security, ARES 2009, pp. 216–223. IEEE (2009)
26. Parrend, P., Frénot, S.: Classification of component vulnerabilities in java service oriented programming (SOP) platforms. In: Chaudron, M.R.V., Ren, X.-M., Reussner, R. (eds.) CBSE 2008. LNCS, vol. 5282, pp. 80–96. Springer, Heidelberg (2008)
27. Pérez, P.M., Filipiak, J., Sierra, J.M.: LAPSE+ static analysis security software: Vulnerabilities detection in java EE applications. In: Park, J.J., Yang, L.T., Lee, C. (eds.) FutureTech 2011, Part I. CCIS, vol. 184, pp. 148–156. Springer, Heidelberg (2011)
28. Qian, H., Andresen, D.: Jade: An efficient energy-aware computation offloading system with heterogeneous network interface bonding for ad-hoc networked mobile devices. In: 15th IEEE/ACIS International Conference on Software Engineering, Artificial Intelligence, Networking and Parallel/Distributed Computing (SNPD) (2014)
29. Qian, H., Andresen, D.: Emerald: Enhance scientific workflow performance with computation offloading to the cloud. In: 2015 IEEE/ACIS 14th International Conference on Computer and Information Science (ICIS), pp. 443–448. IEEE (2015)
30. Qian, H., Andresen, D.: An energy-saving task scheduler for mobile devices. In: 2015 IEEE/ACIS 14th International Conference on Computer and Information Science (ICIS), pp. 423–430. IEEE (2015)
31. Raemaekers, S., van Deursen, A., Visser, J.: Exploring risks in the usage of third party libraries. In: The Goal of the BElgian-NEtherlands Software eVOLution Seminar, p. 31 (2011)
32. Su, Y., Wang, Y., Agrawal, G., Kettimuthu, R.: Sdquery dsi: integrating data management support with a wide area data transfer protocol. In: Proceedings of the International Conference on High Performance Computing, Networking, Storage and Analysis, p. 47. ACM (2013)
33. Vijayakumar, H., Jakka, G., Rueda, S., Schiffman, J., Jaeger, T.: Integrity walls: Finding attack surfaces from mandatory access control policies. In: Proceedings of the 7th ACM Symposium on Information, Computer, and Communications Security (ASIACCS 2012), May 2012
34. Wang, J.J.-Y., Sun, Y., Gao, X.: Sparse structure regularized ranking. Multimedia Tools and Applications, 1–20 (2014)
35. Wang, K., Liu, N., Sadooghi, I., Yang, X., Zhou, X., Lang, M., Sun, X.-H., Raicu, I.: Overcoming hadoop scaling limitations through distributed task execution
36. Wang, K., Zhou, X., Chen, H., Lang, M., Raicu, I.: Next generation job management systems for extreme-scale ensemble computing. In: Proceedings of the 23rd International Symposium on High-Performance Parallel and Distributed Computing, pp. 111–114. ACM (2014)
37. Wang, K., Zhou, X., Qiao, K., Lang, M., McClelland, B., Raicu, I.: Towards scalable distributed workload manager with monitoring-based weakly consistent resource stealing. In: Proceedings of the 24rd International Symposium on High-Performance Parallel and Distributed Computing, pp. 219–222. ACM (2015)

38. Wang, K., Zhou, X., Li, T., Zhao, D., Lang, M., Raicu, I.: Optimizing load balancing and data-locality with data-aware scheduling. In: 2014 IEEE International Conference on Big Data (Big Data), pp. 119–128. IEEE (2014)
39. Wang, Y., Nandi, A., Agrawal, G.: Saga: array storage as a DB with support for structural aggregations. In: Proceedings of the 26th International Conference on Scientific and Statistical Database Management, p. 9. ACM (2014)
40. Wang, Y., Su, Y., Agrawal, G.: Supporting a light-weight data management layer over hdf5. In: 2013 13th IEEE/ACM International Symposium on Cluster, Cloud and Grid Computing (CCGrid), pp. 335–342. IEEE (2013)
41. Wei, F., Roy, S., Ou, X., Robby.: Amandroid: A precise and general intercomponent data flow analysis framework for security vetting of android apps. In: Proceedings of the 2014 ACM SIGSAC Conference on Computer and Communications Security, pp. 1329–1341. ACM (2014)
42. Xiong, H., Zheng, Q., Zhang, X., Yao, D.: Cloudsafe: Securing data processing within vulnerable virtualization environments in the cloud. In: 2013 IEEE Conference on Communications and Network Security (CNS), pp. 172–180. IEEE (2013)
43. Yamaguchi, F., Lindner, F., Rieck, K.: Vulnerability extrapolation: assisted discovery of vulnerabilities using machine learning. In: Proceedings of the 5th USENIX conference on Offensive Technologies, p. 13. USENIX Association (2011)
44. Zhang, H., Diao, Y., Immerman, N.: Recognizing patterns in streams with imprecise timestamps. Proceedings of the VLDB Endowment 3(1–2), 244–255 (2010)
45. Zhang, H., Diao, Y., Immerman, N.: On complexity and optimization of expensive queries in complex event processing. In: Proceedings of the 2014 ACM SIGMOD International Conference on Management of Data, pp. 217–228. ACM (2014)
46. Zhang, S.: Deep-diving into an easily-overlooked threat: Inter-vm attacks. Whitepaper, provided by Kansas State University, TechRepublic/US2012 (2013). http://www.techrepublic.com/resourcelibrary/whitepapers/deep-diving-into-an-easilyoverlooked-threat-inter-vm-attacks
47. Zhang, S.: Quantitative risk assessment under multi-context environments. PhD thesis, Kansas State University (2014)
48. Zhang, S., Caragea, D., Ou, X.: An empirical study on using the national vulnerability database to predict software vulnerabilities. In: Hameurlain, A., Liddle, S.W., Schewe, K.-D., Zhou, X. (eds.) DEXA 2011, Part I. LNCS, vol. 6860, pp. 217–231. Springer, Heidelberg (2011)
49. Zhang, S., Ou, X., Homer, J.: Effective network vulnerability assessment through model abstraction. In: Holz, T., Bos, H. (eds.) DIMVA 2011. LNCS, vol. 6739, pp. 17–34. Springer, Heidelberg (2011)
50. Zhang, S., Ou, X., Singhal, A., Homer, J.: An empirical study of a vulnerability metric aggregation method. In: The 2011 International Conference on Security and Management (SAM 2011), Special Track on Mission Assurance and Critical Infrastructure Protection (STMACIP 2011) (2011)
51. Zhang, S., Zhang, X., Ou, X.: After we knew it: empirical study and modeling of cost-effectiveness of exploiting prevalent known vulnerabilities across iaas cloud. In: Proceedings of the 9th ACM Symposium on Information, Computer and Communications Security, pp. 317–328. ACM (2014)
52. Zhao, D., Zhang, Z., Zhou, X., Li, T., Wang, K., Kimpe, D., Carns, P., Ross, R., Raicu, I.: Fusionfs: Toward supporting data-intensive scientific applications on extreme-scale high-performance computing systems. In: 2014 IEEE International Conference on Big Data (Big Data), pp. 61–70. IEEE (2014)

53. Zheng, C., Zhu, S., Dai, S., Gu, G., Gong, X., Han, X., Zou, W.: Smartdroid: An automatic system for revealing ui-based trigger conditions in android applications. In: Proceedings of the Second ACM Workshop on Security and Privacy in Smartphones and Mobile Devices, SPSM 2012, pp. 93–104. ACM, New York (2012)

54. Zheng, Q., Zhu, W., Zhu, J., Zhang, X.: Improved anonymous proxy re-encryption with cca security. In: Proceedings of the 9th ACM Symposium on Information Computer and Communications Security, ASIA CCS 2014, pp. 249–258. ACM, New York (2014)

55. Zhou, X., Sun, X., Sun, G., Yang, Y.: A combined static and dynamic software birthmark based on component dependence graph. In: International Conference on Intelligent Information Hiding and Multimedia Signal Processing, pp. 1416–1421. IEEE (2008)

56. Zhuang, R., Zhang, S., Bardas, A., DeLoach, S.A., Ou, X., Singhal, A.: Investigating the application of moving target defenses to network security. In: 2013 6th International Symposium on Resilient Control Systems (ISRCS), pp. 162–169. IEEE (2013)

57. Zhuang, R., Zhang, S., DeLoach, S.A., Ou, X., Singhal, A.: Simulation-based approaches to studying effectiveness of moving-target network defense. In: National Symposium on Moving Target Research (2012)

58. Zimmermann, T., Nagappan, N.: Predicting defects using network analysis on dependency graphs. In: ACM/IEEE 30th International Conference on Software Engineering, ICSE 2008, pp. 531–540. IEEE (2008)

# An Abstraction for the Interoperability Analysis of Security Policies

Javier Baliosian[1][(✉)] and Ana Cavalli[2]

[1] School of Engineering, University of the Republic, Montevideo, Uruguay
baliosian@fing.edu.uy
[2] Department of Network Software, TELECOM SudParis, Evry, France
ana.cavalli@it-sudparis.eu

**Abstract.** Complex interactions between two organizations, involving sensible information and resources, requires to honor each organization's security policy. This implies to make compatible and combine different sets of policy rules that were designed for different organizations, and, therefore, different subjects, actions, and objects, classified and organized in different manners. However, finding out what is the security policy that emerges from the combination of all the organization-level policies and the higher-level interoperability policy is not an easy task. In this paper we provide a methodology based on Finite State Transducers to analyse this situation modelling policy-rules, mapping entities, combine them, and automatically generate an interoperability set of security policies.

## 1 Introduction

Policies are often used as a means of implementing flexible and adaptive systems for the management of Internet services, distributed systems, and security systems. Among the different domains where policy-based control has been applied one of the most successful is access control and security. Security policies are usually implemented as sets of rules expressing permissions, prohibitions, and obligations.

When two organizations cooperate and set their systems to exchange data and their users to access each other's information, the interoperability between the systems of both entities must be studied and, in particular, the security of such interoperability is a particularly important issue. Therefore the security policies of both organizations must be analysed and, potentially, modified to fit the cooperation objectives. We understand *interoperability* policies as a set of contracts negotiated between two, or more, organizations applied to control their interoperation. Therefore, as we see it, secure interoperability translates into interoperability of security policies and in this paper we will focus more on this issue. The natural questions to make are: (i) what is permitted if we apply the security rules of two organizations at the same time? (ii) are the obligated actions consistent between them and with the prohibitions of both organizations? and, (iii) is the emerging policy in line with their cooperation objectives?

© Springer International Publishing Switzerland 2015
M. Qiu et al. (Eds.): NSS 2015, LNCS 9408, pp. 418–427, 2015.
DOI: 10.1007/978-3-319-25645-0_30

In order to start analysing policies interoperability, we need a common policy modelling abstraction and a means to draw a correspondence map between two organization's entities and procedures. This means not only to simply translate the entity names, but also to translate their interaction manners, which can be also different amongst different organizations.

Once we have modeled policy-rules using a common abstraction, we can detect contradictions between rules (conflicts) and perform further analyses such as writing the new emerging rules back, in order to visualize and study their conformance with the objectives of the organizations' cooperation.

In this paper we propose a common model based on Finite State Transducers (FST), a type of extended Finite State Machine, in a revised and augmented version of the work presented in [1]. To model policy-rules with this particular type of input/output Finite State Machine, we consider the events and actions of the policy-based system as the input and output alphabet and the input and output languages defined by the FST as the patterns of events and actions that an organization's policy permits, prohibits and obligates, respectively. Some of the theoretical existent work on FSTs and some novel algorithms are used in this work to unite, compose, intersect, and complement policy-rules, and to study the interoperability between security policy-rules sets.

The paper is organised as follows. In Section 2 we present related work on interoperability and secure interoperability, and in Section 3, we present the FST-based model and its theoretical basics. Section 4 presents the description of security rules using FSTs and in Section 5 its application to interoperability analysis. Finally, in Section 6 we conclude and sketch some future work.

## 2   Related Work

The work in [3] propose solutions to specify interoperability security policies without conflicts with the local security policy. They propose an extension of OrBAC (Organisation Based Access Control) model to a called O2O (Organisation to Organisation) model. The development of O2O was motivated by the need to model the management of interoperability security rules between systems and more specifically between secured organizations [4]. This approach based on the O2O model has been compared with previous proposals based on the RBAC (Role Based Access Control) model and ABAC (Attribute Based Access Control) and its advantages have been shown. In [2], the authors proposed methods for automatically derivation of secure interoperability rules. In particular, the authors propose methods to anticipate the security interoperability policy and thus to reduce the policy negotiation steps. The authors defined interoperation contracts to control the aforementioned derivation process of interoperability security policies. There are other works such as [6] and [8], but even if these research works provide interesting solutions to secure interoperability issues, they are limited with respect to the automatic creation of secure interoperability policies. Indeed, one of the main contributions of our paper is to propose a new approach for the automatic creation of secure interoperability policies specification.

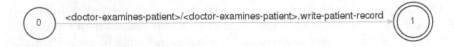

**Fig. 1.** Correspondence between Rule 1 constituents and FST elements.


# 3    Policy Modelling Using $\tau$-Finite State Transducers

As said above, there are many abstractions to model policy rules, however, they suffer from scalability issues. Finite State Transducers have shown several advantages when dealing with large numbers of logic conditions, long strings of symbols and applying pre-processing techniques and heuristics to reduce the complexity of the most expensive inference-related operations.

In this work we consider a policy manager as a transducer that consumes a string of the system events, including context events and actions with pending authorization, and produces a similar string of events that contains the permitted actions, adds the obligated actions, and does not includes actions that were included in the original string but are prohibited by the enforced policy. To depict how the policies are modeled with an example, the Rule 1 below is represented by the transducer depicted in Figure 1, which consumes an event informing that a specific doctor has seen a specific patient and, produces an event that replicates the input (because it is implicitly permitted) plus the action of writing in that particular patient's record. We follow the general convention for FSMs in which State 0 is the initial state and those states represented by a double circle are final. This FST have an additional particularity, the labels on the edges are functions. In particular, for this work, they are Boolean functions defining sets of events instead of a single symbol as in classic transducers. For this reason, there should be a way to specify when an incoming event, lets say "Dr. Gregory House has examined Mr. Walter White", has to be produced, without changes, in the output. With this purpose, an identity flag has been added to the pairs of input/output labels. In the figure, the identity flag is represented with the "<" and ">" symbols.

**Rule 1:** Every time a health professional examines an individual, he or she has to write an entry in the individual's medical record.

The idea of FST labels defining classes of symbols (events in our case) instead only one symbol existed before and was augmented in [1] to use fuzzy membership functions as lables. In this work we use an extension of those concepts, which include predicates as labels and weights that we call $\tau$-FST. It differs from the previous work presented in [1] in the usage of weights on the edges, the generalization of the functions for the labels and registries to facilitate their implementation. Because the focus of this work some of those characteristics are not highlighted in the text below. Additionally, the concept of *semiring* is used for the definitions. Nevertheless, its description is out of the scope of this paper and it is not needed to understand the proposal presented in the following sections. A detailed descriptions of semirings and transducers can be found in [9]. Firstly, we define $\tau$-Finite State Recognizers ($\tau$-FSR), which are needed to define some of the transducers operations.

**Definition 1.** *A* $\tau$*-FSR* $M$ *over a semiring* $(\mathbb{K}, \oplus, \otimes, \overline{0}, \overline{1})$ *is a tuple* $(Q, E, \mathscr{F}, \Pi, S, F, \lambda, \rho)$ *where:* $Q$ *is a finite set of states,* $E$ *is a set of events,* $\mathscr{F}$ *is a set of functions over* $E$, $\Pi$ *is a finite set of transitions* $Q \times \mathscr{F} \cup \{\epsilon\} \times \mathbb{K} \times Q$, $S \subseteq Q$ *is a set of start states,* $F \subseteq Q$ *is a set of final states,* $\lambda$ *is an initial weight and* $\rho$ *a final weight function on the initial and final states respectively.*

Secondly, we define $\tau$-Finite State Transducers ($\tau$-FST) as follows:

**Definition 2.** *A* $\tau$*-FST* $M$ *over a semiring* $(\mathbb{K}, \oplus, \otimes, \overline{0}, \overline{1})$ *is a tuple* $(Q, E, \mathscr{F}, \Pi, S, F, \lambda, \rho)$ *where:*

$Q$ *is a finite set of states,* $E$ *is a set of symbols,* $\mathscr{F}$ *is a set of membership functions over* $E$. $\Pi$ *is a finite set of transitions* $Q \times (\mathscr{F} \cup \{\epsilon\}) \times (\mathscr{F} \cup \{\epsilon\}) \times \mathbb{K} \times Q \times \{-1, 0, 1\}$.[1] $S \subseteq Q$ *is a set of start states,* $F \subseteq Q$ *is a set of final states,* $\lambda$ *is an initial weight and* $\rho$ *a final weight function. For all transitions* $(p, d, r, w, q, 1)$ *it must be the case that* $d = r \neq \epsilon$.

An extension can be defined to let the transducer deal with strings of events in each transition. Regarding the *identity flag* introduced in the definition, it has also its implications in the definition of the *Identity* operation for a given language of events $L$ is $id(L) = \{(w, w) \mid w \in L\}$.

## 4    Writing Rules as $\tau$-FSTs

The FST-based policy model is useful as an analytic tool but not as a policy specification language, for this purpose we use OrBAC [7], a well known policy access framework that includes a high level specification language. OrBAC counts with extensive research and at least three different back-end implementations which makes it a good candidate in order to perform performance and functional comparisons. The details of the integration between MotOrBAC and our FST-based model are out of the scope of this paper. In the following sections we show how policy rules written in OrBAC can be modelled as $\tau$-FSTs. For reasons that will be clearer later in the paper, the modeling strategy is slightly different than the one depicted above. Basically, the action to be authorized or obligated, is disassembled in the Role, Activity, View, and Context components used in OrBAC, which, in this language, correspond with the mos abstract expression of the widely known Subject, Action, and Object. A subject is an particular instance of a role, an action an instance of an activity, and an object an instance of a view. Our $\tau$-FST model for an obligation specified in OrBAC is based on the general obligation automaton described in OrBAC's description [5].

---

[1] The final component of a transition is a sort of "identity flag" used to indicate when an incoming event must be replicated in the output. The negative identity value is to express the obligatory difference between input and output, this is needed to compute the complement of an FST.

## 4.1   Permissions

In a first approach, a *permission* is modelled with a $\tau$-FST that consumes all possible input strings but produces a version of the input string containing only the permitted event patterns. More specifically the subject, the action and the corresponding object are modelled as three different symbols that, without loss of generality, we assume that occur in that order and contiguously in time. Thus, in the context of a system in which everything is prohibited by default, the OrBAC rule `permission(p1,r,a,v,TRUE)` is modelled as the following $\tau$-FST:

$$T_{P+} = \left( id\,(R_P)^* \, \varepsilon \left( \overline{E^* R_P E^*} \right)^* \right)^*$$

where $R_P$ is the $\tau$-FSR that consumes exactly the event string *rav*, $id(X)$ is the identity $\tau$-FST, $\varepsilon(X)$ is a transducer that consumes language $X$ and produces $\epsilon$ always, $^*$ is the *Kleene* closure, and $E^*$ is the language of all possible strings of events.

## 4.2   Prohibitions

Following the modelling idea presented above for permissions, a prohibition is represented by an $\tau$-FST that consumes all possible input strings but produces a version of the input string stripped of the forbidden patterns of events. In the context of a system that permits everything by default, the $\tau$-FST that models the rule `prohibition(p1,r,a,v,TRUE)` is the following:

$$T_{P-} = \left( \varepsilon\,(R_P)^* \, id \left( \overline{E^* R_P E^*} \right)^* \right)^*$$

Because of its simplicity, in this case, and in the case of permission rules above, we present the transducer in a version that accepts a string of any length and many occurrences of the permitted pattern of events. However, later in the paper we will depict stripped down versions that accept only one occurrence of the permitted, prohibited or obligated patterns to keep them legible.

## 5   Interoperability Analysis

As said in Section 1, two organizations willing to interoperate need to negotiate a set of contracts to control their interoperation. In this context secure interoperability translates into interoperability of security policies and the questions we make are: (i) what is permitted to do if we apply the security rules of two organizations at the same time? (ii) are the obligated actions consistent between them and with the prohibitions of both organizations? and, (iii) is the emerging policy in line with their cooperation objectives?

The first obstacle to answer these questions is that the subjects, objects and actions used to define security policies at different organizations may have different names, classifications, and meanings. Therefore, in order to start analysing policy interoperability, we need a common policy modelling abstraction and a means to draw a correspondence map between two organization's entities and procedures. This means not only to simply translate the entity names, but also to translate their interaction manners which can be also different amongst different organizations.

In the section below, we show how to use the composition of transducers to transform the $\tau$-FST representation of rules in order to map their entities and to allow analysing them on a common basis.

## 5.1 $\tau$-FST Composition for Policy Mapping

An $\tau$-FST composition works in the same manner than any other binary relations:

$$R_1 \circ R_2 = \{(x,z) \mid (x,y) \in R_1, (y,z) \in R_2\}$$

This can be seen as a chain of events processing in which the events in the output of the first transducer are used as the input of the second one, with the difference that all the process is modelled by a single FST.

The idea of composition, then, can be used to map the meaning of a policy from one organization to another. To exemplify this, lets consider two hospitals with two similar rules. Hospital H' has Rule 2 and hospital H" has Rule 3, *managing* a medical record includes actions such as *reading*, *writing*, and *signing* one of its entries. However, for H' signing and writing a medical record are things completely different and for H" to sign a medical record is a particular case of writing it. Those rules are modelled as the $\tau$-FSTs $T_{Rule2}$ and $T_{Rule3}$ depicted in figures 2(a) and 2(b) respectively. To describe the composition idea on more simple graphs, we use a simplified representation of those rules in which only one occurrence of the sequence of accepted events, and no other events before or after it, is accepted by the $\tau$-FST.

**Rule 2:** Physicians can manage any medical record.

**Rule 3:** Health Professionals can manage any medical record.

Now, when hospitals H' an H" collaborate, rules from both hospitals have to be considered. For example, a task performed by a physician from H' in H" premises has to be permitted by the rules of both hospitals. However, we need to answer whether a physician from hospital H' is permitted to, for example, write an entry on a medical record at hospital H". To answer this question, we have to compare the rules of both hospitals at a common plane were all the rules speak about the same roles, activities, and views, at least under some given circumstances. Thus, we build a mapping, i.e., a relation, between the names used in Rule 2 and in Rule 3 (e.g., relate physicians to health professionals) for the action of *reading* a medical record; under any other situation that mapping must not be valid. Such a mapping has the shape of the $\tau$-FST $T_{map}$ depicted in Figure 2(c).

The $\tau$-FST $T_{R2\_map} = T_{Rule\,2} \circ T_{map}$ (see Figure 2(d)) models Rule 2 with its output actions written in terms of the entities of H" policy. The $\tau$-FST

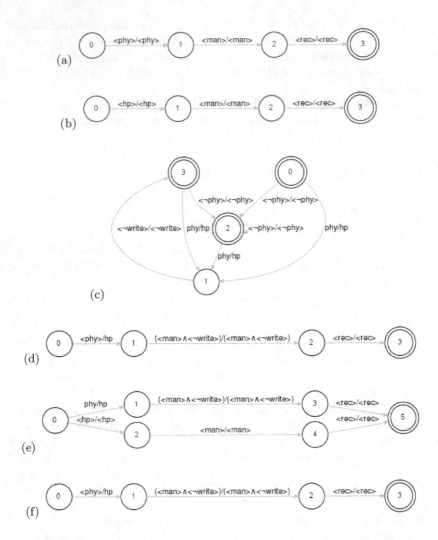

**Fig. 2.** Interoperability Study. (a) FST $T_{Rule2}$ modelling Rule 2. The label *phy* represents the set of *physicians*, *man* represents the class of actions *management* and *rec* the class of objects *medical records*. (b) FST $T_{Rule3}$ modelling Rule 3. The label *hp* represents the set of subjects *health professionals*, *man* represents the class of actions *management* and *rec* the class of objects *medical records*. (c) FST $T_{map}$ which defines a map between the entities of two simple permissions. (d) The $\tau$-FST $T_{R2\_map} = T_{Rule\ 2} \circ T_{map}$. This computation is based on the presumption that $read \rightarrow man$, $man \rightarrow \neg rec$, $man \rightarrow \neg phy$, and $rec \rightarrow \neg phy$. (e) The $\tau$-FST $T_{map\_R3} = T_{map} \circ T_{Rule\ 3}$. This computation is based on the presumption that $read \rightarrow man$, $man \rightarrow \neg rec$, $man \rightarrow \neg hp$, $rec \rightarrow \neg hp$, $rec \rightarrow \neg phy$, $hp \rightarrow \neg phy$. (f) The $\tau$-FST $T_{P_{int}^+} = T_{R2\_map} \cap T_{map\_R3}$. $T_{int}$ is the transducer representing what a subject of H' can do on H" objects when the policies of both organization are applied at the same time.

$T_{map\_R3} = T_{map} \circ T_{Rule} \, 3$ (see Figure 2(e)) models Rule 3 with its input events written in terms of the entities of H' policy. This FST-based mapping does not only creates straight forward name translations between entities but also manages to define a translation that can differ depending on the context or combinations of subjects, objects and actions. We can also think of a translation of the name of a subject depending on the action it is performing or the translation of an action name when it is performed on a particular object and a different one when performed on another.

## 5.2   Interoperability Conflicts Analysis

Once the rules of both organizations are written in a common language of roles, activities, and views, it is possible to start answering the questions on interoperability raised before. To answer the question on what is permitted to do if we apply the security rules of two organizations at the same time, is analogous to find out which are the actions permitted by both sets of rules, which is the same as to compute the intersection of the relations defined by both sets of rules, by computing the intersection of the $\tau$-FSTs that model them.

$\tau$**-FST Intersection.** The intersection of two FSTs is an FST that defines the relation resulting from the intersection of the relations of the two original transducers. FSTs are not always closed under intersection, however, they are closed in the case of $\epsilon$-free letter transducers which we use to model policy-rules in this work. A $\tau$-FST $M = (Q, E, \mathscr{F}, \Pi, S, F)$ is called an $\epsilon$-free letter $\tau$-FST iff $\Pi \in Q \times \mathscr{F} \times \mathscr{F} \times Q \times \{-1, 0, 1\}$.

In this case, the intersection of two $\tau$-FSTs is the intersection of their *underlying* $\tau$-FSRs, that is, the FSR resulting of considering input and output labels on an adge as a single label. The intersection $L(M_1) \cap L(M_2)$ is the language accepted by

$$M = (Q_1 \times Q_2, E, \mathscr{F}, \Pi, S_1 \times S_2, F_1 \times F_2, \lambda', \rho')$$

where

$$\Pi = \{((p_1, q_1), \tau_1 \wedge \tau_2, (p, q)) \mid (p_1, \tau_1, p) \in \Pi_1, (q_1, \tau_2, q) \in \Pi_2\}$$

For example, the intersection of transducer $T_{R2\_map}$ (see Figure 2(d)) with transducer $T_{map\_R3}$ (see Figure 2(e)) is $T_{P_{int}^+}$ (see Figure 2(f)). For more details on how the weights, $\lambda'$, and $\rho'$ are computed see [9]. $T_{int}$ is the transducer representing what a subject of H' can do on H" objects when the policies of both organization are applied at the same time. In this simple case it is easy to see that a *physician* of H' can *read* the *medical records* of H" as if he or she would be a *health professional*. Of course, in the case of any other policy with a realistic number of rules and modelled properly (not in this simplified manner) it would be hard to "read" which actions are permitted, prohibited or obligated under the interoperability scenario. To cope with this problem, we have developed a method to write policies back from their FST representation, however we had to leave it out of this article because space limitations.

The same idea can be used with obligations to answer the second question made before: are the obligated actions consistent between them and with the prohibitions of both organizations? We leave the details of this task out of this paper due to space limitations.

To summarize, the procedure to find out what are the actions that a subject of an organization O' can do on the objects of another organization O", follows the steps below:

1. to model the policies of organization O' as the transducer $T_{O'}$,
2. to model the policies of organization O" as the transducer $T_{O''}$,
3. to model the entity map between O' and O" as the transducer $T_{map}$,
4. to compute $T_{O'\_map} = T_{O'} \circ T_{map}$,
5. to compute $T_{map\_O''} = T_{map} \circ T_{O''}$, and,
6. to compute $T_{int} = T_{O'\_map} \cap T_{map\_O''}$

$T_{int}$ is the transducer which models the set of interoperability policy-rules between O' and O". Please, note that the order in which we present the organizations is relevant.

## 6  Conclusions

In this paper we present a methodology to model security policies with an FST-based abstraction called $\tau$-FST. With their help, we are able to compute what is the security policy that emerges from the combination of all the organization-level policies and the higher-level interoperability policy when two organizations cooperate. We provide a methodology and a set of operations to create rich mappings between entities of different organizations, combine them, and automatically generate an interoperability set of security policies.

To illustrate some of the rules presented in this paper, we use OrBAC as a policy specification language, however, the proposed abstraction is completely independent of that language and can be used to model policies specified in many policy languages.

Future work includes fully integrating the algorithms in a working policy manager, to refine the conflict resolution process using the weights and, possibly, adding learning mechanisms to compute those weights automatically.

## References

1. Baliosian, J., Serrat, J.: Finite state transducers for policy evaluation and conflict resolution. In: Proceedings of the Fifth IEEE International Workshop on Policies for Distributed Systems and Networks, POLICY 2004, pp. 250–259. IEEE (2004)
2. Coma-Brebel, C., Cuppens-Boulahia, N., Cuppens, F., Cavalli, A.R.: Interoperability using O2O contract. In: SITIS 2008: Fourth International Conference on Signal-Image Technology and Internet-Based Dystems, Bali, Indonesia (2008)

3. Cuppens, F., Cuppens-Boulahia, N., Coma, C.: O2O: Virtual private organizations to manage security policy interoperability. In: Bagchi, A., Atluri, V. (eds.) ICISS 2006. LNCS, vol. 4332, pp. 101–115. Springer, Heidelberg (2006)
4. El Maarabani, M., Cavalli, A.: A formal approach for interoperability testing of security rules. In: 2010 Sixth International Conference on Signal-Image Technology and Internet Based Systems, pp. 277–284. IEEE, December 2010. http://ieeexplore. ieee.org/lpdocs/epic03/wrapper.htm?arnumber=5714563
5. Elrakaiby, Y., Cuppens, F., Cuppens-Boulahia, N.: Formal enforcement and management of obligation policies. Data & Knowledge Engineering **71**(1), 127–147 (2012). http://linkinghub.elsevier.com/retrieve/pii/S0169023X11001248
6. Hu, J., Li, R., Lu, Z.-D.: Establishing RBAC-based secure interoperability in decentralized multi-domain environments. In: Nam, K.-H., Rhee, G. (eds.) ICISC 2007. LNCS, vol. 4817, pp. 49–63. Springer, Heidelberg (2007)
7. Kalam, A., Baida, R., Balbiani, P., Benferhat, S., Cuppens, F., Deswarte, Y., Miege, A., Saurel, C., Trouessin, G.: Organization based access control. In: Proceedings POLICY 2003. IEEE 4th International Workshop on Policies for Distributed Systems and Networks, pp. 120–131. IEEE Comput. Soc. (2003). http:// ieeexplore.ieee.org/lpdocs/epic03/wrapper.htm?arnumber=1206966
8. Kapadia, A., Al-Muhtadi, J., Campbell, R.H., Mickunas, D.: IRBAC 2000: Secure Interoperability Using Dynamic Role Translation, May 2000. http://dl.acm.org/ citation.cfm?id=871272
9. Mohri, M.: Weighted automata algorithms. In: Handbook of Weighted Automata, pp. 213–254 (2009). http://www.springerlink.com/index/P872G5Q565H44544.pdf

# Cryptographically Secure On-Chip Firewalling

Jean-Michel Cioranesco[1]($\boxtimes$), Craig Hampel[2], Guilherme Ozari de Almeida[1],
and Rodrigo Portella do Canto[1]

[1] Rambus France, 54 Avenue Hoche, 75008 Pari, France
{jcioranesco,guilherme,rodrigo}@rambus.com
[2] Rambus Inc., 1050 Enterprise Way, Sunnyvale, CA 94089, USA
champel@rambus.com

**Abstract.** As SoCs have become more complex, on-chip interconnect
has transformed into the point of integration for a variety of system
level functions, including security. Integrators have begun to rely on distributed access control hardware to protect resources that are shared
between IP cores executing both trusted and untrusted software. Existing solutions cover enforcement of on-chip access control policies but
they don't secure the programming interface nor the hardware against
possible attacks. As the embedded content increases in theft value, the
on-chip access enforcement will need to consider both software and hardware directed attacks. We introduce a secure on-chip access device that
enables secure and programmable allocation of resources in an SoC by
offering cryptographically signed programming, fault detection and key
integrity. Synthesis results are shown in both ASIC and FPGA implementations.

**Keywords:** SoC security · On-chip firewall · Secure access · Authentication · Fault detection · NoC

## 1 Introduction

The emergence of on-chip-fabric solutions is a natural consequence of Moore's
law. Increasing integration naturally produces greater complexity and hierarchy,
and SoCs have been at the center of this evolution. The evolution of a set of
tools that manage the complexity at the point of integration for these complex
IP blocks has been centered around the on-chip fabric and are now generally
referred to as a NoC or Network-on-Chip. An example of a NoC and its application in a modern SoC is illustrated in Figure 1. Multi-interface integration with
different bus sizes and protocols, in addition to the challenge of floor planning on
a complex SoC have favored the packetization of data over an on-chip network.
On the other hand, bus-based interconnects are very attractive when the system
has difficult timing constraints. This type of SoC architecture is less flexible but
doesn't carry any extra latency due to packet conversion.

Today, the IP cores express their connectivity requirements in the form of
flows which represent the access requirements of a core or a thread. These flows

© Springer International Publishing Switzerland 2015
M. Qiu et al. (Eds.): NSS 2015, LNCS 9408, pp. 428–438, 2015.
DOI: 10.1007/978-3-319-25645-0_31

are used to size and synthesize the network, communicate quality-of-service (QoS) requirements and in a limited way to express the data sharing or non-sharing requirements between a core (or thread) and a resource.

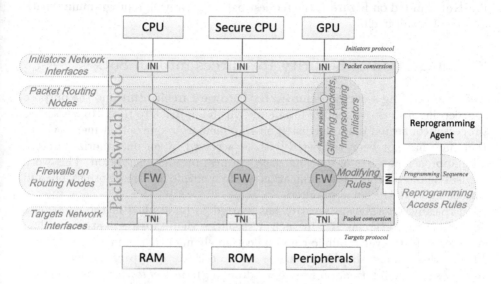

**Fig. 1.** Firewalling in an SoC based on NoC interconnect

These very basic sharing rules are used to configure firewalls that limit an initiator access to a network, a resource, or an address range.

With the introduction of flows that carry special "trusted" status, these firewalls are also being used to create a very rudimentary security barrier between trusted and untrusted flows. This is the beginning of the next significant services that could be offered by NoCs, a heterogeneous multi-core data security integration service.

## 2   Identifying Attack Surfaces on NoCs

Most commons attacks on NoCs are related to QoS considerations and have been well described in previous works [4] [9], but some of them are targeted at data theft. NoC attacks can be classified in three main classes:

- Hijacking: writing to restricted addresses in order to change the system's configuration.
- Extraction of secret information: reading from secure addresses in order to retrieve sensitive data.
- Denial of Service: reducing the system's throughput by replaying or forging request over the NoC.

These attacks are well understood and can be addressed with QoS and fire-walling solutions [9]. However the firewall is only as secure as the hardware and software that implement, enforce and maintain the region control. Regarding SoC firewalling, we can identify three domains where an attack can take place, illustrated in red on Figure 1, the request path, the firewall reprogramming path and the firewall itself.

# 3   Integration of Security Resources into an SoC

Before integrating security resources, the hardware architecture and the purpose for securing it must be analyzed to define which approach to take. [10], A secure processor connected to an untrusted off-chip memory requires that memory content data has not been tampered with or accessed by an unauthorized entity. The approach consists of data integrity verification and encryption. This work focuses on interconnect communication where multiple IP cores, both secure and unsecure, share the same resources.

Typically, information security has started to be studied in the context of communication systems [7]. In such a scenario, there are two entities willing to communicate over a public communication channel that is prone to attacks. Ideally, this channel should have three characteristics: *data confidentiality* (pro-tecting sensitive information from eavesdropping), *data integrity* (ensuring that information has not been modified) and *peer authentication* (verifying that both parties are legitimate). By applying these concepts to a network-on-chip, one can see data confidentiality as protecting memory areas that contain private information with the use of a NoC firewall. In this domain, data integrity makes sure that the access rules are not modified during programming or at rest, while peer authentication allows the firewall to receive programming sequences from an authentic source.

## 3.1   Securing the Request Path

In an ideal world, a NoC could support a full point-to-point authenticated encryption between an initiator and a target. In addition to bringing perfect secrecy through a ciphered communication, this solution could also offer data integrity and authenticity with the addition of an authentication tag. Unfortu-nately, this solution is problematic to implement in an efficient manner within a NoC or an Xbar network. In fact, IP integrators cannot afford the impact on latency and overhead that this solution imposes. Lightweight hardware point-to-point encryption and address scrambling solutions do exist [6] but still add too much latency to be generalized to any application on an SoC. Regarding authen-ticated encryption, the standard defined by NIST, AES-CCB [5], also brings too much overhead for NoC integration.

## 3.2  Securing the Firewall

Firewalling is the easiest solution for implementing on-chip access control. The simplest version of a firewall is a hard-coded look-up table that matches initiator IDs and target addresses with access rights. However, access rights require both security and flexibility, which can only be achieved with a large degree of programmability of the access control rules. Commercial access control IPs exist on the market [1,2] and complex SoCs use firewalling to create on-chip access control [11]. They offer access control over a given address space with reprogrammability. Unfortunately, they do not secure the programming sequence nor authenticate the entity responsible for reprogramming the firewall rules. Moreover, they do not maintain the integrity of the access rules during operation.

Digital signing can secure the firewall programming by ensuring the authenticity of the programming entity, the region and its integrity. This strategy will protect a reprogramming agent from hijacking. By seeding the signature with a cryptographic nonce, replay attacks can also be prevented.

Integrity checking regions per access can ensure the regions have not been tampered with, and can detect a modification fast enough to block the access.

A previous work presented in [9] describes an architecture using multiple security levels on a NoC assuming that secure blocks are capable of defining dynamically new set of rules to different scenarios. Unfortunately it relies on hardware features customized within the NoC, making it less flexible.

# 4  Access Control Firewalling to On-Chip Resources

## 4.1  Overview

Access policies are usually implemented over an address space, so multiple targets can be covered using contiguous global addresses. Figure 2 represents an initiator's view of a partitioned address space of two targets: ROM and RAM. Each initiator has a different set of permissions for the address mapping according to its privilege. Once loaded in registers, an access rule is enforced using combinatorial logic checking of each transaction. The primary goal of the firewall is to allow only transactions from initiators that have correct access rights to a given target.

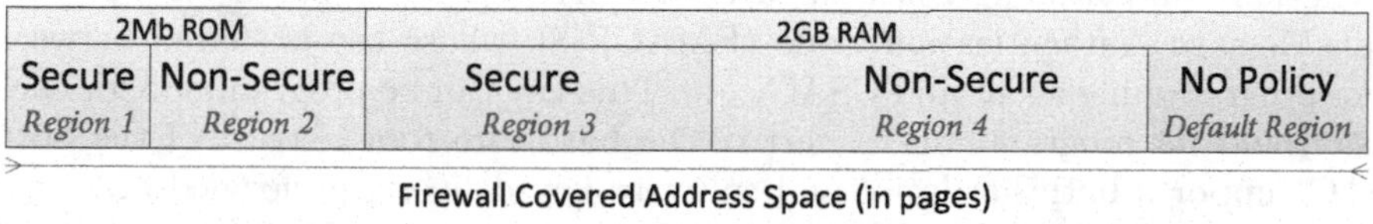

| 2Mb ROM | | 2GB RAM | | |
|---|---|---|---|---|
| Secure | Non-Secure | Secure | Non-Secure | No Policy |
| Region 1 | Region 2 | Region 3 | Region 4 | Default Region |

Firewall Covered Address Space (in pages)

**Fig. 2.** Simple firewall partitioning of an address space covering two targets

## 4.2   Endpoint versus NoC Firewalling

Firewalling at the NoC level presents one major advantage in that the lookup latency is hidden by the packet conversion timing. Indeed, the validity of the access can be checked while the packet is being converted to the target's protocol, thus the access can be granted where the request exits the NoC. An endpoint firewall is a more timing-critical block as it lies at the end of the request datapath (see Figure 3), however the techniques for securing the access rules are equally relevant and can be applied at the endpoint as well as at the ingress of the network.

Moreover, placing the firewall at the ingress or egress of the NoC demands synchronization between the master protocol and the slave protocol, which is usually achieved by registering inputs and outputs [3]. Since mobile applications and IoT devices use NoC for integration, it seems evident that inclusion of the firewall in the fabric itself is optionnal.

## 4.3   Cryptographically Secure Access Control

Cryptographically Secure Access Control (CSAC) is a security layer over the existing hardware management of virtualization of secure/non-secure environments.

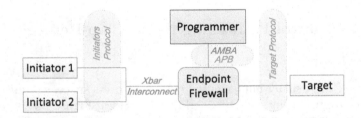

**Fig. 3.** Endpoint firewall that controls accesses from an initiator to a target interface

CSAC implements two security features. First, it cryptographically authenticates the reprogramming agent and ensures the integrity of its reprogramming sequences. Second, CSAC ensures the integrity of the access policies over the SoC by checking and hashing rules per access. CSAC engine is based on a Keyed-Hash Message Authentication Code (HMAC) [8], whose key is shared between the reprogramming agent and CSAC core. This key can be programmed for each session and its programming is part of the hardware root-of-trust of the SoC. CSAC supports both hardware and software key delivery, performed at secure boot of the SoC.

**CSAC Firewall Custom Regions.** A region can be as complex as a system needs it to be. It contains multiple fields, from encoded or decoded initiator access rights, the address space covered by the region from base address to top address range or decoded sub-regions, and specific user bits that can carry data as integrity checks value and other tags. With this flexibility and the scalability of each field's width, the end-user can tailor a CSAC firewall to a specific system use.

CSAC regions can scale up to 128 bits. Figure 4 illustrates an example implementation of a region register with the following fields:

- Disable: disable or enable flag. Encoded on two bits.
- NSR, NSW: decoded access rights per initiators for non-secure read and non-secure write permissions. This field can scale up to 16 bits depending on the number of initiators connected to the CSAC.
- SR, SW: grouped access right for all initiators regarding secure read and secure write for that region. Encoded on two bits.
- BA, TA: base address and top address of the given region. These addresses are given in 4kB pages. This field can scale up to 36 bits according to the address space covered by CSAC.
- Parity: parity bits for the different fields. These bits are continuously checked.
- CRC: CRC12 digest of all regions. This value is checked periodically for detection directed faults.

Each of the fields are scalable as RTL parameters up to the value represented in Figure 4. This enables the user to change or scale region complexity according to the SoC needs.

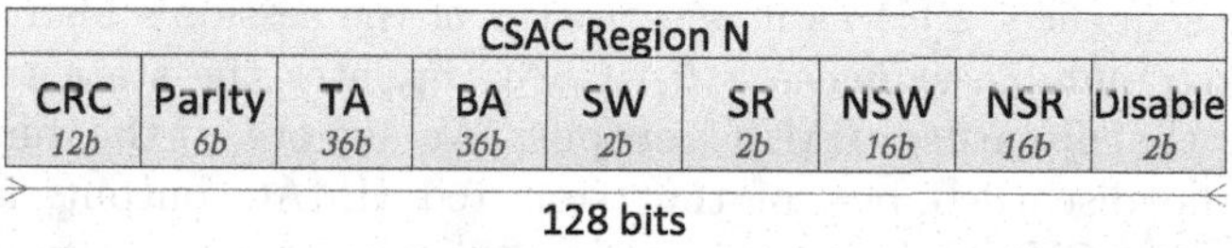

| CSAC Region N | | | | | | | | |
|---|---|---|---|---|---|---|---|---|
| CRC 12b | Parity 6b | TA 36b | BA 36b | SW 2b | SR 2b | NSW 16b | NSR 16b | Disable 2b |

128 bits

**Fig. 4.** Content of a complex CSAC's region

When a request arrives to CSAC, a wrapper decodes the incoming protocol to present CSAC with all the fields required for a region lookup. Depending on the interconnect technology, if an illegal access is detected, the transaction can be blocked at the synchronization node for bus-based interconnect, or at the target socket in the case of a packet switch network. Independently to the illegal and blocked access, an IRQ can be raised to the processor. Some level of reconfigurability regarding IRQ policy is given to the user by programming dedicated registers.

**CSAC Signing Engine.** CSAC signing engine is based on a Keyed-Hash Message Authentication Code (HMAC) using a cryptographic hash function $h$. Let

$K_S$ be the session key, $PR_i$ the $i^{th}$ incoming programming sequence and $SV_i$ the state variable defined hereafter. The HMAC tag of $PR_i$ is given by

$$HMAC(PR_i) = h((K_S \oplus opad)||h((K_S \oplus ipad)||PR_i||SV_i))$$

Figure 5 represents the composition of an incoming CSAC reprogramming sequence. It is composed of eight consecutive APB transactions written to the address of a region. The APB address provides the region number to CSAC, which is used in the signature computation.

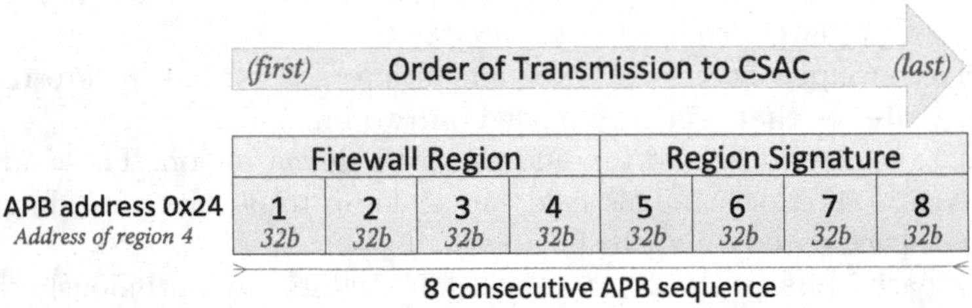

**Fig. 5.** Order of APB sequences of CSAC region programming

**Protection Against Replay Attacks.** To ensure that CSAC is resistant against replay attacks, the region's (access rule) signatures is seeded with a cryptographic nonce. We call this nonce the state variable of the $i^{th}$ incoming programming sequence ($SV_i$) as it is a tracker of the session's history. At each new valid programming sequence $PR_i$, CSAC updates the state variable $SV_i$ with part of the discarded HMAC output. We denote $f$ the function taking part of the discarded bits of the truncated HMAC output, as we have $SV_i = f(K_S, PR_i, SV_{i-1})$. It is evident that this tag becomes a function of all the preceding operations that CSAC has performed during a session and cannot be computed without this knowledge.

$$SV_i = f(K_S, PR_i, f(K_S, PR_{i-1}, SV_{i-2})) = f(K_S, PR_i, f(...f(K_S, PR_0, 0)...))$$

Since the IP does not contain non-volatile memory, the state variable is reset at boot, and initialized with the session key $K_S$ programming. It is important to mention that the register destination address is included in $PR_i$ and thus in the hash computation to avoid any unintended modification on the address bus.

**Key Management Policy.** CSAC security relies on the use of a key for authentication at system level. This key is a secret shared with the authenticated master that reprograms CSAC during operation. As this IP is intended for integration in large SoCs, using non-volatile memory for storing a personalized key should be avoided because it adds extra cost to the chip. Two options are possible for delivering the session key.

- The session key $K_S$ can be loaded through software. The solution used here is the use of a master key $K_M$ hardcoded in the design, the netlist key, and a session key $K_S$ programmed at secure boot within the root of trust with signed code, before non-secure OS and applications are loaded. As, in this solution, there is no personalization of the netlist key among devices, the security relies on a secure boot scheme that will ensure that only the trusted code can load the session key. First the key integrity value is computed for future key integrity checks, then the netlist key is checked for integrity, and then the session key is authenticated and programmed to the key registers using the following signature.

$$HMAC(K_S) = h((K_M \oplus opad)||h((K_M \oplus ipad)||K_S))$$

Note that there is no start variable involved in the signature, so that this step is vulnerable to replay attacks and relying on the secure boot of the systen to perform this operation.
- The session key $K_S$ can be loaded through a hardware key management system, where the security relies on this secure block. The HW KMS will also deliver the session key to the programmer. In this case there is no master key $K_M$.

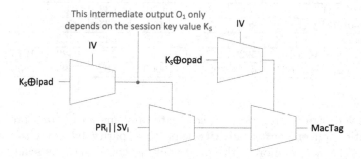

**Fig. 6.** Key integrity checks using HMAC intermediates

Before each signing operation, the key integrity is checked using the embedded hash function using the first intermediate hash computation as represented in Fig. 6. This operation allows us to perform key integrity checks continuously with very little overhead. We truncate this intermediate value to 16 bits and we store in dedicated register during session key programming. Note that this scheme is also used to verify the netlist key $K_M$ before every session key $K_S$ programming.

### 4.4  CSAC Synthesis Results

CSAC was synthesized in five different versions using a digital library with technology node of $45nm$. The synthesis results were obtained with Cadence

Encounter RTL Compiler v13.10. They show the impact of including security features to the CSAC core. Each version was split in two firewall settings: one composed of four regions that provide access rights to six initiators and address a space of 4GB (Table 1); another enabling the use of 14 initiators and covering a target address space of 64GB, with a total of 8 protection regions (Table 2). Results aim at comparing the cost of the enforcement logic and authentication engine. We also created an emulation platform by implementing our solution on a Xilinx ZINQ-700 [12] development board embedding an ARM Cortex A9 MCU core and an FPGA. We created traffic scenarios on the programmable logic using a simple packet-based NoC connecting two initiators, the ARM core, and a DMA to a DDR memory. On the NoC node, we instantiated CSAC IP core to securely partition the 1GB memory. We programmed CSAC region registers in a C++ SW that we compiled on ARM instruction set. FPGA synthesis results are embedded in Table 1 and Table 2.

**Table 1.** Synthesis results of five CSAC designs (4 regions, 6 initiators, 4GB of address space) on a $45nm$ technology node and on Zynq-7000 board.

| Technology | ASIC | | | | FPGA | | |
|---|---|---|---|---|---|---|---|
| Design | Cells | GE | Critical path (ps) | Power (mW) | LUTs Slices | Register Slices | Muxes |
| Basic firewall (a) | 746 | 4461 | 5020 | 0.32 | 417 | 353 | 38 |
| Firewall and parity (b) | 827 | 4760 | 5443 | 0.33 | 441 | 437 | 47 |
| Firewall, parity and CRC (c) | 1729 | 5967 | 5467 | 0.46 | 1103 | 772 | 47 |
| Firewall and HMAC (d) | 5933 | 23156 | 10000 | 2.7 | 2429 | 1973 | 61 |
| Firewall and all features (e) | 6452 | 24677 | 10000 | 2.82 | 3095 | 2350 | 77 |

The base design (a) represents a complete implementation of a firewall with no authentication engine or integrity logic (i.e., parity bits or CRC integrity checking). Design (b) enforces the programming correctness by sending parity bits embedded in the sequence, that will be constantly checked whenever a firewall access request is processed. Design (c) uses, apart from parity bits, a CRC engine that periodically checks the integrity of the protection regions. Design (d) does not implement any enforcement logic in the bits of the protection regions, but authenticates each programming sequence using the HMAC authentication mode in conjunction with the SHA-256 cryptographic hash. The last design, (e), implements all features in the same core.

Tables 1 and 2 show physical synthesis results aiming at a frequency of 100MHz. The gate equivalent (GE) metric was calculated dividing the total cell area of each design by the area of the smallest 2-input NAND gate of the target digital library. In addition to the inherent loss in performance, the security features impact area occupation and power consumption. Power consumption was estimated by the synthesis tool and represents the total power dissipation (dynamic and leakage). The power consumption was calculated by the synthesis tool taking into account an activity profile of the CSAC core and represent an

**Table 2.** Synthesis results of five CSAC designs (8 regions, 14 initiators, 64GB of address space) on a $45nm$ technology node.

| Technology | ASIC | | | | FPGA | | |
|---|---|---|---|---|---|---|---|
| Design | Cells | GE | Critical path (ps) | Power (mW) | LUTs Slices | Register Slices | Muxes |
| Basic firewall (a) | 2203 | 9031 | 7249 | 0.62 | 751 | 823 | 147 |
| Firewall and parity (b) | 2471 | 10082 | 8035 | 0.63 | 810 | 851 | 86 |
| Firewall, parity and CRC (c) | 3026 | 10836 | 7734 | 0.73 | 1689 | 1244 | 181 |
| Firewall and HMAC (d) | 6900 | 27555 | 10000 | 2.79 | 2735 | 2435 | 201 |
| Firewall and all features (e) | 7929 | 30343 | 10000 | 3.17 | 3688 | 2825 | 169 |

average value when the HMAC engine is working. Although the most power consuming module is the HMAC engine, it will be idle most of the time, decreasing significantly the power profile of CSAC.

The CSAC core was designed for only one clock domain. This means that the programming interface needs to work at the same speed as the firewall logic, which can be restrictive in some cases.

By using two clock domains - one for configuration and another for firewalling - CSAC can speed up the firewall logic and avoid NoC clock frequency loss due to security. For example, it can be seen from Tables 1 and 2 that the HMAC SHA-256 engine decreases the performance in designs (d) and (e) by approximately 27%. Since the authentication engine is only used when a new protection region is reprogrammed in CSAC, it does not impact the firewall enforcement logic in a two-clock domain scheme. This technique proves to be helpful when the authentication engine has a significant cost to performance, area and power consumption. In contrast, parity bits and CRC integrity checking relate to both domains because they are enforced when a programming sequence is sent to the core and also when a firewall access request arrives to CSAC. As a result, these two countermeasures do impact the overall performance.

## 5  Future Work

CSAC signing engine uses the NIST recommended hash function SHA-256. Lightweight hash functions should be the object of further research.

Finally, another path for further research is in the application of CSAC principles to memory control systems as memory management units (MMUs). In the case of table look-aside buffers (TLBs), they could contain access right information, thread ID information and embed some additional security features. Ensuring a similar level of authenticity and integrity checking of page tables and TLB entries would require additional work.

## 6  Conclusions

We introduced a novel way of firewalling resources securely in an SoC by cryptographically signing reprogrammed firewall access rules and checking them for modifications or errors during operation. CSAC can be used to efficiently and securely segment address spaces between secure and non-secure initiators. The programmer controlling those partitions can be located on-chip or off-chip and its sequences are authenticated with a very strong collision resistance. In the same way, CSAC is resistant to fault injection/glitching techniques so that a given access policy can be securely maintained. Finally, we point out that CSAC can be also used in broader applications and its principles can be applied (to a certain extent) to memory management units (MMUs).

# References

1. ARM. TZC-400 trustzone address space controller technical reference manual
2. Arteris. Flex NoC interconnect IP
3. Cotret, P., Crenne, J., Gogniat, G., Diguet, J.-P.: Bus-based mpsoc security through communication protection: A latency-efficient alternative. In: 2012 IEEE 20th Annual International Symposium on Field-Programmable Custom Computing Machines (FCCM), pp. 200–207, April 2012
4. Diguet, J.-P., Evain, S., Vaslin, R., Gogniat, G., Juin, E.: NOC-centric security of reconfigurable SoC. In: First International Symposium on Networks-on-Chip (NOCS 2007), pp. 223–232, France, May 2007
5. Dworkin, M.J.: Sp 800–38c. recommendation for block cipher modes of operation: The ccm mode for authentication and confidentiality. Technical report, Gaithersburg, MD, United States (2004)
6. Ege, B., Kavun, E.B., Yalçın, T.: Memory encryption for smart cards. In: Prouff, E. (ed.) CARDIS 2011. LNCS, vol. 7079, pp. 199–216. Springer, Heidelberg (2011)
7. Kocher, P., Lee, R., McGraw, G., Raghunathan, A., Ravi, S.: Security as a new dimension in embedded system design. In: Proceedings of the 41st Design Automation Conference 2004, pp. 753–760, July 2004
8. National Institute of Standards and Technology. FIPS 198–1, The Keyed-Hash Message Authentication Code, Federal Information Processing Standard (FIPS). Technical report (2008)
9. Sepulveda, J., Gogniat, G., Pedraza, C., Pires, R., Chau, W.J., Strum, M.: Hierarchical noc-based security for MP-SoC dynamic protection. In: 2012 IEEE Third Latin American Symposium on Circuits and Systems (LASCAS), pp. 1–4, February 2012
10. Suh, G.E., Clarke, D., Gassend, B., van Dijk, M., Devadas, S.: Efficient memory integrity verification and encryption for secure processors. In: Proceedings of the 36th Annual IEEE/ACM International Symposium on Microarchitecture, MICRO 36, pp. 339–350. IEEE Computer Society, Washington, DC (2003)
11. TI. OMAP543x Technical Reference Manual
12. Xilinx. Zynq-7000 All Programmable SoC

# Enforcing Privacy in Distributed Multi-domain Network Anomaly Detection

Christian Callegari[1,2]([⊠]), Stefano Giordano[1,2], and Michele Pagano[1,2]

[1] Department of Information Engineering, University of Pisa, Pisa, Italy
{christian.callegari,stefano.giordano,michele.pagano}@iet.unipi.it
[2] CNIT, Pisa, Italy

**Abstract.** In this paper, we propose a distributed PCA-based method for detecting anomalies in the network traffic, which, by means of multi-party computation techniques, is also able to face the different privacy constraints that arise in a multi-domain network scenario, while preserving the same performance of the centralised implementation (with only a limited overhead).

## 1 Introduction

The detection of attacks and anomalies in the network traffic has attracted many research efforts in the last years, and some very promising methods, such as those based on the use of Principal Component Analysis (PCA), have been proposed.

Nonetheless, most of these methods are based on a centralised approach that is becoming less and less suitable to the new emerging network paradigms that more and more often require a distributed approach, and, moreover, almost none of them is able to cope with the privacy constraints, typical of such distributed environments.

In this paper we propose a method able to deal with such a scenario. Indeed, our proposal is based on a set of different techniques (namely secret sharing and secure multiparty computation) that allow the probes and the central engine to exchange the traffic data, needed to perform a PCA-based anomaly detection technique, without disclosing any sensitive information on the traffic.

The rest of the paper is organised as follows: Section 2 provides a brief overview of the related works, then in Section 3 we detail the proposed anomaly detection method, whose performance (in terms of detection accuracy, computational complexity, and provided privacy protection) are discussed in Section 4. Finally, Section 5 concludes the paper with some final remarks.

## 2 Related Work

Over the years several solutions have been proposed to detect attacks and anomalies in the networks, as testified by the several surveys on the topic [1][2]. In this context, PCA has emerged as a very promising technique for detecting a wide

© Springer International Publishing Switzerland 2015
M. Qiu et al. (Eds.): NSS 2015, LNCS 9408, pp. 439–446, 2015.
DOI: 10.1007/978-3-319-25645-0_32

variety of attacks [3] [4] and, some recent papers [5] [6] [7] [8] have extended the method, so as to improve the detection performance of the system.

PCA-based anomaly detection techniques appear to be suitable for working on the top of a distributed environment [9] [10]. Instead, as far as the preservation of the privacy is concerned, the only notable work is [11], where the authors first introduce a method that allows a privacy-preserving computation of the principal components (PCs).

## 3    Privacy Aware Distributed Anomaly Detection

In this section we provide a detailed description of the different operations performed by the probes and the central engine to detect of network anomalies. For this purpose, let us refer to a network scenario, where we have $N$ probes distributed in $N$ distinct ASs, each owned by a different ISP, and a single central engine, responsible for the anomaly detection, which can be considered as independent of the different ISPs. Thus, the basic idea is to allow the central engine to perform PCA-based anomaly detection on the whole network traffic, without disclosing any private data of the traffic to the engine itself, while at the same time guaranteeing the same performance that would be obtained by a hypothetic centralised system (able to observe the whole network traffic).

### 3.1    Distributed PCs Computation

At first, the different probes have to collect the traffic traversing their own AS. Given the huge number of traffic flows normally belonging to an AS and the need for providing an efficient and scalable method, each probe $P_i$ (each on his own) aggregates the traffic flows by using a sketch[1]. Thus, for a given time-bin $n$, $P_i$ first computes a sketch $T_{i,n}$, where each bucket contains the quantity of traffic associated to the destination IP addresses that collide into that bucket (note that for the experimental evaluation we have considered $d = 7$ and $w = 512$). Thus, once the probe has evaluated the sketch for all the considered $K$ time-bins, it computes the traffic matrix $Y_i$, whose generic row $j$ is given by the concatenation of the rows of $T_{i,j}$, that is $Y_i(j, \cdot) = (T_{i,j}(1, \cdot), T_{i,j}(2, \cdot), \ldots, T_{i,j}(d, \cdot))$ hence, the matrix $Y_i$ has dimension $K \times m$, with $m = d \cdot w$. Note that the matrix $Y_i$ must have a number of rows that is at least twice the number of columns (the reason will be clear once read the whole procedure), which is, in general, a reasonable requirement given the possibility of tuning, during this "training phase" the number of considered time-bins.

At this point, the traffic matrix of the whole network scenario can be seen as the concatenation of the single "local" traffic matrices $\mathbf{Y} = (Y_1, Y_2, \ldots, Y_N)$, with dimension $K \times (N \cdot m)$ (considering that all the probes have a data matrix of the same dimension). Hence, the first step that has to be realised to determine the PCs is the computation of the covariance matrix $S$

---

[1] Sketches are a family of data structures that use the same underlying hashing scheme for summarizing data.

$$S = \tfrac{1}{K}\mathbf{Y}^t \cdot \mathbf{Y} = \tfrac{1}{K} \begin{pmatrix} Y_1^t \\ Y_2^t \\ \vdots \\ Y_N^t \end{pmatrix} \cdot (Y_1, Y_2, \ldots, Y_N) = \begin{pmatrix} Y_1^t \cdot Y_1 & Y_1^t \cdot Y_2 & \ldots & Y_1^t \cdot Y_N \\ Y_2^t \cdot Y_1 & Y_2^t \cdot Y_2 & \ldots & Y_2^t \cdot Y_N \\ \vdots & \vdots & \ddots & \vdots \\ Y_N^t \cdot Y_1 & Y_N^t \cdot Y_2 & \ldots & Y_N^t \cdot Y_N \end{pmatrix} \quad (1)$$

To this aim, given the need of maintaining the data matrices $Y_i$ private, we apply a Secure MultiParty Computation (SMPC)[2] procedure [13] that allows the probes $P_i$ to compute all the required blocks (also those that would require the knowledge of the other traffic matrices, i.e., all the blocks $Y_i^t \cdot Y_j$ with $i \neq j$), without "really" knowing anything about the traffic matrices $Y_j$.

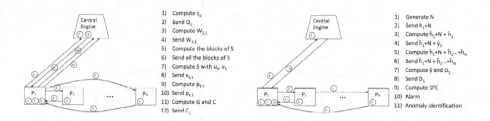

(a) Distributed PC Computation      (b) Distributed Data Projection

**Fig. 1.** Distributed Algorithm

Let us analyse into details how this step is accomplished, also referring to Figure 1(a), where we sketch the procedure for probe $P_i$ (the other probes work analogously). The first step (step 1 in the figure) consists in generating $K/2$ arrays $z_q$, orthogonal to $Y_i$, i.e., $z_q^t \cdot Y_i = \mathbf{0}$, where $\mathbf{0}$ is an array of $m$ zeros. Such arrays are then organised as the columns of a matrix $Z_i$ and the probe computes $Q_i = I - Z_i \cdot Z_i^t$, where $I$ is the identity matrix. Hence, the matrix $Q_i$ is sent to all the probes $P_j$ (step 2 in the figure).

Thus, each probe $P_j$ computes the matrix $W_{j,i} = Q_i \cdot Y_j$ (step 3 in the figure) and sends it back to the probe $P_i$ (step 4 in the figure). At this point, all the probes can easily compute all the blocks of the covariance matrix (step 5 in the figure), by exploiting the fact that:

$$Y_i^t \cdot W_{i,j} = Y_i^t \cdot (Q_i \cdot Y_j) = Y_i^t \cdot (I - Z_i \cdot Z_i^t) \cdot Y_j \quad (2)$$

that, given the property of orthogonality of the arrays $z_q$, leads to

$$Y_i^t \cdot (I - Z_i \cdot Z_i^t) \cdot Y_j = Y_i^t \cdot Y_j \quad (3)$$

---

[2] SMPC [12] is a method that allows parties to jointly compute a function over their inputs, while simultaneously keeping these inputs private.

All these blocks are then sent to the central engine (step 6), that is thus able to "reconstruct" $S$ and correctly compute its eigenvalues $u$ and eigenvectors $v$ (step 7). Given this, the next step consists in determining the $r$ dominant PCs that will be used to define the "normal" subspace. Note that to perform such a step, in principle, it is necessary to project the data matrix $Y$ into the space defined by the PCs, by considering that the project along $v_k$ can be computed as:

$$p_k = Y \cdot v_k \tag{4}$$

so as to evaluate the quantity of energy captured by each PC. But, in our case the central engine does not have any knowledge on the actual value of $Y$, so we have to use a SMPC technique again. To this purpose, we can rewrite (4) as:

$$p_k = (Y_1, Y_2, \ldots, Y_N) \cdot \begin{pmatrix} v_{k,1} \\ v_{k,2} \\ \vdots \\ v_{k,N} \end{pmatrix} \tag{5}$$

(with the number of columns of each $Y_i$ equal to the length of the corresponding $v_{k,i}$), where $v_{k,i}$ represents the $i^{th}$ portion of $k^{th}$ eigenvector (the order of the eigenvectors is determined by the decreasing value of the associated eigenvalues), the one that "would multiply" $Y_i$, and is sent to the corresponding probe $P_i$ (step 8 in the figure). As it is obvious the generic probe $P_i$ computes the quantity $p_{k,i} = Y_i \cdot v_{k,i}$ (step 9 in the figure) and sends it back to the central engine (step 10 in the figure) that can compute the "global" $p_k$ and estimates the associated energy. Iterating the last three steps until $r$ is reached ($r$ is usually evaluated with the scree plot method), the central engine is able to computes all the required PCs, which are then used to form the columns of the matrix $G$ (step 11 in the figure), which, hence, has dimension $(N \cdot m) \times r$.

The final step (step 12) of this phase consists in the central engine sending the matrix $C$ to be used for the data projection: $C = G \cdot G^t$. To this aim the matrix is split into $N$ blocks $C = (C_1, C_2, \ldots, C_N)$, where the generic block $C_i$, which is sent to probe $P_i$, has a number of columns that is equal to the length of the observation $y_i$ (i.e, $m$). Note that $m$ is assumed constant, given that it is simply determined by the dimension of the sketch.

## 3.2    Data Projection

This second phase, corresponding to the detection phase, mainly consists in projecting the observations in the "normal" subspace, described by the dominant PCs, and then evaluating the "residual" energy (i.e., the energy that is captured by the "anomalous" subspace) by computing the Square Prediction Error (SPE) of the projected data. As for the previous phase, we have to take into account the privacy constraints, which mainly mean that we have to keep the observed data of a given probe private (i.e., neither the central engine nor the other probes should be able to obtain them).

To better analyse such a phase, let us refer to Figure 1(b), where we have summarised the whole procedure. In principle given the observation data $y$, projecting them into the "normal" subspace can be achieved as:

$$\hat{y} = C \cdot y^t \tag{6}$$

But, given that the central engine, which is the only entity that knows $C$, does not have any knowledge on the actual value of $Y$, we have to use a SMPC technique. To this purpose, we can rewrite (6) as:

$$\hat{y} = (C_1, C_2, \ldots, C_N) \cdot \begin{pmatrix} y_1^t \\ y_2^t \\ \vdots \\ y_N^t \end{pmatrix} = C_1 \cdot y_1^t + C_2 \cdot y_2^t + \ldots + C_N \cdot y_n^t \tag{7}$$

where the matrices $C_i$ are the blocks of $C$ sent to the probes $P_i$ at the end of the distributed PC computation phase.

Note that, from a first analysis, it can seem that the probe $P_i$ can simply compute $\hat{h}_i = C_i \cdot y_i^t$ and send it to the central engine that can then obtain $\hat{y} = \sum_{1=1}^{N} \hat{h}_i$. Indeed, the central engine is not able to compute $y$, given the knowledge of $\hat{y}$, since the matrix $C$ is not invertible, given that

$$Rank(C) = Rank(G \cdot G^t) \leq \min(Rank(G), Rank(G^t)) \leq r < n \cdot m \tag{8}$$

Nonetheless, by combining this information with some of the equations used to compute the arrays $u_k$, it could be able to obtain $y$, somehow.

Thus, to compute such projections we apply a modified version of the additive Secret Sharing (SS)[3] scheme (step 1 to 6 in the figure). At first, a given probe $P_i$, generates a random number $N_i$ and computes $\hat{h}_i + N_i$, and sends it to the first adjacent probe, $P_{i+1}$, which sums $\hat{h}_{i+1}$ to the received quantity and then sends it to its first adjacent probe. This procedure has to be iterated until the resulting quantity is updated by all the probes and received back by the one that originated it. Thus $P_i$ obtains $\sum_{i=1}^{N} \hat{h}_i + N_i$ and can easily obtain $\hat{y}$ by subtracting $N_i$ (step 7 in the figure):

$$\hat{y} = \sum_{i=1}^{N} \hat{h}_i + N_i - N_i \tag{9}$$

By repeating such process for each probe (note that the procedure can be easily optimised, so as to avoid having too many data exchanges, i.e., the complexity can be reduced from $O(n^2)$ to $O(n)$), each generic $P_i$ obtains $\hat{y}$. If we consider $\hat{y} = (\hat{y}_1, \hat{y}_2, \ldots, \hat{y}_N)$, each probe can compute an array $D_i$, of length $N \cdot m$, whose elements are defined as:

$$D_i(j) = \begin{cases} \hat{y}_j - y_j & \text{if} \quad j \in [(i-1) \cdot m; (i \cdot m) - 1] \\ 0 & \text{otherwise} \end{cases} \tag{10}$$

---

[3] SS refers to a set of techniques that allow a party, called dealer, to distribute a secret amongst a group of $N$ participants, each of whom is allocated a share of the secret.

Such an array is then sent to the central engine (step 8 in the figure), that can compute the "global" SPE, as

$$SPE = || \sum_{i=1}^{N} D_i ||_2 \tag{11}$$

and, by comparing it with a threshold, it decides if an alarm has to be generated or not (step 9 in the figure). In case, the alarm is sent back to all the probes (step 10 in the figure) that will perform the anomaly identification phase (step 11 in the figure) so as to identify the IP flows responsible for the detected anomaly (we do not provide any detail about this phase here, given that it can be performed in any of the ways known in the literature, e.g., reversible sketch [14]).

## 4    System Evaluation

In this section we present an evaluation of the proposed system, taking into account three different aspects: the level of privacy guaranteed by the applied algorithm, the introduced overhead, and the offered performance.

### 4.1    Privacy Aspects

Let us start the analysis, by considering the distributed PCs computation phase, and highlighting how the privacy is guaranteed in the different steps that involve some data exchange:

- during step 2, the knowledge of $Q_i$ does not allow the probes to discover the matrix $Y_i$
- the privacy in (2) is guaranteed by the fact that the matrix $Q_i = I - Z_i \cdot Z_i^t$ is not invertible
- when computing the dominant PCs (step 8-10), the probes send the result of the operation $Y_i \cdot v_{i,k}$ to the coordinator. But, this phase is only iterated until $r$ is reached and, considering that $r$ is usually much smaller than the original dimensionality of the data, the coordinator does not have enough data to compute the actual value of $Y_i$.

Moreover, taking into consideration the data projection phase, we have the following considerations:

- the data exchange in steps 1-6 only involves the transmission of random data, thus do not reveal any information about the data themselves
- the data sent by the probes to the central engine do not reveal anything on the actual data, just being a sort of "projection error".

So, the privacy protection provided by our solution is complete. For sake of completeness, it is worth noticing that the method used for the distributed computation of $S$ has some limitations tied to the quantity $K/2$ of arrays $z_r$ and to the number of data non linearly independent among the probes [13]. Nevertheless, by a deep study of such limitations, we can reasonably conclude that they do not lead to any privacy loss in our application scenario.

## 4.2   Computational Overhead

As it is obvious, the privacy awareness of our solution has a cost in terms of both additional data exchanges among the probes and the central engine and additional operations to be performed.

By analysing the algorithm we can easily notice that the distributed PC computation phase is quite more complicated than if performed in a centralised way. Nevertheless, this is not really significant, given that this phase, roughly corresponding to a training phase, has to be performed only once, before the real "operation" of the system. Instead, considering the detection phase, we can see that the introduced overhead is very limited, being just related to the SS scheme, which is in fact negligible both in terms of computational complexity and data exchange needed.

## 4.3   Detection Performance

The aim of the detection performance evaluation phase is, on one side, to verify the effectiveness of the proposed method and, on the other side, to estimate if, as expected from the theoretical complexity analysis, the introduced overhead is still acceptable for real-time operation. For such purposes, the proposed system has been tested over a well-known public traffic data set, composed of traffic traces collected in the Abilene/Internet2 Network [15]. As far as the effectiveness of the method in detecting the anomalies is concerned, as expected from the theoretical analysis, the system offers the same performance of a hypothetic centralised system. Indeed, the system is able to compute the same PCs that would be computed by a centralised implementation, while fulfilling the required privacy constraints.

Regarding the introduced overhead, the experimental tests have confirmed the complexity analysis, concluding that, considering both the time due to the data exchange and to the additional computation steps, it is such that the method is still suitable to real-time operation. Indeed, the system, implemented over standard general purpose PCs (equipped with an Intel i5 4200 2.6 GHz and 4GB of RAM), is able to process the traffic of a generic time-bin of the provided data set, corresponding to five minutes of traffic of the Abilene/Internet2 backbone network, in about seven seconds. Such a result strongly demonstrates the suitability of the method to real-time operation.

## 5   Conclusion

In this paper we have proposed a privacy preserving distributed anomaly detection scheme based on the use of PCA. The proposed solution, by means of SMPC methods and SS techniques, is suitable for multi-domain network scenarios, where the monitoring probes belonging to a given ISP are not intended to exchange private traffic data neither with the probes of other ISPs nor with the central engine.

**Acknowledgments.** This work was partially supported by Multitech SeCurity system for intercOnnected space control groUnd staTions (SCOUT), a FP7 EU project.

# References

1. Callegari, C., et al.: A methodological overview on anomaly detection. In: Biersack, E., Callegari, C., Matijasevic, M. (eds.) Data Traffic Monitoring and Analysis. LNCS, vol. 7754, pp. 148–183. Springer, Heidelberg (2013)
2. Patcha, A., Park, J.: An overview of anomaly detection techniques: Existing solutions and latest technological trends. Computer Networks **51** (2007)
3. Lakhina, A.: Diagnosing network-wide traffic anomalies. In: ACM SIGCOMM, pp 219–230 (2004)
4. Lakhina, A., Crovella, M., Diot, C.: Mining anomalies using traffic feature. In: ACM SIGCOMM (2005)
5. Chatzigiannakis, V., Papavassiliou, S., Androulidakis, G.: Improving network anomaly detection effectiveness via an integrated multi-metric-multi-link ($m^3l$) PCA-based approach. Security and Communication Networks **2**(3), 289–304 (2009)
6. Callegari, C., Gazzarrini, L., Giordano, S., Pagano, M., Pepe, T.: A novel multi time-scales PCA-based anomaly detection system. In: 2010 International Symposium on Performance Evaluation of Computer and Telecommunication Systems (SPECTS) (2010)
7. Callegari, C., Gazzarrini, L., Giordano, S., Pagano, M., Pepe, T.: Improving PCA-based anomaly detection by using multiple time scale analysis and Kullback-Leibler divergence. International Journal of Communication Systems (2012) n/a-n/a
8. Callegari, C., Gazzarrini, L., Giordano, S., Pagano, M., Pepe, T.: A novel PCA-based network anomaly detection. In: ICC, pp. 1–5 (2011)
9. Liu, Y., Zhang, L., Guan, Y.: Sketch-based streaming PCA algorithm for network-wide traffic anomaly detection. In: Proceedings of International Conference on Distributed Computing Systems (2010)
10. Dusi, M., Vitale, C., Niccolini, S., Callegari, C.: Distributed PCA-based anomaly detection in telephone networks through legitimate-user profiling. In: ICC, pp. 1107–1112 (2012)
11. Zhang, P., Huang, X., Sun, X., Wang, H., Ma, Y.: Privacy-preserving anomaly detection across multi-domain networks. In: FSKD, pp. 1066–1070. IEEE (2012)
12. Cramer, Ronald: Introduction to Secure Computation. In: Damgård, Ivan Bjerre (ed.) Lectures on Data Security. LNCS, vol. 1561, pp. 16–62. Springer, Heidelberg (1999)
13. Karr, A.F., Lin, X., Reiter, J.P., Sanil, A.P.: Privacy-preserving analysis of vertically partitioned data using secure matrix products. Journal of Official Statistics **25**(1), 125–138 (2009)
14. Schweller, R., Gupta, A., Parsons, E., Chen, Y.: Reversible sketches for efficient and accurate change detection over network data streams. In: Proceedings of the ACM SIGCOMM Conference on Internet Measurement, IMC 2004, pp. 207–212. ACM, New York (2004)
15. The Internet2 Network. http://www.internet2.edu/network/

# Short Papers: Mobile and Cloud Security

# De-anonymizable Location Cloaking
# for Privacy-Controlled Mobile Systems

Chao Li$^{(\boxtimes)}$ and Balaji Palanisamy

University of Pittsburgh, Pittsburgh, USA
{chl205,bpalan}@pitt.edu

**Abstract.** The rapid technology upgrades of mobile devices and the popularity of wireless networks significantly drive the emergence and development of Location-based Services (LBSs), thus greatly expanding the business of online services and enriching the user experience. However, the personal location data shared with the service providers also leave hidden risks on location privacy. Location anonymization techniques transform the exact location of a user into a cloaking area by including the locations of multiple users in the exposed area such that the exposed location is indistinguishable from that of the other users. However in such schemes, location information once perturbed cannot be recovered from the cloaking region and as a result, users of the location cannot obtain fine granular information even when they have access to it. In this paper, we propose Dynamic Reversible Cloaking (DRC) a new de-anonymziable location cloaking mechanism that allows to restore the actual location from the perturbed information through the use of an anonymization key. Extensive experiments using realistic road network traces show that the proposed scheme is efficient, effective and scalable.

## 1 Introduction

With the popularity of mobile positioning devices and the wide emergence of location-based services (LBSs), we are witnessing a rapid development of mobile location-based applications. Through location-aware techniques (e.g. GPS, wireless access point), users can acquire personalized services based on their current location. Examples of such services include weather forecast, traffic condition updates, location-based travel services and emergency care. The richness and diversity of location-based services has dramatically improved the quality of life for people. However, these services and benefits also come with a hidden cost: the intrusion of location privacy. For example, knowing the haunts of users during the day time and at nights, an attacker can infer a user's social activities, religious beliefs and political views. Moreover, with the advent of big data and big data analytics, the risk of disclosing location information is further exacerbated as an adversary can correlate the exposed location with information from various data sources to infer more accurate and fine-grained information about individuals.

Various techniques have been proposed to achieve location privacy protection in mobile location-based system. Location anonymization refers to the process

© Springer International Publishing Switzerland 2015
M. Qiu et al. (Eds.): NSS 2015, LNCS 9408, pp. 449–458, 2015.
DOI: 10.1007/978-3-319-25645-0_33

of transforming the exact location of a user to a cloaking area by including the location of multiple other users. A user is considered to be location k-anonymous if and only if her location information is indistinguishable from that of at least $k-1$ other users. However in such schemes, location information once perturbed cannot be recovered from the cloaking region and as a result, users of the location cannot obtain fine granular information even when they have access to it. In several access controlled scenarios, such as when some users of the location have more privileges than the others, it may be desirable to obtain fine granular location information from the exposed perturbed location when the data user has access to the finer granular location information.

During the last several years, many location anonymization techniques [1, 6,8,10,13,20] have been proposed. Most of them were developed as unidirectional cloaking techniques without considering the ability to de-anonymize the perturbed data. In this paper, we propose Dynamic Reversible Cloaking (DRC) a new de-anonymziable location cloaking mechanism that allows to restore the actual location from the perturbed information through the use of an anonymization key. Our proposed mechanism uses an anonymization secret key to uniquely generate a cloaking region which allows the original location data to be restored from the cloaked data using the secret key, However, without the secret key, the original data cannot be inferred even when the adversary has complete knowledge of the cloaking mechanism.

We organize the rest of the paper as follows: In Section 2, we present the required background. In Section 3, we introduce the proposed Dynamic Reversible Cloaking. In Section 4, we analyze the experiment results. We discuss related work in Section 5 and we conclude in Section 6.

## 2 Overview of Concepts and Framework

In this section, we discuss the road network model used for the cloaking process and introduce the conventional location cloaking mechanisms to protect location privacy over road networks. We then define the de-anonymizable location privacy problem and introduce the evaluation metrics used in this paper.

A road network can be modeled as a graph $G = (V_G, E_G)$, consisting of a set of junctions, $V_G$, and a set of road segments, $E_G$. Figure 1 shows an example with 14 junctions and 16 segments respectively. In our work, junctions are defined as the crossover or end points of roads while segments are defined as the direct roads between adjacent junctions. We assume that all mobile users move along the segments. The raw location information of the mobile users is sent with their customizable privacy requirements to a trusted third-party location anonymizer, which transforms the raw location into a cloaking region preserving the required privacy properties, which may then be shared with other untrusted location-based service providers.

The location information of a user is said to be *k-anonymous* if the location information is indistinguishable from the location information of at least k-1 other users. Obviously, the larger the value $k$, the better is the privacy protection that can be achieved. However, large cloaking regions typically provide

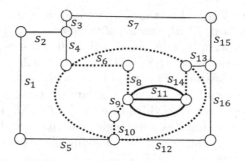

**Fig. 1.** Road network model with de-anonymizable privacy controlled framework

lower utility as it increases the complexity of the operations involved in obtaining an accurate answer to the location-based query [13]. Therefore, to bound the size of the cloaking region, the customizable requirements contain not only the privacy requirement, denoted by $\delta_k$, but also the maximum spatial resolution level, denoted by $\sigma_s$ [13,19], which defines the maximum acceptable size of the cloaking region. The customizable privacy requirements with both the two parameters are organized as the user-defined privacy profile: $(\delta_k, \sigma_s)$.

In the past, several models have been proposed for location anonymization. Random sampling is a basic location cloaking technique that picks segments from the whole graph one by one in a random manner while road-network-based expansion selects adjacent segments of the cloaking region to make the structure of cloaking region tighter [19]. However, to the best of our knowledge, in most existing location privacy-preserving mechanisms, the original exact location information once perturbed in the cloaking scheme cannot be restored to infer finer location information when users have the required access privileges. The focus of our work in this paper is developing a new de-anonymizable cloaking technique that can support privacy control in access controlled scenarios. In such cases, the location privacy of users is protected while allowing only the parties with the required permission to access finer information.

In the proposed de-anonymizable location privacy model, only the data users who possess the permission to access finer information get the secret key to de-anonymize the data. Such data users can de-anonymize the perturbed location using the secret key. A detailed example is shown in Figure 1. The segment $s_{11}$ contains the actual user. Using the secret key, $\{s_6, s_8, s_9, s_{10}, s_{14}\}$ are added to reach the privacy level $\delta_k$. To de-anonymize the cloaking region, the same secret key is used to exactly identify and remove the segments $\{s_6, s_8, s_9, s_{10}, s_{14}\}$ from the cloaking region, thus reducing the perturbed location to the actual segment of the user.

To evaluate the performance of de-anonymizable cloaking scheme, multiple metrics are required. Four metrics are used in this paper.

*Anonymization Time:* The time required to cloak the location information of the user. A shorter anonymization time indicates higher effectiveness.

*De-anonymization Time:* The time required to de-anonymize the cloaking area to get the exact location information of the user. Like anonymization time, a shorter de-anonymization time indicates higher effectiveness.

*Relative Spatial Resolution (RSR):* This metric reflects the relationship between the maximum spatial area defined by $\sigma_s$ and the cloaking area. Specifically, the maximum spatial area is a rectangular area centering on the user. Its lateral and vertical lengths are provided by $\sigma_s = \{ML_l, ML_v\}$. For the cloaking space, its area is also abstracted as a rectangle. The lateral and vertical distances between each pair of segments within the cloaking space are calculated and the largest two values, expressed as $\{CL_l, CL_v\}$, are considered as the lateral and vertical lengths of the cloaking rectangle. Therefore, considering a set of LBS requests with N elements, the RSR is defined as:

$$RSR = \frac{1}{N} \sum_N \sqrt{\frac{ML_l \times ML_v}{CL_l \times CL_v}}$$

Since the RSR is the square root of the ratio between maximum spatial area and cloaking area, a higher value of RSR indicates a smaller cloaking space required to satisfy the $\delta_k$, meaning higher effectiveness.

*Success Rate:* This metric represents the rate of successful cloaking of the requests. For a set $\mathbb{Q}$ of LBS requests, the cloaking area of each query $q$ is represented by $C_q = f(q)$. A parameter $S$ is 1 if the process is successful and 0 if the process is failed. The success rate can be defined as:

$$Success\ Rate = \frac{|\{C_q \mid C_q = f(q), q \in \mathbb{Q}, S = 1\}|}{|\mathbb{Q}|}$$

## 3    De-anonymizable Location Cloaking

In this section, we present the proposed dynamic reversible cloaking algorithm that forms cloaked location regions containing tightly structured segments meeting the required $k$ anonymity level. In this scheme, the anonymization and de-anonymization processes can be considered as two inverse transition strings controlled by the secret key. Specifically, during the two processes, the exchange of segments can be seen as forward and backward transitions between two set of segments, namely the set of segments within the cloaking region and the set of adjacent segments of the cloaking region. Therefore, the two processes are sequences of continuous $n - 1$ forward and backward transitions respectively, which are the inverse of each other. Since there are multiple transition choices, a secret key is used as the transition controller. With the key, both the forward and backward transition strings are determinate and reversible. Without the key, the two transition strings become random and irreversible.

We describe the process with an example presented in Figure 2. For each transition, the number of cloaked segments $|C|$ and adjacent segments $|A|$ are found. For example, suppose in Figure 1, we have $C = \{s_8, s_9, s_{11}\}$ and $A = \{s_6, s_{10}, s_{14}\}$ so that $|C| \leq |A|$. For each addition or removal step, we assign

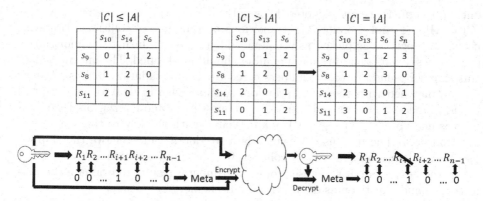

**Fig. 2.** Dynamic reversible cloaking

IDs to all the potential forward and backward transitions between the two sets to distinguish them. These IDs, called transition IDs (TIDs), are organized in a transition table. In Figure 2, $s_8, s_9, s_{11}$ within $C$ and $s_6, s_{10}, s_{14}$ within $A$ are mapped to the three rows and three columns respectively in the order of segment length so that the shortest segments are mapped to the $1^{st}$ row and $1^{st}$ column. The TID in table cell $(i, j)$ associated with $i^{th}$ row and $j^{th}$ column is computed by $((i - 1) + (j - 1)) \bmod |A|$ to make sure no same value is generated in the same row or column. The anonymization key is used to generate a sequence of pseudo-random numbers. The $i^{th}$ pseudo-random number uniquely determines a value for both the $i^{th}$ forward transition and $\{n - i\}^{th}$ backward transition. This value, called picked TID, can be calculated by $p_i = R_i \bmod |A|$ and it is used to select the transition with the TID value same as the picked TID.

However, in the case $|C| > |A|$, since the number of potential backward transitions is larger than the number of available TIDs, the same TID may be assigned to multiple backward transitions, called a collision. Once a collision occurs, the key may fail to distinguish the transitions with same TID and select the backward transition unmatched with the forward transition. In general, collisions during cloaking expansion can be dealt with two approaches. By carefully managing the assignment of TIDs before the anonymization, collisions can be eliminated so that the de-anonymization process can automatically run in a collision-free manner [12]. In this paper, we adopt a different scheme based on using metadata information for collision-resolution. In this approach, the collisions are not eliminated during cloaking expansion but recorded as part of the metadata, which is then used in the de-anonymization process to resolve the collisions. Suppose in Figure 1, we get $C = \{s_8, s_9, s_{11}, s_{14}\}$ and $A = \{s_6, s_{10}, s_{13}\}$. After establishing the table, same TIDs are seen in each column, as shown in Figure 2. To handle such scenarios, in the cloaking process, additional segments, called *null segments* are added to the set $A$ to make $|C| = |A|$. The null segments are not real segments that can be found in the graph and they are conceptual segments used to deal with the collisions during transition. In this example, one null segment is set, denoted by $s_n$. By adding this null segment, we get $|C| = |A| = 4$, and therefore the transitions become free of collisions. However, if the null segment is picked as the next added segment during the anonymization process, that pseudo-random number should be skipped. The information of this skipped pseudo-random numbers is recorded as metadata, which is a binary stream matched with the pseudo-random stream. Each bit is 0 for non-skipped pseudo-random numbers and 1 for skipped ones. After anonymization, the metadata is encrypted by the secret key and shared with the key to the user of the location data. The user uses the metadata to identify and remove the skipped pseudo-random numbers to do a collision-free de-anonymization.

In the next section, we present our experimental results to evaluate the performance and effectiveness of the proposed scheme.

# 4    Experimental Evaluation

In this section, we first briefly describe the experimental setup and then present our experimental results to evaluate the dynamic reversible cloaking algorithm.

## 4.1    Experimental Setup

In our experiments, we use the GTMobiSim mobile trace generator [9] to generate a realistic road network trace on the map of northwest part of Atlanta with 6979 junctions and 9187 segments. 10000 cars are randomly generated along the roads, which then move to random destinations through shortest paths on the road network. We implement three different location anonymization schemes namely random sampling (RS), road-network expansion (RNE) represented by the XStar technique in [19] and our proposed dynamic reversible cloaking (DRC).

## 4.2    Experimental Results

To evaluate the three schemes, we measure the anonymization and de-anonymization time, relative spatial resolution and success rate. Our results show that the proposed dynamic reversible cloaking algorithm is effective and scalable.

We evaluate the effectiveness of the algorithms by varying the k-anonymity level from 10 to 100. Figure 3(a) presents the results of the anonymization time. Higher anonymity level results in longer anonymization time because it requires more segments to be put into the cloaking region. Since the DRC scheme is reversible and generates a stream of pseudo-random values to drive the anonymization process, its anonymization time is higher than the other schemes. However, it continues to have only linearly increasing anonymization time even for higher anonymity levels, thus showing that the scheme is effective and scalable. Figure 3(b) shows values of de-anonymization time for the DRC approach. Here we consider only the DRC scheme as only the DRC scheme can perform de-anonymization. The basic variation trend of the de-anonymization time is

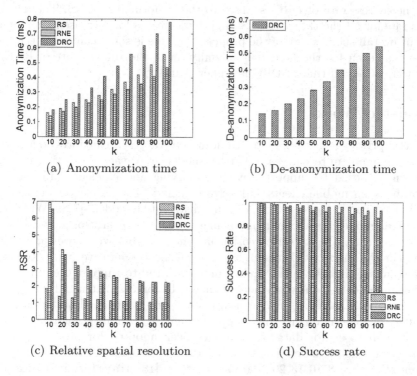

(a) Anonymization time

(b) De-anonymization time

(c) Relative spatial resolution

(d) Success rate

**Fig. 3.** Performance with varying anonymity level

similar as the anonymization time. However, the de-anonymization time for all
anonymity levels is shorter than the corresponding anonymization time as the
anonymization process dynamically adds the null transition to avoid the collisions during de-anonymization. Also, since metadata helps record the collisions, the de-anonymization process directly resolves the collision and it results
in a shorter de-anonymization time. In Figure 3(c), the relationship between
anonymity level and relative spatial resolution (RSR) is given. Instead of pick-
ing segments from the adjacent segment set, RS randomly selects segments from
the whole area defined by the maximum spatial resolution, which gives larger
cloaking region, compared with RNE and DRC. Also, we see that the relative
spatial resolution of DRC is very close to RNE, especially for higher anonymity
levels. Both of the two algorithms pick segments from the adjacent segments
of cloaking region, so the structure of the cloaking region is tighter. In Figure
3(d), success rate for the three schemes with varying anonymity level is measured. Among the three schemes, RS always gets the highest success rate. This
is an inherent feature of RS because it succeeds in all cases unless the number
of users within the whole area defined by maximum spatial resolution cannot
satisfy the required anonymity level. Therefore, the success rate of RS can be
seen as the upper bound of all the anonymimization schemes. Compared with

RNE, the success rate of DRC is closer to the performance of RS. Though the success rate for all the three schemes slightly decreases for increased anonymity level, the overall success rate of the proposed scheme is significantly high. It can be seen that even for the highest anonymity level, the success rate of RNE is higher than 80% and that of DRC is higher than 92%.

## 5    Related Work

As location privacy is gaining more attention, several research efforts on location privacy were made in recent years. Various models of privacy protection systems have been proposed to support privacy-preserving and efficient data communication between mobile clients and servers, including client/server models [4], trusted third party models [5,13,19] and distributed models [7,8]. While the client/server model is simpler to implement, due to the lack of global knowledge in client side, the protection cost is in general higher with lower protection quality. For the distributed model, a decentralized cooperative p2p network is deployed among clients, which requires high overhead to support the infrastructure of communication and movement of clients. In contrast, a trusted third party anonymizer model, such as the one used in our work yields good performance in both query processing quality and computation cost. Various privacy protection algorithms proposed for data privacy have been adopted for protecting location privacy of mobile users. The types of privacy protection algorithms include anonymization [1,5,8,10,13,20], data suppression [18], trajectory inference prevention [2,3,14–16] and encryption [11]. While most of the existing schemes are aimed at preventing the adversary from distinguishing the location of a given user from that of other users, their perturbation techniques are mostly unidirectional and lack the ability to de-anonymize the perturbed information even when a user accessing the information has suitable credentials for obtaining finer information. ReverseCloak algorithms proposed in [12] provide support for multi-level privacy control with the ability to reduce the granularity of the perturbed location based on access credentials. However, in contrast to this proposed work, the approach in ReverseCloak is to perform the location cloaking in a collision-free manner by avoiding the possible segment expansions that may lead to collisions. The cloaking algorithm proposed in this paper takes an alternate approach of allowing collisions to happen during the cloaking expansion process and resolves them with the help of metadata information during the de-anonymization process. While avoiding collisions during cloaking expansion avoids the overhead of metadata management, the approach of collision resolution using metadata can be more efficient in terms of lower anonymization and de-anonymization time overhead.

## 6    Conclusion

In this paper, we present a de-anonymizable location cloaking scheme for protecting location privacy in mobile computing system. Unlike existing location cloaking techniques which are developed as unidirectional location perturbation algorithms, the dynamic reversible cloaking algorithm proposed in this paper can restore the original location information from the perturbed cloaking region when suitable access credentials are provided. Our experiments based on GTMo-bisim show that the proposed cloaking scheme is efficient and scalable. In our future work, we plan to apply the reversible cloaking algorithm developed in this work to protect continuous location-based queries which require continuous exposure of location information leading to possible correlation attacks.

# References

1. Bamba, B., Liu, L., Pesti, P., et al.: Supporting anonymous location queries in mobile environments with privacygrid. In: Proceedings of the 17th International Conference on World Wide Web, pp. 237–246. ACM (2008)
2. Beresford, A., Stajano, F.: Location Privacy in Pervasive Computing. Pervasive Computing, 46–55 (2003)
3. Beresford, A., Frank, S.: Mix zones: User privacy in location-aware services (2004)
4. Cheng, R., Zhang, Y., Bertino, E., et al.: User location privacy in mobile management infrastructures. In: Proc. of Privacy Enhancing Technology Workshop (PET 2006) (2006)
5. Gedik, B., Liu, L.: Location privacy in mobile systems: A personalized anonymization model. In: Proceedings of the 25th IEEE International Conference on Distributed Computing Systems, ICDCS 2005, pp. 620–629. IEEE (2005)
6. Gedik, B., Liu, L.: A customizable k-anonymity model for protecting location privacy (2004)
7. Ghinita, G., Kalnis, P., Skiadopoulos, S.: MobiHide: A mobilea peer-to-peer system for anonymous location-based queries. In: Papadias, D., Zhang, D., Kollios, G. (eds.) SSTD 2007. LNCS, vol. 4605, pp. 221–238. Springer, Heidelberg (2007)
8. Ghinita, G., Kalnis, P., Skiadopoulos, S.: PRIVE: anonymous location-based queries in distributed mobile systems. In: Proceedings of the 16th International Conference on World Wide Web, vol. 19(12), pp. 371–380. ACM (2007)
9. GTMobiSim. https://code.google.com/p/gt-mobisim/
10. Kalnis, P., Ghinita, G., Mouratidis, K., et al.: Preventing location-based identity inference in anonymous spatial queries. IEEE Transactions on Knowledge and Data Engineering 19(12), 1719–1733 (2007)
11. Khoshgozaran, A., Shahabi, C.: Blind evaluation of nearest neighbor queries using space transformation to preserve location privacy. In: Papadias, D., Zhang, D., Kollios, G. (eds.) SSTD 2007. LNCS, vol. 4605, pp. 239–257. Springer, Heidelberg (2007)
12. Li, C., Palanisamy, B.: ReverseCloak: protecting multi-level location privacy over road networks. In: Proc. of 24th ACM International Conference on Information and Knowledge Management (in press, 2015)
13. Mokbel, M.F., Chow, C.Y., Aref, W.G.: The new casper: query processing for location services without compromising privacy. In: Proc. of the 32nd International Conference on Very Large Data Bases (2006)
14. Palanisamy, B., Liu, L.: Attack-resilient mix-zones over road networks: architecture and algorithms. IEEE Transactions on Mobile Computing 14(3), 495–508 (2015)

15. Palanisamy, B., Liu, L., Lee, K., et al.: Anonymizing Continuous Queries with Delay-tolerant Mix-zones on Road Networks. Distributed and Parallel Databases **32**(1), 91–118 (2014)
16. Palanisamy, B., Liu, L.: Mobimix: Protecting location privacy with mix-zones over road networks. In: 27th International Conference on Data Engineering, pp. 494–505 (2011)
17. Sweeney, L.: A model for protecting privacy. International Journal of Uncertainty, Fuzziness and Knowledge-Based Systems, 55–570 (2002)
18. Terrovitis, M., Kmamoulis, N.: Privacy preservation in the publication of trajectories. In: Proc. of 9th International Conference on Mobile Data Management, pp. 65–72. IEEE (2008)
19. Wang, T., Liu, L., Pesti, P.: Privacy-aware mobile services over road networks. Proceedings of the VLDB Endowment **2**(1), 1042–1053 (2009)
20. Xiao, Z., Meng, X., Xu, J.: Quality aware privacy protection for location-based services. In: Kotagiri, R., Radha Krishna, P., Mohania, M., Nantajeewarawat, E. (eds.) DASFAA 2007. LNCS, vol. 4443, pp. 434–446. Springer, Heidelberg (2007)

# First-Priority Relation Graph-Based Malicious Users Detection in Mobile Social Networks

Li Xu[1]([⊠]), Limei Lin[1]([⊠]), and Sheng Wen[2]

[1] School of Mathematics and Computer Science, Fujian Normal University,
Fuzhou, Fujian, China
`xuli@fjnu.edu.cn, putianlinlimei@163.com`
[2] School of Information Technology, Deakin University, Melbourne, Australia

**Abstract.** Mobile social networks (MSNs) consist of many mobile users (individuals) with social characteristics, that provide a variety of data delivery services involving the social relationship among mobile individuals. Because mobile users move around based on their common interests and contact with each other more frequently if they have more social features in common in MSNs. In this paper, we first propose the *first-priority relation graph*, say FPRG, of MSNs. However, some users in MSNs may be *malicious*. Malicious users can break the data delivery through *terminating* the data delivery or *tampering* with the data. Therefore, malicious users will be detected in the process of looking for the data delivery routing to obtain efficient and reliable data delivery routing along the first-priority relation graph. Secondly, we propose one *hamiltonian cycle decomposition of FPRG-based adaptive detection* algorithm based on in MSNs under the *PMC detection model* (the *system-level detection model*).

**Keywords:** Mobile social networks · First-priority relation graph · PMC detection model · Hamiltonian cycle decomposition · Malicious users

## 1 Introduction

A user may be *malicious*, who can break the data delivery through *terminating* the data delivery or *tampering* with the data in mobile social networks (MSNs), which is introduced by combining concepts from two disciplines [5], i.e., social networks [12,16] and mobile communication networks [1]. The MSNs can be viewed as a kind of Delay/Disruption Tolerant Networks (DTNs) [3]. In this paper, we want to detect all malicious users in MSNs under the *PMC detection model* [13] (system-level detection model). Under the PMC detection model, we design one hamiltonian cycle decomposition of the FPRG-based adaptive detection algorithm to detect all malicious users in MSNs. When malicious users are detected, we can choose the reliable data delivery routing without the participation of malicious users under the fundamental framework of the routing.

As far as I know, there is no study about detecting malicious users in MSNs. Detecting malicious users in MSNs is a difficult job due that the number of users

M. Qiu et al. (Eds.): NSS 2015, LNCS 9408, pp. 459–466, 2015.
DOI: 10.1007/978-3-319-25645-0_34

in MSNs is enormous. To overcome the difficulty, we consider the internal social feature of mobile users in MSNs. Considering features have many advantages. First, it avoids the state information collection. Second, the framework of data delivery could be established by considering features and the framework is a regular graph. We use the mathematical model to realize the goal in this paper.

We detect malicious users along the framework of data delivery. Many studies have given schemes to find a preferential data carrier [2, 4, 11, 19]. But they don't consider the internal social features of each user in MSNs. Wu et al. [15, 17, 18] point out the surprising property of being "searchable": Mobile users contact each other more frequently when they have more social features in common. According to the property, each group consists of some users with the same key features in MSNs. In this paper, we define three groups depending on the distribution of malicious users. If all users in a first-priority group are honest, then the group is called as an *honest group*. Otherwise, the group is called as a *dishonest group*.

We detect all malicious users under the PMC detection mode. Because the framework of data delivery is a *hypercube* [14], we can detect malicious users under the system-level detection model. The PMC detection model is one of famous system-level detection models. To realize the goal, we randomly choose a user from a group as the *representative* of the group.

The novelties and contributions of this paper are presented as follows:

• We define a *first-priority relation graph*, say *FPRG*, of MSNs. The FPRG of MSNs is also a basic topology structure for detecting malicious users.

• We propose one hamiltonian cycle decomposition-based adaptive detection for malicious representatives, say *HCD-ADMU-PMC*, based on the FPRG in MSNs under the *PMC detection model*.

• We continuously detect malicious users in any group by the representative of the group or any one honest neighbor user under the PMC detection model.

Organization. The remainder of this paper is organized as follows. Section 2 shows the FPRG and the detection model. Section 3 proposes the cycle decomposition of the FPRG. Section 4 proposes malicious users detection algorithm under the PMC detection model. We conclude our work in Section 5.

## 2 The First-Priority Relation Graph and the Detection Model

### 2.1 The First-Priority Relation Graph of MSNs

We use $G = (V(G), E(G))$ to represent a graph where $V(G)$ is the node-set and $E(G)$ is the edge-set. Let $uv \in E(G)$ be an edge between two nodes $u$ and $v$. For notations and terminology not defined here please refer to [20].

**Definition 1.** *[14] The n-dimensional hypercube $Q_n$ is a graph having $2^n$ nodes labeled from 0 to $2^n - 1$. Two nodes are joined by an edge if their addresses, as binary integers, differ in exactly one bit position. That is to say,*

$V(Q_n) = \{v_1 \cdots v_i \cdots v_n \mid v_i \in \{0,1\}, 1 \leq i \leq n\}$ and $E(Q_n) - \{(v_1 \cdots v_{i-1}v_i$
$v_{i+1} \cdots v_n, v_1 \cdots v_{i-1}\overline{v_i}v_{i+1} \cdots v_n) \mid v_i \subset \{0,1\}, 1 \leq i \leq n, v_i + \overline{v_i} = 1\}.$

In MSNs, users move around and interact at each contact point based on their common social features [15,17,18]. However, usually only a small subset of features is important for routing purposes. The key features in the MSNs are obtained through data mining method of feature extraction. When the social feature is considered, we can choose the routing along the FPRG through groups.

We [8] propose the priority relation graph of MSNs, which is also the basic framework of data delivery routing in MSNs. In this paper, we assume that two groups (nodes) have a *first-priority relationship* when they differ in one feature. We then define the *first-priority relation graph*, say *FPRG*, of MSNs based on the feature, in which any two mobile groups have a first-priority relationship. Each node in the FPRG is called as a first-priority group. More specifically, the FPRG is a general hypercube. Therefore, we also can see that Wu et al. [15,17,18] propose the multi-path routing based on the first-priority relationship.

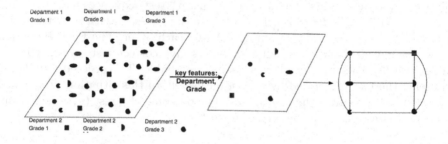

**Fig. 1.** Illustration of the first-priority relation graph of a MSN.

Fig. 1 gives the illustration of FPRG of an MSN. In Fig. 1, each symbol represents a person with two characteristics, and people in the department 1 (2) with grade 1 most preferentially contacts with the people in the department 1 (2) with grade 2 or 3. Moreover, people with grade 1 (or grade 2, or grade 3) in the department 1 most preferentially contacts with the people with grade 1 (or grade 2, or grade 3) in the department 2. Nine solid lines represent nine first-priority relationships among the MSNs.

The proposed FPRG of MSNs is a fundamental framework of the multi-path social feature routing, which guarantees efficient data delivery. We use features of the destination to partition users into groups. This approach is called the *destination-based partitioning*. At each dimension (i.e., feature), we separate users based on whether they have the same features as the one at the destination or not. If they have same features as the one at the destination, then we label 0 at this one bit; otherwise, we label 1 at this one bit. Clearly, the destination-based partitioning group contains users with same key features. This means a general hypercube is "compressed" into a hypercube even though each feature may have many different values.

## 2.2 PMC Detection Model Assumptions

The status of any user is permanent at any a given time. Our object is to accurately detect all malicious users in MSNs. To realize the goal, we firstly want to detect all representatives based on the FPRG. Each representative is assumed to test and to be tested by other neighbors, representatives need to be detected as *honest* or *malicious*. This problem is known as the system-level malicious detection problem. To the best of our knowledge, little attention has been putted on malicious users detection in MSNs involving system-level detection model. The *Preparata, Metze, and Chien (PMC) detection model* [13] is a classical system-level model. We propose some assumptions to correspond the *PMC detection model* [13].

We assume that an honest user always gives the honest answer and a malicious user must give at least one malicious answer after receiving a test-sequence. The test-sequence consists of a lot of problems. All test-sequences have the same size. Under the PMC detection model [13], any two users with a first-priority relationship are capable of performing tests on each other. The PMC detection model assumes an honest user should always give correct test-result, whereas the test result given by a malicious user is unreliable. The ordered pair $(u, v)$ represents the test performed by user $u$ on user $v$. In this situation, $u$ is called the *tester* and $v$ is called the *tested user*. The outcome of a test $(u, v)$ is 1 (resp. 0) if $u$ evaluates $v$ as malicious (resp. honest).

# 3    Hamiltonian Cycle Decomposition of Hypercubes

The $n$-hypercube, for $n > 1$, is a hamiltonian graph [6], i.e., it has an elementary cycle containing all its nodes. Such a cycle is called as a *hamiltonian cycle*. For integer $n \geq 4$, let $f(n) = \lceil log_2(n + 1) \rceil$, then $f(n) \geq 3$. For any given $X_{n-f(n)} \in \{0, 1\}^{n-f(n)}$, let $V(Q[X_{n-f(n)}]) = \{X_{n-f(n)}Y_{f(n)} \mid Y_{f(n)} \in \{0, 1\}^{f(n)}\}$. Then $V(Q[X_{n-f(n)}])$ is a subset of nodes of $Q_n$. Clearly, the induced subgraph $Q_n[X_{n-f(n)}]$ is isomorphic to $Q_{f(n)}$. Therefore, $Q_n$ can be decomposed into a set $\{Q_n[X_{n-f(n)}] \mid X_{n-f(n)} \in \{0, 1\}^{n-f(n)}\}$ of subgraphs, each of which is isomorphic to $Q_{f(n)}$.

A contracted graph $Q_n(f(n))$ is also constructed as follows: $V[Q_n(f(n))] = \{0, 1\}^{n-f(n)}$. Two distinct nodes, say $X_{n-f(n)}$ and $X'_{n-f(n)}$, of $Q_n(f(n))$ are adjacent iff $Q_n$ has two adjacent nodes with the form $X_{n-f(n)}Y_{f(n)}$ and $X'_{n-f(n)}Y_{f(n)}$ where $Y_{f(n)}$ belongs to $\{0, 1\}^{f(n)}$.

**Property 1.** $Q_n(f(n))$ *is isomorphic to* $Q_{n-f(n)}$.

It is well known that $Q_n$ $(n \geq 3)$ contains a hamiltonian cycle, which can easily be constructed recursively. Let $HC_{f(n)}$ be a hamiltonian cycle of $Q_{f(n)}$.

For any given $X_{n-f(n)} \in \{0,1\}^{n-f(n)}$, we design a mapping $\Theta_{X_{n-f(n)}}$ from $V(Q_{f(n)})$ to $V(Q[X_{n-f(n)}])$ as follows: $\Theta_{X_{n-f(n)}} : Y_{f(n)} \mapsto X_{n-f(n)}Y_{f(n)}$ for $Y_{f(n)} \in V(Q_{f(n)})$. Then $HC_{f(n)}$ is mapped onto a hamiltonian cycle of subgraph $Q_n[X_{n-f(n)}]$, which is called a cycle induced by $HC_{f(n)}$ with respecting to $X_{n-f(n)}$, denoted by $HC_{f(n)}(X_{n-f(n)})$. Thus, $Q_n$ contains a set of $2^{n-f(n)}$ disjoint cycles of length $2^{f(n)}$. Based on this, we introduce the following definitions.

**Definition 2.** *Given integer $n \geq 4$. Let $f(n) = \lceil log_2(n+1) \rceil$. Let $HC_{f(n)}$ be a hamiltonian cycle of $Q_{f(n)}$. The collection $\{HC_{f(n)}(X_{n-f(n)}) \mid X_{n-f(n)} \in \{0,1\}^{n-f(n)}\}$ of cycles of $Q_n$, denoted by $HCD(HC_{f(n)})$, is called a cycle decomposition of $Q_n$ induced by $HC_{f(n)}$. Two cycles in $HCD(HC_{f(n)})$ are adjacent iff there is an edge between a node on one cycle and a node on the other cycle.*

## 4   An Adaptive Detection for Malicious Users Under the PMC Detection Model

Wu et al. [15,17,18] propose the multi-path feature routing based on the FPRG in DTNs. However, a user may be malicious. Malicious users can break the data delivery through terminating the data delivery or tampering with the data. Therefore malicious users must be detected through a detection algorithm before giving reliable routing. In this section, our object is to provide a cycle decomposition-based adaptive detection algorithm under the PMC detection model. To realize the goal, we firstly detect all groups by their representatives. If a representative is honest, the representative could continuously detect all users in her/his groups under the PMC detection model. Because the representative and other users in the group are connected with each other. If a representative is malicious, then the group is dishonest group.

In order to describe a detection algorithm for malicious representatives under the PMC detection model, we need the following definitions.

**Definition 3.** *Let $t$ be a syndrome on the first-priority relation graph $Q_n$ of MSNs under the PMC detection model.*

*(1) A test with outcome 0 (resp. 1) will be called a 0-arrow (resp. 1-arrow).*

*(2) A cycle on the first-priority relation graph $Q_n$ is t-zero iff it does not contain any 1-arrow in the obtained syndrome. This cycle is called as a t-zero cycle. Otherwise the cycle is t-nonzero. This cycle is called as a t-nonzero cycle.*

*(3) A cycle is t-guarded if it is t-nonzero but is adjacent to a t-zero cycle. This cycle is called as a t-guarded cycle. Otherwise, the cycle is t-unguarded. This cycle is called as a t-unguarded cycle.*

We start with a general overview of the detection algorithm. Fix $n \geq 7$ and let $f(n) = \lceil log_2(n+1) \rceil$. Therefore, $2^{f(n)} > n$. We consider the cycle decomposition $HCD(HC_{f(n)})$ of the first-priority relation graph $Q_n$ of MSNs, where $HC_{f(n)}$ is the hamiltonian cycle of $Q_{f(n)}$.

**Step one:** we conduct all tests in all copies of $HC_{f(n)}$ in the clockwise direction.

**Property 2.** *In a t-zero cycle of the first-priority relation graph $Q_n$ of MSNs, either all representatives are malicious or all representatives are honest.*

*Proof:* Suppose to the contrary, there exist two consecutive representatives whose status are different. Without loss of generality, we assume that the representative $u$ is honest and the representative $v$ is malicious where $u$ and $v$ are clockwise consecutive representatives. According to the PMC detection model, $t(u,v) = 1$, which contradicts to the $t$-zero cycle.    ■

However, since $2^{f(n)} > n$ for $n \geq 7$, the first possibility is excluded. This enables the diagnosis of all representatives in $t$-zero cycles.

**Property 3.** *Every t-nonzero cycle contains at least one malicious representative, hence there are at most n t-nonzero cycles.*

**Property 4.** *There is at most one t-unguarded cycle in the first-priority relation graph $Q_n$ of MSNs.*

*Proof:* Suppose to the contrary, there are at least two $t$-unguarded cycles. Without loss of generality, assume the cycle $HC_{f(n)}(X_{n-f(n)})$ and the cycle $HC_{f(n)}(Y_{n-f(n)})$ are $t$-unguarded. According to Definition 3, there are at least $2(n - f(n)) - 2$ $t$-guarded cycles. According to Property 3 and the fact of $2(n - f(n)) - 2 > n - 2$ for $n \geq 7$, there are at least $n - 1 + 2$ malicious representatives in MSNs, a contradiction.    ■

**Step two:** we want to detect all representatives on all $t$-guarded cycles on the first-priority relation graph $Q_n$ of MSNs. For each such cycle, we apply representatives of the adjacent $t$-zero cycle as testers.

How many representatives in this unique $t$-unguarded cycle can have all malicious foreign neighbors? We propose the following property to address this problem.

**Property 5.** *In the t-unguarded cycle (if it exists), there is at most one representative, all of whose foreign neighbors are malicious.*

*Proof:* Assume there are at least two representatives, all of whose foreign neighbors are malicious. Since sets of foreign neighbors must be disjoint, the existence of at least $2(n - f(n))$ malicious representatives. Because $2(n - f(n)) > n$ for $n \geq 7$, it yields a contradiction. Hence, the property holds.    ■

**Step three:** it is to detect all representatives of the unique $t$-unguarded cycle on FPRG of MSNs, except possibly $u$, using already detected honest neighbors as testers.

**Step four:** it is to detect the representative $u$, if it exists and has not been detected previously. There are two cases. Either $n$ malicious representatives have been already discovered previously, in which the representative $u$ must be honest, or at most $n - 1$ malicious representatives have been detected, in which the representative $u$ has an already detected honest neighbor on FPRG of MSNs. This neighbor can be used to detect the representative $u$. Thus, a high-level description of the algorithm can be formulated as follows:

---

**Algorithm 1.** A Hamiltonian Cycle Decomposition-based Adaptive Detection for Malicious Representatives under the PMC Detection Model (HCD-ADMR-PMC)

---

**Input:** An integer $n \geq 7$. A hamiltonian cycle decomposition $HCD(HC_{f(n)})$ in the first-priority relation graph $Q_n$ of MSNs. A syndrome $t$ on the first-priority relation graph $Q_n$ of MSNs.

**Output:** A set $M$ of representatives that are detected as malicious.

  1: We randomly choose a user from any group as the representative;
  2: These representatives are vertices of FPRG in MSNs;
  3: Perform all tests in all copies of $HC_{f(n)}$ in the clockwise direction. Identify all $t$-zero cycles. Detect all representatives on these $t$-zero cycles as honest.
  4: Detect all representatives in all $t$-guarded cycles using representatives of adjacent $t$-zero cycles as testers.
  5: Detect all representatives of the unique $t$-unguarded cycle (if it exists), except, possibly, the unique representative with all malicious foreign neighbors. Let already detected honest neighbors be testers.
  6: Detect the last representative, if not detected before.
  7: **return** $M$;

---

## 5   Conclusion

In this paper, we propose one adaptive detection algorithm under the PMC detection model [9,10]. Malicious users detection is to propose reliable routing. The reliable data delivery routing may be proposed in the future.

We may propose another adaptive detection algorithm for malicious users under the comparison detection model [7] in the future. The number of dishonest groups is not large than the number of key features, but the proposed detected algorithm is precise. The pessimism detected algorithms may be proposed to detect more dishonest groups in the future.

**Acknowledgments.** This work was partly supported by the National Natural Science Foundation of China (Nos. 61072080, 61202450, U1405255), Natural Science Foundation of Fujian Province (Nos. 2013J01221, 2013J01222, JA12073), Fujian Normal University Innovative Research Team (No. IRTL1207), and the Hu Guozan Study-Abroad Grant for Graduates of Fujian Normal University.

## References

1. Boldrini, C., Conti, M., Passarella, A.: Contentplace: social-aware data dissemination in opportunistic networks. In: Proc. ACM Int. Symp. Model. Anal. Simul. Wireless Mobile Syst., pp. 203–210 (2008)
2. Bulut, E., Szymanski, B.K.: Exploiting Friendship Relations for Efficient Routing in Mobile Social Networks. IEEE Transactions on Parallel and Distributed Systems **23**(12), 2254–2265 (2012)

3. Fall, K.: A delay-tolerant network architecture for challenged internets. In: Proc. ACM SIGCOMM 2003 (2003)
4. Gao, L., Li, M., Bonti, A., Zhou, W., Yu, S.: Multidimensional Routing Protocol in Human-Associated Delay-Tolerant Networks. IEEE Transactions on Mobile Computing **12**(11), 2132–2144 (2013)
5. Kayastha, N., Niyato, D., Wang, P., Hossain, E.: Architectures, and Protocol Design Issues for Mobile Social Networks: a Survey. Journal: Proceedings of the IEEE-PIEEE **99**(12), 2130–2158 (2011)
6. Kranakis, E., Pelc, A.: Better adaptive diagnosis of hypercubes. IEEE Transactions on Computers **49**(10), 1013–1020 (2000)
7. Lin, L., Xu, L., Zhou, S.: Conditional Diagnosability of Shuffle-Cubes under the Comparison Model. International Journal of Computer Mathematics **92**(2), 230–249 (2015)
8. Lin, L., Xu, L., Zhou, S., Wu, W.: The social feature-based priority relation graph of mobile social networks. In: 2014 IEEE 17th International Conference on Computational Science and Engineering (CSE), pp. 1921–1926. IEEE (2014)
9. Lin, L., Zhou, S., Xu, L., Wang, D.: Conditional Diagnosability of Arrangement Graphs under the PMC Model. Theoretical Computer Science **548**, 79–97 (2014)
10. Lin, L., Zhou, S., Xu, L., Wang, D.: The extra connectivity and conditional diagnosability of alternating group networks. IEEE Transactions on Parallel and Distributed Systems **26**(8), 2352–2362 (2015)
11. Musolesi, M., Mascolo, C.: CAR: Context-Aware Adaptive Routing for Delay-Rolerant Mobile Networks. IEEE Transactions on Mobile Computing **8**(2), 246–260 (2009)
12. Newman, M.E.J., Park, J.: Why Social Networks are Different from Other Types of Networks. PHYSICAL REVIEW E **68**, 036122-1–036122-8 (2003)
13. Preparata, F.P., Metze, G., Chien, R.T.: On the Connection Assignment Problem of Diagnosable Systems. IEEE Transactions on Electronic Computers **EC–16**(6), 848–854 (1967)
14. Saad, Y., Schultz, M.: Topological Properties of Hypercubes. IEEE Transactions on Computers **37**(7), 867–872 (1988)
15. Wang, Y., Yang, W.-S., Wu, J.: Analysis of a Hypercube-based Social Feature Multi-Path Routing in Delay Tolerant Networks. IEEE Transactions on Parallel and Distributed Systems **24**(9), 1706–1716 (2013)
16. Watts, D.J., Dodds, P.S., Newman, M.E.J.: Identity and Search in Social Networks. Science **296**, 1302–1305 (2002)
17. Wu, J., Wang, Y.: Social feature-based multi-path routing in delay tolerant networks, In: Proceedings IEEE INFOCOM 2012, pp. 1368–1376 (2012)
18. Wu, J., Wang, Y.: Hypercube-based Multi-path Social Feature Routing in Human Contact Networks. IEEE Transactions on Computers **63**(2), 383–396 (2014)
19. Xiao, M., Wu, J., Huang, L.: Community-Aware Opportunistic Routing in Mobile Social Networks. IEEE Transactions on Computers **63**(7), 1682–1695 (2014)
20. Xu, J.-M.: Combinatorrial Theory in Networks. Science Press, Beijing (2013)

# A Study of Network Domains Used in Android Applications

Mark E. Fioravanti II, Ayush Shah, and Shengzhi Zhang[✉]

Department of Computer Science and Cybersecurity,
Florida Institute of Technology, Melbourne, USA
{mfioravanti1994,ashah2014}@my.fit.edu, zhangs@fit.edu

**Abstract.** Numerous Android applications use the Internet to share and exchange data. Such data can range from posting simple status updates to private sensitive information such as the users' location or business contacts. Popular Android applications from Google Play have been identified leaking private data to remote third party servers. Existing works focuses on protecting sensitive information from leaving the smartphone, or detecting which applications leak information based on API calls or the permission requests in their Manifest file. In this work, we propose to leverage the combination of static analysis and dynamic analysis to understand ultimately the network domain to which the Android applications are interacting. Network graphs are constructed and demonstrate implicitly the relation of application developers and the network domains used in the applications.

## 1 Introduction

Android has a rich and diverse ecosystem of applications. Recent studies have demonstrated that there are over 1.5 million applications available in Google Play [12] as of May 2015. Although some of those applications need to be purchased, most of them are freely available. Application developers leverage *in-app purchase* or ad engine to obtain revenue. As smartphones are becoming popular and powerful, each device contains a significant cache of sensitive information. Users are interested in maintaining the confidentiality of this information. However, Taintdroid [3] has demonstrated that some popular applications access user sensitive data and send them to remote third party servers.

The seminal work [18] has shown that *INTERNET* is the most popular permission request made by malware samples as well as benign applications. It is desirable to understand how those applications and malware samples use the permission, and what set of network domains are accessed using the permission. The first question has been well studied in the literature. For instance, researchers have proposed to study the permission system used by Android to determine if any privilege escalation could happen [1,4,5,16], or to perform dynamic analysis of the applications at runtime to detect/prevent sensitive data leakage [3,8,9,19]. However, the answer to the second question still remains unclear. In this work, we focus on analyzing the network domains used by Android applications, and

© Springer International Publishing Switzerland 2015
M. Qiu et al. (Eds.): NSS 2015, LNCS 9408, pp. 467–474, 2015.
DOI: 10.1007/978-3-319-25645-0_35

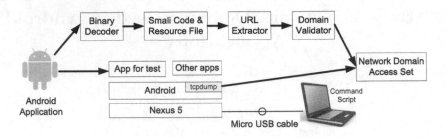

**Fig. 1.** The System Architecture

studying the implication of the results, e.g., potential relationships among the application developers and the network domains.

This work makes the following contributions:

- We successfully combine static analysis and dynamic analysis together to capture accurate and precise network domains used in Android applications.
- Application SMALI files, as well as native libraries are analyzed for any network domain request integration by inspecting the text and extracting the potential URLs referenced by the applications.
- Network graphs are constructed based on the network domains used by Android applications, and implicit relationship among application developers and domains are given.

The rest of this paper is structured as follows. The design and implementation of the proposed network domain analysis framework are presented in Section 2. In Section 3, we provide the evaluation results against popular Android applications obtained from Google Play. Finally we present related works in Section 4 and conclude in Section 5.

## 2    Design and Implementation

Our analysis platform integrates both static analysis and dynamic analysis to provide accurate summary of network domains used by Android application. Figure 1 shows our system architecture. First, we decode the Android application binary into SMALI code and resource files, from which our URL retriever identifies potential network domains. The domain validator will check if the identified network domain is valid or not. If so, it will be added into the network domain access set. Simultaneously, the application binary will be run on an instrumentation platform with automated tools to install, run, execute some commands, and uninstall it. We use *tcpdump* to look through all the network traffic generated by the application during runtime and add those network domains into the access set as well.

## 2.1   Static URL Extraction

Extracting and validating the URLs from an Android application is a multi-stage process. Each application binary is an APK file, a compressed Dalvik EXecutable (DEX) file that runs on the Dalvik Virtual Machine (Dalvik VM). Before the URLs can be extracted, we use the apktool[14] to decompress the APK files to SMALI[6]. The APK file also contains other resources such as icons, images, sound files and Native Libraries which are also examined for strings containing URLs.

**URL Retriever.** URLs are extracted from both the application's SMALI decompiled files and the Native Libraries. First, we use Linux string utility to extract potential URLs from the Native library, and then apply regular expression search on both the SMALI files and those URL-like strings. An intuitive criteria to determine whether a string is a URL, is to check if it begins with *http* or *https*. Although such pattern identifies the *HTTP* requests accurately, in practice provides little information about the domain to which the application was communicating. The string can be in the format of "*http://%s*" or "*http://*" as the developer dynamically assembles or concatenates the string before issuing the HTTP request. Therefore, we modify the URL identification criteria to include strings which are formatted similar to a URL. Unfortunately a large number of strings identified are not valid URLs. Thus, domain validation is applied to identify and remove non-URL strings as to be discussed below.

**Domain Validation.** We parse the Top Level Domain (TLD) and Second Level Domain (SLD) information out of the potential URLs. First, we determine if the potential domain's TLD is within a set of valid TLDs. URLs which are IP addresses are automatically accepted as valid. Second, we perform a DNS query on the potential domain to determine if it is valid. If the response to the DNS query returns with a valid IP address, the domain is considered to be valid. However, if the potential domain does not return with an IP address, the domain cannot yet be rejected as being invalid, as some domain names could be reserved but not used yet. Thus, a second check on potential domains is performed to see if the domain has been registered. If this check also fails, the domain is rejected.

## 2.2   Dynamic Analysis of Network Access

Since some URLs are dynamically constructed, we also integrate an Android GUI testing framework into our analysis platform. We leverage TEMA project [10] (built on top of Android *monkey* [7] event generator) to craft a script including high level commands, e.g., *Drag, TouchScroll, SelectFromMenu, Type*, etc. We run the Android application on Nexus 5 devices, which is connected to our PC where the command script is running on. The scripts are designed to perform main tasks of each application, but it cannot cover all code paths. Therefore, some dynamically built URLs could still be missed from our analysis. Specially for browser applications, the command scripts contain the access request of the URLs extracted from static analysis of the browser's SMALI code, so our script will not incur any extra URL when testing browser applications.

## 3   Evaluation

### 3.1   Collecting Applications

We downloaded android applications directly from Google Play. First, we select top 10 applications from both APP and GAME categories on Google Play, and retrieved their publisher information. Then, we search for the applications developed by those publishers, and in this way, we get more than 1000 applications. We rank them based on reviews and popularity, and finally download 183 applications for our network domain analysis.

### 3.2   Statistics

Static analysis was performed on 183 Android applications, which resulted in 3080 unique domains being discovered. After running each application for 5 minutes in the dynamic analysis platform, additional 52 network domains are identified to be accessed by them. Therefore, we identify 3132 network domains used by those applications.

The application *Opera* browser corresponds to around 400 domains (which is approximately 13% of all of the domains collected). *Android.com* is the most commonly referenced domain by 135 applications. This is not surprising as all of these applications are targeted to the Android platform and make use of existing libraries or components. The other commonly referenced domains do not contain any surprise as well, e.g., ad services, *Google*, *Facebook* and *Akamai Content Distribution Network (CDN)*.

### 3.3   Application Networks

We construct a network graph with individual nodes indicating each application and edges indicating shared domains between two connected applications. It was clear from the graph that applications developed by *Rovio* tend to have strong connections (sharing network domain access), but the remaining applications from other publishers not. We notice that due to some applications using much more network domains, edges indicating commonly used domains among those applications and other applications incur much more interference.

Instead of relying on the total number of shared network domains, we resort to the Jaccard index correlating the number of common domains to the set of all domains the applications using.

$$J(A, B) = \frac{A \cap B}{A \cup B}, \quad 0 \leq J(A, B) \leq 1 \tag{1}$$

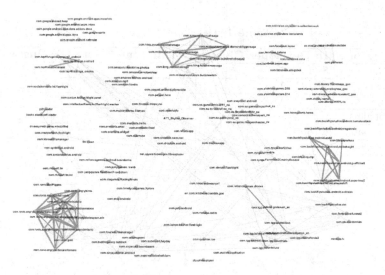

**Fig. 2.** Application Network Graph with Edges based on Jaccard Index

The primary issue with the Jaccard index is that if a pair of applications only contain 1 domain, then the resulting Jaccard index will be 1. Clearly this can't be seen as a strong correlation without other supportive information. To be conservative, we apply a pre-Jaccard index filter, which compares the number of common domains and if the number is less than or equal to 2, the edge is not considered significant. In this way, we can avoid generating a graph consisting of a large number of edges resulting from only 1 or 2 shared network domains. We apply another filter that only shows edges with a Jaccard index larger than 0.5, which means they have more in common than not. The final graph constructed from a pre-filtered Jaccard index is shown in Figure 2.

The Jaccard index based graph clearly highlighted several developer networks. The networks for *Rovio*, *Backflip Studios*, *King*, and *IGG*. It is interesting to note that all of the games from a single developer do not always fall within the same cluster. For example, 4 of *Electronic Art*'s games form two small pair size clusters and the remainder of the developer's games do not cluster. The first cluster of the pair between *Bejeweled Blitz* and *Plants vs Zombies 2*. The second cluster formed by *Tetris 2011* and *Scrabble Free* did not provide any information due to the number of ad libraries included in the game combined with the number of references to *EA* owned domains.

The graph demonstrates that some developers/publishers tend to use the same or similar set of network domains in their applications. Therefore, such behaviour could be leveraged to determine if an application is likely developed by a specific developer. However, it does not rule out the possibility that one application was indeed developed by that developer even if it does not fall into the developer cluster in the graph. Table 1 shows that several notable examples in the graph where applications released by the same developer are not part of a cluster or in the same cluster. *Google* is an example of a developer whose applications are not strongly clustered based on the domains that the applications use.

**Table 1.** Developer Clusters

| Developer | In-Developer Cluster | In-Different Cluster | Unclustered |
|-----------|---------------------|---------------------|-------------|
| King      | 8 (100%)            | 0                   | 0           |
| Rovio     | 11 (91%)            | 0                   | 1 (9%)      |
| Tap4fun   | 4 (100%)            | 0                   | 0           |
| Google    | 0                   | 0                   | 7 (100%)    |
| Facebook  | 4 (80%)             | 0                   | 1 (20%)     |
| Amazon    | 0                   | 0                   | 5 (100%)    |
| Disney    | 4 (80%)             | 0                   | 1 (20%)     |
| Backflip  | 6 (66%)             | 1 (11%)             | 3 (33%)     |

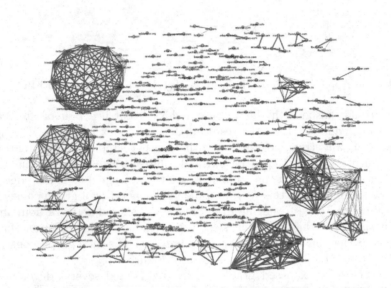

**Fig. 3.** Domain Network Graph with Edges based on Jaccard Index

## 3.4 Domain Name Networks

We also construct another graph where nodes are used to indicate network
domains and edges are used to connect domains which is accessed by the same
application. Again, we use pre-filter Jaccard index same as above and the resulting graph is shown in Figure 3. Domains such as ad services (*Google*, *Flurry*,
*Doubleclick.net*, etc), *Google*, *Facebook*, and *Akamai CDN* are all clustered in
one portion of the graph.

## 4 Related Work

Static analysis has been previously performed on Android applications. Stow-
away [4] mapped application API calls to permissions to determine whether

they are over-privileged. PlayDrone [13] studied Android applications in terms of library usage, repackaged applications, service authentication and etc. Craig et. al [11] studied a collection of popular applications and malware samples to check if Google Play's new auto-update policy could be leveraged to for privilege escalation. A seminal work [18] collected more than 1200 malware samples, and systematically studied different characteristics. In contrast, our work focuses on static analysis to extract URLs and study the network domains used by Android applications.

Researchers have also been applying dynamic analysis to study the runtime behaviour of Android applications. TaintDroid [2] leverages whole system dynamic taint tracking technique to study whether Android applications leak users' private data. VetDroid [16,17] proposed a dynamic analysis platform that studies how permissions are used to access sensitive system resources. [9] applies taint analysis approach to protect users' sensitive data. Our work is fundamentally different in that it is not directly concerned with how the sensitive data is handled within the application or leaked to external sources. Instead, it more focuses on where the sensitive data could be sent. If a malicious application is attempting to harvest sensitive data, it needs to transmit this information to an external recipient. By inspecting the URLs and ultimately the domain names, our work can allow a user to understand where their information could be sent.

Feature extraction and analysis of Android applications with network graphs have previously been proposed. ViewDroid [15] extracted control flows graphs from applications and used the Jaccard index to compare applications to determine if applications are cloned or repackaged. Our work only replies on the URLs and domains contained within an application to determine if two applications are potentially related to each other. Our work differs in that different features are selected and used for the comparison. Moreover, the dual use of the applications and domains as nodes can potentially allow multiple websites to be identified that may be used by the same advertising network.

## 5 Conclusion

Applications have become increasingly popular on the Android smartphone platform and these applications often provide functionality not available from the manufacturer. Various types static and dynamic analysis techniques have been applied on these applications to determine the potential security and privacy risks associated with these applications. In this work, we successfully built an analysis frame that combines both static analysis and dynamic analysis to extract URLs from application SMALI files and native libraries, and then understand network domains accessed by Android applications. The network graphs built based on the analysis results demonstrate the implication among application developers and the network domains used by the applications.

# References

1. Au, K., Zhou, Y., Huang, Z., Lie, D.: Pscout: analyzing the android permission specification. In: Proceedings of the 2012 ACM, CCS 2012, pp. 217–228. ACM (2012)
2. Enck, W., Gilbert, P., Chun, B., Cox, L., Jung, J., McDaniel, P., Sheth, A.: Taintdroid: an information-flow tracking system for realtime privacy monitoring on smartphones. In: Proceedings of the 9th USENIX Conference on OSDI, pp. 1–6 (2010)
3. Enck, W., Gilbert, P., Chun, B., Cox, L.P., Jung, J., McDaniel, P., Sheth, A.: Taintdroid: an information flow tracking system for real-time privacy monitoring on smartphones. Communications of the ACM **57**(3), 99–106 (2014)
4. Felt, A., Chin, E., Hanna, S., Song, D., Wagner, D.: Android permissions demystified. In: Proceedings of the 18th ACM, CCS 2011, pp. 627–638. ACM (2011)
5. Felt, A., Wang, H., Moshchuk, A., Hanna, S., Chin, E.: Permission re-delegation: attacks and defenses. In: USENIX Security Symposium (2011)
6. Google. Dalvik bytecode, November 2014
7. Google. Ui/application exerciser monkey, November 2014
8. Grace, M., Zhou, Y., Wang, Z., Jiang, X.: Systematic detection of capability leaks in stock android smartphones. In: NDSS (2012)
9. Hornyack, P., Han, S., Jung, J., Schechter, S., Wetherall, D.: These aren't the droids you're looking for: retrofitting android to protect data from imperious applications. In: Proceedings of the 18th ACM, CCS 2011, pp. 639–652. ACM (2011)
10. Jääskeläinen, A., Takala, T., Katara, M.: Model-based GUI testing of Android applications. In: Experiences of Test Automation: Case Studies of Software Test Automation, chapter 14, pp. 253–275. Addison-Wesley (2012)
11. Sanders, C., Shah, A., Zhang, S.: Comprehensive analysis of the android google play's auto-update policy. In: Lopez, J., Wu, Y. (eds.) ISPEC 2015. LNCS, vol. 9065, pp. 365–377. Springer, Heidelberg (2015)
12. Statista. Number of apps available in leading app stores as of May 2015 (2015)
13. Viennot, N., Garcia, E., Nieh, J.: A measurement study of google play. In: The 2014 ACM SIGMETRICS, pp. 221–233. ACM (2014)
14. Ryszard, W.: Android apktool: a tool for reverse engineering Android apk files, 2.0.0 rc2 edn., October 2014
15. Zhang, F., Huang, H., Zhu, S., Wu, D., Liu, P.: View-droid: towards obfuscation-resilient mobile application repackaging detection. In: Proceedings of WiSec 2014. ACM (2014)
16. Zhang, Y., Yang, M., Xu, B., Yang, Z., Gu, G., Ning, P., Wang, X., Zang, B.: Vetting undesirable behaviors in android apps with permission use analysis. In: Proceedings of the ACM SIGSAC, CCS 2013, pp. 611–622. ACM (2013)
17. Zhang, Y., Yang, M., Yang, Z., Gu, G., Ning, P., Zang, B.: Permission use analysis for vetting undesirable behaviors in android apps (2013)
18. Zhou, Y., Jiang, X.: Dissecting android malware: characterization and evolution. In: 2012 IEEE Symposium on Security and Privacy (SP), pp. 95–109. IEEE (2012)
19. Zhou, Y., Zhang, X., Jiang, X., Freeh, V.W.: Taming information-stealing smartphone applications (on android). In: McCune, J.M., Balacheff, B., Perrig, A., Sadeghi, A.-R., Sasse, A., Beres, Y. (eds.) Trust 2011. LNCS, vol. 6740, pp. 93–107. Springer, Heidelberg (2011)

# Detecting Malicious Activity on Smartphones Using Sensor Measurements

Roger Piqueras Jover [✉], Ilona Murynets, and Jeffrey Bickford

AT&T Security Research Center, New York, USA
{roger.jover,ilona,jbickford}@att.com

**Abstract.** Mobile devices have long been targets of malware attacks, exploiting the inherent trust that users place in them. They possess unique features, such as continuous internet connectivity, the ability to make premium phone calls and send premium SMS messages, storing sensitive information, and programmatically turning on the camera or microphone. Compromising these features opens up new attack possibilities and enlarges revenue streams for attackers. Despite various existing solutions for detecting mobile malware through binary analysis techniques, mobile malware infections have steadily been on the rise. This paper presents a novel system for detecting the malicious behavior based on smartphone sensor measurements. The system identifies various unique trigger events that should only occur via user action, such as sending SMS messages or turning on the camera or microphone, and determines whether the user initiated them. It can detect various categories of malware, including spamming botnets, premium service fraud, and spyware. The initial version of the prototype is implemented by modifying the default Android SMS messaging app to show that malware sending malicious messages can be detected based on smartphone sensor measurements.

## 1 Introduction

Mobile devices have become an integral part of our daily lives; we rely on them to send and receive email, communicate with family and friends, perform financial transactions, and much more. Due to the inherent trust users place in these devices, as well as the various amounts of sensitive features and personal information stored on them, it is no surprise that mobile devices have become targets of complex malware attacks. New attacks and revenue streams for malicious actors, unseen in the desktop space, are enabled by the unique features of smartphones. Continuous internet connectivity, the ability to make premium phone calls and send SMS messages, and programmatically turning on the camera and microphone are often leveraged in malware infections, and used to expense fraudulent charges to customer accounts. Usually customers find out about such infections only when they receive and inspect their bill at the end of the month.

Over the last couple of years, numerous new malware implementations have been identified. These malicious applications are usually designed to perform

© Springer International Publishing Switzerland 2015
M. Qiu et al. (Eds.): NSS 2015, LNCS 9408, pp. 475–487, 2015.
DOI: 10.1007/978-3-319-25645-0_36

mobile fraud (i.e. fraudulent premium service subscription [2]), assembly of malicious botnets [3], spyware [27] and ransomware [20].

Due to the increasing amount of mobile security threats, various solutions have been proposed in order to protect user devices. Though many security companies provide mobile variants of their anti-virus software, they typically use common signature-based techniques which malware authors can easily circumvent by using encryption and packing techniques [14]. App stores themselves are attempting to protect users by scanning applications for malicious content before posting them, but recent work has shown the feasibility of subverting the app store review process, thereby compromising the integrity of the app store itself [22]. In fact, Google's own App Verification Service, introduced in Android 4.2, was shown to detect only 15% of 1,200 malware samples previously released to the public [16]. In many cases, users are able to sideload applications or use alternative app markets, bypassing these protections all together.

Alternatively, host based behavioral detection engines, that can detect these sophisticated type of threats, are simply infeasible to deploy on current mobile devices due to their heavy resource requirements, restrictive sets of APIs, and limited energy constraints [9]. By using standard machine learning techniques, malicious mobile applications can be successfully detected [24], however they require a significant amount of available labeled data (i.e. recent known malicious applications) to have an acceptable false positive and false negative rates.

Instead of detecting malicious binaries, this paper takes an alternative approach, derived from the idea disclosed in [17], proposing a system to detect the malicious behavior itself. Previous work has detected malicious behavior by inspecting all API calls of a mobile system [10]. Alternatively, we identify a small subset of unique *trigger events* that should only occur via a user action such as sending SMS messages, making a phone call, turning on the camera or microphone, etc. By analyzing data from the various sensors of a mobile device at the time of one of these sensitive actions, our system detects whether it was user initiated or not. For example, sending an SMS message is almost always initiated by a user pressing the send button within their messaging application. Turning on the microphone is always initiated by the user making a phone call or starting a voice recording application. If the system identifies that a sensitive action occurred in the background without user consent, we alert the user and identify the application performing the suspicious action.

Related work has also leveraged sensors on smartphones for similar applications [19,25,26]. These proposals implement an access granting functionality based on sensor measurements. As such, users acquire OS permissions to perform an action by performing a gesture or, alternatively, this permission acquisition occurs implicitly by the sensing of the user's movement when placing a phone call. The system introduced in this manuscript also leverages sensor data but for a different application, instead of implicitly or explicitly granting permission to the user to access certain OS calls, it provides online malware detection leveraging all the available sensors on a smartphone.

In order to assess the feasibility of the proposed system, we developed an initial prototype specifically for the use case of malicious SMS messages. The goal is to detect various types of different malware such as SMS spamming botnets and premium SMS fraud applications. By means of modifying the native Android 4.4 messaging application, smartphone sensor measurements are collected and analyzed. It is shown that malicious outgoing SMS messages can be detected with high accuracy by means of a very short sensor data capture. The promising results indicate the viability of the overall proposed system, both in terms of implementation as well as performance.

The remainder of this paper is organized as follows. Section 2 describes the operation and design of the malicious behavior detection system, providing details on the trigger events under analysis and the sensor data being leveraged. Section 3 presents the implementation details and performance results of the prototype built for the use case of malware sending text messages. Finally, Section 4 concludes the paper.

## 2    Sensor-Based Detection of Malicious Activity

The evolving threat of smartphone malware requires pro-active techniques to protect users. Current strategies against mobile malware are reactive. Malicious apps are pulled from the markets once they have infected many users and, in some instances, charged for fraudulent services. This not sustainable or scalable giving the constant flux of new malware samples seen in the wild, with reports of 700000 new malware instances in the first quarter of 2014 alone [8].

Researchers have shown ways to bypass the security review process of app markets [22], which makes it feasible for fraudsters to publish new malicious applications frequently. Although there are known techniques for malware detection, signature-based detection by antivirus fails to detect the majority of new malware instances [6]. Despite eventual detection and forensic analysis to update the anti-virus signatures, this delay results in thousands of infected devices and legitimate customers with erroneous charges in their monthly bills. Other novel sophisticated approaches for malware and spyware detection involve great deals of traffic analysis and deep packet inspection (DPI) at either the network or the device itself [11]. On one hand, this potentially conflicts with privacy preserving laws and customers often do not feel comfortable having their traffic monitored. On the other hand, endpoint-based DPI suffers of strict computational requirements and battery drain on mobile devices. However, network-based algorithms can successfully detect malware infections without requiring DPI [12].

This paper introduces a technique for detection of malware and spyware infections on mobile devices. The proposed method is local, running on the mobile device, but with very low computation load, negligible battery drain and no traffic inspection. The main novelty of the malware detection algorithm is that it does not aim to detect malicious applications, but the actions - i.e. a very small subset of API calls - that occur as a result of a malware infection. This is done by capturing a very small sample of data from the mobile device sensors at the

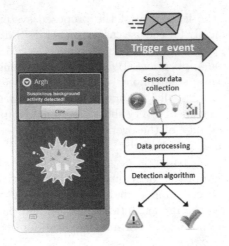

**Fig. 1.** Sensor-based detection of anomalous activity

time of these actions, and applying a decision tree-based detection. As a result, this system is able to determine whether certain activities, such as an outgoing text message to subscribe to a premium service, are a result of the interaction of the user with the User Interface (UI) or a suspicious event that occurred in the background. The implementation of this system is similar to the implicit permission granting system described in [25], which also proposed to collect sensor measurements at specific actions (i.e. placing a phone call and NFC tapping). Instead of preventing malicious access to sensitive resources, our system takes an alternative approach by notifying the user when malicious behavior has been detected, aiming to minimize the impact of false positives.

Sensor-based detection of malicious activity is a challenging task. Arguably, one could determine, for example, whether a text message was typed and sent by the user, if the system could collect data *while* the SMS is being written. The sensor readings when typing follow a simple pattern and can easily be detected by an algorithm [21]. However, this is not possible in our scenario because it would require to constantly monitor sensor measurements to determine when a message is being typed, which would result in severe battery drain. Our challenge is to determine whether an action was user triggered or not with sensor data captured *right after* the API call occurred (e.g. an SMS was sent).

## 2.1 System Description

The proposed detection system consists of the following steps: sensor data collection upon trigger event, sensor data processing, extraction of features, classification and detection. The overall system architecture is described in Figure 1. Note that there is also an extra off-line stage, not depicted in the figure, which collects training data and defines the detection algorithm.

A number of trigger events are defined. These are actions, i.e. API calls, that can be executed both interacting with the UI or programmatically and, if executed without the user's consent, could be leveraged with a malicious intent. In fact, many of them are common important elements in the operation of known instances of malware. These suspicious actions trigger the system to capture a short sample of sensor readings. The captured data is processed in order to extract features. Based on these features, the system determines with high accuracy whether the user did perform the action that triggered the suspicious event or it was executed without the user's intent/knowledge.

As an example, Figure 1 depicts the case of an SMS sent to a premium number. The API call `sendTextMessage` from the `SmsManager` class - in the case of an Android device - triggers a sample from the sensors to be taken. Features are extracted from this sample and, applying a previously trained and defined classification algorithm, it is determines whether the user sent that message through the UI.

## 2.2   Trigger Events and Malware Detection

The great majority of known malware instances aim to generate a revenue or perform some sort of Internet fraud. The common modus operandi of such type of malware is often initiated with either an SMS to a premium number or an outgoing traffic flow to a suspicious domain. Other malware families provide fraudsters with a network of infected devices to, for example, send spam messages [4]. In this case, the infection results in both outgoing flows to a central Command and Control (C&C) host and a large amount of outgoing SMS messages to unknown destinations. Malware infections also often try to spread by sending text messages to known contacts with a link to trick the recipient to install the same malicious app.

Other families of malware are leveraged to create botnets of computing devices in order to perform network scanning, launch attacks or even mine Bitcoin [7]. In this case, these botnets of smartphones also rely on outgoing flows to C&C hosts. Other types of malware leverage infected mobile devices for click fraud activities [1]. Moreover, researchers have argued the potential threat of malicious spyware applications activating the microphone or the camera without the user knowledge and consent [27].

Given the characteristics of the main types of mobile malware seen in the wild, the *trigger events* that can be monitored in the proposed malware detection engine are: *outgoing SMS, outgoing suspicious IP flows and activation of the camera or microphone.*

Recent studies report that an average of 6 billion SMSs are sent per day in the US [5]. Given the number of active cellphone lines in the US, this results in an average of about 19 SMS per day per person. Therefore, all outgoing SMSs could be considered *trigger events* without, in average, resulting in high battery drain due to the activation of the sensors. One could also configure the system to only analyze outgoing SMSs to unknown numbers (not present in the contact list) in order to minimize the number of times a sensor data sample is taken. However, this configuration would fail to detect certain types of malware that spread and contact numbers in the contact list. Users with malware-free devices would rarely, if not ever, have the system querying the sensors due to a suspicious outgoing SMS. Although, for example, a spamming malware infection would potentially result in many sensor activations and, thus, increased battery drain, a security alert would prompt on the phone only after the first message.

Following the same intuition, not all outgoing data flows should be analyzed, as these occur very frequently and their analysis would result in severe battery drain. Consequently, data traffic *trigger events* can be defined as outgoing IP flows to either blacklisted domains or non-whitelisted domains. Outgoing IP flows can also be specifically monitored for third party applications.

## 2.3   Device Sensor Sample Capture

The sensors typically available in modern smartphones are:

- Kinetics: Gyroscope (X,Y,Z) and accelerometer (X,Y,Z).
- Position: Orientation (X,Y,Z).
- Environment: Light sensor, barometer, proximity sensor.
- Connectivity: Connection status {none, 2G, 3G, LTE, WiFi}, Bluetooth status {on, off}, GPS {on, off}.
- (Optional) Location: GPS coordinates, cell id of serving cell (cellular), SSID of serving access point (WiFi).

The proposed malware detection system can leverage all of these sensors, but it could also be implemented with a subset of these sensors. The design of the system is flexible and modular, such that other potential new sensors in future smartphones can be added. Moreover, this method can be used in other personal connected devices. For example, wearable connected devices, Internet of Things (IoT) embedded devices, network-connected cars, etc.

Both for kinetics and position sensors, data from the 3 axes (X,Y,Z) is collected. Location sensors, such as the Assisted Global Positioning System (A-GPS), can be used optionally, mainly given its high battery drain. Alternatively, one could log, with marginal increase in battery drain, the cell id of the base station to which the phone is connected to or, in the case of WiFi, the Service Set Identifier (SSID) of the serving access point (AP). This id could then be mapped to an online repository of known locations of cell towers and WiFi APs or used by itself as a feature for the detection algorithm.

Sensor data is captured for a very short duration, up to just a few seconds, in order to further minimize impact on battery life. Moreover, other than the activation of the camera and the microphone (for an application other than a phone/video call), all the trigger events are linked with an outgoing communication. Note that, when the phone is in a connected state actively transmitting or receiving data, the battery usage is the highest and it is mainly due to the actual radio communication component of the phone [15]. The battery consumption due to the activation of the sensors for a few seconds is negligible compared to the battery drain of the active Radio Frequency (RF) front end itself.

Each *trigger event* results in the capture of a sample of sensor data, from which features are extracted. The detection step of the system processes the extracted features and determines whether the *trigger event* was initiated by the user. This step is executed as a decision-tree-based classification algorithm, which is defined in an off-line training stage.

## 2.4   System Operation and Deployment

The specific algorithm for activity classification and malware detection, for example the conditions and branches of a decision tree-based detection, is dynamic and can be either individual per user or global for all users. A cloud-based host in charge of defining the initial algorithm and periodically training it, though the classification is implemented and evaluated locally on the device. This cloud-based host is constantly fed new data from the mobile devices, such as false positives. For example, assuming that a system prompt/alert was shown upon an anomaly being detected, false positives could be manually discarded by the users, labeled and automatically reported to the central host. Further tuning of the detection algorithm with labeled data of false positives would strengthen the system.

Based on this architecture, the central system would periodically push an updated detection algorithm to the mobile terminals. The algorithm could also be updated in the event of, for example, the user purchasing a new smartphone equipped with a new type of sensor.

Due to its implementation, the proposed system has certain limitations. The main one is the fact that a smart piece of malicious software could send SMSs or open an outgoing IP flow to a blacklisted domain only when the user is about to send a legitimate SMS. Although this is possible, the only way for the malware to know when the user is about to send, for example, a legitimate SMS would be to constantly monitor the sensors. This way, the malware could be tuned to detect when the user is taping a message and then send its malicious payload. However, this would require the malware to constantly monitor the sensors, resulting in very rapid battery drain that would alert the user of something anomalous in the device.

## 3   Prototype

In order to determine the potential viability and performance of a sensor-based malware detection system, we implement a prototype on an Android Motorola Moto X smartphone. This initial implementation is aimed specifically to detect when a text message is being sent programmatically without the user's consent/knowledge, which could be useful in, for example, detecting the presence of premium SMS fraud applications and spamming botnets [2, 4].

## 3.1    Implementation

The initial prototype collects sensor information when SMS messages are sent. Instead of modifying the API framework itself, we simulated this exact functionality by modifying the official Android 4.4 messaging application, obtained from the official AOSP source code repository. This allows us to create labeled sensor data generated on user initiated SMS messages, as well as randomly simulated malicious messages in the background.

We add a new class to the messaging application, called the `SensorSampler` which enables the various sensors on the phone for a 10 second time period and logs sensor measurements to a file. The 10 second samples are taken to asses the performance of the detection algorithm for various window durations, as short as 1 second and as long as 10 seconds, as in a final implementation one would intuitively encounter a tradeoff between a short (i.e. 1 second) sample with minimum battery drain but with lower detection accuracy and a longer (i.e. 10 second) sample with higher accuracy but higher battery drain.

By grepping through the messaging application's code base, we located the point at which the `sendTextMessage()` API call is made. Here we add code to spawn an `IntentService` and log the sensor readings in the background. We have an additional long lived background service that randomly records sensor measurements to a separate file, in order to represent messages not initiated by the user. We label these samples as malicious messages. Time stamps for each message sent are recorded as well, for correlation during the results stage.

The data samples were collected from real users for a period of 2 weeks, during which they communicated normally via SMS with friends and relatives. Samples of real SMSs are thus taken at all situations, conditions, positions and orientations of the phone. In parallel, malicious samples are samples of sensor data taken at random times throughout the day. As a result, malicious samples include any type of context, such as while the phone is in a pocket, in a bag while walking, and more challenging scenarios such as playing a game or browsing the Internet.

The recorded sensor measurements are used for analysis, to determine if user-initiated SMS messages can be identified using machine learning techniques. Although, as discussed in Section 2, the sensor samples can only be captured right after the API call occurred, the results obtained by the prototype do indicate that it is feasible to detect malware infections with good accuracy and false positive rates with the processing of such *after the fact* captures.

## 3.2    Detection Algorithm Training and Performance

Measurements of each coordinate $X$, $Y$ and $Z$ coming from kinetics and position sensors, as well as light sensor measurements, are treated as unevenly spaced time series. A total of 109 time and frequency domain features including 92 kinetics, 13 position and 4 light sensor features are extracted from each window of 1 to 10 seconds from the beginning of the time series [1]. A detailed overview of

---

[1] In order to compute FFT, the unevenly spaced time series are first interpolated.

**Table 1.** Features extracted from kinetics, position and light sensors

| Sensor | Time-domain | Frequency-domain | #features |
|---|---|---|---|
| Gyroscope | Mean, standard deviation, mean absolute deviation for $X$, $Y$ and $Z$, the overall magnitude, and correlations between axes. | Principal frequency, spectral energy, first 5 components of FFT and magnitude, X-Y-Z freq-domain entropy and correlations between axes. | 46 |
| Acceleration | | | 46 |
| Orientation | | | 13 |
| Light | Mean, standard deviation, mean absolute deviation and range. | | 4 |

the feature extraction methods for accelerometer measurements is presented in [18, 23]. In our work, features are also extracted from time series corresponding to orientation, gyroscope and light measurements. Table 1 summarizes all the extracted features.

To detect which SMSs were initiated by malware, we used logistic regression, support vector machines, functional, alternating, random trees and random forest classifiers based on the features from each of the ten time windows individually. The overall performance of the random forest classifiers was superior to the rest. To improve the false positive rate even more the random forest classifiers trained on the features for each of the ten windows are fused.

To detect which SMSs were initiated by malware, we used logistic regression, support vector machines, functional, alternating, random trees and random forest classifiers based on the features extracted for each of the ten time windows individually. The overall performance of the random forest classifiers was superior to the rest of the classifiers and thus this was the chosen classifier for the prototype implementation. To improve the false positive rate, several random forest classifiers trained on the features for each of the ten windows are fused. A classification rule is then presented as a linear combination of ten classifiers with weight coefficients found from minimization of the total prediction error on the training dataset, where false positive errors have a higher weight $W_{FP}$ than false negative weight $W_{FN}$. The random forest uses a random subset of features to generate multiple decision trees from a sampled training set with replacement. The prediction is then determined by the majority rule of the generated decision trees. The Waikato Environment for Knowledge Analysis (WEKA) data mining tool [13], which implements these decision trees, shows that 82 features have a positive information gain with respect to the indicator whether a message was sent by a user or a malware. Out of the top 20 features there were:

**Table 2.** Classification results for different sample durations and combining all samples

| Sample length | 1 | 2 | 3 | 4 | 5 | 6 | 7 | 8 | 9 | 10 | combined |
|---|---|---|---|---|---|---|---|---|---|---|---|
| False Positive | 0.126 | 0.146 | 0.097 | 0.126 | 0.097 | 0.126 | 0.146 | 0.107 | 0.136 | 0.117 | 0.077 |
| False Negative | 0.10 | 0.112 | 0.129 | 0.086 | 0.069 | 0.095 | 0.078 | 0.129 | 0.121 | 0.103 | 0.103 |
| Accuracy (%) | 88.58 | 87.21 | 88.58 | 89.49 | 91.78 | 89.04 | 89.04 | 88.12 | 87.21 | 89.04 | 90.86 |

- Frequency domain features: 1st, 4th and 5th components of FFT, the magnitude of the first five components and the spectral energy of $Y$ axis of acceleration.
- Time domain features: pairwise correlations between axes of gyroscope, mean and standard deviation for all axes of orientation and acceleration.
- Light features: mean, standard deviation and range.

Let the random forest classifiers for time windows $1, \ldots, 10$ be classifiers $1, \ldots, 10$, respectively (i.e. classifier $k$ is the classifier for the time window of k seconds), and let $x_{ki} \in \{0, 1\}$ be the prediction of classifier $k$ for testing record $i \in \{1, \ldots, n\}$, where $x_{ki} = 0$ if classifier $k$ predicts record $i$ as user initiated SMS, and $x_{ki} = 1$ if it predicts the record as malware initiated SMS. Let $y_i \in \{0, 1\}$ be an actual label of data record $i$ ($y_i = 0$ and $y_i = 1$ if record $i$ is user and malware initiated SMS, respectively). To improve the false positive, the data labels are regressed with respect to the predictions of the ten classifiers:

$$\widehat{y}_i = \sum_{f=1}^{10} w_f x_{1i}, \tag{1}$$

where $\widehat{y}_i$ is the prediction of data label $y_i$ and $\sum_{f=1}^{10} w_f = 1$. The regression coefficients $w_f$ are found by the least squares method

$$\min_{w_f, \alpha} \sum_{i=1}^{n} \left( W_{FP} I_{\{\widehat{y}_i > \alpha\}} + W_{FN} I_{\{\widehat{y}_i <= \alpha\}} \right) \left( I_{\{\widehat{y}_i > \alpha\}} - y_i \right)^2$$

$$\text{s.t.} \quad \sum_{f=1}^{10} w_f = 1, \tag{2}$$

where $I_{\{.\}}$ is the indicator function equal to 1 if the condition in curly brackets is true and zero otherwise.

The goal of the proposed system is to detect malware activity on smartphones while minimizing the number of false positive alerts the user receives. Thus, we assign $W_{FP} = 0.7$ and $W_{FN} = 0.3$.

The data set consists of 309 SMSs initiated by a user (using the device over several days) and 348 randomly simulated malicious messages, as described in Section 3.1. Two thirds of the data were used to train the algorithms and one third to test them. Table 2 shows predictions of the ten classifiers and of their optimal linear combination on the testing dataset. The "accuracy" column in Table 2 shows the proportions of the total correct classifications. The model based on the 5 second samples has the highest accuracy, while the combined model has the lowest false positive. Regardless, the frequency of false positive alerts will usually be very low, especially if sensor measurements are done only in the event of an outgoing SMS to a number not in the user's phone contact list. Recent research shows that a contact list-based model can reduce malware detection false positives [12].

Note that all the performance results in Table 2 are for the detection of a single malicious SMS. The great majority of malware instances will send multiple SMS messages, which will result in an overall higher malicious activity detection accuracy.

The algorithm performance results show that it is possible to achieve good detection accuracy, which meets the battery life preservation requirements highlighted in Section 2. The results of the initial experiments presented in this paper indicate that indeed smartphone malware activity could potentially be detected by analyzing sensor data measurements.

## 4    Conclusions

This paper introduces a smartphone malware detection system, which aims to detect the malicious activity, as opposed to the malware infection itself. This system leverages smartphone sensor measurements to determine whether a specific *trigger event* occurred due to the user's input or programmatically by a malicious application. These *trigger events* are API calls and other actions that should not occur without the user being aware of it, and are commonly malware-triggered actions.

An initial prototype, implemented by modifying the native Android 4.4 messaging app, is designed to detect malicious text messages generated by a malware infection. Processing sensor measurements from the gyroscope, accelerator, orientation and light sensors, a classification algorithm is able to detect a malicious outgoing message with high accuracy. The promising results validate the potential feasibility of an overall malicious activity detection engine on smartphones based on sensor measurements, which will be part of our future work. We plan to extend the prototype to additional *trigger events* and sensors.

## References

1. Chinese mobile malware powers click-fraud scam. The Register, February 2011. http://goo.gl/Jgmxmx
2. Security Alert - Android Trojan GGTracker Charges Premium Rate SMS Messages. The Lookout Blog, June 2011. http://goo.gl/oo5oQZ
3. Android spam scam is first smart phone botnet. cNet, July 2012. http://goo.gl/hyX1rF

4. Security Alert - SpamSoldier. The Lookout Blog, December 2012. http://goo.gl/7lkRM
5. SMS Usage Remains Strong In The US: 6 Billion SMS Messages Are Sent Each Day. Forrester Research, June 2012. http://goo.gl/WvTTGM
6. Study: Mobile Antivirus Apps Fail the Spyware Test. Time Magazine, July 2013. http://goo.gl/xzQRFR
7. Google removes Bitcoin mining Android malware from Play. Threat Post, April 2014. http://goo.gl/M9VMwW
8. McAfee Threats Report: Third Quarter 2013. McAfee Labs (2014). http://goo.gl/y5uAfv
9. Bickford, J., Lagar-Cavilla, H., Varshavsky, A., Ganapthy, V., Iftode, L.: Security versus energy tradeoffs in host-based mobile malware detection. In: Proc. 9th Conference on Mobile Systems, Applications and Services (2011)
10. Bose, A., Hu, X., Shin, K.G., Park, T.: Behavioral detection of malware on mobile handsets. In: Proceedings of the 6th International Conference on Mobile Systems, Applications, and Services, pp. 225–238. ACM (2008)
11. Burguera, I., Zurutuza, U., Nadjm-Tehrani, S.: Crowdroid: behavior-based malware detection system for android. In: Proceedings of the 1st ACM Workshop on Security and Privacy in Smartphones and Mobile Devices, pp. 15–26. ACM (2011)
12. Giura, P., Murynets, I., Jover, R.P., Vahlis, Y.: Is it really you?: user identification via adaptive behavior fingerprinting. In: CODASPY 2014, pp. 333–344. ACM (2014)
13. Hall, M., Frank, E., Holmes, G., Pfahringer, B., Reutemann, P., Witten, I.H.: The weka data mining software: an update. ACM SIGKDD Explorations Newsletter 11(1), 10–18 (2009)
14. Hamlen, K.W., Mohan, V., Masud, M.M., Khan, L., Thuraisingham, B.: Exploiting an Antivirus Interface. Computer Standards and Interfaces, November 2009
15. Huang, J., Qian, F., Gerber, A., Mao, Z.M., Sen, S., Spatscheck, O.: A close examination of performance and power characteristics of 4g lte networks. In: Proceedings of the 10th International Conference on Mobile Systems, Applications, and Services, pp. 225–238. ACM (2012)
16. Jiang, X.: An Evaluation of the Application Verification Service in Android 4.2. http://www.csc.ncsu.edu/faculty/jiang/appverify/
17. Jover, R.P., Murynets, I.: Malware and anomaly detection via activity recognition based on sensor data, May 7, 2015. US Patent 20,150,128,265
18. Kwapisz, J.R., Weiss, G.M., Moore, S.A.: Activity recognition using cell phone accelerometers. ACM SigKDD Explorations Newsletter 12(2), 74–82 (2011)
19. Li, H., Ma, D., Saxena, N., Shrestha, B., Zhu, Y.: Tap-wave-rub: lightweight malware prevention for smartphones using intuitive human gestures. In: Proceedings of the Sixth ACM Conference on Security and Privacy in Wireless and Mobile Networks, pp. 25–30. ACM (2013)
20. Lookout. U.S. targeted by coercive mobile ransomware impersonating the FBI, July 2014. http://goo.gl/uh0a6a
21. Miluzzo, E., Varshavsky, A., Balakrishnan, S., Choudhury, R.R.: Tapprints: your finger taps have fingerprints. In: Proceedings of the 10th International Conference on Mobile Systems, Applications, and Services, MobiSys 2012, pp. 323–336. ACM, New York (2012)
22. Oberheide, J., Miller, C.: Dissecting android's bouncer. In: SummerCon (2012)
23. Preece, S.J., Goulermas, J.Y., Kenney, L.P., Howard, D.: A comparison of feature extraction methods for the classification of dynamic activities from accelerometer data. IEEE Transactions on Biomedical Engineering 56(3), 871–879 (2009)

24. Rieck, K., Trinius, P., Willems, C., Holz, T.: Automatic analysis of malware behavior using machine learning. Journal of Computer Security **19**(4), 639–668 (2011)
25. Shrestha, B., Mohamed, M., Borg, A., Saxena, N., Tamrakar, S.: Curbing mobile malware based on user-transparent hand movements. In: Pervasive Computing (PerCom 2015) (2015)
26. Shrestha, B., Saxena, N., Harrison, J.: Wave-to-access: protecting sensitive mobile device services via a hand waving gesture. In: Abdalla, M., Nita-Rotaru, C., Dahab, R. (eds.) CANS 2013. LNCS, vol. 8257, pp. 199–217. Springer, Heidelberg (2013)
27. Templeman, R., Rahman, Z., Crandall, D.J., Kapadia, A.: Placeraider: Virtual theft in physical spaces with smartphones. CoRR, abs/1209.5982 (2012)

# A Game Theoretic Framework for Cloud Security Transparency

Abdulaziz Aldribi and Issa Traore[✉]

The Department of Electrical and Computer Engineering,
University of Victoria, Victoria, Canada
aaldribi@uvic.ca, itraore@ece.uvic.ca
http://www.isot.ece.uvic.ca

**Abstract.** Over the past few years cloud computing has skyrocketed in popularity with the IT industry. Connected to this growing popularity is an increasing level of concern over the security of the cloud computing infrastructure. Despite this concern, cloud providers do not disclose any information about their security precautions. With no information on the security precautions, a provider's clients cannot be certain that their applications are safe from attack. Furthermore, clients are not granted access to the network level of the system to implement any of their own security features.

In this paper we approach cloud security transparency constraints from a game theoretic perspective. Specifically, we model the security transparency problem as a dynamic non-cooperative game theoretic problem, whereby the provider and client are modelled as the players in the game. A theoretical analysis through which the provider or client can compute his/her best strategy to reach the Nash equilibrium is presented.

**Keywords:** Cloud computing · Cloud security · Transparency · Game theory

## 1 Introduction

Cloud computing solutions are rapidly increasing in popularity within the IT industry. However, security still remains a major concern for cloud adopters and potential clients [1]. Despite the great level of concern for security, most cloud providers offer little to no assurance of precautionary measures to their clients. The reason may be the opposing interests of the provider and the client with respect to security transparency. For the provider, increasing security transparency essentially means making their security implementations more visible to the client [2]. Transparency poses problems for the provider. For instance, if a client has malicious intent, they would have detailed knowledge of the system. Providers often service multiple clients on a single server; providers will not disclose any information to one client that could compromise the others. This poses the question of how clients can trust their provider's security setup with such

© Springer International Publishing Switzerland 2015
M. Qiu et al. (Eds.): NSS 2015, LNCS 9408, pp. 488–500, 2015.
DOI: 10.1007/978-3-319-25645-0_37

little information on it. If a client has customers, and is responsible for their sensitive information, the client cannot reassure their customers of the security precautions taken by the provider without any information.

In this paper, we employ game theory to investigate analytically and help formulate and analyse approaches to security transparency in cloud computing. In particular, we present a theoretical model through which the client and provider can compute their best strategy to reach the Nash equilibrium to enter into a contract. To our knowledge this is the first work in the literature that applies game theory to decision making to solve the security transparency issue of contracts.

The rest of the paper is sectioned as follows. A coverage of related work is given in Section 2. Section 3 reflects on the motivation behind this paper based on a theoretical gaming approach to security transparency in cloud computing, and it presents the analytical results. Finally, the paper's conclusion is provided in Section 4.

## 2   State of the Art

Despite no directly related work to security transparency in cloud computing, there have been multiple attempts to improve it. We list two examples of these attempts. The first allows the clients to conduct limited cloud monitoring and penetration testing on the VM they are deployed on. The second example takes the approach of suggesting security disclosure principles for the initial contract between a provider and a potential client. By disclosing limited security information, hopefully a potential client would be satisfied with the precautions a provider has taken.

### 2.1   Amazon Web Services

Amazon Web Services (AWS) has recognized the problem in security transparency between client and provider and have made strides towards limited network monitoring for their clients. If a client submits a formal request, AWS will allow limited penetration testing. To do this AWS requires the client submit a start and end date of their testing, only use approved testing tools,and not impede the performance of the resources, since they are sharing them with other clients [3]. Another option that AWS offers for monitoring is called "Cloud Watch". Cloud Watch is an Amazon developed tool that allows clients to monitor their VMs' resource usage and other customizable metrics. Cloud Watch is a subscription based tool which charges by the hour or per metric [4].

### 2.2   Sun Microsystems

In 2009, Sun Microsystems published a paper on "Cloud Computing with Transparent Security" [5]. In the paper, Sun proposes implementing a certain set of transparency standards that a provider must meet in their initial sign up contract. Sun recommends that the provider disclose common security policies and practices but withhold details of their architecture. In the paper, they also recognize some key benefits of increasing security transparency:

- improved trust from the client, potentially resulting in faster adaptation
- helps provider to better understand and manage customer expectations related to security
- educe the amount of time and resources spent, by the provider, reassuring clients of potential risks (eg: AWS frequently needs to respond to client requests for penetration testing)

Although this idea gives a good basis for the initial contract, we believe that it would not increase transparency enough to give client's peace of mind. The only way for a client to fully trust a provider's security setup is to allow them to implement or control a portion of it.

# 3  Analyzing Transparency Constraints Using Game Theory

Game theory as a mathematical notion provides a set of tools to analyse and model interactive decision making situations between agents with conflicting interests. It is also defined as the study of how the ultimate result of a competitive circumstance is decided on by the action of the players involved in the game, based on the purposes and preferences of these players, and on the strategy that is used by each player [6]. In this section we take advantage of Game Theory to obtain the best security transparency decision in Cloud Computing.

In subsection 3.1, the importance of security in cloud computing for both provider and client is discussed using game theory. The interaction between the provider and the client regarding transparency in cloud security is presented in subsection 3.2. The concept of Nash equilibrium is presented in subsection 3.3 for transparency in cloud security and we address how game theory can help decision makers with that. This section closes with subsection 3.4 by studying the effect of mixing a game strategy if it is used to sign the contract between provider and client if the provider is willing to ensure transparency to the client.

## 3.1  Dominance "from Prisoner's Dilemma Game [7]"

In game theory, a game (G) contains three components (P,S,U), where P is the set of players, S is the set of strategies, and U is the set of payoff functions. In the game in this section all players are assumed to be rational, which means their choice will be according to the outcome they prefer most since they know their opponent's choice. There are two strategies for every player, X and Y; strategy X is said to dominate strategy Y if the outcome resulting from X is better than the outcome resulting from Y. Therefore, since all players are rational they will never choose to play a dominated strategy. Discovering which strategies dominate will lead the rational player to choose only one of their strategies.

This example illustrates the dominant strategy, and it has been presented here to show how security is very important for both the cloud provider and client to enter into a contract:

Player 1 ($P_1$) : is a cloud provider
Player 2 ($P_2$) : is a client
Provider offer → ($High, Low$) Security
Client will → ($Buy, Don't buy$)

They are considering entering into a contract from a cloud service for a period of time. The cloud service provider has two security level options to provide to the client: High or Low. A low security option is not a viable option for the provider since the chance of breaching security is high and that will cost too much if it happens. High security is the only desirable option for the client, thus the contract will not be signed if the provider chooses to provide a cloud service with low security. The client has to choose 'Buy or Don't buy' according to the level of security that is provided by the cloud service provider. However, the level of security put into the contract cannot be verified by the client.

**Table 1.** Dominance strategy: High - Low security game between a cloud provider P1 and a client P2

| $P_1$ \ $P_2$ | Buy | Don't Buy |
|---|---|---|
| High | A,a | A,b |
| Low | B,c | C,a |

The payoff matrix of the game's dominance strategy is shown in Table 1 for two different types of strategies, where the following variables are defined:

- A and a represent the most preferred outcome for $P_1$ and $P_2$, respectively;
- B and b represent the second most preferred outcome for $P_1$ and $P_2$, respectively;
- C and c represent the least preferred outcome for $P_1$ and $P_2$, respectively.

In the matrix, the possible payoffs for $P_1$ and $P_2$ are presented as variables to show it in a general form. Player 1 chooses a row, either High or Low, and Player 2 chooses one of the columns Buy, Don't buy.

In this example "High" is a strategy that dominates the "Low" strategy for the cloud provider. Regardless of whether the client chooses to buy or not, the provider always prefers to provide high security protection. Therefore, since the client believes that the cloud provider is rational and always prefers a High security level, they will choose buy and enter into a contract with the cloud provider. Therefore, "Buy" is a strategy that dominates the "Don't buy" strategy for the client.

In the remainder of this section we will formulate the game and present the expected utility for both the cloud provider and client if they would like to sign a contract. If $(P_1)$ chooses "High" the payoff will be (A) and if the client chooses "Buy" which dominates "Don't buy", then the payoff for both provider and client is (A,a), resulted from playing (High,Buy) strategies, which always dominates "Low, Don't buy" strategies.

In this example "High" strictly dominates "Low" for $(P_1)$ and "Buy" strictly dominates "Don't buy" for $(P_2)$. Here we can see what the expected utility is for both the cloud provider and client if they would like to sign a contract, and what is best for them.The first two equations are the expected utilities for client if buys the service or not:

$$EU_{buy} = 0.5 \times a + 0.5 \times c \tag{1}$$

$$EU_{Don't\ buy} = 0.5 \times b + 0.5 \times a \tag{2}$$

The folowing equations are the expected utilities for provider if provides High or Low security

$$EU_{high} = 0.5 \times A + 0.5 \times A$$
$$EU_{high} = A \tag{3}$$

$$EU_{low} = 0.5 \times B + 0.5 \times C \tag{4}$$

Let $\sigma$ donate the probability that a player plays a particular pure strategy, then we finds the expected utility if it provides High or Low security to the provider, and Buy or Don't buy for the client. The client's expected utility of playing "Buy" can be written as pure strategy as a function of the provider's mixed strategy:

$$EU_{buy} = \sigma_{high} \times a + \sigma_{low} \times c \tag{5}$$

The client's expected utility of playing "Don't buy" as a pure strategy is:

$$EU_{Don't\ buy} = \sigma_{high} \times b + \sigma_{low} \times a \tag{6}$$

Now we are looking for a mixed strategy from the provider that leaves the client indifferent situation between his/her pure strategies. In other words, we want to find $\sigma_{high}$ and $\sigma_{low}$ such that:

$$EU_{buy} = EU_{Don't\ buy} \tag{7}$$

This implies the following:

$$\sigma_{high} \times a + \sigma_{low} \times c = \sigma_{high} \times b + \sigma_{low} \times a \tag{8}$$

And since

$$\sigma_{high} + \sigma_{low} = 1 \tag{9}$$

then

$$\sigma_{low} = 1 - \sigma_{high} \tag{10}$$

We get

$$\sigma_{high} \times a + (1 - \sigma_{high}) \times c = \sigma_{high} \times b + (1 - \sigma_{high}) \times a$$
$$\sigma_{high} \times a + (c - c \times \sigma_{high}) = \sigma_{high} \times b + (a - a \times \sigma_{high}) \tag{11}$$
$$2 \times a \times \sigma_{high} - c \times \sigma_{high} - b \times \sigma_{high} = a - c$$

$$\sigma_{high} = \frac{a - c}{(2a - c - b)} \tag{12}$$

By substituting $\sigma_{high}$ into $\sigma_{high} + \sigma_{low} = 1$ we get

$$\sigma_{low} = 1 - \left( \frac{a - c}{(2a - c - b)} \right) \tag{13}$$

So if the provider chooses high security with probability $\frac{a-c}{(2a-c-b)}$ and low with probability $1 - \left( \frac{a-c}{(2a-c-b)} \right)$ then the client will earn the same payoff for selecting either to buy or not as a pure strategy.

Now it is possible to calculate a mixed strategy for the client that leaves the provider indifferent between his two pure strategies:

$$EU_{high} = \sigma_{buy} \times A + (1 - \sigma_{buy}) \times A \tag{14}$$
$$EU_{low} = \sigma_{buy} \times B + (1 - \sigma_{buy}) \times C \tag{15}$$

$$EU_{high} = EU_{low} \tag{16}$$

This implies

$$\sigma_{buy} \times A + (1 - \sigma_{buy}) \times A = \sigma_{buy} \times B + (1 - \sigma_{buy}) \times C \tag{17}$$

Which gives:

$$\sigma_{buy} = \frac{A - C}{B - C} \tag{18}$$

$$\sigma_{Don't\ buy} = 1 - \left( \frac{A - C}{B - C} \right) \tag{19}$$

So if the client chooses to buy with probability $\frac{A-C}{B-C}$ and not to buy with probability $1 - \left( \frac{A-C}{B-C} \right)$ then the provider is in-between providing high security and low security as a pure strategy.

## 3.2   Transparency in Cloud Security

In this example we apply the same previous game strategy to find out if the contract will be signed or not and whether the client requests security transparency from the provider. All players are assumed to be rational, which means their choice will be according to the outcome they prefer most since they know their opponent's choice.

The cloud service provider has two security transparency level options to provide to the client More or Less. The Less security transparency option is the preferable option for the provider since the main concern of the provider is to protect the cloud from any chance of breaching security. More security transparency is the only desirable option for the client who would like to protect his data from any security issues, thus the contract will not be signed if the provider chooses to provide cloud services with less security transparency. The client has to choose Buy or Don't buy according to the level of security transparency that is provided by the cloud service provider.

**Table 2.** Utility matrix of $P_1$ and $P_2$ dependent on the transparency level

| $P_1$ \ $P_2$ | Buy | Don't Buy |
|---|---|---|
| More | C,c | C,b |
| Less | B,c | A,a |

Table 2 illustrats the outcome of the provider and client, if they sign or not the contract, depends on the transparency level. In this example "Less" is a strategy that dominates the "More" strategy for the cloud provider. Regardless of whether the client chooses to buy or not, the cloud provider always prefers to provide less transparency in the security for the client for protection reasons. And since the client believes that the cloud provider is rational and will always prefer less security transparency, then the client will prefer not to sign a contract with that provider. Therefore, the rationality of both players leads to the conclusion that the provider will provide less security transparency and as a result the contract will not be signed.

In this section we will formulate the game and present the expected utility for both the cloud provider and client if they would like to sign a contract. The expected utility for the cloud provider is expressed as:

$$EU_{More} = 0.5 \times C + 0.5 \times C$$
$$EU_{More} = C \tag{20}$$

$$EU_{Less} = 0.5 \times B + 0.5 \times A \tag{21}$$

And the expected utility for the client is given by:

$$EU_{Buy} = 0.5 \times c + 0.5 \times c$$
$$EU_{Buy} = c \tag{22}$$

$$EU_{Don't\ buy} = 0.5 \times b + 0.5 \times a \qquad (23)$$

By solving these equations, it is possible to figure out what the best for provider is to ensure high or low security transparency, and whether the best option for the client is to sign the contract(i.e. buy) or not.

Now let us use sigma ($\sigma$) to represent the probability that a player plays a particularly pure strategy.

Let us find the expected utility of providing more or less security transparency for the provider, and whether to sign the contract or not for the client.

$$EU_{Buy} = \sigma_{More} \times c + \sigma_{Less} \times c \qquad (24)$$

$$EU_{Don't\ buy} = \sigma_{More} \times b + \sigma_{Less} \times a \qquad (25)$$

We want to find $\sigma_{More}$ and $\sigma_{Less}$ such that:

$$EU_{Buy} = EU_{Don't\ buy} \qquad (26)$$

This corresponds to:

$$\sigma_{More} \times c + \sigma_{Less} \times c = \sigma_{More} \times b + \sigma_{Less} \times a \qquad (27)$$

And since

$$\sigma_{More} + \sigma_{Less} = 1 \qquad (28)$$

Then

$$\sigma_{More} = 1 - \sigma_{Less} \qquad (29)$$

Which implies:

$$(1 - \sigma_{Less}) \times c + \sigma_{Less} \times c = (1 - \sigma_{Less}) \times b + \sigma_{Less} \times a \qquad (30)$$

This gives:

$$\sigma_{Less} = \frac{b - c}{a - b} \qquad (31)$$

So if the provider chooses less transparency with probability $\frac{b-c}{a-b}$ and more transparency with probability $1 - \left(\frac{b-c}{a-b}\right)$, then the client will earn the same payoff for selecting either to sign or not to sign the contract.

### 3.3    Transparency in Cloud Security using Nash Equilibrium

From the previous examples, knowledge of the dominating strategies by players will give them advice on how the game could be played. However, this is not always the case with all games that they have dominating strategies, thus it will be difficult for players to play the game if there is not enough advice on all outcomes. Therefore, the players need a more general strategy, which is the main concept of Nash equilibrium. Nash equilibrium recommends an action profile for each player so that no single player has an incentive to deviate from its current optimal strategy and cannot obtain a higher payoff, assuming that each player follows the recommendation since both of them are rational [8]. From the previous example, we will examine the utility outcome for both provider and client if the provider is willing to provide more security transparency to the customer. Also, the client can change the game by giving him the right to cancel the cloud service contract if the security transparency is less than expected.

**Table 3.** Utility matrix of provider and client which leads to Nash equilibrium

| $P_1$ \ $P_2$ | Buy | Don't Buy |
|---|---|---|
| More | A,a | C,b |
| Less | B,c | B,b |

Table 3 is the utility matrix of provider and client that shows the resulting game; it is clear that the most preferred outcome for both provider and client is for more security transparency to be provided and the contract to be signed by the client. Also, since the client has the opt out option in the contract, his or her second preferred outcome will be not to sign or even cancel the contract if the provider changes the transparency level.

In this game there is no dominating strategy for either the provider or client. Instead, there are two Nash equilibria: one of them is the strategy combination (less, don't buy). The second one is the strategy combination (more, buy); this strategy is in equilibrium since the player $P_2$ prefers to sign the contract when the transparency is more and player $P_1$ prefers to provide more transparency if the client will sign the contract. Both Nash equilibria are logical options for the provider and client on how to play the game. Since Nash equilibrium strategies are chosen by the players, they will rationally stay with their strategies and will not change.

Now, this game can be formulated and the expected utility presented for both the cloud provider and client if they would like to sign a contract. The expected utility for the cloud provider can be expressed as:

$$EU_{More} = 0.5 \times A + 0.5 \times C \tag{32}$$

$$EU_{Less} = 0.5 \times B + 0.5 \times B = B \tag{33}$$

And the expected utility for the client is given by:

$$EU_{Buy} = 0.5 \times a + 0.5 \times c \tag{34}$$

$$EU_{Don't\ buy} = 0.5 \times b + 0.5 \times b = b \tag{35}$$

By solving these equations, it is possible to figure out which options are the best for the provider and the client. For the provider, the choice will be between high or low security transparency,while for the client it will be about whether to Buy or Do not buy. Let us find the expected utility of providing more or less security transparency by the provider, and signing the contract or not by the client.

$$EU_{Buy} = \sigma_{More} \times a + \sigma_{Less} \times c \qquad (36)$$

$$EU_{Don't\ buy} = \sigma_{More} \times b + \sigma_{Less} \times b \qquad (37)$$

We want to find $\sigma_{More}$ and $\sigma_{Less}$ such that:

$$EU_{Buy} = EU_{Don't\ buy} \qquad (38)$$

This corresponds to

$$\sigma_{More} \times a + \sigma_{Less} \times c = \sigma_{More} \times b + \sigma_{Less} \times b \qquad (39)$$

And since

$$\sigma_{More} + \sigma_{Less} = 1 \qquad (40)$$

We have

$$\sigma_{More} = 1 - \sigma_{Less} \qquad (41)$$

Which gives:

$$(1 - \sigma_{Less}) \times a + \sigma_{Less} \times c = (1 - \sigma_{Less}) \times b + \sigma_{Less} \times b \qquad (42)$$

By solving this equation we get

$$\sigma_{Less} = \frac{a - b}{a - c} \qquad (43)$$

So if the provider chooses less transparency with probability $\frac{a-b}{a-c}$ and more transparency with probability $1 - \left(\frac{a-b}{a-c}\right)$,then the client earns the same payoff for selecting either to sign or not to sign the contract.

## 3.4  Transparency in Cloud Security Using a Mixed Strategy

Not every game in strategic form always has a Nash equilibrium that makes each player definitely choose it. Therefore, the player may decide to choose one of these pure strategies randomly with certain probability. A mixed strategy is the idea that when the player randomizes his strategy selection, any finite strategic form of the game has equilibrium if a mixed strategy is allowed.

In this example, a mixed strategy is applied to transparency in cloud security, assuming that the cloud provider is willing to provide transparency in security to the client and the client will sign the contract. The main concern for the provider is that if the client performs malicious activities, they may attack the provider cloud or other client's services. Therefore, the provider would like to be sure that the client follows the regulations and does not intend to violate them.

In this scenario the provider has two strategies, either to monitor (Moni) the client activities which will cost the provider, or to rely on the contract regulations (don't Moni) and assume that the client will not violate them. For client strategies, if he or she intends to carry out malicious activity (Malic) and gets caught by the provider, which will cost him or her too much by either paying money and/or being put in jail. The alternative for the client is to perform normal activities ( denoted Nor ).

**Table 4.** Utility Matrix for Mixed strategy

| $P_1$ \ $P_2$ | Nor | Mal |
|---|---|---|
| don't Mo | A,b | C,a |
| Mo | C,b | B,c |

Table 4 shows the resulting game. The main difference in this game compared to the previous games is that this game does not have equilibrium in pure strategies. Since the most preferred outcome for provider comes from choice that is different from client choice (similarly for the client). Therefore they will not remain on one choice.

For example, if the provider chooses not to monitor the activities of the client, assuming that the client will be using the transparency features normally, now if the client chooses to behave normally the outcome will be in the provider's favour which is (A,b). However, if the client turns out to be an attacker and his or her activities become malicious, the provider will lose too much and the outcome will be on the side of the client (C,a). If the provider chooses to monitor and the client performs malicious activities, that will result in them getting caught by the provider and the outcome will be worse for the client (B,c).

By visiting all cases, the provider would strongly prefer for the client to behave normally and not perform or intend any malicious activities, but this is not always the case. Therefore, the provider will monitor the client's activities if it is felt that the types of activities are risky. If the provider always chooses not to monitor the client's activities, then this will turn out to be a dominating strategy and the client will perform malicious activities which results in a unique equilibrium. From Table 4, this game has no equilibrium in pure strategies, since if the provider is not willing to change their choice and if it is not monitoring, the most preferred outcome for the client without doubt would be to perform malicious activities.

Since this game is a kind of a mixed strategy, the players should maximize their worst outcome against all possible choices of the other players. For example, a mixed strategy for the provider in this game is to monitor the client activities with a certain probability. This monitoring probability could be used to find out what will lead to equilibrium. If the probability of monitoring the client activities is very low, then the client will get outcome (b) for behaving normally, while a better outcome (a) will be gained if he or she changes their behaviour to be malicious. On the other hand, if the probability of inspection is much higher, then the expected outcome for the client if he or she behaves in a malicious way is the worst outcome (c), thus the client will behave normally to improve his or her outcome and become (b). If the provider knows when the client will be indifferent, this means they know when the client will possibly randomize between his or her strategies for behaving normally or maliciously, since both of these strategies give the same outcome.

In this last part, we will find the probability that makes the client indifferent.

$$EU_{Nor} = \sigma_{don't\ Mo} \times b + \sigma_{Mo} \times b \tag{44}$$

$$EU_{Mal} = \sigma_{don't\ Mo} \times a + \sigma_{Mo} \times c \tag{45}$$

We want to find $\sigma_{don't\ Mo}$ and $\sigma_{Mo}$ such that:

$$EU_{Nor} = EU_{Mal} \tag{46}$$

This corresponds to:

$$\sigma_{don't\ Mo} \times b + \sigma_{Mo} \times b = \sigma_{don't\ Mo} \times a + \sigma_{Mo} \times c \tag{47}$$

And since

$$\sigma_{don't\ Mo} + \sigma_{Mo} = 1 \tag{48}$$

Then

$$\sigma_{don't\ Mo} = 1 - \sigma_{Mo} \tag{49}$$

Which implies:

$$(1 - \sigma_{Mo}) \times b + \sigma_{Mo} \times b = (1 - \sigma_{Mo}) \times a + \sigma_{Mo} \times c \tag{50}$$

This gives:

$$\sigma_{Mo} = \frac{b - c}{c - a} \tag{51}$$

So if the provider chooses to monitor the client activities with probability $\frac{b-c}{c-a}$ and does not monitor with probability $1 - \left(\frac{b-c}{c-a}\right)$, then the client earns the same payoff for selecting either to behave normally or to perform malicious activities in the cloud or for other clients.

From all the previous case studies, techniques from game theory have been applied to help formulate and analyse the conflict between the cloud provider and client to reach an agreement, and for more transparency in security to be obtained by the client.

## 4   Conclusion

Security is one of the primary concerns with cloud computing. The provider that successfully assures clients that their applications are safe will be the provider that gains more clients. in this paper, techniques from game theory have been applied to help formulate and analyse solutions to security transparency that the provider could offer to the client, who would require more transparency in security to sign the contract. Moreover, through equilibrium analysis of the transparency security game, the provider can gain a deeper understanding of client strategies. As has been discussed in this article, the application of game theory with incomplete and imperfect information is an emerging field in security transparency in cloud computing, with no papers published so far.

From our research, it is clear that providers want to gain clients' trust. If clients trust their provider, they will recommend their provider. Building strong relationships between the clients and the provider is vital to cloud computing, and we believe this relationship can be achieved by giving clients a bigger sandbox to play in.

**Acknowledgement.** This research is supported by the Qassim University and the Ministry of Edu- cation of the Kingdom of Saudi Arabia.

# References

1. Gens, F.: IT cloud services user survey.pt.2: Top benefits and challenges, IDC eXchange (2008). http://blogs.idc.com/ie/?p=210
2. Pauley, W.A.: Cloud provider transparency: an empirical evaluation. In: Security and Privacy, vol. 8, pp. 32–39. IEEE Press (2010)
3. Penetration Testing. http://aws.amazon.com/security/penetration-testing/
4. AWS CloudWatch Cloud-based Server Monitorin. http://aws.amazon.com/cloudwatch/
5. Micro, S.: Building Customer Trust in Cloud Computing with Transparent Security. Sun Micro White Paper (2009)
6. Midha, S., Sharma, A.K., Sikka, G.: A survey on wireless sensor network clustering protocols optimized via game theory. ACM SIGBED Review **11**, 8–18 (2014)
7. Kreps, D.M., Milgrom, P., Roberts, J., Wilson, R.: Rational cooperation in the finitely repeated prisoners' dilemma. Journal of Economic Theory **27**, 245–252 (1982)
8. Nash, J.: Equilibrium points in n-person games. Proceedings of the National Academy of Sciences **36**, 48–49 (1950)

# Short Papers: Application and Network Security

# Let's Get Mobile: Secure FOTA for Automotive System

Hafizah Mansor(✉), Konstantinos Markantonakis,
Raja Naeem Akram, and Keith Mayes

Information Security Group, Smart Card Centre, Royal Holloway,
University of London, Egham, UK
{Hafizah.Mansor.2011,RajaNaeem.Akram.2008}@live.rhul.ac.uk,
{K.Markantonakis,Keith.Mayes}@rhul.ac.uk

**Abstract.** Over-the-air (OTA) firmware update is available in some systems such as mobile networks. Security plays a vital role to ensure that the firmware update process is successful despite possible threats against it. Therefore mobile devices may be useful to support the OTA firmware update process for other devices such as those used for automotive applications. Using a mobile device as a tool can offer added security features as well as giving flexibility to the process. Automotive security is of high importance as it is critically related to the safety and reliability of the vehicle. We propose a secure OTA firmware update (FOTA) protocol to offer flexibility to the firmware update process, while meeting the required security requirements. The protocol was formally analysed using Scyther and CasperFDR and no known attack was found.

**Keywords:** Firmware update · Over-the-air · Electronic Control Unit · Formal analysis · CasperFDR · Scyther

## 1 Introduction

A security module such as an attack resistant microcontroller has a very small trusted code base. Hence it is possible to design, test and verify its operation so that a firmware update is not required. However, for more complex electronic assemblies and embedded systems, firmware update is a common and necessary requirement.

Firmware update is therefore an important feature in the life cycle of many embedded systems. Depending on the infrastructure in place, the firmware update can take place via over-the-air (OTA) or over-the-wire (OTW). However, in the automotive industry, security plays a very important role to ensure the safety and reliability of the car. The Electronic Control Unit (ECU) is the microcontroller used as a building block to control the operation of a car. In modern cars, there can be up to 70 ECUs to control different operations [5]. If any of the ECUs are attacked, the safety of the car and passengers may be at risk.

© Springer International Publishing Switzerland 2015
M. Qiu et al. (Eds.): NSS 2015, LNCS 9408, pp. 503–510, 2015.
DOI: 10.1007/978-3-319-25645-0_38

## 1.1   Problem Statement

Firmware updates of automotive subsystems are security critical, but there is yet to be a secure solution that can be accessible to all the involved entities. A secure solution with flexibility in the process is important to ensure its acceptance, especially by the users.

## 1.2   Contribution

The contributions of this paper are as follows:

1. We propose a secure OTA automotive firmware update protocol with the use of a mobile device. The mobile application to conduct the firmware update ensures the authentication of the parties involved and the confidentiality of the firmware.
2. We provide analysis of the OTA firmware update protocol using Scyther [2] and CasperFDR [7].

## 2   Related Work

The E-safety Vehicle Intrusion Protected Applications (EVITA) [4] proposed an architecture using Hardware Security Modules (HSM). Different HSM levels are used for different security functions required by the different ECU modules [8]. There are three types of HSMs namely full HSM, medium HSM and light HSM. Full HSM is used in the Central Communication Unit (CCU) module, which is the ECU module responsible for Vehicle-to-X (V2X), i.e. Vehicle-to-Infrastructure (V2I) or Vehicle-to-Vehicle (V2V) communications. Medium HSMs are used for advanced ECUs (gateways, head unit, engine control) in the in-vehicle networks. Light HSMs are used for sensors and actuators communications. Firmware Update Over-the-Air (FOTA) in the EVITA project [6] uses the diagnostic tool at workshop. This process requires the car to be at the workshop to initiate the update process. Flach et. al proposed CARMA for personalised tuning [3]. The CARMA is a mobile application on the Android operating system that can be used to change a few parameters of the engine (on a single ECU) to improve the car performance, but security was not the main consideration.

## 3   The Secure FOTA Protocol

We decided to choose the architecture with the mobile device as an interface of the FOTA process.

### 3.1   Goals

In this section, we consider the requirements for each entity involved in the FOTA protocol.

1. The OEM is required to (a) distribute the updated firmware with confidentiality. (b) store updated information related to the car, for example, versions of firmware, parts ID and associated cryptographic keys. (c) ensure secure communication between the OEM and car via the mobile device (including authentication).
2. The mobile device is required to (a) pass the encrypted firmware from the OEM server to the car. (b) authenticate parties involved (OEM and car) in the update process. (c) pass information from the car to the OEM server and vice versa. (d) store the old encrypted firmware from the car as a backup.
3. The ECU is required to (a) authenticate the OEM through the mobile device. (b) pass an encrypted version of old working firmware to the mobile device prior to the installation of the update. (c) receive the encrypted version of firmware from the OEM server (through the mobile device), decrypt it and install it. (d) inform to the OEM server if any ECU has been replaced via the mobile device.

## 3.2   Protocol Notations and Assumptions

In this section, we discuss the protocol notations and assumptions.

**Table 1.** Protocol notation

| | |
|---|---|
| oem | original equipment manufacturer |
| ccu | central communication unit |
| ecu | electronic control unit |
| md | mobile device |
| $id_x$ | ID of entity x, x=OEM, mobile device, CCU or ECU |
| $pk_x$ | public key of entity x, x=OEM, mobile device, CCU or ECU |
| $sk_x$ | private key of entity x, x=OEM, mobile device, CCU or ECU |
| $K_{Nb}$ | session MAC key between MD-CCU-ECU |
| $K_{Na}$ | session MAC key between OEM-MD |
| $\{M\}_k$ | message M is encrypted with key k |
| $sign_{sk}\{m\}$ | message m is signed with private key sk |
| $MAC_K\{m\}$ | MAC of message m using key K |
| ts | time stamp |
| $psk_{ecu}$ | pre-shared symmetric key of ECU (shared between OEM and ECU) |
| $psk_{fek}$ | pre-shared firmware encryption key (shared between OEM and ECU) |
| $psk_{unlock}$ | pre-shared symmetric key to unlock the ECU into reprogramming mode (shared between OEM and ECU) |
| $Frm_{old}$ | old working firmware |
| $Frm_{new}$ | new firmware (to be updated) |

**Assumptions.** A number of assumptions are made as follows: (a) Cryptographic keys between the OEM and cars (Central Communication Unit (CCU) and ECUs) are preloaded during the manufacturing stage. CCU is the central unit that stores all the keys for all ECUs in the same network. All external communications to the car must go through the CCU. (b) HSM-based ECUs are used, i.e as proposed in the EVITA project. (c) A mobile application will be used to conduct all the mobile device's functions for the OTA firmware update protocol. (d) The mobile application is used for an individual car, i.e one car per mobile device. (e) All ECUs are known to the OEM, i.e the cryptographic keys are pre-loaded before the ECUs are distributed in the market for parts replacements. (f) Every car has a barcode that can be scanned to obtain the car's details. (g) The ECUs and CCUs are tamper resistant. (h) The communication channel between the entities is vulnerable to attacks.

## 3.3   Protocol Description

The mobile device is seen as a tool to receive notification of available update and the firmware update itself. When an update is available, the car manufacturer notifies the car owner through the mobile application. The car owner will download the updated firmware into his mobile device. At a later convenient time, he would be able to download and install the firmware into his car ECU from his mobile device.

**Registration.** First, we consider the registration process for all the involved parties. In this proposal, we consider the car manufacturer is the trusted party maintaining the registration and the application server for its firmware updates. During the installation and registration, the mobile device will obtain the cryptographic keys for further communications. The required keys are OEM server public key, CCU public key and ECU public key (to verify the signatures of OEM, CCU and ECU respectively). The OEM server and the car will obtain the mobile device's public key. Whenever an ECU is replaced, the mobile device will be updated with the new parameters (will be discussed in 3.3). (a) Mobile device: Firstly, the mobile device needs to install the application, which will be available from the application store. Once the application is installed into the mobile device, the public key of the OEM is obtained. (b) OEM: The unique identification of the car (eg. could be the vehicle identification number, VIN) will be obtained. From the car identification number, the car parameters such as the make, model and year of manufactured are obtained. These parameters are important to be able to receive the correct update from the OEM server. This can be done conveniently by scanning the barcode of the car using the mobile device's camera (this is outside the scope of this paper). In this phase, the public key of the CCU and all ECUs' identifications are obtained. The parameters are stored in the mobile device to be later transported to the OEM in order to get the relevant updates.

**Notification.** This phase is required to ensure the ECU gets the correct update. There are two options to get the update. The mobile user can manually check whether any update is available or be automatically notified by the OEM.

**Download to Mobile Device.** When a new firmware update is available, the update is downloaded into the mobile device in an encrypted version using

**Table 2.** Protocol description: OEM-MD Download phase

(1) MD → OEM : $id_{md}||\{K_{Na}\}_{pk_{oem}}||ts1||sign_{sk_{md}}\{id_{md}||\{K_{Na}\}_{pk_{oem}}||ts1\}$
    OEM → MD : $id_{oem}||ack||ts2||sign_{sk_{oem}}\{id_{oem}||ack||ts2\}$

(2) MD → OEM : $id_{md}||RequestDL||id_{ecu}||ts3||MAC_{K_{Na}}\{id_{md}||RequestDL||id_{ecu}||ts3\}$

(3) OEM → MD : $id_{oem}||\{psk_{unlock}\}_{psk_{ecu}}||ts4||MAC_{K_{Na}}\{id_{oem}||\{psk_{unlock}\}_{psk_{ecu}}||ts4\}$
    MD → OEM : $id_{md}||ack||ts5||MAC_{K_{Na}}\{id_{md}||ack||ts5\}$

(4) OEM → MD : $id_{oem}||\{Frm_{new}\}_{psk_{fek}}||ts6||MAC_{K_{Na}}\{id_{oem}||\{Frm_{new}\}_{psk_{fek}}||ts6\}$
    MD → OEM : $id_{md}||ack||ts7||MAC_{K_{Na}}\{id_{md}||ack||ts7\}$

a firmware encryption key ($psk_{fek}$). The (encrypted) key to unlock the ECU $psk_{unlock}$ is also transferred to the mobile device. Refer to Table 2. (1) The OEM and mobile device will establish a secret session key, $K_{Na}$. This session key $K_{Na}$ is generated by the mobile device and securely shared with the OEM. It will be used for MAC computations during the whole OEM-MD download phase. The mobile device will sign the message of $id_{md}$, encrypted $K_{Na}$ and timestamp. $K_{Na}$ is encrypted with the OEM public key. The OEM will verify the signature, decrypt the $K_{Na}$, store it and send an acknowledgment. (2) The mobile device sends a request for the firmware download, RequestDL. It is concatenated with the identification of the respective ECU ($id_{ecu}$), time stamp and the MAC. (3) The OEM verifies the MAC and sends the key to unlock the ECU into reprogramming mode ($psk_{unlock}$). The key is encrypted with a pre-shared key between the OEM and ECU ($psk_{ecu}$). The mobile device verifies the MAC, stores the encrypted $\{psk_{unlock}\}_{psk_{ecu}}$ and sends an acknowledgment. (4) The OEM then sends the firmware ($Frm_{new}$) encrypted with the pre-shared firmware encryption key ($psk_{fek}$). The mobile device verifies the MAC, stores the encrypted firmware and sends an acknowledgment.

**Download and Install.** Refer to Table 3 for this phase. Once the new firmware is downloaded in the mobile device, the user can choose to conduct the update at

**Table 3.** Protocol description: MD-ECU Download and install phase

(1) MD→CCU  : $id_{md}||\{K_{Nb}\}_{pk_{ccu}}||ts8||sign_{sk_{md}}\{id_{md}||\{K_{Nb}\}_{pk_{ccu}}||ts8\}$
    CCU→ECU : $id_{ccu}||\{K_{Nb}\}_{pk_{ecu}}||ts9||sign_{sk_{ccu}}\{id_{ccu}||\{K_{Nb}\}_{pk_{ecu}}||ts9\}$
    ECU→CCU : $id_{ecu}||ack||ts10||sign_{sk_{ecu}}\{id_{ecu}||ack||ts10\}$
    CCU→MD  : $id_{ccu}||ack||ts11||sign_{sk_{ccu}}\{id_{ccu}||ack||ts11\}$

(2) MD→ECU  : $id_{md}||\{psk_{unlock}\}_{psk_{ecu}}||ts12||MAC_{K_{Nb}}\{id_{md}||\{psk_{unlock}\}_{psk_{ecu}}||ts12\}$
    ECU→MD  : $id_{ecu}||ack||ts13||MAC_{K_{Nb}}\{id_{ecu}||ack||ts13\}$

(3) ECU→MD  : $id_{ecu}||\{Frm_{old}\}_{psk_{fek}}||ts14||MAC_{K_{Nb}}\{id_{ecu}||\{Frm_{old}\}_{psk_{fek}}||ts14\}$
    MD→ECU  : $id_{md}||ack||ts15||MAC_{K_{Nb}}\{id_{md}||ack||ts15\}$

(4) MD→ECU  : $id_{md}||\{Frm_{new}\}_{psk_{fek}}||ts16||MAC_{K_{Nb}}\{id_{md}||\{Frm_{new}\}_{psk_{fek}}||ts16\}$
    ECU→MD  : $id_{ecu}||ack||ts17||MAC_{K_{Nb}}\{id_{ecu}||ack||ts17\}$

a later convenient time. This is an advantage if the car has no long range wireless communications of its own. (1) The mobile device and car will establish a session key $K_{Nb}$. This session key $K_{Nb}$ is generated by the mobile device and securely shared with the car (CCU and ECU). It will be used for MAC computation during the whole MD-ECU download and install phase. The mobile device will sign the message of $id_{md}$, encrypted $K_{Nb}$ and timestamp. The $K_{Nb}$ is encrypted with the CCU's public key, concatenated with time stamp and the mobile device signature. The CCU will verify the signature, decrypt the $K_{Nb}$ and store it. It will then encrypt $K_{Nb}$ with the ECU's public key, concatenated with time stamp and the CCU's signature and send to ECU. ECU will verify the signature, decrypt the $K_{Nb}$, store it and send an acknowledgment. (2) The mobile device transfers the encrypted unlock ECU key, ($\{psk_{unlock}\}_{psk_{ecu}}$) to the ECU. It is the key to unlock the ECU to enable reprogramming mode. The ECU has its own unlock key, which is only known to itself and the OEM. The ECU will verify the MAC and decrypt $\{psk_{unlock}\}_{psk_{ecu}}$. If it is the correct key, the ECU will change into reprogramming mode. Else, the process will stop here. (3) The ECU transfers the old firmware ($Frm_{old}$) to the mobile device. This firmware is encrypted using the pre-shared $psk_{fek}$, concatenated with time stamp and MAC. The currently working firmware in the ECU ($Frm_{old}$) is transferred to the mobile device in encrypted version to ensure its confidentiality. This will be used as a backup for rollback if the installation of the new firmware fails. The mobile device will send an acknowledgment to the ECU once all the blocks of the encrypted $Frm_{old}$ is received. By transferring the old firmware to the mobile device as a backup, it avoids doubling the memory size in all ECUs. (4) The ECU receives the encrypted firmware update $\{Frm_{new}\}_{psk_{fek}}$ from the mobile device. After the MAC is verified, it will decrypt the firmware and install the updated firmware to the flash of ECU block by block. The firmware is encrypted with a pre-shared firmware encryption key. Only the ECU is able to decrypt the firmware. For every block of installed firmware, the chain of hashes are computed and verified. Any error will terminate the update process and the process will restart again. After three trials, the ECU will rollback to its previous version. If the rollback fails, an error message will be indicated on the mobile application. A replacement of an ECU maybe suggested if there is any issue with memory failure.

**ECU Replacement.** If any of the ECUs are replaced, the key update protocol needs to be established to ensure further firmware updates on the ECUs are possible. (1) The mobile device (through the CCU) will request the new ECU information (RequestID). The ECU will give its ID to the mobile device (through the CCU). (2) The mobile device will request the OEM to verify the authenticity of the ECU (RequestVerifyID). It is concatenated with the $id_{ecu}$, time stamp and its signature. (3) The OEM will verify the ECU's ID and will ask CCU to conduct further verification. It will send a random number ($rnd$), $psk_{ecu}$ and $pk_{ecu}$, encrypted with CCU's public key to the mobile device. The mobile device will pass this message to the CCU. (4) The CCU will decrypt the message to obtain the $rnd$, $psk_{ecu}$ and $pk_{ecu}$. It will then pass $rnd$ and its $pk_{ccu}$ to the

**Table 4.** Update/ ECU replacement phase (between OEM-MD-car)

(1) MD→ECU   : $id_{md}||RequestID||ts1$

  ECU→MD   : $id_{ecu}||ts2$

(2) MD→OEM   : $id_{md}||RequestVerifyID||id_{ecu}||ts3||$

       $sign_{sk_{md}}\{id_{md}||RequestVerifyID||id_{ecu}||ts3\}$

(3) OEM→MD   : $id_{oem}||\{rnd, psk_{ecu}, pk_{ecu}\}_{pk_{ccu}}||ts4||$

       $sign_{sk_{oem}}\{id_{oem}||\{rnd, psk_{ecu}, pk_{ecu}\}_{pk_{ccu}}||ts4\}$

  MD→CCU   : $id_{md}||\{rnd, psk_{ecu}, pk_{ecu}\}_{pk_{ccu}}||ts5||$

       $sign_{sk_{md}}\{id_{md}||\{rnd, psk_{ecu}, pk_{ecu}\}_{pk_{ccu}}||ts5\}$

(4) CCU→ECU : $id_{ccu}||rnd||pk_{ccu}||ts6$

  ECU→CCU : $id_{ecu}||\{\{rnd\}_{psk_{ecu}}\}pk_{ccu}||ts7$

(5) CCU→MD   : $id_{ccu}||ack||ts8||sign_{sk_{ccu}}\{id_{ccu}||ack||ts8\}$

ECU. If the ECU is authentic, it will be able to produce the correct $\{rnd\}_{psk_{ecu}}$ and pass the value (encrypted with the received $pk_{ccu}$) to the CCU. The CCU will decrypt and verify the value sent by the ECU with the precomputed value. (5) The CCU will acknowledge the authenticity, and send an acknowledgment to the mobile device.

### 3.4   Formal Analysis

The proposed protocol is formally analysed using Scyther and CasperFDR tools to verify its correctness. Scyther performs an automatic analysis of security protocols in a Dolev-Yao style model, for an unbounded number of instances [2]. CasperFDR tool uses Communication Sequential Process (CSP) files to be analysed using Failure Divergence Refinement (FDR) [7].

**Formal Analysis Using Scyther.** The scripts can be found in Scyther input scripts. The default verification setup was used (i.e five as the maximum number of runs, typed matching and to find the best attack with ten maximum patterns per claim). The results for all the claims made are verified as "Ok" in the "Status" and "No attacks within bounds" in the "Comments". This means that no attack was found within the bounded statespace, but there can possibly be an attack outside the bounded statespace [1].

**Formal Analysis Using CasperFDR.** Due to space constraints the scripts and associated details are presented in CasperFDR input scripts. All the specifications made are verified and no attack was found for all the assertions.

## 4    Conclusion

In the automotive industry, a secure firmware update process is crucial for safety reasons. This paper proposes a secure OTA firmware update protocol with the use of a mobile application for the automotive systems. The proposed mobile application will ensure the authentication of all parties involved in the update process and confidentiality of the firmware. However, even if the mobile application is compromised, it cannot reveal the unencrypted firmware and associated secret/ private keys. The benefits of the proposed solution are that the phone/ application are used as a pipe (without retaining any secrets) and the phone cannot perform any undesired operations on the encrypted firmware. The FOTA protocol was analysed using Scyther and CasperFDR and no attack was found. Our further work includes implementation of the proposed protocol, the development of the mobile application and exploration of lifecycle management scenarios. Examples of lifecycle cases to be explored are phone change, loss or theft, the use of the mobile application by mechanics to service multiple cars and the change of car ownership.

## References

1. Cremers, C.: Scyther User Manual, draft edn (February 2014)
2. Cremers, C.J.F.: The scyther tool: verification, falsification, and analysis of security protocols. In: Gupta, A., Malik, S. (eds.) CAV 2008. LNCS, vol. 5123, pp. 414–418. Springer, Heidelberg (2008)
3. Flach, T., Mishra, N., Pedrosa, L., Riesz, C., Govindan, R.: Carma: towards personalized automotive tuning. In: Proceedings of the 9th ACM Conference on Embedded Networked Sensor Systems, pp. 135–148. ACM (2011)
4. Henniger, O.: EVITA: E-Safety Vehicle Intrusion Protected Applications. Technical report, EVITA (2011)
5. Henniger, O., Apvrille, L., Fuchs, A., Roudier, Y., Ruddle, A., Weyl, B.: Security requirements for automotive on-board networks. In: 2009 9th International Conference on Intelligent Transport Systems Telecommunications, (ITST), pp. 641–646. IEEE (2009)
6. Idrees, M.S., Schweppe, H., Roudier, Y., Wolf, M., Scheuermann, D., Henniger, O.: Secure automotive on-board protocols: a case of over-the-air firmware updates. In: Strang, T., Festag, A., Vinel, A., Mehmood, R., Rico Garcia, C., Röckl, M. (eds.) Nets4Trains/Nets4Cars 2011. LNCS, vol. 6596, pp. 224–238. Springer, Heidelberg (2011)
7. Lowe, G.: Casper: A compiler for the analysis of security protocols. Journal of Computer Security **6**(1), 53–84 (1998)
8. Wolf, M., Gendrullis, T.: Design, implementation, and evaluation of a vehicular hardware security module. In: Kim, H. (ed.) ICISC 2011. LNCS, vol. 7259, pp. 302–318. Springer, Heidelberg (2012)

# VICI: Visual Caller Identification for Contact Center Applications

P. Krishnan[✉] and Navjot Singh

Avaya Labs, 211 Mt. Airy Rd., Basking Ridge, NJ 07920, USA
{pk,singh}@avaya.com

**Abstract.** In this paper, we present VICI, a system for auditing and authentication in contact center scenarios. The technique we present exploits the widespread use of smartphones and other camera-enabled devices to allow a user (caller) to upload their picture, which can be verified automatically or by an agent before processing a transaction. The method can be configured for different levels of security, ensures that the image(s) are *fresh*, and relies on the computational complexity of image processing. We present our technique, the various configurable options available to the system/agent, and describe a prototype implementation of our system.

**Keywords:** Authentication · Biometrics · Security · Contact center · CRM

## 1 Introduction

An important component of customer service is to allow customers to contact the business to solve their problems. For example, in banking, customer transactions can be as simple as verifying an account balance, or more complex, like performing a wire transfer. A central component of these interactions is verifying the customer's credentials. Typically, the verification process is performed either in an automated way or by a customer service agent. In most situations, the business verifies what the customer *knows* (e.g., a password, PIN, or personal questions), what the customer *has* (e.g., numbers on a card, account statement) or uses 2-factor authentication (e.g., via sending a one-time-password to a cellphone the customer has). To improve the quality of the authentication, businesses use layered security, especially driven by risk models, where multiple techniques are used to increase the strength of the authentication.

While the above mentioned methods are reasonable for many situations, they still do not establish that the interaction is happening with the customer as opposed to somebody who knows information about the customer. There are several situations in which legal requirements and company policy require a higher level of authentication. As a simple example, consider retirement accounts (e.g., 401k accounts in the United States). These accounts are considered individual accounts, and even spouses are not allowed to make transactions on these accounts without explicit permission from the account holder. This is, in spite of the fact that, the spouse may have all the personal information and might even have access to the user's devices. Another area where

© Springer International Publishing Switzerland 2015
M. Qiu et al. (Eds.): NSS 2015, LNCS 9408, pp. 511–518, 2015.
DOI: 10.1007/978-3-319-25645-0_39

enhanced authentication may be required involves access to insurance and medical information and medical follow-ups, where only the patient or a pre-designated individual can participate in relevant discussions.

## 1.1      Using Biometrics

A well-studied and effective technique for authentication that verifies the user more explicitly is biometrics [1,2,3]. In many situations, biometrics provides an additional layer in the layered security architecture. Several aspects can be used for authentication using biometrics, e.g., (multiple) fingerprint(s), iris, face, and voiceprint. Amongst these, iris and fingerprint typically require either specialized equipment or security embedded in end-devices for effective use. Voice biometrics are currently used in contact centers, and provide reasonable performance [4] when the speech phrases used for authentication are reasonably long.

**Facial/Visual Identification.** Given the widespread presence of cameras in connected consumer devices, facial identification is a very promising and orthogonal technique, and something we explore in this paper. A typical flow for the facial identification process is shown in Figure 1. Assume, for now, that the contact center (business) has a profile picture of the customer (user) in their database. During the online authentication phase, a fresh image of the user is obtained and compared against the image in the database. There are three main parts to the system: (i) having a database of customer profile pictures (ii) obtaining the caller image during or at the start of the transaction, and (iii) comparing the two images (the database image against what is obtained from the customer in the online phase). We examine these three parts below.

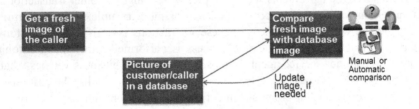

**Fig. 1.** A typical facial identification process

    Seeding the database can be done in many ways: either at the time of customer acquisition (e.g., account opening), from other trusted databases, or during a customer interaction itself as shown in Figure 1.

    The *verification system* compares the acquired image against the database image to determine a match. Image comparison is a well-studied problem and *not* the emphasis of our paper. The comparison could be automated or done by a human. Automated facial recognition is a heavily studied and ongoing research area [5]. Automated facial recognition is complex and its accuracy is dependent on many factors not in the contact center's control (e.g., lighting, background, orientation) [6]. However, it is believed that humans have an uncanny ability for face identification. There are some interesting studies [7] that show that humans reach a decision about image matching in two seconds or less and in some situations automated techniques may perform better than humans, especially for matching unknown faces. Many contact center scenarios we have discussed allow human intervention, and in our work we propose the use of a system that *melds automated and human recognition* to get the best of both worlds. To distinguish this aspect from automated facial recognition, we label our process *visual identification*. In effect, our system can use known facial verification techniques [5] and (optionally) blend its results with a trained human agent's perception to reach a decision on success. For transactions that require customer-agent interaction, visual identification only uses a few seconds of the agent's time.

The remaining part of the process and the main focus in this paper is how to obtain a fresh image of the caller. By *fresh*, we mean that the image presented is not a stored image that can be easily faked by the sender to represent the customer. Our goal is to build a system, VICI, for visual identification that allows a facial image to be sent from an un-trusted remote device without specialized hardware at the user end, while ensuring with high probability that the image received can be trusted and is fresh.

In Section 2, we describe the idea behind VICI, our technique to obtain a fresh image from a remote end-user. We describe the VICI system, options and issues in Section 3, present our prototype implementation in Section 4 and conclude in Section 5.

## 2      VICI: Visual Caller Identification

The core idea in VICI is to request an image from the user. To ensure that the image is fresh, the user is presented with a gesture challenge, e.g., "tilt your head and hold a finger to your forehead while taking the picture." The image of the user performing the gesture is then presented to the verification system (automated+agent) to compare against the database image to ensure they match. Effectively, the gesture request provides a nonce [8] for the security of the transaction. The main idea of VICI is shown in Figure 2.

Conceptually, the VICI technique is verifying the participation of the person whose image is obtained and, along the lines of the CAPTCHA technique [9], ensuring that the gesture is easy for a human to perform but difficult for an automated system to generate. However, unlike CAPTCHA, the verification while easy for a human may be difficult (using current techniques) for automated algorithms.

In the following discussion we describe the VICI system that builds on this core technique to provide a set of configurable options that allows the contact center to tune the security of the transaction. For example, the basic VICI system could use a single image to audit and authorize the user (as opposed to only the user credentials) for higher value transactions. The other aspects we describe below can be used to tune the security for more risky transactions.

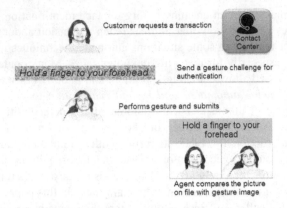

**Fig. 2.** The VICI authentication flow.

# 3     VICI: Building a System

To take the basic VICI concept from Section 2 and make it usable and tunable in a
contact center system requires several components. These include, among others, a
method to evaluate transaction risk (which will be provided by business process systems but also influenced by the VICI system), techniques to prevent an adversary
from pre-creating the gestures or creating them on-the-fly, and allowing the user to
choose a device to perform the transaction. The system can choose from these available options to adjust the security based on perceived risk.

**Gesture Types and Entropy.** The security of the technique increases with the entropy of the nonce. This includes the database of available gestures, and the difficulty of
the gestures to be generated by automated means. Some examples are shown in Figure 3. Some gestures involving the teeth, tongue, hair and sometimes the lips and eyes
of the user (e.g., put out your tongue or wink) are known to be hard to visually model
in computer graphics [10]. The gestures could use combinations to make them more
unique (e.g., hold up two fingers of your left hand while looking down). The gesture
database can be updated and refined over time. The database is expected to be large
but finite. However, a key to getting a large set of gestures is via combinations and
using multiple images or a sequence of images as we will see below.

**Fig. 3.** Example gestures for use with the VICI system

**Multiple Images or a Short Video.** Given a database with $m$ gestures, a method to significantly increase the total possible combinations is to request a sequence of images with one of the $m$ gestures. A combination of $k$ images will provide a possible set of $m^k$ possible gesture combinations. The value of $m$ and $k$ can be adjusted to derive the desired security.

The concept of multiple images can instead be implemented using a short video that may be recorded at the client device and uploaded to the authentication system. When using a video, there are several additional tools available to the system. For example, an interesting gesture that reflects in the captured video in a unique way is changing the perspective: either asking the user or the camera to be moved. The range of motion that could be requested is also larger with videos. Another technique is to include voice in addition to image(s) and ask the user to speak a phrase. Even without the voice, the lip movement matched to the requested phrase provides freshness information. With voice, the verification system could layer voice biometrics to further enhance the security. With video, the automated component of our verification system could find the face and evaluate if certain requested movements are taking place.

As a simple example, a $k$ digit random number from the alphabet $\{0\ldots5\}$ could be generated, and the user could be asked to hold up successively between 0 and 5 fingers in addition to performing a certain gesture involving the face. The value of $k$ can be adjusted for increasing the number of available unique gesture combinations.

**Presenting the Gesture to the User.** How the gesture is presented to the user can further aid in improving the solution's security. Since the challenge is expected to be interpreted and enacted by a human, the challenge can be presented as a CAPTCHA [9] to make it more difficult for a machine to interpret it. Another method in the repertoire is to present the desired challenge as an image or short video to the user. Repeating a (simple enough) action seen in an image or video is relatively simple for a human to do, but quite complicated to be interpreted and re-created by a machine.

**The Timeliness Constraint.** For each gesture $i$ in the database, we can maintain information about the typical time $t_i$ taken by a user to perform the gesture. After the gesture $i$ has been presented to the customer, both the server and the client can count down for $f(t_i)$ time, where the function $f(.)$ provides an allowance in $t_i$ for the user to record their gesture (and could be user-specific). If the upload is not obtained within $f(t_i) + \Delta t$ time at the server, where $\Delta t$ accounts for the round trip communication latency, the image is considered unreliable, and the process is adjusted to obtain additional images. The process is depicted in Figure 4. The system can also adapt to the frequency and pattern of unreliable images.

**Real-time Transaction.** Our solution thus far assumes an ongoing online transaction between the client device and the server with occasional uploads from the client to the server. It is also possible, for additional security, to have a real-time session established between the client device and the server (e.g., via WebRTC [11]). In this case, the real-time media is sent from the client to the server with timely recording of the media done at the server. Doing so makes it less susceptible to client manipulation.

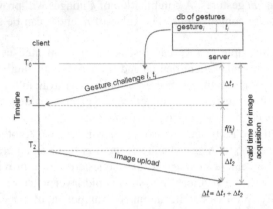

**Fig. 4.** Enabling the timeliness constraint

**Adaptation.** Based on the ongoing session, the risk level of the transaction can be continually evaluated and fed into any other input that evaluates risk. The parameters from VICI that contribute to the risk of the transaction include deviations from the timeliness constraint, and any deviations in the verification process (e.g., absence of face in image or confirmed significant difference between the acquired and database images). This can contribute to higher levels of challenges (type of gesture, increased number of images, escalation to video or audio+video and activating the real-time transaction module).

**Contact Center Agent Considerations.** While the customer could be given reasonable time to provide their image, the matching process is relatively quick. A human requires just a couple of seconds to compare two images [7]. The human element of the verification system could be done by a contact center agent and can be done while the customer waits in queue or is talking to an agent. The image/video acquisition can be done prior to customer-agent interaction (e.g., when a customer is in a wait queue).

## 4    Prototype Implementation

We built a prototype of the VICI system, and describe two implementations here. The first used html5 and the second used WebRTC [11] for acquiring the media.

### 4.1    Images/Video Using html5

In this implementation, we had a customer call into a contact center using a smartphone. The system then generated and sent an authentication URL via SMS to the smartphone. When the user clicked on the URL, an html5 session was established between the smartphone and the web server. The server chose a challenge at random from a database, embedded it as a CAPTCHA, and presented it to the user. A local timer was started at the client. The customer could click to upload their image. Javascript and Ajax provide the method for implementing the timeliness constraint.

For image/video acquisition on the smartphone we used standard html5 media capture tags. When the call was routed to the agent (using available contact center routing software), the agent was provided a pop-up to verify the presented image with the database image.

## 4.2    Image Sequence Using WebRTC

For experimenting with image sequences, remote video and real-time transactions, we used the WebRTC framework. This restricted us to Android smartphones or desktops with browsers that supported WebRTC.

In this case, the user started their interaction on the web and initiated an authentication session. This invoked the WebRTC channel, and with user permission, the local video was acquired using getUserMedia() and shown to the user. They were presented with a challenge (coded using a CAPTCHA). The signaling was done using websockets. It was now possible to provide a sequence of requests for images with different gestures, and get a snapshot of the image in the user's browser canvas. The acquired image was uploaded to the server. The contact center agent could, before being connected to the customer, access the uploaded images and determine a match.

The WebRTC implementation can allow for media to be recorded at the contact center server or at the client device.

## 4.3    Comparing and Evaluating the Two Prototypes

Depending on the type of device, either the html5 or the WebRTC method can be activated. With WebRTC, the media is available natively inside the browser context and allows pushing of instructions and media, countdown of timers, and acquisition of images/video to happen in parallel, with the user fully aware of each of these activities. The html5 media capture tag, however, is supported in most smartphone browsers as opposed to the limited support of WebRTC in certain desktop browsers and Android smartphones today.

In a limited user study, we checked our system with a small user group for a contact center-like interaction. The ad-hoc SMS method for starting the authentication was viewed very favorably. The gestures had to be reasonable and were thought useful for high value transactions. The time for face verification (by agent) matched previous studies: a couple of seconds to match with great accuracy. A more detailed user study (of both end users and agents) is being planned to help better understand the viability of VICI.

# 5     Conclusion and Future Work

In this paper, we have studied the problem of user authentication and use of biometrics for user validation. Amongst the common biometrics available, a user's voice and face are most accessible, and the face allows a mixture of human and machine involvement for verification.

We have presented VICI, a visual identification system for use by businesses in contact centers to authenticate callers and audit transactions. By challenging a user with a gesture or sequence of gestures, the image/video is verified to be fresh. The verification system combines automated and human verification to compare the presented image/video against a profile picture.

The VICI system incorporates additional techniques like image sequences, use of short videos, potential layered use of voice biometrics, timeliness constraints and use of real-time transactions to further manage risk. These techniques can structure the transaction in a layered security model to achieve the required level of security.

There are several interesting avenues for further exploration; for example, automated methods for generating a gesture database, and automated verification including gesture and partially occluded face verification. Extended user studies on use of this technique would be an interesting avenue for exploration.

# References

1. Jain, A., Hong, L., Pankanti, S.: Biometric Identification. Comm. of the ACM **43**(2), 91–98 (2000). Biometrics Consortium homepage. http://www.biometrics.org
2. O'Gorman, L.: Comparing passwords, tokens, and biometrics for user authentication. Proceedings of the IEEE **91**(12), 2019–2040 (2003)
3. Ratha, N.K., Connell, J.H., Bolle, R.N.: Enhancing Security and Privacy in Biometrics-Based Authentication Systems. IBM Systems Journal **40**(3) (2001)
4. Markowitz, J.A.: Voice Biometrics. Communications of the ACM **43**(9), 66–73 (2000)
5. Zhao, W., Chellappa, R., Phillips, P.J., Rosenfeld, A.: Face Recognition: A Literature Survey. ACM Computing Surveys **35**(4), 399–458 (2003)
6. Phillips, P.J., Flynn, P.J., Scruggs, T., Bowyer, K.W., Chang, J., Hoffman, K., Marques, J., Min, J., Worek, W.: Overview of the face recognition grand challenge. In: Proc. IEEE Computer Vision & Pattern Recognition, vol. 1, pp. 947–954 (2005)
7. O'Toole, A.J., Phillips, P.J., Fang, K., Ayyad, J., Penard, N., Abdi, H.: Face Recognition Algorithms Surpass Humans Matching Faces Over Changes in Illumination. IEEE Trans. on Pattern Analysis and Machine Intelligence **29**(9), 1642–1646 (2007)
8. Cryptographic nonce. http://en.wikipedia.org/wiki/Cryptographic_nonce
9. von Ahn, L., Blum, M., Hopper, N., Langford, J.: Captcha: using hard AI problems for security. In: Biham, E. (ed.) EUROCRYPT 2003. LNCS, vol. 2656, pp. 294–311. Springer, Heidelberg (2003)
10. Pighin, F., et al.: Synthesizing realistic facial expressions from photographs. In: ACM SIGGRAPH 2006 Courses (2006)
11. WebRTC 1.0: Real-time communication between browsers, W3C Draft. http://www.w3.org/TR/webrtc/, http://www.webrtc.org

# Performance Analysis of Real-Time Covert Timing Channel Detection Using a Parallel System

Ross K. Gegan[1][(✉)], Rennie Archibald[2],
Matthew K. Farrens[1], and Dipak Ghosal[1]

[1] Department of Computer Science, University of California, Davis,
Davis, CA 95616, USA
rkgegan@ucdavis.edu
[2] AT&T Labs, 2600 Camino Ramon, San Ramon, CA 94583, USA

**Abstract.** As network data rates continue to increase, implementing real-time network security applications requires a scalable computing platform. Multicore and manycore parallel processing systems provide a way to scale network security applications. The focus of this study are network covert timing channels (CTCs) that provide secret communication between hosts by modulating the inter-packet delays of an overt application. In this paper, we present an implementation of a parallel CTC detection tool in a Massively Parallel Processing Array (MPPA) architecture. We examine the effectiveness of our tool for detecting model-based CTCs using parallel implementation of four common detection techniques, namely, the Kullback-Liebler Divergence (KLD), Kolmogorov-Smirnov (K-S), regularity and first order entropy tests. We evaluate the performance of the algorithms using classification rates and study the scalability by varying the number of cores. Results show that while parallelization provides benefit, the scalability is limited by the memory available in each core and the ability to stream in large number of flows to different cores.

**Keywords:** Covert Timing Channel (CTC) · Massively Parallel Processing Array (MPPA) architecture · CTC detection · Experimental analysis

## 1 Introduction

Covert timing channels (CTCs) belong to a class of communication methods that exploit the timing and/or ordering of authorized overt communication as a carrier for secret messages. Examples of overt carriers for timing channels include the seek time of a hard disk head, time between phone calls, or inter-packet delays (IPDs) of an IP packet stream. There are two broad classes of network traffic based timing channels, IPD timing channels and combinatorial

This research was supported by NSF grant CNS-1018886.

timing channels. The latter employs packet ordering in one or more network flows to embed the secret message. In this study we consider IPD based timing channels, where the sender modulates a covert message into the IPDs of a single IP packet stream. The receiver observes the packet arrival times and using a shared code-book, decodes the covert message.

CTCs have a variety of malicious uses, including the theft of sensitive data and anonymous communication between botnets [16]. Therefore, it is important to quickly detect CTCs in network traffic. Detecting CTCs requires packet inspection and processing. The processing is required not only on individual packets but also on sequences of packets and across flows. Performing these functions at very high network line rates (10 Gbps now and soon scaling up to 40 to 100 Gbps) is critical to safeguarding enterprise networks. Solutions based on the use of Field Programmable Gate Arrays (FPGAs) and/or multi-core CPUs have limitations with regards to performance, flexibility, power, and programmability. In this study, we propose to investigate the effectiveness of Massively Parallel Processing Array (MPPA) architectures to scale packet processing and analysis tasks to meet the CTC detection challenges presented by next generation high-speed networks. We provide background on existing covert timing channel detection and disruption techniques, then evaluate the performance of four basic detection tests — the Kullback-Liebler Divergence, Kolmogorov-Smirnov, time-domain regularity and first order entropy tests) — using the Tilera TilePro64 MPPA architecture [17].

We obtained the detection results for two common types of CTCs model-based covert timing channels (MBCTCs) and time-replay covert timing channels (TRCTCs)[1]. The results match previous results [5] and verify their results. In addition, our tests show that our tool can handle traffic at rates up to 2 Gbps. Results show that while parallelization provides benefit, the scalability is limited by the memory available in each core and the ability to stream in large number of flows to different cores. The initial implementation of this detection tool should serve as a framework for future real-time detection of different covert timing channels as well as other network security applications.

The remainder of the paper is organized as follows. In Section 2 we discuss the CTC detection methods that we have considered in our study. In Section 3 we discuss details of the MPPA architecture and the design challenges and solutions to implement the CTC detection methods. In Section 4 we discuss the experimental results. Finally, in Section 5 we give the conclusions and the future work.

## 2   Covert Timing Channels and Detection

In this paper, we consider a subset of network covert timing channels (CTCs) in which the sender modulates a covert message into the inter-packet delays (IPDs) of a packet stream. The receiver observes the inter-packet delays, and using a shared

---

[1] Due to space limitations, we only present the results for MBCTCs. TRCTC results can be found in [18].

code-book, decodes the data. There are two main varieties of covert timing channels active CTCs and passive CTCs. To transmit a message, active CTCs must create extra traffic, while passive CTCs do not. There are advantages and disadvantages to either approach. Typically, passive CTCs are more difficult to detect, while active CTCs are faster. Both types require the sender to use a hijacked machine. In addition, passive CTCs have a smaller capacity, because they must rely on the packet rate of the real application traffic [10].

A few common active types of network traffic based CTC include IP CTCs (IPCTC), Time Replay CTCs (TRCTC), and Model Based CTCs (MBCTC). Although our experiments included multiple types of CTCs, this paper only includes the MBCTC results. MBCTCs attempt to copy the properties of legitimate traffic by fitting the covert channel to a statistical model which most closely matches the actual traffic. The channel uses a filter to send outgoing traffic to an analyzer which determines the distribution model to use, such as Poisson, Gamma, or Weibull distribution. Then, the channel uses the selected model's inverse distribution function to encode the message. On the receiver's side, the message can be decoded using the model's cumulative distribution function. As a result, MBCTCs have a distribution very close to legitimate traffic, making shape-based detection difficult. In addition, MBCTCs can further complicate detection by periodically changing the parameters of the model or using a new model [5].

## 2.1   Detection Tests

Although techniques such as fuzzy time [7] and the network pump [8] can reduce the capacity of a CTC, they are not applicable to all covert channel systems. In particular, these techniques may significantly modify the inter-packet delays, which may be undesirable, particularly for applications such as VoIP which require QoS guarantees on jitter and end-to-end packet delays. Rather than relying on an underlying disruption mechanism, the network administrator might prefer to first detect a CTC, and then block it, either through selectively adding random noise or blocking the flow entirely. We considered four tests, the regularity test, the entropy test, the Kolmogorov-Smirnov (K-S) test, and the Kullback-Liebler Divergence (KLD) test, to detect CTCs. We test for regularity using the method developed in [2]. The entropy test measures the amount of randomness in the flow's distribution. The entropy should be larger in MBCTCs than legitimate traffic, so we can assume a CTC exists if the entropy is above a certain threshold [5].

The entropy value, or the E Score, is given by [5]

$$E\ Score = -\sum_{i=1}^{n} P(x_i) \log P(x_i) \tag{1}$$

where $P(x_i)$ refers to the probability of the inter-packet delay sample taking the value $x_i$. We determine the first-order E Score by distributing the observed inter-packet delays into equal sized bins, which are then used in the equation. A more complex test based on the entropy test, the corrected conditional entropy (CCE) test, has been shown to reliably detect a variety of CTCs [5]. However, the complexity of the CCE test, requiring the construction of a Q-ary tree, makes it unfeasible for our current setup. In [5], the test took 16 milliseconds on an Intel Pentium D 3.4Ghz processor [5]. Given the relatively low performance (866 Mhz) of the individual TilePro64 cores and the need to perform the detection tests at high rates, we decided against including the CCE test [17].

The Kolmogov-Smirnov test referred to at the KS test, reports the maximum distance between two probability distributions. The KS test score (KS Score) is given by [5]

$$KS\ Score = Max|S_1(x) - S_2(x)| \qquad (2)$$

where $S_1$ and $S_2$ refer to two distinct distributions. One advantage of using the KS test is that the distribution type does not matter, meaning it works equally well regardless of the traffic type used to create the distribution. The Kullback-Liebler Divergence test referred to as the KLD test, measures how much one distribution diverges from another. The KLD test score (KLD Score) is given by [5]:

$$KLD\ Score = D_{KL}(P||Q) \qquad (3)$$

$$= \sum_{i=0}^{n} P(i) \log \frac{P(i)}{Q(i)} \qquad (4)$$

where $P(i)$ is the legitimate distribution, while $Q(i)$ is the distribution for the inter-packet delays we test. A large KLD Score indicates a big difference between two distributions, meaning a covert timing channel might exist. Finally, we use the regularity test, which measures the change in IPD variance. The Regularity test score referred to as the R Score, is given by [5]:

$$R\ Score = STDEV(\frac{|\epsilon_i - \epsilon_j|}{\epsilon_i}, i < j, \forall i, j) \qquad (5)$$

For some CTCs, the distribution patterns do not change much over time, giving a lower R Score than legitimate traffic. However, most CTCs routinely update their encoding scheme, making the R Score more similar to legitimate traffic [5].

## 3    Implementation

In order to scale real-time network security application for higher and higher link data rates, we must rely on parallel processing devices with multiple cores. There are three common varieties of multi-core parallel processing devices Field-programmable gate array (FPGA) based, Graphical Processing Units (GPU) based, and Massively Parallel Processing Array (MPPA) based. While GPUs contain a relatively large number of processing units, they are not typically implemented in systems other than PCs. Compared to MPPA architectures, GPUs require much more power and OS support in order to operate. GPUs also require each core to run the same set of code, while MPPA architectures can each run independent code. FPGA based architectures have numerous disadvantages compared to MPPA architectures. FGPAs usually require designers to write code in a low-level, gate oriented language (VHDL). Furthermore, FGPAs require the designer to pay attention to many details not inherent to algorithm development, such as timing constraints and clock propagation. In contrast, MPPA architectures have some of FGPAs positive traits, like being able to run multiple logical blocks simultaneously, and pipeline operations across processors. Importantly, MPPA architectures provide excellent I/O performance, since the processors on the periphery of the chip communicate directly with the I/O devices. For these reasons, we have selected an MPPA architecture to implement our security application.

For our experiments, our objective was to measure the relative real-time effectiveness of different covert timing channel detection tests, as well as study how adding cores could improve the detection performance. We used a Tilera TilePro64 NIC to monitor incoming traffic in real-time and run our detection tests. The Tilera TilePro64 has 64 identical cores called tiles each containing their own processor and cache, consisting of an L1 (16KB instruction and 8KB data) and 64KB L2 cache. The total RAM available on the card is 8 GB, and each tile's processing speed is 866 Mhz. For high-speed I/O, the card includes two 10 GBps Ethernet XAUI interfaces. Although we used a 10 Gbps interface, the packet replay program tcpreplay [15] could not replay traffic at very high speeds while accurately maintaining the relative packet timings. Consequently, the data rates used in our experimental study were lower than 10 Gbps.

### 3.1 Implementation of the Detection System

To perform our detection experiments, we used two machines, a sender machine which replays traffic samples, and a receiver machine hosting the TilePro64, which runs our detection tool. Using tcpreplay, the sender machine replays the CTC injected traffic samples to the receiver at various rates. Meanwhile, our detection tool runs on the NIC, monitoring the incoming traffic for CTCs for a set period of time. The tool uses a built-in Tilera hash function to distribute the incoming flows evenly across the individual cores. For each incoming packet in an individual flow, the cores will calculate the IPD using the previous packet's arrival time. The IPDs are stored and used to update a set of five bins representing the traffic's timing distribution. Once a core has gathered enough IPDs, it performs the covert timing channel detection tests. We vary the IPD threshold in our experiments, but it is typically set to 1000 IPDs, because only those flows containing at least 1000 IPDs have been injected with CTCs. When the test period ends, the detection tool reports the final results the true and false positive rates, as well as the detection time data.

### 3.2 Design Challenges and Solutions

Implementing the CTC detection methods on the TilePro64 posed many design challenges owing to various architectural constraints as well as issues related to traffic traces used in the experimental analysis. In the following subsections we highlight a subset of key challenges and our solutions.

**Memory Constraints and Optimization.** A major challenge was ensuring that the detection tool could handle large amounts of traffic at high data rates without dropping packets. Additionally, since each core in the TilePro64 has limited memory, it was important to make sure that the implementation of the detection method did not require too much memory. Our detection tool attempts to discover CTCs in the incoming traffic flows by calculating the IPD distributions for each flow and comparing the detection test results to a threshold value based on the training data. Considering that at a 10 Gbps rate, each packet must be processed in under 67.2 nanoseconds, this task requires swift calculations on each new packet, even at lower data rates. Since a single core cannot handle all the flows, we parallelize the work. Most schemes took too much time processing each flow, resulting in a large number of packet drops. Since communication between cores was too time consuming, the most effective method was to distribute the flows evenly across the cores. The TilePro64's built-in hash functions distribute packets based on flow, and as a result each core receives a roughly equal subset of the total flows.

For each incoming flow, a core must store some information to complete a detection test. In particular, each core holds a hash table storing the five bin distribution values, the previously received packet's timestamp (for calculating IPDs), and the total packet count for each flow. We used a basic hash function [9] to determine a packet's flow. Since the information is typically not needed for longer than 2ms after calculating the distribution, we can replace the hash entry on a conflict, preventing the core from running out of memory.

Overall, we wanted each core to perform the minimum amount of work. Therefore, we needed to find a way of reducing the number of flows tested without missing any potential CTCs. Looking at internet traffic profiles, we find that 80 percent of flows contain no more than 20 packets [12]. We assumed that large flows are most likely to contain a CTC, and significantly reduced the number of flows each core processes by separating the large Elephant flows from the small Mice flows [13]. Our code uses the Sample-and-Hold technique [13], which calculates a random value for each new packet, so every incoming packet has a small chance − 3% in our case that its flow will be stored. Therefore, the large flows are stored with a larger probability than the small flows, reducing the total data stored and thereby addressing the core memory constraint.

**Evaluating Performance Using Small Anonymized Packets.** We obtained multiple anonymized traffic traces from the CAIDA repository [18]. The traces correspond to captures taken from an OC-192 link in San Jose, consisting primarily of HTTP traffic. One capture was used to create our training statistics, such as the legitimate traffic distribution for HTTP traffic, as well as the E score, KS Score and KLD Score results for each individual flow. The training data also determined the bin sizes used to create the inter-packet delay distributions. In another CAIDA traffic capture, we injected MBCTCs into 10% of the flows containing more than 1000 packets. To accomplish this, we first created capture files for each eligible flow, then use a script to change their IPDs, thereby creating sets of legitimate and CTC flows. The flows are then merged back together to form a capture file we use for the experiments, selecting a small percentage of the merged file's flows to contain covert timing channels.

One challenge faced was deciding how to handle our sample's small packet sizes. Since the CAIDA repository traffic is anonymized, the packets contain only the headers. Processing traffic consisting solely of 64 byte packets is the most difficult case to handle in real-time [11]. For 64 byte packets at 10 Gbps, the Tilera TilePro64 Ingress Packet Processor (IPP) at times has no more than 50 cycles to process the incoming packet. Furthermore, a recent paper by Lee et al. [11] shows that most hardware timestamps cannot accurately represent the inter-packet delays for 64 byte packets when replaying traffic at 1 Gbps. Since larger packet sizes are associated with larger data rates [14], our experiments use an estimate for the data rate of non-anonymized traffic. We estimate the data rate by multiplying the rate which tcpreplay reports by the average HTTP packet size (512 bytes [4]), then dividing by 64.

## 4    Results and Discussions

Our experiments were performed using tcpreplay to replay a CTC injected traffic trace to a receiver machine hosting the Tilera TilePro64. The trace consisted primarily of HTTP traffic. A legitimate traffic trace was used to determine the legitimate IPD distribution, while the another was injected with CTCs for use in the experiments. Table 1 provides a description of the flows contained in the CTC injected trace file used in our experiments.

**Table 1.** Sample traffic statistics. Large Flows are those containing at least 1000 packets.

| Sample | Total Packets | Total Flows | Large Flows | Legitimate | CTCs |
|--------|---------------|-------------|-------------|------------|------|
| MBCTC | 33581932 | 631089 | 3377 | 3056 | 321 |

### 4.1    Rate of Classification Curves

The effectiveness of a classifier can be judged by the area under the ROC curve which plots the True Positive as a function of the False Positive. The larger area under the ROC curve, the more effective is the test. In our experiments, the true positive rate is the percentage of CTCs correctly identified, and the false positive rate is the percentage of eligible flows misclassified as CTCs. The classification rate tests were performed by running the detection tool without a threshold, allowing all eligible flows to be captured by the Tilera NIC. Once the detection period ends, we compare the scores against a set of score thresholds and print the detection rates. This method keeps the replayed traffic's data rate consistent across runs while forming the ROC curves. The classification results for the different tests are shown in Figure 1. We also examine how the classification rate varies based on the number of IPDs tested. These results are shown in Figure 1(f).

MBCTCs fit the channel's IPDs to a statistical model, making the distribution similar to legitimate traffic and more resistant to shape-based detection tests[5]. Although legitimate traffic's average R score will be larger, the test's large standard deviation makes it a poor metric. In addition, the refitting algorithm makes the regularity similar for samples containing more than 100 packets [5]. The legitimate traffic scores were calculated using 2500 sample flows captured on the Tilera network card at 25.96 Mbps (estimated 207.68 Mbps), while the covert traffic scores were calculated using 150 CTC flows.

**Table 2.** Detection test scores for legitimate flows versus covert flows in the MBCTC capture file.

| Test Score | Legitimate Mean | Legitimate SD | CTC Mean | CTC SD |
|---|---|---|---|---|
| E Score | 0.51 | 0.15 | 2.10 | 0.52 |
| KLD Score | 0.28 | 0.11 | 1.66 | 0.59 |
| KS Score | 0.17 | 0.04 | 0.59 | 0.18 |
| R Score | 1941 | 1654 | 131 | 1191 |

Comparing the scores in Table 2, we see that MBCTC traffic will typically have larger E Scores, KLD Scores, and KS Scores, and smaller R Scores compared to legitimate traffic flows. We can detect CTCs by looking for large disparities between the observed score and the score for legitimate traffic. For example, large E Scores indicate the existence of a covert channel. Comparing the rates, we see that the entropy test (Figure 2a) most reliably detects MBCTCs, followed by the KLD test, the KS test, and the regularity test. The KLD test measures the relative entropy between two distributions, which could explain its relative success. Previous results by Gianvecchio et al. [5] have shown the effectiveness of entropy-based measurements for detecting MBCTCs. The same paper also shows the KS and regularity tests to be poor classifiers [5]. Since MBCTCs mimic legitimate traffic distributions, the two distributions will be very similar. Therefore, the KS test's method of identifying large distances between distributions is ineffective for detecting MBCTCs. The regularity test requires around 40% false positive rate among large flows before performing better than guessing, most likely due to the large standard deviation in R Scores.

Figure 1(e) shows the entropy test's rate of classification curve when measuring the detection rates at the fastest traffic rate we could achieve using tcpreplay (232.18 Mbps, estimated at 1.86 Gbps). The relative effectiveness of the detection tests remains the same, but the rates are universally lower testing at a high rate. This can be attributed to the decreased accuracy caused by replaying

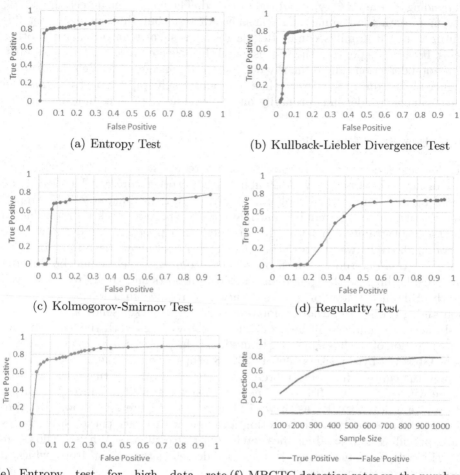

(a) Entropy Test

(b) Kullback-Liebler Divergence Test

(c) Kolmogorov-Smirnov Test

(d) Regularity Test

(e) Entropy test for high data rate (1.86 Gbps)

(f) MBCTC detection rates vs. the number of IPDs used to calculated the E score.

**Fig. 1.** (a) - (e) MBCTC ROC curves for different detection tests. (f) The impact of varying the number of IPDs tested.

the traffic sample at the highest possible speed. At lower rates, tcpreplay can accurately reproduce the capture file's relative packet timings, but replaying the traffic at higher rates alters the timing [15]. Since the inter-packet delays change, the detection test scores also change, reducing the test accuracy.

In Figure 1(f), we show how varying the number of required IPDs affects the detection rates of the entropy test at a set threshold (E Score $>= 2.07$). Increasing the number of IPDs tested generally improves the test accuracy, although the true positive rates may decrease along with the reduced false positives. The trade-off between sample size and detection time must be considered carefully depending on the CTC type and the test used. The more time detecting a CTC, the more data the channel can transmit. All tests but the regularity test finish in around 0.10 milliseconds. Regularity takes slightly longer than the other tests, because we perform the test using all the collected IPDs, not the five bins. The total detection time primarily depends on the incoming traffic's date rate — higher rates reduce the average time. Previous results [5] demonstrate that the ideal sample size depends primarily on the test and channel complexity.

## 4.2  Benefit of Parallelization

Real-time detection of covert timing channels requires us to handle a large number of flows simultaneously. Although a single worker core can handle all the flows in our sample when replayed at 27.18 Mbps (estimated 217.45 Mbps), higher rates of traffic require multiple cores to prevent packet drops due to memory constraints. To parallelize our detection program, we distribute the incoming flows between cores using the TilePro64's built-in hash function. The hash function determines which bucket an incoming packet should be directed towards, hashing on the source and destination ports and IP addresses, as well as the Ethernet Mac address. Each bucket is mapped to a worker tile queue, containing the packets waiting for processing. If a bucket sends a packet to a full queue, the packet will be dropped. Ideally, we want each tile to handle an equal portion of the flows in order to minimize the packet drops. At an estimated 1.86 Gbps (64-byte packets sent at 232.18 Mbps, the maximum rate we could replay the capture file using tcpreplay on our hardware), a single tile working alone will only receive 20% of the packets. Using seven tiles reduces the packet drop rate to less than 1% as shown in Figure 2(a). Figure 2(b) shows that similar results are obtained when testing a sample with larger packet sizes at this rate, providing additional justification for our rate estimates. When the flows are distributed evenly, increasing the tiles used decreases the packet drops, which in turn increases the detection rate.

## 4.3  Summary of Results

Our results demonstrate that using more worker cores reduces the time packets spend in a queue, reducing packet drops. The decreased packet drops increase the accuracy of the tests. Our sample size experiments demonstrate a trade-off between detection test accuracy and detection test time. Using more IPDs increases the accuracy, but also increases the time required to identify a flow. While the only effective MBCTC classifier we tested was the first-order entropy test, the detection rates for the other tests match those found in previous experiments [5]. Our results show that these tests can be performed quickly (less than 1 ms) and previous papers have shown their effectiveness for detecting other CTC varieties not included in this first implementation [3][5][1].

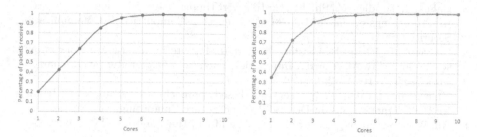

(a) Percentage of MBCTC sample packets (b) Percentage of BigFlows.pcap packets received at an average rate of 232.18 Mbps received at an average rate of 1943.71 Gbps (an estimated 1.86 Gbps)

**Fig. 2.** Increasing the number of cores handling flows reduces the number of packets dropped, improving detection test performance.

## 5 Conclusion and Future Work

Through our experiments, we have demonstrated an initial implementation of a real-time parallel covert timing channel detection program. Although only the entropy test proved effective, our classification tests produced detection rates similar to a previous CTC detection paper[5] verifying their results. In addition, our program shows some benefits provided by using a massively-parallel processor for detecting anomalous network flows. Future experiments should explore alternative parallelization methods. Although all the techniques we tested can be performed on a single-core, more complex tests require too much time for our tool at high rates. Parallelizing the algorithms could make tasks such as constructing the Q-ary tree for the CCE test more feasible. Since different CTCs require different detection methods, one notable way to improve on our design would be to duplicate incoming flows and send them to separate groups of cores detecting different types of covert channels. Our experiments have shown that less than 10 cores are necessary to handle incoming flows at rates around 2 Gbps without packet loss. This gives us an opportunity to utilize the remaining cores to perform other detection tests. Ideally, each group of cores could also perform multiple detection tests simultaneously. One alternative would be performing CTC detection using a GPU instead. Our detection tool should serve as a framework for future covert timing channel research.

## References

1. Archibald, R., Ghosal, D.: A comparative analysis of detection metrics for covert timing channels. Computers & Security (2014)
2. Cabuk, S.: Network covert channels: Design, analysis, detection, and elimination. Ph.D. dissertation, Purdue University, West Lafayette (2006)

3. Cabuk, S., Brodley, C., Shields, C.: IP covert timing channels: design and detection. In: Proceedings of the 2004 ACM Conference on Computer and Communications Security (2004)
4. Caetano, M., Vieira, P., Bordim, J., Barreto, P.: International journal of computer science and network security. International Journal of Computer Science and Network Security **10**, 13–20 (2010)
5. Gianvecchio, S., Wang, H.: An entropy-based approach to detecting covertchannels. In: IEEE Transactions on Dependable and Secure Computing, Vol. 8(6) (2011)
6. Hu, W.-M.: Reducing timing channels with fuzzy time. Journal of Computer Security 1.3, 233–254 (1992)
7. Kang, M.H., Moskowitz, I., Chincheck, S.: The pump: a decade of covert fun. Computer Security Applications Conference, 21st Annual. IEEE (2005)
8. Kolosovskiy, M.: Simple implementation of deletion from open-address hash table. arXiv preprint arXiv:0909.2547 (2009)
9. Kothari, K.: Mimic: an active covert channel that evades regularity-based detection. Comput. Netw. 57(3) (2013)
10. Lee, K.S., Wang, H., Weatherspoon, H.: Phy covert channel: can you see the idles. In: USENIX symposium on Networked Systems Design and Implementation (NSDI), April 2014
11. Matta, I., Guo, L.: Differentiated predictive fair service for tcp flows. In: Proc. ICNP 2000, Osaka, Japan, November 2000
12. Psounis, K., Ghosh, A., Prabhakar, B., Wang, G.: Sift: A simple algorithm for tracking elephant flows, and taking advantage of power laws. In: 43rd Allerton Conference on Communication, Control and Computing (2005)
13. Schultz, M., Crowley, P.: Performance analysis of packet capture methods in a 10 gbps virtualized environment. In: 2012 21st International Conference on Computer Communications and Networks (ICCCN). IEEE (2012)
14. tcpreplay developers. tcpreplay website (2014). http://tcpreplay.synfin.net/trac/wiki/tcpreplay
15. Thyer, J.S.: Covert data storage channel using ip packet headers. SANS Institute (2008)
16. Tilera. Tilera tilepro64 overview (2014). http://www.tilera.com/sites/default/files/productbriefs/
17. CAIDA. CAIDA Data (2014) http://www.caida.org/data/overview/
18. Gegan, R.: Parallelized Real-Time Covert Timing Channel Detection. Master's Thesis, Computer Science Department University of California, Davis (2015)

# Detecting Malicious Temporal Alterations of ECG Signals in Body Sensor Networks

Hang Cai and Krishna K. Venkatasubramanian[(✉)]

Department of Computer Science,
Worcester Polytechnic Institute, Worcester, MA 01609, USA
{hcai,kven}@wpi.edu

**Abstract.** Electrocardiogram (ECG) sensor is one of the most commonly available and medically important sensors in a Body Sensor Network (BSN). Compromise of the ECG sensor can have severe consequences for the user as it monitors the user's cardiac process. In this paper, we propose an approach called *SIgnal Feature-correlation-based Testing (SIFT)* which is used to detect temporal alteration of ECG sensors in a BSN. The novelty of SIFT lies in the fact that it does not require redundant ECG sensors nor the subject's historical ECG data to detect the temporal alteration. SIFT works by leveraging multiple physiological signals based on the same underlying physiological process (e.g., cardiac process) – arterial blood pressure and respiration. Analysis of our case study demonstrates promising results with ~98% accuracy in detecting even subtle alterations in the temporal properties of an ECG signal.

## 1 Introduction

Emerging Body Sensor Networks (BSNs) have demonstrated great potential in a broad range of applications in healthcare and wellbeing. The fact that BSNs collect sensitive data and provide valuable information to caregivers and users makes them attractive targets for tech-criminals to exploit. One such threat is *sensor compromise*, which we define as the unauthorized modification of sensor output (i.e., measurement) to relay incorrect patient health data to the base station. The modification of sensor output can be done in several ways including installation of malware on sensors that modify the readings [2], and inducing arbitrary signals into sensor circuitry leading to erroneous readings [8].

Electrocardiogram (ECG) is one of the most widely deployed sensors on individuals. Any compromise of ECG sensor or surreptitious alteration of the sensor output can pose extreme consequences to a person's health from missed diagnosis and delayed treatment. In general, compromising an ECG sensor in a BSN allows the adversary to alter its signal in two possible ways: (i) *temporal* alteration, which modifies the timing information of ECG complex (e.g., interbeat-interval); and (ii) *morphological* alteration, which modifies the shape of the ECG. In [1], we proposed a method to detect the morphological alterations of ECG signal in BSNs. In this paper, we present a complementary work on detecting temporal alterations of ECG sensor output due to adversarial compromise.

© Springer International Publishing Switzerland 2015
M. Qiu et al. (Eds.): NSS 2015, LNCS 9408, pp. 531–539, 2015.
DOI: 10.1007/978-3-319-25645-0_41

Temporal alterations can be used to modify a regular ECG signal to imply atrial fibrillation (irregular heart rhythm) or atrial tachycardia (abnormally high heart rhythm) or vice-versa.

Recent years have seen some work in the domain of anomaly detection in BSNs. These approaches have tried to adapt sensor-redundancy-based methods for detecting faulty sensors in BSNs [3,5,7,12]. Such BSNs naturally require considerable sensor-redundancies, where multiple sensors of the same type (e.g., accelerometers) measure the same limb movement. However, they might not be applicable when we consider ECG sensors, since for usability reasons typically there is only one ECG sensor in a BSN. Alternatively, history-based anomaly detection approaches have also been proposed in [13]. However, the human body is too dynamic for the past to effectively determine the current patient state at all times.

In this regard, we present a novel methodology for detecting temporal alteration of ECG sensor output in a BSN called **SIgnal Feature-correlation-based Testing (SIFT)**. It works by generating a subject-specific model by correlating their ECG sensor output with synchronously measured arterial blood pressure (ABP) and respiration (RESP) signals. As ABP measures the same physiological phenomena as ECG — the cardiac process, consequently, the inter-beat intervals in ECG and inter-systolic peak intervals in ABP are highly correlated. Further, both ABP and RESP signals affect the ECG inter-beat intervals through the autonomic nervous system [4,11], which is reflected in the observation of several frequency-domain features in inter-beat-interval sequence, ABP and RESP signals. Therefore, any alteration of the temporal properties of ECG signal by an adversary, if not reflected as a commensurate change in the ABP and RESP signals, is considered as evidence of compromise. The analysis of SIFT demonstrates promising results with ~98% accuracy in detecting even subtle ECG signal alterations for both healthy subjects as well as subjects with cardiac conditions.

## 2   Problem Statement and System Model

Formally speaking, let $x$ be the signal the adversary is trying to alter, then the goal is to find a means of detecting if this signal $x$ has been temporally altered to $x'$, solely-based on a set of reference signals $Y = \{y_1, y_2, ...y_n\}$ such that, each $y_i$, where $1 \leq i \leq n$, shares certain common features with $x$, either in the time or frequency-domain or both. In our case $x$ is the ECG signal, while $Y$ is a set with $n = 2$ elements: ABP signal and RESP signal.

In terms of the **system model** we assume the BSN is comprised of a number of wearable medical sensors capturing physiological signals from patients, especially the ECG, ABP and RESP sensors. These sensors continuously collect health and contextual data at regular intervals and forward it over a *single-hop* network to a highly capable base station for further processing. Our ECG compromise detection system is deployed at the base station.

In terms of the **threat model** we assume the primary goal of adversaries is compromising the ECG sensor and temporally altering its output using side-channel attacks such as [8]. Once the ECG sensor is compromised, it may generate erroneous output at any time. We assume that ABP and RESP sensors are secure and will not be attacked.

## 3   SIFT: An Approach for ECG Temporal Alteration Detection

In this section, we introduce our approach to the detection of temporal alteration of ECG sensor output called **Signal Feature-correlation based Testing (SIFT)**. Figure 1 shows the basic operation of SIFT. It consists of three steps: (1) feature generation, (2) training, and (3) detection.

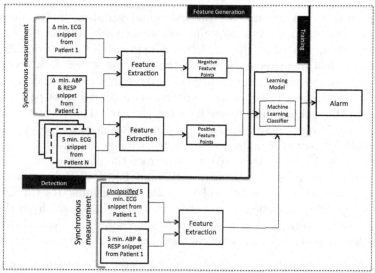

**Fig. 1.** Signal Feature-correlation based Testing for the Detection of Temporal Alteration of ECG Sensor Output

**Feature Generation.** We view compromise of ECG sensors, with the intention of providing incorrect data about the subject, to manifest itself as *temporal changes* in the output ECG signal. Temporal changes are associated with the interval between two consecutive R-peaks being misreported. Therefore, we first transform the ECG signal into a series of inter-beat-intervals by detecting the R-peaks and calculating the time difference between two consecutive R-peaks. The RR-tachogram thus produced forms our *candidate signal*. We then extract feature points from this candidate signal with two other *reference signals* derived from ABP and RESP signals. These feature points will then be used to train a subject-specific model and used to detect ECG alterations. In all, we extracted a set of 13 features from candidate and reference signals, which can be classified into two categories: (1) *Time-Domain Features*, which include (i) correlation coefficient of the RR- and SS-intervals obtained from ECG and ABP snippets; (ii) average RR-interval duration; and (iii) average SS-interval duration. (2) *Frequency-Domain Features*, which include (i) difference in frequency at which Mayer wave is observed in the power spectrums of RR-tachogram and SBP signal; (ii) difference in frequency at which the RSA wave is observed in the power spectrums of RR-tachogram and RESP signal; (iii) highest, lowest and average power in LF band of magnitude squared coherence (MSC[1]) between RR-intervals and SBP signal; (iv) highest, lowest and average power in HF band of MSC between RR-intervals and RESP signal; and (v) total number of peaks in the LF and HF bands of MSC between RR-intervals and SBP signal and RR-intervals and RESP signal, respectively.

**Training.** In order to account for the individual variation in the physiological processes, we build a *subject-specific* model for each subject on whom we tested our system. To train the models, we first extract the aforementioned 13-dimensional features from $\Delta$ minutes (the time for which data needs to be collected to train the model) of synchronously measured ECG, ABP and RESP signals from the same subject and label these as negative class points (which indicates the three signals are from the same patient). The feature extraction is done using sliding window of size $w < \Delta$, which is moved over the three synchronously measured signals. Each $w$-sized window of data thus produces one feature point for the system. We then extract the aforementioned features using snippets from ECG signals with ABP and RESP signals from different patients and label these as positive class points (which indicates the ECG signal is from the different patient but ABP and RESP signals are from the same patient). Once the negative and positive points are collected, we feed them into a machine learning classifier to generate a subject-specific model.

**Detection.** After model training stage is completed, we can use the trained model for a subject to decide if any newly received snippet of ECG signal has been temporally altered or not. Again, we use feature generation method for $w$-sized long synchronously measured ECG and ABP and RESP snippets to generate a feature point, and then feed this feature point to our subject-specific model. Then the model will output a label for this feature point as negative or positive. If the point is deemed positive, we raise an alarm. Note that we have to set $w$ to a value greater than or equal to 5 minutes because it is the recommended duration needed to produce clear Mayer and RSA waves [9]. This means SIFT needs at least 5-minutes of subject data to be able to determine signal alteration.

---

[1] Magnitude squared coherence (MSC) is the measure of spectral coherence and measures the causality between the two signals. The MSC of two signals signal $x(t)$ and signal $y(t)$ is defined as follows: $C_{xy}(f) = \frac{|P_{xy}(f)|^2}{P_{xx}(f)*P_{yy}(f)}$, where, $P_{xx}(f)$ and $P_{yy}(f)$ denotes the power spectral densities of signal $x(t)$ and signal $y(t)$ respectively, and $P_{xy}(f)$ denotes the cross power spectral density of these two signals.

Developing alternative mechanisms for reducing the time needed to generate alerts (i.e., $\Delta$) is part of our future work for this project.

# 4    Validation

Our goal with the validation was to demonstrate two things: (1) the ability of our approach to detect changes in the temporal properties of ECG signals induced by an adversary, and (2) the inability of an attacker to deceive SIFT using synthetic ECG signals derived from historical ECG data from a subject.

**Dataset.** We collected 28 subjects' data from the MIT PhysioBank Fantasia and MGH databases [6]. The Fantasia database is made up of healthy subjects, while the MGH database mainly contains data from subjects with specific cardiac conditions (i.e., ailment). We categorize these subjects into three types: (1) *Normal* subject type indicates subjects who did not suffer from any cardiac conditions and had normal sinus rhythm ECG, which consists of 6 males and 7 females with an average age of 44.46 (std 25.52). (2) *Abnormal* subject type indicates subjects with consistent tachycardia or bradycardia, which consists of 4 males and 2 females with an average age of 61.4 (std 19.25). (3) *Mixed* subject type indicates subjects whose ECG signal showed both normal as well as tachycardia or bradycardia rhythms, which consists 5 males and 4 females with an average age of 44.78 (std. 20.39).

**Detection Results.** In our experiments, we select Naive Bayes as our classifier to train the model. We set $\Delta = 60$ minutes and $w = 5$ minutes to produce the feature points. Furthermore, we compared the results of SIFT with an approach that analyzed historical RR-intervals to detect ECG alteration at any given time. This case is represented by the label **RR-only** in the results.

Figures 2, 3 and 4 show the box-plots for balanced accuracy (BAC), false positive (FP) and false negative (FN) rates of our detection system. In terms of detection accuracy, we can see that RR-only is reasonably accurate (average BAC of ∼87.41%). However, it has a considerably higher spread (compared to our approach). The RR-only approach performs best for subjects in the Abnormal set mainly because subjects in this set displayed unhealthy ECG (the variations of the RR-interval in this group is considerable high) and therefore it was easy to detect changes to these. In the case of Normal subject type the variations of box plot were much larger because the variations of the RR-interval is comparably smaller. Finally, in the case of the subjects in Mixed set the performance was worst both in terms of median BAC as well as the spread because subjects in this set exhibited ECG that was both normal as well as abnormal rhythms.

However, we can see that using SIFT the detection performance and spread is considerably better than using RR-only approach in terms of median BAC, FP, FN. For *Normal* subject type, our approach provides 98.46% BAC on average with average FP at 2.44% and FN at 0.65%. Not surprisingly the performance degrades a bit when we consider subjects with cardiac conditions. For the *Mixed* subject type, the average BAC of SIFT is 96.39%. However, the average FP

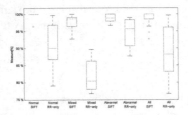

**Fig. 2.** Balanced Accuracy Rate for Our Approach and RR-only features

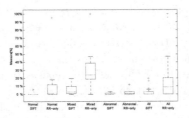

**Fig. 3.** False Positive Rate for Our Approach and RR-only

increases to 6.06% with the average FN at 1.15%. We suspect the reason for this increase is twofold: (1) on detailed examination of the data, some of the subject's ECG, ABP and RESP signals had considerable measurement errors, and (2) to a lesser degree, physiological signals of subjects in the Mixed set display both normal and abnormal rhythms and this decreases the classifier performance. In the future, we plan to work on improving the proposed system to reduce the second category of errors. For the *Abnormal* subject type, where the subjects display consistently tachycardia or bradycardia, we found the average BAC to be 98.81% with FP and FN at a much better 1.26% and 1.11%, respectively. These results demonstrate that our approach can accurately detect temporal alterations in ECG signal without sensor redundancy and considers the current state of the subject in its operation. Additionally, our approach can distinguish even subtle ECG signal temporal alterations for both healthy and unhealthy subjects. By subtle changes we mean when an adversary replaces an ECG snippet with another very similar one. For example, an actual ECG snippet with normal sinus rhythm being replaced with an ECG snippet from another person with normal sinus rhythm.

**Attacks Using Synthetic ECG.** We add another layer of analysis to the capability of our approach in detecting ECG compromise by evaluating if it can be fooled by using synthetic ECG signals obtained from generative models parameterized with a subject's own ECG data. In this regard, we used ECGSYN [10] a well-known synthetic ECG generator, which has been shown to generate clinically relevant synthetic ECG signals given a set of input parameters. We trained the ECGSYN model with actual subject's ECG data collected over a number of

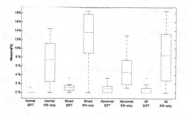

**Fig. 4.** False Negative Rate for Our Approach and RR-only

intervals from 5 minutes to 20 minutes from the dataset used to train the subject-specific model. This simulates the case where the attacker knows a portion of the ECG signals used to train the subject-specific model and uses it to alter the current ECG signal. Based on our experiments we find that if we use 10 minutes ECG data to train the ECGSYN model, we were able to detect the alteration of ECG (replacement of actual ECG with synthetic ECG from ECGSYN) in 91.07% of the cases, giving us FN at 8.93%. Not surprisingly, the FN goes up to 9.82% and the accuracy drops down to 90.18% as the amount of data available for training the ECGSYN model is doubled to 20 minutes. Despite the extreme assumption of the attacker having access to a portion of the same data as our approach has trained its model, the approach works with over 90% accuracy. This result shows that our approach is robust even to an adversary who have access to a subject's ECG data.

## 5  Related Work

Most of the work in this domain has been on detecting faulty sensors in wireless sensor networks. However, most of the fault detection schemes are based on two main assumptions: (1) the network has a large number of sensors with identical functionality deployed, and (2) for a given stimulus, the sensors in the same neighborhood should have the similar sensed values. Given these assumptions, the approaches cluster the nodes into different "subnets" according to their location and compare the similarity of the sensor readings with others nearby based on a pre-defined threshold. In recent years, researcher have tried to adapt these redundancy-based methods to the domain of BSNs [3, 5, 7, 12]. Almost all the work done for BSNs requires considerable sensor redundancies, i.e., motion monitoring BSNs. Useful as these solutions are for detecting faults with motion sensors, they might not be applicable when we consider physiological sensors in a BSN, as typically there is only one sensor of a particular type. Finally, in [1], a method to detect only the morphological alterations of ECG signals was proposed. As stated before this work is complementary to our work and needs to be used in conjunction with our work here to provide a full ECG compromise detection system.

## 6    Conclusions

In this paper we presented SIFT, a novel methodology to detect temporal alteration of an ECG sensor output using its correlation with arterial blood pressure and respiration signals. Analysis of our approach demonstrated promising results with ~98% accuracy in detecting even subtle ECG modifications. In the future, we plan to extend this work in the following directions: (1) reducing the minimum time for which data needs to be collected for effective training of the SIFT, (2) implement SIFT on an actual BSN system to evaluate its performance, (3) investigate ways to overcome our assumption that reference signals are not compromised, by using reference signals that are collected from more trustworthy sources such as the base station.

## References

1. Cai, H., Venkatasubramanian, K.K.: Detecting malicious morphological alterations of ECG signals in body sensor networks. In: Proceedings of the 14th International Conference on Information Processing in Sensor Networks, pp. 342–343. ACM (2015)
2. Clark, S.S., Ransford, B., Rahmati, A., Guineau, S., Sorber, J., Fu, K., Xu, W.: Wattsupdoc: power side channels to nonintrusively discover untargeted malware on embedded medical devices. In: Proceedings of USENIX Workshop on Health Information Technologies, vol. 2013 (2013)
3. Duk-Jin, K., Prabhakaran, B.: Motion fault detection and isolation in body sensor networks. Pervasive and Mobile Computing 7(6), 727–745 (2011)
4. Fink, G.: Encyclopedia of Stress, Three-Volume Set, vol. 1. Academic Press (2000)
5. Galzarano, S., Fortino, G., Liotta, A.: Embedded self-healing layer for detecting and recovering sensor faults in body sensor networks. In: 2012 IEEE International Conference on Systems, Man, and Cybernetics, pp. 2377–2382, October 2012
6. Goldberger, A., Amaral, L.A.N., Glass, L., Hausdorff, J.M., Ivanov, P.C., Mark, R.G., Mietus, J.E., Moody, G.B., Peng, C.-K., Stanley, H.E.: Physiobank, physiotoolkit, and physionet: Components of a new research resource for complex physiologic signals. Circulation 101(23), 215–220 (2000)
7. Kim, D.J., Suk, M.H., Prabhakaran, B.: Fault detection and isolation in motion monitoring system. In: 2012 Annual International Conference of the IEEE Engineering in Medicine and Biology Society (EMBC), pp. 5234–5237. IEEE (2012)
8. Kune, D., Backes, J., Clark, S., Kramer, D., Reynolds, M., Fu, K., Kim, Y., Xu, W.: Ghost talk: mitigating EMI signal injection attacks against analog sensors. In: 2013 IEEE Symposium on Security and Privacy (SP), pp. 145–159, May 2013
9. Malik, M., Bigger, J.T., Camm, A.J., Kleiger, R.E., Malliani, A., Moss, A.J., Schwartz, P.J.: Heart rate variability standards of measurement, physiological interpretation, and clinical use. European heart journal 17(3), 354–381 (1996)
10. McSharry, P., Clifford, G., Tarassenko, L., Smith, L.: A dynamical model for generating synthetic electrocardiogram signals. IEEE Transactions on Biomedical Engineering 50(3), 289–294 (2003)
11. Pitzalis, M.V., Mastropasqua, F., Massari, F., Passantino, A., Colombo, R., Mannarini, A., Forleo, C., Rizzon, P.: Effect of respiratory rate on the relationships between rr interval and systolic blood pressure fluctuations: a frequency-dependent phenomenon. Cardiovascular Research 38(2), 332–339 (1998)

12. Sagha, H., del R Millan, J., Chavarriaga, R.: Detecting and rectifying anomalies in body sensor networks. In: 2011 International Conference on Body Sensor Networks, pp. 162–167 (2011)
13. Zahra, T., Mohsen, S.: A trust-based distributed data fault detection algorithm for wireless sensor networks. In: Proceedings of International Workshop on Internet and Distributed Computing System (2008)

# Author Index

Printed in the United States
By Bookmasters